How to Start and Operate a Mail-Order Business

How to Start and Operate a Mail-Order Business

FOURTH EDITION

Julian L. Simon
University of Maryland, College Park
and
Julian Simon Associates, Economic Consultants,
Chevy Chase, MD

with contributions by
Paul Bringe, John Caples, David Ogilvy,
and Victor Schwab

McGraw-Hill Book Company
New York St. Louis San Francisco Auckland
Bogotá Hamburg Johannesburg London Madrid
Mexico Milan Montreal New Delhi Panama Paris
São Paulo Singapore Sydney Tokyo Toronto

Library of Congress Cataloging-in-Publication Data

Simon, Julian Lincoln
  How to start and operate a mail-order business.

  Bibliography: p.
  Includes index.
  1. Mail-order business.   1. Title.
HF5466.S54 1987   658.8'72   86–10508
ISBN 0–07–057531–2

1 2 3 4 5 6 7 8 9 0 DOC/DOC 8 9 3 2 1 0 9 8 7 6

ISBN 0-07-057531-2

The editors for this book were William Sabin and Nancy Young,
the designer was Naomi Auerbach, and the production supervisor
was Teresa F. Leaden. It was set in Baskerville by Williams Press.
It was printed and bound by R. R. Donnelley and Sons Company.

The fourth edition of *How to Start and Operate a Mail-
Order Business*, in its many examples, shows that both
men and women have been successful in mail order, and
it has endeavored to give both sexes a balanced
treatment. However, much of the material quoted and the
several chapters contributed by others were written when
it was the generally accepted practice to use the pronouns
he and him generically. We assure our readers that in
these cases no offense is intended.

*For Rita again, and now also for
David, Judith, and Daniel*

Contents

Preface

The *main purpose* of this book is to teach you, a newcomer to the mail-order business, what you need to know to make money in mail order. This includes those of you want want to start a business from scratch. It also includes business people who now sell retail or through salespeople, and who want to utilize the mail-order selling method to increase their profits or to expand their operations.

The step-by-step organization of this book is tailored to newcomers to mail order. It tells you what to do first, second, and third. It teaches you exactly how to proceed from one stage to the next, until you are reaping the profits you want.

Choosing a product is the first and crucial decision you must make. Therefore, we tackle that problem first. I show you the real "professional method" that is the secret of the big operators who find one profitable product after another.

This book teaches you the *business* of mail order and the *business decisions* a mail-order operator must make. This is unlike most previous books about mail order, which have concentrated on how to write advertising copy. But copywriting and artwork skills are only valuable to you as a mail-order operator if you can make sound decisions about what to sell and where to sell it. Furthermore, art and copy talent can be obtained from advertising agencies and free-lance specialists. But there are no specialists to help beginners in mail order with their business decisions. That's what this book is designed to do.

The *second purpose* of the book is to collect in one place the important facts and data that will be of interest and help to experienced mail-order operators. I've tried very hard to separate *proven facts* from mere opinions and old wives' tales, which is not always an easy task.

The *third purpose* is to describe the mail-order business to students of business, especially those interested in small business. More than any other business, a mail-order business can use the basic ideas of managerial economics and statistics. Therefore the mail-order business can be a model for people in other kinds of businesses. Furthermore, students will gain by the how-to-do-it approach even if they have no intention of going into mail order.

How to Use This Book

Begin by flipping through the book. Study the table of contents. Browse around to find out just what is in the book, and where. Read Chapter 2, "What is the Mail-Order Business?" to give you some background on the industry you want to enter.

Then *study* Chapter 3, "The Professional Method of Finding Products," and Chapters 4 and 5. If you are already in another line of business, those chapters will help you evaluate your product for mail-order selling. If you are starting from scratch, Chapters 3 through 5 will make it relatively simple to solve the problem of what to sell *profitably*. And you don't even need to have a bright idea!

Make no mistake about it—Chapters 3, 4, and 5 are the key to the mail-order business. They teach newcomers to select products in the same way the big operators do. Read these chapters again and again, and then begin to follow the instructions. If you *really* want a mail-order business, you must follow through the steps in those chapters.

Once you are satisfied that you have selected one or more salable products, read Chapter 6 to make sure that your products may be sold by mail. Then read Chapter 7 on mail-order strategies which will help you prepare a road map for the sale of your products. Chapter 7 will also direct you to the other chapters in the book that will be most helpful in solving your particular problems. Your further study will depend upon your choice of type of business, product, and general strategy.

Anyone who has completed eighth grade and has a knowledge of arithmetic has enough education to understand the ideas in this book. Nevertheless, some of it may seem hard going sometimes. And I say, let it be a little difficult. If a reader is not hardworking enough to plow through this book, he or she probably is not diligent enough to make money in mail order.

(It is sad but true that a dullard or a lazybones will not make money in mail order any more than he or she will make money in farming or selling insurance or running a flower shop. The sooner some of the dreamy fortune seekers quit kidding themselves, the better for all.)

Mail order requires specialized knowledge, which this book will help you gain. Ignorant beginners who *intend* to stay ignorant are surely wasting their time and money. Even those of you who tackle the business with plenty of intelligence and energy may get hurt until you learn what mail order is all about.

There are two important sources of knowledge about mail order, and you must learn from both. The first source is your observation of other mail-order businesses. Chapter 3 tells you how and what to observe. A unique advantage of this business is that it is easier to learn the inner workings of a mail-order firm than those of any other type of firm. You don't need to work there or spy on them. All you need to do is to watch their advertisements. Much that is important about the operation of any mail-order business is revealed to you by its advertising.

Books and articles about mail order are the second source of mail-order knowledge. This book rounds up for you most of the important general mail-order knowledge. But you must also read other books. Of the books mentioned along the way and in Appendix B, buy or borrow as many as you have time to read. It will be the best investment you can make in your mail-order future.

There are two important reasons for reading what other writers have written about mail order: (1) Some books cover specialized aspects of mail order that cannot be covered here. And (2) you must constantly refresh your memory. Even old-time professionals never stop their mail-order education.

Don't let the length of this book scare you. You don't need to read many chapters right away. Instead, you will refer to them as you need them. And when you are operating successfully and you need some special answers, you may even feel that the book is too short and doesn't contain everything.

Here's a piece of general advice. Get to know people who are already in the mail-order business. You will soon learn which mail-order businesses are in your area. Call the owners, and ask if they will talk with you. Don't be shy; tell them what you want. Probably they will be hospitable. The mail-order business can be a lonely one, and mail-order people, like all of us, like to give advice. If you seem sensible and willing to listen, they'll be glad to spend some time with you, to your great advantage.

How This Book Is Written

The *general* advice in the book about how to proceed step by step to build a mail-order business is based on my own experience in mail order. Business economics and marketing provide the background theory.

The *specific* facts include my own data, plus whatever I have been able to glean from every publication I could lay my hands on. It is paradoxical that the mail-order business lives on statistical information, yet very little analysis of mail order has been done. That is why I have collected every fact about mail order I could find.

The casual reader may grow impatient with such apparent trivia as a list of recommended abbreviations of state names. But any one such trivial point might be worth more than the price of the book to a new or old mail-order operator. Mail-order people learn by costly experience. If I can reduce that cost of experience, I will consider it a contribution.

Many of the specifics in the book are "only common sense." But the application of common sense takes time. Time costs money and mistakes cost money. I hope this book saves you both, and starts you on the path to profit and pleasure.

Recent Developments

Though the principles of successful mail-order operations are the same as always, this edition contains several new chapters on recent developments in the mail-order business.

By far the most important recent development of interest to the small mail-order firm, or to the person about to enter the mail-order business, is the availability of computers and programs that will service the small mail-order firm at low cost and without having to develop their own program from scratch. This revolution is not yet complete, and the next couple of years will surely bring exciting improvements. But by now I can write a chapter telling you how you can buy a computer and program which will handle most of your needs, if not all of them, at a price that any operating mail-order business can afford to buy—in fact, cannot afford *not* to buy—well less than $10,000.

This new Chapter 30 first introduces you to the basic ideas that you need to know about computers and programs for your purposes. It discusses what the ideal system will do for you, and it gives you a checklist for acquiring a system. It also examines how two programs now available for personal computers stack up against a detailed checklist. Chapter 30 is the only such discussion in print anywhere. In my opinion, it alone is worth the price of the book, and I'll bet that you agree when you use it to help you get started with a computer system. (I don't ordinarily make such an enthusiastic statement about my own writing, but it seems warranted in this case.) Another improvement in this edition, stemming from a recent development in the field, is that lists of direct-mail list brokers, mail-order consultants, and mail-order advertising agencies do not need to be included, as they were in earlier editions. This is because the classified advertising sections in *Direct Marketing, Zip, Catalog Age,* and *Direct Mail List Rates and Data* carry excellent lists of such persons and organizations because most of these organizations advertise there. And there are even fuller lists in Zip's annual December issue, *Who's Who of Direct Marketing.* These periodical listings are far more up-to-date than a book can be. Therefore, it is a pleasure to turn this task over to them. This and other emendations from earlier editions have provided the space to treat other topics in greater depth than has been possible in the past.

Still another welcome change is the improvement in the data concerning mail-order sales and the related industries. In the earlier editions of this book, it seemed worthwhile to pull together whatever data of this sort that existed, so as to make them available to all who were interested. But now one can find excellent presentations of Arnold Fishman's sophisticated data in the July issue each year of *Direct Marketing* and in another set of estimates in publications sold by Maxwell Sroge, Inc. These new sets of data are brought up to date each year, which a book cannot do, of course, so I am glad to turn the job over to them.

Still another recent development is the growth in catalog sales, which now is far-and-away the most important aspect of mail order. Along with this growth has come much more attention to treating subgroups of customers separately. That is, instead of mailing all customers the same number of catalogs each year, customers who are better prospects receive more frequent mailings, and persons who do not buy for a long time are trimmed from the list with greater efficiency.

One major development since the first edition has been the entry into the business of major firms such as Bell & Howell, J.C. Penney, Singer Sewing Machines, and others who see a great future in the mail-order business. (But don't worry about competition from them.) Another important development has been the use of the computer in direct-mail operations for eliminating duplicate names, and for creating personalized letters.

Perhaps the most important recent development has been the spectacular overall growth in size and sophistication of this business that some people had formerly thought was going out of style. More about these changes later.

Another recent development in the business is the use of the fancy new name, "direct marketing." One of the advantages of this term is that it does not exclude telephone selling, as does the name "mail-order business." But the main purpose of the new name is to impress potential investors with a new, exciting image of the business. Since most people don't know the name "direct marketing," we'll stick to "mail-order business."

The most important economic idea in the mail-order business is the *estimated value of a customer*. This idea is now discussed at much greater length than in the first edition. The readers who wish to deepen their knowledge of related topics may want to read Chapters 4 through 7 in my *Applied Managerial Economics* (Prentice-Hall, 1975). And as long as I'm recommending my own books, you might find some help in my *The Management of Advertising* (Prentice-Hall, 1971) and in *Basic Research Methods in Social Science* (Julian L. Simon and Paul Burnstein, 3d ed., Random House, 1985).

Debts for the First Edition

It is time to thank Gil Totten for teaching me how to think about advertising at the beginning of my career, and Joseph Phelan for his demonstration by example that an artist can and should think hard and straight about business problems.

Jan Schick typed this manuscript with a maximum of efficiency, intelligence, and accommodation, all of which I appreciate. My mother, Mae G. Simon, cheerfully typed the first draft of the manuscript, braving the worst of the dangers of a treacherous handwriting. Lawrence Miller gave helpful assistance in the final stages of preparing the manuscript.

The following people graciously read chapters of this book, and made helpful comments from their expert knowledge:
Paul Barris
Orlan Gaeddert
Glen Hanson
John Maguire
Jack Sawyer
Victor Schwab
Morton J. Simon
Robert Wolfson

Debts for the Second Edition

The preparation of this new edition brings the pleasurable obligations of additional acknowledgments. The first and foremost acknowledgement is to the skilled and enthusiastic participation of my mother, Mae G. Simon. Stanley J. Fenvessy contributed material on duplication processes, and Peter Hoke of *Direct Marketing* was kind enough to give permission to reprint various excerpts in the text. In our discussions, Philip Harvey and Linda Mews and I arrived at many new ideas. Sylvia Farhi typed with her usual competence, intelligence, and initiative.

Debts for the Third Edition

I am pleased and grateful to be able to acknowledge help with this third edition from Paul Bringe, John Caples, and Robert Kestnbaum, who all contributed chapters. Their wisdom is as good as one can find in the mail-order business. Bruce Holocek and Dan Richards also contributed useful comments and facts.

Debts for the Fourth Edition

Ed Burnett read the third edition from cover to cover. Drawing upon his extensive knowledge and keen insight into all aspects of direct marketing, he furnished me with a comprehensive set of comments which were of great value in preparing the fourth edition. Too few people in this world are so generous as to devote time and energy to help someone else's book in this fashion, especially someone whom they have never met. Ed also supplied a set of his writings on related subjects, and I drew frequently upon that material, as noted in the text. I shall be in Ed's debt for this selfless gift.

Lloyd Merriam helped me understand the Response computer program, and he discussed with me the characteristics of an ideal program for the personal computer in mail order.

Bill Sabin has been an ideal editor, pushing me at just the right times to get this edition done properly. And Nancy Young copyedited the manuscript uncommonly well.

Picking up with an old friend in a new way is always fun. My oldest friend (from when we were 6), Donald Benjamin, gave me the benefit of his enormous experience and knowledge in the printing business, and he read Chapter 21 with a keen eye. He corrected assorted errors, and he brought the data in the chapter up to date, for which I am most grateful.

Once again my mother, Mae G. Simon, has helped me with various matters in the preparation of the manuscript, with her usual large amounts of character and determination. I will miss her greatly in preparing the next edition, and it hurts that she did not live to see this edition in print.

Stephen Moore has once more turned his hand to a new set of research tasks, especially going through the manuscript and noting items that needed changing from the prior edition.

And with Gratitude to Many Others . . .

It has given me great satisfaction that many people have read the first, second, and third editions of this book. And a fair number of those readers have written me about their progress, mentioning that the book helped them start successful businesses and avoid costly mistakes. That is the kind of reaction that makes any writer feel good. I've also met many nice people through this correspondence. And it is very gratifying that the book continues to help enough so that this new up-to-date edition is needed.

The preface to the first edition begins with the hope that the book will help you make money in mail order. I'll end this preface with the same hope for your success—and with the additional wish that you will also enjoy your adventure and success in the mail-order business.

Julian L. Simon

1

The Possibilities of Mail Order

Who Can Make Money in Mail Order? / Can You Start Small and Part-Time? / Can You Still Make a Fortune in Mail Order? / Can You Make a Nice Living without Much Capital to Invest?

Who Can Make Money in Mail Order?

It is possible to start from scratch and be earning a million dollars a year—I said "earning" and not "sales volume," mind you—inside of 10 years. For example, in February 1983, I received a letter from which the following is extracted:

> In 1973, my partner and I determined to go into the mail-order business. At that time, we had been manufacturer's representatives for 12 years and were very tired of building up sales volume for others and then losing the territory to an idiot son-in-law or because the sales manager was jealous of our income. . . .
> It occurred to me that if I were going to be in the mail-order business, perhaps I should make a study of it. I had always been a good student so that it was kind of fun to trek down to the main library and to go through the card files looking for appropriate reading material. Among the many books that the library had, was your 1968 1st edition. I read it from cover to cover while sitting at the library and then went to my

local bookstore to order a copy. I have subsequently read it perhaps a dozen times. I really did learn the basics of the business from that book. . . .

From that first order on March 4, 1974, my business has grown to one which I feel will do $15,000,000 in this current fiscal year.

The author of the letter, R., told me that the $15 million of annual sales provides him an annual income in excess of a million dollars a year. And his business is a highly stable, repeat-order business conducted at a high ethical standard, giving R. an excellent standing in his community.

So—it can be done.

An official U.S. government booklet on establishing a mail-order business says:[1]

With a little determination and sagacity, the average person can easily master the principles of selling by mail. A principal requirement is good common sense and a mind made up to build a business. . . . As well suited for women as for men. . . . Age only a secondary consideration. . . . Advanced schooling helpful, but not essential.

And in this book you will be reading some astonishing success stories of men and women who started businesses at their kitchen tables with a few hundred dollars and from that start built businesses grossing millions.

All true! But let me add, loud and clear and repeatedly, so no one can miss it: *Mail-order success is only a dream to many people who get interested in it.* Fast-money mail-order "deals" fan the delusion of quick, easy fortunes. But few people who come to mail order have the necessary characteristics to make a go of it.

Robert Baker checked eighty-seven mail-order advertisers and found that only ten were advertising 5 years later.[2] He also found that only 27 percent of 500 advertisers had run ads the previous year.

Baker's figures, though not scientific, are helpful in pulling you down from the clouds. And of course you should remember that even the biggest firms in the mail-order business and in the economy as a whole expect to succeed with only perhaps one out of four ventures that they try out.

And why should the mail-order business be easy? It may well be the most desirable business in the world to be in. As with all good things, the fight to get a piece of it will not be easy.

The government booklet is right in saying that you don't need to be brilliant or well-educated to succeed in mail order. Many remarkably successful operators had little formal schooling. And some of the smartest professors at the world's major universities have made suggestions to me at parties ("I have a great idea for mail order") that would casue them to go broke in no time at all. Successful mail-order operators have studied mail order and know it inside out. That's about all the education they need. And that's about all the education you need for *your* success.

Can You Start Small and Part-Time?

One of the great advantages in starting up a mail-order business is that you *can* start part-time. There is no store to open in the morning, no interference with your present job.

Furthermore, it is usually *wise* to start part-time. Mail order is a rough, tough business, and you can't learn it overnight. Learning will be much less painful if your livelihood, and that of your family, doesn't depend on immediate success.

And you have an *advantage* if you start part-time. As you will learn later, one of the important skills in mail order is to be able to move fast on the basis of skimpy evidence. Part-time operators don't need to move so fast, and therefore they can move more surely. Their slower pace helps keep them from making wrong and expensive guesses.

Here are a few examples of businesses that were started part-time but grew to be sizable enterprises.

According to a story in *The Washington Post* on February 4, 1985 (Washington Business, p. 1)[3]

> Three years ago, Eileen B. Claussen was looking for a swing set for her two children. "We quickly found there was no single local place we knew of where we could buy good swings," she said. Not only was there a limited selection of sets at area stores, but those that were being offered were of poor quality and too expensive.
>
> So, on top of her full-time job in the federal government, Claussen decided to become an independent mail order dealer for two swing-set manufacturers, operating out of her home. "We had a phone and a post-office box—that was all."
>
> Today, Claussen's part-time venture had grown so much that Turtle Park Toys sells not only swing sets but also a wide variety of educational toys, promoted in a 32-page catalogue. Business—which is "now well into six figures"—has increased so much, that Claussen has had to move the operation from her home to a small three-room office on Wisconsin Avenue. She still has her full-time job, doing most of her work "between 10 and 12 at night." Her mother handles the bulk of the day-to-day operations.

"We thought we were doing well the first year, but between the first and third catalogue, sales have increased five times." she said. Demand from local customers has been so great that Turtle Park Toys has opened its office to the public for a few hours a week so its loyal clientele can buy items on the spot instead of through the mail.

In 1974, William Crutchfield, whose hobby was restoring Porsches, found that there was no place where he could buy good quality audio equipment for the cars. Therefore, he set up shop in his mother's basement. By 1983, his sales revenues were more than $15 million, which puts him well up into the 250 biggest mail-order firms in the United States, according to Maxwell Sroge's book, *Inside the Leading Mail Order Houses.*

Also in 1974, Arni Nashbar combined $1,000 capital with his hobby of bicycling. The story about him in *DM News* was headed "Mail Order Bicycle Firm with $1,000 Start-Up Grossed $6.5 Million in Last Fiscal Year," and it all happened in 10 years. The rest of the story continued as follows:[4]

NEW MIDDLETOWN, OH—An advertising man who enjoyed bicycling decided, in 1974, to invest $1,000 in an attempt to convert his hobby into a profitable mail order business. The resulting company, now Nashbar Associates, Inc., grossed $6.3 million in sales in the fiscal year ended Oct. 31, 1983, and the firm anticipates sales to jump to $7.5 million for 1983–84.

The company has grown completely through mail order stimulated by direct response advertising and the catalog that was developed and expanded in the evolutin of the venture.

Catalog costs for 1983–84 have been projected at $300,000. The figure will cover five mailings during the year. . . . An additional $120,000 has been budgeted for the company's space advertising. An inventory of $800,000 is planned, she stated.

The firm's first advertisement was 2 1/2″ × 5″ in the August 1974 issue of *Bicycling.* It was hand-drawn, with drawings of the 12 accessories the new company—Bike Warehouse—was offering. . . . The company operated at a loss that first year. . . .

Bike Warehouse operated out of the basement of Arni Nashbar's advertising agency in Boardman, OH, a suburb of Youngstown. Offered were such bike accessories as lights, water bottles, locks and cables, tools and T-shirts with the names of major brands of bicycles. The selling point was low prices. . . .

The ad brought in 166 orders and the money was immediately reinvested in the company. Bike Warehouse had a loss of $2,200 at the end of its first year. . . .

A six-page catalog using brown ink on white paper was included with the merchandise sold starting in November 1974. . . .

The first catalog had cost $541.52. In 1978, 45,000 were printed at a cost of $3,000, using different color inks.

Lee Wildeman started Holiday Gifts, Inc., while running a laundry, and didn't go into mail order full time until 3 years later.[5] He began with one ad in *House & Garden* for the Melody phone, which plays a tune while you ask someone to wait on the telephone. Because that ad succeeded, he continued in business, losing a few hundred dollars the first year. He didn't make a profit his first 3 years but after 10 years he was spending $450,000 a year in magazine advertising alone, which indicates that the size of the business has grown to a good many millions of dollars by now—from a part-time start.

Ex-GI Sam Lauderdale and his wife Mary Lauderdale were in college. Mary's mother sent her a pecan fruitcake which someone suggested to them was good enough to sell. They started advertising by sending 500 letters to prominent people in nearby Texas towns. After 25 years in business they had accumulated a very profitable list of 27,000 people, 12,000 of whom buy regularly and about 11,000 of whom buy amounts ranging from $50 to $4,000 yearly for gifts.[6]

One last example: Larry Newhouse and his wife Madeleine started selling costume-jewelry rings from their kitchen table with a $1,500 investment.[7] During the day Larry was a salesman selling jewelry. In the evening he made up orders in his basement. Five years later the sales of their firm, House of Camelot, were over $3 million yearly.

Some mail-order ventures can continue to be profitable part-time hobbies. A special skill that you can sell by mail—bookbinding, for example—can be a perfect mail-order product.

Or, you can run a small mail-order business part-time if you spend some time developing an item for which there is a limited appeal. (Successful items with wide appeal cannot remain small. Big competitors will find you out, horn into the field with their versions of the product, and steal your market.)

An example of a limited-market ad: "CIGARETTES—Make 20 plain or filter-tip for 9¢. Facts free. . . ." That ad has appeared almost word for word for years—an unquestioned profit-maker. But because of the small size of the operation (the ad runs in only a few magazines) and small profits, it can continue relatively safe from competition.

Another example of a limited-market is that of Lee Mountain, who from his base in the little town of Pisgah, Alabama, has been buying and selling used correspondence school courses and educational books since 1919. You can find his little classified advertisements in the classified columns of many such magazines as *Popular Science and Sports Afield.*

Limited-market mail-order businesses need not be small in size. L. L. Bean has been selling hunting, camping, and fishing equipment by mail for 65 years. In 1985 the firm had a list of 1,649,159 customers who had purchased something from them in the previous years, and it had grossed many tens of millions of dollars.

Can You Still Make a Fortune in Mail Order?

How about the story of R. on page 1, earning an income of a million dollars a year less than 10 years after he started with the help of this book? Sears, Roebuck and Montgomery Ward are not the only great success stories in mail order. Fortunes have also been made in recent years. Examples include Hudson Vitamin, Spencer Gifts, Sunset House, and many more.

It is possible to pyramid your winnings and get rich fast in mail order because you can increase your market tremendously in a great hurry. A retail store can increase its patronage only slowly. It takes time for its reputation to become known and for customers to become steady patrons. In mail order, however, if you find a very profitable item, you can spread into a great many media very rapidly.

In case you worry about there being too much competition, read this squib written almost a century ago in 1900: "Of course it is not so easy to succeed in the mail-order business now [1900], as it was a few years ago, when there was much less competition. This is especially true in case the business is started and conducted along the same lines as followed by scores of other mail dealers."[8]

Many, many fortunes have been made since then, and even more will be made in the future. In fact, the prospects in mail order now are probably better than ever.

An example is Arthur S. De Moss and National Liberty Insurance Company. In 1959 insurance agent De Moss got interested in selling health insurance by mail. He offered low rates to people who do not drink alcoholic beverages. In his first year he made a profit of $55,000—and in a little more than 10 years the company was earning *$20 million.*

Furthermore, the high profit margin above the product cost for most mail-order products means that you can earn a huge return on your investment if your advertising is successful. As an example, read this letter from a Los Angeles advertising agency specializing in mail-order advertising to *Golf World:*

> Enclosed is our check in the amount of $195.89 to cover the full page ad for the XXXXX Book Co., less agency discount and 2% discount. This was the ad on the book, XXXXX, by XXXX. We thought you would be interested in knowing that as of this date the ad has pulled exactly 1187 orders.

If XXXXX's figures are correct—this letter was sent out by *Golf World* to help boost space sales, and you should therefore give credence to it only with caution—these are my guesses as to the profit results of the ad:

```
1,187 orders in 3 weeks
1,187 orders estimated after first 3 weeks
2,374 × $2.98 = gross revenue                                    $7,074.52
   Less: Advertising                            $  195.89
         Estimated cost of books, shipping, etc.   1,600.00
         Total cost                                              1,795.89
         Gross profit                                           $5,278.63
```

Needless to say, this ad probably will not pull as well in other media. Successes like this one are all too rare.

Two other examples: (1) An ad for the book *How to Collect from Social Security at Any Age,* ran in *Parade.* The cost of the ad was $33,214, and the sales generated were $228,492. The costs of printing and mailing the book probably were about $25,000 to $40,000— which leaves a tidy profit. Of course this offer will not do this well very often, if ever again, but even with a much lesser response there is a profit.[9] (2) In 1963 Martin Faber started Film Corporation of American, a mail-order photo finisher and film seller, with a cash investment of $1,000. By 1973 sales were $44 million, and pretax earnings were somewhere between $4 and $5 million (of which taxes took about half). The firm operated in several foreign countries, and it sold to 18 million families in the U.S., about one family of four in the country.[10] (And now? Out of business!)

On the one hand, it is no snap to make a fortune in mail order. Competition is keen. If you show signs of doing well, competition finds it easy to imitate you and cut into your market. And once you are really in business, you face all the problems of any other business: personnel, stock, housing, taxes, and the rest. Bankruptcies and reorganizations of several large mail-order firms should convince you that mail order is no easy-magic way to make money.

R. H. Macy went into the mail-order business in a big way for a while. But eventually Macy's got out.

Furthermore, you can't make a huge fortune unless you have the necessary capital to use as leverage. Even if you *know* you have a tremendous winner, you must have cash or credit to purchase stock, advertising, and printing. Even if your winner is terrific, you can't make a fortune in a hurry just by plowing back earnings. By the time you have a respectable stake your competition will have swamped the market.

A Few Other Examples of
Successful Mail-Order Businesses

Here are a few more examples of mail-order businesses, to give you some idea of what mail-order businesses are. In this section, and elsewhere where actual businesses are named, I stick to facts that are in print, rather than give examples of businesses I have worked with because that way there is no danger of giving away trade secrets.

This section is based on the facts about mail-order businesses given in the lists of mail-order buyers that are offered for rent in *Direct Mail Lists, Rates and Data* (DMLRD),[11] together with data compiled by Arnold Fishman and published in *Direct Marketing's Annual Guide to Mail Order Sales* (July 1985).

1. Lands' End has a list of 1.2 million people who bought clothes, luggage, and shoes from them in 1984, with an average unit of sale of $65 and with many customers who bought more than once during the year. From that information I would guess a total of well upward of $100 million in yearly sales.

2. Lane Bryant had in the 12 months preceding May 1985, 1.4 million buyers for its clothes that are sold to large and tall women, with an average unit of sale of $50. In 1984 sales were $150 million.

3. Harry and David is the name of a firm in Bedford, Oregon, that sells fine foods, including fruits, and that has a fruit-of-the-month club. They offer for rent a list of 660,000 people who were buyers of their products in the 12 months preceding May 1985. The average unit of sale is $60, and ad annual sales were $45.6 million.

4. One of the most active, respected, and biggest mail-order businesses in the country is the Fingerhut Corporation. They sell all kinds of merchandise, but especially apparel, home furnishings, appliances, and merchandise related to automobiles. Their list of paid buyers who purchased on the installment plan in 1984 contains 2.2 million names. The average unit of sale was $50. Revenues were $512 million. And Fingerhut is now owned, along with eight other mail-order companies, by American Can.

And there were dozens more firms with annual sales over $25 million yearly—including L. L. Bean ($300 million)—without even mentioning Sears ($2.8 billion), J. C. Penney ($1.7 billion), and so on.

These selected examples of big mail-order firms don't truly represent what the business is about, however. Let's take a random sample of mail-order firms by taking the first firm listed alphabetically in the first category of merchandise in the alphabetical listing of merchandise categories in DMLRD—until we get tired. For example:

1. The first alphabetical category is "Almanacs and Directories," and the first listing is Concord Reference Books. In 1983 there were 61,411 buyers of a national directory of addresses and phone numbers, with an average unit of sale of $30.

2. The first category under B is "Babies," and the first firm listed is American Baby, Inc. There is no information on buyers, so let us pass on to the next firm, American Bronzing Company, which metalplates baby shoes and other keepsake items. In 1983, there were 89,000 buyers. The average unit of sale was $21.00.

3. The first category under C is "Children," and the first firm listed is Abracadabra Magic Shop, which sells novelties mostly to boys, ages 8–13. Their total list as of 1983 was 20,000, which included both buyers of goods (average unit of sale $15) and buyers of their paid catalog ($1 or $2).

4. The first category under D is "Dogs and Pets." The first mail-order firm listed is Dunn Supply. It sells bird-dog and horse equipment and outdoor apparel and has a list of 74,245 persons who purchased in the last 12 months, with an average unit of sale of $74. So this "unknown" company selling a very specialized line of goods must have grossed more than $50 million last year. This is not an untypical story for mail-order business.

5. The category under E is "Education and Self-Improvement," and the first listing is Advanced Learning Systems which offers a list of 48,294 persons who either purchased or inquired about its audio tape programs on personal growth, health, and so on. They do not indicate how many of these persons actually bought.

6. The first categoy under F is "Fashions." Abercrombie & Fitch, a long-estblished retail firm before it went into the mail-order business, offers a list of 25,000 persons who purchased sportswear, outdoor equipment, and various other "upscale" merchandise in the last 12 months, with an average unit of sale of $95.

How many mail-order firms are there? Four list firms have compiled lists of mail-order houses. One list includes 9,900 firms, the second includes 9,345, the third list includes 7,500, and the fourth list includes 6,400. The lists probably differ in the smallest firms that they list. (For information about the total dollar volume of the mail-order business, see the next chapter.) But these numbers do not include the large number of non-mail-order firms that do some selling of their product using mail-order methods. How many of these there are, no one has any idea. (The fact that there are approximately 425,000 active mailing permits does give some indication, though of course this figure includes many firms that do not sell by mail order but only advertise by direct mail; it also includes many nonprofit mailers.)

A good many other examples of mail-order firms are found in Appendix F, some with bits of their history.

An example of success in marketing industrial rather than consumer products by mail is that of Revere Chemical.[12] For many years, Revere sold building and ground maintenance materials through salespeople. Then they went into mail order seriously with ads in business magazines and direct mail, offering ice-melting material as the main attraction. In 10 years they developed 100,000 customers, and they became much bigger in volume than the business had become in the previous 53 years.

Can You Make a Nice Living without Much Capital to Invest?

There are also many small mail-order businesses, netting their owners a nice living, that started from scratch with practically no capital (a few hundred dollars, maybe). Many of these businesses originally depended upon some special skill or knowledge of the owner: hat restoring, playing cards for collectors, bee supplies. Many of these businesses were built slowly, as customers were gained and kept. There is a cosmetics firm in California from which all my aunts have bought by mail ever since one of them visited the store in 1927. And in the last few pages you read the examples of Lee Wildeman, the Lauderdales, the Newhouses, and Martin Faber, all of whom started their businesses with roughly $1,000 or less.

Another example: Arizona lawyer James E. Grant began part-time, selling Arizona legal forms to other lawyers and office-supply firms. In his first year of part-time work he grossed $50,000, and when last heard from he was about to go into the business full-time.

These small mail-order businesses that make nice livings yet neither grow big nor die off usually are too small to attract much competition. But "small" could mean an income of $50,000 to $100,000 per year.

Some of these successful small firms are tied to retail or manufacturing operations. The people who successfully sell wrought-iron furniture by mail probably could not survive if they had built solely as a mail-order business.

Other small mail-order businesses scratch out a specialized corner in a profitable market—perhaps by straight price appeal. There are several successful operators who operate this way in the photographic supplies market. But take my word for it: This is a rough way to make money. The competition is extremely tight, and woe to the inefficient!

In mail order, more than in any other business, you must be able to go it alone. You must be able to do without people with whom to talk things over. There is no boss, of course. But there is also no competitor nearby, nor are there any face-to-face customers, or salespeople coming by to sell you. And unlike doctors or lawyers or plumbers who go into business for themselves, you can't just sit in your office until something happens. Nothing will happen until you make it happen.

So—you need real gumption and self-reliance. This is one reason why a part-time start may be wise. While you have an outside job, you have financial and social support to keep you going.

Still, the mail-order business has a wonderful advantage for one who wants to go into business for oneself; it is relatively cheap to get into business long enough to find out whether your plan is profitable. To open up and test out a restaurant may require $40,000 and 2 years. You can test many mail-order products for $100 or $1,000, though $10,000 may be necessary to test a large, repeat-order business.

This is the long and short of it: Mail order is a terrifically desirable business, and it has many advantages. Because it is so desirable it is also very competitive and tough. And trying to find "one great item" is not the way to solve the problem, as we shall explain later.

2

What Is the Mail-Order Business?

Why Do People Buy by Mail? / How Big Is Mail Order? / Mail Order Is Booming / Who Can Use the Mail-Order Method? / Everybody Loves Mail Order—Even Those Who Hate It / Portrait of One Mail-Order Segment

"Mail-and-phone-order" or "telemail-order" should be the name of this branch of business, rather than just "mail-order business." But historically it has been "mail-order business" and so it will probably remain, despite industry attempts to relabel it "direct marketing," which would include house-to-house selling.

When we talk about "the mail-order business," we mean all businesses that deal with customers at a distance, without face-to-face selling. We also include the appropriate departments of firms that do some business at a distance, e.g., the mail-selling and telephone-selling activities of stores.

Firms that sell over the telephone resemble mail-order businesses, too. The selling techniques they use are like mail-order techniques, those of direct mail in particular.

Department stores have for many decades received many of the orders for their newspaper-advertised goods by telephone. And now Sears, Roebuck finds that fully 90 percent of the business generated by its catalogs comes by telephone instead of mail.[1]

Until recently, the high cost of long-distance telephone calls, direct or collect, discouraged both buyers and sellers. But now the cost of these calls has fallen, compared with other costs. And there are convenient methods of having buyers call direct with an 800 number, as seen in the Books by Phone ad shown in Figure 2-1. The Bell System now has 200,000 WATS lines connected on which inbound calls are paid for by the firm receiving the calls. And according to Ed Burnett, more money is spent on telephone marketing nowadays than on direct mail (though not including other media such as magazines and television).

Businesses that sell through agents recruited by mail are in the mail-order business, too. Fuller-Brush started that way. In 1913 Fuller used tiny classified ads in *Popular Mechanics* magazine.

When you think of mail order, you probably think first of Sears, Roebuck, the correspondence schools, and book and record clubs. But don't forget the magazines, from *Reader's Digest* and *Time* to the *Journal of Marketing*, all of which sell subscriptions by mail. For example, the magazine *Bon Appétit* formerly distributed 150,000 of its 450,000 copies through liquor stores, but in 1976 the new publisher decided to cut out that practice. He went to direct-mail sales, and he was able to raise circulation back to 400,000 within a year, with further increases to come, and at a very satisfactory cost.[2] Magazine subscription sales are perhaps the biggest mail-order operation of all. They account for 9.6 percent of all the direct mail that is sent out each year in the United States. (Next come general mail-order houses with 4.5 percent, book publishers with 3.4 percent, and newspaper publishers with 3.4 percent. But don't forget that direct mail only takes in a *part* of the mail-order business.)[3]

And keep in mind the fancy foods, prescription eyeglasses, artists' supplies, auto accessories, motors and generators, chemicals, and the hundreds of other categories of goods sold effectively by mail (see Appendix G).

Specialty goods were always big in the mail-order business. But in just the last few years, there has been a stunning turn away from the huge general catalogs—the "big books"—and toward specialty catalogs. As late as the 1970s, there were still the Big Five with their huge general catalogs—Sears, Montgomery Ward, Spiegel, Penney, and Alden's. But Alden's closed up its operation, Spiegel shifted entirely to specialty catalogs from its big book, and in 1985 Montgomery Ward shocked the entire mail-order community by announcing that it was discontinuing its big book because of a succession of heavy losses.[4]

It is important that when you think about possibilities for your mail-order business, you should *not* restrict yourself to those products

For people who love books but hate shopping...

or who arrive breathlessly at the bookstore just after closing time...or who don't live near a bookstore at all...or who get discouraged when the first store they try is out of stock:

1. Call toll-free any hour of the day or night from anywhere in America.

2. Ask for any books you've been wanting to read but too busy to buy.

3. Charge it to your BankAmericard, Master Charge, American Express or Diners Club credit card.

BOOKS BY PHONE

Shipped within 48 hours. Postage and handling $1 no matter how many books you order at once.

800-832-9100

Out of N.Y. State 800 645-9000 • Long Island 516 549-1300

Figure 2-1 Direct marketing with telephone ordering.

narrowly thought of as "mail-order produts." Remember that there is *some* truth in the old saying that "if it can be sold, it can be sold by mail." And if you already have a business of your own of almost any kind, you should consider doing some of your business by mail—

even if you only hang up a sign that says "Packages Mailed Anywhere in the World," as the candy and novelty shops do, or "Meals To Go" if you run a restaurant. (Later, we shall discuss your choice of product at length.)

Why Do People Buy by Mail?

Some people genuinely like to buy by mail. Many get a thrill from waiting for the mail carrier to bring their packages of goodies. But most people buy through mail order because a mail-order merchant makes them an offer of merchandise or price that no store nearby can match, or because no salesperson calls on them to sell the product. Mail-sold novelty goods are seldom available in nearby stores. Sex books are available in book stores but can be bought by mail without embarrassment.

Very little mail-order merchandise competes on a price basis with merchandise sold through nearby stores. Actually, selling by mail is often an *inefficient* and *expensive* sales technique. Staple merchandise usually can be sold cheaper over the counter in a retail store than it can be sold by mail. The retail merchant can operate on a gross margin of 60 percent down to 20 percent, while mail order usually operates on a margin of 60 percent or more.

But mail order can usually compete very well on products for which a salesperson makes *outside* calls for the firms selling the item. The cost of an outside sales call may be anywhere from $20 to $1,000; sales calls to businesses now average an astonishing $200 (in 1985), according to a McGraw-Hill survey (though remember that McGraw-Hill is a publisher and has a stake in having advertising look good by comparison). Sales can often be made by mail at considerably less cost than that.

The Small Business Administration classifies mail-buyers in the following way.[5]

1. Those interested in novelties. They want something different from their neighbors. These people look over magazines for items that appeal to them. Frequently they find products, relatively inexpensive, of novel appearance and design.

2. Those pursuing a hobby or some particular line of interest. Included here are such groups as home gardeners, stamp collectors, how-to-do-it enthusiasts, and many others.

3. Those who buy by mail as a matter of convenience. They find it easier to buy by mail and especially so if they live in a location removed from adequate shopping facilities. Often they send away for merchandise to benefit from a wider selection. They fill much of their staple goods needs in this way.

4. Those who buy by mail for what they consider a price advantage. They look over mail-order catalogs and also the advertisements of stores in their area or farther away to make comparisons and selections in the same manner that women shop for bargains in the local store.

Many people in the mail-order business have suggested that the increase in the number of women who have 9 to 5 jobs, and who therefore have less time to go shopping, accounts for the recent boom in the mail-order business. Maybe so, but I think that this is only one factor among many that are responsible for the increase in Americans' (and Europeans') desire to buy by mail and telephone. Better mail-order selling has helped and so have credit cards, but people's good experiences with buying by mail may be most important of all.

How Big Is Mail Order?

It is difficult to make a reasonable estimate of how much merchandise is sold by mail or telephone each year, because so much mail-order business is done by firms whose primary business is not by mail, or by firms that don't think of themselves as being in the mail-order business. There are no government indices that measure the amount of business done by mail or telephone.

The most reliable estimate seems to be that of Arnold Fishman. He calculates that in 1984 consumer products worth $54.1 billion and business products and services worth $31.6 billion were sold through mail order and that $29.7 billion of charitable contributions were obtained through mail order. Leaving aside the charitable contributions, mail order accounted for goods and services worth $85.7 billion.* To put that in perspective, the $54.1 billion of consumer products was about 4 percent of retail sales and about 1.5 percent of the GNP, and about $228 was spent on mail order by the average U.S. resident. And mail order has been growing faster than has the

---

* These estimates exclude all in-store sales and personal selling but they do include orders placed by telephone or electronically. The estimates do not include sales induced by telephone solicitations, as I understand the matter.

economy as a whole.[6] In the fiscal year 1985, 37 billion pieces of third-class direct-mail advertising were mailed.[7]

Fishman's estimates of the numbers of businesses and the volume of sales in dollars in various specialty mail-order industries are shown in Tables 2-1, 2-2, and 2-3. (The reason why the total number of businesses is so much larger than other estimates of the number of mail-order businesses in the U.S. is that these tables include magazines, newspapers, and cable television firms.)

Selling by telephone is another huge industry which might well be considered part of the mail-order business but which is not discussed in this book. Telemarketing, as it is called, accounts for about $90 billion in sales as of 1985, according to *Zip* magazine (January 1985, p. 53).

Table 2-1. Specialty Consumer Products

	Sales ($MMs)	Businesses (No.)
Animal care	550	100
Apparel	2,220	530
Audio-video	300	270
Automotive/aviation	340	340
Books	1,975	—
Collectibles	1,350	520
Consumer electronics science	740	260
Cosmetics/toiletries	300	120
Crafts	570	730
Food	780	600
Gardening	640	370
Gifts	1,140	470
Hardware/tools	320	190
Health products	940	280
Home construction	170	320
Housewares	570	630
Jewelry	420	150
Magazines	4,150	5,000
Multiproducts	2,160	150
Newspapers	2,600	1,700
Photographic products	430	100
Records	470	—
Sporting goods	1,360	1,070
Stationery	220	90
Tobacco	50	40
Toys/games/children's products	300	290
Computer software	375	—
Total	24,940	14,320

Table 2-2. Specialty Vendors: Consumer Services, Nonfinancial

	Sales ($MMs)	Businesses (No.)
Astrology/occult	70	40
Auto clubs	1,230	20
Cable TV	6,320	5,000
Cultural events	480	—
Educational	150	40
Home study	300	—
Insurance	5,700	—
Photofinishing	320	—
Sports events	600	—
Total	9,470	—

In addition to the marketing of cable TV ($6.3 billion) through mail order, other consumer service sales segments are prime segments for mail order:
• Auto clubs ($1.23 billion) entirely supported by mail-order sales generation
• Cultural events ($.48 billion) and sports events ($.60 billion) with mail and phone orders as substantial source of sales (20–40 percent)

Table 2-3. Specialty Vendors: Consumer Services, Financial

	Sales ($MMs)	*Businesses (No.)	*SIC codes
Brokerage, discount (commissions)	520	120	6,411
Brokerage, no-load mutual funds (fees)	1,300	290	6,411
Credit card security services	90	3	—
Insurance	5,700	100	6,311
Total	7,610	513	—

* Standard industrial classification codes

Mail-order consumer financial services sales of $7.61 billion are dominated by insurance (75%) and no-load mutual fund brokerage (17%).

Mail Order Is Booming

When I wrote the first edition of this book in the 1960s, people—even those in the business—said that mail order was declining. But since then—especially in the last 10 or 15 years—it has become clear that the mail-order business is booming, and that it has a very rosy future.

Expenditures for direct-mail advertising rose from $266 million in 1936 and $919 million in 1950, to $11.8 billion in 1983.[8] The number of pieces mailed rose from 10 billion in 1952 to 29 billion in 1979 (perhaps 2 billion containing advertising).[9] And a large proportion of direct mail is mail-order advertising. Increased costs of postage, printing, and other expenses must be taken into account, however, and the dollar figures are not adjusted for inflation.

According to the *Statistical Abstract of the United States,* the number of establishments classified as "mail-order houses" (which includes only catalog sellers for the most part), rose from 2,550 in 1958 to 7,400 in 1982, and the total dollar sales rose from $1,986 million to $10.9 billion in 1982.[10] These totals apply to only a small part of the industry such as Sears, Roebuck and J. C. Penney, but the rate of increase is interesting.

Consumer mail order is very much in our minds because we see advertisements and catalogs so frequently in our homes. Business and industrial mail order is also extremely important, too, however, for the entire economy as well as for the sellers and buyers, and it has been increasing in size very rapidly. It is difficult to develop meaningful statistics about mail-order sales to businesses because they are so intertwined with all other sales; for example, much of the supplies that IBM sells might properly be classified as being sold by mail order. But with other types of office supplies and stationery there is no confusion, and the quantities sold by mail order are increasing rapidly in their importance. Furthermore, in my judgment this represents the best set of opportunities for newcomers. And one can get into selling products such as specialized janitor supplies with relatively little expense.[11]

Specialty catalog businesses have been growing especially rapidly, and they now constitute the largest segment of mail order. The number of firms mailing catalogs rose from about 4,000 in 1981 to about 6,500 in 1984, and the total number of catalogs mailed out is close to 3 billion. Sears alone sent out about 360 million catalogs in 1985, up from 300 million 5 years earlier—which is more than 10 percent of all the catalogs mailed in the U.S.! But please notice that nowadays more than half the number of these catalogs (though not that large a proportion of their total pages) are *specialized* catalogs, an important pointer to trends in mail order. In fact, Sears now mails more than 50 different catalogs, whereas in the past it had just its one big book.[12]

In the past decade or so, J. C. Penney started a catalog operation from scratch and has reached a billion dollars in sales. Singer Company and Bell & Howell are other major firms that got into the mail-order business in a big way in the past 10 or 15 years. After seeing successes like these, many other big companies have begun to move into mail order and direct marketing. The oil companies including Mobil, Citgo, Phillips, Shell, and Exxon began to exploit their credit-card lists in a big way, selling such items as cookware sets and recording equipment. General Mills was impressed by the fact that a few years ago the most active stock on the American Stock Exchange was New Process, a mail-order seller of clothing. So General Mills proceeded to buy some big existing catalog firms: LeeWards (hobby craft and needlework), Eddie Bauer (outdoor goods), Talbots (women's clothing), H. E. Harris (stamps), and Bowers and Ruddy Galleries (rare coins).[13] In the 3 years prior to 1985, Bloomingdale's went from zero to $60 million in sales, mailing twenty separate specialty catalogs.[14] General Mills has started up a subsidiary named Thomas Garroway, Ltd., to sell fancy foods by mail, and they have also bought up several existing large mail-order firms.

Xerox now sells children's books, and Avon has been selling women's clothes and now is experimenting with a mail catalog of its regular merchandise, as is Fuller Brush.[15] W. R. Grace sells cheese, and American Airlines sells luggage. Of course RCA and CBS have been heavily in the mail-order record and tape business for years. By 1978, half of the biggest fifty corporations in the U.S. had mail-order divisions.[16] (But not all these biggies do well when they come into mail order, or do better than people starting from scratch. For example, in a previous edition of this book I noted that Kent Cigarettes had just introduced the Kent Gallery, selling novelties in mass-media magazines. I haven't heard much of that venture since then. General Foods came in like a lion with Fabrizaar, but now is quiet as a lamb.

L. L. Bean is a big story all by itself. Its sales rose 58 percent between 1981 and 1983, the last date for which I could obtain data. Bean sends out 12 catalogs a year to their best customers, a total of 55 million catalogs in 1983. In 1984 their sales had reached almost $300 million—a lot of money for a firm that started out selling outdoor gear alone.[17]

Even Nelson Rockefeller became interested in mail order not long before his death in 1979. He set up a mail-order and retail operation to sell reproductions of the paintings and sculptures in his huge personal collection.[18]

A research firm undertook a trade study of catalog buying and forecast an annual rate of growth of 8 to 12 percent. "In short, we conclude that there will be a continuing strong trend toward shopping at home."[19] And a major new trend is for catalog shopping to become a serious rival for specialty stores among city people. Neiman-Marcus and Sakowitz, two famous Texas stores, are leading examples of stores which see much of their future in catalog sales, and they are expanding swiftly in that direction. (But life is not a bowl of cherries, even for the biggies. Sakowitz had to file in court for reorganization as protection from creditors in 1985, though this may be mainly a retail-store problem. And Montgomery Ward lost so much money in mail order that Mobil shut its catalog operation down in 1985.)

From a financial point of view, too, mail-order companies are doing well. The after-tax profit-to-sales ratios of publicly held mail-order companies have been higher in recent years than the profit-to-sales ratios of comparable major retailers.[20]

The future of the mail-order business abroad is bright, too. American companies are starting operations abroad to take advantage of this. According to Fishman, 50 percent of Time, Inc.'s total mail-order volume is outside the United States, and the Franklin Mint does 30 percent outside the U.S. European mail-order firms are nothing to sneeze at, either. For example, Schickedans in West Germany had sales of over $2 billion in 1982, to be compared with Sears' $3 billion in the much larger United States. Total sales outside the United States were $29.3 billion, to be compared with $54.1 billion in the United States, broken down as follows:

	Sales ($Bs)
Europe	
Austria	.400
Belgium	.269
Denmark	.106
Finland	.339
France	3.240
Italy	.538
Netherlands	.480
Sweden	.568
Switzerland	.558
United Kingdom	3.589
West Germany	7.855
Non-Europe	
Canada	2.809
Japan	6.814
Australia	1.759
Total Non-U.S.	29.324
United States	54.135

Japanese mail-order sales grew a hefty 11 percent in fiscal year 1984.[21]

The trend of mail-order operating costs is not at all unfavorable, either, despite the rapid increase in postage and the consequent screams of direct-mail and mail-order operators. The reason is rapid technological advance in the printing industry. And we can expect a continuation of this pleasant trend in the future.

Who Can Use the Mail-Order Method?

The "mail-order business" is far broader than the layman usually thinks it to be. Mail order is really a *method* of doing business—or even of doing something other than business—rather than just a branch of business. Anyone who wishes to induce others to respond to an offer should think about the mail-order method. It boils down to advertising to potential customers, asking them to respond (usually with money, but sometimes with other things you want of them, such as their time), and then doing what you promise them you will do in return. Here follow a few examples of less well-known uses of the mail-order method.

1. *Increasing the size of a college student body.* The following story tells how Beloit College has succeeded in the competition that has arisen recently to get more students:[22]

   According to Census Bureau estimates, the number of 18-year olds in the country will peak this year, then decline as much as 18% in the early- to mid-1980s. In addition to this shrinking of the pool of college-age students, there is apprehension that with tuition and other costs on the rise, more students will decide to forgo traditional four-year college careers.

   Among the more vulnerable schools are liberal-arts colleges such as Beloit that already are losing prospective students to institutions offering more-specialized training.

   In the coming battle, Beloit College, situated in southern Wisconsin 100 miles northwest of Chicago, has a major advantage: It has already fought one such battle; in fact it is still fighting it. The increase in freshman enrollment this term to 293 from 200 may mean that the tide has turned but the battle goes on. Beloit's total enrollment has dropped 35% in the last six years, to 894 students today. . . .

   In 1977, the year it attracted only 200 freshmen, the college reorganized its admissions office and named a new director, John W. Lind, a Beloit graduate who had been in charge of financial aid. For six months, the admissions office held meetings with every department in the college to learn about their programs and find out what kind of jobs their graduates were getting. At the same time, Mr. Lind was working on his strategy for going after students.

Like many colleges, Beloit relies on the Student Search Service of the College Entrance Examination Board as a major means of identifying prospects. For a fee, the service provides the names of college-bound high-school students on the basis of how well they did on their Scholastic Aptitude Tests, where they live, what they intend to study in college or a number of other factors. Beloit bought 97,000 names of prospects starting college this past fall and, from an initial mailing, received responses from about 5,000.

"Our premise was to be as individual and personal with prospective students as possible," Mr. Lind says. One approach was to do a lot of personal letter writing to students who showed interest in Beloit. But the admissions office also turned to the telephone to chat with potential applicants and their parents around the country. The calls started at the end of October and continued through May, with an average of five or six people, including faculty volunteers, on the telephone at least one night a week.

"That as much as anything was responsible for our success," Mr. Lind says. "Students were being inundated with mail and not reading it. We felt we were doing them a service. If we called and they weren't interested, we would thank them, drop them from our file and not go back. But many times we found students interested in programs we're strong in, and we got a lot who applied and enrolled."

The result was a 12% increase in applications and a class of 293 freshmen last September, the largest in four years. Many of the freshmen say it was Beloit's personal approach that tipped the balance in the school's favor.

2. *Fund-raising for charities.* This has always been a mail-order activity. In the past few years, political fund-raising has taken on increased importance due to the new federal election-contribution laws; the letter from then-President Gerald Ford is an example. Now direct-mail political fund-raising is seen as a fundamental—and to some, frightening—part of the political scene. More discussion of this type may be found later in this book.

Consider this 1975 news story:[23]

(Date line Matthews, Ala., Jan. 23)—Democrats running for President make pilgrimages to Morris Dees's house these days. . . . His colleagues in the McGovern campaign of 1972 called him a "bona fide genius" for building up a computerized file of several hundred thousand small contributors and then milking that list inventively—some would say unmercifully—for all the money his candidate needed. At a postage and printing cost of roughly $3 million, Mr. Dees's intricate, persistent come-ons netted about $20 million for the McGovern campaign from almost 700,000 citizens—the record to date in popular political fund raising.

Twenty-five miles up the road in Montgomery, Governor George C. Wallace seems well started on a comparable direct-mail triumph. With the help of Richard A. Viguerie of Falls Church, Va., king of the right-wing (usually Republican) mailing lists, the undeclared Wallace campaign will have spent over $2 million on roughly 13 million "prospect letters" by the middle of this year to identify a core of 250,000 contributing supporters. And even if the Wallace campaign simply breaks even on that preliminary project, mail professionals say it will yield something better than money: a friendly base for re-solicitation. . . .

The man the candidates ask is Mr. Dees, 38 years old, a gentleman farmer and civil rights lawyer who lives comfortable here off the mail-order fortune he amassed selling birthday cakes, cook books and encyclopedias in his twenties.

By 1977 the pace of political fund-raising was even faster. "In 1977, $28.2 billion, or 80 percent of all contributions received by nonprofit organizations, was raised through direct mail. This includes religious, professional, educational, charitable, and public-interest organizations."[24] The fund-raising-by-mail organization has taken on political power and influence of its own: As *The Wall Street Journal* reports on Viguerie.[25]

Clearly, Mr. Viguerie (pronounced VIG-ur-ree) is a man who thinks big. Right now, he is riding a conservative wave that he thinks is sweeping the country. His fund raising and influence over a variety of right-wing causes and candidates have earned him the nickname "godfather of the New Right"—a nickname he doesn't seem to mind. Striding through his elegant offices in suburban Falls Church, Va., he explains briskly, "We're trying to build a movement here."

Using computers and sophisticated direct-mail techniques, Mr. Viguerie in the past several years has collected millions of dollars from the public for conservative causes and candidates; this year alone, he says, he expects to raise $25 million to $35 million. His allies in the conservative movement—and there are many—say he is a genius who speaks to and for a large body of Americans. His critics—there are lots of them, too—say that his work has also furthered the interests, both in political power and in profits, of Richard Viguerie.

Mr. Viguerie just smiles. He's lucky, he says, because "my avocation is also my business."

Millions of people who have never heard of Mr. Viguerie have probably seen examples of his handiwork: fund-raising letters. Some such letters come in the name of candidates like Jesse Helms, the conservative Republican Senator from North Carolina, or Avi Nelson, who lost to Sen. Edward Brooke in the Massachusetts Republican primary. Other letters bear the names of political groups such as the Committee for the Survival of a Free Congress of the National Conservative Political Action Committee.

The 1984 political campaign was the most active for direct-mail fundraising, and unless the election laws are changed, we can expect even more of this kind of mail-order activity.

3. Magazines, such as *Business Week* and *Advertising Age,* have set up their own mail-order operations to sell books and other items directly from their own advertising pages.

Everybody Loves Mail Order —Even Those Who Hate It

It is fascinating to see how the extraordinary efficiency of the mail-order business is used even by those who have no interest at all in the mail-order business for its own sale.

Item 1: If Consumers Union does not hate advertising with a passion, it certainly has never shown any affection for it. Yet Consumers Union spends a huge chunk of its total budget in direct-mail and display advertising solicitations to get new members and to sell subscriptions of its publications, *Consumer Reports* and *News Digest* (Figure 2-2).

Item 2: The U.S. Treasury entered the mail-order medallion business as of 1980.[26]

WASHINGTON—The Treasury decided it will sell a planned series of gold medallions by direct-mail order once Congress provides the funds to produce them.

The medallions, called for by legislation passed last year, will give more Americans the chance to buy Treasury gold. At the Treasury's monthly gold auctions, the minimum purchase is a 300-ounce gold bar, or more than $69,000 at 1st year's average price of $230.17 an ounce. The medallions, to be sold at market prices plus costs, would come in half-ounce and one-ounce sizes.

A Treasury official said the agency decided to sell the medallions by direct mail—rather than by auction or through distributors—so that more individuals could buy them. The Treasury also plans to limit the quantity that individuals, corporations, dealers or banks may buy, but it hasn't set the limit yet.

The official wouldn't estimate how much the mail-order system would cost. He said details are being held up pending Congress's appropriation of funds to produce and distribute the medallions. The law authorizing the sale requires that medallions totaling one million ounces of gold be produced and offered for sale in each of the five calendar years beginning in 1980.

Figure 2-2

Item 3: Communist ideology denounces advertising as a vicious capitalistic device. It is therefore with a certain glee that I notice the managers of the USSR's magazine *Soviet Life* using a very American aggressive mail-order campaign to sell their product to the capitalistic running dogs in the United States. And darned if they aren't doing a good job of it, too. Somewhere between 42,000 and 48,000 copies sold each month—most of these 53,000 or 54,000 copies that are sold—are sold by mail, whereas only between 2,000 and 5,000 are sold on newstands. *Soviet Life's* promotion campaign won a top award given by the Philadelphia chapter of the Direct Marketing Association.[27]

Portrait of One
Mail-Order Segment

To give you a more detailed idea of a single segment of the mail-order business—though a particularly vigorous segment, to be sure—let's review some data (taken from a defunct publication, *List Letter*, as of a few years ago) on the scope of the business done by the firms that sell the horticultural products that are sold to home gardeners:

Rayner Brothers. . . . Family-owned, 57-year old business which specializes in strawberries, blueberries, fruit trees and small fruits . . . Customers purchase average of $56 through the catalogue, 290,000 1979–1983 buyers & inquirers. . . .

Stark Brothers. . . . A nursery and fruit business which first opened in 1816. Now 100% direct mail generates ⅔ of the company's business. Their customer is the amateur, backyard gardener who purchases an average $45 order. 1,000,000 buyers . . . 150,000 last 12-month buyers. . . .

Vermont Bean Seed Co. . . . This vegetable and wild flower seed catalogue was put on the market in spring '82. It reaches serious, large-scale gardeners and farmers who buy by the pound, not the packet. Vermont Bean Seed Co. does research on seeds for colder climates and shorter growing seasons, and most of their customers come from the northern half of the country. The buyer is 100% direct mail generated and pays an average $23 per order. . . . 30,677 1982 buyers . . . 61,000 1980–1982 buyers . . . 19,000 1982 inquirers.

Michigan Bulb. . . . This slim, 4-page mailer offers home gardeners low prices. A large spring mailing of 9.5 million and a fall mailing of 5 million brought an average $12 sale. This is a low ticket, high volume nursery and bulb house. The list is 50% direct mail generated through sweepstakes promotions. The remainder comes from space ads in mag-

azines, newspapers and Sunday supplements. Continuations with insurance offers, general merchandise and multi-magazine users, according to the owners. 550,000 fall buyers . . . 900,000 spring buyers. . . .
Garden Way Market Place. . . . These names were generated through a sweepstakes offering garden related prizes. Names referred by entrants were sent a Marketplace piece. Average age: 45. Median income: $22,000. 90% men. The spring emphasis is on gardening; the fall catalogue covers home improvements, 53,583 1982 fall Sweepstakes inquiries & referrals . . . 139,934 1982 spring Sweepstakes inquiries & referrals. . . .
George W. Park Seed Co. . . . This well-known seed, bulb and accessory catalogue has been in business for over 100 years. Buyers are home gardeners who spend an average of $15 with many repeat orders. Seeds from Park will be riding along on the Columbian Space Shuttle this year. . . . 538,924 spring 1982 buyers . . . 62,337 fall 1982 buyers. . . .
Burpee. . . . Said to be the largest seed catalogue in the country and perhaps the world. . . . Burpee boasts of the greatest brand recognition in the industry, and mails three times a year. Buyers are home gardeners with a median income of $24,000. Average sale: $25–$30. 2,140,192 1980–1982 mail order buyers. . . .
Savage Farm Nursery. . . . This is a 100% direct mail generated list of buyers of trees and other plants with an average $24 sale. 168,841 active buyers . . . 50,000 1981–1982 buyers. . . .
Henry Field. . . . 95% direct mail generated catalogue buyers. Mostly homeowners with above average-sized gardens. Average order: $20. Buyers are mostly from the South. 400,000 projected spring 1983 buyers. . . .
Jackson & Perkins Co. . . . These 100% direct mail generated buyers spent an average of $40 on roses, fruit trees and other gardening items. Mostly rural and suburban customers for this high ticket catalogue. 251,329 previous 6 months' buyers . . . 798,652 last 18 months' buyers. . . .
Kelly Brothers Nurseries. . . . A wide variety of nursery stock in this catalogue attracts home owners interested in purchasing trees, shrubs, bulbs and other landscaping items for their yards and gardens. They spend an average $25. . . . 180,221 1980–1982 buyers . . . 340,702 1980–1982 inquirers. . . .
J.W. Jung Seed Co. . . . A young upstart by some nursery standards, this nursery and seed house was founded in 1907. It prides itself on providing quality stock at reasonable prices. Average sale: $21. . . . 160,428 1982 buyers . . . 386,542 total buyer file. . . .
Garden Way Publishing Book Buyers. . . . These people bought an average of $10 worth of Garden Way home "how to" books and "Country Wisdom" bulletins. Subjects include: vegetable gardening, cooking and preserving, alternate energy, building, livestock raising and country living. Median income: $24,500. Mostly homeowners, average age of 30 years. 82,053 1982 book buyers . . . 103,980 1981 book buyers. . . .
Garden Way Research. . . . Buyers of at least one of three products: a $100 garden cart, a $300 workbench, or a $300 kitchen work center.

Median income: $30,000. Average age: 48. Most live in suburban or ex-urban areas. 57,610 1982 cart buyers . . . 56,368 1980–82 Workbench buyers and inquirers . . . 33,750 1982 Kitchen Work Center buyers and inquirers . . . 248,995 cart inquirers. . . .

Farmer Seed & Nursery Co. . . . Started in 1888, the catalogue was originally printed in both English and German. The nursery developed strains of stock at the University of Massachusetts specifically designed for the Northern Midwest's shorter growing season. Their customer is a home gardener, aged 45–50, in the $10,000 to $30,000 income range who spends an average of $21 with Farmer Seed. 132,000 1980–1981 buyers . . . 46,000 1982 buyers. . . .

Wayside Gardens. . . . A high ticket, quality nursery generating an average $38 order through 50% direct mail and 50% space ads. . . . 161,044 1980–1982 buyers . . . 151,475 paid catalogue requests. . . .

J.E. Miller Nurseries Inc. . . . Miller's Planting Guides and catalogues specialize in hardy fruit trees, fruit vines and ornamental trees and bushes. Buyers are large property owners predominantly from the Northeast, who spent an average of $35–$40. . . . The list is 95% direct mail and 5% space ad generated. 426,092 1981–1982 buyers/inquirers . . . 99,905 1982 buyers . . . 116,151 1982 inquirers. . . .

Twilley Seed Co. . . . Twilley started as a family-run business in 1934. The company is still run essentially the same way, with a stronger emphasis on the home gardener. Their customers are 40% consumers and 60% small market growers, who buy an average of $35. . . . The catalogue has recently added more color and increased the number mailed out. . . . 32,216 1981–1982 buyers . . . 12,245 1976–1980 buyers. . . .

Gurney. . . . An old (1866) family-run seed and nursery catalogue which includes a surprise "thank you" gift to each mail order buyer. Gurney sells to small town rural customers in their 50s, who have larger than average gardens. 92% are homeowners and most live in the Northern U.S. Average order: $20. . . . Continuations with merchandise, political fundraisers, charity and publication offers. 925,000 projected spring 1983 buyers. . . .

White Flower Farm. . . . Buyers on this list have either paid a $5 catalogue fee or made an average purchase of $50. . . . 55,986 last 12 months buyers. . . .

Earl May Seed and Nursery. . . . 64-year-old seed catalogue. . . . Customers paid an average of $13 through direct mail. . . . 180,000 1981–1982 buyers. . . .

Spring Hill. . . . A mail order garden center and nursery since 1849. . . . Average sale: $31. . . . 550,000 last 12 months' mail order buyers. . . .

Burgess. . . . Average sale from these home gardeners: $20. . . . 750,000 projected 1983 buyers. . . .

Harvest Nursery. . . . Catalogue of plants, trees, seeds, fruits and accessories has an average sale of $18.50. All customers have responded by mail to space ads and catalogue offers. 255,000 1982 1st–3rd quarter buyers . . . 63,000 1982 4th quarter hotline. . . .

Joseph Harris Seed Co. . . . This flower and vegetable seed catalogue started in 1879. Today, the average buyer is a homeowner who spends $16.75. . . . 138,801 1981–1982 mail order buyers. . . .

Van Bourgondien Brothers. . . . Specializing in Dutch and domestically grown bulbs and perennials. Average order is $35. . . . 125,000 fall/ spring 1982 buyers. . . .

Roto Crop. . . . Buyers of home garden compost bins and shredders who spend an average of $60. Sales generated through space ads in gardening magazines and some direct mail. 53,247 1976–1982 buyers. . . .

De Jager Bulbs. . . . Buyers of bulbs of every kind with an average $40 sale. . . . 33,015 1979–1982 mail order buyers. . . .

Herbst Brothers. . . . Space ads in family magazines generated names of amateur gardeners who buy seeds from the Herbst catalogue. . . . The average sale for this company, founded in 1876, is $20–$25. . . . 26,096 last 12 months' buyers. . . .

Lakeland Nurseries. . . . This nursery specializes in novelty gardening items. 100% direct mail generated suburban and rural buyers who pay an average of $23. . . . 664,189 1981–1982 mail order buyers . . . 284,787 1982 mail order buyers. . . .

R.H. Shumway. . . . Primarily a seed catalogue. Customers are 100% direct mail generated, purchasing an average of $27 worth of seeds, bulbs and gardening accessories. . . . 36,729 1982 buyers. . . .

Brittingham Plant. . . . This 38-year-old farm specializes in strawberries and small fruit plants. In 1977, they established a mail order catalogue for the serious gardener. Average sale: $15. . . . 17,941 1982 buyers & catalogue requests. . . .

Bountiful Ridge. . . . This berry and fruit and nut tree catalogue mails out once a year in November. . . . 160,000 1979–1982 buyers. . . .

Breck's. . . . Specializes in Dutch bulbs. . . . Average sale: $32. . . . 650,000 12 months' mail order buyers. . . .

Grace's Gardens. . . . This catalogue is billed as the "world's most unusual seed catalogue." . . . 40,000 1981 buyers/inquirers. . . .

Vaughan-Jacklin. . . . A 104-year old company selling bulbs, plants, roses, vegetable seeds and supplies. . . . Average sale: $2 to $20. . . . 98,226 1982 buyers. . . .

Encore House Nursery. . . . Respondents to space ads selling house plants, small fruit plants, vegetables, cactus and trees. Average sale: $10.50. . . . 384,000 1982 1st–3rd quarter buyers . . . 129,000 1982 4th quarter buyers. . . .

3

The Professional Method of Finding Products

Types of Mail-Order Marketing / "The Method":
Take Off Your Thinking Cap / Theory behind
"The Method" / Why This Unlikely Business
Principle Holds True / Step by Step—How to
Find and Evaluate Successful Products /
Developing Markets: How to Make a Slow Horse
Run Fast

The most crucial chapters in the book for you are Chapters 3, 4, and 5. Read them through several times. Be sure you are familiar with everything that is in them.

Everyone who has ever dreamed the American dream wants a nice, cozy mail-order business for his or her own. Preferably you'd like a mail-order business you can run with your left hand, from your hammock, and between fishing trips.

The sad truth is that if you ever do find a dream product that sells like hotcakes, at a fantastic profit, the dream won't last much longer than it takes you to quit your steady job and get used to easy living. Competition will pour in so fast, squeezing your profit margins, that you'll be half drowned before you know it.

But the sad truth can also be your key to success in mail order. That's what this chapter is all about.

Now I'll say for the first time something that will be repeated many more times in the book in order to improve the chances that you'll come to believe it: For most people, the best bet is a specialty catalog business. And perhaps the best opportunities within this category lie in selling goods to businesses rather than to consumers.

Types of Mail-Order Marketing

Before you go looking for a mail-order product, you had better decide which general type of operation you are interested in. The important types are one-shot items (don't try it because few succeed); correspondence courses; specialized catalogs of repeatedly bought items (a good bet); the general catalog business, especially gifts (enticing, but a money-losing trap for beginners); commercial and industrial products (my most frequent recommendation to people); and mail order through agents (particularly big in Great Britain). More about each type now follows.

One-Shot Items

This is everyone's idea of the mail-order business. You advertise in magazines or by direct mail, and you either sell enough of the advertised product right from the ad to make a profit, or you lose money (Figure 3-1).

The advantage of a one-shot product is, first, that you know *immediately* whether you succeed or fail. You don't pour money into a business for a year before finding out it won't work. The one-shot product also gives you back your investment in the shortest possible time. This means that one-shot items have the greatest get-rich-quick potential.

But one-shot items are also the toughest, most competitive business in all the world. It is easy for *you* to get into business, and it is just as easy for your imitators, who will jump in just as soon as they detect you are making a pile—a fact that is hard to conceal in mail order.

As Paul Bringe says:[1]

> If you are in a business where every new customer brings an immediate profit *you are in a dangerous business.* The fast buck boys will be swarming in on you soon. There are few who have the courage to invest in future customers—and that's just what makes such an investment a wide open opportunity for the man who looks ahead.

HOW TO GET RICH
THE LAZY MAN'S WAY

I used to work hard. The 18-hour days. The 7-day weeks.

But I didn't start making big money until I did less—a lot less.

For example, this ad took about 2 hours to write. With a little luck, it should earn me 50, maybe a hundred thousand dollars.

What's more, I'm going to ask you to send me 10 dollars for something that'll cost me no more than 50 cents. And I'll try to make it so irresistible that you'd be a darned fool not to do it.

After all, why should you care if I make $9.50 profit if I can show you how to make a lot more?

What if I'm so sure that you *will* make money my Lazy Man's Way that I'll make you a most unusual guarantee?

And here it is: I won't even cash your check or money order for 31 days *after* I've sent you my material.

That'll give you plenty of time to get it, look it over, try it out.

If you don't agree that it's worth at *least* a hundred times what you invested, send it back. Your *uncashed* check or money order will be put in the return mail.

The only reason I won't send it to you and bill you or send it C.O.D. is because both these methods involve time and money.

And I'm already going to give you the biggest bargain of your life.

Because I'm going to tell you what it took me 11 years to perfect: How to make money the Lazy Man's Way.

O.K.—now I have to brag a little. I don't mind it. And it's necessary—to prove that sending me the 10 dollars . . . which I'll keep "in escrow" until you're satisfied . . . is the smartest thing you ever did.

I live in a home that's worth $250,000. I know it is, because I turned down an offer for that much. My mortgage is less than half that, and the only reason I haven't paid it off is because my Tax Accountant says I'd be an idiot.

My "office", about a mile and a half from my home, is right on the beach. My view is so breathtaking that most people comment that they don't see how I get any work done. But I do enough. About 6 hours a day, 8 or 9 months a year.

The rest of the time we spend at our mountain "cabin." I paid $30,000 for it—cash.

I have 2 boats and a Cadillac. All paid for.

We have stocks, bonds, investments, cash in the bank. But the most important thing I have is priceless: time with my family.

And I'll show you just how I did it—the Lazy Man's Way—a secret that I've shared with just a few friends 'til now.

It doesn't require "education." I'm a high school graduate.

It doesn't require "capital." When I started out, I was so deep in debt that a lawyer friend advised bankruptcy as the only way out. He was wrong. We paid off our debts and, outside of the mortgage, don't owe a cent to any man.

It doesn't require "luck." I've had more than my share, but I'm not promising you that you'll make as much money as I have. And you may do better; I personally know one man who used these principles, worked hard, and made 11 million dollars in 8 years. But money isn't everything.

It doesn't require "talent." Just enough brains to know what to look for. And I'll tell you that.

It doesn't require "youth." One woman I worked with is over 70. She's travelled the world over, making all the money she needs, doing only what I taught her.

It doesn't require "experience." A widow in Chicago has been averaging $25,000 a year for the past 5 years, using my methods.

What *does* it require? Belief. Enough to take a chance. Enough to absorb what I'll send you. Enough to put the principles into *action*. If you do just that—nothing more, nothing less—the results *will* be hard to believe. Remember—I guarantee it.

You don't have to give up your job. But you may soon be making so much money that you'll be able to. Once again—I guarantee it.

The wisest man I ever knew told me something I never forgot: "Most people are too busy earning a living to make any money."

Don't take as long as I did to find out he was right.

Here are some comments from other people. I'm sure that, like you, they didn't believe me either. Guess they figured that, since I wasn't going to deposit their check for 31 days, they had nothing to lose.

They were right. *And here's what they gained:*

$260,000 in eleven months
"Two years ago, I mailed you ten dollars in sheer desperation for a better life . . . One year ago, just out of the blue sky, a man called and offered me a partnership . . . I grossed over $260,000 cash business in eleven months. You are a God sent miracle to me."

B. F., Pascagoula, Miss.

Made $16,901.92 first time out
"The third day I applied myself totally to what you had shown me. I made $16,901.92. That's great results for my first time out."

J. J. M., Watertown, N.Y.

'I'm a half-millionaire'
"Thanks to your method, I'm a half-millionaire . . . would you believe last year at this time I was a slave working for peanuts?"

G. C., Toronto, Canada

$7,000 in five days
"Last Monday what I learned on page 83 to make $7,000. It took me all week to do it, but that's not bad for five day's work."

M. D., Topeka, Kansas

Can't believe success
"I can't believe how successful I have become . . . telephone order taker for a fastener company in Chicago, Illinois. I was driving a beat-up 1959 Rambler and had about

"*. . . I didn't have a job and I was worse than broke. I owed more than $50,000 and my only assets were my wife and 8 children. We were renting an old house in a decaying neighborhood, driving a 5-year old car that was falling apart, and had maybe a couple of hundred dollars in the bank.*

Within one month, after using the principles of the Lazy Man's Way to Riches, things started to change — to put it mildly.
- *We worked out a plan we could afford to pay off our debts — and stopped our creditors from hounding us.*
- *We were driving a brand-new Thunderbird that a car dealer had given to us!*
- *Our bank account had multiplied tenfold!*
- *All within the first 30 days!*

And today . . .
- *I live in a home that's worth over $250,000.*
- *I own my "office". It's about a mile and a half from my home and is right on the beach.*
- *I own a lakefront "cabin" in Washington. (That's where we spend the whole summer — loafing, fishing, swimming and sailing.)*
- *I own two oceanfront condominiums. One is on a sunny beach in Mexico and one is snuggled right on the best beach of the best island in Hawaii.*
- *I have two boats and a Cadillac. All paid for.*
- *I have a net worth of over a Million Dollars. But I still don't have a job . . ."*

$600 in my savings account. Today, I am the outside salesman for the same fastener company. I'm driving a company car . . . I am sitting in my own office and have about $3,000 in my savings account."

G. M., Des Plaines, Ill.

I know you're skeptical. After all, what I'm saying is probably contrary to what you've heard from your friends, your family, your teachers and maybe everyone else you know. I can only ask you one question.

How many of them are millionaires?

So it's up to you:

A month from today, you can be nothing more than 30 days older — or you can be on your way to getting rich. You decide.

Sworn Statement:
"On the basis of my professional relationship as his accountant, I certify that Mr. Karbo's net worth is more than one million dollars."

Stuart A. Cogan

Bank Reference:
Home Bank
17010 Magnolia Avenue
Fountain Valley, California 92708

Joe Karbo

Joe, you may be full of beans, but what have I got to lose? Send me the Lazy Man's Way to Riches. But don't deposit my check or money order for 31 days after it's in the mail.

If I return your material — for *any* reason — within that time, return my *uncashed* check or money order to me. On that basis, here's my ten dollars.

Name _____

Address _____

City _____

State _____ Zip _____

© 1978 Joe Karbo

Figure 3-1 Rare examples of successful one-shot products—don't try it.

Figure 3-1 (Continued)

Not only do successful one-shot items draw direct competition, but they also get indirect competition. The catalog houses like Spencer Gifts, Sunset House, and Walter Drake leap on any inexpensive novelty sold through mail-order advertising, and they insert the item into their catalogs. The cost of selling a single item through a catalog is considerably less than one-shot selling costs, and therefore you can't stand catalog competition for long. Furthermore, catalog merchants can saturate a market.

You never really build a *business* when you sell one-shot items. You do not have a loyal clientele of people who come back and back just as long as you are in business. The one-shot merchant's business dies 3 months after the last ad is run.

There are two types of one-shot items: (1) explosive fads that sell furiously in full-page ads till the market is saturated and (2) one-shot staples. The staples never have a big enough market to make big ads pay off, but some of them go on and on, year after year, in 1-, 2-, and 3-inch ads.

What is generally true of one-shot items is especially true of the explosive fads. If you really are looking for a quick million, that's where to cast your eye. But beware the fantastic odds even if you are a thoroughly experienced mail-order person. Note also that even if you hold a patent on an item, there isn't one product in 10 years that will support a whole mail-order business. It takes many items to do that. The one-shot dealer is constantly discarding old products.

And yet—there are one-shot success stories. Ed Stern got interested in prescription drugs when a member of his family suffered from some side effects of a drug. He tried to find a book for consumers on the subject, and when he couldn't, he wrote one himself: *Prescription Drugs and Their Side Effects.* He sold more than 70,000 through mail-order ads in TV Guide (his first test medium), *Redbook, Parade,* and other magazines and newspapers. He also sold about that many in stores.[2] But, Stern is director of mail-order sales for Grosset and Dunlap, who published the book for him. And the book is not strictly a one-shot deal, because Grosset includes package inserts with Stern's book that sell another medical book, which increases the total take-in.

Correspondence Courses and Other High-Priced Inquiry-and-Follow-up Propositions

Correspondence courses are like one-shot items in this respect: You expect to make only a single sale to the customer. But correspondence courses are different from inexpensive one-shot products in most other respects.

Correspondence courses and other high-priced merchandise are never sold directly from display advertisements, and they seldom are sold from a cold-canvass direct-mail piece. Instead, they are sold by a series of letters sent to people who have been induced to inquire for more information by display ads.

Furthermore, correspondence courses cannot usually be bought wholesale by you. They require careful and expensive preparation by the firm that sells them by mail. Other high-priced merchandise also usually requires more work to obtain supplies than does low-priced merchandise.

For these reasons, it is not quite so easy to put this type of merchandise on the market. And therefore the successful operator won't be swamped so quickly with imitating competitiors, and profits are sheltered for a while.

Specialty Catalog and Other Repeat-Order Businesses

Most mail-order businesses that are successful for a long time sell a line of specialty products that the customer buys again and again: cigars, uniforms, office supplies, etc. (see Figures 3-2 and 3-4.) Almost always, they "lose money" on the first order from the ad, but they make their profit on the second or tenth sale to the customer.

The strength *and* the weakness of a repeat-line mail-order business is that it requires more capital and more courage to get started. It takes more time and money before you can tell whether or not you're going to make a success. You can't cut your losses as quickly in a repeat-line business as you can with one-shot items.

But because you must risk more to get into business, you have greater protection from competition once you're established. It is just as tough for *them* to get in. Furthermore, your customers are an ever-growing asset that your competition can't reach. The customers are your business, and no one can ever take that away from you as long as you serve their needs well.

Repeat-line businesses are also more profitable, I believe, if operated carefully and sensibly. A rule of thumb is that the harder and more costly it is to break into a line of business in which some firms are operating profitably, the higher the profits will be once you have broken in.

Figure 3-2 Examples of successful repeat-order businesses.

Figure 3-3 More examples of successful repeat-order businesses.

Figure 3-4 Some other successful businesses.

A catalog is almost always part of a repeat-purchase business. But the catalog need not be large or elaborate at first; it can start small and plain and go from there, as discussed in Chapter 24.

Repeat-purchase businesses usually obtain their first orders from a customer at a "loss"—that is, the sale by itself does not cover the expense of advertising and goods. But you make up the "loss" on subsequent sales. It takes patience to wait for the later sales to make up for the initial loss, but you must think of this as a necessary process of investment.

Best of all is what Joffe calls a "self-liquidator," an item that will continue to bring in new customers and yet pay for itself immediately. Joffe tells us that Mack the Knife has been a successful self-liquidator for his firm (Henniker's), which he follows up with his specialty-and-gift catalog.[3] And I'd guess that the "Tidi-File" in Figure 3-5 is a self-liquidator for Frank Eastern Company, which sells a full line of office supplies.

Within the category of specialty repeat-order businesses, I recommend that you pay special attention to businesses that sell to other businesses and to institutions. An example is the line of products sold to shop courses in high school, a catalog page of which is shown in Figure 3-6. The reason is that these mail-order businesses tend to be less skillful at present, because the field is newer, and therefore the competition is less severe.

The General Catalog Business

This section is about Sears, Roebuck, of course, and also the novelty catalog people like Spencer Gifts, Sunset House, Brookstone, and several others.

Forget this type of business. At least for now. That's my best advice for all newcomers to mail order.

Mail Order through Agents

Many firms that employ house-to-house canvassers as their sales force recruit these agents exclusively through mail-order ads in magazines and newspapers together with follow-up mailings to those who inquire. Firms selling Christmas cards, cosmetics, fire extinguishers, and shoes are good examples. The agents and the firm never meet in person. All business between them is done by mail.

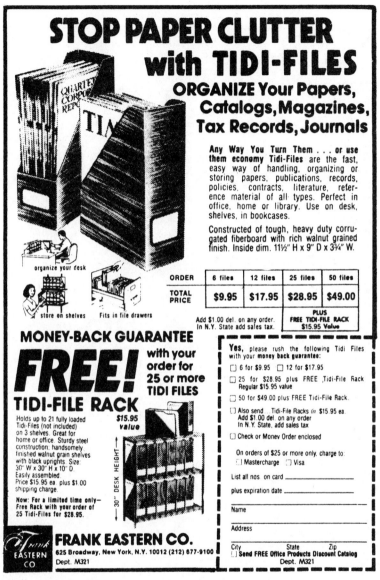

Figure 3–5 A self-liquidation advertisment in The Wall Street Journal.

You are not likely to tackle this aspect of mail order unless—through other outlets—you already sell a product that is adaptable for this type of mail-order operation. And that's another long story that we won't tell here.

PEGS

Country Peg

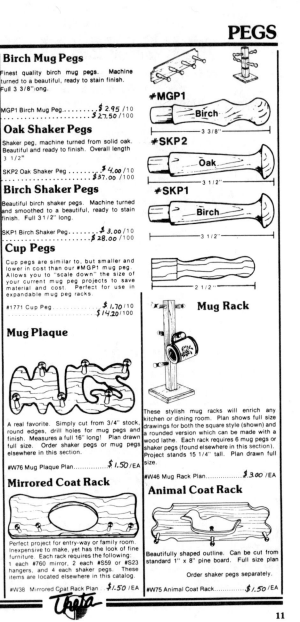

—3 3/8"—

Our new peg is designed for use in country coat racks as well as for all other coat peg applications. Features 2 piece construction to reduce cost plus allows you the flexability of substituting your own 1/2" dowel for special projects where a longer peg might be needed. Peg ball and shank sold as a set, but comes unassembled. Simply glue ball to shank.

#1770 Country Peg .... $.16/EA
.... $13.00/100
.... $113.50/1000

Owl Coat Hanger

A cute little owl shaped project to use for a coat, hat or even necktie rack. Measures 10" high. Order moving eyes and shaker pegs elsewhere in catalog. Plan drawn full size.

#W39 Owl Coat Hanger Plan........$1.50/EA

Jiggle Eyes

Plastic "jiggle" type eyes can be used on an assortment of projects. Sold in packages of 100 eyes. Available in 4 sizes.

#88060 6mm 1/4" Jiggle Eyes ... $1.40/100
#88010 10mm 3/8" Jiggle Eyes . $1.70/100
#88120 12mm 1/2" Jiggle Eyes $2.00/100
#88020 20mm 4/5" Jiggle Eyes .$4.10/100

Mirrors

Very high quality mirrors for use in our #W20 mirror planter plan, #W2l mirror sconce plan, and #W38 mirrored coat rack plan.

#776 2 1/4" x 9" Mirror $1.50/EA
#763 5 1/2" x 12" Mirror $2.50/EA
#760 7 1/2" x 12" Mirror $3.00/EA

Birch Mug Pegs

Finest quality birch mug pegs. Machine turned to a beautiful, ready to stain finish. Full 3 3/8" long.

MGP1 Birch Mug Peg.........$2.95/10
.... $27.50/100

Oak Shaker Pegs

Shaker peg, machine turned from solid oak. Beautiful and ready to finish. Overall length 3 1/2"

SKP2 Oak Shaker Peg $4.00/10
....................$37.00/100

Birch Shaker Pegs

Beautiful birch shaker pegs. Machine turned and smoothed to a beautiful, ready to stain finish. Full 3 1/2" long.

SKP1 Birch Shaker Peg.......$3.00/10
.... $28.00/100

Cup Pegs

Cup pegs are similar to, but smaller and lower in cost than our #MGP1 mug peg. Allows you to "scale down" the size of your current mug peg projects to save material and cost. Perfect for use in expandable mug peg racks.

#1771 Cup Peg............. $1.70/10
.... $14.20/100

Mug Plaque

A real favorite. Simply cut from 3/4" stock, round edges, drill holes for mug pegs and finish. Measures a full 16" long! Plan drawn full size. Order shaker pegs or mug pegs elsewhere in this section.

#W76 Mug Plaque Plan................$1.50/EA

Mirrored Coat Rack

Perfect project for entry-way or family room. Inexpensive to make, yet has the look of fine furniture. Each rack requires the following:
1 each #760 mirror, 2 each #S59 or #S23 hangers, and 4 each shaker pegs. These items are located elsewhere in this catalog.

#W38 Mirrored Coat Rack Plan .$1.50/EA

#MGP1 Birch —3 3/8"—

#SKP2 Oak —3 1/2"—

#SKP1 Birch —3 1/2"—

—2 1/2"—

Mug Rack

These stylish mug racks will enrich any kitchen or dining room. Plan shows full size drawings for both the square style (shown) and a rounded version which can be made with a wood lathe. Each rack requires 6 mug pegs or shaker pegs (found elsewhere in this section). Project stands 15 1/4" tall. Plan drawn full size.

#W46 Mug Rack Plan................$3.00/EA

Animal Coat Rack

Beautifully shaped outline. Can be cut from standard 1" x 8" pine board. Full size plan

Order shaker pegs separately.

#W75 Animal Coat Rack..............$1.50/EA

11

Figure 3-6 Page of products sold to high schools for shop courses.

Commercial and Industrial Products

Some commercial products are sold by firms that sell only by mail. Office supplies are an example. But a good deal of mail-order sales of commercial and industrial products is handled by manufacturers or wholesalers who also sell through a sales force.

One-Shot Items Will Be Our Examples

Throughout the book we shall talk mostly about one-shot items, but only because they make the clearest examples and demonstrations of mail-order techniques. *Everything* that applies to finding a good one-shot item applies to repeat lines and other aspects of mail order. And I *strongly advise* that you not try to build a business that is based on one-shot, sold-from-the-ad products.

"The Method": Take Off Your Thinking Cap

Proof First. Before telling you what 'The Method' is, I'll try to prove it to you with real examples. And I'll try to ram the lesson home by making you work through the experience.

Below and on the following pages you will find classified ads A, B, C, and D and display advertisements E and F. Each advertisement is for a different product. Your problem is to decide (1) whether D or E brought in more dollars and (2) which two of the four classified ads did best.

All the ads were written by the same copywriter, so you need not concern yourself with the *quality* of the ads. D and E appeared in the same issue of the *National Enquirer,* and the ad that did better had by far the worse position on the page. A, B, C, and F all appeared in *Popular Science* classified. The classifications they ran under were not the crucial factor. This experiment took place several years ago, but the principles have not changed.

Advertisement A

"MAKE YOUR OWN WILL." Forms. Instruction Booklet $1. (Guaranteed!)

Advertisement B

HARMONICAS. Excellent imported chromatic harmonica now only $3.95. Satisfaction guaranteed. Catalog free.

Advertisement C

"HOMEBREWING . . BEERS . . WINES!" Instruction Manual $1. (Guaranteed!)

Advertisement D

"SECRETS of Poker and Dice." Tested book teaches winning in honest games. Odds. $1. (Guaranteed!)

Advertisement E

**$2.98 CONTRAPTION
SQUELCHES SOUND
OF TV COMMERCIALS**

Mad at loud, nasty TV commercials? Now with AD-SQUELCH you can shut up those advertisers that annoy you.

AD-SQUELCH is a brand-new contraption that allows you to shut off, & turn on, TV sound right from your chair. The picture stays on. Works with any TV set made in U.S. Hangs out of sight when not in use.

To install AD-SQUELCH on your set, first open the back with All-model screwdriver included in kit. Then make two connections that a 7-year-old child can do in 3 minutes. That's all!

Complete AD-SQUELCH contains everything necessary to equip your set, plus simple, step-by-step, illustrated directions.

Lean back & enjoy your TV without extra-loud, unpleasant commercials. Send $2.98 to-day to XXXXXXX.....................AD-SQUELCH mailed postpaid same day order received. Complete Satisfaction Guaranteed or Money Refunded.

Tear Out and Mail To-day

Advertisement F

Made your decisions? These are the answers:

F outpulled E by a ratio of 15 to 1. E was one of the most complete fiascos of all time, while F was a success. (Actually, the paper's typographer set up F in a terrible format. The ad did well *despite* the bad typography.)

A and C were profitable ads. B and D would have to have pulled 3 to 4 times as much as they did to become really profitable.

Unless you know the mail-order business, it is unlikely that you picked the winners. But experienced mail-order operators would probably have got them all right—*without thinking hard, and without guessing.* They would know for sure.

The mail-order operators' secret is this: They would recognize that F, A, and C offer products that have been, and are now, sold successfully by mail. They know that they are sold successfully because they have seen ads for them repeated again and again over long periods of time. But the E, B, and D products are not now being offered repeatedly by anyone.

The principle of the theory is: *Do what is being done successfully.*

The first corollary of that principle is: *Never innovate, never offer really new products.* It's as simple as that.

The second corollary is: *Offer your product in a similar manner and in exactly the same media as the innovator,* at least until you know the situation intimately. At that time you may test new copy against the old, and you can use additional media to *add* to your schedule.

The words of authority never *prove* anything. But the words of a man who has demonstrated success can be very persuasive. So I quote John D. Rockefeller: "When you hear of a good thing—something already working for the other fellow—don't delay but get in while you can."

Theory behind "The Method"

The artist in you that thrills to novelty, boldness of thought, and "creativity" will point to the good new ideas that have made people rich. The examples you will give are true and well known. But the number of people who have sunk big chunks of their lives into schemes that failed badly is not known. And the failures vastly outnumber the successes. Few of us can afford the time that it takes before rare success turns up for us. (Don't forget that each person who backs a losing scheme is always quite sure he or she has a winner. But, of course, the losers are not as smart as you are!)

It may be true that the total *amount* made by winners exceeds the *amount* lost by losing schemes. This would explain why large corporations can afford to try many new schemes. But only large corporations have the time and money resources to wait through a great many tries until a winner appears.

My personal experience should help prove what I have said. This is the story of how I learned this secret.

Before I went into mail order, I had a fine college education, service in the Navy as an officer, plus experience working in one of New York's top advertising agencies selling by direct mail and in the advertising promotion department of a huge Madison Avenue publishing house. I had received the degree of Doctor of Philosophy in Business Economics. Furthermore, I had been an advertising consultant to, among other firms, one of the biggest department store chains in the United States.

Then I decided to go into the mail-order business for myself. I read every available book but found little to help me. I talked with everyone I could find, some of the most learned and most successful people in the country. I asked each one of them what I should sell.

Finally, I had a list of four major product lines to try. And I went full steam ahead!

Sounds as if I was perfectly prepared, doesn't it? Maybe you can guess what happened—a complete *bust!*

One after the other, the products proved unsuitable for mail order. I hadn't lost much money. (I didn't have much to start with.) But I was bewildered and discouraged. Where should I go from here?

But I knew that *some* operators had the knack of finding successful products. So I went back and studied the operations of the most successful mail-order dealers. I studied them, and studied them, and studied them until . . . *finally I knew.* I had found out what the top money-making mail order—many of whom *had never finished high school*—knew all along.

And it was so easy! How I regretted the time I had wasted. All my education and experience did me no good in learning the secret of "The Professional Method." In fact, even now I have trouble convincing professor friends of mine that the secret is real—that is, until I show them the *results.*

The Method turns off some people, those who get their kicks from being far-out and who want to live the artistic life. For them, innovation is of value for its own sake, as is often the case in art and science. But unlike (bad) art and science, the yardstick in business is not how new and different and esthetic the idea is, but rather how well the idea works and how much money it makes.

But this does not mean that the mail-order business does not provide an outlet for your creativity. When I was a child, one of my mentors annoyed me greatly by telling me to emulate this or that very diligent, well-behaved "good boy" who did all his homework and chores and was superrespectful to his elders and their words. One reason the mentor's advice bugged me was the use of the word "emulate," which I felt was just a fancy word for imitate or copy. When I checked the dictionary, I found that emulate means to *do something similar to but better than* the person or act being emulated. That didn't make me any happier with my mentor, but it does provide the perfect word for this section on The Method.

Your aim with The Method should not be to just *copy* what someone else is doing, but to grasp the central principle of a successful operation and to find better ways of putting that principle into operation—that is, to emulate the particular successful mail-order business you have your eye on. And out-and-out copying is not likely to be successful, as we shall see.

Why This Unlikely Business Principle Holds True

The *first* reason why the emulation principle works so well is that both the mail-order industry and business as a whole do a great deal of trial-and-error experimentation. Much of this experimentation is carried on by people highly qualified to do it. All this trial-and-error investigation makes it highly unlikely that a single innovation by a nonprofessional will find a wide and profitable market.

Your chances are better when the innovation requires specialized knowledge, such as that of a chemical engineer or of an airplane pilot or of a biologist. But anyone can dream up a new kind of can opener. The chances against your making a fortune with a new kitchen gadget are astronomical.

The *second* reason why emulation works is the outsider's lack of information. Newcomers to mail order don't know what has been tried and found to fail. They don't know what the market needs. And the newcomer doesn't have information with which to project the profit potential of a totally new product.

The *third* reason why emulation works—*especially* in the mail-order business—is that the first person to sell a product has very little advantage over those who follow. The pioneer has less advantage here than in almost any other line of business because it is so easy and cheap for mail-order competitors to duplicate the product and its advertising. The barriers to entry against competitors are low indeed. So the time advantage of the leader is only a matter of months. That's why the one-shot mail-order business is such a tough competitive field.

The *fourth* reason why the emulation principle works—also peculiar to mail order—is that a mail-order campaign is remarkably open to inspection by all who care to look. Reading all the likely magazines and checking the mail sent to major mailing lists will tell you much of what you need to know about a competitor's campaign. There is little in the way of trade secrets that the leaders can keep hidden. What was learned by the sweat of their brows and costly experimentation, you can learn free and at ease.

And *fifth*, the emulator even has an *advantage* over the leader. The leader had to bear the cost of testing until he or she found the most effective copy and the media that would pay out. You, the emulator, then follows as closely as is consistent with business ethics. You can explode into a great many media just as soon as you have tested your copy, and this means that you will reach peak volume much faster than the originator did.

It may be that the market is too small for both of you, though this is not true very often. Perhaps you have developed better copy or a better offer than the leader, and you are able to force him or her out. But if your test ads are well done and your results are only borderline, you'd better seek another product.

The only advantages the leader has over emulators are: (1) The leader has already developed tested copy and has information about the relative performance of the various media, and (2) the leader's development costs are "sunk," so that, in a true economic sense, cost for future operations will be less than that of followers. Like any other lower-cost producer, the leader can last longer in a struggle than can higher-cost producers.

Those are the reasons why the best mail-order product for you to market is a presently successful product. The same reasons also show that the media you should expect to use are exactly the media used by the leader. You will first use the media that the competition uses most heavily—in terms of space or frequency—because those are the media in which the leader's (and your) payout will be greatest.

In this chapter I have tried to be as blunt as I can be in saying: If you try to sell any *new* mail-order product or service—that is, a product or service that you don't know is now being sold successfully in mail order—the odds are very strongly against you. At the very same time, I can safely tell you that if you operate intelligently and efficiently you have an excellent chance of making good in selling whatever products and services successful mail-order firms are now selling. Even though I have tried to make this message crystal-clear in previous editions, I still get phone calls and letters from readers who say: "But you still haven't told us how to find a successful product." So maybe I better look for another way of explaining what's going on here.

Let's say that a friend of yours is thinking about opening a retail business. What kind of a store would you advise your friend to open? Or better, how would you advise your friend to go about finding out what kind of store to open? I think that you might look around your city, or in other towns, to see which kinds of retail stores seem to be doing well. You might look especially closely at those which have been growing particularly fast recently. You might then reason that since they are doing well, your friend might also do well in the same line. If your friend instead began to think up ideas for a new sort of retail store that is not now operating successfully—a rope store, say, or a store to sell old beer cans—I think that you might look skeptically on the venture and think that the odds of success are low. Of course, some new ventures that have never been seen before come to do well in each decade—yogurt stores and ice cream stores and sneaker stores in the last decade, for example. But for each such new success like those, there must be many that failed. The odds simply are much greater against such a totally new venture than in starting a store of the same sort that others now are operating successfully.

You might say, however, that in the retail business one has to have a lot of capital to get started, and that keeps out every Tom, Dick, and Harry who might want to do the same thing that others have done successfully, a barrier to entry which allows opportunity to be there. And you might say that the small capital requirement is the reason that you want to go into the mail-order business. The fact of the matter, however, is that there is a barrier to getting started in the mail-order business, too, though it perhaps is not as visible as the need for capital in opening a store and stocking it with inventory. As I have emphasized throughout the book, almost all successful mail-order businesses sell a line of *repeat* goods. Therefore you must invest in getting customers who will buy from you again and again, and that needs capital, just as for retail stores. Perhaps more important in the mail-order business, however, is the investment of time and thought that is needed to begin small and gradually learn and build on your mistakes. This may mean starting with a classified ad or two, or a small display ad somewhere, working part-time, and gradually building your personal skills and your tested advertising sales methods for the business. It is this requirement of go-slow patience and trial-and-error learning which keeps most people out of the mail-order business—or at least keeps them from operating successfully in the mail-order business. It is also this factor which keeps it from being so competitive that no one can make any money at all.

I hope that this explanation, by analogy to retail stores, makes clearer why I recommend to you that you look for opportunities among products and services where there is already evidence of successful mail-order activity.

A Big Difficulty of The Method

When you try to emulate a successful operation, you must be sure that you learn *all* the essential facts about the operation you are emulating—or you may find yourself in big trouble. Stone tells the story of how one copycat drowned.[4]

> Years ago, when I was a principal of National Research Bureau, we had a division which sold collection stickers to business men by mail. We

sold millions and millions of collection stickers. I bragged about this to a Texan once, and it wasn't six months later that he started a company to sell collection stickers by mail. He copied us "right off the page." In less than a year this Texan was hopelessly bankrupt.

There was just one thing I neglected to divulge when I was bragging to this Texan. I neglected to tell him *we lost money on every collection sticker order.* He didn't know we "bought" new customers in volume with our collection sticker offer so we could sell Christmas greeting letters to those same customers at a substantial profit.

As an individual you want to reap the profits yourself, and now. So follow The Method and leave the new concepts for others, or until later.

Step by Step—How to Find and Evaluate Successful Products

The first step to finding successful products is to get hold of a copy of *Standard Rate & Data,* "Consumer Magazine and Farm Publication" section, and write to every magazine listed in it with circulation over perhaps 100,000 in these classifications: Men's, Romance, Women's, Sports, Almanacs, Mechanics and Science, Motion Picture, Fraternal, Religious and Denominational, Exposure, Fishing and Hunting, Gardening, Newspaper-Distributed Magazines, Health, Home Service and Home, TV and Radio, Veterans, Business and Finance, plus every single farm magazine. There are other mail-order media, but these will do for a start. Give yourself a company name, and write to each magazine for a sample copy and a "rate card."

Look through each magazine you receive, and for each one make notes on an index card of the types of products sold in it. You should be learning that there are hundreds of magazines you have never seen in all your well-bred, high-thinking life. And those magazines of which you are not aware are probably the best mail-order media of all. They carry a tremendous proportion of the one-shot products we are using as our examples here. For goodness sake, do not limit yourself to the Home Service magazines. Much of the advertising they carry is amateurish and unsuccessful, and much more is of products and lines that are tough for a newcomer to sell successfully.

Keep your eye on the classified sections, too. There is much to be learned from classified.

Next, go to a back-date magazine shop, and buy 100 back copies of *Popular Science, Workbasket,* farm magazines, *House Beautiful,* and low-life men's and women's magazines—especially the latter. Not only are the "gray matter" low-life magazines important, but you can't find them in any library.

Now you should begin reading ads in earnest. Don't try to form conclusions. Just look and look and look at all kinds of mail-order ads. At first you will think there are 100,000 products on the market. But soon the various ads will become familiar. Then you will recognize the addresses of some companies offering several different products.

You are making progress when you recognize *most* of the ads you see. And you will have learned almost enough when you can recognize the layout styles of the important mail-order firms. By that time you will know that there are relatively few products and advertisers on the market and even fewer big and successful companies that have been around for several years.

Of course, the successful products are the ones that you recognize as appearing again and again over a period of years and in a great many magazines. The most successful among the successful are those that even run ads in the slow summer months.

(Why do once-successful products disappear? Some go off the market because the Federal Trade Commission or the Post Office Department finds them fraudulent or deceptive. Others, some full-page-ad products, may exhaust their fads after a while. Many do not really disappear, but reappear intermittently.)

Next, get acquainted with the direct-mail mail-order offers. Get a few friends to save all the direct mail they get. Write to every single free offer, or offer of information, that you come across in the magazines, especially in one full issue of *House Beautiful.* This means writing for *hundreds* of catalogs and offers. And try to find some products you want to buy or try by mail. Buy some things by mail that you wanted anyway. Don't be afraid to accept offers of a free trial or offers to refund your money if you're not satisfied. You'll get your money back, just as you'll give it back once you're in the mail-order business.

Important: Use a different set of first initials in the name you sign for each firm you write to, and keep a record of which initials went where and on which date you received it. Then record which offers you receive addressed to which initials, and the date. Your initial code will then teach you which lists are rented to whom, very important information later on. The card below is an edited example from our files.

G. H. Smith

Sent to
  Miles Kimball Company, Sep 1, 19—HOUSE BEAUTIFUL

Rented by:
  Publishers Clearing House, Jan 21
  American Home Magazine, Feb 12
  Saturday Evening Post, Mar 31
  Publishers Clearing House, July 18
  etc.

Study the direct-mail offers the same way you studied the magazines. Then, one way or another, get your hands on a copy of Standard Rate and Data Service, Inc.'s *Direct Mail List Rates and Data* (DMLRD). This wonderful publication is a gold mine of information for the person who wants to learn about the mail-order business, and it is indispensable for the mail-order operator who gets new orders from list solicitations. DMLRD is a compilation of data on a high proportion of the important lists. The lists that interest the person who wants to learn about mail order are the lists of mail-order *customers* of various firms. You can learn how many customers a firm has had, and the average unit of sale in dollars, which tells you a great deal about the firm. More about this publication later.

Getting your hands on a copy—even a back copy, which will be sufficient for the beginner's needs—can be tough unless you're prepared to fork out the $170 (1985) subscription price for the six bimonthly editions. Some big libraries have a copy. Or you can try to look at a copy belonging to a mail-order business or an advertising agency in your area. Maybe you can persuade your local library to buy it. So you'll have to scrounge. But try *somehow* to get your hands on a copy of DMLRD.

Study the lists being offered for rent, and the *size* of the lists. This will give you further information on the number of firms in any line, and the amount of business they do in the various products. These data will also be important later on when you wish to estimate the profit potential for various product lines.

All this time you should be watching the mail-order section of your Sunday newspaper, examining the magazines that come into your hands, and keeping a sharp ear for mail-order offers on the radio.

Appendix G in the back of the book contains a long sample list of successful mail-order lines.

Two Storied Exceptions

If you are not convinced by what I said about the humdrum emulation method being the best way to find successful products, here are the stories of a couple of exceptions that you can use to prove that I'm all wet. (But don't say I didn't warn you of disaster if you try to follow their examples.)

Al Sloan[5] is the fellow behind the famous Bell & Howell camera promotions. Way back in the 1930s, he began by developing an arrangement with jewelry stores by which he sold them circulars that had the store's merchandise on one side and Sloan's merchandise—boudoir chairs, comforters, and the like—on the other. And Sloan's merchandise was also offered as a premium—as a gift, or for $1— if the customer bought any of the jewelry store's merchandise from the circular. Sloan "syndicated" the offer across the country, and hence Sloan is known as the pioneer of this sort of deal. And he also worked up a deal that sold hundreds of thousands of sets of Wearever aluminum as premiums, using the same store-circular strategy.

The deal that made Sloan famous in the mail-order business was an extension of his syndication method—the sale of a $150 movie camera for Bell & Howell in coordination with gasoline companies and others who had large lists of customers with solid credit. Traditional mail-order people doubted that the deal would work because, until then, big-ticket consumer items had never been sold this way. But Sloan's deal pulled fantastically—selling $50 million worth in 2½ years—and enriched everyone connected with the deal.

Now Sloan has a new deal in the works, a centrifugal paint sprayer, which he is selling in conjunction with such major firms as Fingerhut's, World Book, and an oil company; it is reported doing well.

But—here's the other side of the coin. Disaster overtook even as experienced and talented an operator as Sloan. This was the report in the trade press in 1972:[6]

"The syndicators of merchandise programs have sustained impossible losses for mysterious reasons," Al Sloan of Whitney-Forbes, Inc. told this reporter last week in Chicago, during visit with Sloan in Michael Reese Hospital. Syndication pioneer said he has mounted 14 promotions in the last four years. Each tested carefully to oil company active and inactive charges. Based on tests, continuation to full lists indicate substantial profits. Instead, says Sloan, sustained loss of almost $2 million. Test projections considered timing (seasons), recession factors. Showed this reporter detailed results, by product promotion, by accounts. Continuation often halved test results. Most often because inactive portion of lists failed. Problem many sided. Sloan's system was to supply all up-front promotion money with commission to oil company. Not uncommon to risk million dollars based on the successful test.

Continuation brought losses due to insistence of clients to run inactive accounts, the major client interest and ahead of hefty commissions earned on a percentage of sales, whether effort was profitable or not. According to Sloan reactivated customers, secured through merchandise mailings, worth better than $400 per year in gas, oil and tires to oil companies. Thus no risk mailing syndicator's offer even to bad list. Other side of problem: unused merchandise committed and made based on test and unexpected continuation results. Mistakes in box car figures, tens of thousands of unsold units."

Joe Sugarman is another such story and—relax—Sugarman's story has strictly an upbeat ending as of this date. Here are excerpts from a front-page *Wall Street Journal*[7] article on Sugarman:

Back in 1971, when electronic pocket calculators were still primitive and costly, an advertising man named Joseph Sugarman figured he could make a pile of money selling the little gadgets through the mails.

Mr. Sugarman raised $12,000 with the help of friends, persuaded Craig Corp. to let him market its calculator, and mailed out 50,000 fliers extolling the new product. "I lost my shirt," he recalls. But then the manufacturer dropped the price to $180 from $240. Mr. Sugarman wrote a new ad, mailed it to a million peiple and hit the jackpot.

"I made $20,000 in 10 days," he says, and by the end of 1972, he had done "a half-million dollars in volume, grossed $100,000 and netted $50,000." As sales took off, giant retailers such as Sears, Roebuck and Montgomery Ward took an interest in the Craig calculator, and they, too, began selling it.

In the seven years since then, the 40-year-old Mr. Sugarman has done his mail-order number on dozens of other electronic gadgets, ranging from burglar alarms and home pinball machines to remote-control model speedboats. In every case, his methods have remained the same: pick an emerging product, plug it with ads in general magazines and special brochures, and distribute it through the mail. His company, JS&A National Sales Group, once occupied his basement but now employs 50 people in modern offices. The company's annual sales are approaching $50 million, and its profits provide Mr. Sugarman with an enormous mansion and a matching ego. . . .

"I like gadgets," Mr. Sugarman says. He is a connoisseur of gadgets who carefully selects for his largely upper-income, male clientele an array of toys that look nifty and do nifty things. "Maybe you're just looking at a guy who has good taste," he says in explanation of his knack for picking winners.

Mr. Sugarman scrutinizes a product's styling, which can make or break it on the marketplace. One reason he agreed to sell a $150 Japanese-made "jogging computer" this year was its "space-age styling" and "digital read-out," he says. The machine consists of a platform on which the jogger runs in place and a sleek console that measures the pace and "distance" of the jog and prints the results on a lighted screen.

But Mr. Sugarman has more than any eye for styling. One of his merchandising tricks is to infuse a product with a timely marketing angle. "Someone offered me a small walkie-talkie in the middle of the CB craze," he recalls. "Instead of using the walkie-talkie idea, I focused on the mini-CB angle" and called the product the "Pocket Com." In the three years since he introduced it, Mr. Sugarman has sold 250,000 Pocket Coms. . . .

Not all of Mr. Sugarman's efforts succeed, however. He got caught with a $1,500 laser-beam mousetrap, brought to market in April 1977. The gadget detected the presence of a mouse with a laser beam, which activated a spring-loaded wire trap. The device was mounted on a polished walnut base that could be "handsomely displayed in any office, board-room, or rodent-infested area," Mr. Sugarman said in his ad. Unfor-tunately, he didn't sell a single one. Mr. Sugarman said he was trying to test the adage that "if you build a better mousetrap, the world will beat a path to your door." Not always, apparently.

Financially speaking, Mr. Sugarman's biggest flop was a $250,000 loss he sustained in 1975 on a "checkbook with a brain," a $40 electronic device that recorded savings deposits, checking balances and the like. Mr. Sugarman has concluded that people would rather write such in-formation in their checkbooks by hand.

Another noteworthy flop was "Mickey Math," a Mickey Mouse cal-culator. "I thought I had the next 'pet rock,' " Mr. Sugarman says. He now believes that the product flopped because a calculator "is a pretty serious product. People don't buy it for a joke."

Developing Markets: How to Make a Slow Horse Run Fast

You *may* be able to increase the size of the market and force the volume of a product much higher than your competitors have managed to do. In this section we shall discuss ways of developing proven products. But heed this warning: Do *not* count on expansion potential when you estimate the size of a product's market unless you are already a highly skilled mail-order operator. These are some ways you can develop or increase the size of a market:

1. *Advertise classified products in display advertising.* Some firms that advertise in classified have insufficient skill, initiative, or capital to push out into display, and an enterprising firm can take advantage of this. For example, coin catalogs have been successfully sold in

classified for years. Then a big operator began to sell coin catalogs in full-page ads in dozens of magazines, spending hundreds of thousands of dollars in advertising.

But—many of the firms that use classifieds are wise birds that *also* use display or that have found out from hard experience that display advertising won't work for their purposes.

2. *Another way to increase a market is by personalizing items with the customer's monogram or initials.* This is actually a special case of increasing a market by improving the desirability of the product offer. But be careful—personalizing can be costly.

3. *Search through old magazines (10 to 40 years old) for products that were once sold successfully but that outlived their fads.* Sometimes you can bring these products back to life. But sometimes their market has died with them because times have changed and Americans no longer are interested in the product.

4. *Find successful mail-order products in English magazines and transplant the ideas to this country.* Again, be careful: the British and Americans are very different in many ways.

5. *Sell a product similar to existing products.* If one outfit successfully sells a franchised business to clean rugs, for example, you might consider selling a franchised business to clean walls.

6. *Upgrade a successful book or short correspondence course.* The "Little Blue Books" of Emanuel Haldeman-Julius represent a gold mine of tested mail-order material. The subject matter of many of the books he originally sold for 5 cents can be amplified and upgraded into full-scale mail-order successes. (But be sure not to copy his material!) Read Haldeman-Julius's book, *The First Hundred Million*,[8] the best book ever written on the technique of choosing and selling books by mail order, if you can lay your hands on a copy (it is out of print).

4

More about Finding Products to Sell

Follow Your Hobbies into Mail Order / From Stores to Mail Order / If You Are Already in the Mail-Order Business / Buying a Business

Chapter 3 discussed how to find products if you are starting from scratch. In this chapter we'll talk about how to exploit some special advantages you may have—hobbies, a retail business, connections with others who have products to sell, and so on.

Follow Your Hobbies into Mail Order

A path to mail-order success that many successful operators have used—even starting with nothing but the legendary kitchen table— is to capitalize on your knowledge of, and interest in, one of your hobbies. Let's consider some examples:

1. Pat Baird started Ships Wheel Inc. because she always loved the sea and boating. She had had a heart attack and needed an activity to keep her busy. Her first step was a single ad for four items in *Yachting.* At that time she did her paperwork on the kitchen table

and stored her inventory in the garage. Now her items fill an 80-page catalog, of which Ships Wheel sends out hundreds of thousands, or millions, or copies each year. Many of the items—drinking glasses for example—are personalized. A big success any way you look at it, out of Pat Baird's hobby interest.[1]

2. Jean Shramm had an aunt who ran a "doll hospital," and Mrs. Shramm got fond of the dolls. She and her husband had a real-estate office in Vermont, so she borrowed some dolls from the aunt and put them on display shelves in the office, withdrawing $500 from her savings account to finance the early stock. People bought the dolls. So she next decided to sell by mail order and borrowed $2,000 from the bank. Eventually the business grew so much that she sold it to a major corporation.[2]

3. Ewing Hunter had been a Ferrari auto buff for years. In 1973 he found it difficult to obtain the owner's manuals and parts manuals for a Ferrari he bought. So he decided to reproduce and sell manuals himself. He invested only enough for some brochures and $250 in postage. In 6 months he was grossing $1,000 per month. Five years later the firm was grossing perhaps $1 million annually, largely on parts sales. (An interesting feature of the business is that people pay $2 for the catalog.)

4. The following 1985 newspaper story is not untypical:

"If all we wanted to do is make money, we should have opened a liquor store," said Martin Paule, one of the three owners of Deva, a mail order clothing company in Burkittsville, Md., near Frederick.

Deva—which means angel in Sanskrit—is a most unusual mail order company by almost any standard. Its highest aim is not to make money—although it doesn't shun profits—but to bring serenity and peace to its customers and nearby communities, according to its owners.

Thus, the catalogue that Deva prints to promote its loose-fitting, free-spirited clothes is spiced with sayings of a philosophic nature. "Deva is a community of the heart," the catalogue says on one page. "We know that miles are no distance to the spirit. . . ."

"We think we're a little bit strange, but that's the beauty of being in business for yourself," Paule said. Paule founded Deva seven years ago with Nancy and John Coker. The three had been trying to establish a metaphysical bookstore in Los Angeles when John Coker's parents asked him to help with the family business in Frederick.

The three liked Frederick, though they quickly concluded it was not right for their bookstore. But by chance, the partners met a group of people recently returned from India with a batch of free-flowing, Indian-made clothes.

Through local sewing stores, Nancy Coker found women who were interested in sewing clothes at home, using Deva's patterns and pure cotton fabrics. Business began to take off, and the firm now has 13 full-time employees as well as the founders.

Initially, Deva sought customers through advertisements in such magazines as the Yoga Journal and the Vegetarian Times. But success at local craft fairs convinced company officials that there was a much broader market for their clothes, which include such items as draw-string "lotus" trousers, the "shepherdress," and the "kismet cloak." Now, the company advertises in mass-market publications, such as Smithsonian and Ms. magazines.

Today, Deva sells about $700,000 in clothing a year (some of it made by other manufacturers) and is earning a profit.[3]

From Stores to Mail Order

Few people who start in mail order from scratch would decide to sell airplanes or farms. But if you are already in one of those businesses, you may decide that you can increase your volume by mail-order selling.

Remember: We are *not* talking about ordinary direct mail that so many firms use to *help* them close deals. We're talking about mail-order deals in which the customer is first contacted with printed material, and in which the whole transaction takes place without face-to-face meeting.

Businesses that may not be practical to *begin* purely for a mail trade may be very profitable to expand by mail. The art-supplies business is a good example. You would require a stock of perhaps $100,000 to back up a mail-order business—expensive indeed. But if you are a large retail dealer in art supplies, you already bear the cost of the stock, and you do not need to charge any of that cost to the mail-order operation as you would if you sold by mail only.

Shoes, sporting goods, lamps, and rugs are other examples of the same principle—retail businesses which lend themselves to mail order. There is still another good reason why an established retailer or manufacturer may find it profitable to develop a mail-order operation. Mail-order advertising can stimulate the sale of goods through regular outlets, too. Book publishers often find that a mail-order campaign will increase sales of books in stores by between 100 and 400 percent. This means that in such a case the mail-order sales campaign can bring back mail-order sales at an apparent loss and still be profitable to the business as a whole.

In some cases retailers have shifted over completely from retail to mail order, as seen in this report.[4]

SHOES FOR HARD TO FIT WOMEN

Starting with retail stores in Greater Boston area, [Hill's] branched out into direct mail six years ago. The operation has been so successful there is a possibility that only one retail store will remain and all efforts will be concentrated on mail. With 120,000 mail customers now, the market can become much larger, since all sizes of shoes are carried, including regular sizes. Lawson Hill Jr., president, says he can carry 118 different sizes vs about 19 for a regular retail store. He stocks over 15,000 different pairs of shoes. Two major mailings are made each year to 1.5 million names each time. . . . Hill is an advocate of "scientific marketing" and describes the formulation of his catalog in these terms, using "eye flow" pages. His average sale is $22 and the average order is for 1½ pairs of shoes.

And traditional department stores have begun to participate in what many think is a "new marketing revolution," as these examples suggest:[5]

Neiman-Marcus, a Texas-based department store, has developed a mail-order operation that is highly personalized; that offers an intensely edited selection of merchandise, frequently exclusive and of high quality. . . . Saks Fifth Avenue published a Christmas catalog for the first time in 1972, and Bloomingdale's in New York City mailed a catalog recently for the first time in over 20 years. Harrod's of London has long published catalogs.

The most impressive case is that of J. C. Penney. This was the story as of 1973:[6]

The J. C. Penney Company is the second largest merchandise retailer in the United States. Our total sales in our 1973 fiscal year will be over $6-billion. We are second to Sears Roebuck. But unlike Sears and Montgomery Ward who started in the catalog business and later added stores, we began with our stores. Mr. Penney opened his first store in 1903. He called his early stores the Golden Rule Stores. Each store manager was a partner in the Company. *Today* we have 1,700 Penney Stores.

We did not enter the catalog business until 1963, when we purchased a small regional catalog company to get us started.

Today we do about $500-million with our catalog in 40 states and are well on our way to becoming national. Sears Roebuck today does well over $2-billion in catalog sales. So you can see we have a little way to go.

We operated our catalog business at a loss for eight years until we earned our first profit in 1971. The obvious question we were asked during those difficult years was: "why?" Why did we believe it was so necessary to bring in a catalog operation in which we were willing to invest for so long a period?

There are several answers, which provide good testimony to the importance of the catalog as an example of direct marketing. First we saw it as a way to increase our share of the market. We were unwilling to concede that important segment of the market to Sears, Wards, and others.

Second, our best judgment, backed by some hard research facts, told us that just as our store business would help us get a catalog business started, a catalog would help build volume in our stores.

Finally, there were good indications that direct marketing by means of a catalog was a rapidly growing business, fitting more and more into changing lifestyles of Americans. If catalogs were to become increasingly important in the future of retailing, we certainly didn't want to stand by and watch.

By 1984, Penney's direct-marketing sales were $1.9 billion.[7]

A nice example of how mail-order selling can be used to take advantage of an existing product you control is the success of selling Bob Dylan's comeback tour in 1974:[8]

The times, Bob Dylan is telling us, they are a'changin'.

And he's also telling us something about advertising. In his first concert tour in eight years, the young poet-songwriter-performer is demonstrating the power of advertising. It seems that his 21-city tour had a sellout capacity of 650,000 seats (at between $9.50 and $10.50 a ticket).

To fill those seats with denim and corduroy-clad bottoms, the tour promoters ran a newspaper ad once in each tour city last December. According to the latest estimates, these one-time-only ads pulled between 2,000,000 and 3,000,000 mail orders.

And here is an example of how a clothing retailer branched out into mail-order selling.[9]

HOW CASEY JONES RAILROADED US INTO MAIL ORDER BUSINESS

If you look in the New York Times or National Observer lately, you might see our ad for a "Casey Jones 5-Piece Outfit." It looks like a railroad engineer's outfit in little boy's sizes. It is made of sturdy denim ticking. And each ad pulls around 60 orders. At an average of $19 each. Or a total of $1,140. . . .

Those of you with a good memory had read of many examples of retail stores growing many times their size through mail order. Why not us? Why not our retail store? . . .

We leafed through our newspaper ads for the previous year. One item pulled so well we repeated it often. Each time we appealed to the same audience . . . and each time it drew mail, phone and in-person orders. The item: the above-mentioned dungaree set by Oshkosh B'Gosh, manufacturers of men's sturdy work clothing. Would this item pull as well in a national ad as in a local ad? Why not? People are people. . . .

You must have exclusivity in your presentation that cannot be knocked off by someone else. But Oshkosh is available to other stores. It is not sought out by many specialty shops since they make only this one item in a huge and diversified men's line. But it *could* be bought by other stores. And promoted.

What would make it *ours* alone? Something added. What do you associate with a train conductor? A lamp. A train. A whistle. We leafed through a wholesale toy catalogue and found a marvelous four-inch hardwood whistle. Great. We added the bandana made by Oshkosh and we now had an "exclusive 5-piece set." We named it "The Casey Jones Set."

As an added fillip, we offered to monogram the name on the jacket for an extra $2. . . . We knew our customer sought out gift items. Something different . . . and for children. We geared our advertising a month or two before Christmas. We selected our first media buy, the National Observer whose reader profile closely matches our existing customer. The Observer can be bought by regions. (We recommend you test with the region nearest you first. Cost is about half the national $4.10 per line rate.) We bought the Eastern edition first. It pulled well enough to try for the national circulation (half-a-million).

The two ads sold a total of 153 sets.

Here's what that figure means in terms of money made:

Eastern edition	$ 109.80
National edition	246.00
Cost of set ($8. × 153)	1,224.00
Cost of set and ads:	$1,579.80
Total sales (153 × 18) =	$2,754.00
Less expenses	1,579.80
Net profit	1,174.20

Each order included an extra $1.00 for postage which took care of mailing charges. More than half included the monogramming $2.00 fee which means an *extra* $100 profit.

In 1967, bar owner Eddie DiNicolantonio got interested in message-printed T-shirts. In 8 years he built up Printed Sportswear, selling to stores in the Atlantic City area. Then he thought to sell to businesses by mail rather than in person, and within a few months he had the makings of a successful operation.[10]

Lou Burnett has owned a golf course near Interstate 76 in Georgia for 19 years. A few years ago the golf pro at a local military installation began to eat into Burnett's pro-shop sales of clubs and other equipment with what Burnett considered unfair price competition. So Burnett began to advertise even lower prices in local newspapers, then in regional media, and finally in national magazine classified ads. Soon he had done so well that he was ready to sell the golf course and concentrate on the mail sales alone.[11]

Small manufacturers also can develop successful mail-order businesses with products they have formerly sold through other channels. For example, Burton Bank had manufactured men's slacks for 25 years, starting in 1948. After selling his slacks business in 1975, he tried selling just a single item—the "bush jean" or "bush short"— by mail-order. He ran one ad in the *National Observer,* made a good profit, and within a year he had a twelve-page catalog of men's and women's wear and did half a million dollars in business the first year.[12]

"But I haven't got a store or a product," you may wail. OK, but maybe you can hook up with someone who *does* have a store or a product, to your mutual benefit. How about making a deal with the fellow who sells tires for foreign cars in your town? Sell those tires by mail out of his inventory. Or the aggressive camera dealer in town who has lots of interesting specials? Or the "war surplus" dealer down the road? Or golf clubs? And so on. Look around, use your imagination, and be willing to walk in and suggest the idea. Almost anyone will hear you out when you have a deal like this to propose. But you'll have to be very careful about the price you agree on with the retailer—it will have to contain much less than his usual margin, once past the trial stage. And eventually he will have to be competitive with the price you can get from the original manufacturing source, though allowing for the overhead which the retailer saves you from having to provide yourself.

If You Are Already in the Mail-Order Business

If you are already in a mail-order business, you almost surely are actively looking around for new products to sell in order to keep growing and to increase your profit. Of course you have an enormous advantage over your situation when you were first starting out in business. But the odds still are strongly against any single new idea panning out. Luckily for you, in the mail-order business you can try out new ideas at relatively low cost until you find ones that work.

The guiding principle, if you are already in the mail-order business, is to develop new ventures that take advantage of some existing features of your present business. The most important possibilities are: (1) your customer list, (2) your shipping and warehousing capacities, and (3) any special skills of your staff that may be underutilized during some periods of the year.

Selling new—though related—products to your old customers is the basic tried-and-true method of mail-order growth. Haband started out selling neckties; now their main business is pants and shoes. Richard Sears started with watches, and by now Sears, Roebuck has branched out into almost everything. You can expand your offerings by increasing the size of your catalog or by increasing the number of mailings to customers. Either way, however, remember that the new merchandise must appeal to similar sorts of people as your existing merchandise does; otherwise you are not taking advantage of your customer list (except for their trust in you, which is a help), in which case you are little better off than starting from scratch.

Taking advantage of the firm's knowledge of a market, its skills, and its facilities is a bit less obvious than taking advantage of the customer list, so let's consider an example:[13]

> The company is Chap Stick in Lynchburg, Virginia. For many years we have handled Chap Stick's mail-order companies, the principal one being Blair Quality Products. Blair is an Avon-like business. Its dealers sell toiletries and cosmetics to their friends and neighbors. There are no field managers; however, the Blair dealers are, in fact, simply mail order customers of the company. Blair recruits its dealers through advertising in *TV Guide*, and in the big circulation movie and fan magazines. But Blair dealers cannot be recruited profitably in *Glamour, Cosmopolitan, Mademoiselle* or *Seventeen*.
>
> But those magazines comprise a huge market. How could Chap Stick develop a new business for this market? Well, let's add two other factors to the equation. Chap Stick Company has an excellent and flexible consumer-oriented computer operation. Secondly, the Chap Stick Company has a superb capability for manufacturing cosmetics, packaging them, and mailing them to individual customers. Analyze these strengths—and the media market—and you might well come up with Chap Stick's new business—the Kenneth Beauty Program.
>
> Chap Stick was brought together with Kenneth, the famous hairdresser and beauty expert. Drawing on Kenneth's strong ideas about beauty, Chap Stick put together a highly individualized 40-page beauty-guidance report, printed by computer at relatively low cost. This report is uniquely the customer's own. She answers about 50 questions which are fed into the computer, and gets a highly personal one-of-a-kind analysis.
>
> We sell the Kenneth Beauty Program for cash—using a very editorial-looking ad which incorporates a full page questionnaire. Buyers get a periodic newsletter, which is—of course—a vehicle for selling the Kenneth line of cosmetics.

If you already sell a product, these are some of the factors to consider when you decide whether to market your product through mail order:

1. Do any of your competitors sell by mail? If they do, your problem is almost solved. If they don't, don't let their example stop you.

2. How many customers do you have who *now* buy from you only by mail? If you already have a good many people or firms on your books who have moved to other parts of the country or whom you never see, and who still buy from you, then you probably have a product that lends itself to mail order.

3. These rules of thumb may be helpful:

    a. Is the product light in weight per dollar of sales price? Mailability is very important if you are to obtain a profitable return. Books are ideal because of the cheap postage rate they enjoy.

    b. Can you get a high markup on the cost to you? Three-to-one is a familiar formula, but there are too many situations to which it does not apply. Don't be hamstrung by the formula. On a big-ticket item the ratio can be much smaller and still make money for you.

    c. Is it a product that is not readily obtainable in stores near most consumers?

    d. Can the sales appeal be communicated on paper? Perfume is hard to sell by mail because prospects want to smell before they buy.

    e. Will you have to offer credit? Do you have the capital and the organization to offer credit terms?

    f. Do outside salespeople sell your product? Examples: insurance, industrial equipment, commercial supplies. All are sold both by outside salespeople and through mail order.

    g. Is your product a regular seller year after year? The effort and money necessary for a mail-order campaign are often too great for a novelty item that will soon have no market.

Finally, you must determine whether or not your product will sell by mail by actually *testing* it. But since you already sell the product, you have the great advantage of knowing your product and what aspects of it appeal to customers; you also have stock to fill test orders with. Chapter 26 tells you how to make the necessary tests.

Buying a Business

Buying an already going mail-order business is another way to get started, of course. Chapter 32 discusses that subject in detail.

5

Which Products
Are Best for You
to Sell

*Profit-Potential Estimates / How Much Investment
Will It Require? / Is the Product Strictly Legal? /
How Long Does It Take to Make Money? /
Specialty and Novelty Products / Why Is a
Profitable Mail-Order Product Profitable? / Testing
the Potential of the Product Line You Choose / A
Closing Note*

By now you should have started making a list of products that you
know are being sold successfully and that might be possibilities for
you. Our job in this chapter is to narrow that list down to the five,
one, or no product(s) that are right for your interests, your capital,
your background, and your energies.

Profit-Potential Estimates

One of the most important factors that you must consider when
choosing a product is its profit potential. It is not enough that you
can make a high *percentage* of profit on your advertising investment.
You must also be able to invest enough money in advertising so that
the *total profit* return is great enough for your desires, and great

enough to repay your investment of energy and time in organizing the project.

For example, this ad has run for over 30 years, month after month, practically without change: "Earn money evenings, copying and duplicating comic cartoons for advertisers." Ordinarily, any ad running for many months will draw competitors like flies to honey. But the cartoon-duplicating ad runs in only a few classified sections, and hence, no matter how profitable each ad might be, the total profit each month will not amount to much. This may explain why there is no competition.

Of course, if there is no competition, it may also mean that there is only room for one firm. It may be that the market cannot be widened with new kinds of product offers, by finding new media, or by using display ads.

Cardmaster ads for hand postcard duplicators are another example of a long-running ad that has probably drawn little competition because of a too-restricted market. Cardmaster does use display ads, however, which puts it in a much bigger profit class than cartoon duplicating. Or it may have the market to itself because it can obtain the merchandise more cheaply than anyone else can. But that would be unusual.

Many more of these limited-profit product situations occur in specialized and trade markets.

What you seek, then, is a product that can generate enough volume so that it can also generate considerable profit. You can estimate a product's market and its volume and profit potential by searching out the media where the product's ads presently appear. Add up the dollars spent for space in a given month and you will have an underestimate, because you will never manage to find all the insertions.

Estimating the volume of a product sold by a given firm through direct mail is much harder, because you have no easy way of determining how many and which mailing lists are being used. This is one more good reason why the beginners should stick to magazine advertising to generate customers until they have some experience.

How Much Investment Will It Require?

You must make an estimate of the expenditure of time, energy, and money required for developing the product and the campaign to sell it by mail. Then compare the time-and-energy expenditure to the estimated profit to see if the profit is worth the investment of your time.

For example, selling a law-study course may be profitable and interesting to you. But unless you can think of a shortcut, the development of the course and the backup texts will require vast resources of time and money.

To sell wallet-size photo duplicates, you need either photographic equipment or a connection with a firm that will do your processing. A photographic plant may well cost more than you want to invest, and lining up a reliable connection may be difficult to arrange.

Remember, though, that the greater the costs in time and money for you to get into a particular line, the harder it is for future competitors to get in, too. So a hard-to-begin product line may offer you some protection and security.

Is the Product Strictly Legal?

A large proportion of one-shot mail-order items advertised at any one time are close to the line of legality, some on one side of the line, some on the other. Sooner or later many will be forced out of business by the Federal Trade Commission or the Postal Service, while others will be assaulted by the Better Business Bureau.

What is legal and what is illegal are discussed in the next chapter. In brief, you will remain on safe ground if

1. The buyers get from you exactly what even the most gullible of them expect to get.
2. The customers don't feel gypped.
3. Every word and picture you put in your ad is true in spirit as well as in letter.
4. Your product is neither pornographic nor obscene.
5. The product is not a lottery or gambling scheme of any kind.
6. The offer is not a "chain" scheme in which your customers make money by doing the same thing you do.

Be especially careful of drug products and of plans and equipment designed to make money for the purchaser.

There are two good reasons why you should not imitate others in venturing to the edge of what is legal:

1. The experienced shady mail-order operators, together with their legal advisors, have spent a long time learning what they can get away with. Even then, the biggest of them have been caught and thrown in jail. As an inexperienced newcomer, you're the gal or guy who is *sure* to get hurt.

2. Perhaps more important, you may be surprised to find that you have a powerful conscience when you least expect it. Before carrying out a sharp scheme, you may feel, like P. T. Barnum, that it's a game to fleece the suckers that are born every minute. But after the deal is done, you may feel terrible remorse and guilt that you never anticipated. A sharp scheme has wrecked many a person.

Don't laugh at what I say as being naive. Please don't take a chance. Sell a product you can respect, in a manner you will not be ashamed of.

How Long Does It Take to Make Money?

If you settle on a repeat-business item—as I hope you will—you must also think about how *long* it will take for your customers to return you a profit and what else can be sold to them. The longer it takes to get into the black ink and the greater the capital you need to start, the greater the risk you are taking, but the more valuable and secure your busines if all goes well.

Specialty and Novelty Products

Despite everything I have said up until now, you are going to be interested in novelty and specialty products. Since that's the way it is, I'll tell you a success story. But remember that there are few success stories like this one.

> In 1951 Leonard Carlson started Sunset House with one mail-order item: a $1 name-and-address rubber stamp. Then he developed a catalog of novelty items such as a nose-hair remover and an electric toilet-seat warmer, getting new customers mostly from ads in a wide variety of magazines. In a little more than a decade, Sunset House sales hit $10 million, and now are far more than that.[1]

Sounds easy, doesn't it. Sure, Sunset House makes money. But for every Sunset House that has made it big in the mail-order specialty business, there must be a hundred people who have failed because they did not have a good nose for specialty mail-order items, or because they could not handle the advertising and business end.

Why Is a Profitable Mail-Order Product Profitable?

I have already argued that at first you should never ask or try to answer this question. All you need to know is that an item *is* already a good seller for someone else. Forget about *why* it is, or is not, a good mail-order item—at first.

Nevertheless, if you stay in the mail-order business for a while, or even if you don't, you will probably get involved in considering whether an untried mail-order product will be a winner.

This idea should help you to understand mail-order products: Except for novelty, repeat, and catalog items, most items that can profitably be sold by mail can also be sold profitably by an *outside* salesperson.

This is the reasoning behind the idea: Outside selling and mail-order selling are both expensive methods to sell goods, figured as a proportion of sales. Only those items that continue to support a high markup are good for mail order.

Repeat-order and catalog mail-order businesses have a much lower cost of selling because the largest expense arises from making a *new* customer.

Here are some questions you can ask yourself about a product if there is no competition to guide you:

1. How many media (or, for direct mail, how many lists) do I expect to be able to use profitably?

2. Are these media large?

3. How much will it cost to stock the product and prepare the advertising?

4. Will I be able to use only tiny ads, or bigger ads also?

If the product falls into one of the following classes, it has a very poor mail-order prospect:

1. Standardized and branded goods, unless you can offer a substantial price advantage.

2. Goods whose characteristics are hard to communicate in ads, e.g., perfume (except "knock-offs" of famous perfumes) and high-style women's dresses (at least for beginners).

3. Goods sold on a small profit margin, e.g., coffee and food (except gourmet food).

4. Goods that don't lead to profitable repeat sales.

If you are considering a product to be sold through sales agents, consider John Moran's checkoff list of the requirements of an agent-sold item.[2]

1. Must appeal to agent
2. Must appeal to agent's customers
3. Little investment for agent
4. Not seasonal
5. No choice of size or color (but shoes do well, and dresses)
6. Light weight
7. Easy for agent to carry samples
8. Not obtainable in stores
9. No breakage or spoilage
10. Very high commission

Testing the Potential of the Product Line You Choose

Never think that you have "found a product line" until you have successfully tested the product, the offer, and the copy. Until then, all you have is an idea, and it is exceedingly unwise to invest much time or energy in a product line that is only at the idea stage.

The actual mechanics of testing are fully described in Chapter 26. But these points are relevant here:

1. *It is customary to run test advertisements* before *you have the merchandise.* This allows you to beat a hasty retreat with small loss if your ad doesn't pull. Return the money and letters as "out of stock" but with some kind of present so that the "buyers" are left happy. When the late Bennett Cerf was still president of Random House, one of the largest U.S. publishers, Cerf's practice was to make small test mailings "to determine whether or not a given book is worth publishing at all or possibly to determine how to price a book

or how to package it or how many copies to print."[3] This may not be the nicest practice in the world, and you must conduct yourself in accordance with both general fairness and with the new FTC regulations on this subject (see Appendix B).

One of the great virtues of mail order is that you *can* put your toe into the water and test the business fully without getting in up to your neck. This is not the case with any other kind of business I know of.

2. *Mediocrity of results is the most likely test outcome.* Chances are you'll get neither a runaway winner nor a dud. The professional is the person who can tinker with a so-so proposition and make a winner of it.

3. *Failure of an ad can mean that the product or the offer or the copy or the medium is at fault.* But a clear failure is most likely to be the fault of the product or the medium.

A Closing Note

Now I'm going to sound like a fortune-teller. The best way to find a good mail-order product is to *have another* good mail-order product already. This isn't just double talk. It's my guess that successful mail-order people have files of dozens of good products that they don't have time or capacity to develop at the moment or that are too big or too small for them to tackle.

What this should mean to you, however, is the importance of getting into business with *some* product. Even if your first product is not tremedously profitable, it will at least lead you to evaluate other products, and that is the way you will find better products.

So—think of your first venture as an investment in getting into business. And if you're willing to work on a thin margin, almost *any* already proven product will do for you. You can then compete successfully because you won't be charging for salary or overhead, or demanding a profit margin, as your established competition will be. You can't go on that way for very long, of course, but it's a way to break in.

6

What You May
and May Not Do
in Mail Order

*Why Is the Law So Important in Mail Order? /
What They Used to Get Away With / What Is a
Racket? / Special Products You May Not Sell by
Mail / Penalties for Illegal Acts / How to Check
on Legality / The Mail-Order Rule of Fulfillment*

Don't, DON'T, *DON'T* skip this chapter. Don't make the mistake of thinking that it doesn't apply to you. Sooner or later—probably sooner—you will understand why I make this appeal so strong.

A quick example to make you see how important this chapter is: I might have advertised this book by saying, *"You, too, can earn money in mail order"* or *"Make $20,000 yearly in mail order."* I have not used those headlines for two reasons:

First, I know they might get me in trouble with the law; and second, I would feel bad about misleading some people about how easy it is to make money in mail order.

But if I *had* used those headlines, there is a good chance that some legal agency (probably the Federal Trade Commission) would have jumped on me sooner or later. No matter what the legal outcome, I would be caused trouble, and aggravation, and a big money loss.

Here is a recent news story that dramatizes some of the rackets and some of the trouble that one can get into:[1]

Bill Manning, 62, a retired electrician in Lyford, Texas, was looking for a way to cushion his savings against inflation. Last summer, he got a brochure from an Arizona-based firm named DeBeers Diamond Investment Ltd. Thinking he was dealing with the South African diamond giant, Manning mailed off a check for $5,000. He was still waiting for his diamonds in November when DeBeers—which has no connection with De Beers Consolidated Mines of South Africa—filed for bankruptcy, with the FBI at its heels. Now, Manning is queued up with other disgruntled investors, hoping someday to recover his savings.

DeBeers is one of dozens of mail-order diamond firms under investigation in three states for allegedly defrauding investors of hundreds of millions of dollars. Buoyed by soaring prices for fine gems, diamonds have emerged as the latest investment scam. . . .

In New York, the state attorney general's diamond task force has focused on Diamond Resources Corp., a now-defunct Manhattan firm that allegedly passed off zirconium chips as real gems. Three company officials are convicted felons, and sources say Donald Nixon, nephew of the former President, made several $50,000 telephone sales for the firm. Nixon's attorney denies his client was connected with the firm, but concedes that "he may have called some of his friends to see if they would be interested in purchasing diamonds. . . ."

I am *not* a lawyer, and I have *not* studied the law of mail order carefully. Therefore, what I say here is not legally precise or perfectly accurate. It does not deal with the subtleties that are the very essence of legal practice. I shall try to tell you in a *business* terms how I think the law affects you as a mail-order merchant.

If you have any doubts whatsoever about the legality of a plan of action, refer immediately to *The Direct Marketer's Legal Adviser* by Robert J. Posch, Jr., or to *The Law for Advertising and Marketing* by Morton J. Simon. (No relative, we have never even met.) If you can't find a *definite* answer there, you might—if you are a good researcher—look at *The Law of Advertising* by George and Peter Rosden or consult the sources mentioned in those books;[2] better yet, see a lawyer. Don't make a move until you are sure the move is within the law.

Why Is the Law So Important in Mail Order?

An unscrupulous or overzealous operator can cheat the public more successfully (until the law puts a stop to it) in the mail-order business than in almost any other line of trade. There are several reasons for this.

Unlike a retail store owner, you as the seller of one-shot items do not have to depend upon the goodwill of satisfied customers. You have the money whether or not the customer grumbles. A satisfied customer does you no more good than an unsatisfied customer.

Even unconditional guarantees do not remedy the situation. Many dissatisfied customers will not trouble themselves to wrap and mail a piece of shoddy merchandise to get back $2 or $5.

A dissatisfied customer of a local store will tell his or her neighbors about being cheated. Not only will the store's business suffer, but the store owner will have to face the loss of personal reputation among the neighbors. Someone may even punch the proprietor in the nose.

But the dissatisfied mail-order customer has no good way of getting back at unscrupulous mail-order operators—except by reporting them to the authorities. And the mail-order person's neighbors seldom know the exact nature of his or her business. So this important community control of a businessperson's actions does not exist in mail order.

The mail-order seller has great control over what the buyer knows about the product. The buyer cannot ask sharp questions of the seller or examine the merchandise carefully. The advertisement tells buyers exactly what the *seller* wants them to know, and nothing more. This increases the possibility of a cheated customer.

That's why you *must* know about what you can and can't do in mail order.

And it's not just dishonest people who get into legal trouble in mail order. Anyone can get carried away with the desire to make a sale.

What They Used to Get Away With

The majority of mail-order operations are, and always have been, respectable. They are respectable because of the law, because of the conscience and ethics of most mail-order operators, and because many of them sell repeat items that demand a satisfied customer.

But 80 and more years ago when mail order was a brand new way of doing business, the law did not have sufficient remedies against hanky-panky. The laws that worked to regulate face-to-face business dealings were inadequate to deal with business at a distance by mail. And so, sharp operators ran wild.

Verneur E. Pratt told the following stories.[3]

One ad, for example, offered a "Steel Engraving of George Washington" for 50 cents. The copy beneath the headline described the excellence of the engraving, the beautiful, deep, rich color used, and the fact that the paper was deckled on all four edges. In return for his 50 cents, the buyer received a two-cent stamp.

Another well-known example was that of the "Patented Cigarette Roller" that rolled with equal ease either round or oval cigarettes. It was made entirely of metal, heavily nickel-plated, with only one moving part. It fitted the vest pocket and was so simple that it could not get out of order. In return for $1.00 the buyer received a three-inch nickel-plated spike. The instructions read: "Lay either a round or oval cigarette upon the table, pushing the spike directly behind it, upon doing which you will find the cigarette to roll easily and with almost no effort."

Every statement in the copy was true. The bilked customer merely placed his own interpretation upon it, and his curiosity as to how the device would roll the cigarettes led him to part with his dollar bill.

In the advertisement for the "Patent Potato Bug Killer" stress was laid on the fact that "$1 equips you to kill all the potato bugs in a ten-acre field." In return for the dollar, two little slabs of wood were sent, accompanied by ironically elaborate instructions as to how to pick the bugs off the vines with fingers, laying them down on one slab, pressing the other firmly down upon the bug, and thus quickly and efficiently extinguishing its life.

Another mail-order ad was headed "$3.95 for this 5 piece Wicker Set." The illustration showed a handsome, sturdy wicker table, a settee, two straight-backed wicker chairs, and a rocker. The copy, after extolling the virtues of the materials used, guaranteed the set to be "exactly like the illustration." When the set arrived, the discomfited buyer found it to be in truth exactly the same size as the illustration.

And some 80 years ago, Samuel Sawyer related this yarn.[4]

A manufacturing concern, in Connecticut, produced an interesting little novelty in the form of a sun-dial enclosed in a watch-case. It was the same size as a gentleman's watch and when the case was opened, revealed the dial by which time could be determined from the sun, in the good old-fashioned way of our forefathers. This article was produced and supplied at wholesale for a few cents to any concern that wanted to buy.

One New Yorker conceived a bright idea. He had an illustration made of the article in such a manner that anyone who glanced at it could naturally say it represented a nice watch. Then he prepared an advertisement describing "the new timekeeper; warranted for twenty years, not to get out of order," and called it a timekeeper, which was true enough, and by the general language of his announcement led the reader to believe that a watch could be obtained with a subscription to a cheap periodical. . . .

People showered their complaints upon the police and postal authorities, but as there was really nothing in the advertisement which described the article as a watch, the authorities were afraid to undertake legal action. . . . No misstatement in language could be found by the district attorney and no prosecution ever went very far, but the promoter of this scheme was compelled to submit to columns of unpleasant newspaper exposures. . . .

What Is a Racket?

By now the situation has changed drastically. As always, the law may be slow, but it eventually finds ways to deal with the injustice. Today, practically any shady mail-order proposition is within the long reach of one or another branch of the law.

The law covers a lot of ground. For example, telling the literal, technical truth is not enough. You may be in the wrong for what you don't say: For example, in most cases you must reveal that imported goods are made abroad.

You may fall into the clutches of the law because your ad *suggests* an untruth, even if it doesn't say it. And you can err by hiding the truth away in small print or big words or in many other ways.

Fraud, false advertising, and deceptive advertising constitute the likeliest problem you must avoid. Here are some general guides:

- "Fraud" means "taking money under false pretenses," but almost anything that a jury thinks is a "racket" will qualify to get you into jail.

- Your advertisement must not fool even "gullible" people, or "ordinarily trusting people." The test is not what a *university graduate* would find in an ad, or even a *reasonable person*. If you fool any substantial portion of *your public*, you are in the wrong. And what counts is not your actual words, but what people believe after they have read your ad.

  Some kinds of exaggeration may be permissable, however. You can probably get away with saying that a cheap dress is "the most beautiful dress in the world." But that probably will not be successful advertising practice.

- Good intentions on your part *may* save you from going to jail—if you can prove your good intentions—but they will *not* prevent the Postal Service or the Federal Trade Commission from shutting down your operation. That is sufficiently painful, and sufficiently costly, so that you should make every effort to prevent its happening.

- Your advertisement *can* be illegal even though the customer is not obviously injured. For example, if you get the customer to write for full further information by misleading him or her, you are outside the law even though the information you send is perfectly truthful in describing the product. An example is advertising a correspondence course in a "Help Wanted" column.

- Whether or not your ad is legitimate is *not* obvious from the content of the advertisement itself. Other evidence may be necessary. For example, perhaps you advertise that your correspondence course on bicycle repairing will teach people how to earn $10 an hour. Whether the ad is legitimate depends upon how many bicycle repairers make $10 per hour and how many graduates of your course actually do so.

Here are some specific examples of mail-order operations that the law gets after. These examples are all taken from just one of the Postal Service's press releases, stating that it had upheld complaints for false advertising through the mails.[5]

> Jay Norris Corp., Freeport, N.Y., charged with marketing a "Lincoln-Kennedy" coin—a Lincoln penny upon which a profile of President Kennedy had been stamped—under the pretense that the Treasury Department had minted the coin.
> National Opportunity Research Service, Princeton, N.J.; charged with selling $10 memberships in an organization which promised members an opportunity to earn up to $10,000 in return for each one dollar investment, and to buy merchandise at 35 percent below wholesale.
> James Allen, of Atlanta, Ga., for advertising a $6.95 "scientifically evolved" plan guaranteed to help persons lose as much as 22 pounds within a week by means other than caloric dieting.
> Hartford Publishing Corp., Denville, N.J., for promoting a weight reduction program called the "Digital Diet Method" which consisted only of a diet booklet.
> Greenland Studios, Miami, Fla., for the sale of a massage band guaranteed to firm up muscles and significantly reduce sagging skin.

And here's another one:[6]

> American Consumer (Philadelphia, PA) has been charged with 1,000 counts of mail fraud in Federal District Court in Philadelphia, by U.S. Attorney Peter F. Vairs. The charges could cost the company $1,000 per count or $1 million if the government's case prevails. The firm which is reported to have sales of $32 million annually was indicted for its "Cross of Lourdes" promotion. The company's promotion said that the $15.95 item had been dipped in holy waters at Lourdes, the site of 58 miracles and had been blessed by Pope Paul VI in the Vatican. In another action before the Pennsylvania Bureau of Consumer Protection, the company signed a consent decree and paid a fine of $45,000 for

marketing a tomato plant which promised to produce tomatoes by the ton. Consumer was also hit for a walnut tree promotion that offered a $3.95 tree which would produce 3,000 walnuts.

Please notice in the above examples that, in addition to some firms that I never heard of and that may be new small ventures, there are two huge mail-order outfits being attacked by the U.S. Postal Service— Greenland Studios and Jay Norris—each of which sells many millions of dollars worth each year. This should teach you that you may *not* feel legally safe even if you do the same thing that the big firms do. Both you *and* the big firm may get clipped by the law—although I think it is fair to say that if a large firm and a small firm do the same thing, the small operator is in *more* danger from the law. The reason is that the legal agencies expect that the small operator will be more likely to give in because he can less well afford to pay for a lawyer. Larger firms, in contrast, often count on their lawyer's being able to stall the government until they reap most of the profit— and then go out of business (in which case the court is asked to drop the case as no longer being material).

An example of how the law sometimes discriminates against the little guy is the sale of *will forms*. Despite the fact that there is nothing illegal about selling or advertising them in a proper fashion, the Federal Trade Commission has had a standing rule that sellers of will forms are told to cease their selling. If you begin to sell them, you will sooner or later get a letter from the Federal Trade Commission that will frighten you out of your wits. The FTC knows that the threat will probably work even if the agency cannot back up the threat. But at the same time the largest novelty firms go on advertising and selling will forms year after year. How about that for justice? But then, it is not yet a perfect world.

Correspondence schools that promise students good jobs, and insurance plans that misrepresent the insurance, are two major classes of mail-order activities that are presently under attack by the law. Work-at-home schemes are always in trouble. The owner of one of the largest, whose ad read "Part time, work home, mailing our catalog" went to jail for 5 years a few months before I wrote this.

Read what the Chief Postal Inspector has written about work-at-home schemes, one of the most common mail-order-business frauds:[7]

WORK AT HOME SCHEMES

"Send just $1—Find out how you too can earn $25 a week addressing envelopes at home during your spare time," promised an ad running in dozens of newspapers across the country. Fortunately, postal inspectors moved quickly against this bogus scheme. Within a few weeks 13,000 letters, all containing dollar bills, were returned to the senders stamped: "Fraudulent—Return to Sender." The scheme was phony because today large mailers rarely "job-out" envelopes for manual addressing. The promoters were sentenced to long prison terms for mail fraud.

In many advertised schemes the victim receives something for his money, but it may be useless. One promoter advertised a booklet on how to make more money for one dollar. The pamphlet merely explained that honesty and leadership are among the necessary traits for success. It also invited the reader to take a course in self-improvement, at additional cost. A $2 booklet promising to show one how to attain wealth, revealed that hard work is the secret. For a dollar another company promised information on job oppportunities. All it furnished were a few classified ads clipped from a newspaper.

Many work-at-home mail-addressing jobs are actually chain-letter schemes. In answering the ad promising such work the victim may receive a letter saying that a dollar will bring additional information and material for making money addressing mail. After sending a dollar a person may receive identical copies of the same letter he answered.

One "work-at-home" promoter started a small operation which rapidly grew into the largest and most complained-about promotion of this type in the United States. Beginning with a sure-fire method for applying a velvet-like finish to any material, he soon branched out into enterprises involving silk-screen printing, miniature trees, moulding machines for making plastic novelties, tropical fish, and other activities which might appeal to those seeking work in their home. He and his office manager were convicted of mail fraud and sentenced to prison.

A fraud artist preyed on invalids, shut-ins, and others in need of extra income by charging $3 for "instructions" which guaranteed large incomes from addressing envelopes and clipping newspapers. His victims lost an estimated $300,000 to this promoter before complaints developed and postal inspectors investigated. He was sent to prison.

Do not make the mistake of assuming that because you see ads for an offer that it is legal. Often ads will run for quite a while until the authorities get around to chasing them down. Here is a list of offers which postal authorities say they often investigate:

Classified directory solicitations to simulate billings for listings in established directories

Distributorships

Endless chains
  Chain letters
  Referral plan (selling, etc.)
  Pyramid selling

Estates (missing heirs)

Franchises

Gambling
  Lottery dealer (includes distributors or agents of sweepstakes, etc.)
  Turf tipsters

Home improvement (includes aluminum siding, remodeling, fall out shelters, etc.)

Insurance

Investments
 Oil and gas leases
 Stocks

Job opportunities (sale of information purporting to lead to employment—domestic and foreign)

Loans
 Debt consolidation
 Mortgage

Literary
 Manuscript
 Song promotion

Matrimonial (lonely hearts)

Medical
 Body ailments (includes devices, vitamins, drugs)
 Cosmetics
 Hypnotism
 Reducing (including chin straps, vibrating gadgets, drugs)
 Sexual (devices and stimulants)

Merchandise
 Coins
 Nursery (trees, plants, evergreens, etc.)

Real estate
 Improved
 Unimproved (sale of submarginal land for homesites, vacation resorts, etc.)

Schools
 Correspondence courses
 Diploma mills

Solicitations
 Begging letters
 Charity
 Religious cults

Vending machines

Work at home
 Addressing envelopes
 Clipping newspapeers
 Sewing baby shoes

Without comment I reproduce in the following pages a couple of direct-mail offers—$100,000.00 Club and The Letter (Figures 6-1 and 6-2)—that may fit into one or more of the above categories. Another interesting news story is the following about the Pallottine Order:[8]

> The Baltimore-based Pallottine mission mailed almost 100 million appeals like that last year. According to professional fund raisers, the order's solicitation could have brought as much as $8 million to $15 million in contributions. But the fathers reported that less than $500,000 was actually sent to starving, sick or naked children at the order's missions in 22 foreign countries. . . . the Pallottines have built up a massive mail-order operation which has sent as many as 5 million pieces a day, at a cost of more than $100,000 in postage.
> The business is run from a heavily guarded warehouse that contains computerized mailing lists, automatic typewriters and high-speed envelope stuffers. The Fathers have kept a low profile by sending most of their solicitations out of state. Some of the Pallottines' appeals include offerings of ball-point pens, calendars and prayer cards. But the *pièce de résistance* is a flashy "Free Pallottine Sweepstakes," offering 237 prizes including two Plymouth Furies. . . .
> Although the Pallottines' Baltimore mission runs one of the largest charity mail-solicitation campaigns in the U.S., the 2,200-member Roman

Catholic order has a religious exemption from disclosing its financial records. Last week, however, Baltimore Archbishop William Donald Borders ordered an audit of the Pallottines' mail-order empire by an out-of-state accounting firm—and promised to make the results public.

The best way to learn what is legitimate and what is not is to read the weekly Federal Trade Commission Report and the monthly Post Office Enforcement Report. Write your congressional representative to ask for them.

Here are some specific things to watch out for:

- Medical and drug products usually need *scientific* proof that they will work. Testimonials from satisfied users are not enough to prove that your product relieves a disease. Many diseases go away by themselves, and your product may get false credit in the user's mind. You need *clinical* evidence, scientific *experimentation*, or *chemical* evidence, furnished by qualified people.

- Recently the Federal Trade Commission suppressed a business that sold a plan to increase height, though the seller claimed to have scientific evidence of the *possibility* of its doing so.

- Be triply careful of such words as "cure," "banish," and "remedy" when selling drugs. See the literature mentioned at the end of the chapter for further information.

- In a company name you can't use such words as "Laboratory," "Manufacturer," "Refiner," etc., unless you really perform those activities. And names that suggest nonprofit organizations, such as "Institute" and "Bureau," are highly suspect, as are the words "U.S.," "Federal," or "Government."

- Guaranteeing a refund to dissatisfied customers probably does not keep you safe from the charge of defrauding your customers. (I say "probably" because the law does not seem to be clear on this point.)

- Phony prices are illegal. For example, you can't say "formerly sold at $10.98" unless a *substantial number* were really sold at that price. However, there is no restriction on your charging as high a price as you like for anything you sell.

- Testimonials must be true. You are as responsible for the correctness of a statement you quote from a customer as if you made the statement yourself.

Enroll Me Today

The $100,000.00 Club

I UNDERSTAND WITH THE ENCLOSED $25.00 MEMBER-
SHIP FEE I AM AUTOMATICALLY ENROLLED IN THE
$100,000 CLUB. SEND ME MY CERTIFICATE OF MEMBER-
SHIP WITH ALL OF THE BENEFITS AND PRIVILEGES.

NAME _____

Please print for fast delivery.

ADDRESS _____

TOWN & STATE _____

ZIP CODE _____

TELEPHONE _____

ENCLOSED FIND MY TWENTY-FIVE DOLLARS ($25.00)
(Make Check or Money Order payable to: J. MORGAN HUGHES)

RETURN TO SENDER Not Interested

AFFIX
21c
Postage

(For ½ Ounce)

AIR MAIL

J. Morgan Hughes

Dear Friend,

    I am inviting a limited number of people to become members of a very unusual club. I can promise you adventure, excitement and out of the ordinary benefits beyond your wildest dreams. One of the numerous benefits will be the opportunity to profit by $100,000 during your first year of membership. You buy nothing, you sell nothing you just have fun. Impossible?

    Your receiving this letter was not a matter of chance. You were among a select group of people throughout the world that I chose to receive this letter. Why? Because, unless I am wrong you possess certain qualities not found in the majority of people. These qualities are a necessity to this club to provide a secret strength. Once you learn this strength, I can assure you that you will never reveal it to anyone.

    Let's say I have misjudged you, that you live a dull everyday existence. That adventure is not part of your makeup. That the "unusual" is for the other guy. That the thrill of making a lot of money doesn't give you a "kick."

    If this is true and I have misjudged you, there is no point in wasting your time reading any further. For those who are mildly curious please read on, for as I wrote this letter a short time ago when I fit the unadventuresome category myself. I lived each day in a high pressure business, seeing little of my family and friends and seeing nothing of the world except on occasional TV. How has this changed?

    Let me tell you an incredible, but true story.

    As you may remember some time ago in history a man from Cuba, named Fidel Castro, formed a new government and purged his country of all businesses, night clubs, gambling casinos, and persons that did not suit his needs for a new peoples Cuba.

    One of the thousands of persons caught in Castro's purge escaped to this country but was somehow separated from his family during the escape. Arriving here he was penniless and left with little hope of ever seeing his family again.

    Perhaps it was fate that brought this man to me. I gave him a job with my company. He was promoted rapidly as he seemed to have a talent for business and a winning way with other employees. During the next two years we became good friends and he began telling me of his past life and all he had accomplished as a successful business leader in Cuba. He was the principal owner of seven night clubs and casinos. He vaguely told me how he and a small group of men had almost overnight acquired their first casino; then how this same group multiplied their efforts to practically monopolize the casino industry in Cuba.

Figure 6-1 Don't touch an offer like this one.

The LETTER...

URGENT!

This is the most important letter you will ever read!
Please spare me five minutes right now. It is in your interest!

You can
earn up to $813,800 in the next 50 days*

Based on 5% return as described in detail on other side

... and reach up to seven million people in direct mail for a very low investment!

Dear Reader,

This is no joke and in the next five minutes I will prove it to you. You can make this much, and perhaps even more, since the only limit is your own initiative . . .and it's all perfectly *legal!*

At various times through the years, you have probably received a few "chain letters," all of them asking you to send $2 to someone, for nothing of value in return. It probably occurred to you that if you continued the letter by mailing out duplicate copies to other people, these people would likewise not really want to send you money for nothing of value in return.

But, you *do* know how appealing the *multiplying power* of a "chain letter" can be. I am now going to tell you about a most fantastic *"Co-op Advertising Program" that has all the multiplying power* of a "chain letter" but *is perfectly legal!*

This *"Co-op Advertising Program"* offers the people you send *this* letter to a *double incentive* to send you their two dollars! The first incentive is the valuable report that they will be buying. The second incentive is that the *same report they buy from you can be resold by them* to people they send this letter to. As a result, *your offer is legal!*

Please read the four "advertisements" on the back of this letter. Each one of them offers a unique and valuable *one-page* report of useful money-making information that took years of time and money to obtain. These reports are exclusive and *not available anywhere else!* No matter how knowledgeable and experienced you may be, you will find a wealth of information and new ideas in each report that you can't afford to ignore! You owe it to yourself to purchase these reports *for the valuable knowledge they contain*, which is well worth the two dollars . . .but remember, by buying the four reports advertised on the reverse side, you will also be buying *the right to reproduce and sell them* to other people, by your participation in this novel *"Co-operative Advertising Program."*

The one-page reports that you will be buying *can be easily duplicated* at a cost of as little as 5¢ each, by Xeroxing (photocopying) or inexpensive offset printing (remember, you will be reselling them for $2 each). And there is no need to duplicate a large supply initially until you begin to receive orders for your reports. Even if you have never been in the mail-order business, this is an easy, legitimate way for you to get started and possibly make up to $10,000 to $1,000,000 in a very short amount of time with a very small investment of time and money!

HERE'S HOW THE ENTIRE DEAL WORKS!

❶ Order the four reports from the advertisers printed on the reverse side of this letter by sending *each* of them $2 plus a self-addressed stamped return envelope (to get a faster reply). When you receive the four reports, you may then duplicate them *and offer them for sale to others* (I will show you how in a moment). Be sure to *ask for each report by title when ordering* since each advertiser sells all four reports, *as you will shortly be doing too.*

❷ Using your home or office typewriter, type *your* name and address and the names and addresses of the *first three* advertisers printed in the "Co-op Advertisers Ad Section" on the reverse side of this letter (those selling Reports #1, #2 and #3). With scissors or a razor blade, cut out your name and address and the other three names and addresses that you typed and neatly paste *your* name and address *under ad #1* (you'll be selling Report #1). Paste each name and address down one position. The original name and address now printed in the number four position will no longer be used. *Example:* Let's say the four advertisers on the reverse side are (1) Smith (2) Jones (3) Edwards (4) Blake. You will type your name and address in where "Smith's" name and address now appears. "Smith" will move down to #2. "Jones" will move down to #3 and "Edwards" will move down to #4. "Blake's" name will be eliminated. *Don't worry about "Blake."* He was once in the number one position *and has possibly received several hundreds of thousands of dollars by now.* So don't worry about "Blake." It's your turn now!

❸ After neatly pasting in *your* name and address in the #1 position and the names and addresses of the other three advertisers into positions 2, 3 and 4, take the letter to an offset printer (listed in the Yellow Pages of your telephone book) and tell him to run off 500 copies (or more if you wish). Do not make any other alterations of this letter as you may harm its "pulling power."

Figure 6-2 Another "don't touch" offer.

Page 2

❹ You then mail out 500 (or more) copies of this letter (with your name and address in the number one position) to friends, relatives, smart business people in your local telephone directory, or to names of mail-order buyers or opportunity seekers that you can rent cheaply from mailing list brokers (listed in your Yellow Pages under mailing lists).Use your business skills to choose the most productive lists since this is the key to making a profit! You can be in the mail with 500 pieces for about $165, including postage. You can mail less than 500 if you are low on funds just to get started, or until the money starts to roll in, which should take only a week or ten days.

*HERE'S HOW YOU CAN MAKE THOUSANDS OF DOLLARS

After carefully following the instructions above, you mail out your 500 letters (with your name and address in ad position #1). With a 5% response, 25 of the five hundred people to whom you mailed this letter will send you two dollars each (that's $50) for Report #1 and they should also continue mailing this letter by mailing out five hundred letters each (25 x 500 each). Remember, each of *those 12,500 letters will have your* name and address in the number 2 position selling Report Number Two for $2. Now those 12,500 letters may pull in a 5% response, or 625 new people, each sending you two dollars for Report #2 (that's $1,250 total) and if each of *those people continue the letter by mailing five hundred each, this will increase the circulation of your ad to 312,500* (625 x 500 letters each). Your name will now be in the number 3 position, selling Report Number Three at $2. Now a 5% return would produce *15,625* new people, each sending you $2 for Report Number Three (that's *$31,250.00* for you) and if each one of those people continues the letter by mailing five hundred letters each, the circulation will be over seven million (*7,812,500* to be exact). And finally, with your name and address in the number four position, selling Report Number Four for $2, a 5% return would produce *390,625* new people, each sending you two dollars for Report Number Four (that's *$781,250.00* cold cash for you). This would bring the total money you would receive to a whopping $813,800. Not bad for an initial investment of *$165!* What percentage of new people your mailing will pull will depend on the mailing list that you use. Many lists will pull less than 5%. Some "hot" mailing lists can pull *more* than 5%, which will mean more money for you! Even only a *1%* return would bring you *$1,560.00*, nearly 10 times your investment on only 500 pieces mailed (or *$15,600.00* if you mail 5,000 letters). As you can see, *it's hard not to make money!*

So *get started now!* Time is wasting. If *you* do not want to seize this opportunity *which knocks this once,* give it to someone else who will (maybe you can get them to share it with you for telling them about it after they start rolling in the dough). *Don't do what you've too often done and let this chance for real big money go by. If there is something you do not understand, please* **Read This Letter Again.**

——— CO-OP ADVERTISERS AD SECTION ———

Send $2 to each of the four advertisers whose names and addresses appear below. Order each report by its title, and enclose a stamped self-addressed envelope for each report. You have the unconditional right to copy and resell these reports.

1 **REPORT #1   HOW TO MAKE BIG MONEY IN YOUR SPARE TIME** $2.00
   One-page report on making big money working out of your home.
   EQUAL OPPORTUNITY
   ⬆ (Your name and address will go here when you reproduce this letter.) ⬆

2 **REPORT #2   HOW TO RAISE $10,000 OVERNIGHT** $2.00
   One-page report on raising $10,000 in 24 hours or less.
   PROFITS UNLIMITED

3 **REPORT #3   HOW TO GET RICH ENJOYING YOURSELF** $2.00
   One-page report—how to make big money while letting other people do the work.
   MR. LES BENNETT

4 **REPORT #4   GETTING LOANS, LEASES, MORTGAGES & CREDIT FAST** $2.00
   One-page report teaches you how to borrow without co-signers, red-tape, collateral, etc.
   MR. Z. FOLI

Each Report carries a 7-day money-back guarantee, if returned with self-addressed stamped envelope.

Remember, you now have a chance to get in on this early. As this spreads in the weeks ahead, others can beat you to the punch. You'll never forgive yourself if someone you know makes a fortune right under your nose. Don't let that happen. *Join us now and* **"get in on the ground floor."** *Opportunity seldom knocks twice!*

Legal Notice & Disclaimer: We cannot and do not represent or guarantee how much profit you will make, or indeed that you will make any profit, by participating in this plan. There is no condition that you purchase anything from us. You may freely reproduce our reports or use this sales technique to sell your own merchandise if you choose to.

[Reprint this letter]

Here goes an unlawyerlike statement of how you can test whether your advertisement or offer is free of fraud or deceptive advertising. You are safe if

1. Your customers get from you exactly what the most gullible of them expect to get.
2. The customers don't feel gypped.
3. Every word and picture in your ad is true in spirit as well as in letter.

Customers can be dissatisfied without feeling gypped. For example, a month after buying from you their taste may change, and they may no longer like the style or design of your product. They won't be happy, but they won't feel cheated.

Customers may also be dissatisfied at some later time because they come across an opportunity to buy for less. They will then be dissatisfied, but our society generally recognizes that it is not theft to charge as much as the traffic will bear as long as you stick to the truth.

It may help you evaluate the honesty of your offer if you consider the information that the potential consumer *needs* to evaluate your offer. The less information about the product the customer has to start with, the more responsibility you have to inform the customer completely.

As examples, compare selling fabric by the yard to home sewers with selling a patent medicine. As long as you don't lie about the quality, width, pattern, or type of yarn in the fabric, home sewers have plenty of knowledge to decide whether to accept your offer. Furthermore, as soon as they receive and examine the goods, they can tell whether you really told them the truth. So you can take some liberties in puffing the beauty and quality of your merchandise.

But potential consumers of a patent medicine are neither scientists nor doctors and therefore have no way of testing whether your medicine will help them or even whether it is any good for anyone. Customers do not usually understand the difficult and subtle scientific tests of a drug's efficacy, and they can easily be swayed by misleading evidence. Customers may believe testimonials of people who *thought* the medicine helped them, without considering that many patients get well even if they only take sugar pills.

Furthermore, consumers may not have sufficient information to evaluate your product until long *after* their purchases. Correspondence courses and money-making plans are good examples: The purchaser must often try them out for quite awhile before finding out whether they are helpful or worthless.

Sawyer long ago wrote accurately about what is and is not legitimate:[9]

> To explain what I mean, let me give you a few brief examples. First I write this lying statement:
>
> *"Our stogies are made of pure Havana tobacco."*
>
> That's a lie because the stogies are made of Virginia tobacco.
>
> Here is a sample of evasion that might be used if deemed necessary:
>
> *"Smoke some of our stogies, then smoke the best 15 cent Havana cigar you can buy and we believe you will like our stogies better."*
>
> That's an ingenious evasion. You've probably become so used to Virginia tobacco that it suits you better than Havana and you assume that everyone else will think likewise.
>
> Some persons might criticize your opinion, but nobody can successfully accuse you of deceiving if you train yourself to believe what you suggest. The first statement may bring you to jail, the second never can. In fact, this very expression would tend, by psychological operation, to lead a person to think the same as yourself (after he had smoked a box of stogies at one cent each) that they tasted better than Havanas.
>
> I repeat, tell the exact truth whenever and wherever you can. If you feel that it is necessary to your success to make a strong statement, use ingenuity and don't put yourself in a position where you can be proved a downright liar under cross-examination.
>
> To cover the principal argument of your ad, and yet tell the strict truth without the slightest bother from your conscience as to black or white lying, you can say:
>
> *Our stogies are made of Virginia tobacco and after smoking a box of them, we believe you will continue their use, even though you have been accustomed to smoking 15 cent Havanas.*
>
> . . . The same idea will apply to any commodity. I have simply undertaken to show the difference between a deliberate lie, a unique and legal evasion, and an ingeniously told actual truth. Even the statement I have given as truthful is as a salted and buttered baked potato compared to a raw potato, but the advertiser who cannot at least write up his goods with some enterprise, better try another line of trade.

Times are different now, though, and much of what got by when Sawyer wrote would not pass muster now. Standards are higher now, I'm glad to say. Bringe describes the standard which we are now aiming for (but don't always reach)—that the advertising should simply not deceive.[10]

THE USES OF DOUBLE SPEAK

What is it? It's the statement that appears to say one thing but gets through to our mind with quite another message. "Nine out of ten doctors use aspirin," when sandwiched in a block of copy for Bayer Aspirin, seems to say that the aforesaid doctors are using the advertised product. Here is a headline on an investment service ad:

WHEN THESE 22 STOCKS SPLIT
The Number of Shares Held Could Double or Triple

Seems like a big promise, doesn't it? Seems to point to a speculative killing. Yet it is a simple statement of fact that promises nothing.

"Clients in nine states depend on our ability to create advertising which gets measurable results at the lowest possible cost."

The sleeper word in that statement is "measurable." It could mean one order or one thousand. The reader, looking for the big promise and wanting it, interprets the word as pie in the sky and will impatiently brush aside the truth *even when he knows it.*

You would not use such deceptive statements in your mail? Any statement you permit your reader to twist to fit his emotional needs can be a deceptive statement for him.

Special Products You May Not Sell by Mail

Lotteries.   Straightforward gambling schemes are forbidden of course. But also be careful of any "contest" idea because many of them are found to be forms of lotteries.

Pornographic and Obscene Literature, Films, Etc.

Chain Schemes.   These are money-making plans in which your customers are taught to make money in the same way you do. Example: you sell them a plan to sell the same plan to other people. Such schemes are illegal.

New Drugs.   This includes all drugs that are not standard, well-accepted medical remedies. You may not sell new drugs without special permission from the Food and Drug Administration.

Penalties for Illegal Acts

Several agencies of the federal or state governments can jump on you, and they each have different procedures and penalties. Your likeliest sources of trouble, in this order, are listed below.

■ *U.S. Postal Service.* Postal inspectors have the power to arrest you, with the probability of trial and jail. However, first offenses of a minor nature, by basically honest people, are often handled with a Fraud Order. This is an order from Washington to your local post office to stamp "Fraudulent" on incoming mail and return it to the sender.

Postal inspectors also have the authority to suppress your illegal business by getting you to sign a statement that you will go out of business and by authorizing the post office to stamp "Refused. Out of Business" on the mail and return the mail to the senders.

As Jerome Beck puts it,[11]

There are really two mail fraud statutes. One fines you up to $1,000 and can put you away for up to five years for each violation. Here, the government has to prove you intended to defraud. The other statute has a more gentle penalty—it just puts you out of business. And for this the government only has to show falsity, not intent. All your good intentions are irrelevant.

■ *Federal Trade Commission.* After giving you a chance to state your case and to appeal it, the Federal Trade Commission can order you to cease your illegal practice. No penalty is attached to most cease-and-desist orders, but if you violate the order, you may be fined. Some orders—e.g., those against dangerously false drug advertising—may carry an immediate penalty.

■ *Food and Drug Administration.* This organization has the power to stop you, or to fine and jail you, for false statements on the *labels* of drugs, cosmetics, and foods. Under some circumstances, advertising may be considered a label.

■ *State Fraud Commissions.* Most states have bodies with police power over advertising. However, they are less likely to be heard from than the U.S. Postal Service or Federal Trade Commission.

■ *Direct Marketing Association.* It maintains a "Mail Order Action Line" that accepts consumers complaints and attempts to get satisfaction for the consumer if it feels the complaint is warranted.

■ *The National Better Business Bureau.* Though not a government agency, it has the power to hurt you. It can collect information about an operation it believes is illegal or unfair, and it can disseminate that information to media in which you wish to advertise. The media might then refuse to accept your advertising.

Pay attention to this: Even if a doubtful scheme does not land you in jail, the effects can be disastrous. Here are the things you can lose:

1. You can lose the lawyer's fees to fight your case. Even in the unlikely event that you come out clean, it will take you a long time to make up what you have to pay your counsel.

2. You can lose the heavy investment of time, energy, and money required to set up a going business. Nothing is more discouraging than to slave and spend until finally you see a neat profit coming in, only to have to close up shop by order of the law. This is a losing proposition no matter how you look at it.

3. You can lose your self-respect and your pleasure in the mail-order business. Don't shrug your shoulders at this. Many a good person has found out with terrible regret that what seemed like a prank wound up as a terrible burden on the conscience. Don't think you can play footsie with the public without coming to feel guilty and losing your esteem for yourself. Few happenings can cause more misery and unhappiness.

How to Check on Legality

Here are some ways to find out if your offer is legal:

- *Don't Assume That What Others Do Is Legal.*   Some of the advertisements you see will eventually be squelched by the authorities. Others are prepared by very slick operators who know the law well, employ smart lawyers, and are not frightened of going to jail. If you try to imitate them, you will either play too safe and make no money, or you will go too far and land in trouble.

- *Use Your Common Sense about Whether Your Offer and Advertisement Are Honest.*   Show the ad to friends and ask them what they think it means. If they are misled by the ad, rewrite it. If you are ashamed to show the ad to friends because of your good name, then the offer is probably shady and illegal.

- *Get Information.*   Write to the Federal Trade Commission and ask for the Trade Regulation Rule on Mail Order Merchandise of 1975, from the Federal Register of October 22, 1975, and November 5, 1975, and for their weekly "News Summary." Write to the Information Service of the Post Office and ask for their monthly bulletin "Enforcement Action—Fraud and Mailability." Do this today, and by the time you are ready to go into business, you will have learned a great deal about what is legal and what is not.

Call or write the Council of Better Business Bureaus, 1150 17th St. N.W., Washington, D.C. 20036 or 845 3d Ave., New York, NY 10022. Ask if they have had any complaints about the concerns that will be your competitors.

You may request opinions about the legitimacy of your product, your offer, or your advertisement from the Federal Trade Commission, the Food and Drug Administration, or the Attorney General of the United States, all in Washington. Make sure that your request is routed to the appropriate addressee. Do *not* ask your local post office head for an opinion. He or she is prevented by regulation from doing anything more than to refer you to the appropriate section of the regulations.

- *Check with a Lawyer.* Try to find a lawyer who has experience with advertising and marketing problems. If you select a general practitioner, he or she may appreciate your referring him or her to the sources below.

- *Read and Research.* A fine new help for mail-order people has recently appeared, a book by Robert J. Posch, Jr., entitled *The Direct Marketer's Legal Adviser.* Posch covers the most important legal topics relevant to operating mail-order firms, and he also provides what seems to this layman as an excellent set of references for those of you (or your lawyers) who want to go even deeper. The only shortcoming I can find with this book is that it does not cover illegal and unethical businesses, but it is instead written for the legitimate businessperson. That's fine. But even the most decent people have been known to temporarily stray off the reservation, and they need to be reminded of the limits of decency and the law.

You may want to consult these other books, though some may require that you can find your way around a law library:

The Law for Advertising and Marketing, Morton J. Simon, and the *Advertising Truth Book,* which Simon wrote for the Advertising Federation of America.[12]

Honesty and Competition, George J. Alexander, Syracuse University Press, 1967.

Trade Regulation Reporter, a Commerce Clearing House publication.

Do's and Don'ts in Advertising Copy, National Better Business Bureau.

"The Regulations of Advertising," *Columbia Law Review,* vol. 56, p. 1018, November 1956.

Postal Frauds and Crimes, Mack Taylor (1931).

The Law of Advertising, George and Peter Rosden, New York: Mathew Bender, 1974.

Carefully read the statement, in Appendix B from the 1954 *Federal Trade Commission Annual Report.* It is a good summary of what you can and cannot do.

The Mail-Order Rule of Fulfillment

Even the most honest and ethical mail-order operator can fall afoul of the law by simply being insufficiently attentive to shipping merchandise on time. You must ship the merchandise within 30 days of receiving the order or you can be penalized up to $10,000 for each violation, unless you clearly tell the prospective customer that the order will take longer than that to arrive. This requirement has four parts, as summarized by Posch:[13]

1. You must not solicit any order unless you have reasonable basis to believe that you can fulfill it on time.

2. If a delay occurs, "you must send a postage-paid return notice to the buyer clearly and conspicuously offering the buyer the choice to either cancel the order and receive a full and prompt refund or extend the time for shipment to a specified revised shipping date."

3. If you still cannot ship at the end of the first delay period, "you must notify the buyer of the additional delay. You may request the buyer's permission to ship at a future date or even at a vague, indefinite date . . . . If the buyer remains "silent" . . . then you must treat the order as cancelled and return a refund promptly."

4. Certain state laws have tougher special provisions.

Be careful. Firms have been penalized as much as $200,000. For more details on the Mail Order Rule, see Appendix B.

7

Strategies of Mail-Order Selling

*Which Media to Use for Your Test? / Direct Mail
versus Display Advertising / The Advantages and
Disadvantages of Classified Advertising / Selling
through Agents versus Other Mail-Order
Methods / Joint Venture ("Syndication") versus
Going It Alone*

By this time I assume you have selected a product. Either it is a
product that you already sell at retail, or it is a product you decided
upon after following the procedure in Chapters 3 through 5. If you
have not yet decided on a product, you should go back and follow
the instructions in those chapters.

But you're not in business yet! You won't *really* be in business until
you have tested a particular ad for your product in one or more
media—and obtained successful results!

The greatest thing about the mail-order business is that you can
reserve final judgment until you have the best possible evidence for
your decision to go full steam ahead. Generally you can't know whether
a retail store or other kinds of business will succeed until you have
invested $5,000, $15,000, or $50,000. But in mail order you hold
back all but $50 or $500 of your stake till you almost *know* your
business will succeed.

You can't get off so cheaply if you choose to sell a line of repeat-
order goods or a line of catalog items. In that case, you must test

not only the pull of your original ads, but you must also test the subsequent reorders from your customers. Chapter 22 tells you how to calculate. In any case, your original ad or mailing will not break even on repeat-order goods. The amount you "lose" on that first ad is your investment in the customer list which will form the backbone of your business.

Selling by inquiry—and—follow-up requires somewhat more investment than a one-shot item. One of the biggest correspondence-course operators budgets $20,000 to test a new correspondence course; $10,000 of that is for the writing of the course, and $10,000 is for testing ads. But if you have time and the knowledge to do your own work, you can get by with far, far less. The *out-of-pocket* expense to me in setting up a correspondence course of mine was much less than $500.

Selling through agents also requires more testing investment than one-shot sales but less than a catalog business.

Your problem now is how to spend your $50 to $500 wisely so that you can get a positive test. You must draw up a blueprint for your mail-order selling effort. You want to make the blueprint as successful as you can, right from the start.

The three most important decisions you must make, in the order of their importance, are decisions about

1. The *type* of media to use and the specific media in which you will place your test ads

2. The proposition you will offer

3. The copy and layout of your ad

Which Media to Use for Your Test?

If you choose a product that is already sold by several competitors, your choice of media in which to test is obvious. Advertise in exactly the same magazines that your competitors advertise in *most frequently* and with the *biggest ads.* That's where your best chance of success is.

Some mail-order people advise against testing in the most promising media. They say that you are likely to get inflated expectations of how your product will sell. They have a point in their argument.

But I believe in trying the very best media first because even if you have only a mild success there, and you can never improve your technique, you have found a *small* profit anyway, a profit you can tap again and again.

Besides, it is much less painful to test various offers and copy if you make a couple of bucks at the same time, instead of having to shell out of your pocket for each test.

If your product is *not* being sold by mail by competitors, then choose media in which *similar* products are advertised. If you intend to sell garden furniture, go where other furniture or garden advertisers are—maybe to magazines like *House Beautiful* or the garden section of *The New York Times.*

If you have a new correspondence course to teach a skilled trade, go where other trade correspondence courses are advertised—maybe to magazines like *Popular Science,* or the *Premium Men's Group* magazines or *Specialty Salesman.*

If you have a new type of low-cost insurance offer (not likely for a beginner), try the mailing lists used by advertisers of auto insurance, casualty insurance, and life insurance. A good list broker can steer you to those lists.

Still in the dark? If your product is so different from anything else on the market (and it should *not* be), you may not even know whether to use direct mail, display advertising, or classified advertising. The following sections will teach you the advantages and disadvantages of the three basic mail-order media.

You may test television, radio, matchbook covers, and other exotic media—but only *after* you are successful in the basic types of selling channels.

If you sell a line of goods by catalog, there are two ways you can test whether an item should become a permanent part of your catalog—as permanent as anything can be in the mail-order business.

1. Insert a 2- or 3-inch ad into mail-order media with which you are well acquainted—perhaps a regional edition of *The Wall Street Journal* or a Sunday newspaper supplement or *The New York Times Magazine*—for a quick test. After several such tests of different items, you will learn what a set of results in that medium indicates about the probable pull of the items in your own catalog.

2. Or, run the product in one edition of your catalog. This is the fairest test of all, of course. Its only disadvantage is the time it takes to obtain results.

Direct Mail versus Display Advertising

Before we begin comparing direct mail to display advertising, a word about classified advertising: If your offer even remotely lends itself to classified advertising, *try classified first*. Only after you have tested classified and taken advantage of its possibilities, should you go on to *either* direct mail or display.

Now let's continue on the assumption that you either have done what you could with classified, or that classified does not lend itself to your offer. When should you use direct mail? The answer is *not* "always," as some beginners in mail order think. In fact, direct mail is not the first medium you should think of for products. I think you should first consider whether your offer will sell profitably in display ads. If it seems to be a toss-up between display and direct mail, try display first. Here are reasons for trying display first:

1. Testing is cheaper in display. For $200 to $300 total cost for space *and* preparation, you can often get an accurate idea of whether a product will succeed. But preparation costs alone, for the simplest direct-mail piece, will be many times as expensive. And as noted in Chapter 22, you must test *several* direct-mail lists before you can have any confidence in the results.

2. Testing is also more *informative* in display. Some magazines are very general in appeal, partly because of their huge circulation—Sunday supplements and the "shelter" magazines, for example. Unless your offer is very specialized, you can rest assured that poor results in a very general medium are not due to an idiosyncrasy of the medium, as might often be the case with lists.

Use direct mail if your competitors use it. Their success promises your success. That is the basic logic of this entire book.

Use direct mail if you can shoot at prospects with a rifle instead of a shotgun. (That is the favorite metaphor of the direct-mail enthusiasts.) If your product has much greater appeal for some groups of people than it does for others, and if your potential customers can be identified by any external characteristics and a list of them is available, then you should consider using direct mail.

For example, if you want to sell a course on raising children, any general magazine *may* be satisfactory. If you sell a book on Catholic religious instruction, Catholic magazines deliver the audience you want. But if you sell a teaching device of special interest to priests who head Catholic schools, you will probably use direct mail (unless Catholic educators also have their own magazine).

Compiled lists are the most specialized of all. Lists of mail-order buyers are not so specialized except with reference to the product they bought originally. A list of customers who buy cheese by mail is tremendously specialized for another cheese company (which isn't likely to be able to rent the list). It is much less specialized for gift sellers, though the list may nevertheless be a very profitable list for them.

Industrial and commercial lists are very specialized, of course. Businesses that sell to a particular industry will generally use both direct mail and the trade magazines. But direct mail is far more essential to them. Trade-magazine space costs are very high compared with space costs in consumer magazines, and that narrows the gap between display and direct-mail costs.

Direct mail is also more flexible for the form of the copy message, the timing of the message, the addressee of the message, the length of the message—and also the infinite combinations of the form of the "package," the color, and so on. Direct mail is also much more satisfactory for repeat-order businesses.

Office supplies are a favorite product sold by direct mail to *many* industries and trades. Economic information services are another very successful direct-mail product to businesses.

Any *particular* nonfiction book is an extremely specialized item. Few books on special topics in anthropology or mathematics are likely to have a wide general audience. There is seldom a magazine circulation that corresponds perfectly with the focus of the book—even an anthropology or mathematics journal, though they may be good media anyway. Furthermore, the publisher can do the necessary *complete* selling job only in direct mail. That's why publishers of specialized nonfiction use direct mail so much.

Use direct mail only if you expect to get at least a $10-size order out of the average customer, including all future purchases—$20 may be a more sensible figure—and at least $30 to $50 total sales to the average customer over time. These amounts are based on

1. The minimum costs to get a mailing into the mail (perhaps $150 to $250 per thousand, in 1980)

2. The highest rates of response you can possibly expect in any large-scale mailing

For example, correspondence-course sellers seldom are willing to pay more than $1, $2, or $3 at most for inquiries from display ads. But to get inquiries at such low costs from direct-mail solicitation, they would need to obtain a response of around 10 percent—which is very unlikely, indeed.

But if you can afford a much higher inquiry cost and if the specialized prospects cannot be obtained through magazines, direct mail might be the way to go.

You are more likely to use direct mail to develop new customers if you sell a "repeat item." Repeat items obviously produce more revenue in the long run than items that the customer never buys again, and therefore a new customer is worth more to you. In fact, if you sell a repeat item, you usually expect to lose money on the first order (if you count in the cost of developing the customer, as you should).

Repeat-item catalog houses use direct mail to solicit for all orders after the first, of course.

Use direct mail when you have a story to tell that is too long and complicated for a display ad. Use direct mail when your product requires illustration, especially in color. There are virtually no limits to the methods you can use to tell your story in direct mail.

Catalogs are an example of a form of *material* that can be carried by direct mail but not by magazines.

Sometimes you don't want the whole world to know about a special proposition you are offering to some part of your market. Magazine publishers, for instance, sell some subscriptions at full price and others at a cut rate. If they offered cut-rate deals in display ads, no one would ever renew a subscription at the full rate.

The relative privacy of direct mail provides *some* screen from the prying eyes of your competitors. The display advertiser does business in a fishbowl and is often eaten by predatory cats.

Direct mail can search a limited geographical area for customers, and most periodicals cannot. A manufacturer of fire alarms developed a lovely small-area technique. First he saturates a town to develop leads for his "sales engineers." Then he sends circulars to the immediate *neighbors* of each family that buys, telling the neighbors to ask the person who purchased what he or she thinks of the fire-alarm system. This follow-the-leader method helps instill confidence in the product.

After saturating each town, the sales force moves on like an infantry company following an artillery barrage. This is a great way to use direct mail.

Some advertisers use both direct mail *and* display advertising to develop new contracts. Firms that sell through agents also seek prospects through direct mail because only a few magazines reach a heavy proportion of potential agents. Novelty and gift-catalog firms often use both display ads and direct mail. The moral to the story is that you should use *every* medium that will return you any profit on your investment. Only in that way can you maximize your earnings.

In two important ways, direct mail is *easier* to use than display advertising:

1. The time lag between mailing and getting enough returns for accurate predictions is much less than the lag between placing your ad in a magazine and getting predictable returns from it (though newspapers can be even faster). This means you can make more money *quicker* in direct mail than in display advertising. And you recover your investment quicker.

2. Some direct-mail advertisers will scream to high heaven that I'm wrong about this, but—direct-mail *testing* is much more accurate than display-ad testing (except for split-run copy testing). From any set of results in reasonable numbers, the direct-mail advertiser can get a much better idea than the display advertiser about what will happen when the original advertising is repeated to new names on the same list.

Yes, it is true that the results ordinarily will fall off when you go back to a list after a test because the test was not done clearly enough. But the direct-mail advertiser can take account of that in the calculations. Seasonal effects can also be allowed for.

The display advertiser, however, is at the mercy of changes in the position of the ad in the magazine, more or less competition, better or worse editorial matter, timing of the ad, and many other factors. The display advertiser never does as well on the second insertion either (all else being equal), but he or she has more trouble estimating the drop-off than does the direct-mail advertiser.

The greater predictive power of direct-mail results means that the direct-mail advertiser can often—though not always—proceed more rapidly, with greater confidence, than can the display advertiser.

These two advantages are *not* reasons for choosing to use direct mail. Whether or not you use direct mail *must depend on the product.* There may, however, be reasons for choosing a product that can be sold by direct mail.

The Advantages and Disadvantages of Classified Advertising

The *advantage* of advertising in classified columns is that, for almost any product, a dollar spent in classified advertising will bring back more profit than a dollar spent in any other space unit. That is a fact, proved many times. Chapter 16 shows a comparison of the effectiveness of classified against other space units. That is why so many advertisers who use display ads—and even full-page ads—also continue using the humble classified columns. Correspondence schools almost all use both display and classified.

Furthermore, many large firms got their start with their original ads in classified columns. Fuller Brush began with classified.

You can't generate large volume and create a big business in classified columns alone, however. You may not think so at first, but the number of places in which you can run profitable classified is small, and this restricts your business badly. Few classified advertisers can invest even $1,500 per month in classified. Most of them are limited to a much smaller expenditure by the lack of productive media.

A small budget means a small possible profit. You'll have to be a very efficient and clever mail-order dealer to net an honest $750 on a $500 advertising expenditure.

This limitation also explains why classified advertising is not used by many firms that *should* use it. An advertising agency's 15 percent commission on $500 doesn't look very big compared with the work involved in billing and handling the paperwork. So agencies do not recommend classified to their clients. This problem can be solved profitably for everyone concerned by increasing the agency's commission on classified (perhaps as high as 30 percent) or by paying the agency on a fee basis or by cutting the agency in for a fixed percent of the total volume on the gross profit. Until very recently, this was considered unethical by advertising and media people, but practices are changing now.

Classified is an excellent place for the mail-order novice to begin. You can test products and gain invaluable practical experience with very small amounts of capital. Anybody can afford to risk $10 for a test ad in a million-circulation magazine. The thrills and experience will be worth that much even if the first attempt, or the first five attempts, are total busts.

The novice who advertises in classified does not have to arrange for typography, layout, or art work. In classified, you *can* get into the mail-order business with an ad written on scrap paper and sent directly to the magazine.

Most classified advertisements offer free information to develop inquiries. Direct sales are seldom made from classified ads. The reason is obvious: It is rare that you can tell enough about a product in ten words or twenty words so that the potential customer (1) wants the product, (2) understands what it is, and (3) knows how much it costs and where to order.

However, it is relatively easy in a small number of words to whet a person's desire for further information. And since the reader risks no money, he or she does not need to be convinced of your reliability in order to inquire. In your follow-up letter you have plenty of time to describe the product in detail and to convince the prospect that you are honest and reliable and that the product or service is a good buy. Chapter 25 describes in detail the follow-up letters you should send in response to inquiries.

Some products are sold directly from ads *as well as* through inquiries—often next to one another in the same magazines—by different firms. And neither forces the other out of business. These are usually information manuals (employment information, how to start a credit business, etc.) that sell for $2 to $5 directly from the ad, or for $10 and up from follow-up letters to inquirers.

Most successful classified ads are of these types:

1. Ads for agents to sell products house to house. This is a more complicated business than other types of mail order.

2. Ads to produce inquiries for books, correspondence courses, and other information. This includes all "homework" schemes.

3. Ads that sell pamphlets directly from the ads.

Few classified ads are for repeat products, though recently some catalog operators have begun to use classified ads to generate inquiries for their catalogs.

Selling through Agents versus Other Mail-Order Methods

There are two basic ways that you can use agents as part of a mail-order operation:

1. Your agents can go out and find prospects for your goods, and sell them directly. This method is used for those types of mail-order products that almost necessarily require the use of agents: men's shoes and suits, for example, and cosmetics for women. These products require deomonstration to induce the customer to buy.

Direct salespersons get a commission of up to 60 percent of the sale price on their sales.

2. A second method is to have a sales force close leads in person that you have *developed by mail.* Encyclopaedia Britannica, major insurance firms, and top correspondence schools use this method. So do smaller outfits like Enurtone (a device to prevent bed-wetting).

A salesperson can generally double the number of sales you can close by mail alone, and the commission runs from 5 to 15 percent. Usually a product must sell for at least $50 to $100 to make this method profitable.

Either method of selling through agents is somewhat more complicated than other types of mail-order methods, and they usually involve a larger investment and greater preparation. You not only have to develop the advertising to sell the final customer, but you must also develop the selling campaign to convince prospective agents that they should sell your product for you.

But don't underestimate the potential of selling through agents. Many of the largest mail-order firms work through sales agents. One expert in this field recently estimated that there are a million agents in the country who make a full-time living selling for mail-order firms, and lots more who work part-time.

Joint Venture ("Syndication") versus Going It Alone

There are business situations in which it is best to undertake the entire venture yourself. But there are also situations in which it makes sense to share the burden. There has been considerable increase in the number of joint ventures, especially among relatively big businesses. The most frequent form of cooperation has been between (1) owners of firms with large mailing lists of affluent customers—for example, the owners of credit-card lists, such as the oil companies and finance companies such as American Express; (2) producers of expensive home equipment, such as cameras and table recorders; and (3) the mail-order campaign developer.

A typical division of labor, as described by Bell & Howell's Direct Mail Marketing Division, is as follows:

EACH MAILING IS A 3-WAY JOINT VENTURE

1. *Manufacturer Provides*
   * Product that works
   * Shipments per scheduled requirements
   * Product and market information and assistance on ongoing basis

2. *Campaign Development Organization Provides*
   * Development of product idea and total package (with testing)
   * Creative development (and testing)
   * Advertising printing and production services
   * Contract sales of mailing commitments
   * Procurement of inventory in advance of mailing requirements
   * Drop-shipping services
   * Client and consumer order handling, customer and product services
   * Returned merchandise service

3. *Mailing Client (or Third Party) Provides*
   * List and list maintenance
   * Total mailing cost and printing and postage
   * Order receipt and screening
   * Credit clearance
   * Debt collection service

In the past, firms were leery of joint ventures for fear of being cheated by partners. But American businesses have increasingly learned that it pays not to worry about getting the last penny that is coming to them and therefore to be more free and easy about engaging in joint ventures. If you are in a situation in which the other party really brings to an enterprise some assets or skills which you do not possess, a joint venture can be a very good deal indeed.

8

The Tactical Decisions in Mail Order

Sell from the Ad or from Follow-ups? / What Price Should You Set? / Refunds, Guarantees, Trial Offers, and CODs / Credit Cards / Installment Credit versus Cash on the Barrelhead / Should You Solicit Telephone Orders?

These are the important decisions you must make about the selling proposition:

1. Whether you will try to close the sale
   a. Directly in your ad or letter
   b. By the inquiry-and-follow-up technique
   c. Through agents
2. What price you should set
3. What kind of trial offer or credit terms you will extend

There are many promotional tactics that can increase the number of orders that you get, including

1. A time limit on the offer. This prevents procrastination, but it may turn off the buyer.
2. Sweepstakes and contests. These are effective but expensive, and you must be careful with the law.
3. Credit terms and postponed payments, such as "Bill me only upon receipt." Credit costs you money, and it increases bookkeeping and hassle.
4. Sale prices, "prepublication" prices, closeouts, and so on.
5. Bonuses and/or premiums for large orders or for orders paid with cash.
6. Most powerful of all is the free trial and/or iron-clad money-back guarantee.

Sell from the Ad or from Follow-ups?

Offers priced at $50 or over usually cannot be sold directly from a display ad. For a purchase involving a lot of money, the prospect needs a longer sales pitch than you can deliver in a space ad. You need a follow-up direct-mail piece to do the job.

The standard technique for merchandise priced over $25 or $50 is either (1) to run display advertising offering further information and then to follow up with direct mail, or (2) to solicit with direct mail only.

If you use the two-step display-plus-follow-up technique, don't show the price in the ad. This is because, like a good encyclopedia salesperson, you don't want to scare the prospect away before you have had the opportunity to make the prospect want the product very badly.

Ordinarily your first direct-mail piece to a prospect will aim to make the sale. However, some products require such elaborate and expensive sales presentations that you can afford to send your direct-mail pieces only to prime prospects. If so, your first letter is just a canvass technique to obtain really hot prospects. Then you send these prospects the full presentation. The famous Southern Roofing direct-mail campaign first canvassed for inquiries. Those people who returned the inquiry card then got follow-up letters which contained full information.

What Price Should You Set?

The basic rule is that you should pick the price at which you will make the most money.

The way to find that "best" price is to test many different prices.

A manual can sell as a book for $8.95 or $15.95. Or the same information in a slightly different format can go for $39.50, $49.50, $69.50, $99.50, or even $249.50. Whether you sell for $8.95 versus $15.95 or $49.50 versus $69.50 will be a matter for testing. But whether you sell the item as a book or as a correspondence course is a more basic strategic question.

The price of a mail-order item depends relatively little on the wholesale cost to you, but it depends heavily on the costs of advertising and selling it.

How to Test for the Best Price

To choose the best price, you must know how to figure the profit you make at that price. Here's how to figure the profit you make on a single ad:

1. Add

    a. Advertising cost

    b. Cost of merchandise, including labor, postage, and other incidental costs

2. Subtract from total dollars received

3. The difference is your profit on the ad

Here is an example: Packages of a dozen ball-point pens cost you 80 cents per order to ship, including all merchandise and handling costs except advertising. You run two ads, each costing $200, which are identical except for the price advertised. Ad A asks $2, ad B asks $3.98:

Ad A

Pulls 300 order @ $2—total revenue	$600	
Cost—300 × 80¢ for merchandise		$240
Advertising cost		200
		$440

$600 – $440 = profit of $160

Ad B

Pulls 130 order @ $3.98—total revenue	$517.40	
Cost—130 × 80¢ for merchandise		$104.00
Advertising cost		200.00
		$304.00

$517.40 − $304 = profit of $213.40

The $3.98 price listed in ad B is clearly the more profitable price of the two.

This simple example shows you that the offer at almost twice the price does *not* need to pull twice as many inquiries to be more profitable.

If the purpose of your advertisement is to create customers for your other products as well as to sell the product that you have advertised, then you must figure differently. Very often you will be willing to sell a product at a lower price, and to take less profit directly from the ad, in order to increase the number of customers added to your list.

The correct way to figure the price in this repeat-business case is to add the future dollar value of the customers to the immediate profit of the ad. Chapter 9 teaches you how to figure the dollar value of customers.

This is how one mail-order operator broke down his costs for a "typical article," probably a printed manual, that sold for $2.98 a few years ago.[1]

Product and postage	$0.45
Overhead—5%	0.15
Shipping container	0.06
Shipping label	0.02
Instruction sheet	0.02
Order processing	0.15
Reserve for refunds—5% of sales	0.15
Bank charges	0.05
	$1.05 = total merchandise costs

At a selling price of $2.98, any ad that brings in orders at an average advertising cost of less than $1.93 makes a profit on this article. In other words, if a $50 ad brings 32 orders (for $95.36), the average advertising cost is $50 divided by 32, or $1.56 each. The profit per order is $1.93 less $1.56, or 37 cents each.

How to Guess the Best Price

In your first test ad, you should try the price that has the best possibilities. The following observations should help you pick a price. But please notice that they are all very old by now, and the prices have been much outmoded by inflation. (If you double or triple them, they may make sense in 1986 terms.) But these observations are still the best we have, dated or not.

1. Victor Schwab said in 1950 that $2 or $1.98 is the lowest price at which you can make money without follow-up sales.[2] Schwab may be generally right about that, but I myself made many happy thousands of dollars selling products for a buck a throw. That includes manuals and merchandise, too. Of course the cost of the goods, plus postage, must be under 25¢.

On the basis of split-run tests (described in the next section) Schwab found[3]

> $2 did 62.2 percent better than $2.50 (product sold to women)
>
> $1.98 did 87.7 percent better than $2.75
>
> $2 did 26.7 percent better than $4 plus free premium (7 months of a magazine versus 12 months of the same magazine)

2. Harold Preston found in 1941 that a $1 or $2 price would outpull a fractional price (such as 98 cents or $1.98), probably because it is easy to mail one or two dollar bills.[4] But above $2 he found that fractional prices do better.

Preston certainly is right at the $1 level. But more firms use $1.98 than $2, which makes me think $1.98 may be generally better. Preston made his observation four decades ago, and more families use checks now than they did then.

Catalog houses even use fractional prices under $1. Their customers usually buy several items at a time, however; hence their situation is different.

Even-dollar prices also have the advantage of getting you more cash and fewer checks. The bank charges you to cash checks, and you have *clerical costs*, no matter how small the check is; so they are undesirable. But this is less important now than it used to be because such a large proportion of the population have checking accounts and credit cards.

(CAUTION: A few mail-order operators think that the hard-to-trace cash dealings in mail order make a perfect setup to beat the Internal Revenue Service. It isn't so. One very famous mail-order man shot himself because he was discovered by the tax people to have had $40,000 in small change in his safe. You'll live a happier and freer life if you play it straight with the government and with yourself.)

3. Verneur Pratt observed that "large mail-order houses (like Sears and Montgomery Ward) consistently cut prices on standard goods, the values of which are known, and make up the loss by selling 'blind merchandise at long-profit prices.' "⁵

4. Competition doesn't always set the price. As of 1965, two firms had sold hypnotism manuals successfully for years in tiny classified ads. One sold for $1, the other for $2. Some customers must obviously have thought they would be getting a better product for $2, even though the ads gave them no reason to believe that was true. Two other firms have sold hypnotism manuals at $1.98 and $3.98, respectively, in display ads.

5. It usually holds true that even if your product is printed material, where cost is small relative to the advertising cost, you generally will need returns greater than one and one-half times the cost of an ad to make money directly from the ad.

Furthermore, overhead is always higher than you think it is. You'll be lucky to make a profit if your advertising, plus your goods, costs you more than 70 percent of your revenue.

6. Offering several qualities, or several different sizes, is very often a successful pricing policy. In some cases such a policy cannot lose, as, for example, when you are offering sampler packages. A fancy-tea firm first tried out a catalog at 25 cents versus a sampler package of three teas for $1. The latter worked better. But then the owner got the idea of offering *both* the catalog *and* the samples in the same ad, and that did much better than either price offer alone. Then he also tried a $3 sampler *together with* the 25 cent catalog and $1 sampler, and the combination was still another improvement. Eventually, after a great deal of testing of differenct combinations, he found that a 25 cent catalog and samplers at $1, $3, and $6 was best of all in terms of long-run profit. And it makes sense that you usually gain by adding an optional higher-priced offer. It does not reduce the total number of orders, and at least some people will want the higher-priced package (though sometimes not enough to make the offer worthwhile).

Refunds, Guarantees, Trial Offers, and CODs

The terms of the offer can have a terrific effect on your sales. It is very important that you choose the most *profitable* terms. And the offer that pulls the most orders is not necessarily the most profitable.

The Refund Offer. It is a practically unbreakable rule in mail order that you must guarantee satisfaction or money back. Even if you don't want to offer a guarantee, many advertising media will accept your advertisement only if you agree to do so.

It is true that some people will return goods. Some people even are cranks about returning goods. Others will find interesting ways to sting you. And none of us likes to part with money that has once been paid over to us.

Nevertheless, you will almost surely wind up with more *profit* overall by making the refund offer. The extra sales will more than counterbalance the refunds you pay out.

Once in a while you may offer a product on which returns are so high that you lose money. If that happens, it's usually because the product is rotten, and that should be an indication for you to pull it off the market until you can improve it.

Returns can be quite high and the offer still can make money. Booksellers who offer a 7-day free trial without payment of any sort expect 20 percent of the books to be returned and 20 percent more not to be paid for. They can still wind up in the black.

Returns can be very small if customers are truly satisfied. In the 1960s I sold thousands upon thousands of a tiny sixteen-page booklet that cost under 3 cents to print—for $1 a booklet. I offered an unconditional guarantee of satisfaction with no time limit. I received exactly one request for a refund—from an apologetic fellow who said he had bought another copy months before.

There are several types of guarantees you can make. You can offer money back within 7 days, within a month, or within a full year. You can offer double-your-money-back, too. The strength of the guarantee will affect the pull of the ad as well as the number of returned orders. If you have a really strong product, make the strongest possible guarantee.

If the number of returned orders you get on the strongest possible guarantee is significantly large, your final decision will depend upon a *test* of the various refund-offer plans.

If you offer a full-year guarantee, you don't need to wait a whole year to find out how many returned orders you will get. How fast they come back depends upon the product and how long it takes customers to give it a real trial. But in any case, you can almost always count on more than half the returns coming back within a month of receipt.

When you make your guarantee, emphasize in your ad that if your customers want their money back, they'll get their money back. A money-back guarantee always seems a little too good to be true. And readers are suspicious that you will find some excuse not to refund. Write your guarantee as powerfully as you can to put that fear to rest. "Iron-clad." "Unconditional." "Legally binding guarantee." "No questions asked."

CODs.   No matter how powerful your language is, country shrewdness makes people want to keep a tight hold on their money till they are *sure.* That's where the COD comes in. They are willing to pay extra to be sure that you won't run off with their money without sending the goods. This is especially true for mail order over television and radio. People have less faith in the spoken word than in the printed word.

Offering the COD option will increase your response, compared with "Sorry, No CODs," especially if you word it strongly enough. Lately the fashion has been to say "Free 7-day trial" when you mean that the customer orders by COD and has the right to return within 7 days.

Even on installment deals, COD can help. Schwab quoted a test in 1950 in which a $2 COD first payment did 23 percent better than $1 cash in advance.[6]

COD mailing charges cost money to everyone, of course. It costs the buyer more. And it costs you, too, in clerical costs, plus the COD and postage costs for refusals of orders. Until recently, most firms that sell articles for $2 to $10 offered COD, so it obviously has paid for most firms. Recently there seems to have been a considerable decline in the use of CODs, perhaps because so many people now pay with checks and credit cards, about which they feel some greater safety than with cash.

As of 1953, Baker estimated that for shopping-section items, COD refusals averaged 5 to 8 percent of orders shipped.[7] For less expensive merchandise than that which Baker talked about, the refusal rate will be less. And like everything else in mail order, the COD refusal rate will vary among customers from different media.

CODs are particularly important for TV or radio advertising.

Push the prospects hard to send cash with order. Emphasize the high cost of COD and that you prepay postage for cash with order. Even offer an extra premium for cash payment.

Many firms that sell articles for $4 and up—and sometimes for $2 articles—ask for $1 deposit on COD shipments. The seller keeps the deposit if the COD is refused. That way the seller can't lose by the shipment even if it is refused. The deposit also cuts the refusal rate. But I've never seen data showing that the deposit method is more profitable overall.

A 1960s *Esquire* newsletter suggested five ways to reduce COD refusals.[8]

1. *State the terms of your offer clearly.* Don't say "$2.95 plus a few cents postage," the customer may think a "few cents" postage means six or eight cents. But 18 cents postage plus 40 cents COD* is not just "a few cents." Phrase your offer this way: "Only $1 postpaid, or COD for $1.38." The customer knows definitely how much money to have ready when the package arrives. This not only cuts down refusals but stimulates cash orders by offering a saving for cash payment.

2. *Ship the merchandise the same day the order arrives, if possible.* If you delay for three or four days, the customer may be out of the city, may change his mind, or may have spent the money on something else. It's always a good idea to ship the merchandise while the customer is hot.

3. One advertiser switches COD's into cash in this manner: "Check here if enclosing your remittance. We pay the 58 cents postage and COD fees. Same 7 day return privilege." When the customer knows what saving can be made by sending cash, your cash sales will increase and COD refusals decrease.

4. *Acknowledge COD orders* and let the customer know how much money to have ready for the postman. You can do this with a postcard, filling in the exact amount of money needed.

5. *Ask for a deposit with the original order.* This reduces refusals to a minimum. When the customer has some money invested in the merchandise, it is very unlikely that he will refuse the shipment.

The Trial Offer. Schwab ran a test on a $4.68 encyclopedia of "Send No Money" versus "Send $1" COD. "Send No Money" pulled 10 percent better.[9] That suggests to me that after all the costs and revenues were calculated, the "Send No Money" offer would come out ahead.

People like to keep their money in their hands until they have the goods. They also like to delay their final purchasing decision as long as they possibly can. The trial offer is designed to get around the

---

* The COD rate is now considerably higher.

reluctance that people have to commit themselves. The trial offer gives people the feeling that they have maximum freedom to return the merchandise after they have examined it.

People also seem to prefer to delay payment even when the commitment is made. Think how many times you have said "Bill me later" even when you knew the purchase was final.

Here are Stone's figures on delayed-payment offers, relative to a rating of 100 for cash with order: Cash with order and free gift for trying the product, 144; "Bill me" (open account), 177; "Bill me" and free gift for trying, 233.[10]

Here are some figures that show the power of the trial offer, from Schwab's tests.[11]

1. A 5-day examination before payment versus cash on the line. The full-examination offer pulled better by 60, 98, 24 and 34 percent in four tests.
2. A 10-day examination before payment versus COD. The approval offer *pulled* 62.6 percent better (this was a $2.50 article).
3. A 7-day-approval examination versus COD, on a $1.98 offer. The 7-day approval did 28 percent better.

Naturally, what you *really* care about is the amount of *profit* you wind up with. Just because a trial offer pulls more requests doesn't mean you make more that way. That means that you must make a careful calculation to evaluate whether you are better off with or without the trial offer.

According to Paul Grant, firms that ship on approval average 65 percent payment, 20 percent returns, and 15 percent nonpayment.[12] These figures probably apply to merchandise priced higher than that studied by Schwab, and therefore they are probably more conservative.

You can also raise your rate of profit by offering an extra discount, premium, or other throw-in. Grant gives us these observations:[13]

1. A five percent discount for promptness in ordering (usually with a two-week limit) usually increases the number of orders from 2% to as high as 9%.
2. An offer to prepay parcel post postage on products weighing from four pounds, up, usually results in bringing orders more quickly (with the same two week limit) and has been known to increase orders as much as 4%.
3. Where a choice of COD or cash is given the purchaser, an offer to pay postage on cash orders results in a higher percentage of cash receipts ranging from 3% to as high as 10%, depending upon the weight of the product and the distance it is to be shipped.
4. A 5% discount instead of prepaid postage . . . has approximately the same effect on increase in the number of orders.

5. Offering a desirable giveaway in consideration for a prepaid order or for orders received in a limited time has been known to increase the number of orders from 2% to as high as 8%.

In each case the question is whether the tactic that gets you more orders and gross revenue also brings in more *net* revenue.

Credit Cards

Credit cards enable people to buy on credit. And if you accept credit-card purchases, you *will* increase the volume of your business, both in numbers of orders and in size of orders.

Credit-card sales have truly exploded, rising by a factor of *60* from 1967 to 1979, from $86 million to $60 billion.[14] Now a mail-order firm can refuse to accept them only at a high cost in lost sales. Perhaps 10 to 15 percent of mail-order sales go through credit cards, and "catalog sales run, on the average, 25%–50% larger when credit cards are offered."[15] The price you must pay to the credit-card firm—or the bank for VISA and Master Charge—varies from situation to situation, but generally the bank cards cost you much less, so you might consider accepting only them.

Installment Credit versus Cash on the Barrelhead

Every top mail-order operator agrees that you *must* offer installment-payment terms to sell almost any article priced over $10. (One high-class catalog operation sells up to $20 without credit, successfully. This proves that there *is* an exception to every rule. But the exception doesn't, in turn, *prove* this or any other rule.)

You will prefer to get cash immediately, of course. So you offer a substantial discount (maybe 10 percent) for immediate payment. Five to ten percent of your customers will take you up on that discount. Later in the series of payments you will again offer discounts for immediate payment of the full *balance*. That will help get the cash, too.

You'll have to sweat for the rest. The minute a due date passes, you must send out the first letter in your collection series. And you must keep on following up with collection letters until it's no longer any use.

If you sell a correspondence course priced at $50 or up, you will eventually receive perhaps 60 percent of the total billings. Charles Atlas eventually collected in full from 73 percent of the purchasers of his $20 course. Higher-priced correspondence schools figure they are doing well if 60 percent of the purchasers pay up in full. The installment contract should be written by a lawyer, then put into simple English by you and checked by the lawyer. The contract usually holds the purchasers liable for the *entire sales price* even if they stop taking a correspondence course.

Merchandise with a relatively low markup—shop tools, jewelry, home furnishings—and high-markup printed material present different problems. The low-markup merchandise has real value to you if it is returned in default. For high-markup stuff, your problem is to extract as much money as you can from delinquents and forget about merchandise returns. Your chief weapon will be a series of collection letters. The letters should range from polite to stern. Their actual composition is crucial. Write your letters from samples that other mail-order firms use or from models in books of collections letters.[16]

You will have to tinker around to find the best intervals between letters. Best intervals for various products can range from *1 day* to more than 3 weeks.

Bringing suit for your money seldom pays unless the sale price is well into the hundreds of dollars.

Collection agencies *may* help you. Since you pay them only if they succeed in collecting, you can't lose anything. But chances are they won't see much prospect of collecting your accounts, and therefore they won't work on them.

Should You Solicit Telephone Orders?

Ever since telephones found their way into people's homes in large numbers, people have been ordering merchandise by telephone that they otherwise would have ordered by mail or in person. This meant that catalog firms such as Sears, Roebuck and Montgomery Ward set up telephone-order catalog facilities in all large cities, increasing the proportion of business in cities relative to rural business. (By now Sears does 85 percent of its mail-order business by telephone or at catalog desks.)[17] The coming of the telephone also made city department stores partly into mail-order-type operations, as many people called in their orders generated by advertisements instead of going to the store in person. (Notice the difference between *ordering* by telephone from space ads and *soliciting* business by calls initiated by the seller.)

In the 1970s, a new phenomenon appeared on the market: firms selling major appliances by phone orders on a drop-ship basis (that is, they maintain no inventory and, of course, no store). As *The New York Times* described it,[18]

CONSUMER NOTES

Buying-by-Phone Outlets for Appliances on Rise. First you could buy appliances in department stores, then discount stores, then catalogue stores and now you do not need any stores at all. Telephone discount buying of large appliances and TV sets has suddenly become popular. It works simply. You call a number, the voice at the other end says hello, you tell the voice what appliance you want and its model number, the voice gives you a price, you say, "O.K., I'll take it," you get a delivery date and when it's delivered, you pay the truck driver in cash or certified check.

In most of the telephone operations, you are talking to an outfit with no retail store and no warehouse—just contacts with large distributors of brand-name appliances. When you call, the phone discounter looks up the price in his warehouse book, and when you order, he phones the order to his supplier, who delivers directly to you.

Telephone ordering makes credit more of a problem, because you don't get cash with an order. The discount houses work on a cash-on-delivery basis, but other credit arrangements are preferred by most firms that sell by telephone.

A boost to telephone ordering comes from collect phone calls, and—even more—from the 800 system whereby a customer dials directly and you pay. You can see this device at work in Harry and David's ad in Figure 8-1. (Notice how the ad suggests calling to save time; the Books-by-Phone operation described in Figure 2-1 is built on that device.)

Telephone ordering obviously is on the rise; think about it when you plan your business.

Another phenomenon—a more important one to the mail-order business—is telephone ordering from outside the local telephone area. This innovation has occurred partially because of the decrease in long-distance telephone rates relative to people's incomes. For example, L. L. Bean of Freeport, ME has been selling hunting and fishing equipment by mail since 1913. In recent years the volume of telephone calls has been increasing rapidly:[19]

Figure 8-1

We have 8 girls on telephones for incoming orders, and they keep busy. Of course, when they are not taking telephone orders they have other work to fill in the time. However, during Christmas season they are on the phone taking orders all the time.

Telephone ordering is generally preferred by many customers. But in addition, telephone ordering makes possible increased service:[20]

On telephone orders, [L. L. Bean gets] all kinds of cases where they are leaving for an upcoming [trip] or someone has a birthday and they have to have the merchandise shipped quickly. . . .

There is so much service involved in handling our phone orders that the order taker has to know the products, or at least be in touch with one of our people that they can transfer the problem to. Also, the customer wants to know whether the item is in stock, if we can ship quickly, and we have to be able to give them that kind of service.

9

Calculating the Dollar Value of a Customer

Introduction

How much is it worth to you to get an additional customer? The calculation of the answer to this question is the most important calculation a mail-order merchant makes.

The calculation of the value of a customer may be done more precisely in the mail-order business than in any other line of business. And yet, there are many (even many successful) mail-order firms that have never made this calculation correctly, as may be seen in the interviews with mail-order firms frequently reported in *Direct Marketing*.

This chapter is not easy reading. But please don't skip it. At least read until the last example. Knowing the value of a customer is crucial because this information helps you find the break-even point for the number of responses to a space advertisement or mailing-list campaign that are necessary for you to make money rather than lose money. Once you have correctly calculated the value of a customer, you only need to estimate the number of new customers you will get from the ad or mailing (and know the cost of the space ad or the mailing) to decide if that space ad or mailing should be undertaken.

The "value of a customer" is the total *profit* he will bring you. Not the *volume*, mind you, but the profit. You certainly would not pay me $2 to bring you a customer who will give you $10 in volume but only $1 in profit. But if you had a high-margin business and $10 volume gave you $4 profit, you *would* pay me $2 to bring you in a customer who would spend $10. In *fact*, you'd be willing to pay me almost $4 for him or her. (The sophisticated readers among you will recognize that "present value" is a more precise term than "profit." The value of a customer also is a present-value concept. And the decision whether or not to accept an advertising opportunity involves some other elements left out in this chapter so as not to obscure the central point.)

Three elements enter into the calculation of the dollar value of a customer: (1) The dollar amount of revenue ("gross revenue") you expect to get from the customer in each year; (2) the cost to you of filling the order; and (3) your "cost of capital"—that is, the worth to you today of a dollar in net revenue next year or 2 years from now.

There are good customers and poor customers, and obviously the good customers are worth more than the poor customers. But we're talking now of *average* customers. When you first get a *new* customer, you can't tell whether he or she will be a good customer or not.

For a one-shot deal—say, a camera sold by Bell & Howell from a Diners Club list mailing—the calculation of the value of a customer is reasonably simple. The revenue from the first sale is all that Bell & Howell will get from the customer. And the costs of the camera are relatively easy to figure because they will all be incurred immediately. And you do not need to know the "cost of capital" because all the revenues and costs will occur within a short time, and there is no "interest" to be paid while waiting for your money. So the value of a customer to Bell & Howell is simply the sales price minus the cost of goods sold and the cost of servicing the order. (Notice that the cost of the advertisement that solicits the customer is *not* included in this calculation of the value of the customer.)

Even in this simple case one can err badly by forgetting some important costs, a matter which will be taken up in the next chapter. In this chapter we'll assume that the costs are figured correctly.

The main complication in calculating the dollar value of a customer arises when a substantial portion of your business is repeat business— as is the case for almost all successful mail-order businesses. When a substantial number of customers buy more than one time, the value of a customer derives not only from her first purchase but also from the subsequent purchases she is likely to make. If you ignore the subsequent purchases, you will arrive at a wrong calculation, too small a customer value. That will cause you to forgo some valuable customer volume, and it may actually lead you to decide that a whole line of business is unprofitable when in fact it is profitable. For example, if magazine publishers did not include repeat business in their value-of-a-customer calculations on subscription campaigns, they would never solicit *any* subscriptions by mail.

We'll proceed with several examples. We'll begin with the simplest possible example of a typist who solicits business by advertising. Next we'll go on to a common sort of repeat-business situation, a mail-order sewing-supplies firm. Then we'll wind up with a calculation from a magazine's subscription campaign that looks more complicated but still is fundamentally the same.

The Value of a Customer to Various Businesses

Let's begin with a very simple example—the case of a typist who wants to get typing work to do at home. The reason for beginning with such a simple case is that the method needed to handle this kind of problem is straightforward and almost obvious. Yet it is the same method needed for major mail-order advertising campaigns.

Assume that Judith wants to make money typing at home. She realizes that she must advertise in order to obtain jobs. The question is: Where and when should she advertise?

We must begin by collecting some information. Does Judith type fast enough to make a profit? She announces to us that she must net at least $3.75 per hour from typing. Next we must find out whether she can type fast enough to earn at least her "opportunity cost" of $3.75 per hour. Judith wisely *experiments* to determine her cost of production. She clocks herself typing some average material and determines that she can do five pages per hour on the average. If we assume for the moment she will charge the going rate for average-quality work—$1.20 per page in this town—she can hope to gross $6 per hour, not counting any possible costs of advertising promotion.

A notice on a college-dormitory bulletin board is Judith's first advertising. In the first week she gets one call, which results in her typing a four-page paper. On this evidence, she sensibly concludes that while the bulletin-board notice may produce some business, it will not produce *enough* work to keep her busy. This is frequently the case for advertisers. A particular advertising vehicle may produce business very cheaply—in this case, at practically no cost at all—and may therefore be very profitable. But advertisers must also use less efficient advertising vehicles to get more business and increase *total profit.*

Judith now considers placing advertisements in both the college daily and the town newspaper. At this point, she must begin to think in a more businesslike way. Which of the two papers is likely to bring in the most business per dollar of cost?

One source of information about an advertising vehicle's potential is observation of what other firms—other home typists, in this case— are doing. Judith observes that there are many advertisements for home typists in the college newspaper's classified section but just one ad in the town newspaper. She therefore wisely decides to imitate the other typists, and she places a classified advertisement in the college paper.

Now that Judith has run her advertisement in the college newspaper for a week's trial, she must calculate whether the advertising is profitable or not. Judith paid out $7.50 for the week's classified advertising, and she obtained two customers from it. She can directly link the customers to the advertising for these reasons: (1) She has not publicized her services in any other way; and (2) when they called, both customers said they had read her advertisement in the paper. One customer's business amounted to $9 worth; the other's was $3. This required a total of 2 hours' typing. Judith then figured this way:

Production expenditures:		
2 hours' labor × $3.75	$7.50	
Advertising expenditures	7.50	
Total cost		$15.00

The total cost of $15.00 exceeded her first week's sales of $12. Hence she figured that the advertising was a losing proposition and she decided to advertise no more.

But the following week one of her customers returned with another $6 worth of business, reducing the apparent loss on the initial advertising. Clearly Judith must somehow take account of the long-run effect, the *repeat* sales that the advertisement generates.

What is needed here is an estimate of how much business our home typist can expect to get from an *average customer in the long run.* But instead of waiting many months to collect this information, Judith wisely consults a friend who is experienced in home typing. Her friend tells her that on the average, a customer yields $30 worth of business before leaving town or graduating or buying a typewriter or otherwise ceasing to patronize the typist. Some customers provide less than $30 worth of business, of course, and others more; $30 is an average. Judith can now estimate that her first week's advertising brought in $60 worth of business (two customers multiplied by the $30 long-run estimate for the average customer), and she can now figure the overall profitability of the advertising this way:

Total sales (gross revenue)	$60.00
Production expenditures for $60 business:	
10 hours × $3.75	37.50
Sales minus production cost	22.50
Advertising expenditure	7.50
Sales minus production cost minus advertising cost	15.00

The advertising now is seen to be profitable because the sales revenue less the production cost exceeds the cost of the advertising. So the typist decides to rerun the advertisement in the next issue of the college newspaper. So we see that correct figuring leads to a decision opposite to that of her earlier naive figuring.

The value of a customer enables us to quickly determine whether any given advertisement is above or below the break-even point of profitability. The value of a typing customer can be estimated as sales minus labor expenditure. That is, $30 − (5 × $3.75) = 11.25. The labor cost is estimated at 5 hours on the basis of the experimental data which showed that Judith types an average of five pages per hour. The concept of the value of a customer is then used this way: Any unit of advertising that produces customers at a cost of $11.25 or less per customer is profitable; otherwise, it is unprofitable. For example, Judith's original advertisement produced two customers estimated to be worth a total of 2 × $11.25 = 22.50, for an advertising expenditure of $7.50. This suggests that her first advertisement was profitable.

In the following weeks the repetitions of her advertisement produced an average of only $1\frac{1}{2}$ new customers per week, but since the value of $1\frac{1}{2}$ customers (1.5 × $11.25 = 16.88) is considerably greater than the $7.50 weekly cost, the advertising still is profitable on the average, indicating that she should continue to run the advertisement.

The value of a customer provides a standard against which to compare the results from any medium as well as any advertisement.

Before we leave Judith, our home-typing friend, and move on to more complex problems, a few of her other management decisions deserve to be mentioned.

Other decisions for the home typist are *how large* an advertisement to run, and *how many* advertisements to run in various media. These decisions depend on the extent to which she really wants to set up a business. If she wants to do no more than obtain work for herself for 8 hours a day or less, these questions may not arise. But if she really wants to start a business, employ other typists, and job out the work, she will need to run bigger advertisements and more of them. The decision rule in every case is the same as before: Does the added unit of advertising produce enough customers so that, when multiplied by the long-run value of a customer, the cost of the added unit of advertising is exceeded?

Now let's move on to the actual (but camouflaged) case of Home Sewing, Inc., a firm that sells sewing materials by mail. Home Sewing obtains customers with a special introductory offer at $3 in space advertisements. Its records show that 30 percent of those introductory customers buy again from the line of regular merchandise. And on the average, 40 percent of customers who buy regular merchandise once, buy a second time; 40 percent who buy a second time, buy a third time, and so on. The average size of subsequent orders is $10. Home Sewing figures that the total costs of servicing a customer (the goods, shipping, and everything else except the cost of advertising) amount to 70 percent of the sale price for the introductory offer and 50 percent thereafter. The average time between orders is 6 months, and over that period the cost of money to the firm is 10 percent, so $1 received 6 months hence is worth about 90 percent of $1 (90 cents) now.

The value of a new customer to Home Sewing can be figured as follows: ($3 introductory-offer revenue − .70 × $3 cost to the firm of introductory offer) plus (.3 probability of repeating from introductory offer) times ($10 second-order revenue − .50 × $10 cost of second-order) times (.9 to allow for the cost of money over half a year) plus (.4 × .3 probability of repeat from second order) times ($10 third-order revenue − .5 × $10 third-order cost) times (.9 × .9 to allow for the cost of money over two 6-month periods), and so on for subsequent periods.

That is,

$$\text{Value of new customer to Home Sewing} = (\$3 - \$2.10) + .3\,(\$10 - \$5) \\ (.9) + (.4 \times .3)(\$10 - \$5) \\ (.9 \times .9)\cdots = \$.90 + \$1.35 \\ + \$.49 + \cdots \\ \approx \$2.74$$

So the value of an additional customer to Home Sewing is about $2.74. Actually, the value is considerably higher because subsequent

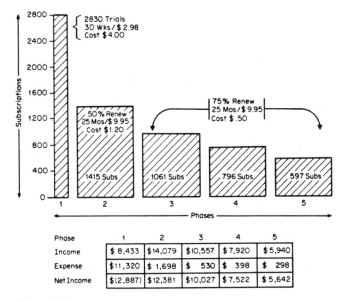

Phase	1	2	3	4	5
Income	$ 8,433	$14,079	$10,557	$7,920	$ 5,940
Expense	$11,320	$ 1,698	$ 530	$ 398	$ 298
Net Income	$(2,887)	$12,381	$10,027	$7,522	$ 5,642

Figure 9-1

orders have not been figured in. But it is clear from inspection of the figures that the value now of additional future orders is really quite small—so small that their calculation is hardly worthwhile.

Now let us see how the value of a customer changes if one of the elements is different. Let's say (as actually happened) that this firm found on further inspection that the reorder rates were higher than originally thought—the reorder rate is really 40 percent (that is, .40) from the introductory offer to the second order, and 49 percent (that is, .49) for subsequent reorders. The value of a customer then is

$$\text{Value of a customer} = (\$3 - \$2.10) + .4(\$10 - \$5)(.9)$$
$$+ (.49 \times .4)(\$10 - \$5)(.9 \times .9) \cdots$$
$$= \$.90 + \$1.80 + \$.80 + \cdots$$
$$\approx \$3.50$$

For practice, let us calculate the value of a customer to Home Sewing under a third set of conditions. Assume, the firm found that its costs for subsequent orders were only 45 percent rather than 50 percent. So

$$\text{Value of a customer} = (\$3 - \$2.10) + .4(\$10 - \$4.50)(.9)$$
$$+ (.49 \times .4)(\$10 - \$4.50)(.9 \times .9) \cdots$$
$$= \$.90 + \$1.98 + \$.88 + \cdots$$
$$\approx \$3.76$$

Before the death and resurrection of *Life* a few years ago, its circulation director supplied excellent data on *Life*'s circulation advertising results, summarized in Figure 9-1. Like every other magazine and like other repeat-business mail-order firms, *Life* could never have been profitable if it had depended on the revenue from the first orders. For the sample shown, in the first year the apparent "net loss" was $2,877. But by the end of 5 years, the operation had become a profitable investment in balance.

Assume for the moment that fulfillment costs of producing and distributing the magazine equaled the revenue from advertising—a pretty good assumption for mass consumer magazines. Then figure out how much *Life* could afford to spend for each new customer in this way:

1. Subscription revenue from an *average* customer during the "life" of the customer equaled

$$(\$8,433 \times .94 + \$14,079 \times .70 + \$10,557 \times .48 + \$7,920 \times .31 + \$5,940 \times .20) \div 2830 = \$9.36$$

The meaning of the dollar amounts in the above calculation—$8,433 and $14,079 and so on—is clear; they are the revenues received in each period from the customers originally obtained by this mailing. The dollar amounts in items 2 and 3 below will be similarly clear. But the meaning of the decimal multipliers—.9, .51, .3, and .20—is not so obvious. These are the "discount factors"—the opposite side of the coin from the "cost of capital"—that allow for the fact that sums of money in the future are worth less than the same sums of money in hand now. That is, a dollar that you will receive in 6 months is worth less than a dollar now, and I assume that for *Life* it was worth about 90 cents, corresponding to an annual discount factor of roughly (but not exactly) .8. And if the annual discount factor is about .8, the discount for the $10,557 to be received 31 months from now is about (but not exactly) .51.

The sum of the revenues to be received in each period, each multiplied by its appropriate discount factor, is the "present value" of the stream of revenues. Further discussion of this concept, which is probably the most important general concept in business decision making, may be found in any college text on finance.

It is very easy to forget about the discount factor and simply add up the dollar amounts in each period. But this is quite erroneous. In fact, I made this mistake in earlier editions of the book, despite my explaining just above in the typist example that we must discount sums in the future to know their meaning in the present. Ignoring discounting in *Life*'s case leads to a falsely large value of a customer, which would lead *Life* to use many mailing lists which are really not profitable while thinking that they are profitable, an expensive mistake indeed.

2. The total cost of soliciting *renewals* for a group of customers divided by the number of original customers in the group equaled

$$(\$11,320 \times .94 + \$1,698 \times .70 + \$530 \times .48 + \$398 \times .31 + \$298 \times .20) \div 2830 = \$4.33$$

The above calculation shows the present value of the expenditures that the firm will make, following the initial solicitation expenditures in the initial period, in order to induce the customers to renew their subscriptions.

3. The most that the magazine should have spent to get a customer was

$$\$9.36 - \$4.33 = \$5.03$$

The above calculation shows the present value of the *net revenue* in each period—the difference between gross revenues and expenditures in that period—except for the initial period when we deal with the solicitation expenditures (spent to obtain the customers) separately from later expenditures and revenues, each net revenue multiplied by the appropriate discount factor. This is the value of a customer to *Life,* putting aside the roughly offsetting factors of advertising revenue and the cost of producing the magazine. This value of a customer tells *Life* how much it is worth to acquire an additional average customer.

Once more let me repeat that we have simplified all the computations of the value of a customer in this section by ignoring advertising revenue and the cost of fulfillment—producing, mailing, overhead, etc.—on the grounds that the two amounts are of about equal value and have opposite effects on the computation. In a real calculation they must be taken care of in an explicit fashion.

Note how, after the trial-period renewal, *Life* customers fell away at about 25 percent *each* year. It will be true for practically every mail-order business that a constant *percentage* of a group of customers will drop out each year. Once you have estimated the customer fall-off rate for 1 year for your business, you have a terrifically valuable tool for future planning.

Here is a more recent report on *Bon Appétit* magazine[1]

> Mr. Knapp calculates that his advertising cost per subscription runs
> between $3.50 and $4.50 from magazine ads and between $7 and $8
> from direct mail. Rather high for a magazine with a $7.95 annual
> subscription rate, you say. But you have to know that publishers expect
> to make their money on renewals.

How to Estimate Repeat Rates

But, you ask, how does one know what the repeat rates will be?
Sometimes the repeat rate is very easy to learn, sometimes a bit
harder. An easy example: Once I sold monthly flower subscriptions
by direct mail. After the first experimental month, I immediately saw
that fifteen of twenty-five (60 percent) of my introductory-offer customers signed up for another month at the regular rate. And at the
end of the second month, I found that eleven of fifteen (about 73
percent) bought again. That was enough information for me to make
a rough estimate of how the business would do in the future. Of
course my samples were small, and at first I had no evidence yet
about subsequent repeats after the first repeat. But after a few more
months I had accumulated solid evidence from bigger samples, and
I had information about the repeat rates after the first repeat. My
initial estimates were not far off, and they certainly were accurate
enough to work with.

Now let's take the camouflaged case of a fishing-equipment firm,
Doog and Doog. These are two friends of mine who have been in
business for about 4 years as of the date we are making the analysis—
March 1986. Doog and Doog had never estimated their repeat rates
as of the date they called me in as a consultant. But they had kept
all their old orders in boxes. So we sorted out all the customers whose
names started with B or R, as a rough way of taking a sample of the
buyers who had *first* ordered merchandise in January, February, and
March of 1983. (We could tell which customers were ordering for
the first time because they were buying the introductory offer. All
the other B and R orders we put aside.) Then we checked to see
how many times each of them ordered again. We found that of the
110 first-time buyers who ordered merchandise in January through
March of 1983 and who had names beginning with B or R the
following were the repeat-purchase records:

No. of repeat buyers	No. of times reordered	No. of orders
26	1	26
12	3	24
4	3	12
3	4	12
1	5	5
46		79

[You may think that it was a lot of work and cost a lot of money to go back through 3 years' worth of old orders to get this information. It was a bit of a nuisance, and now the firm has learned that it makes sense to keep records in better form; in their case, the Doogs are now ready for a modern computerized system (see Chapter 30). But even so, the total cost of studying the back orders was only a few hundred dollars, and the information gained is worth much more than that to Doog and Doog in future added profit.]

If the firm has kept good records of customer purchases in the past, the job is much simpler. If your records are on index cards, you should take a random sample of, say, 300 people who first bought between 3 and 5 years ago, and you should study their purchases over 3 years from the date of first purchase. (Use a longer period if the firm's repeat business extends a very long time, as is the case with magazine subscriptions.) If the firm's records are on the computer (as I hope yours will be), the firm can even work with all the customers in that category with no extra effort.

The best way to take a fair random sample from index-card records is as follows. To make things simple, we shall assume that the future ends after 3 years. Anything you take in after that is gravy, a margin for error. For several economic reasons this won't distort our calculations very much.

If you have been in business over 3 years, the figuring is a breeze. All you have to do is take a sample of people who bought from you over 3 years ago, and see how much they purchased in the first 3 years after you first heard from them. Use a ruler to make a mark at equal intervals in your customer files so that there are *300 equal intervals.* This saves you the trouble of counting off the cards. Take the first customer's card *over 3 years old* that comes after each mark. (If your records are computerized, you instruct the computer to make the calculations from every customer's record.)

If you have been in business only a short time, you can *estimate* the same data by first figuring out how the average customer's purchase frequency drops as time goes on. Then you project the effect for a 3-year period. Better yet, get some help from a statistician on this. Actually, this procedure is especially vital for new businesses. It is only in this way that you can accurately decide whether you are making or losing money.

IMPORTANT: You *must* sample *both* the customers who are still active *and* those who are now in your inactive or "dead" file. If, by some unfortunate accident, you have thrown away the records of inactive customers, you will need a procedure slightly more complicated than we have space to describe here. Any statistical consultant should be able to set up a satisfactory procedure for you in a few hours.

I can't tell you the *exact* size of the proper sample for your business. But 300 customers should be more than enough in most cases, and a sample a little too big won't cost you much extra.

The value of a customer then is calculated as follows:

1. Take a *fair* (random) sample of the names of 300 customers—active and inactive—who first bought over 3 years ago.

2. Multiply the total amount purchased in each year by your average "profit margin" or "order margin"—that is, the proportion of the sales dollar that is left over after paying for the cost of goods sold, mailing, and other fulfillment expenditures.

3. Multiply each amount arrived at in step 2 by the appropriate discount factor to show its value in the present.

4. Sum up the discounted amounts arrived at in step 3.

5. Divide by 300 to get the present value of the average customer.

Figuring the value of a customer is a bit more complicated when you sell through a catalog, partly because you are not likely to know in advance how many catalogs you will be sending the customer each year, how big the catalogs will be, and therefore the amount of sales to the customer. But by the same token, having a sound estimate of the value of a customer is especially important for a catalog operator. So don't let the extra complexity scare you off.

The figure you come out with is the amount it is worth to you to *get a customer onto your books.* Never lose an opportunity to get a customer for anything less than that cost. (I am here assuming that the firm has gotten past the point at which it has extreme difficulty raising capital, and, hence, it does not need to trade off "growth" or profit versus "safety.")

The most amazing part of the value-of-a-customer concept is that so few thoughtful, successful, and otherwise capable businesspeople understand it or use it fully. As Ed Burnett puts it:

Since few understand the importance of the 2nd order, too few mailers spend enough time, effort, and grey matter on getting more of their one-time customers to become 2 & 3 time buyers. Very few premiums for example are utilized for sale No. 2, when sale No. 1 has in part been induced by just such an added bonus. All too many mailers fail to ask their customers, even their multiple customers, for the favor of being given a name or two of friends who might like to receive the same offer. (And when some get such friends-of-friends they simply mail them like any other prospect list, which is deadly—instead of linking the names of customer and friend, which is personalization at a very high and very effective level.)

The procedure described here should not cost you more than $1,000 at 1986 prices including clerical time, no matter how big your list is. (And if your business has progressed to the point at which the customer records are computerized, the job is even less expensive.) I practically guarantee that the information will increase your future profit by many thousands of dollars, if your business is any size at all.

Using the Value of a Customer

The most obvious point—that one *must* use the value of a customer as the criterion, and as the *only* criterion—is sometimes overlooked. For example, a successful auto dealer quit his direct-mail auto sales campaigns after a postage increase, without even checking the results of his campaign. But when he realized that the sale of even a single car would justify a good many thousand letters, he began to reconsider. The moral: Always keep the value of a customer in mind.

The dollar value of a customer is used in decision making as follows: You should run any advertisement or list for which the expected result of this multiplication [(number of customers) times (value of a customer)] is greater than the cost of the ad or mailing. But if the cost of the ad is greater than the expected number of customers multiplied by the value of a customer, the ad or mailing should not be done.

Remember that you are interested not only in the *frequency* of reorders, but also in the *dollar amounts* of reorders. Calculate the dollar size of reorders *separately* for first reorders, second reorders, etc. In the example above, the amount of the reorder is the same for each reorder, but in many cases the amount is different, averaging higher (or, less often, lower) with subsequent purchases.

Remember that from the expected *revenue* of a customer, you must subtract the *cost* of servicing these orders, or else your calculations will overstate the value of a customer. The next chapter takes up the subject of estimating those costs appropriately and accurately.

Often it is useful to refine the calculation of the value of a customer to take into account the value of the particular first order. This refinement can be worthwhile because customers tend to vary much more in the size of the first order than in subsequent orders, and because the money from the first order is received immediately and hence has higher value to you per dollar than future revenue.

Here is an example of how the calculated value of a customer depends upon the first-order size for the sewing-materials firm:

Table 9-1

If first order is	Firm can pay, to get the order
$ 3.00	$3.00
3.50	3.20
4.00	3.45
4.50	3.65
5.00	3.90
5.50	4.10
6.00	4.35
6.50	4.55
7.00	4.80
7.50	5.00
8.00	5.25
8.50	5.45
9.00	5.70
9.50	5.90
10.00	6.15

It is amazing and sad to see how much profit mail-order firms forgo by not correctly estimating and using the value of a customer. For example, a large mail-order shoe firm was asked about its mailing-list rental policy.[2]

Q. What rate of returns from your mailings do you consider a good point?

A. We happen to break even at 1.8%. We rent anything that goes over that. By break even, I mean it pays off in the first mailing. We don't rent a list that pulls less than that because it goes into a loss position and we don't like that. Although in a long test, it might be worth doing, we like to have short-term profits.

Q. In other words, you won't take a 1.5% return and hope you get repeat orders which will then make it worthwhile?

A. We do not have to do this right now. I think it might be acceptable, but not necessary.

I am absolutely sure that if this firm took into account the value of the customers after the initial order, it would greatly increase its profit by renting more lists and increasing its volume.

Another example: A firm that sells correspondence courses had been making no distinction between the potential value of future equipment and course purchases by those who had actually purchased and those who had only inquired. When these different values had been calculated, they immediately indicated changes in advertising patterns that would increase profits by a quarter of a million dollars per year.

The value of a customer also shows up in a lawsuit against a firm that stole a customer list. The thief got 4,000 customers, who purchased an average of $100 the first year, with a decay rate of 20 percent a year and a net margin of 35 percent, so the value of the stolen customers could be reckoned as:

$$(\$100 \times 4{,}000 \times .35) + \frac{1}{1 - .20} (\$100 \times 4{,}000 \times .35)\, .85 + \cdots$$

It would be appropriate to take account of expected increases in unit sales in the future, in this case.

This chapter and the next one are not easy reading. However, it is important to read them for two reasons: (1) I think I know a fair amount about all the topics covered in this book. But I am more of a specially qualified expert on the economic calculations of mail order than on any other topic. (2) These calculations are more likely to make the difference between losing money and making money than any other mail-order decisions you will make.

10

Calculating Mail-Order Costs and the Order Margin

The Engineering Method / The Overall Expenses Method

The previous chapter said that knowing the value of a customer is crucial in making decisions about which advertisements and lists to run. But, to calculate the value of a customer correctly, it is necessary to know the cost of servicing the customer (*all* the costs of merchandise, shipping, and so on, but excluding the costs of the advertising itself). When those costs are subtracted from total sales, the remainder is called the "order margin" or "gross order margin." This chapter shows how to calculate those costs.

A small, but (to me) painful, story illustrates how the wrong cost calculations can lead to the wrong decision. This concerns what are known as "sunk costs." The adage goes, "Sunk costs are sunk," which means that after you expend money for something—whether it is for research and development, for typography, or for an alteration to a building—you should, from that moment and forevermore, put that expenditure out of your mind and out of your calculations. The notion of trying to "recapture" sunk costs leads to disastrously bad decisions. Furthermore, the price at which you buy something—a car or a stock or some inventory—should not be allowed to have any influence on the price at which you sell it, or on any other business decision.

Of course it is very difficult psychologically to ignore past expenditures, and to really treat sunk costs as sunk. And accountants may mislead you into thinking that you must take sunk costs into account. This is because the business of accountants is to look backward, to "account for" what happened in order to appraise success or failure, and also to keep track of the business for tax purposes. But decisions are forward looking, and the kind of thinking that is appropriate for looking backward is totally inappropriate for forward-looking decision making.

One day I sat with an executive of the firm that had published a book of mine, the firm being one of the three biggest book publishers in the United States. (I consider that concealing its identity is an act of mercy.) I asked why the firm did not continue with a mail-order advertising campaign that had just been tested to sell the book. The executive told me that the advertising campaign was not profitable. I was curious, and we examined the figures. The test showed that the publisher could expect to sell copies at the mail-order price of $8.95 for an average advertising expenditure of about $3. I said that in view of the production expenditures necessary for printing additional books—only about $1.25 or $1.50 per copy because the book had already gone through two printings, plus small expenditures for handling and mailing—the advertising campaign clearly *was* profitable. But the executive said no, we had to add in the "overhead" of several dollars, which meant that the advertising campaign would then be below the break-even point. When I asked what the "overhead" charge was for, he replied that it was the standard charge the firm's accountants insisted be applied to all such decisions. He said the overhead covered executive salaries, editing, physical plant, and so on. He agreed with me that additional advertising for this book, that had already been produced, would not increase the firm's need for editors, and so on. But nevertheless, he insisted on including that "overhead" charge in the calculation, and hence the campaign was not continued. The result was that both the firm and I wound up a lot worse off then we could otherwise have been—a bad decision because of bad reckoning of costs.

Ed Burnett makes the same point in the context of a decision about whether a test of your offer with a particular mailing list should be considered to be a success or a failure. (When he says "bookkeeper" he means the accountant.)

A good way to go broke in Direct Mail is to evaluate each marketing test like a bookkeeper. You must keep in mind that bookkeepers are bean-counters, not marketers, and you must never let their counts, however accurate, obscure the marketing reality disclosed by your test or tests.

In the first place the bookkeeper looks at all costs, including the "sunk" costs of creation, typesetting, art, copy, graphics, photos, layout, pasteups, while the marketer puts these aside. (You might think of such "sunk" costs as part of research and development, for if no mailing is ever printed or mailed such costs have no possible way to be retrieved through amortization by a successful series of mailings.)

Your bookkeeper looks at an initial cost of a test mailing and points out the cost is $500/M, the gross sales [total sales volume] only $700/M, the gross profit $400 [gross sales of $700 minus fulfillment expenses of $300], and hence a "loss" of $100/M [gross profit of $400 minus mailing costs of $500]. The marketer looks at the same figures and declares it a great success. How? He figures the cost of the continuation @ $310/M [because the sunk costs are sunk, and do not need to be made again, and because the large mailing is cheaper per thousand than the test mailing], gross sales through selected continuations at $800/M [because you will improve your offer], gross profit $450/M, gross profit per M in the mail $140—and licks his chops over the hundreds of thousands of likely names available.

Now let us talk about the methods of estimating costs correctly. One is the "engineering" method, and the other is the "total expenses" method. We'll take them up in that order.

The Engineering Method

The *engineering* method of estimating the costs of servicing orders is as follows: You calculate how much of everything is needed for the average order: how many items multiplied by the price of the items, how many minutes of labor multiplied by the price of labor per minute, the average cost of mailing, and so on. The sum of the individual cost elements for an average order is the cost of the average order. The estimates of the physical quantities of resources used are made by actual physical examination of each of the inputs—for example, counting the number of orders each worker handles per hour.

The engineering approach is most appropriate in a situation in which you sell only one kind of merchandise—for example, only watches or only magazines—so that all the costs apply to the single line of business. In such a situation you know exactly how much building rent, say, is relevant to each watch or magazine subscription, on the average. But where you sell watches *and* books *and* fishing boots, it is difficult or impossible to know what the cost of building rent, say, is for the sale of the average watch or the average pair of boots.

The main point to remember in estimating costs by the engineering method is *not to forget any important costs*. The costs of the merchandise and the direct labor in handling and the shipping cost are obvious, unforgettable, and easy to estimate. But what about such costs as the following?

1. Returned merchandise—costs of shipping and of damage to merchandise

2. Merchandise that must be replaced because it arrived damaged at the customer's address

3. Bad debts

4. Lost shipments

You must estimate how often these events will occur and then apply an appropriate proportion of the cost to each order.

Then there are costs which apply to each order but which you may not be able to relate to any particular order. These include

1. Bank charges

2. Management costs

3. Indirect labor, such as truck drivers and supervisors

Many mail-order novices have figured that they were making a profit on every individual order, but then, at end of the year, have found that they had lost money altogether—usually because they did not take account of all these nonobvious costs.[1]

The categories of expenditures that must be taken into account vary from business to business. The types of expenditures for a fairly typical specialty catalog business are shown in Table 10-1.

The Overall Expenses Method

In situations in which you sell a variety of merchandise, you must adopt another approach. You must calculate the *average profit margin* (aside from advertising costs), based on the firm's overall expenses over some period of time. This method is complex but it has some

Table 10-1. Mail-Order Firm's Income and Expense Summary, October 31, 1979, with Respect to Production-Cost Decision

	(1) 1 month ended October 31, 1979	(2) 12 months ended October 31, 1979	(3) Adjusted October figures	(4) Year-adjusted yearly figures (Col. 3 × 9)	(5) Future-adjusted yearly figures (Col. 4 adjusted)	(6) Future-adjusted yearly figures for sales volume of $375,000	(7) Future-adjusted yearly figures for sales volume of $500,000
Income:							
Sales	$31,652	$143,924	$31,652	$284,868	$284,868	$375,000	$500,000
Interest							
Expenses:							
Salaries	3,426	21,329	4,000	36,000	41,000	51,250	65,600
Contract labor	16	467	75	675	See "Salaries"	See "Salaries"	See "Salaries"
Postage	2,534	12,562	2,200	19,800	19,000	24,700	33,200
Advertising	11,291	51,541	Not relevant	Not relevant	Not relevant	Not relevant	Not relevant
Advertising production	4,732	5,678	100	900	900	1,000	1,200
Merchandise purchased	8,905	36,632	8,000	72,000	80,000	104,800	140,000
Printing	297	9,752	0	9,752	10,000	13,000	17,500
Packing	473	1,400	475	4,275	See "Salaries"	See "Salaries"	See "Salaries"
Office supplies	112	1,357	112	1,008	1,000	1,310	1,750
Travel	11	611	50	450	450	500	600
Rent	228	1,898	228	2,052	3,500	4,200	5,250

Taxes	473	1,304	300	2,700	2,700	
Telephone	145	1,187	120	1,080	1,080	
Bank charges	26	408	35	315	315	
Freight	26	332	30	270	270	
Dues and subscriptions	11	162	15	135	135	
Professional services	132	566	50	450	450 = \$5,130	
Personnel relations	0	174	20	180	180	
				= \$5,130	6,400	8,192
Total expenses (excluding owner's salary)	32,838	147,360	Not relevant	Not relevant	Not relevant	Not relevant
Total expenses less advertising	21,547	95,819	152,042	160,980	207,160	273,292
Total expenses less advertising ÷ total sales	68%	67%	53%	57%	55%	55%

advantages. First, it automatically ensures that you don't forget any nonobvious costs. And second, it lays the basis for estimating how costs change as the overall volume of the business changes.

Let's consider the disguised example of a firm selling drug products through mail order.[2]

The owner wanted to know what her total costs, aside from advertising, would be at the present sales volume and at higher and lower sales volumes, so that she could determine how many dollars of sales per dollar of advertising expenditure an advertisement had to produce in order for her to break even. For example, assume that she is considering the possibility of an advertisement in *Esquire* magazine that would cost her $400, and from which she would expect $1,000 in gross sales. Should such an advertisement be run? Would it be profitable? The answer obviously depends upon whether the cost of servicing the orders is greater or less than the $600 difference between gross sales and advertising costs—in percentage form, ($1,000 − $400)/$1,000 = 60%. That is, she needs to know the ratio of order-servicing costs to total sales so she can use it as a rule of thumb in deciding whether or not to run various advertisements. The newness of her business (now ending its second year) complicates the estimation process because it takes time to learn how best to run a business and to know what major expenditures are necessary at various intervals of time.

Let us examine columns 1 and 2 in Table 10-1 which show the firm's expenditures for October 1979 and for 12 months ending October 1979. First we shall attempt to estimate what the costs would be next year for a yearly sales level that is approximately the level represented by sales in the last month, October 1979. As our first approximation, we begin with the sum of the expenditures for the month, $32,838, from which we substract October advertising expenses of $11,291 (because we want to know how much she can *afford* to spend for each advertising opportunity and break even or better) to get $21,547. This suggests that nonadvertising expenses would be $21,547/$32,838 = 66%. The ratio of order-servicing costs to total sales is $21,547/$31,652 = 68%.

But perhaps this month is not typical. So we inspect the figures in more detail to see if any of the entries are unusually high or low. Here we must be especially careful not to fool ourselves, because one is much more likely to notice the categories that are unusually *high* because of one-time expenditures but to forget the categories that are unusually *low*. For example, we notice that taxes in October are almost half the last year's total, because a twice-yearly property tax was paid that month. Therefore, that category should be lowered a bit to predict the tax level over a full-year period. The same is true of advertising production; a yearly catalog's preparation costs were paid for in October. On the other hand, "contract labor" (daily-wage occasional labor) was unusually low in October, because a lot of packaging work—which is usually done with day labor (contract labor)—was done in September, and, hence, this category should probably be raised for predictive purposes.

A good way to get clues about unusual expenses is to look for categories whose proportion of total expenses is different in the short period (the month, in this case) and in longer periods (the past year as a whole, in this case). For this reason, one would generally prefer to work only with the whole year's expenditures; things tend to even out over a longer period. But in the case of a fast-growing business such as this one, in which the pattern of costs has been changing rapidly over the year, one cannot have the luxury of looking only at the full year, but must instead inspect the shorter recent periods as well.* In the light of the expenditures during the last 12 months, the expenditures for October are now adjusted as shown in column 3 to estimate a "representative" period's expenditures.

When estimating the yearly total from the 1-month figure, one must remember seasonality. December and the summer months are very low for the mail-order business, whereas October is a very good month. October is apt to represent perhaps one-ninth of the total year's sales, and we therefore multiply the adjusted monthly income and expenses by 9 to get estimated yearly figures. The resulting estimated yearly expenditures for the current-level expenses are as shown in column 4.

The next step is to translate the accounting categories into categories that are closer to the firm's operational-decision-making cost categories. For example, it does not matter for future decisions if the everyday routine operations of handling orders were done last year by weekly salaried workers or by daily-wage workers; what matters is what the total sum paid for those operations is likely to be next year. Therefore, the categories "contract labor" and "packing" are combined with the estimated proportion of "salaries" that goes to pay for the direct labor in physically handling orders. We estimated that to be about $1,800 for October and 9 × $1,800 = $16,200 for a year at a sales volume of 9 × $31,652 = $284,868 per year.

---

* To make the point vivid for those readers who have never been in business, imagine how you would predict your next year's personal expenditures from your expenditures during last week only. Notice how unusual last week was—but then, *all* weeks are unusual.

Next, we make some allowance for the fact that the firm is still learning how to conduct its business efficiently; its expenses should therefore be lower in the future than until now, sales volume and other things being equal. Therefore, we create an estimated *future* expenditures schedule for the same sales volume, based on our notions about how such learning and other changes will affect expenditures. That schedule is shown in column 5 of Table 10-1. That column suggests that costs would be 57 percent of sales volume at this sales level in the future.

Now we must prepare estimated cost schedules for other possible sales volumes. (These estimates are summarized in Table 10-1.) First, however, let us clarify a point that the firm's owner raised. She said, "If I run just one more advertisement, the resulting sales volume will cause no increase in the rent, the bookkeeper's salary, and so on. Therefore, all those expenditures should not be included as costs when we are figuring out the break-even point to be used for deciding which advertisements to run." What she said is partly correct; if *one* more small advertisement is run and sales volume is therefore $500 more than otherwise, rent and similar fixed expenses would not change perceptibly. But a significant change in the break-even rule of thumb would affect not just one advertisement but many, and might raise or lower sales volume by, say, a third or a quarter. Therefore, we must calculate costs for possible sales volumes that are *significantly* higher (and lower) than at present. And if sales volume rises by a third, the rent will probably go up, as will the salaries for bookkeeping and similar "indirect labor." Wrong handling of this rather subtle matter could lead to too low a break-even percentage for costs, too much advertising, and lowered profitability.

Starting with the estimated future costs at present sales volume, we make our best guesses of how all the input factors—direct labor, postage, rent (a tough judgment), indirect salaries (another tough one), and so on—would differ between the present sales volume and other possible sales volumes. These estimates for the other sales levels are shown in columns 6 and 7, each one leading to a break-even cost-proportion estimate for that particular sales volume. The firm can then proceed to figure how much its expenditures for advertising must be in order to obtain that much sales volume; this is also the amount of advertising consistent with the cost-proportion rule of thumb given by the cost estimate for that level of sales. The firm can then select that level of advertising (and sales) that promises the highest total profit. And the cost-proportion rule of thumb that accompanies that level of sales volume is the one that should be used.

To summarize this estimation of future cost for an ongoing firm at different sales volumes: First, the actual expenditures were calculated in the current short period from the accountant's income-and-expense statement as a first-approximation level of costs for the sales-volume level in the current short period. Then the categories in the short period (a month, in this case) were examined for unusually high or unusually low entries in the light of the longer period's figures, and adjustments were made to make the short period more representative. Then the categories in the accountant's income-and-expense summary were rearranged into categories that more closely resemble operational-decision-making categories. Then the cost figures for that basic level of expenditures were adjusted for expected future changes in costs such as learning, technological, and economic changes. Last, the adjusted cost schedule for the present level of sales was used as the base to estimate costs at other possible levels of sales on the basis of how each of the categories would be different at every other level of sales (see Figure 10-1).

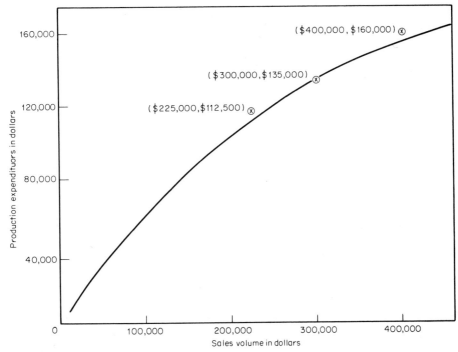

Figure 10-1

This example has its special characteristics—a relatively new and fast-growing firm—and the procedure will not be quite the same for other sorts of firms. But the fundamental approach should be the same: estimation of base values for present sales levels, adjustment for future changes, and estimates at other sales levels.

11

How to Key Your Advertisements

How to Key a Magazine Advertisement / How to Key Direct Mail

How to Key a Magazine Advertisement

These are the jobs that the key and address in a mail-order ad must do:

1. *The key must indicate clearly which ad the customer is answering.*
2. *The key must be easy to identify by clerical help.* What *not* to do is illustrated by advertisers who used to key on the back of the coupons. The editorial or advertising matter was different for each coupon, all right. But the clerk who recorded the key had to remember the back of each coupon, or compare it with a sample. That was a slow, expensive process. And some people send in the coupon pasted to a sheet of paper!
3. *The key must make it easy for magazines to advance the key each month.* This gives you a separate record for each issue. Some advertisers key by using only a different name in each magazine. This practice is not wise unless you already know the results from the magazines so well that you don't need a monthly record.

4. *The key must make it easy to tabulate returns in your media records.* This means that you need some sort of alphabetical or numerical code in the key.

5. *For classified ads only: The key must use minimum word count.* The best system for classified ads that include a post office box number will be a single block of numbers using one of the key systems described below.

There are many methods of keying. You can use "Drawer," "Department," "Studio," "Room," or similar words, followed by the actual code. If you sell several products, you can use a different introductory word from the list above. This will ease your keying problems and will speed the job of sorting the mail.

You can also use different street numbers if you live in a small town, and if you get the postmaster's permission. Or you can address the mail to different first names. (But if you are asking for money in the ad, you will need to stick to one name so you can deposit checks easily.)

The crucial problem is: What letters and numbers shall make up the key?

This is the solution I have found best: A typical key is "71-F223" as in "Samco, Drawer 71-F223, Hoboken, N.J.," the third ad in a series in *Field & Stream.*

"Drawer 71" is the number of the post office box.

"F22" stands for the magazine, and it is established by referring to an alphabetical list of magazines. *Field & Stream* is the twenty-second magazine alphabetically among the Fs. (If a magazine is alphabetically between 1 and 9, it gets redesignated with a number from 91 to 99.) I use the *Standard Rate & Data* index list, but you can use any list.

If the magazine is not on the list, it is designated 81, 82, etc. Or you can start your list with every other number, and fill in the spaces with unlisted magazines.

The "3" is for the third issue. The fifteenth issue becomes "F2215."

The major virtue of this system is that it permits records to be kept in the order in which keys are listed, and still be in nearly alphabetical order. This eases the record keeping and tabulating in a great many ways that you won't appreciate until you have tried other keying systems.

This system also meets the other requirements cited above.

It *is* possible not to key each issue separately. This procedure saves some clerical labor in tabulation. But it loses much information that is extremely valuable unless you already have several years of experience with the media in question.

The crucial things in keying are:

1. *Don't forget to key.*
2. *Key correctly.*

It is usually in the very first ads for a product that you omit the key or you duplicate keys, because you have not yet set up a complete system. And unfortunately, it is those first ads that give you the most valuable information that your records can supply. *So don't forget to key,* and *key correctly.*

Writers on mail order often state flatly that a post office box number produces fewer orders than a street address. But I have never seen any *evidence* on this. It is *probably* true that if you ask for money in the ad, and if the ad is small enough to look insubstantial, a *high* box number in a big *city* might reduce response. But other than that, I'll bet it doesn't matter *what* address you use.

The lower the number of the box or drawer, the better. In general, a low number sounds impressive and old, while a high number sounds anonymous. But more than that, a number in two digits makes some kinds of keying easier than three or four digits (one digit is even easier).

How to Key Direct Mail

Direct-mail keying is easier than periodical keying because the customer does not need to write down the key. You print or stamp the key on either the return envelope or the coupon that the customer sends back—a different key for each list you test. You can also code the key to show the date sent out as well as other useful information. If you cannot have the key printed, or if you should happen to forget to key until it is too late to catch the printer, you can key by fanning the coupons or business response envelopes and then drawing a broad stripe with a wide marker at various places on the envelopes. You can also cut nicks into the paper in various places. But it is best not to forget to print the key and avoid hassle reading it later on.

You should ensure that you code a separate key on every variation of mailing that you send out. You can never have too many separate keys; your computer will take care of the dirty work of sorting them for you. Later on you can lump together the results from several keys if you want to analyze them together. But you can never separate the results of several variations if they come in with the same key.

The key of the original source of the customer *must* be retained with the customer's records forever. You should most definitely not substitute the key for a subsequent catalog or mailing for the original key; rather, you should *also* keep the information on the subsequent keys along with the full information on the later orders. More about this in Chapter 30 on computer programs.

An alphabetical key is still best, for the reasons mentioned above.

If you use a two-step selling system, you often want to key the follow-ups so you can know how many dollars each medium finally produces. The commonest and easiest system is to type the original incoming key onto the address label for the follow-ups. The address label is then placed on the order coupon, and it is arranged so that it shows through a window envelope. The date of receipt is also typed onto the address label in most cases.

As you examine samples of direct mail, you will notice examples of other types of keys.

12

How to Start a Classified-Advertising Business

The First Steps to Classified / The Terms of a
Classified Offer / How to Write a Classified Ad /
How Long Should the Classified Ad Be?

This chapter is about advertising in the classified columns of magazines. This topic is seldom mentioned at all in discussions of mail-order advertising, but it can be a first-rate way to get into business. The classified sections of nationally distributed newspapers like the *National Enquirer, The Wall Street Journal,* the *National Observer,* and *The New York Times* are good for some mail-order offers. Many weekly farm newspapers are also excellent for mail order. With few exceptions, newspaper classified columns will not pay off for mail-order advertisers. Some correspondence courses, books, and book-finding services are exceptions to the rule, however.

The arena of classified includes far more than a few magazines like *Popular Science,* however. There are over 300 magazines that are good classified media, most of which you have never heard of.

The page from the classified section in the 1979 *Grier's Almanac* shown in Figure 12-1 and the section from *VFW* magazine in Figure 12-2 contain examples of mail-order businesses that use the classifieds, though some of these offers are of less overall value than I wish they were.

The First Steps to Classified

Your first step toward a classified mail-order business is the same first step we talked about in Chapter 3. *Examine the media and the competition.* Write a postcard to every medium you can find that carries classified, asking for a sample copy of the magazine and rates for *classified* advertising. Rate information on classified is omitted from some rate cards and from some *Standard Rate & Data* listings.

Then get hold of the back issues of magazines from back-date magazine shops. Or, you can examine the back files of *Popular Science, Workbasket, Popular Gardening, Popular Photography,* and others at your nearest public library.

In the list of classified media in *Consumer Rate & Data,* you will note Charlton Boys' Comics Group, Charlton Crossword Group, Charlton Girls' Comics Group, Charlton Puzzle Group, etc. These are groups of many magazines whose classified sections are sold together by Charlton Publishers, a firm in Derby, CT. You cannot buy classified space individually from the magazines in those groups. These and other groups are an important part of the classified mail-order industry because of their tremendous circulation.

Clip the classified pages out of the magazines and file them alphabetically. At the same time, make up a 3- by 5-inch file card on each magazine, noting on the card the products and firms advertising in it that interest you. Don't spend much time thinking about what you're doing until you have looked at the classified pages of at least fifty different media. Then you can begin to consider what looks good and what doesn't. You are, of course, looking for the ads and products that appear in many media and over a long period of time. Those are the *successful* products.

Pay most attention to the magazines whose cost is *highest* per word. That's where the gravy is. If you can't use the expensive magazines successfully, your operation will be tiny potatoes at best.

Your product need *not* appeal to everyone; it need *not* be able to run profitably in all media. If you have an offer that will be successful in most of the farm magazines, you are in good shape. On the other hand, if your offer will be profitable only in the automobile-magazine classifieds, the volume will probably be too small to justify your investment of time.

The Terms of a Classified Offer

Judging from the time-tested behavior of classified advertisers, it usually is not wise to charge the inquirers even a postage stamp for

YOURS FREE! WHOLESALE CATALOG filled with Motorcycle. Snowmobile, Small engine parts and accessories. Low, Low prices Manufacturer s Supply, Box 157GA, Dorchester, WI 54425

RINGS, JEWELRY priced 130% below retail price. Catalog, $1.00 (refundable) Anka-GR, 95 Washington, West Warwick, RI 02893

CARNIVOROUS PLANTS

CARNIVOROUS AND WOODLAND terrarium plants Catalog 25¢ Peter Pauls Nurseries, Canandaigua, NY 14424

CHAIN SAW PARTS

SAVE TO 40% on first quality, guaranteed. Chain, Guidebars, Sprockets, Sharpening Equipment for all makes saws. Also Small Engine Parts, Service Tools. Free Catalog. Write today Zip-Penn, Dept. A22, Box 6329, Erie, PA 16512

COINS

INDIANHEAD & LINCOLN Cents 33 Different, 1883-1949—$2.99 Catalog--25¢ Edel's, Carlyle, Illinois 62231

SEND 50¢ for 5 "S" wheat cents and price list Jacobs Coins, POB 532-A, Mableton, Ga 30059

EARLY AMERICAN COINS before Nineteen Hundred—Solid investment. Half cent $15.00, Indian cent 60¢, Large cent $4.50, Two cent piece $4.95. Three cent piece $5.50, "V" Nickel 75¢, Half dime $7.00—All with clear dates. Satisfaction Guaranteed—Postpaid Detroit Coin Co., 1764 Penobscot Bldg., Detroit, Mich. 48226

CURIOS

VAN VAN OIL—$1.00. Incense and other items Curios, 436 Front St., Memphis, Tenn. 38103

DO-IT-YOURSELF

MAKE YOUR OWN TRAPS, CAGES! 2500 Cage Clamps, Clincher $14.95. 999 picture pet hobby supply catalog $1.00 Stromberg s, Pine River 46, Minnesota 56474

JAPANESE BEETLE TRAP. Commercial bait milk jug Plans $2.00. Bill Gazaway, Rt. 4, Alpharetta, Ga 30201

EARTHWORMS

MAKE MONEY FAST raising Fishworms, Crickets. We teach you how to raise and sell. FREE LITERATURE Breeder Redworms— 1,000-$8.95, postpaid Carter Worm Farm—9, Plains, Georgia 31780

BIG MONEY Raising Fishworms! Redworm Breeders 1,000-$6.95, 2,000-$13.50. 5,000-$30.00. African Nightcrawlers 1,000-$12.95. Postpaid with instructions. Seymour Sales. Bronwood, Georgia 31726

EDUCATION, SCHOOLS, INSTRUCTIONS

DETECTIVE CAREER. Rewarding, exciting. Free information. Universal Detectives. Box 8180-GA, Universal City, Calif. 91608

UNIVERSITY DEGREES by mail! Bachelors, Masters, PhD's. Free revealing details. Counseling, Box 317-GA2, Tustin California 92680

HIGHLY EFFECTIVE Specialized Home Study Courses. Over 70 categories to choose. Advance rapidly! Diploma awarded. Our 33rd Year! Free literature. Cook's Institute, Desk 12, Box 20345, Jackson, MS 39209

CIVIL SERVICE Test Preparation home study course. Job Security may be yours by preparing for coming examinations. Write. National Training Service, Inc., Box 160, Haddonfield, N.J 08033

LEARN SEWING MACHINE repairing. A profitable trade, Easy to learn. Free details. Sewing Center, 187 GR, Rochelle, Ga. 31079

FINISH HIGH SCHOOL at home quickly! See our advertisement page 58! Academy Senior High School.

EMPLOYMENT OPPORTUNITIES

OVERSEAS EMPLOYMENT—$15,000 – $50,000+. Free information! Employment International, Box 29217-MO, Indianapolis, Indiana 46229

FEMALE HELP WANTED

TEAR OUT THIS AD, mail with name, address for big box of home needs and cosmetics, FREE to reliable men and women. Tell and show friends, make good money spare time taking their order. Write today. BLAIR, Dept 341JA, Lynchburg, Va 24506.

GENEALOGY

ANCESTOR HUNTING? Trace Your Family Roots The Easy Way! Details Free. Lokadex Library. Box 8948-G, Rochester, NY 14624

GINSENG

GINSENG! $50 POUND. Have seeds, roots Goldenseal. For complete growing, marketing information write F B Collins, B16, Viola, Iowa 52350.

GINSENG, SEEDS, roots, books for sale Write for prices Roots 'O' Gold, RR2, Box 74, LeCenter, MN 56057

GOVERNMENT SURPLUS

GOVERNMENT SURPLUS DIRECTORY. Buy 250,000 different items (including Jeeps) low as 2¢ on dollar! Most complete information available—$2.00 Surplus Disposal, Box 19107-MO, Washington DC 20036

OFFICIAL UNITED STATES DIRECTORY— Unequalled!!—Tells Everything!!—Jeeps—$37.22!!—Cars—$22.50!!—Agri-Machinery!!—Livestock!!—Forage!!—400,000 Listings—Your Immediate Area!!—$2.00—(Includes G-Lands Info-Guide!) United States/Great Lakes Information Surplus Depository. P.O.B 807-FM. Marshfield, Wisconsin 54449 (Copyright 1979)

JEEPS—$59.30!—Cars—$33.50!—200,000 items! Government Surplus. Most comprehensive directory available tells how, where to buy—Your area—$2.00—Moneyback Guarantee—Government Information Services. Dept GI-4, Box 99249, San Francisco, California 94109 (433 California)

GREETING CARDS

REQUEST FREE: 1979 Scripture-text Card Folder. Special Offer Write, Box 81 (A), Roanoke, Va 24002

HEALTH ITEMS, INSTRUCTIONS

UNDERSTAND YOUR HAY FEVER & Asthma Problems 6 Basic Principles 25¢ for Booklet Write Nephron Corporation, Dept XXAA Tacoma, Washington 98401

NATURE'S ANSWER against Heart Attack, Arthritis, Diabetes, Cataract. Free information Provoker Press, St. Catharines—223, Ontario L2R 7C9

NERVOUS—Write for free literature how John Winters approached this problem. Address Orbacine, Dept A-94, 2 Overhill Road, Scarsdale, N Y 10583

HEMORRHOIDS (Piles)? Take Melrose for permanent relief. Used effectively for 50 years Guaranteed. An Herbal medicine. $4.75 for one month's treatment Robert S Moser Druggist, P.O.Box 8863, Asheville, N.C 28804

ARTHRITIS. Please send for Paul McCoy's remarkable true life story about his complaint. It's free. Address Norkon, Dept A-94, 2 Overhill Road, Scarsdale, N.Y. 10583

WANT BEAUTIFUL FINGERNAILS? Simply brush on famous formula. Guaranteed. Send $1.50 Phoebe,Box 221G,New Canaan,Ct 06840

FOR HEALTH & Happiness. Send $2.00 to H & H, P O. Box 1701-GA, Kissimmee, Fla 32741 You'll be glad you did

EDGAR CAYCE Recommended Products Specialists in hard-to-find herbal remedies mentioned in the Cayce readings. Current pricelist free on request. Heritage Store, Box 444-GA, Virginia Beach, VA 23458.

HOW TO STOP SMOKING. Guaranteed method $2. Path Research A107, Box 1060, Orangepark, FL 32073

OVERWEIGHT? In controlling weight, mind-power beats dieting, pills or will-power. Amazingly easy! You simply relax, listen and lose. Two cassettes and booklet. $25.00 (Refundable) RELAXED LEARNING, INC., 30-C South El Camino, San Mateo, Ca. 94401

MY ARTHRITIS

MY ARTHRITIS has been completely wiped out. To receive our proven, safe, money back guaranteed plan, send 15 cent stamp. Raney's Medical Research, Box 104, Drasco, AR 72530.

THUMB SUCKING? If someone you know wants to stop and can't, let us help. Safe, simple, rewarding method. Proven effective. Send $8.00 for complete kit. postpaid. Thumbs Up, 70 E. 96 St., New York, N Y 10028.

HEARING AIDS

SAVE UP TO 50% OFF comparable aids. Buy direct. 30 Days FREE Trial. No Salesman will call. Low Battery Prices. LLOYD S, Dept GLC, 128 Kishwaukee St., Rockford, Ill. 61104

FREE HEARING AID Catalog Save ½ by mail! Write MONEYSAVER$, 9530GRA Langdon, Sepulveda, Ca 91343.

HONEY

PURE, NATURAL HONEY. $14.00 gallon Postpaid. Sample jar $1.50 Ellison's, 205 Oak Drive, Belton, South Carolina 29627

INVENTIONS, PATENTS WANTED

IDEAS, INVENTIONS, NEW PRODUCTS needed by innovative manufacturers. Marketing assistance available to individuals, tinkerers, universities, companies with feasible concepts. Write for Kit-GAL, IMI, 701 Smithfield, Pittsburgh, PA 15222

JEWELRY

GENUINE INDIAN JEWELRY/Handcrafts/Findings/14K Gold Chains. Wholesale Details $1.00 (Refundable). Lange/GA, 6031 North 7th St., Phoenix, AZ 85014

BIG PROFITS—Jewelry! Lowest Wholesale Prices Free List CCCC Conover, N C 28613.

LIVE BAIT

MAKE MONEY FAST raising Fishworms. Crickets. We teach you how to raise and sell FREE LITERATURE Breeder Redworms—1,000—$8.95, postpaid Carter Worm Farm—2, Plains, Georgia 31780

SELLING ENTIRE Farm Red Wigglers! Majority Breeders! Special! 3,000-$9.95, 5,000-$15.95. 10,000-$26.95. African Crawlers 1,000-$12.95. Postpaid with instructions. Beatrice Worm Farms, Dawson, Georgia 31742

GOLDEN MEALWORMS, 1,000/$3.50 Giant Mealworms, 1,000/$12.00. 2,000 to 5,000, $11.00 per 1,000. 6,000 to 10,000, $10.00 per 1,000. Mableton Mealworms, 5539 Andrews, Mableton, Ga. 30059

GOLDEN MEALWORMS 1,000—$5.00 with raising instructions. Georgia-Anne Farms 2, Plains, Ga. 31780

LOANS BY MAIL

SECRET LOANS by Mail. Borrow $100 to $5000 for any good reason in absolute privacy. No endorsers, no co-signers Fast Service Write Dial Finance, Dept. 3727, 340 S W. Eighth Street, Des Moines, Iowa 50309

BORROW $25,000 "OVERNIGHT". Any purpose. Keep indefinitely! Write Success Research, Box 29263-MO, Indianapolis, Indiana 46229.

MAGIC TRICKS, JOKES

FREE! World's Leading Novelty Catalog. 1600 Funmakers, Jokes. Science, Sports, Hobbies. Bargains Johnson-Smith, C-54, Mt Clemens, Mich 48043.

MISCELLANEOUS

CHRISTIANS, CLERGYMEN, SCHOLARS! Illustrated map of Palestine. 500 descriptive words $2 C. Brewer,1298 Carr, Memphis, 38104

EVERYONE! VETERANS! Collect Now! From Government. Five special reports! 25¢ Guaranteed! Grandcees, GR79, Hamilton, Ga 31811

WHO ELSE Will Be Successful? Booklet $1.00 Success,Drawer P. Lexington, N C 27292

NEW-CAR-TRUCK pricing wheel calculates invoice cost w/in 005! Send $3.00 Buyers Guide, 2511 SW 410, SA, TX 78227

PECAN HALVES-WALNUTS-Sliced Almonds! Three-Quart Sampler, $9.95 Postpaid! Canecreek Farm, Box 2727-GA,Cookeville,TN 38501

FREE BAR of luxury soap each $5.00 order Catalog. Soap Source, P O. Box 4009-K Greenwich, CT 06830

Figure 12-1 Classified section in Grier's Almanac.

Figure 12-2 Classified section from VFW magazine.

further information. Asking for a coin or stamp severely cuts down the number of inquiries. It is undoubtedly true that the people who do send the coin are the best prospects. Nevertheless, you will do better to obtain the lesser prospects and try to sell them, too. The coins or stamps that you get will usually not be a significant source of revenue, and the extra wordage in the ad necessary to ask for a dime or a quarter may cost you more than the coins you get. But most important, the request for a coin cuts responses greatly.

However, you will find it profitable to ask for a small sum if you offer an expensive catalog that many people would like to have even if they are poor prospects. If your catalog costs you a dollar or two, you can't afford to send a copy to people who would like to look at its pretty pictures but who never intend to buy. You ask for payment *not* because of the value it represents, but because it helps you separate the good prospects from the poor ones. Sears, Roebuck accomplishes this *not* by asking for a coin (many years ago they sold their catalogs for sums up to 50 cents), but by insisting that a person be a *proved customer* before receiving their expensive general merchandise book.

Prices

As a very general rule, $1 is a better price than either 50 cents or $2—in *classified* and for printed products whose cost is low. From my own experience I have found that you will not make twice as many sales at 50 cents as at $1 and in that case $1 is more profitable than 50 cents. I have also found that $1 gets considerably *more* than twice as many sales as $2, enough more to make the $1 price best.

CAUTION: My experience should be only a *suggestion* to you. The opposite results will occur for some kinds of products. You must *test* various prices for your own product and offer.

Remember that the more the product costs you to make and mail, the more you must get for it. But the price does *not* go up in proportion to the costs. See Chapter 8 for a full discussion of how to set the best price for your product.

When reckoning your costs and revenues, don't forget the value of the names of your customers or inquirers. Satisfied customers can later be sold other products, and each customer's name then becomes very valuable. And even if you yourself *never* try to sell anything to the customer again or even if the prospect has never bought from you, the name has value and should *never, never* be thrown away. You can convert names into money either by renting the list or (more likely for beginners and small businesses) selling the names. See Chapter 22 for a discussion of lists, list brokers, and how to sell or rent lists.

How to Write a Classified Ad

We shall go into some detail on this topic, because the art of writing classified ads is not covered in the books that discuss display-advertising copy.

What is true of *all* advertising copy is *especially* true for classified writing: You as the copywriter must be absolutely precise and economical with the words and language you use. Every fuzzy or useless word takes a chunk out of potential profit. A single word that is not true to its mark and completely clear may turn potential customers away from the ad.

That's why writing classified ads is superb training for creating all types of advertising. The head of a large and important agency once voiced the wish that all his high-priced copywriters had had a 6-months' apprenticeship in writing classified ads at the start of their careers.

Furthermore, the same elements that make up a successful full-page ad must also go into a good classified ad. The order in which these elements, in general, appear in a classified ad follow:

Element 1: Gaining the Attention of the Reader. This is less of a problem with classified advertising than with display ads. Potential customers actively read a particular classification in the classified pages, usually in the order in which they appear, and they tend to read or skim almost every ad. Nothing you can say in your classified ad will attract readers who are not already looking through that particular classified section. Those who do read the classified section are almost a captive audience, and you don't have to use showmanship tricks to attract them to your ad.

Nevertheless, your ad must compete with the other ads for readers' fullest attention as they skim through. You must try to attract that large portion of the readers who might not read *through* your ad carefully.

Attracting attention is done in display ads by the headline, the layout, and the artwork. Your classified ad has no artwork and no layout other than the standardized block of type. The whole job of leading readers into and through your ad, therefore, must be done by the first word (or words) in the advertisement. The first word or words are set in capitals, and the *best* first words will be those that are most exciting and interesting to the potential purchasers of your product.

The principles of writing the lead words of the classified ad are exactly the same as the principles of writing the headline of a display mail-order ad. The lead words will go right to the heart of the product, and they will never tease or be cute. A successful classified ad will never contain a general appeal like "Have Extra Fun with Your Family."

Element 2: The Promise.   If the product is a manual or course on self-improvement or making money, the classified ad will contain the "big promise" or "emotional appeal" that is the key element of many mail-order display ads. This promise must have more power to attract the reader than any other words: "$70–$100 Weekly Possible," "Giant Arms," "Second Income from Oil," etc.

Element 3: Telling What the Product Is.   If the product is solid, *tangible* merchandise, the classified ad will dive right into an exciting description of the product, or it will name the product in the lead words. "Jeep Parts," "Patent Searchers," "Socialist Books," and "Accordions" are examples. The heading of the classification also serves the function of naming some products quite precisely: "Cameras and Photo Supplies," "Farms, Acreage, and Real Estate," "Music and Musical Instruments."

Element 4: Calling to the Prospect.   Many kinds of products use the lead-word technique of calling out to potential prospects: "Inventors," "Writers," "Bookhunters." If the classification heading performs this function, calling out to the reader will probably not be successful or necessary in the individual advertisements.

Element 5: Description of the Product.   After the lead words, the good classified ad will contain whatever descriptive words are necessary to tell enough about your product to make the prospects want it *and* to convince them that you are telling the truth and are reliable. All that can sometimes be done in just three words. More about that later.

Element 6: The Price.   This is only if you are trying to make direct sales.

Element 7: A Call to Action.   This could be "Write today" or "Send." Some ads can do without the call to action; others benefit from it.

Element 8: A Guarantee. This is if you are making direct sales. I have found, in every single test I have run, that the guarantee increases my profit. But some other advertisers evidently don't agree, because they don't include a guarantee in their ads.

Element 9: The Key and the Address. You will find instructions on keying in Chapter 11. Never use more than a one-word name: "Violinco" will do just as well as "Violin Company" and saves money. Omit "Street" and street numbers if the postmaster will give you permission. After a while you can omit your address completely if you live in a small town. In a fair-sized city you can use a single block of letters for your post office box and key.

Steps in Writing the Classified Ad

These are the actual steps that I follow in writing a classified ad. I can only recommend them to you as one man's method. Your approach may be different, but you should be covering the same ground.

1. Study the ads of your successful competitors.

2. In the order in which they come into your head, scribble down every word or idea or group of words that would help you to sell the product if you had all the space you wanted. In addition to all the words about your product, include all the classic selling words: "News," "New Discovery," "Bargain," "Free," "Save," etc. Include every important word that is in your competitor's ads.

3. Write down your lead word (or words). Your first ads will have the best chance of success if your lead words express the same *idea* as your most successful competitor's ads. (But use *different* words.)

4. Using your list of important words and phrases, write the best ad you can, without trying to make the ad short or concise. Just make sure that you have in the ad everything you think must be in it, in the correct order. Include every "selling idea" that your successful competitors have in their ads.

5. Then hone and polish the ad. Try for the most powerful and evocative words that you can find. It is amazing the difference that a single word can make. I found that the words "Manual" and "Book" brought in *twice as many* orders as did "Instructions" in an ad for a how-to-do-it booklet I was selling. Every experienced mail-order person has at least one story like this.

6. Squeeze out every single *extra* word. Keep in mind that one extra word can cost you $500 in a year's time. Use figures instead of words ("50¢" for "fifty cents"). Leave out "the," "a," "an." But don't abbreviate because a short word costs you as much as a long word. Long words help because they make the ad look bigger.

   Use as much punctuation as possible to make the ad look exciting and big. Use quotation marks ("New Discovery"), dots ("Quick . . . Cheap . . . Powerful"), exclamation points (Now!!!).

   Remember that publishers generally count each letter or group of letters as a word. ("Department J" is two words.) Hyphenated words usually count as two words, also. ("Do-It-Yourself" is three words.)

7. After that, you're on your own. You will have to test new words and new ideas to see if they increase your returns. Test action words like "Write today." Test extra description words. Test new lead words. Test leaving out various words and ideas. Test everything, and keep testing till you have really profitable copy. Then test some more. See Chapters 4 and 13 for instructions on how to test.

How Long Should the Classified Ad Be?

When asked how long an ad should be, advertising people like to paraphrase Abraham Lincoln's famous remark: The ad should be long enough to do the job. The advice is sage but not very helpful except to point out that the best length for an ad differs from situation to situation.

Properly, the length of an ad is determined by these two factors:

1. *The ad must be long enough to tell the basic story.* If any crucial element is left out, the ad will fail completely. For example, if you do not include enough description of the product so that readers understand what it is you are selling, you make no sales at all. Telling the reader what the product will do *for* him or her may be a crucial element. Telling him or her that the product is new may also be crucial.
2. *"The more you tell, the more you sell."* Assuming that all the crucial elements are present, further sales talk will increase sales to *some* extent. The problem is to determine *how* much more than the crucial elements it is profitable to pile into the ad.

Not only does each extra sales word increase your sales somewhat, but the sheer size of an ad affects its selling power. In other words, even if you just added neutral dummy words like "the," "and so forth," "Now Now Now Now," etc., you would probably increase sales somewhat. But dummy words seldom (perhaps never) increase sales *sufficiently* to make them profitable.

You can find the best size of your particular ad only by actual testing. Try an ad 50 percent longer than your basic ad. Try another ad 100 percent longer. Try a third ad that leaves out some of the elements in your basic ad. Then calculate which ad is most profitable. Then and only then will you know the best size.

If you find the bigger ad is more profitable, try an even bigger ad. If the smaller ad is more profitable, try an even smaller ad.

This is how you *calculate* which is the most profitable advertisement:

1. Figure how much you net on each *sale*, exclusive of advertising cost. Take everything into account, including labor, but *exclude advertising cost*. If a pamphlet sells for $1, and printing, binding, etc., costs 10 cents, outgoing postage 6 cents, clerical labor (including your own) 5 cents, reserve for refunds 3 cents, labels, envelopes, and other costs 8 cents, adding to 32 cents, then $1 less 32 cents equals 68 cents net, exclusive of advertising cost.

2. Determine how many *more* orders the bigger ad brings in than does your basic ad, and multiply by the 68 cents net. (In other words, if the big ad brings in 80 more orders than the little ad, multiply 80 $\times$ .68, which equals $54.40.)

3. Calculate how much more the bigger ad costs than the basic ad. (In other words, cost of big ad minus cost of small ad.)

4. If the cost in step 3 is less than the extra net in step 2, then the bigger ad is more profitable than the smaller one.

You should understand very clearly that an ad twice as long (and therefore twice as costly) as your basic ad definitely does *not* have to bring in twice as many orders to be more profitable. Wrong figuring will lead you to lose much profit. The *only* correct way to figure is the way set forth above.

13

How to Test and Run Classified Ads

Where and How to Test Your Classified Offer and Advertisement

We assume that by now you have chosen your product and have decided whether you will offer it in one step or two steps. You have selected the price you will try first. Next you must find out whether your product will make money, and how and where it will make the most money. In other words, you need to place "test" ads.

This section discusses how, where, and when to place test ads, and how to interpret their results. The following sections discuss how to classify an ad, and how to run multiple ads.

How to Place a Classified Ad

By now you should have rate cards for all the classified media. Chapter 14 tells you how to read the rate card to find out the cost per word, where to send the ad, and when the closing and publication dates are. That section also tells you how to read information from the *Standard Rate & Data* publications.

Chapter 31 tells you how to set up an advertising agency through which you can receive credit and place ads at a discount. It also tells you how to choose an advertising agency that will help you with your ads.

But at the beginning it will be sensible to send your ads directly to the media, at full card rates. You can simply type (or write, if necessary) your advertisement and instructions for proper classification, and send it in with your check to the magazine. The magazine will take care of the rest for you.

If you want to get really professional, or if you want to try to establish your own "house" agency, you can have standard (AAAA) forms printed up by offset, for perhaps $15 for a thousand (two sides). See Chapter 31 for more information about how to go about it. Figure 13-1 shows a filled-out copy of the standard form.

The Quick Test

Time is important. You are always in a hurry to find out how good your product is so that you can quickly increase your volume to profitable levels. Therefore, you want to test your ads in media that will give you quick information about how good your offer is.

Capper's Weekly, Grit, and the *National Enquirer* are favorite testing media for classified advertisers. In *Capper's* you can reliably test any offer for the farm market. *Grit* gives you a test of rural, small-town, family readers. The *National Enquirer* tests the less stable, thrill-seeking, alienated portions of the lower economic classes who are also the readers of the important exposure, romance, men's detective, etc., magazines.

The virtue of these test media is that no more than 2 or 3 weeks elapse between the time you place the ad and the time the ad appears. And within a week of publication you have sufficient results to predict accurately how your test will turn out (see Chapter 14 for details on how to predict quickly). Compare this with the requirement of some media for copy 3 months before publication, and from which the returns come in so slowly that another 2 months may elapse before you have enough data to draw a conclusion.

ORDER BLANK FOR PUBLICATIONS
(COPYRIGHT OCTOBER 1956)

JULIAN SIMON ASSOCIATES

NEWARK, N. J.

☐ IF CHECKED HERE THIS IS A SPACE CONTRACT

☒ IF CHECKED HERE, THIS IS AN INSERTION ORDER

TO PUBLISHER OF SATURDAY REVIEW
25 West 45th Street
CITY AND STATE New York 36, New York

NO 1759

DATE November 3, 19

PLEASE PUBLISH ADVERTISING OF (advertiser) Customblend Company
FOR (product) Coffee

SPACE	TIMES	DATES OF INSERTION
Classified	2	Next two open issues (Dec 3 and 10?)

FREE COFFEE Booklet. "All About Coffee". Sampler: Eight quarter-pounds originating different countries $2.75 (guaranteed!).
Customblend, 28-CSR22, Millburn, New Jersey

POSITION
Personal

COPY KEY Key CSR23 second insertion CUTS

ADDITIONAL INSTRUCTIONS

RATE
$.55 per word, 19 words

LESS AGENCY COMMISSION 15 PER CENT ON GROSS LESS CASH DISCOUNT 2 PER CENT ON NET

SAMPLE ONLY

JULIAN SIMON ASSOCIATES PER Julian L. Simon
NEWARK, N. J.

Order Blank for Publications Copyright October, 1956. American Association of Advertising Agencies, Inc. (OVER)

Figure 13-1

Many of the farm papers have relatively short closing dates, and some of them are good test media for general products.

How Much to Spend for Tests

Chapter 26 gives you the full story on testing. Read it before starting your advertising campaign.

You must understand that the information you get from a test is worth money. It is often profitable and necessary to run a test ad even if you have to send back all the money you receive. And it is common practice, though perhaps not strictly ethical, to place ads before you have the merchandise.

Your test must produce enough results so that the conclusions you base on the ad will be fairly accurate. A rule of thumb: You must usually spend at least $50 in advertising for your first classified test of a product *or* an offer or a piece of copy. That means two $25 tests, one $50 test, etc., for each offer *or* piece of copy, etc. A smaller test volume than that will not give you enough information about whether even to test further.

How to Interpret Test Results

So you have placed your test ads, and the results are coming in. On the basis of the partial results, you estimate the total orders or inquiries you will receive. Use the tables in Chapter 14 to make that prediction.

Remember that the prediction will not be perfect. First of all, the tables are imperfect. Furthermore, you should modify the tables for classified advertising because responses tend to come in faster for classified than for display ads (perhaps because it is easier to cut out a display ad and save it for awhile).

Your results may be higher or lower than they "should" be because of sheer chance (see Chapter 26 to figure how accurate your prediction is likely to be). You must also take into account the seasonal variation from month to month when interpreting your test results.

Then you must decide, on the basis of your predicted results, whether the test is a success or a failure. Chapter 14 will help you decide. These are some very rough rules of thumb:

1. If you are selling a manufactured product for $5 to $25, you must take in at least 3 times the cost of the advertising. (I hope that this and the following rules of thumb do not mislead you by

focusing your attention away from the all-important "order margin," the difference between the selling price and the costs of the merchandise and other costs of filling the order.)

2. For printed products in which the cost of the material is very slight, dollar results more than twice the cost of advertising should be solidly profitable. Under 1½ times the cost of advertising you will probably lose money.

3. Fifteen cents per inquiry is a fair cost for a $2 to $3 item.

4. A dollar per inquiry is a fair cost for a $50 item or for agents.

These rules of thumb assume that you can improve your advertising and your offer after you run your test ads.

Calculating the success or failure of a repeat-sale product is more complicated. Chapter 22 tells more about this.

You should also make an adjustment in your projection to account for the fact that media like the *National Enquirer* and *Capper's* will both pull more volume per dollar than most other media you will use. (That's why they carry so much classified advertising.)

The Second Round of Testing

Many people have lost their shirts because they went pell-mell ahead with a full campaign on the basis of one or two test ads. Don't let it happen to you.

If your first ad (or ads) makes you think that your offer is profitable, you should then expand your schedule to run perhaps 3 or 4 times as much advertising (measured in dollars) as your first test. Go into several different *kinds* of magazines that may be good prospects, rather than stick to one type. For example, if you tested in *Capper's,* don't stick to farm magazines when you retest. If it seems at all sensible to do so, try perhaps *Popular Science, Successful Farming, Grit,* and *Sports Afield,* in addition to several state farm magazines. If your offer looks definitely profitable, follow the instructions in the rest of this chapter.

Where to Run Your Ads

Let's assume you have already tested your offer in two or more of the magazines mentioned in the previous section. The results are promising, and you now want to make some real money by advertising in every medium that will be profitable.

Your next move is to test the various *categories* of magazines that seem promising for your offer. Here are category breakdowns that you can use:

Men's mass-circulation magazines (including Debonair Men's Group, Magnum Men's Group, Premium Men's Group, Victory Men's Group)

Women's mass-circulation magazines (including Ideal Women's Group, Reese Women's Group, MacFadden Women's Group)

General (including Quality Fraternal)

Better men's magazines (including Mechanics and Fishing and Hunting magazines)

Farm magazines and papers

Specialty and hobby magazines

Salesman's magazines

Magazines under 50,000 circulation

Try magazines under 50,000 circulation *last.* They give you the least profit for your time and labor. They seem to work for some offers. But wait until you know your offer is thoroughly profitable before trying them.

If you have an item that appeals to men, try the better men's magazines before the "mass" men's magazines because their closing dates are shorter.

If your offer pays off in the one or two magazines you test in any category, advertise in *all* the magazines in that category immediately. If you are a more cautious person, advertise in the best half of the magazines in that category (those magazines with the biggest classified sections). But never place an ad until you have examined the classified section of that magazine and found that it contains similar advertisements.

At the same time that you are spreading your offer into all the magazines *within* groups, test out other groups. A profitable offer will make money in some very unlikely places. Some offers to women have done very well in the mechanics and fishing and hunting magazines (under "Of Interest to Women").

At all times keep your eye on the big magazines or groups of magazines. The few big media are worth 10 or 20 times as much attention you pay to other media.

When to Run Your Ad

Some months of the year are better for mail order than others. Chapter 15 gives you a table that helps predict how good the various months will be for products that are not themselves seasonal. (Swimming equipment will naturally do better in spring and summer than in fall and winter, and you would not use the table for such a product.)

The most general ranking of the months, from best to worst, is January, February, March, October, November, September, August, April, May. December is worst for some offers, not quite so bad for others.

Remember that the figures in Table 15-1 in Chapter 15 refer to *issues of magazines* and not to the number of replies you will receive in *calendar months*. For example, the May issue may do far worse than the September issue, but you may get more replies from *all* your ads in May than in September. Remember also that the issue month refers to the date the magazine really appears on newsstands and in mail boxes and not to the "cover date" of the magazine, which is meaningless.

Unless your ads are pulling very well indeed, you probably should schedule no ads from May to August, and none in December unless you have a gift item. If you figure you can make money on the ad even if replies are only *half* of what they are in the best month, then it is safe to plan ads for the low months.

The summer is worse for one-shot items than for repeat or two-stage-inquiry propositions because the media cost is only a small part of the total selling cost for a follow-up business. The other costs—follow-up letters, postage, labor—will remain more or less proportional to replies received, all year round. So, the smaller your media advertising is as a percentage of total selling cost, the safer it is to keep on advertising during the summer.

CAUTION: Be especially careful your first summer in the business. Taking losses can be very discouraging, indeed.

How Often to Run Classified Ads

It is generally true that if your offer is good enough to make any profit at all, it will be profitable to run the ad in every consecutive issue of *monthly* magazines, with the exception of the low months.

Don't worry about results dropping off in monthly magazines. If there is any drop-off, it will be slight, and results will soon reach a plateau. New competition is a much greater danger for you than drop-off, and you must grab your profit while the field is still relatively clear.

The reason why classified ads are so immune to drop-off is that only a small portion of the readership reads the ad in any one issue. Each issue leaves the reservoir of potential customers almost untouched. The slight decline in that reservoir is offset by the changing readership of the magazine.

Here's why it pays to run in every issue even if there is some drop-off. Compare these two plans of action, assuming that drop-off is *much greater* than it will be for most classified ads:

Issue	1	2	3	4	Total profit
Plan A cost	$20.00	Not run	$20.00	Not run	
Plan A net revenue*	50.00				
Plan A profit	30.00	Not run	30.00	Not run	$ 60.00
Plan B cost	20.00	$20.00	20.00	$20.00	
Plan B net revenue*	50.00	45.00	42.50	42.50	
Plan B profit	30.00	25.00	22.50	22.50	$100.00

* By "net revenue" I mean the amount that is left after all costs except advertising have been subtracted. It is analogus to "order margin."

You can see that Plan B earns $100 profit while Plan A earns $60 profit, even though Plan A's rate of return on the invested capital is higher.

Furthermore, in view of the small amount of drop-off in the monthly magazines, you can run the same ad over and over again *without changing it.* An additional reason for not changing the ad is that the attention-getting element is what you usually change in display ads, and this element is a less important part of the classified advertisement.

Drop-off will be least in magazines that are sold mostly on newsstands. If you run a classified ad so large that drop-off might be a factor, the potential trouble spots will be in *all-subscription* magazines like fraternal publications and regligious magazines.

I have found no sign of appreciable drop-off for a ten-word ad I ran in *American Legion Magazine* for many consecutive months, even though it is 100 percent subscription. (The results were standardized for seasonal variation in this comparison.)

"Till-Forbid" Orders and When to Use Them

Placing an insertion order for an ad takes quite a little clerical time for you, and for the magazine, too. The paper shuffling, typing, and filing consume enough time so that if you had to make a new insertion each time an ad ran, it would not be economical to run any ads that cost less than perhaps $10 per month, and the profit on all ads would be cut sadly.

The situation is much the same at the magazines.

The "till-forbid" order solves this problem. Once you have tested your offer and your copy enough to feel sure that they are profitable, you then tell the magazine to run the ad *automatically* each month until you tell them to stop ("till-forbid," or "TF"). Each month they push the key number forward in accordance with instructions you give them.

Not only does this procedure save you the cost of labor, but it saves advertising costs as well. Because repeating a TF order saves them money, many magazines pass on the savings to you by giving you a discount on repeated insertions of the same copy.

It is not wise to place TF orders until you are *quite sure* that your offer and copy are as good as you can get them. Not only is it laborious to kill a lot of TF orders and to place new ones, but you may make costly mistakes of duplication and omission.

How to "Classify" a Classified Ad

The idea behind classified ads is that the classified section is like a department store. People look at the department (classification) which carries the particular product they are interested in. A woman who wants to buy a cow looks under "Livestock," and a man who wants to make extra money looks under "Business Opportunities."

That's why it is important to place your ad under the classification that most of your potential customers will look at.

The best classification to try first is the classification that your competitors use. Don't make the mistake of thinking that that classification is "occupied." (Notice that competitors use different classification headings in different magazines.) Once you are well established, you can test other classifications. Your competitors don't have *all* the answers, either. (But they must know how to learn by experience and be right *most* of the time or they would be out of business.)

When there is not enough competition to provide guidance for you, or when you are testing media in which the product is new, you must use your common sense. Look for the *special* interest of the product. You will find that it pays to run a product under a specific relevant heading rather than under a more general heading of "miscellaneous." For example, a hypnotism manual will do better under "Hypnotism" rather than under "Books and Education" or "Miscellaneous." The specific heading will do better even though the overall readership is lower. In Table 13-1 you can see that the readership in the "Tobacco, Smokers Supplies" heading is only two-thirds of that in "Miscellaneous." But those who sell tobacco have evidently found that the former category is better for them.

Table 13-1. Readership in Some Classified Categories[1]

Readex Survey in Popular Mechanics	
Tobacco, smokers supplies	12%
For sale—miscellaneous	16
Wanted—miscellaneous	12
Miscellaneous	18
Personal	12

These figures also suggest that if your common sense tells you that your offer belongs under *either* "Personal" or "Miscellaneous," you should try "Miscellaneous" first.

If the magazine has no heading that is specific for your product, ask them to put one in. The heading acts like a very powerful lead word. The magazine may ask you to pay extra for the special heading, and often it is worth the extra cost.

If two headings are quite similar—"Money-Making Opportunities" and "Business Opportunities," for example—try first one, then the other, to see which does better.

If two classifications seem otherwise alike, the one that comes first in the classified setion has an advantage. "Additional Income" comes first in *Spare Time* and is better for some products than "Business Opportunities."

Because of the position advantage, some publishers alternate the order in which the classifications appear from month to month. But some of these publishers will honor a request if you name two alternate classifications and specify "whichever comes first."

You should also see to it that magazines give you a fair shake in putting you before your competitors a good part of the time. But don't expect to rate with the competitor who has run steadily for years until you have proved you are a steady customer, too.

I offered a product every single week in *Saturday Review.* I alternated between "For the Gourmet" and "Personals." The results continued to be quite satisfactory. I did not test this alternation against keeping the ad under one heading each week. But since the ad pulls equally well under each heading, we could not *logically* expect any possible improvement from staying under one heading only.

The equality of results under the two headings is curious and interesting. It could be due to one of these factors:

1. The product is not extremely specialized or really relevant to gourmets.

2. The *Saturday Review* readers could be such avid classified readers that they read *all* classified ads.

3. Sheer scientific coincidence could explain it, too.

Extra Gold from the Classified Mine

As we said before, the great disadvantage of classified is the limited number of media available in which a given offer can make a profit. And so, classified advertisers must make maximum use of the most profitable media by running two or more ads under different headings in the same issues.

You can increase your profit by running two or more ads *if, and only if,* these conditions hold for a magazine:

1. The magazine must carry three or more full pages of classified ads. The mechanics and fishing and hunting magazines and *Workbasket* are some of the few magazines in this category.

2. The magazine must have over 300,000 circulation, preferably much of it in newsstand sales.

3. Previous insertions of the ad must have pulled almost *twice as many* replies as the ad needed to break even. This figure includes a slight margin to allow for imperfect calculation of response.

The second ad will *not* double your response, and the third ad will not *triple* it. Two ads should produce perhaps 1½ times the response to a single ad. The reduced response to the second ad is partly the result of placing the second ad under the second choice of classification headings.

Until you have considerable experience with your offer, and with classified advertising generally, you will be wise to run a second ad only in magazines in which other advertisers run more than one ad.

Some multiple-ad advertisers use the same wording in all the ads, while others use different copy. If different wordings are equally good, they stand an increased chance of attracting more total readers. But you must *test* several times to be sure that the second piece of copy is as good as the first.

Multiple insertions may also be used as a means of testing copy. You run both ads in two successive issues, reversing the classifications under which they appear. For example, the first month copy A runs under "Business Opportunities," and copy B runs under "Educational." In the second issue they reverse: Copy B runs under "Business Opportunities," and copy A under "Educational." Then you can compare to determine which copy is better and which classification is better.

14

Display-Advertising Procedure and Testing

How to Place an Ad / Exploratory Testing of
Your Offer / How to Estimate Results Quickly /
Have You Got a Winner? Standards for
Decision / The Second Stage of Testing

So you have a product and an offer that you think will do well in magazine display advertising! You think you're ready to get into print and into business. This chapter will guide you in your next steps.

We shall not discuss the arts of writing copy and laying out ads. Constructing display ads calls for competent professional skill. Amateur dabbling just won't get by. One solution is to use the services of an advertising agency. (See Chapter 31 on picking a *mail-order* advertising agency; avoid ordinary non-mail-order advertising agencies like the plague.) Or else you must make yourself into a copywriter of semiprofessional skill.

Some of the best mail-order copywriters that have ever lived give you their famous wisdom on the subject in Chapters 17, 18, 19, and 21. But no short lesson can teach you to write good mail-order ads. If you want to learn how, get hold of *at least two* of the books listed below, and *study* them thoroughly. ("Study" means much more than "read." It means "read many times with very close attention.") And then you will need practice and more study to learn your trade. But your results will be worth it.

These time-tested books were written by truly great mail-order copywriters:

John Caples, *Tested Advertising Methods*[1]

Victor O. Schwab, *How to Write a Good Advertisement*[2]

These three volumes can help you give yourself a fine general education in writing advertising:

Clyde Bedell, *How to Write Advertising That Sells*[3]

G. B. Hotchkiss, *Advertising Copy*[4]

David Ogilvy, *Confessions of an Advertising Man*[5]

This chapter will include all the reported results of mail-order display-ad tests that I could find in writing or in my own records and that are reasonably sound and valid.

How to Place an Ad

If you use an agency, and if your account is sizable, an advertising agency will handle many or all of the technical problems for you. But the beginner—who needs help the most—has only a small account to offer an agency, and hence gets little service from the agency. Therefore, whether you set up your own house agency, or whether you have an outside agency, you must know how to produce and place an ad.

Getting to be an agency is simple in principle, and not much harder in practice. All you need is a supply of insertion orders and stationery, plus recognition and credit from the media.

Remember to choose an agency name distinct from your mail-order firm name in order to maintain the fiction of a separation. The media have no desire to ferret out the connection, because it might cost them business. But everyone concerned must join together in maintaining the phony appearance of agent and client.

Gaining recognition and credit with media is a bootstrap operation; if one magazine thinks that other media have given you credit, it will, too. So you have to develop a list of references. The newspapers are toughest on credit, perhaps because they have to wait longer for their money.

Start by merely sending off your ads, on regular agency forms, to the media you choose. If the magazine questions you, offer to pay in advance. That will end most squawks.

Once you have placed ads in several media, either on credit or with cash on the barrelhead, you can use those media as references. Just tell other magazines the names of the media in which you have placed ads. In a relatively short time, you will be able to satisfy all but the toughest credit managers.

I do not suggest that you seek recognition from the various media associations because I assume your assets are too limited to make a good showing. But if you can deposit a chunk of money in a separate checking account, and if you can claim some experience in marketing and advertising, you might try for formal recognition.

To place an ad you must know how to read a rate card. Reading a rate card and the *Standard Rate & Data* listings is confusing at first, but it is really quite easy. Two rate cards are shown in Figures 14-1 and 14-2.

The *Spare Time* rate card in Figure 14-1 practically duplicates its *Standard Rate & Data* listing.

The rate card in Figure 14-2 offers a group composed of four magazines: *Bronze Thrills, Jive, Hip,* and *Soul Confessions.*

The items of special interest to you are explained below.

The Cost per Agate Line. There are fourteen agate lines to the inch. Notice that the cost per line decreases as you take larger units of space. Some magazines offer much greater discounts than others do.

The price of space is theoretically the same to all comers. However, "distress covers"—covers that remain unsold at the last minute—are sold at a cut price to major mail-order advertisers. Other special deals are also made from time to time. Be sure to inquire if any "remnant" space is available at a large discount.

There are also discounts for repeated insertions in many magazines.

Theoretically, the price of space remains the same all year round. But the publishers are well aware that mail-order results drop off drastically in the summer, and many of them offer special summer rate reductions. Three insertions for the price of two is a common inducement to advertise in the months with poorer responses.

Size of the Circulation. Usually you will decide about a magazine without considering the circulation, solely on the basis of the other ads it carries. If, however, your product requires merely huge numbers of readers, examine the ratio of cost-per-line/circulation. Fifty cents per line per 100,000 readers is the going price for totally unspecialized, low-class magazines, good for many mail-order products. Specialized

SPARE TIME 5810 West Oklahoma Avenue, Milwaukee, Wisconsin 53219 414/543-8110

1 PERSONNEL
Publisher and Advertising Manager—Harvey R. Kipen
Production Manager—Betty C. Hinz
Editor—Stan Holden

2 REPRESENTATIVES and/or BRANCH OFFICES
Chicago, Illinois 60611
919 N. Michigan Avenue
Telephone (312) 787-4545

3 COMMISSION AND CASH DISCOUNT
a. 15% to recognized advertising agencies.
b. 2% cash discount on display advertising, only if paid within 10 days from date of invoice. Net 30 days. No agency commission after 30 days.
c. Bills rendered date mailing of an issue begins.

4 GENERAL
a. Rates subject to change without notice except on contracts which have been accepted and acknowledged by the publisher.
b. Advertising which is objectionable or misleading in the opinion of the publisher is not accepted.
c. Orders with special conditions such as positioning or editorial are not accepted.
d. No frequency discount.
e. Rates based upon complete material furnished. All production work required such as art, keyline, typesetting, photography billed at cost plus 15%.

5 DISPLAY ADVERTISING RATES
1 page (429 lines) $3,100.00
2/3 page (286 lines) 2,335.00
1/2 page (214 lines) 2,015.00
1/3 page (143 lines) 1,460.00
1/6 page (70 lines) 755.00
1 inch (14 lines) 160.00
2 pages facing 6,045.00
2 pages facing, black and standard red 6,445.00

Advertisements other than standard units charged for on the following basis:
7-69 lines $11.45
71-142 lines 10.75
144-213 lines 10.15
215-285 lines 9.35
287-428 lines 8.15
Over 429 lines 7.20

6 COLOR
Red, per page, extra $250.00
Red, smaller units, extra 200.00
Special color, per page or less, extra 300.00
Four colors, per page, extra 750.00

7 INSERTS
Post card $5,100.00
First post card and ad page facing 8,240.00
Other past card positions with ad page facing 7,890.00
Add $200.00 for second color, standard red, page facing.
Add $550.00 for four colors, page facing.

Post card inserts are 5" deep x 6" wide, printed in two colors, both sides. Subject to availability of companion card.

8 BLEED
Bleed requirements: 8¾" wide x 11¼" deep. Type matter must be at least ¾" away from edge. No extra charge.

9 COVERS AND SPECIAL POSITIONS
All orders ROP. Bigger space users get cover positions or other special positions requested on a rotating basis at no extra charge.
Split runs not available.

10 CLASSIFIED
$3.50 per word. Minimum 15 words—$52.50. First line set in Caps. All copy set solid without display, leaded or blank spaces. Name, address and numbers must be included in word count. Zip code does not count as word. Cash with order unless placed by recognized advertising agency. No cash discount.

11 CONTRACT AND COPY REGULATIONS
a. Advertisers and advertising agencies assume liability for all content of advertisements including text, representation and illustrations and also assume full liability for any claims against the publisher arising therefrom.
b. Cannot guarantee proofs for correction if copy is not received by closing date.
c. Publisher does not assume responsibility for errors in key number and no allowances or deductions are given should such errors occur.
d. Cash with order unless credit has been established.

12 MINIMUM DEPTH—ROP
1 column, 7 lines; double column, 14 lines.

13 MECHANICAL REQUIREMENTS
a. Publication trim size: 8" x 10⅞"
b. Standard units in inches:

	Width	Depth
Full page	7½ x	10¼
2/3 page	5 x	10¼
1/2 page (vertical)	3⅝ x	10¼
1/2 page (horizontal)	7½ x	5
1/2 page (double column)	5 x	7½
1/3 page (vertical)	2⅜ x	10¼
1/3 page (double column)	5 x	5
1/6 page	2⅜ x	5

c. Width of column: 2⅜"; double column, 5".
d. Depth of column: 143 lines.
e. Pages are 3 columns, 429 lines to a page.
f. Kind of printing: offset.
g. Publisher assumes no responsibility for materials un-called for 6 months after date of insertion.

14 ISSUANCE, CLOSING AND CANCELLATION DATES
a. Published nine times a year: January, February, March, April, May, August, September, October, November (monthly except June, July, and December).
b. Issued 1st of month.
c. Closes 1st of month preceding. For example: March issue closes February 1. Mailing begins March 1.
d. Cancellations not accepted after closing date.

15 CIRCULATION INFORMATION
a. Character of circulation: Men and women known to be interested in income opportunities, interested in selling (spare time or full time), starting a business of their own, franchise openings, profitable sidelines. Current respondents to a wide variety of Direct Selling and Start-Your-Own-Business offers.
b. Sources of circulation: names drawn for each issue from carefully selected lists of persons who have answered specific ads.
c. Locality of circulation: national.
d. Rates based upon a guaranteed circulation of 300,000 copies per issue.
e. Publisher will provide copies of postal receipts upon request.
f. Subscription: 9 issues (one year) for $4.00; single copy, 50¢. Mailed free to selected readers.

16 MISCELLANEOUS
a. Established 1955.
b. Published nine times a year by The Kipen Publishing Corp., 5810 W. Oklahoma Ave., Milwaukee, Wisconsin 53219. Harvey R. Kipen, president.
c. Member: Direct Selling Association; Direct Marketing Association; Third Class Mail Association.

SPARE TIME
Money Making Opportunities

Guaranteed circulation of 300,000 copies per issue

RATE CARD NO. 16

Issued May, 1985 Effective August, 1985 Issue

Published Nine Times A Year

January
February
March
April
May
August
September
October
November

Monthly Except June, July and December

5810 West Oklahoma Avenue, Milwaukee, Wisconsin 53219 414/543-8110

Figure 14-1

NATHAN KATZ ASSOCIATES · *Publishers' Representatives*
P. O. BOX 9005, 8700 BOULEVARD EAST, NORTH BERGEN, N. J. 07047

SPECIAL MAIL - ORDER RATES

Published monthly - consisting of five (5) titles
BRONZE THRILLS - SOUL TEEN - JIVE - HIP - SOUL CONFESSIONS

Circulation - 550,000

Rates: Page - $1,000.00   Column: $375.00   Inch: $70.00
II Cover: - $1,125.00   III Cover: $1,250.00   IV COVER : $1,500.00

Issue		On Sale		Closing		
March	1979	February	1979	December	5,	1978
April	1979	March	1979	January	5,	1979
May	1979	April	1979	February	5,	1979
June	1979	May	1979	March	5,	1979
July	1979	June	1979	April	5,	1979
August	1979	July	1979	May	5,	1979
September	1979	August	1979	June	5,	1979
October	1979	September	1979	July	5,	1979
November	1979	October	1979	August	5,	1979
December	1979	November	1979	September	5,	1979
January	1980	December	1979	October	5,	1979
February	1980	January	1980	November	5,	1979

Printed Offset: Page: 7" x 10"   Column: 2-1/4" wide

---

1 – General Advertising
a. One inch (14 agate lines) . $ 47.00
   One col. (140 agate lines) . . 300.00
   Two col. (280 agate lines) . . 570.00
   Full page 800.00
   2nd and 3rd Covers – BW . . 900.00
   4th Cover (2 colors) . . . 1,200.00

Inside pages: color rates on request.
   Bleed: 10% extra.
b. Inserts – on application.
c. Cover positions non-cancelable.
d. Minimum size of advertisements, 14 agate lines (one Inch).

e. Six (6) time insertion 5% discount.
   Twelve (12) time insertion 10% discount.
f. No cancellations or changes accepted after forms are closed.

---

2 – Reading Notices   Not accepted.

---

3 – Commission and Cash Discounts
a. Agency commission 15%.

b. Cash discounts 2%.

c. Cash discount date 10 days from date of invoice.

---

4 – Mechanical Requirements
a. Body of book and covers printed on offset press.
b. Depth of column 140 lines.
c. Three columns to page.
d. Page type space 10 in. deep x 7½ in. wide.
   Double column width – 5 in.

Single column width – 2-3/8 in.
e. Copy material required for offset press production. Supply original art and velox prints of all halftone illustrations and 4 slick proofs. For covers requiring one or more colors other

than black that contain no tints or halftones, color separations with register marks and color indications clearly marked, accepted.
f. Closing dates – 5th of 3rd preceding month. (Sept. closes June 5th and monthly thereafter.)

---

5 – Circulation
a. Location of circulation – U.S., possessions, Canada, South and Central America, newsstands and chain stores.

b. On sale 5th of month and monthly thereafter.)

c. Monthly guarantee 335,000 based on yearly average.

---

6 – Miscellaneous
a. We reserve the right to refuse any advertisement we deem unsuitable.
b. Established 1957.
c. We assume no responsibility for errors in key numbers

and will allow no deductions on this account.
d. Rates guaranteed for three issues.
e. Publishers – Good Publishing Co., 1220 Harding St., Fort Worth, Texas 76102.

f. Advertising representatives – Nathan Katz Associates, 7214 Bergeline Ave., North Bergen, New Jersey 07047. Tel. (201) 869-2219. New York (212) 755-1324.

Figure 14-2

magazine may get as much as $3.20 per line per 100,000 (*Popular Photography*, for example) as of 1974—but astonishingly, this rate has not changed in more than 10 years.

Type of Circulation—Newsstand or Subscription. Magazines whose circulation is almost entirely by subscription distribute almost the same number of copies every month, whereas newstand magazines sell fewer in summer. The readers of subscription magazines are the same people, month after month. Different people buy at newsstands from month to month, increasing the relevant circulation for the mail-order advertiser who advertises in consecutive months. Still another difference is that returns come in slower for newsstand magazines.

Method of Printing. *Spare Time* is printed letterpress and requires a plate, or you can send copy instead. *Complete Women's Group* specifies offset and requires reproduction proofs or material that is "ready for camera."

Width of Column. The column width determines the layout you must send. But it also affects how much you pay per inch. The wider the column, the fewer the inches of space you require to tell your story.

Editorial Mention. Item 4 on the *Spare Time* card in Figure 14-1 is interesting. It suggests how prevalent is the practice of making deals for editorial mention along with the advertising space purchased.

Advertising Representatives. Many mail-order magazines solicit advertising through independent agents known as publishers' representatives. Work through them whenever possible.

Closing Date and Publication Date. The actual publication date is important because it determines whether the month will be good or poor for mail orders. The lag between the closing date and the publication date is the period that you will have to wait for results from the medium.

If you have a small ad, you can sometimes get the ad into a magazine after the listed closing date. Call the representative to find out if the issue is still open, or send the order in, specifying the exact issue you want to be in, even if it is past the closing date.

Exploratory Testing of Your Offer

Even though you know that competitors are making money with offers, you can't be sure that your ad will make money until you try it. Even if you run in the same media that they do, you may not make money if (1) your ad is inferior to theirs, or (2) the market is too small to support all of you.

Some mail-order firms have checked on the power of their advertisements compared with their competitors' by running ads identical to the competitor's—changing only the name and address—and comparing the results to their own ad's results. This practice is either unethical or illegal, however.

Ideally you will run your first ad in a medium that (1) is used by your competitor and (2) has a short closing date so that you can get quick results. The time of the year doesn't matter much because you can use the information in Chapter 15 to predict how the ad will do in other months of the year on the basis of any month's results.

How do you find the media in which the competition runs ads? By intensive study of mail-order media, of course.

The competition may not run in any short-closing medium, however, and you still need a quick test. So you will run a test in a short-closing medium anyway. The results will still give you a good idea of how effective your ad is.

The best short-closing media for your product will depend on the offer, of course. If the product is a novelty or style item, the magazine sections of the Sunday papers will be a likely bet. The Sunday magazine sections of *The New York Times, Family Weekly,* and the *Chicago Tribune* are the standard test media for such outfits as Spencer Gifts, Sunset House, and Walter Drake; *Family Weekly* is a favorite test medium for many mail-order firms. See *Standard Rate & Data* for the names of other Sunday newspaper magazines. The closing date for these magazines is 2 to 4 weeks before publication.

Other kinds of offers will do better in the regular mail-order sections of the Sunday papers, *Capper's Weekly* (which has a special low test-rate), *Grit,* or the *National Observer.*

The *National Enquirer* is the favorite testing place for off-color or "private" offers related to sex, hypnotism, patent medicines, etc.

The Sunday papers are extremely discriminating about the ads they accept. They find many mail-order propositions objectionable and refuse to carry them. However, if *The New York Times* accepts your proposition, most of the others will, too. So sometimes it pays to try the *Times* first and convince them. Then you're in.

Your first ads will probably be bigger than later ads because you don't want to risk leaving anything out of the ad that might cause a flop. After you have found a successful combination, you can sharpen up and compress your copy, find the most economical layout, and generally refine the ad.

Your first ad should be *approximately* the size of the competing ads. In other words, if the competition runs 4-inch, one-column ads, you will probably run 3- to 6-inch ads, rather than a full page or a 1-inch ad.

Your exploratory ads will probably be all type and no artwork if the product is a book, or a course, or anything else that doesn't absolutely require a picture to sell it. All-type ads can almost always do a *satisfactory* job, though artwork may make the ad much more profitable. Your test media usually will set all-type ads for you without extra charge. Artwork, plates, and typographer's type for a fancier ad often cost more than it pays to spend while you are still in the experimental stage.

How to Estimate Results Quickly

If you had all the time in the world, mail order could be almost a sure thing for you. At each step along the way you could wait until you were absolutely sure you had enough information before taking the next step. Of course you would always take the risk that just when you were finally about to go ahead full steam, a faster-footed competitor would swing in and pick up all the marbles.

Mail-order professionals don't wait to proceed until they are sure. They can't afford to. They have to get plenty of ads running in a short time so that they can produce volume and profit. They therefore must take risks by acting on insufficient information.

A person's ability to take risks smartly *and* boldly determines how well he or she will do in mail order. The person with no guts doesn't have to be so shrewd to make money, but will only make peanuts. The person with guts and bad judgment will lose his or her shirt. Only the operator with courage and good judgment can make a pile. In this respect mail order is like all other businesses, but careful study brings an especially big payoff in mail order.

This gives an advantage to the beginner who enters the mail-order business in his or her spare time. The beginner can take much more time between steps than the person who depends on mail order for bread and butter. The extra information you gain by taking plenty of time offsets your lack of knowledge and experience—at least partly—and gives you a fighting chance to make money (a little bit, anyway) while you serve your apprenticeship.

First you must estimate, when a small part of the returns are in, how well an ad will have pulled when *all* the returns have come in. Then you must estimate how well the ad will do in future insertions in the same medium and in other media, based upon the guess in the first part of the estimate.

Now we shall talk about how to guess the total results on the basis of the early results. Remember that, like any other scientific estimate, the estimate must be only approximate. The accuracy of the guess will depend upon the amount of information you have available, and upon how shrewd you are at considering all the pertinent circumstances.

Table 14-1 summarizes the prediction tables given by several writers on the mail-order business. The elapsed time in each case dates from the day the first inquiry is received, except as noted. The numbers indicate the total percentage of responses received by the end of a time period.

Baker says that many of his clients report faster returns than the figures he shows. By my findings he seems very slow, too. Cates's data are old, so don't rely on them very much.

Sumner says that the method of distribution has a particularly large effect on return rates in the women's service-magazine category. He shows these data:[6]

	10 days	30 days	60 days	90 days	1 year
Subscription	32.9	66.5	82.0	88.3	98.4
Newsstand	13.3	51.4	81.7	87.0	97.8

In each of the schedules in Table 14-1, the figure given for "first week" means the number of returns in hand on the seventh day that returns came in.

But things are not so simple. The "first day" can mislead you. Frequently, an employee of a publication writes for the offer weeks before the magazine has been distributed. Many mail-order people believe that when this happens, it is an infallible omen of good results. Maybe, but it certainly fouls up your prediction schedules. You can ignore returns that come in prior to magazine distribution. But remember that the distribution date varies from month to month by

Table 14-1. Time Rates of Returns—Cumulative

Media	1st wk.	2nd wk.	4th wk.	8th wk.	26th wk.	52nd wk.
TV						
Baker[7]	82	96	99	100		
Radio						
Baker[7]	80	94	99	100		
Daily newspaper						
Grant[8]	90					
Baker[7]	42	78	95	98	100	
Cates[9]	70	95	99	100		
Stone[10]	74	90	96			
Sunday news supplement						
Baker[7]	35	65	79	89	99	100
Graham[11]		(33% in first 4 days)				
Sumner[12]		(50% in first 4 days)				
Stone[10]		(90% by end of third week)				
Sunday predates (preprints)						
Graham[11]		(50% in first 10 days)				
Sunday comics						
Stone[10]		(90% by end of second week)				
Weeklies						
Baker[7]	21	41	65	82	96	100
Graham[11]	33					
Simon (H. K.)[13]	30					
Cates[9]	41	78	96	100		
Segal (Alexander)[14]		(20% in first 2 days, 33% in first 3 days, 50% in first 4 days)				
Biweeklies						
Baker[7]	15	30	60	77	93	100
Fraternal monthlies						
Baker[7]	7	28	61	83	99	100
Simon (J. L.)[15]		35	67			
Monthly magazine shopping section						
Baker[7]	7	33	65	85	100	
General monthly magazine						
Grant[8]			60	75	96	
Baker[7]	5	18	45	68	91	100
Graham[11]		(50% in first month)				
Kestnbaum[16]	11	35	55	81		
All-newsstand monthlies						
Baker[7]	4	13	26	57	87	100
Segal (Alexander)[14]	25	(50% in 30 days)				
All-newsstand bimonthlies						
Baker[7]	1	4	12	36	80	100
3rd-class direct mail						
Segal (Alexander)[14]	33	66	80	91		100
3rd-class direct mail to business firms						
Stone[17]	49	81	(87% in third week)			

as much as 10 days. Remember also that some magazines mail their subscription copies over a period of many days. The magazines that go to direct salespeople (e.g., *Spare Time*) mail over a 15-day period.

Another difficulty is that the rate of accumulation varies from vehicle to vehicle within the same category. Table 14-2 shows the variation in patterns among five monthly magazines.

Returns vary by *type of product*. John Moran asserts that the higher the unit of sale, the slower the returns,[18] but I've seen no statistical evidence of this.

Returns may vary by *size of ad*. I have observed that classified returns come in faster than display ads. A possible explanation: The bigger the ad, the easier it seems to be to clip it out and save it.

I'd suggest placing little faith in a prediction based on other people's schedules until you reach the point that should produce 50 percent of the returns. Once you have run ads for your own product, you will have the most accurate information for your purposes. The second time you run an ad in a magazine, you should know within the first week or two how well the ad will pull. Another good trick is to compare the highest-return days of the two insertions. This high day will occur fairly early for non-newsstand media, usually. The comparison is usually not as accurate as a comparison of several weeks' totals, because it is based on relatively few returns. But it avoids the problem of when the "first day" is.

Table 14-2. Patterns of Cumulative Percent of Total Inquiries Received in Monthly Magazines

Week no.	Publication A	Publication B	Publication C	Publication D	Publication E	Average
1	7.6	13.2	10.6	11.8	8.3	11.0
2	24.7	33.8	36.7	31.1	48.3	35.0
3	41.4	41.8	52.2	43.8	63.3	47.6
4	53.6	48.9	59.0	51.1	68.9	54.9
5	62.4	56.9	63.3	60.1	71.4	61.9
6	65.8	66.2	78.5	75.5	74.1	72.2
7	73.0	72.0	81.0	80.1	80.0	77.3
8	80.6	76.0	84.0	82.7	82.8	80.9
9	85.4	80.1	86.2	85.6	86.9	84.4
10	88.2	84.2	88.4	87.9	90.1	87.4
11	90.1	87.8	90.6	90.8	93.7	90.4
12	93.2	90.3	92.4	94.9	96.9	93.5
13	95.7	93.5	94.7	96.9	98.4	95.9
14	96.8	95.7	96.8	98.5	98.8	97.4
15	98.9	99.2	98.9	100	100	99.5
16	100	100	100			100

SOURCE: Robert Kestnbaum in John Dillon (ed.), *Handbook of International Direct Marketing* (New York: McGraw-Hill, 1976, pp. 125–153).

Have You Got a Winner?
Standards for Decision

Say you ran an ad in a Sunday newspaper magazine, and by 12 days after publication you have more than enough returns to cover all investments, including the cost of merchandise sold. In other words, returns for a week and a half bring you over the break-even point.

You then know that the ad will make a profit. And if you wait a reasonable length of time until you place your next ad, if the season is just as good, and if everything else is the same, a repeated ad in the same medium should also bring you a profit.

But you don't make much money running your ad in just one magazine. How will your ad do in other places?

There are a few experienced mail-order people who have enough know-how and guts to jump immediately into a wide range of media based on incomplete returns from a few test ads. But if you try this, you'll lose your shirt.

The amateur has an advantage because she or he isn't in such a big rush to use all available capital, and therefore she or he can play safer than the professional.

Some first-test media can yield deceptive results. For example, offers tested in the *National Enquirer* sometimes do *twice as well* as they do anywhere else. In that case, you should proceed with extreme caution in entering other media unless the *National Enquirer* results are *more than twice the break-even point.*

On the other hand, tests in Sunday supplements will often give poorer results than will the shopping sections in the "shelter" magazines (for example, *House Beautiful*). That's why the shelter magazines run so many more mail-order ads than do the Sunday supplements. So, even if your test results in the Sunday supplement are only "almost profitable," you *may* have a winner elsewhere—especially if you can improve the ad.

The Second Stage of Testing

Your next step will be to insert your ad in two or more additional media, probably of different types. How to choose the *categories* is discussed in Chapter 15. As more results come in from your test ad that make you surer that you have a winner, and as the amount of profit seems to be higher than your early estimates, go into more categories and more media.

15

Profitable
Display-Advertising
Operation

This chapter is about the decisions you must make after you have run a successful test.

Where to Advertise

Are Your Chores Done? Long ago you should have written to every mail-order magazine for a sample and a rate card. You should also have made a card file containing an entry for each magazine. The card should show how much mail-order advertising the magazine carries and the kinds of products that are advertised there. Soon you'll be using that file over and over again, so check that it is complete.

Which Categories of Magazines
Will Make Money for You?

The general answer to picking categories is the same as the answer
to everything else in mail order: Go where the competition is, because
that's where the profit is. Read through your sample copies again,
looking for the ads of your competitor.

Here is an illustration of how being a follower and emulator can
help you and why you should not fear the presence of competition
in media: As I was writing the first edition of this book, I was in the
midst of developing a correspondence course for the mail-order market. My thinking was as follows:

> Right now I'm in no rush to market the course. One competitor has
> come a little way into the market. And I am glad to see him, because
> he is thoroughly professional and will do much of the job for me. He
> will test out media and product offers, and find out just how much of
> a market there is. If he does very well, I'll speed up my project. If he
> does poorly, and gets completely out of the market, I'll take stock again—
> perhaps run a few tests—with an eye to dropping the project. If I didn't
> want to write this course for the fun of it, I would have waited to start
> it until I saw how the competition did.

The rest of this section discusses the situation when you can't just
follow your competition—either because your product is somewhat
new or because your competitor hasn't developed her media schedule
fully enough. (Be suspicious, though. The competitor is smart, too,
and likes profit. If the competitor is not advertising widely, there
may be good reason for it.)

Look at the mail-order magazines on the newsstand and elsewhere.
Quite a few, aren't there? Some will produce a profit on your particular
offer; some will not. Your problem is to find out which will and which
won't.

Testing the magazines one by one would be difficult and time-
consuming. What you can do, instead, is to consider the various
categories, one by one, using one magazine to test a category.

When we talk about categories, we shall use the *Standard Rate &
Data* classification.

First you select the categories in which your offer has the best
chance of success, using your judgment. Then you run your ad in
the best prospective medium within each category. (That is, within
each category you would probably pick the medium with the most
mail-order advertising.)

After the results are in, you will know which categories *will* work for you. Then you will place ads in every magazine in the categories which test out profitably. You will probably also place ads in a few of the magazines in more questionable categories, and if they pull well, you can then try the others.

For the time being, place no more ads in those categories that did not show a profit. But don't forget about them entirely. You may later come back to one or more of them successfully, either because you have improved your copy, or because the magazine you tested was not representative of the rest of the group, or because your original test went astray by chance.

Remember that you cannot infallibly choose categories for your product by the names of the categories or by their readership. Men's products have been sold profitably in women's magazines, and vice versa.

In each category, some magazines will produce better for you than will others. And it makes sense to try the best prospects first, because that way if your test is not successful, you will lose as little as possible. You can't know in advance which magazine in each category will be best for your product. But as a general guideline, it makes sense to try the magazine that carries the most mail-order advertising. In addition, Table 15-1 shows Stone's list of the best prospects in a few important general groupings, as of 1984.[1]

During this second stage of testing, if you wish to test the largest magazines, you should consider running in only one of their *regional editions* to reduce the possible loss of the test. If your product has any regional appeal (for example, camping in the West), by all means test that region. But you should recognize that aside from special regional advantages, your test is likely to produce somewhat poorer results than will running in the entire national edition, because regional ads tend to be placed in the back of the magazine where ads produce less well than in the front. And regional ads cost 10 to 50 percent more per thousand readers than the national rate.

All decisions described above should be considered in the light of seasonal variation, of course.

Most of the time you will stick to media on our list. There may be times when you have a very specialized product (i.e., by definition, a product that appeals only to a narrow group of people). In that case you *may* successfully go into magazines that carry little or no mail order. An example: Electroplating kits appeal to the hot-rod set, and they are sold successfully from some automobile magazines that carry no other mail-order advertising.

Table 15-1. Basic Consumer Magazine Categories*

Demographic	Category	Sample publications
Dual audience	General editorial/ entertainment	*Grit, National Enquirer, National Geographic, New York Times Magazine Section, Parade, People, Reader's Digest, TV Guide*
	News	*Time, Newsweek, Sports Illustrated, U.S. News & World Report*
	Special Interest	*Architectural Digest, Business Week, Elks, Foreign Affairs, Hi Fidelity, Modern Photography, Natural History, Ski, Travel & Leisure, Wall Street Journal, Yankee*
Women	General/service/ shelter (home service)	*Better Homes & Gardens, Cosmopolitan, Ebony, Family Circle, Good Housekeeping, House Beautiful, House & Garden, Ladies' Home Journal, McCall's, Redbook, Sunset, Woman's Day*
	Fashion	*Glamour, Harper's Bazaar, Mademoiselle, Vogue*
	Special interest	*Brides, MacFadden's Women's Group, McCall's Needlework & Crafts, Parents*
Men	General/ entertainment/ fashion	*Esquire, Gentlemen's Quarterly, Penthouse, Playboy*
	Special interest	*Cars, Field & Stream, Mechanix Illustrated, Outdoor Life, Popular Mechanics, Popular Science, Road & Track, Sports Afield*
Youth	Male	*Boys' Life*
	Female	*Teen, Young Miss*
	Dual audience	*Scholastic Magazines, National 4-H News*

* For big-ticket items, try *The Wall Street Journal.*

What about Newspapers?

In some countries, such as Great Britain, newspapers are the main display mail-order medium. But in the United States, newspapers have only been a very secondary medium, except for Sunday supplements. Recently, however, Media Service Corporation of Cleveland has announced a plan to reduce the cost and increase the flexibility of national newspapers' mail-order campaigns. And it is certainly fast-acting. If you're interested, you'll have to check on this.

Do All Magazines in the Same Category Pull the Same?

In general you can expect magazines in the same category to be more like one another than like magazines in other categories. But there can still be great differences among magazines that are listed together and that seem similar.

Here is an unusual (and perhaps unbelievable) example of different results in the same category. These are the results of the same ad in three similar salesman's magazines, as reported by publication Z, of course:

Publication	Ad cost	No. orders	Volume
X	$520.00	106	$1,002.50
Y	487.50	88	511.50
Z	422.00	1,132	7,772.05

When prospecting for new media, or shopping among media for the best magazine for your test, keep an eye on the cost-per-agate-line per 100,000 readers. For many kinds of offers, you want just circulation and more circulation. One dollar per 200,000 circulation is a basic, low-line rate.

But don't forget to look at the width of the column. A wide column means you get more advertising space per inch.

For low-class magazines especially, space is generally bought through publishers' representatives rather than directly from the magazines. It is preferable to work through them in order to gain their goodwill, advice, and assistance.

When to Advertise

Remember this principle first and always: The best months for your product may run entirely contrary to the general findings for most products. Of course you won't be enough of a darn fool to advertise bathing suits in the winter. But other products have less obvious, but just as significant, seasons that have nothing to do with general buying trends. Every month in the year is the best month for *some* types of offers.

Whether or not your product is the gift type will affect its seasonality. Gifts hit a peak before Christmas, of course. Much of the merchandise advertised in the "shelter" magazines is gift merchandise. Examine

Table 15-2. Mail-Order Linage in *House Beautiful*

Month	1951		1952	
	Number of ads	Linage	Number of ads	Linage
January	90	658	87	5,786
February	188	12,982	183	12,032
March	175	11,564	209	13,486
April	213	15,434	270	18,928
May	278	18,922	306	21,114
June	249	15,680	256	16,888
July	104	6,876	126	8,228
August	91	6,412	109	7,776
September	221	15,524	260	17,244
October	431	30,720	490	36,223
November	887	62,338	986	68,871
December	531	35,694	530	34,424

SOURCE: *House Beautiful* Research Service, reported in Robert A. Baker, *Help Yourself to Better Mail Order*, Printers' Ink Publishing Co., Inc., New York, 1953, p. 85.

the data in Table 15-2. But it is *not* true that, because there are 10 times as many ads in November as in January, *House Beautiful* ads will *pull* more than 10 times as well in November as in January. They won't. A *small* drop in expected returns will lead *many* wise advertisers to stay out because the small drop is enough to change a profit into a loss.

Products that do not serve as gifts don't do so well just before Christmas. And money-making offers do wonderfully well in January.

Just as soon as you have seasonal data on your product, use your own data as a guide rather than refer to the general results. Your own data are always *much* more accurate for your purposes than anyone else's data can be.

Table 15-3 compiles data from several reports that rank the months for general display advertising from best to worst.

I hope you're a little confused at the differences between the various rankings of the months. Your confusion should teach you this: While there are some *general* seasonal principles, eventually your decision must depend upon your own product and your experience with that product.

The frequency of appearance of newspaper preprint inserts, which are expensive and on which the advertiser usually keeps very close records, tells us something about the amount of response in various seasons. Stone kept track of the number of inserts for 1 year. In January there were six preprint inserts, in February six, March two, April none, May none, June one, July seven, August five, September seven, October fourteen, November six, and December one.[2]

Table 15-3. Month Rankings for Mail-Order Advertising

Month	Baker[a] (mostly novelties probably)	Moran[b]	Fate Magazines[c] (book advertisers)	Stone[d] (direct mail)	Grant[e] (mostly money-making offers, probably)	O. E. McIntyre, Inc.[f] (from magazine and book publishers)	Stone[g] (space advertising)
January	3(96)	3	1(100)	1	1 (100)	1 (100)	2 (98)
February	4(92)	1	9(76)	3	2½(98)	3 (85)	1 (100)
March	7(83)	2	8(77)	2	4½(96)	8 (78)	4 (91)
April	8(79)	7	4(80)	6	10½(67)	10 (71)	8 (80)
May	9(69)	9	12(65)	10	12 (58)	11 (70)	10 (77)
June	12(60)	10	11(68)	11	9 (71)	12 (69)	12 (71)
July	11(65)	11	5(79)	12	8 (75)	6½(80)	10 (77)
August	9(69)	8	3(82)	9	6½(83)	2 (86)	6½(83)
September	4(92)	5	6(78)	5	2½(98)	4½(81)	10 (77)
October	1(100)	4	2(87)	7	4½(96)	9 (76)	4 (91)
November	1(100)	6	6(78)	4	6½(83)	4½(81)	4 (91)
December	6(87)	12	10(74)	8	10½(67)	6½(80)	6½(83)

Note: Index numbers for relative pull are given in parentheses. Highest = 100.
[a] From Robert A. Baker, *Help Yourself to Better Mail Order*, Printers' Ink Publishing Co., Inc., New York, 1953, p. 71.
[b] From John Moran, *The Mail Order Business*, MBA Business Associates, Syracuse, NY, 1949, page not known.
[c] From *Fate* Magazines, promotional literature, undated.
[d] From Robert Sonte, *Successful Direct Mail Advertising and Selling*, Prentice-Hall, Englewood Cliffs, NJ, 1955, p. 59.
[e] From Paul Grant, L. W. Mail Order Survey, page not known.
[f] From O.E. McIntrye, Inc., "Best Seasons for Direct Mail," *Media/Scope*, September 1963, p. 27.
[g] From Robert Stone, "Where to Start, How to Test, in Direct Response Magazine Ads," *Advertising Age*, Oct. 22, 1973, p. 119.

Over the years, International Correspondence Schools has amassed a wealth of advertising statistics. Their seasonal fluctuation is considerably greater than indicated in any list shown above. International Correspondence Schools' advertising boss has said that "during the best month of the year our inquiry cost is one-half that of the worst month of the year."

Yet International Correspondence Schools advertises the year round. Why? Because they and the other large correspondence schools are not pure mail-order organizations. Their direct-mail literature is not expected to close the sale. The inquiry names are sent on to salespeople in the various localities, and it is they who close the sale.

Salespeople have to eat and to work, summer as well as winter. So even though summer inquiries cost twice as much to obtain, the correspondence schools are willing to pay through the nose anyway, in order to give the salespeople work year round, and hence maintain their organization intact. (But don't weep for the correspondence schools. They make it up in winter.)

The extent of the seasonal fluctuation also depends on the type of circulation a magazine has. The more copies it distributes by subscription, the less we expect the mail-order sales to fluctuate from month to month. Like readers of subscription magazines, readers of newsstand magazines purchase less by mail during the summer. But the *number* of newsstand readers *also* drops during the summer, whereas the number of *subscription* readers stays much the same.

Remember that we are *not* talking about sales in *calendar months.* We are talking about total returns to issues that appear in particular months. It is easier to understand why May is so relatively poor and August so relatively good if you understand that the May issue is in readers' hands in June, July, etc. (the summer doldrums). The August issue has much life left in the lively fall. The fact that direct mail does worse in June and July than in May supports this reasoning.

However, my own data suggest that the general seasonal patterns shown above indicate something about calendar-month sales as well as about issue months. In other words, May is a poorer calendar month than September, which is just as summery.

The seasons of nature are not the only factors that can affect the pattern of sales. Human events can make a dent, too. During the first month of the Lindberg kidnapping, returns were reported to slump 30 to 70 percent. Pearl Harbor also reduced sales volume drastically. There isn't anything you can do in advance about cataclysms. But understanding their effect can help you interpret your test results.

It would make sense for magazines to drop their advertising rates during the summer, and some do. (You will get offers of one-third off for summer issues.) But too few magazines show the good sense to drop their rates, or perhaps they believe it is important to be a one-price store.

How Often to Repeat a Winning Ad

How often you can repeat your ad in a single medium depends upon these factors:

1. The size of the ad

2. The medium and its readership (especially how much of the circulation is from newsstands)

3. How many other magazines the ad is running in

4. The number of ads run by your competitors

5. The type of product

6. The profitability of your ad

Running several different ads rather than the same ad, in an attempt to prevent results from dropping off, poses issues that are similar.

We shall consider the above factors one by one. But first let's put one more bullet into an old myth that refuses to die (perhaps because it is to the advantage of some people to keep it alive). The myth is "cumulative advertising effect." The effect does not exist, most especially in mail order.

There is no doubt that two insertions have a greater total effect than one insertion. But the implicit notion in the cumulative-advertising-effect argument is that two insertions have *more than twice* the effect of one insertion. Not only is there no evidence for this, but every single report by mail-order people shows that the second insertion *never* pulls better than the first, unless the results are confused by seasonal changes.

The first scientific book about advertising, *Analytical Advertising*, by W. A. Shryer, was mostly a factual polemic against the cumulative-effect notion. On the basis of a huge amount of data, Shryer flatly concluded: "The first insertion of a tried piece of copy in a new medium will pay better, in every way, than any subsequent insertion of the same copy in the same magazine."[3]

Table 15-4. Results of a Magazine Subscription Campaign*

Date run	Medium	Cost of advertisement	No. of subscriptions	Cost per subscription
March	*Technical World*	$ 40.00	51	$ 0.79
April	*Technical World*	40.00	20	2.00
Feb. 19	*Saturday Evening Post*	250.00	338	0.72
Mar. 6	*Saturday Evening Post*	250.00	181	1.38
March	*Circle*	30.00	10	3.00
April	*Circle*	30.00	3	10.00
Feb. 19	*Literary Digest*	45.00	58	0.74
Mar. 19	*Literary Digest*	62.50	35	1.80
Feb. 3	*Chicago Journal*	12.00	17	0.71
Mar. 3	*Chicago Journal*	27.00	13	2.07
Feb. 6	*Chicago Examiner*	90.00	258	0.35
Feb. 27	*Chicago Examiner*	90.00	94	0.95
Mar. 6	*Chicago Examiner*	90.00	57	3.60
Mar. 13	*Chicago Examiner*	90.00	25	1.60
Feb. 6	*New York American*	112.50	131	0.85
Mar. 6	*New York American*	112.50	71	1.38
Feb. 13	*Chicago Inter Ocean*	15.00	20	0.75
Mar. 6	*Chicago Inter Ocean*	33.75	29	1.16
Feb. 15	*New York Journal*	49.00	62	0.79
Mar. 8	*New York Journal*	112.50	53	2.12
Feb. 27	*San Francisco Examiner*	30.00	67	0.45
Mar. 20	*San Francisco Examiner*	42.50	9	4.71
Feb. 27	*Minneapolis Journal*	11.00	21	0.52
Mar. 13	*Minneapolis Journal*	24.75	2	12.37
Mar. 27	*Minneapolis Journal*	24.75	1	24.75
Feb. 27	*Philadelphia Times*	12.00	22	0.55
Mar. 20	*Philadelphia Times*	27.00	3	9.00
Feb. 27	*Los Angeles Examiner*	10.00	16	0.62
Mar. 13	*Los Angeles Examiner*	22.50	11	2.22
Feb. 27	*Chicago Tribune*	30.00	72	0.41
Mar. 20	*Chicago Tribune*	67.50	9	7.50
Feb. 27	*Boston Post*	20.00	32	0.63
Mar. 13	*Boston Post*	45.00	7	6.42
Feb. 20	*St. Louis Post-Dispatch*	20.00	38	0.52
Mar. 13	*St. Louis Post-Dispatch*	45.00	26	1.73
Feb. 20	*Cincinnati Enquirer*	18.00	24	0.75
Mar. 20	*Cincinnati Enquirer*	40.50	8	5.05

*No better data available despite the age of this analysis.
SOURCE: William A. Shryer. *Analytical Advertising*, Business Service Corp., Detroit, 1912, pp. 82–83.

(Mind you, I am not saying that the second insertion has no effect. A person who sees the ad twice *is* more likely to buy than the person who sees it *only* once. But many of the very best prospects purchase from the *first* insertion, skimming the cream of the market.)

The data in Table 15-4 show the results of a popular magazine's campaign to secure subscriptions. The data are from Shryer and are more than half a century old, but they are as useful now as when they were first published.

Notice that in every case the cost of inquiries from the second insertion was *substantially* higher than from the first insertion. Average costs per inquiry were $0.85 from the first insertions, $1.91 from second insertions. The third insertion was so unprofitable that it was tried only once. Part of the drop-off from the first to the second insertion might have resulted from the declining mail-order season as the winter and spring went on, but this would not have explained the bulk of the results.

Here is the way to calculate the most profitable frequency scheduling for your ad. Of course your estimates of the responses to the series of ads with different frequencies cannot be exact. But make the best estimates you can and then calculate as shown in Table 15-5, working with net sales (gross sales less advertising cost less cost of merchandise and other costs).

We see, in the calculation in Table 15-5, that it is most profitable to advertise every month in this case, even though the results in *any particular* month will be lower than if you advertised less frequently. In other cases, however, the calculation may show that you will make the most total profit by advertising every other month or twice a year.

Effect of Size of Ad on Repetition. A small ad can be rerun more frequently than can a big ad. Schwab estimates that a second insertion of a full-page ad within 30 to 90 days of the original insertion will pull 25 to 30 percent less than the original insertion. The third insertion within a short period will drop to 45 to 50 percent of the original insertion. Schwab claims that a wait of 6 months to a year is required before the repeat insertion will do as well as the first insertion.[4] These estimates apply to *identical* advertisements and not to different copy.

The same *small* ad can run month after month in *some* media and continue to be profitable. However, even classified ads can suffer a drop-off, too. I ran a classified ad in *Western Farm Life* in two consecutive issues of the little all-subscription twice monthly. The second insertion pulled just 80 percent of the first insertion. A third insertion a month later pulled less than 50 percent of the first insertion. A fourth insertion 2 weeks later pulled 37 percent of the first insertion. Until I stopped them, subsequent insertions took a beating, ranging from 32 percent to 4 percent of the original insertion. We were bucking a seasonal trend, but the trend could account for only a small part of the effect.

Table 15-5. How to Choose the Optimum Frequency of Advertising

	Jan.	Feb.	Mar.	Apr.	May	Jun.	Jul.	Aug.	Sep.	Oct.	Nov.	Dec.	Total net sales	Advertising cost	Profit or loss
Alternative A: Advertise each month	$100	75	60	55	53	51	50	50	49	49	49	49	$690	12 × $40 − 10% = $432	$258
Alternative B: Advertise bimonthly	$100		80		70		65		63		63		$441	6 × $40 − 5% = $228	$213
Alternative C: Advertise twice in the year	$100						98						$198	2 × $40 = $80	$118

However, the same ad in the *Saturday Review* ran almost indefinitely, week after week, changing only its classification. After an initial not-too-sharp drop-off that coincided with the seasonal trend (I can't estimate the drop-off accurately because there was a copy change), the ad hit a plateau and pulled the same gratifying results week after week.

Neither *Western Farm Life* nor *Saturday Review* is typical of classified sections. *Western Farm Life* is all-subscription, twice a month. *Saturday Review* is also almost all subscription, biweekly. Therefore, their results are not samples of classified advertising generally. The differences *between* them might be explained by the greater amount of classified carried by *Saturday Review*.

It is easy to understand why big ads should suffer greater drop-off than small ads if we consider the difference in the number of people who "notice" the ads. About 4 percent of the readership of *Popular Mechanics* will "notice" a 1-inch ad, while anywhere from 20 to 60 percent will "notice" a full-page ad. The second month it runs, the small ad can put itself before the eyes of 96 percent of the prior audience who never saw the ad before, and almost 4 percent will again "notice" it (assuming no change in readership). But the big ad has used up a very substantial chunk of its audience.

Furthermore, except for completely subscription magazines, far more than 4 percent of the readers of any issue will not have *read* the previous issue. (But keep in mind that the people who "notice" an ad are not a random sample of the readership. Rather, they are those people who have the highest perception for a product and the greatest likelihood to buy.)

Subscription versus Newsstand Circulation. It stands to reason that if exactly the same people see every issue of a magazine, the drop-off must be greater than if there is a turnover of readership. The more newsstand copies sold, the greater the turnover, and hence the less the drop-off.

This effect will be greater upon big ads than upon small ones, of course.

Number of Media Used. The pool of magazine readers in the United States is huge. But it is not limitless. If you insert a big enough ad often enough in enough magazines, you can certainly reach the point at which the returns will decrease. This is akin to the saturation concept of general advertisers.

It is unlikely that the returns to a *small* ad will be much affected by the number of magazines in which it runs.

Competition.   Competitors move in if they sniff the pungent aroma of a golden goose. The competitors can kill your goose if they deluge the media with ads. Their potential customers are your potential customers, too.

But the appearance of competition does not automatically mean that you must fold your tent and quit. Sometimes competitors will try to enter your business, then fail and leave you in peace; this may happen because they cannot learn to operate as efficiently as you do, or because they do not discover some essential aspect of the business (see the example of the collection stickers in Chapter 3). Another reason why the arrival of competitors may not be a disaster is that they may not affect your sales as badly as one would expect. For example, one firm I have worked with introduced an old but never mail-ordered product to the market. I did not believe it would succeed—and it did, anyway, going from nothing to $1.4 million yearly gross and $160,000 yearly profit in the first 5 years. Then, when the firm did succeed, I worried about competition. And competition did enter and has remained. But the effect on the response to this firm's ads has not been disastrous, even when a competitor's ad ran on the same page.

In most mail-order situations, moreover, you are competing mostly against inattention and inertia in your audience rather than against other advertisers.

Fads and Repeat Items.   Some products are of interest once in the lifetime of a customer. A book on karate is an example. Other products are repeat sellers—clothes, for example. Still a third type are products that people are likely to get interested in only at special times in their lives—specialized correspondence courses are one such item.

It is more likely that you can "force" the market for karate books than for clothes or correspondence courses. And once you have forced the market, it takes a couple of years for the market to recover. Products that you can "force" are like fad products. This is the only possible explanation for the waves of saturation ads for such commodities as karate books that roll in for a year or two, then disappear for a while. (However, many propositions that disappear drop out because the government muscles them out, and not because the market is temporarily exhausted.)

How Profitable Is the Ad?   Just as with classified ads, you should repeat a *very* profitable display ad more often than a borderline ad—despite the continuing drop in returns to the profitable ad. As we proved in the classified discussion, you will almost always make more total profit by running two insertions at less than maximum results than you will by running one insertion that gets you maximum results.

Not only will your own profit be greater, but you have a better chance of keeping competition out if you run your ad more frequently. The competition may be attracted by apparent success as shown by your frequency of insertions. But when the competitors run a test ad, the results will be lower under the frequent-insertion plan, just as yours are. And so the results appear less attractive to them, and they are not so likely to continue competing.

What about running *different* ads instead of the same ad, in an attempt to foil the drop-off effect? If you run full-page ads, it certainly pays you to follow the example of such experienced advertisers as International Correspondence Schools, who run several different ads each season. But the advertiser who runs small ads or classified ads will find it too costly and too time-consuming to work with several ads. Instead, you will run the same ad at such intervals as you find profitable, trying out new ads from time to time to see if they beat the standard ad.

Customary repetition intervals for small ads are (1) every issue in monthlies that are largely sold on newsstands, (2) not quite so often in all-subscription magazines, and (3) every month or every 2 months in Sunday supplements.

Shryer gave us the sound rule of thumb that the interval between insertions should be long enough for the earlier ad to pay out its break-even costs. This is on the conservative side.

Before we leave the subject of repetition, here are a couple of inspirational notes:

- A full-page Sherwin Cody ad pulled 225,000 inquiries, 11,000 orders, and $328,500 in a 10-year period. This ad has never really been changed in over 30 years, though many ads have been tested against it.[5]

- La Salle Extension University's basic 1-inch ad occupied $300,000 worth of space and produced $3 million in sales over 25 years. (Several years after those figures were collected, the ad is still going strong.)[6]

Free Advertising: The Potential of Editorial Mentions

Many mail-order products appeal to the pipe dreams and unrealized hopes held by many people. Not in so many words, of course, because government agencies will crack down. But the nature of those pipe dreams is such that the imagination seizes on vagueness in the ad to create its *own* belief.

Examples of these pipe dreams include "Reduce Weight Quick," "Be Irresistibly Sexy" (both men and women), and "Increase Personal Efficiency Miraculously." Among the most notoriously powerful of the pipe dreams are "Get Something for Nothing" and "Get Rich Quick without Risk."

Some mail-order people have used the idea of "free ads" (editorial mentions) to appeal to the get-rich-quick dream of people who want to get into mail order. Seems wonderful, doesn't it? Ads for your products in the best magazines without costing you a cent!

There is some truth in the appeal, of course. New and interesting products are real news, and readers *are* sufficiently interested so that dozens of magazines really do have "shopping sections." An example of an editorial mail-order section appears on the left side of the *Family Weekly* page shown in Figure 15-1.

"Editorial mentions" are mostly given to consumer products publicized in the shopping sections of consumer magazines. But such editorial mentions are really just one type of the general public relations art of crashing the editorial columns of the media.

It is standard procedure for manufacturers of new industrial products to obtain free write-ups of products in business and trade publications. Information on new products is one of the most important types of news that a professional magazine can print, and editors are anxious to receive such publicity notices.

Book reviews are another form of "free advertising." Book review editors seek out those books which will be of most interest to their readers.

News of products that are being offered for the first time to jobbers or dealers is another important type of "free advertising." You should always consider the possibility of merchandising a new product through dealers as well as by mail order.

We shall concentrate on the problem of obtaining editorial mentions for consumer mail-order products, however.

How to Obtain Free Editorial Mentions

You obtain editorial mentions by sending a news release plus a sample and a photograph to the editors of shopping sections of magazines whose readers might be interested in your products.

Figure 15-1 Example of editorial-mention page, *Family Weekly.*

The news release itself should be in the form of a letter that tells the editor about your product and asks for publicity. Along with the news release, or within it, you include a product write-up which is suitable for publication in the magazine. The write-up is not the same as an advertisement. Rather, it should resemble editorial material, and especially the editorial material in the shopping section of the particular magazine to which you are writing. Naturally, you will not write a separate release for each magazine, but it may be good policy to create a separate news release and product write-up for each different *type* of magazine. The release should organize the important facts and present them in such a way that the editor of the shopping section can write up your product with a minimum of time and trouble.

The best way to learn what should be in a write-up is to study the editorial mentions in the "shelter" magazines (*House Beautiful,* etc.).

If your product is really very desirable, the magazine will create good copy from the raw material you send them. But you are even better off if you hire a professional public relations person, or an advertising agency with experience in this line, to do the job for you.

You should indicate in the write-up, or in the news-release letter, that a money-back guarantee goes with the product. Shopping-section editors want to protect their readers and themselves. The guarantee makes them feel protected, in addition to increasing your sales.

Remember that a news release must contain *news*. The purpose of shopping sections is to tell readers about *new* products. So emphasize *news* in your letter and write-up.

Your write-up should not sell too hard. Some magazines want only the bare objective facts, while others give you more leeway in praising your product.

Key the address in each write-up so that you know from which magazine the orders come. That will be valuable information for you when you are deciding where to purchase advertising. (Chapter 11 tells you how to create keys.)

A sample of the product will help you obtain editorial mentions. But whether or not you send a sample, the photograph you send should do a good job in showing off your product. Eight- by ten-inch glossy photographs are customary, and they are not too expensive when you order them in quantity. Be sure to hire a good photographer.

Perhaps the most important part of the job of obtaining editorial mentions is to send your news release to the right magazines. You are just wasting your time and postage if you send a news release on fishing equipment to a magazine that goes to new mothers. Study the magazines to see if your product will fit the readers.

Read the following words of wisdom from *Esquire,* one of the important shopping-section magazines:[7]

WHY PRODUCT RELEASES GET REJECTED

A lot of product publicity is inept and amateurish, consequently much of this material is filed in editors' wastepaper baskets. It's amazing how many releases are mailed indiscriminately to publications without regard to their editorial compatibility with the magazine.

Some are so poorly written, so badly organized and so lacking in information that they are completely unusable. Many editors will not risk eye strain trying to read releases that come in on fourth, fifth or even sixth carbons! Product photos, too, are of such poor quality or so unimaginative that a self respecting editor cannot possibly publish them. Releases often make ridiculously exaggerated claims. Some sound like technical manuals; the writer obviously doesn't understand what the product can do or how it is applied and cannot explain the same in plain, simple English.

Here are several suggestions that can be helpful in getting you better product publicity:

1. Put your news in the first three lines of your release.
2. Limit your adjectives.
3. Know your publications.
4. Don't ask for tear sheets (copies of the page on which it runs).
5. Don't mention advertising possibilities.
6. Get to know the editors to learn their problems.
7. Don't make an old product sound new.

And let's add number 8, perhaps the most important: Make your press release believable. Don't exaggerate, don't fake it. *Be credible.*

Obtaining editorial mentions is not as easy as it seems. It requires a public relations effort, and the public relations campaign is just as risky as an advertising campaign.

Furthermore, a large proportion of editorial mentions for mail-order products are given to *advertisers.* Much shopping-section space is "sold" just like advertising space—only more cynically. Advertisers and media sometimes make deals which provide for one editorial mention for each four ads, one for two, or even one for one.

If you have a truly new and interesting product, you *may* get a *start* with editorial mentions. Don't let what I say discourage you. A friend of mine with absolutely no experience in mail order recovered with editorial mentions most of a $20,000 investment in a product he invented. But sooner or later you must start paying for display space just like anyone else, if your business is to prosper.

Per-Inquiry (PI) Deals in
Display Advertising

A "PI"(per-inquiry) deal is one in which the advertising medium obtains inquiries or orders at its own address, and then "sells" the inquiries or orders to advertisers at a fixed rate per inquiry or per order. Advertisers pay only for the inquiries or orders turned over to them.

Of course this sounds fine to you—the advertiser does not have to risk a cent. But it is easy to arrange PI deals only when you have a tested and proven advertisement and offer. And very often you can make more money with a tested offer by buying space outright. Furthermore, many magazines want no part of PI deals.

Today, PI deals in the United States are made mostly on television and radio advertising. But there is a fair amount of PI deals in magazines, too. Berkey Photo Film, a film processor, is a major mail-order operator, for example, and arranges a considerable amount of PI deals with print media. It figures as follows:[8]

> Here is an example. Let's assume that we can afford to pay $5 per gross order to achieve our required profit. Now, if the literature cost approximates $4 per thousand and we feel, based upon past performance, that we'll pull two orders per thousand, we can afford to pay the publication $3 an order. (Calculation: 1) $4/M ÷ 2 orders/M = $2 per order to pay for the literature: 2) $5 allowable per order less the $2 per order (from above) = $3 per order).
>
> We would then negotiate a $3 P.I. rate.

Reports from England say that PI deals are common there. A major advertising firm says that[9]

> [We] are buying space on cost per order received basis (we've just bought a double page spread in the magazine with a circulation of 4 million purely on a cost per converted sale basis!), on a free test insertion basis and of course by the use of remnant space.
>
> We've even persuaded a number of publications to re-run ads—free of charge—if the result has not been acceptable in comparison with previously agreed targets.

16

The Display Advertisement

*What Almost Every Good Ad Contains / Appeal
and Copy / Layout and Artwork / How Big
Should an Ad Be? / Where Is the Best Place in
the Magazine for Your Ad to Be?*

You must either learn mail-order copywriting from experience plus
one of the top-notch books referred to earlier, or use an agency.
There are no short-cuts to the vitally important art of creating ads.
That's why this book makes no attempt to teach you how. But we
will provide some facts and figures to aid your judgment.

What Almost Every Good
Ad Contains

Here are some *facts* about mail-order ads and their selling power:

1. *The power of a single word can be incredible.*   In an eleven-
word classified ad, the offer of a "book" or "manual" pulled nearly
twice as many dollar bills as did the offer of "instructions" (as mentioned earlier).

2. *Never write a classified ad without a guarantee in it. And never
forget to play up the guarantee in a display ad.*   The extra word
may increase your cost almost 10 percent in a classified ad, but in

my experience it also increases the returns perhaps 20 percent—even when no one uses the guarantee.

Don't be afraid of refund demands even if the product is information that can be read and then returned—as long as the merchandise is good and customers don't feel gypped. Charles Atlas offered to return the first payment after 7 days, or to return payment in full plus 6 percent after completion, to dissatisfied customers. Only 1 percent are reported to ask for their money back.

On the other hand, I know of a firm that sold a shoddy money-making manual for $2 and offered a money-back guarantee. The 20 percent who wanted refunds made the operation a losing venture.

3. *Always offer the customer a chance to trade up to "deluxe" models and/or an opportunity to purchase accessory merchandise.* Schwab quotes these results of comparative split-run tests:[1]

   a. Choice of three types of products did better than one model by 19.7 percent and 30.4 percent in two tests.
   b. Choice of six did 52.6 percent better than choice of four, and 261.8 percent better than one model.
   c. Choice of two did 52.9 percent better in number of orders and 25 percent better in dollars than one model.

Maybe the effectiveness of choices is that they lead people to ask, "Which one?" rather than "Should I?" A classic closer of face-to-face salespeople is "Which model would you like?" or "What size, please?" However, such speculation is unnecessary, even though it is fun. What counts is the oft-demonstrated useful effect of offering the choice.

4. *These are ways to encourage quick action:*[2]

   Time limit

   Limited supply

   Prices about to rise

   Combination offers

   Cut-price leaders

   Copy technique

Incentives to quick action get more total orders. If the potential customer waits awhile, his desire to buy very often cools off.

If you use any of these devices, keep them truthful or the Federal Trade Commission may get you.

5. *Harold Preston gives us this quote on colorful language:*[3]

Victor O. Schwab, a leading authority on mail selling, advises you to use words in your headline that the public doesn't expect, "words that *stop* the casual reader—startle him—grip his eyes and his interest."

Mr. Schwab cites such words as "Pushover," "Ain't," "Don't Belly-Ache," "Scatter-brain," "Weasel," "Hog," "Skunk," as eye-arresters that substantially increased the returns from advertising in which they were used. Words like "Bunk," "Bosh," "Gee," "Phooey," are in the same class. . . . By changing the conventional salutation of a letter to "Yousah, Yousah," I tripled the returns of a subscription campaign.

6. *Use as many testimonials as you can.*   People must believe before they'll buy.

Testimonials are a powerful means of inducing belief. If you wait around for completely unsolicited testimonials, you'll be gray before you have a handful of testimonials, even if you're giving gold nuggets away free. You can obtain "unsolicited" testimonials by writing to your customers some time after the sale, saying that you appreciate their patronage and asking if you can help them further. This kind of courtesy and conversation stimulates some of them to write you chatty letters in which they will say nice things about your product.

But remember that you can't stretch the truth by using testimonials. Any statement in a quoted testimonial must be as true as if you yourself make the statement. Recheck Chapter 6 on what you can and can't do with testimonials. (While I'm talking testimonials, I'd appreciate hearing from any of you who are willing to write me comments—even criticism. It won't be for quotation, unless you so indicate, but rather to help me when I again write about mail order. You can address me in care of the *publisher.* As I said in the preface to this edition, the many letters I received from the previous editions have been a great satisfaction to me. And I have been able to help some of the people who wrote me about their mail-order problems. So I will welcome hearing from you.)

Here is evidence of the importance of belief and trust from a split-run test: Using an unknown firm name brought in 77 orders to each 100 orders pulled by the identical ad *signed* by a well-known company.[4]

Appeal and Copy

"Appeal" is what advertising people call the basic selling idea of an ad. If the ad emphasizes how the product will make money for the purchaser, money making is its appeal. If the ad suggests that the product will make a woman devastatingly beautiful, the appeal is sex. And so on.

The best way to pick an appeal is the same as the best way to pick a product and a media schedule. Use the same appeal as your successful competitor—at least to start with.

Gather all the information you can on the words and ideas other people use to sell the product. Before I sat down to write copy for a book on hypnotism, I not only read the competitor's ads, but also examined hypnotists' listings and displays in the classified phone directory, read book jackets, and pored over hypnotism catalogs and brochures. I jotted down every selling idea I could find in all that reading and used it for my material.

Following the competition will take you a long way, but to make the most money, you must also be a leader. Like any other kind of a leader, however, you must not leap too far from where the pack is at any one time. Instead, you make changes gradually on the basis of your analysis and your hunches about which appeals can be emphasized. Of course, there are occasional exceptions to this rule— the stories of Al Sloan and Joe Sugarman that were told earlier in the book. But such exceptions do not disprove the rule that most successful mail-order operations develop from well-established trade practices.

The only way to determine which appeal is best for a product is to test. Testing methods are described in Chapter 26.

The Headline "How to Fix Cars—quickly, easily, right" sold 20 percent more books than exactly the same headline with the word "Repair" in place of "Fix"[5]—which already was a very successful ad.

Schwab's split-run tests for his clients produced these results:[6]

- "Reducing" did 138 percent better than "Relieving Nervous Tension," and 266 percent better than "Improving Your English." (However, this was a test of three *different* books as well as different appeals, which makes the test less conclusive.)

- "Sex" did 211 percent better than "Succeed in Business," and 223 percent better than "Selection of Vocation."

- "Newness" improved an ad 75.4 percent and 79 percent in two tests.

How to Qualify Prospects

To "qualify" prospects means to weed out poor prospects who cost you money for catalogs and direct mail, but at the same time to keep the attention of the good prospects.

Here is a list of ways Moran suggests for qualifying prospects:[7]

1. Make a headline selective.
2. Reduce emphasis on free offer in headline and copy.
3. Charge for booklet.
4. Ask for age, sex, occupation, etc.
5. Make it obvious that booklet is a sales piece.
6. Show that product has limited use to a special few.
7. Eliminate coupon.
8. Insert stipulations, restrictions, etc., in coupon.
9. Show the price.

Layout and Artwork

Coupons

A coupon is a crucial part of almost every mail-order ad that is big enough to contain one. The only time the coupon is omitted is when the advertiser wants to qualify prospects very strictly and not make it too easy for them to respond.

Notice that most advertisers who run even a 4-inch ad find it profitable to spend *one-quarter of the advertising cost* just for the coupon area. That's how important the coupon is in increasing responses!

The coupon makes it "easy to order." The prospects don't have to think what to say or how to write it. All they do is fill in their names and addresses, and perhaps check a box or two. That's why 70 to 85 percent of responders will use the coupon.

The coupon suggests *action,* and it also seems to suggest getting something free or at a bargain rate. The coupon itself attracts many readers to the ad. Many years ago general advertisers suffered a fad of testing their copy by couponing ads for free booklets and other giveaways. They soon quit the practice when they found that the rate of response depended as much on the size of the coupon as it did on the excellence of the copy.

Some advertisers use a coupon that is too small for anyone to use. Nevertheless, it has much of the effect of a coupon in increasing response and it saves space. Inquirers write their names and addresses in the margin of the page next to the coupon.

Some advertisers use a heavy dashed border around the entire ad (see Figure 16-1). "Tear Out and Mail Today" at the bottom of the

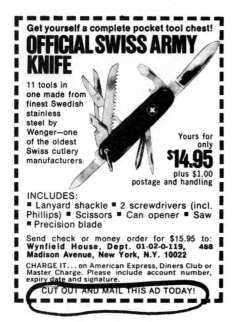

Figure 16-1 Example of saving coupon space.

ad is also used frequently. The whole ad looks like a coupon even though there is no room for name or address. I have found that this device gives a good boost to small ads composed entirely of type.

The list below is Henry Musselman's checklist of important items in the coupon for a *direct-mail piece*.[8] The list is just as valid for display ads.

Leave room for complete name and address.

Require only a fill-in for sizes, colors, etc.

State the proposition clearly.

Tell prospect just what to do.

Convenient size and shape.

Keyed to denote source.

Re-state the guarantee.

Stand out from rest of ad.

If premium is offered, the offer is included in coupon.

In full-page ads, put the coupon at the outside bottom of the page. Some advertisers who drive terrifically hard for inquiries—e.g., the Duraclean rug-cleaning franchise ad—seem to have success with making the coupon the dominant element in the ad's layout—either at the top, as shown in Figure 16-2, or by turning the coupon sideways, or by similar gimmicks to make the coupon stand out visually. (In his recent best seller, David Ogilvy triumphantly trumpets as a recent Madison Avenue discovery this well-known mail-order device.[9])

Points of Interest about Layout and Art

Readers usually pay more attention to editorial matter than to advertising, and they have more faith in it. The "reading notice" tries to take advantage of that fact by making the ad look like the adjoining editorial columns. The headline must also look like "news." Figure 16-3 illustrates a reading notice.

Some media charge extra for "readers." Others do not accept them because they regard them as undesirable.

General advertising strives for an esthetic quality in advertising, and perhaps wisely so. The general advertiser aims at a huge audience with whom its reputation is precious. The general advertiser therefore cannot afford to irritate its potential customers with unpleasant ads.

But mail-order firms have different requirements for an ad. Many successful mail-order ads look crowded, vulgar, and garish—called "buckeye" by the trade. The buckeye format creates "excitement" and uses space to the utmost.

Split-run tests comparing a "busy" layout to a balanced and artistically unified layout showed that the "busy" layout did 111 percent better, 68 percent better, and 30 percent better than the artistic layout, in three tests.[10] (But Bruck Holocek tells me that in the hobby field, busy ads do not do best, in his experience.)

Baker points out that the "busy" layout technique uses lots of gimmicky "spot art": scissors on top of the coupon, a hand pointing at the guarantee, one-sentence claims thrown all around the page.[11] Figure 16-4 is a good example.

So—don't let any "fine artist" sell you a bill of goods about how your ad is ugly and should be beautified. You're liable to find that as artistic satisfaction increases, profits sink.

Artwork can often be obtained cheaply and efficiently from "clip books" that contain a variety of standard artwork elements. One such book is *Instant Art for Mail Order Operations,* sold for $15 (1979 prices) by Crain Books, 740 Rush Street, Chicago, IL 60611.

Special inserts into magazines cost more than ordinary full-page ads, but some are worth the added freight. According to Stanley Rapp, reply cards increase returns by 3 to 6 times for some advertisers,

Figure 16-2 Example of prominent coupon.

2 to 3 times for others of his clients (probably including record clubs).[12] Figure 16-5 is such an insert.

About *color* in ads: Split runs indicated that color outpulled black and white by 182 percent, 83 percent, 224 percent, and 26 percent for a *home-decoration* product.[13] So for *that* product, color was worth the usual 50 percent surcharge. But a marriage book would undoubtedly not get the same benefits from color as a home-decoration product.

How Big Should an Ad Be?

Mail-order advertisers figure the size of an ad this way: They increase the size of their ads in each medium until a further increase costs more than the increase in revenue produced.

Figure 16-3   Example of a "reading notice" ad.

Figure 16-4 Example of a "busy" ad.

Figure 16-5 Example of an insert card.

There are some types of mail-order products that *demand* large space. For example, a 4-inch ad may pull *more* than 4 times as much as a 1-inch ad for *some* products. This usually occurs when it is impossible to tell a full advertising story in less than the 4 inches.

Four inches may be the "natural" space unit for that product. A half-page may be the "natural" unit for other products. The famous Charles Atlas course found that the ad had to be at least one column by 98 lines (7 inches) in order to show Atlas' picture effectively. Small space was no good for that offer.

Generally speaking, however, the published evidence is overwhelming that increasing the size of an ad will *not* increase the returns in proportion. For almost every mail-order advertiser who cares to use them, classified ads are far and away the most productive medium—often 3 times as productive, dollar for dollar, as the most effective display space. A full-page ad will practically never pull twice as many orders as a half-page ad. La Salle Correspondence University has never found *any* display ad that performs as well as its 30-year-old 1-inch ad.

More than 70 years ago Shryer found, when selling his correspondence course on starting and managing a collection agency, that the cost of inquiries went like this:

Classified 5 lines	30¢ per inquiry
7-line display	53
16-line display	70
56-line display	76
half-page display	92

In many cases the five-line classified ad made more *total profit* than did the fifty-six-line ad in the same medium.[14]

This effect still holds in our day, and for many kinds of products. An agency man who serves many mail-order clients writes: "Many small space users find their most efficient use of space ranges between 28 and 50 lines."[15]

But it *is* economical and rational to increase the size of the ad as long as the profit from the increased orders is greater than the increased cost of the space. If a quarter-page costs $400 and returns *net* a profit of $200 on sales of $800, a half-page ad *may* net a profit of $250 on sales of $1,400. If that is the case, it pays you to run the half-page ad.

The advertisers who run large ads are those who pull very successfully in small space. They are the advertisers who (by definition) face a large potential market. The large ad demands that a large percentage of the medium's audience have an active interest in the product.

John Caples wrote[16]

> If the reader of a publication does not have a corn, your full-page ad, no matter how attractive, will not sell him a corn remedy. On the other

hand, if the reader does have a corn that is bothering him, he will be stopped by the one-word headline, CORNS, in a small ad. Since you cannot predict when the readers' corns will be troublesome, you are better off with a small ad in every issue of a publication than with a big ad once in a while.

And Robert Baker ventured to qualify the relationship, saying: "If the item is of genuine interest to 25 percent or more of a particular medium's readership, you can effectively use as much as a full page. But if your item is of limited interest, probably you should confine yourself to small units."[17]

Mail-order advertisers cannot increase their total profit by running more small ads instead of fewer larger ones. There are always too few media that will pay out a profit, and the trick is to use each of them to the limit. That is why, unlike general advertisers, the mail-order person does not fix a budget and then spread it over the various media. Instead, you should keep spending as long as it is profitable to do so. If medium A will make more with a big ad than a small one, then the big ad should run in that medium. That decision will stand independent of decisions about media B through Z. (This principle also explains why it sometimes pays to advertise in months that are half as productive as the best months.)

As a practical matter, then, you will begin with the smallest ad that can do a complete selling job, and gradually increase the size of your ads until your profit begins to diminish.

Some magazines give discounts for larger space units that make it profitable to run larger ads. The discounts are huge in some magazines. You can sometimes purchase a whole page of a three-column magazine for little more than two columns would cost. On the other hand, the discounts in other magazines are not worth bothering about. The smaller the discount, the smaller the ad you will run.

The discounts almost always mean you should use even units of space, however. Use a full column instead of almost a full column. You get more space and actually pay less.

"But then," you say, "why do some of the biggest and smartest firms in the country run full-page ads in *Reader's Digest* and *Time?*"

There are several parts to the complicated answer. This is one of the possible reasons: Repeated surveys have shown that a half-page gets 55 to 60 percent as many *readers* as does a full page. But in a huge study, Rudolph found that a half-page produced almost 70 percent as many *coupons* as a full page.[18]

National advertisers want *readers*. Mail-order firms want *coupons* (and money). That's part of the reason why mail-order firms advertise differently than auto and soap manufacturers do.

Furthermore, the biggest advertisers are not always the smartest advertisers. A big firm can often get away with stupidity that would break a small, competitive producer. And a big national advertiser can't measure its successes and failures as accurately as a mail-order firm can.

One Big Ad versus Several Small Ones

Pratt sometimes found it "profitable, where several items are to be sold, to advertise them separately in the same periodical on different pages, rather than combine them in one advertisement."[19] But production problems are greater with several ads, and you may forgo important bulk-space discounts.

Some large mail-order firms do both: During a single month they may take a full page to display many products together and also run fifteen small ads all over a magazine like *True Detective*.

Where Is the Best Place in the Magazine for Your Ad to Be?

The position of an ad on the page (if it is smaller than a full-page ad) and the location within the magazine can affect the ad's pulling power. You need to know which spots are best for two reasons:

1. To make a more accurate judgment of how well the copy is pulling

2. To request the best space

If you run a small ad, you have little control over where the ad runs. Mostly it's potluck where the layout person will fit you among the big ads and editorial features. However, when you become a steady customer and develop a good relationship with a magazine or its advertising representative, they may heed your request for a favorable spot.

Observations of people's eye movements suggest that the upper part of the page does better than the lower part, and that the outside of a page is better than an inside column. Dollar results confirm it. My data for a 3½-inch ad show that the outside top corner does 15 to 30 percent better than the inside bottom corner next to the gutter (the inside of the page where the magazine is stitched or pasted together).

Results based mostly on full-page ads indicate that right-hand pages are slightly better than left-hand pages. Inquiry results for La Salle Extension show that the right-hand page pulls 10 percent better than the left.[20] Readership surveys range from no difference to 10 percent difference.[21]

La Salle Extension also finds that the front pages of a publication average 40 percent better than the back pages.[22] From readership surveys, Daniel Starch figures the front as 10 percent better than the middle or back.[23] Victor Schwab says it is better to be well forward on a left-hand page than on a right-hand page far in the back of the book.[24] However, small-space advertisers may find it more advantageous to be in a back-of-the-book shopping section than to be in the front of the magazine.

The back cover is almost universally acclaimed as the best position, and it therefore costs more than inside pages. One mail-order writer says it produces three orders to two for the average inside page.[25]

This is Schwab's list of the best locations, in descending order: back cover, page facing second cover, pages 3, 5, 7, page facing inside back cover.[26]

Stone recently estimated the strength of full-page ad locations, relative to the first right-hand page indexed at 100, as follows:[27]

First right-hand page	100
Second right-hand page	95
Third right-hand page	90
Fourth right-hand page	85
Back of front of book (preceding editorial matter)	70
Back of book (following main body of editorial matter)	50
Back cover	100
Inside third cover	90
Page facing inside third cover	85

It is better to be near editorial matter than near other advertisements, as a general rule. Coupon ads don't do so well on the inside front cover because people don't like to cut the cover.

Segal says that a gutter position cuts results 20 to 40 percent on the average, and sometimes up to 80 percent.[28] He finds narrow-column books are the worst for gutter positions. Sumner estimates that gutter position cuts returns by 50 percent.[29]

17

How to Write Potent Copy

by David Ogilvy

David Ogilvy surely is the world's best-known advertising man, and he may well be the most respected. Although he made his fame in general advertising, he never ceased to use mail-order methods, and to proclaim that the mail-order approach to copy is the heart and soul of all good advertising.

Headlines

The headline is the most important element in most advertisements. It is the telegram which decides the reader whether to read the copy.

On the average, five times as many people read the headline as read the body copy. When you have written your headline, you have spent eighty cents out of your dollar.

If you haven't done some selling in your headline, you have wasted 80 per cent of your client's money. The wickedest of all sins is to run an advertisement *without* a headline. Such headless wonders are still to be found; I don't envy the copywriter who submits one to me.

A change of headline can make a difference of ten to one in sales. I never write fewer than sixteen headlines for a single advertisement, and I observe certain guides in writing them:

From David Ogilvy, *Confessions of an Advertising Man*, Atheneum, NY © 1963 by David Ogilvy Trustee. Reprinted by permission of Atheneum Publishers.

1. The headline is the "ticket on the meat." Use it to flag down the readers who are prospects for the kind of product you are advertising. If you are selling a remedy for bladder weakness, display the words BLADDER WEAKNESS in your headline; they catch the eye of everyone who suffers from this inconvenience. If you want *mothers* to read your advertisement, display MOTHERS in your headline. And so on.

Conversely, do not say anything in your headline which is likely to *exclude* any readers who might be prospects for your product. Thus, if you are advertising a product which can be used equally well by men and women, don't slant your headline at women alone; it would frighten men away.

2. Every headline should appeal to the reader's *self-interest.* It should promise her a benefit, as in my headline for Helena Rubinstein's Hormone Cream: HOW WOMEN OVER 35 CAN LOOK YOUNGER.

3. Always try to inject *news* into your headlines, because the consumer is always on the lookout for new products, or new ways to use an old product, or new improvements in an old product.

The two most powerful words you can use in a headline are FREE and NEW. You can seldom use FREE, but you can almost always use NEW—if you try hard enough.

4. Others words and phrases which work wonders are HOW TO, SUDDENLY, NOW, ANNOUNCING, INTRODUCING, IT'S HERE, JUST AR-RIVED, IMPORTANT DEVELOPMENT, IMPROVEMENT, AMAZING, SENSA-TIONAL, REMARKABLE, REVOLUTIONARY, STARTLING, MIRACLE, MAGIC, OFFER, QUICK, EASY, WANTED, CHALLENGE, ADVICE TO, THE TRUTH ABOUT, COMPARE, BARGAIN, HURRY, LAST CHANCE.

Don't turn up your nose at these clichés. They may be shopworn, but they work. That is why you see them turn up so often in the headlines of mail-order advertisers and others who can measure the results of their advertisements.

Headlines can be strengthened by the inclusion of *emotional* words, like DARLING, LOVE, FEAR, PROUD, FRIEND, and BABY. One of the most provocative advertisements which has come out of our agency showed a girl in a bathtub, talking to her lover on the telephone. The headline: *Darling, I'm having the most extraordinary experience . . . I'm head over heels in DOVE.*

5. Five times as many people read the headline as read the body copy, so it is important that these glancers should at least be told what brand is being advertised. That is why you should always include the brand name in your headlines.

6. Include your selling promise in your headline. This requires long headlines. When the New York University School of Retailing ran headline tests with the cooperation of a big department store, they found that headlines of ten words or longer, containing news and information, consistently sold more merchandise than short headlines.

Headlines containing six to twelve words pull more coupon returns than short headlines, and there is no significant difference between the readership of twelve-word headlines and the readership of three-word headlines. The best headline I ever wrote contained *eighteen* words: *At Sixty Miles an Hour the Loudest Noise in the New Rolls-Royce comes from the electric clock.**

7. People are more likely to read your body copy if your headline arouses their curiosity; so you should end your headline with a lure to read on.

8. Some copywriters write *tricky* headlines—puns, literary allusions, and other obscurities. This is a sin.

In the average newspaper your headline has to compete for attention with 350 others. Research has shown that readers travel so fast through this jungle that they don't stop to decipher the meaning of obscure headlines. Your headline must *telegraph* what you want to say, and it must telegraph it in plain language. Don't play games with the reader.

In 1960 the *Times Literary Supplement* attacked the whimsical tradition in British advertising, calling it "self-indulgent—a kind of middle-class private joke, apparently designed to amuse the advertiser and his client." Amen.

9. Research shows that it is dangerous to use *negatives* in headlines. If, for example, you write OUR SALT CONTAINS NO ARSENIC, many readers will miss the negative and go away with the impression that you wrote OUR SALT CONTAINS ARSENIC.

10. Avoid *blind* headlines—the kind which mean nothing unless you read the body copy underneath them; most people *don't*.

Body Copy

When you sit down to write your body copy, pretend that you are talking to the woman on your right at a dinner party. She has asked

---

* When the chief engineer at the Rolls-Rouce factory read this, he shook his head sadly and said, "It is time we did something about that damned clock."

you, "I am thinking of buying a new car. Which would you recommend?" Write your copy as if you were answering that question.

1. Don't beat about the bush—go straight to the point. Avoid analogies of the "just as, so too" variety. Dr. Gallup has demonstrated that these two-stage arguments are generally misunderstood.

2. Avoid superlatives, generalizations, and platitudes. Be specific and factual. Be enthusiastic, friendly, and memorable. Don't be a bore. Tell the truth, but make the truth fascinating.

How long should your copy be? It depends on the product. If you are advertising chewing gum, there isn't much to tell, so make your copy short. If, on the other hand, you are advertising a product which has a great many different qualities to recommend it, write long copy: the more you tell, the more you sell.

There is a universal belief in lay circles that people won't read long copy. Nothing could be farther from the truth. Claude Hopkins once wrote five pages of solid text for Schlitz beer. In a few months, Schlitz moved up from fifth place to first. I once wrote a page of solid text for Good Luck Margarine, with most gratifying results.

Research shows that readership falls off rapidly up to fifty words of copy, but drops very little between fifty and 500 words. In my first Rolls-Royce advertisement I used 719 words—piling one fascinating fact on another. In the last paragraph I wrote, "People who feel diffident about driving a Rolls-Royce can buy a Bentley." Judging from the number of motorists who picked up the word "diffident" and bandied it about, I concluded that the advertisement was thoroughly read. In the next one I used 1400 words.

Every advertisement should be a *complete* sales pitch for your product. It is unrealistic to assume that consumers will read a *series* of advertisements for the same product. You should shoot the works in every advertisement, on the assumption that it is the only chance you will every have to sell your product to the reader—*now or never.*

Says Dr. Charles Edwards of the graduate School of Retailing, at New York University, "The more facts you tell, the more you sell. An advertisement's chance for success invariably increases as the number of pertinent merchandise facts included in the advertisement increases."

In my first advertisement for Puerto Rico's Operation Bootstrap, I used 961 words, and persuaded Beardsley Ruml to sign them. Fourteen thousand readers clipped the coupon from this advertisement, and scores of them later established factories in Puerto Rico. The greatest professional satisfaction I have yet had is to see the prosperity in Puerto Rican communities which had lived on the edge of starvation for four hundred years before I wrote my advertisement. If I had confined myself to a few vacuous generalities, nothing would have happened.

We have even been able to get people to read long copy about gasoline. One of our Shell advertisements contained 617 words, and 22 per cent of male readers read more than half of them.

Vic Schwab tells the story of Max Hart (of Hart, Schaffner & Marx) and his advertising manager, George L. Dyer, arguing about long copy. Dyer said, "I'll bet you ten dollars I can write a newspaper page of solid type and you'd read every word of it."

Hart scoffed at the idea. "I don't have to write a line of it to prove my point," Dyer replied. "I'll only tell you the headline: THIS PAGE IS ALL ABOUT MAX HART."

Advertisers who put coupons in their advertisements *know* that short copy doesn't sell. In split-run tests, long copy invariably outsells short copy.

Do I hear someone say that no copywriter can write long advertisements unless his media department gives him big spaces to work with? This question should not arise, because the copywriter should be consulted before planning the media schedule.

3. You should always include testimonials in your copy. The reader finds it easier to believe the endorsement of a fellow consumer than the puffery of an anonymous copywriter. Says Jim Young, one of the best copywriters alive today, "Every type of advertiser has the same problem; namely to be believed. The mail-order man knows nothing so potent for this purpose as the testimonial, yet the general advertiser seldom uses it."

Testimonials from celebrities get remarkably high readership, and if they are honestly written they still do not seem to provoke incredulity. The better known the celebrity, the more readers you will attract. We have featured Queen Elizabeth and Winston Churchill in "Come to Britain" advertisements, and we were able to persuade Mrs. Roosevelt to make television commercials for Good Luck Margarine. When we advertised charge accounts for Sears, Roebuck, we reproduced the credit card of Ted Williams, "recently traded by Boston to Sears."

Sometimes you can cast your entire copy in the form of a testimonial. My first advertisement for Austin cars took the form of a letter from an "anonymous diplomat" who was sending his son to Groton with money he had saved driving an Austin—a well-aimed combination of snobbery and economy. Alas, a perspicacious *Time* editor guessed that I was the anonymous diplomat, and asked the headmaster of Groton to comment. Dr. Crocker was so cross that I decided to send my son to Hotchkiss.

4. Another profitable gambit is to give the reader helpful advice, or service. It hooks about 75 per cent more readers than copy which deals entirely with the product.

One of our Rinso advertisements told housewives how to remove stains. It was better read (Starch) and better remembered (Gallup) than any detergent advertisement in history. Unfortunately, however, it forgot to feature Rinso's main selling promise—that Rinso washes whiter; for this reason it should never have run.*

5. I have never admired the *belles lettres* school of advertising, which reached its pompous peak in Theodore F. MacManus' famous advertisement for Cadillac, "The Penalty of Leadership," and Ned Jordan's classic, "Somewhere West of Laramie." Forty years ago the business community seems to have been impressed by these pieces of purple prose, but I have always thought them absurd; they did not give the reader a single *fact.* I share Claude Hopkins' view that "fine writing is a distinct disadvantage. So is unique literary style. They take attention away from the subject."

6. Avoid bombast. Raymond Rubicam's famous slogan for Squibb, "The priceless ingredient of every product is the honor and integrity of its maker," reminds me of my father's advice: when a company boasts about its integrity, or a woman about her virtue, avoid the former and cultivate the latter.

7. Unless you have some special reason to be solemn and pretentious, write your copy in the colloquial language which your customers use in everyday conversation. I have never acquired a sufficiently good ear for vernacular American to write it, but I admire copywriters who can pull it off, as in this unpublished pearl from a dairy farmer:

> Carnation Milk is the best in the land.
> Here I sit with a can in my hand.
> No tits to pull, no hay to pitch,
> Just punch a hole in the son-of-a-bitch.

It is a mistake to use highfalutin language when you advertise to uneducated people. I once used the word OBSOLETE in a headline,

---

* The photograph showed several different kinds of stain—lipstick, coffee, shoe-polish, blood and so forth. The blood was my own; I am the only copywriter who has ever bled for his client.

only to discover that 43 per cent of housewives had no idea what it meant. In another headline, I used the word INEFFABLE, only to discover that I didn't know what it meant myself.

However, many copywriters of my vintage err on the side of underestimating the educational level of the population. Philip Hauser, head of the Sociology Department at the University of Chicago, draws attention to the changes which are taking place:

> The increasing exposure of the population to formal schooling . . . can be expected to effect important changes in . . . the style of advertising. . . . Messages aimed at the "average" American on the assumption that he has had less than a grade school education are likely to find themselves with a declining or disappearing clientele.[1]

Meanwhile, all copywriters should read Dr. Rudolph Flesch's *Art of Plain Talk.* It will persuade them to use short words, short sentences, short paragraphs, and highly *personal* copy.

Aldous Huxley, who once tried his hand at writing advertisements, concluded that "any trace of literariness in an advertisement is fatal to its success. Advertisement writers may not be lyrical, or obscure, or in any way esoteric. They must be universally intelligible. A good advertisement has this in common with drama and oratory, that it must be immediately comprehensible and directly moving.*

8. Resist the temptation to write the kind of copy which wins awards. I am always gratified when I win an award, but most of the campaigns which produce *results* never win awards, because they don't draw attention to themselves.

The juries that bestow awards are never given enough information about the *results* of the advertisements they are called upon to judge. In the absence of such information, they rely on their opinions, which are always warped toward the highbrow.

9. Good copywriters have always resisted the temptation to *entertain.* Their achievement lies in the number of new products they get off to a flying start. In a class by himself stands Claude Hopkins, who is to advertising what Escoffier is to cooking. By today's standards, Hopkins was an unscrupulous barbarian, but technically he was the supreme master. Next I would place Raymond Rubicam, George Cecil, and James Webb Young, all of whom lacked Hopkins' ruthless sales-

---

* *Essays Old and New* (Harper & Brothers, 1927). Charles Lamb and Byron also wrote advertisements. So did Bernard Shaw, Hemingway, Marquand, Sherwood Anderson, and Faulkner—none of them with any degree of success.

manship, but made up for it by their honesty, by the broader range of their work, and by their ability to write civilized copy when the occasion required it. Next I would place John Caples, the mail-order specialist from whom I have learned much.

These giants wrote their advertsements for newspapers and magazines. It is still too early to identify the best writers for television.

18

More on Copy
by Victor Schwab

*Victor O. Schwab was President of Schwab &
Beatty, Inc., New York City, an advertising
agency that handled probably a larger volume of
mail-order advertising than any other American
company.*

Mail-order advertising's a tough job. A successful mail-order advertisement has to go all the way—producing good inquiries or orders
in sufficient quantity, without the aid of salesclerks, actual inspection
of the merchandise, point-of-sale display, or any other supplementary
help. That means that such advertising must be carefully planned.
For a mail-order advertisement is not simply an advertisement with
a coupon or a "buried offer" tacked on the end. Every element in
it is integrated, painstakingly constructed from the top down. It has
a tough job to do—and how well it does it depends upon its appeal,
headline, body matter, subheads, and the offer made. Now let's break
down each of these components, starting with the selection of appeals.

Copy Appeals

Here is a check list of some of the major copy appeals—the advantages
that people want to gain through the use of the products they buy:

> *Better health.* Greater strength, vigor, endurance; the possibility of
> longer life

From Roger Barton (ed.), *Advertising Handbook*, Prentice-Hall, Inc., Englewood
Cliffs, NJ, 1950, 1978.

More money.   For spending, saving, or giving to others

Greater popularity.   Through a more attractive personality or through personal accomplishments

Improved appearance.   Beauty; style; better physical build; cleanliness

Security in old age.   Independence; provision for age or adversity

Praise from others.   For one's intelligence, knowledge, appearance, or other evidences of superiority

More comfort.   Ease; luxury; self-indulgence; convenience

More leisure.   For travel, hobbies, rest, play, self-development, and the like

Pride of accomplishment.   Overcoming obstacles and competition; desire to "do things well"

Business advancement.   Better job; success; "be your own boss"; reward for merit

Social advancement.   Moving in better circles; social acceptance; "keeping up with the Joneses"

Increased enjoyment   From entertainment, food, drink, and other physical contacts

People also want to:

Be good parents	Appreciate beauty
Have influence over others	Be proud of their possessions
Be sociable, hospitable	Be creative
Be gregarious	Acquire or collect things
Express their personalities	Be efficient
Resist domination by others	Win others' affection
Satisfy their curiosity	Be "first" in things
Be up-to-date	Improve themselves mentally
Emulate the admirable	Be recognized as authorities

And they want to save: Money, time, work, discomfort, worry, doubts, risks, embarrassment, offense to others, boredom, personal self-respect, and prestige

This specific list can be summarized in two broad generalizations. Here is the *plus* generalization:

Show people—in words, or pictures, or both—what they can save, gain, or accomplish with your product—how it will *increase* their mental, physical, financial, social, emotional, or spiritual stimulation, satisfaction, well-being, or security.

And here is the *minus* generalization:

Show people—in words, or pictures, or both—what risks, worries, losses, mistakes, embarrassment, drudgery, or other undesirable conditions your product will help them to avoid, lessen, or eliminate— how it will *decrease* their fear of poverty, illness or accident, discomfort, boredom, and the loss of business, personal, or social prestige or advancement.

Headlines

Now we come to headlines. The most profitable advertisements usually lead off with a headline that holds out the product's specific promise to do something that people want done for them—or, negatively, to end some condition that people want to get rid of. It isn't enough to cram appeal into the *body* copy. It's the headline that gets people into the copy; the copy doesn't get them into the headline.

Briefly, the purpose of the headline is to call out a phrase or a sentence that will *stop* people, and will make as many of them as possible say, "I want that!"; or at least, "What *is* that? Tell me more!"

As far as the "tell me more" part of it goes, an advertisement with even mediocre, or actually poor, copy can do a fairly good job— provided the headline itself is strong, using the right appeal to present a product that does a job that people want done for them.

On the other hand, copy that is really superlatively fine won't even get the chance to go to work unless the headline pulls people into it. Some of the most tremendous flops among advertisements contain body matter filled with strong, appealing copy. But it just wasn't "capsulized" into a good headline.

Ten Successful Headlines

Here are ten successful mail-order headlines, with the reasons that I believe explain their effectiveness:

PROFITS THAT LIE HIDDEN IN YOUR FARM

1. Strong acquisitive appeal.
2. Starts with a powerful keynote word.
3. The idea of "profits that lie hidden" (or money wastes and losses that may be retrieved, perhaps very easily) can be even more attractive to the reader than the idea of working, perhaps very hard, to produce an increased *new* profit.

4. Headline taps (in addition to the money appeal) the more subtle human emotion of hating to lose or "pass up" any part of a profit or advantage that is already existent, waiting to be grasped to the full.

5. Not indefinite as to "the" or "a" farm; it's *your* farm. A direct challenge.

HOW TO WIN FRIENDS AND INFLUENCE PEOPLE

1. Words like How To, An Easy Way To, Why, New Way To, and Which of These, suggest *news*, or a shortcut to some desired accomplishment; make people want to read the copy that follows. If headline were changed to "Win Friends and Influence People," then it would become simply a wall-motto, a piece of trite advice.

2. Strong basic appeal. We all want to win friends and influence people, both in our social lives and in our business careers.

HOW I MADE A FORTUNE WITH A "FOOL IDEA"

1. Again the "desire-to-read" beckoning of a "how" headline.

2. We always like to hear about other people and their experiences. This advertisement is evidently going to tell us an apparently interesting and human one.

3. Paradoxes excite interest.

4. Hits a lot of people, bull's eye. Almost everyone has had a cherished money-making idea that others have thought "foolish" or "impractical" or "up in the clouds."

5. Sympathy for the "underdog," and human interest in his "turning the tables" despite the ridicule of others.

DO YOU MAKE THESE MISTAKES IN ENGLISH?

1. Question form of headline is often the best device of all to get people into the copy.

2. A "right between the eyes" challenge that is difficult to ignore.

3. The "You" reference application comes quickly and pointedly.

4. The word "These" is vitally important in this headline. Gets the reader into the copy in order to discover which particular mistakes he may be making. Compare it with "Do You Make Mistakes in English?", an implied criticism of the reader, without any strong pull for reader to get into the copy.

THE MAN WITH THE GRASSHOPPER MIND

1. An immediate association with himself leaps to the mind of the reader.

2. We want to check at once on the personal parallel. What are the symptoms? Starting things one never finishes? Jumping from one thing to another? Evanescent enthusiasms, resolutions, jobs? How much am I like him? It's not a good trait. So what did he do about it? What can I do about it?

3. People, what they are, and what they do, are irresistibly interesting. "I want to read about this person; doubly so, because he is (or was) evidently somewhat like me."

4. Headline, although negative in nature, strikes home more accurately and dramatically than would a positive one based upon the opposite of the trait referred to.

IT'S A SHAME FOR *YOU* NOT TO MAKE GOOD MONEY . . . WHEN THESE MEN DO IT SO EASILY.

1. Attention-value of the colloquialism, "It's a Shame."

2. The "You" angle is there quickly and strongly, and also is made comparative and competitive with other people.

3. Appeal itself is of course good. Most of us want to make good money as easily as possible.

4. The "These," again—to get reader into the copy.

DOES YOUR CHILD EVER EMBARRASS YOU?

1. Question headline.

2. Direct; challenging; common circumstance that brings up flood of recollections. "How can such experiences be avoided in the future?"

3. "Your"—"You."

4. Strong selfish appeal. Often overlooked is the frank fact that parents are, *first*, individuals; second, parents. The kind of reflection that the actions of children cast upon the personal standing, prestige, and self-esteem of their parents is an important copy angle to remember.

A LITTLE MISTAKE THAT COST A FARMER $3,000 A YEAR

1. Very arresting. What farmer wouldn't be eager to find out what the "little mistake" was?

2. A narrative of the experience of another person—and, even more interesting to its farm-paper readers, of another farmer.

3. Somewhat paradoxical and therefore awakens even greater curiosity. "How could it be a 'little' mistake and still cost him so much money? What was it? How did he find it out? How did he correct it? I wonder if I am making that mistake. Maybe the ad will also tell me of some others that *I* may be making?"

THOUSANDS HAVE THIS PRICELESS GIFT—BUT NEVER DISCOVER IT !

1. Strong in curiosity value. "What is this 'gift'? Why is it 'priceless'? If 'thousands' have it perhaps *I* may be one of them. I want to find out !"

2. The "undiscovered" angle is also appealing. Most people have the conviction that they have hidden talents and abilities that others have never discovered, and which they themselves have never developed or displayed to a world that is inclined to underrate or misjudge them.

THE CRIMES WE COMMIT AGAINST OUR STOMACHS

1. "The Crimes We Commit" phrase has good attention-value in itself.

2. Whole idea of the headline "starts where the reader is"—because it is merely a more intensified and dramatic way of expressing the average person's opinion that he very often gives his own digestive processes some pretty rough treatment. So, since he has had the same general idea himself, he is ready to go along with you and wants to find out more about it.

3. This *rapport*, between the theme of the advertisement and the common opinion of its readers, makes the "Our" equal in effect to "Your."

Now analyze these headlines yourself. Here are some other successful mail-order headlines. Go back over the headlines just listed, keeping in mind the factors that were isolated and discussed, and see how many of these same specific factors (and also general similarities) you will find in this second list:

Thousands Now Play Who Never Thought They Could !

Advice to Wives Whose Husbands Don't Save Money—by a Wife

Why Some People Are Never at Ease among Strangers

Imagine Harry and Me Advertising Our Pears in *Fortune!*

Why I Cried after the Ceremony

He Made the World Blush with Shame !

The Child Who Won the Hearts of All

The Secret of Making People Like You

I Teach Music a Funny Way!

The Only Sure Way to Avoid Embarrassment

Are You the Kind of Guest People Like to Invite?

How a New Discovery Made a Plain Girl Beautiful

Why Some Foods Explode in the Stomach

Whose Fault When Children Disobey?

Suppose This Happened on YOUR Wedding Day!

Put Your Name on This Payroll!

Are You Ever Ashamed of Your Child?

Are We a Nation of Low-Brows?

A Startling Memory Feat That You Can Do

Do YOU Do Any of These Embarrassing Things?

Why Good Dancers Are Popular

The Most Interesting Man I Ever Met

How to Get Rid of an Inferiority Complex

Body-Matter Copy

Now we come to the body matter of a successful mail-order advertisement. First we'll discuss the quantity of copy; then the quality.

Quantity of Copy

The LONGER your copy can hold the interest of the greatest number of your readers, the likelier you are to induce MORE of them to act at once.

That is why you find that the copy in mail-order advertisements is usually long—particularly in those that pull for orders rather than for inquiries. The sludge of human inertia is so terrific that, unless *(and usually even though)* the quality of the copy—or the inherent power of its basic appeal—may be way above average, too small an amount of it cannot motivate that sludge into immediate mail-order action.

Mail-order advertisers have found an astonishingly direct relationship between the mere number of words used in an advertisement and the general effectiveness of that advertisement. They have found that, unless the copy is *exceptionally* fine or *exceptionally* bad, these ratios of resultfulness in relation to copy-length are fairly constant.

If the copy is exceptionally fine it may accomplish the desired result even though it may not be so long as the copy in another successful advertisement on the same proposition. But the production of copy that is exceptionally fine does not occur often enough to risk cutting *all* copy arbitrarily, merely to "make it shorter." Copy, on the average, is more likely to be either fair or good, rather than either bad or fine. Therefore, the law of averages makes it safer for mail-order advertisers to run copy that is free of at least the *one* risk of being too short to impel the reader to act at once.

Quality of Copy

The more interesting your copy is to people, the longer you can hold them. If you can get your reader interested, and keep him interested, he will read what you want to tell him. That brings us to the *qualitative* factor in mail-order copy—*how* to make your copy hold your reader's interest longer.

Therefore, "interest" is our vital key-word in getting longer copy read.

Now, what *subject* interests your reader most? Himself—and his family, of course. And so your most effective copy-subject is—what your product will *do* for your reader, or for his family. It is amazing how much copy people will actually read if it continues to point out good consumer benefits. The continuously interesting presentation of strong and specific consumer-benefit sales points gets longer copy read—and the results justify and reward its use.

19

Caples on Copy
by John Caples

John Caples may be America's most experienced advertising man. His mail-order ads include such classics as the best-known, most-quoted ad of all time, "They Laughed When I Sat Down at the Piano." He has written four valuable books on advertising.

About Headlines

1. *The headline is the most important element in most advertisements.* Headlines make ads work. The best headlines appeal to people's self-interest, or give news. Long headlines that say something outpull short headlines that say nothing. Remember that every headline has one job. It must stop your prospects with a believable promise. All messages have headlines. In TV, it's the start of the commercial. In radio, the first few words. In a letter, the first paragraph. Even a telephone call has a headline. Come up with a good headline, and you're almost sure to have a good ad. But even the greatest writer can't save an ad with a poor headline. You can't make an ad pull unless people stop to read your brilliant copy.

2. The best headlines appeal to the reader's self-interest or give news. Examples: "The secret of making people like you." "Do you have these symptoms of nerve exhaustion?" "Announcing a new fiction-writing course." "How a new discovery made a plain girl beautiful."

---

3. Sometimes a minor change in a headline can make a difference in pulling power. A mail-order ad for a book on automobile repair had this headline: "How to repair cars." The pulling power of this ad was increased 20 percent by changing the headline to read: "How to fix cars."

4. Recasting a headline can make a big difference in response. Here is the headline of a couponed ad selling retirement annuities: "A vacation that lasts the rest of your life." Here is the headline of an ad that pulled three times as many coupons: "A guaranteed income for life." The losing headline attempts to be clever by calling retirement a vacation. The winning headline is a straightforward promise of a benefit.

5. Long headlines that say something are more effective than short headlines that say nothing. A book publisher had difficulty selling a book with the title, "Five Acres." The book was transformed into a best-seller by changing the title to: "Five Acres and Independence." Another publisher had a book titled "Fleece of Gold." The sales of the book were more than quadrupled when the title was changed to"Quest for a Blonde Mistress."

6. Writing headlines, the copywriter should try to break the boredom barrier. "How I became a star salesman" was the headline of a successful ad for a course in salesmanship. The pulling power of the ad was increased by changing the headline to "How a fool stunt made me a star salesman."

7. Attract the right audience. Do not use a headline or opening sentence that merely shouts "Hey You" or "Attention Everybody." Be selective.

Use a headline that attracts prospects—prime prospects—persons who will buy your product or service if your copy is convincing.

I recall two ads I wrote for a retirement income plan. Both ads were designed to get coupon leads for salesmen. One ad had a selective headline "How we retired on a guaranteed income for life."

The other ad had a more general headline "A vacation that lasts the rest of your life." I thought: That vacation headline is clever.

It has a poetic sound. It may do well.

Both ads were tested in the *New York Times Sunday Magazine Section*. I learned a lesson.

The ad "How we retired on a guaranteed income for life" pulled more than twice as many coupons as the ad "A vacation that lasts the rest of your life."

Here are two more examples of successful headlines. Note that the very first words reach out and grab prime prospects.

(a) Car insurance at lower cost if you are a careful driver.

(b) The deaf now hear whispers.

Here are two prospect-grabbing headlines that were printed on direct-mail packages:

(a) If you are eligible for Medicare . . . here is important news.

(b) Now, at last—a brand new magazine exclusively for apartment dwellers like you.

8. Ads that involve the reader are effective. For example, the best-pulling ad for a book of etiquette showed a picture of a man walking between two women. Headline: "What's wrong in this picture?" A successful ad for a course in interior design had this headline: "Can you spot these 7 common decorating sins?"

9. Straightforward ads usually outpull "cute" ads. Two couponed ads soliciting subscriptions for a daily newspaper were tested by mail-order sales as follows:

First ad—headline: "Take it from me, this is the newspaper for you." Illustration: Picture of a smiling newsboy offering the reader a copy of the *Los Angeles Times.*

Second ad—headline: "How to get the *Los Angeles Times* delivered to your home." Illustration: None. Just headline and copy.

Results: Ad No. 2 outpulled Ad No. 1 by 190 percent.

10. A book could be written on the subject of appeals but it is safe to say that *self-interest, news,* and *curiosity* always have been, and continue to be, powerful motivators.

Here is a successful correspondence-school headline that combines both news and self-interest: "Announcing a new course for men who want to be independent in the next 10 years."

Here is a famous curiosity-arousing headline for a book on etiquette: What's wrong in this picture?

Here is a successful headline that combines both self-interest and curiosity: How I made a fortune with a "fool idea."

11. You can sometimes combine two successes to make a super success. For example: Seven ads for house paint were tested for pulling power. Here are the headlines of the two most successful ads:

- "New house paint made by (name of manufacturer)."

- "This house paint keeps white houses whiter."

These two headlines were combined as follows: "New house paint made by (name of manufacturer) keeps your white house whiter."

A campaign with this theme sold more house paint than any previous campaign.

About Pictures

12. Use pictures that sell. Avoid far-fetched pictures that fail to identify your product or service. I recall an ad for air travel in which the main illustration was a picture of a camera.

Another time I saw an ad for a camera which featured a picture of an airplane. The writers of these two ads should have exchanged illustrations.

13. As a rule, a good picture is one which shows your product or service in use. For example, the best-pulling illustrations in Retirement-Income ads are pictures of happy couples sitting on a beach.

In an ad for a bicycle, a picture of a boy riding a bicycle shows the product in use.

The winning illustration in a series of tests for house paint ads was a picture of a man painting a house.

14. Don't forget the pulling power of a picture of the product itself. Book club ads show pictures of books.

Record club ads show pictures of records. Jackson & Perkins, rose growers, show pictures of roses.

About Copy

Hold the Audience

15. After you have stopped your prime prospects with your headline or picture, you must find a way to hold their interest. One way to do this is to use a first paragraph which continues the idea expressed in your headline. Example:

(Headline) Learn Piano
(First Paragraph) Play popular song hits perfectly. Hum the tune. Play it by ear.
No teacher—self-instruction. No tedious practice. Just 20 brief, entertaining lessons, easily mastered.

Another method is to quote an authority. Example:

(Headline) HOW TO WIN FRIENDS AND INFLUENCE PEOPLE
(First Paragraph) John D. Rockefeller, Sr., once said: "The ability to

deal with people is as purchasable a commodity as sugar or coffee. And I will pay more for that ability than any other."

Ad writers can take a tip from magazine article writers who often hold the readers' interest with a dramatic opening paragraph. Here is the beginning of a recent article on fat reducing:

> One of the heaviest patients I ever treated was a 360-pound man who had to squeeze sideways through my office door.

Here is the opening sentence of an article on deodorizers:

> The hit of the annual Chemical Show held in New York City a few months ago was a pair of skunks housed in a plastic cage.

16. In a direct mail letter, your opening sentence can perform the function of a headline by making an attractive offer. Here is the opening sentence of a direct mail letter selling hospital insurance: You are cordially invited to apply for the first 30 days of coverage for only 25¢.

Body Copy

17. Write your copy to the sixth-grade level. Simple language is not resented by educated people. And simple language is the only kind that most people understand. When you read over your copy, say to yourself: "Will this be understood by my barber or by the mechanic who fixes my car?"

18. What you say is more important than how you say it. Mail-order advertisers do not use expensive artwork or fancy language.

19. Two forces are at work in the minds of your prospects. (1) Skepticism, and (2) the desire to believe. You can do your prospects a favor by giving them evidence that what you say is true. Your client will also benefit by getting increased response.

20. Specific statements are more believable than generalities. An example of a specific statement is the famous slogan for Ivory soap: "99 44/100% pure."

21. When writing copy, don't merely tell your prospect the benefits he will get by buying your product or service. You should also tell him what he will lose if he doesn't buy.

22. Put your best foot forward in your copy. A copywriter asked my opinion of an ad he had written. He said, "I saved the best benefit till the end and used it as a punch line in the last paragraph." I said, "Put your best benefit in the first paragraph. Otherwise, the reader may never get to your last paragraph."

23. Avoid humor. You can entertain a million people and not sell one of them. There is not a single humorous line in two of the most influential books in the world—the Bible and the Sears, Roebuck catalog.

24. If you want to drive home a point, you should say it three times. For example, suppose you are making a free offer. At the beginning of your copy, say, "It's free." In the middle of your copy, say, "It costs nothing." At the end, say "Send no money."

25. Long copy sells more than short copy. The more you tell, the more you sell.

26. *Write long, boil it down.* Write more copy than you need to fill the space. If you need 500 words of copy, begin by writing 1,000 words. Then boil it down to a concise, fact-packed message.

27. Your ad must not only be truthful, it must be believable. Here are ways to accomplish this:

(*a*) Tell how long the company has been in business. A recent Jackson and Perkins ad said: Our 100th Year . . . 1872–1972.

(*b*) Include testimonials from satisfied customers.

(*c*) State approval by experts—(Examples: Good Housekeeping Seal of Approval. . . . Won Gold Medal Award).

(*d*) Give proof of popularity—(Examples: More than 12,000 sold. . . . 700 letters from delighted customers).

Testimonials Increase Sales

28. Include testimonials in your ads. Two ads for a financial publication were split-run tested in *Reader's Digest*. The ads were identical except that one contained four brief testimonials buried in the copy. The ad with the testimonials produced 25% more sales. Some of the most successful mail order ads have been built entirely around testimonials. Examples: "I was a 97 pound weakling," "How I improved my memory in one evening."

29. Localized testimonials in local media are especially effective. Seven couponed ads for a public utility were tested in New Haven newspapers. One ad featured a testimonial from a New Haven woman. This ad outpulled all the others. A newspaper campaign featuring local testimonials for a packaged laundry soap raised the sales of the soap from fourth place to first place.

About Sales Boosters

Offer a Guarantee

30. Offer a free trial or a money-back guarantee. And spell out your guarantee. The word guarantee has been used so many times that it has lost much of its force. Here is a classic example of a spelled-out guarantee:

> "This is my own straightforward agreement that you can have my coaching material in your hands for 10 days examination and reading before you make up your mind to keep it. You are to be the sole judge.
> "You can return the material for any reason, or for no reason at all, and your decision will not be questioned. Your refund check will be mailed to you in full by the very next mail. This agreement is just as binding as though it had been written in legal terms by a lawyer."

Prove It's a Bargain

31. If the facts warrant, you should prove that your proposition is a bargain. Examples:

> (a) A recent Doubleday Bargain Book Club ad contained a certificate with this heading: This Value Certificate is worth up to $63.25 in Publishers' Editions.

> (b) A recent Columbia Record Club spread in TV Guide said: Any 14 records $2.86.

> (c) One advertiser dramatized his low price by saying: Only 15¢ a day. Another said: Only 10% above wholesale price.

> (d) Some advertisers build up the value of their propositions. The publisher of a business periodical said: $20 spent for a year's subscription may save you $2,000. A manufacturer said: One gallon of this floor wax covers the average kitchen floor about 30 times.

Give a Reason to Act Now

32. You can often improve the pulling power of an ad by setting a time limit. Retail advertisers increase sales by setting a cut-off date. *Reader's Digest,* in selling subscriptions, frequently uses such phrases as, "Return this card before Oct. 31."

33. If the price is going up, say so. If the supply is limited, say so. Use action words (Examples: Act at once. Don't put it off. Delay may be serious. Order today.)

Offer a reward for promptness. For example, in a current Book-of-the-Month Club ad featuring a 10-volume set "The Story of Civilization," there is a small picture of a book entitled "The Lessons of History by Will and Ariel Durant." The test alongside the book says: A copy will be included free, with each set sent to new members who enroll at this time. Pub. price $5.

34. You should ask for action at the end of your ad. Tell the reader what you want him to do. Sometimes it pays to offer a reward for action. In selling a 10-volume world history, the Book-of-the-Month Club offers a free book "to new members who enroll at this time."

Make It Easy to Act

(a) Offer a booklet or sample.

(b) Offer a free trial.

(c) Offer a free cost estimate.

(d) Offer an easy payment plan.

(e) Tell how to order or get information by telephone. A Finance Company increased telephone replies by including in their newspaper ads a panel containing a picture of a telephone and these instructions: For quick information on loans, telephone MAin 2-4500 and ask for Miss Miller and just say, "Please tell me how I can get a loan."
The name "Miss Miller" was changed to a different name every time a new ad ran. This made it possible to tell which ads pulled best.

(f) Use a coupon or business reply card. Make the coupon or card easily accessible. Not long ago, Reader's Digest in their sub-

scription ads, started using reply cards which are lightly held in place by a sawtooth, die-cut edge.
This device gives the reader the easiest-to-tear-out reply card in the world.

Summing Up

The next time you write a direct response ad or letter ask yourself these questions:

1. Does the headline (or envelope copy) attract prospects?

2. Does the illustration attract prospects?

3. Does the opening paragraph hold the prospect's interest?

4. Does the ad contain news? Does it appeal to self-interest? Does it arouse curiosity?

5. Is the copy believable?

6. Does the copy prove it's a bargain?

7. Is it easy for the prospect to act?

8. Has the prospect been given a reason to Act Now?

20

The Direct-Mail Piece, Postage, and Results

By now you have found a product or a line of products that you have chosen to sell. And you have tentatively decided the terms of the offer you will make: price, credit, etc.

As in other media, in direct mail the offer is most important of all in bringing about success or failure. The choice of good lists is next most important. Copy and the "letter package" are the third important factor in success or failure. Despite this order of importance, most mailers spend a disproportionate amount of time preparing and testing copy and the physical characteristics of the mailing, when they would do better trying to improve their offers and the lists they use.

In this chapter we are not specifically discussing the follow-up letters sent to inquirers stimulated by space advertising. Much of this chapter does apply to follow-ups, of course, but Chapter 25 discusses that special problem in detail.

This chapter is about "cold" mailings that offer your product to rented or purchased lists, or to your own list of customers.

The Mailing Piece

So you have decided to try direct mail with your offer! This is a quick summary of how you proceed. Each step is spelled out in detail later.

First, you must select a few lists to test (usually with the help of a list broker). The test lists will be your guess as to the best possible lists available. More about that later. Second, you work up a mailing package—a good, standard type of copy and package—also discussed on the next few pages. And next you mail your package to a test portion of the list you selected. Read Chapter 26 to determine how big a test you should use.

Then you sit back to await the results. A section in this chapter teaches you how to predict the total results before they are all in. Compare the *predicted* returns against your costs to establish whether you have a success or a failure. Another section discusses the proper accounting techniques for this comparison.

A success? Go back to the list you tested, and mail either a much larger test, or the entire list. Chapter 26 helps you make that decision. And start testing other lists in order to widen your scope and increase volume.

General Principles of What to Send

This section will not try to teach you to write direct-mail copy, or to create direct-mail layouts and packages. Those lessons are well taught by

Robert Stone, *Successful Direct Marketing Methods*[1]

The Robert Collier Letter Book[2]

Yeck and Maguire, *Planning and Creating Better Direct Mail*[3]

Study these books. Even if you hire outside help, you will need as much expertise of your own as you can develop.

The very best short introduction is the article by Robert Stone in the *Advertising Handbook.*[4]

Many of the principles of display copy apply to direct-mail copy, of course. Testimonials improve results. Premiums improve results. Time limits improve results.

The results you get *can* be influenced *very greatly* by what you write in the letter and brochure. And it is difficult to identify good copy without testing. As an example, consider this experience of Bringe's:[5]

WHAT YOU SAY FIRST MAKES A DIFFERENCE

An eight-way test of 2,000 mailing packages, identical except for the lead line, mailed on the same day to the same state, brought some interesting variations. With the winning mailing as 100, the rest pulled 93, 90, 88, 84, 81, 78 and 62. Of course tests of 2,000 pieces do not give a very high predictability factor. But in this case 38% fewer orders from the worst of the lot compared with the winner could be the difference between a successful business and bankruptcy.

It demonstrates how a small difference in presenting an idea can make a big difference in results. Nine people tried to rank the packages before they were mailed. Three put the worst letter first. Four put the best letter last. None guessed the second or third correctly. Which demonstrates that the customer who pays for the product is the only reliable judge of effective copy.

This section will try to give you some *facts* about direct-mail packages that apply for mail order. Many of them come from tests run by the National Research Bureau.

The proper use of the graphic arts is crucial in direct-mail mail order. Chapter 27 tackles that subject.

The Elements of the Best Direct-Mail Packages

There are no hard and fast laws about which elements will make up the best direct-mail package. But subject to innumerable variations and exceptions, most direct-mail people agree that the best direct-mail piece will consist of either (1) letter, reply card (or coupon and reply envelope), outer envelope; or (2) letter, brochure or circular, reply card, outer envelope.

The letter is the single most crucial part of the package. No salesperson would ever walk into an office, slap down a presentation, and expect the prospect to do the rest of the selling. Sending a brochure or circular without a letter does just that—aside from the inevitable exceptions to mail-order rules, a brochure or circular by itself is not a good package.

Brochures and circulars work best when your product requires illustration.

Other Offers in the Package

Every direct-mail seller eventually gets the idea of increasing revenue by adding extra offers in the package. And with that idea comes the dream: "If it costs me no more to mail ten offers than one. . . ."

Sometimes you can increase revenue in this fashion. In fact, a catalog is just a big bunch of offers. But your original offer will never pull quite as well when you include other offers with it.

Whether or not it is profitable to add further offers to your offer is a question you must test for yourself.

You must test everything important, of course. Chapter 26 tells you how to make the tests. But you must also be discriminating about *what* you test. Don't waste your time testing hand-sealed versus machine-sealed envelopes, or Remington versus IBM typewriter face. Save your testing energy for the big and important things: price, extra offers, presence or absence of a brochure, etc, . . . and above all, lists.

The Letter

Write as much copy as you need to write. Never cut your sales argument short because you think the prospect won't read that much. Successful sales letters often run to four and six pages, outpulling shorter letters. In general a two-page letter outpulls a one-page letter, if you can find that much to say about the offer.[6]

But don't be wordy. Say only what you must say, and nothing more.

A good *letterhead* is very important. The best letterhead fits the spirit of the letter. The National Research Bureau found that a letterhead specially designed to fit the offer usually outpulls a "standard" letterhead, and that two-color letterheads outpull one-color letterheads.[7]

The quality of the paper *may* matter, but sometimes does not. Moran reports a *Standard & Poor's* test in which cheap paper pulled the same number of returns as expensive paper.[8] (This test, unlike so many others, was large enough to be reliable.) Usually 20-pound stock is quite satisfactory, except for letters to professional groups.[9]

Make the letter as interesting to read and look at as possible. Avoid any repetitive regularities in style. Use plenty of subheads, indentations,[10] underlinings, capitalization of paragraphs, handwritten interjections, and even spot art to jazz up the appearance. But never make the letter so jazzy that it cheapens the product. Good taste, experienced taste suited to the market, the price, and the product, is your only guide.

A two-color letter usually may outpull a one-color letter.[11] Furthermore, B. M. Mellinger says that the second color almost always proves to be worth the extra cost.[12] But nowadays big mailers find that colored paper is seldom worth the extra cost. Instead, they frequently use colored ink.

A two-page letter on two separate sheets is definitely better than two sides of the same sheet.[13]

Automatically typed letters are used more and more. The purpose is to make each letter seem individual. Of course you can't fool lots of people. But at least, as Paul Bringe says, [14]

> [D]on't let the repairman keep your machine in too good shape. If your letter is perfect it defeats the personal touch you want to create. Try to make your automatic letters look as though Sadie the Steno labored over them. If your machine is perfect you will help your cause by slipping a small error in somewhere. People make mistakes and personal letters should look as though they came from people.

Computer Letters

Every once in a while in the mail-order business, there comes along a truly new and successful idea. The computerized letter is one such idea. It was pioneered by *Reader's Digest* in 1967 and produced terrific returns at first. By now the novelty has worn off, and the results, though often good, are very seldom sensational.

The principle of the computer letters is its *personal* quality. The best sales letter is a very personal one, a direct person-to-person message from seller to buyer. But when there are a great many potential buyers, the seller cannot afford to sit down and write each one a personal letter in longhand. That's why various printing processes are used. But computer letters can produce a more personal quality than ordinary printed letters, and at much lower cost than individually typed letters.

There are two basic types of computer letters, the "fill-in" letter and the completely computerized letter. The "fill-in" device uses letters that are printed except for the spaces to be filled in; in this, it differs from the older print-and-type letters only in that (1) the "fill-in" is done mechanically and hence is cheaper, and (2) other blanks than just name-and-address salutation are filled in. A large proportion of the time, this just means that the addressee's name is sprinkled throughout the letter, usually at the end of paragraphs (because of the differences in lengths of names).

The completely computerized letter is completely typed by the computer. It takes advantage of the firm's knowledge about the potential customer's business, personal background or type of previous orders, size of factory, and so on, to produce a letter that really is fitted to the particular reader. The reader then can feel that the letter is not the same impersonal solicitation going to thousands of persons or firms. But of course this sort of letter requires that the mailer have available much information about the potential buyer, and that the information be in such a form that the computer has access to it. A good example of such a situation is that of fund-raising campaigns that have information on computer cards or tape about the individual's prior contributions. The person who receives the letter then can be reminded of his or her own past contributions.

One large user of computer letters was a firm which sold individualized coats of arms. The letter said that a coat of arms was available for your particular name. This sometimes had its amusing side. For example, a man who was the president of a company and whose name came out of the computer as "George W. Schiele Pres" was written to as follows: "Good news for the Pres Family. Did you know that the family name Pres has an exclusive and particularly beautiful Coat of Arms?"[15]

Computer letters can improve results markedly in some business situations, but they are not magic. They are just one more tool among the mail-order person's bag of devices. If you reach the point of considering the use of computer letters, you might do well to consult a couple of consultants to get their advice (which may differ markedly in cost and wisdom; that's why it pays to talk with more than one consultant). And as with doctors in past centuries, your chance of obtaining benefit rather than harm from the encounter is not always high.

In Chapter 22, computerized political fund-raising letters are discussed, some of which brought considerable criticism to President Ford for being in poor taste because they were phony—apparently personally signed, but really not so.

Repeat Letters

Sometimes a list pulls so well the first time around that it pays to mail to the same list again. What should you mail then?

Nation's Business tested to find the best method. An original mailing to a list of 20,000 which got excellent results was followed up the next month, but the follow-up was split into four groups of 5,000. Here are the results:

1. Simulated carbon copy of original letter with memo attached—same offer—77% of the original return.
2. A different letter reminding about the first mailing—same offer—52%.
3. A different letter containing the same offer, but making no mention of the original mailing—65%.
4. A completely different letter with a different offer, no mention of original mailings—50%.

The conclusion: A good *offer* is worth repeating.[16]

The Brochure or Circular

Brochures and circulars come in such a remarkable number of sizes and shapes that I know of no valid generalizations about the best-pulling styles. Distinctions between brochures and circulars and booklets are not clear, either. What we call a "circular" is usually short—one, two, or four pages. If it is longer, we call it a "brochure" or "booklet." "Booklet" usually suggests that it contains other information than just your sales pitch. And we usually think of a brochure as a very fancy selling piece.

A two-color circular outpulls one color regularly.[17] Four-color circulars are sometimes worth the money. And a circular separate from the letter will usually do better than a letter-circular combination.

A typeset circular costs more than a typewritten circular but is worth it. And a reply coupon on the circular adds extra returns.[18]

Testimonials are powerful no matter where you use them—in the letter or in the circular. They add all-important credibility. Some advertisers devote entire brochures to testimonials. Naturally, this technique will work best when the reader has some doubts about claims made in the letter. Most testimonials are not spontaneous. Some are solicited outright with questionnaires. Other "unsolicited" testimonials are obtained by writing customers a chatty letter that expresses your hope that they are satisfied and asks if you can help them further. If they are truly satisfied, a gratifying number of testimonial letters will follow.

Outer Envelopes

In a recent test of self-mailers versus envelope-enclosed packages, the extra cost of the envelopes was much more than recovered in extra orders.

The envelope should be used for copy whenever possible. A catalog house claimed to sell more from the envelope copy than from the best page in the catalog. Most well-tested magazine circulation efforts use copy on the envelope; the example of a subscription solicitation for *Mother Earth News* is shown in Figure 20-1. But keep the envelope bare of copy if taste demands it in your particular line of business.

The National Research Bureau claims that illustrated envelopes are effective when used properly.[19]

Preston recommended the baronial sizes, rather than conventional envelopes.[20] A 500,000-letter, test to women showed the baronials to be more than worth the extra cost. Preston observed informally that baronials are worth their cost to men, also.

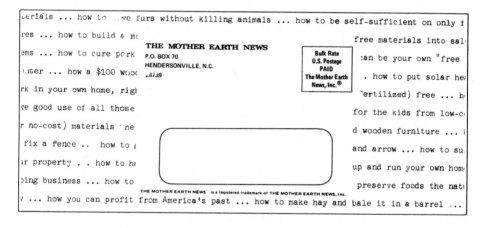

Figure 20-1 Example of envelope copy.

Odd shapes and oversized envelopes are generally reported to be effective, subject to cost and post office regulations that make most odd shapes illegal. They are especially effective in a series of letters to the same people.

Coupons, Order Cards, and Reply Envelopes

The most important fact about coupons and reply envelopes or reply cards is: *Always* include one or the other in *every* mailing. The theory is, "Make it easy to order." Evidence is abundant that return envelopes and order cards increase returns substantially, far more than their extra cost. Baker estimates an average 5 to 10 percent increase for the reply envelope.[21] Musselman says a coupon "increased sales 22%."[22] And Bringe notes:[23]

> With the qualification of "generally speaking" I can tell you that filling in the full name and address of your reader on the reply card will increase your response. Telling your reader to return the card without signature or initials will also increase response.
>
> Case in point is a list cleaning request for a client's newsletter. Response is close to 50% as compared with 12% on a previous try. The only variable was a filled in card as against no fill in.

I have found that 98 percent of those who respond will use business-reply envelopes, and 92 percent will affix stamps and use *ordinary* reply envelopes. The rest will use their *own* envelopes.

Business-reply envelopes versus ordinary reply envelopes is not a clear issue. Innumerable advertisers have tested one against the other, and yet some use each, with the preponderance of mailers using business-reply envelopes. Some mailers don't use the business-reply envelopes because they are (sometimes irrationally) annoyed by nuisance returns of empty envelopes.

Some advertisers may misread their first results because of the greater number of respondents who use plain envelopes *rather* than ordinary reply envelopes. This *could* lead to misevaluation of tests in favor of business replies. When I took account of this factor on a test that I ran, business replies were just about a break-even proposition against ordinary reply envelopes.

The higher the unit cost of your item, the more profitable business-reply envelopes are—usually, and with the exception of high-priced items.

Save 33%: imported goose feather pillows Sale $10

NAME _____

ADDRESS _____

CITY _____

STATE _____ ZIP _____

PLACE
POSTAGE
STAMP
HERE

Bamberger's

Post Office Box 13076

Philadelphia, Pennsylvania 19199

Dept. of Accounts

Figure 20-2a

To get a business-reply permit and number, just fill out the free permit application at the post office. You then pay 45 cents for each business-reply envelope you receive.

Mailers should consider the wide variety of trick reply-envelope forms available for various purposes. These include outgoing self-mailers that convert into reply envelopes, and "wallet" replies that are basically order forms.

I'd suggest careful testing before using any expensive trick envelope for long runs.

The reply envelope is an important carrier of sales messages for many firms. Department stores such as Macy's use their reply envelopes with monthly bills to sell shirts, sheets, and similar merchandise. An example is seen in Figure 20-2 for a major Newark department store,

EUROPEAN CRUSHED GOOSE FEATHER PILLOWS
FOR CUSTOM SLEEPING COMFORT: *REG. $15,* SALE $10

Enjoy new heights of sleeping comfort. Select the support
you need and the sleeping angle you prefer. Low, for soft
sink-in comfort; medium, for average support or high, for
over-stuffed firmness. The natural feathers stay fresh and
fluffy with a feather-proof cotton ticking. Jumbo 20x28"
finished size fits standard or over-sized beds.

Regularly $15 . . . . SALE $10

#302 4-74

Please send me the following:

Pillow Ht.	Quantity	Size	Price	
				Merch. total _____
				Sales tax _____
				Total am't _____

Account no._____

M.O. ⃝ ⃝ Check enclosed
Name_____

Address_____Apt. no_____

City_____State_____Zip_____

Please use this section for address correction:
Account number_____

Name_____

New address_____Apt. no_____

City_____State_____Zip_____

PHONE (201) 565-4444 OR YOUR LOCAL BAMBERGER NUMBER OR WRITE BOX 176, 131 MARKET ST., NEWARK, N.J. 07101.
AT ALL BAMBERGER STORES. SORRY NO C.O.D.'s. WE'LL DELIVER AS SOON AS POSSIBLE BUT PLEASE ALLOW 2 WEEKS
FOR DELIVERY. WHEN ORDERING BY MAIL ADD SALES TAX REQUIRED BY THE STATE OR LOCALITY
WHERE MERCHANDISE WILL BE DELIVERED. DEPT. 59

Figure 20-2b

Bamberger's. Other firms have worked out deals with subscription
agencies that supply reply envelopes with magazine-subscription sales
copy on them. The reply envelope is such a powerful medium for
this type of selling because it is always "close to the money" and
rarely gets thrown away.

Color and design of the reply envelope can affect the results. Moran
quotes data showing that a gaudy reply card outpulled a plain card
twenty-two to fourteen and green outpulled brown six to four. (No
reliability estimate on either figure; suggestive but inconclusive data.)

An illustration on the reply care may increase returns. And "guarantee stubs" for the purchaser to rip off and keep as a receipt may
increase response, too.[25]

Repeat the *proposition* on the coupon and order card. Leave plenty of room for name and address, and leave space for "State." You will be surprised by the number of people who expect you to know where they live without their telling you.

Offer an opportunity to trade up on the coupon or reply card. Add a checkbox for "Morocco binding $9.98" or "2 sets $14.95." A substantial number of purchsers will usually take advantage of the deluxe offer, quantity offer, or offer of allied merchandise.

Sometimes it pays to throw in extra reply cards, with a note: "Pass them along to your friends." One advertiser found that ten cards was the best number to include with his particular proposition.

Catalogs

Catalogs—which are covered in detail in Chapter 24—really are much more than direct-mail pieces. They are more like stores assembled in a book and (usually) delivered by mail. The world of catalogs ranges from mimeographed eight-pagers of tiny firms selling used books to the fantastic productions of Sears, Roebuck and the other giants, from consumer-novelty catalogs like those of Sunset House to those of major industrial firms selling generators and tractors. Catalogs really deserve a whole chapter to themselves. Maybe they will get one in the next edition of this book.

Many of the decisions about a catalog are similar to decisions about direct-mail pieces: how much color, what kind of artwork, what kind of gimmicks (free gifts and contests, for example), delivery methods (parcel post, United Parcel Service, truck, etc.), coupons and rider forms, whether to include a letter (always yes, and make it "wrap-around," a four-page piece that goes outside the catalog), and, of course, copy.

But there are also some decisions and characteristics that are special to catalogs. One such decision concerns the placement of merchandise in the catalog; generally it makes sense to put the best sellers up front. Another decision is the length of the catalog; the general answer to this question is to include all those items—and *only* those items—that more than pay their own costs of paper, printing, artwork, and postage. The same answer applies to the question of which merchandise to include.

The most important special characteristic of catalogs is that you can measure with perfect accuracy the relationship between the advertisements in the catalog and the sales of each product. The smart catalog firm takes full advantage of this information, checking closely and keeping tabs on each item to see which to drop or give less space or move to the back, which to move to the front or give bigger space. Total revenue (or even better, net revenue) per square inch of catalog space is the heart of catalog management.

Types of Postage

Very few mailers find that first-class postage pays for itself. Many find that third class even pulls just as many orders, at a lower cost.

Metered mail generally does just as well as, or better than, stamped mail. Prospects are not as much against business mail as many observers think. A "designed imprint" pulls as well as metered mail.

Here are the results of an interesting test of the effectiveness of different types of postage, as quoted by Paul Bringe.[27]

> Four groups of 75,000 pieces each were mailed. Group A—No. 9 colored window envelope with bold teaser line on face, printed third class indicia. Group B—same but with third class stamp rather than indicia. Group C same but with first class stamp. Group D—No. 9 white window, return address on flap, "First Class Mail" printed on face, commemorative first class stamp.

	Orders pulled	*Relative cost per order*
Key D (equals 100)	100	100
C	89	112
A	75	101
B	70	110

> The first class mailing that *looked* like first class (D) brought the most orders at the lowest cost.

Replies to *inquiries,* however, are generally sent first class. A prospect's enthusiasm cools off quickly if he or she doesn't hear from you soon after writing. Grant states that inquiries "lose 1 percent" for each day not answered.[28]

How to Estimate Results Quickly

The art of predicting total results from partial returns is discussed at length in Chapter 14. Here are some rules of thumb for *direct mail*—showing the percentage of responses you can expect. The "first day" is the day the first reply comes back, *not* the day of mailing.

Robert Baker

6th day	13th day	27th day	8th week	26th week
35%	72%	89%	96%	100%

SOURCE: Robert A. Baker, *Help Yourself to Better Mail Order*, Printers' Ink Publishing Co., Inc., New York, 1953, p. 73.

Ken Alexander (Segal)

5th day	8th day	15th day	23rd day	29th day
33%	52%	72%	77%	81%

SOURCE: Ken Alexander (pseudonym for Alexander Segal), *How to Start Your Own Mail-Order Business*, Stravon Publishers, New York, 1950, page not known.

Robert Stone
(To business lists rather than consumers; 1st replies on 5th day after mailing)

1st day	2d day	5th day	6th day	7th day	8th day	9th day
8.06%	16.08%	29.96	37.20%	48.60%	59.16%	68.48%

12th day	13th day	14th day	15th day	16th day	19th day
74.01%	77.21%	81.26%	83.06%	84.13%	87.21%

SOURCE: Robert Stone, *Successful Direct-Mail Advertising and Selling*, Prentice-Hall, Englewood Cliffs, NJ, 1955, p. 50.

American Heritage
(Mailed on Friday, one-half of responses on or before 2d Friday following)

Paul Grant
(From old customers)

1st week	2d week	3d week
52%	85%	90%

(From "cold" prospects)

1st week	2d week	3d week
46%	80%	89%

SOURCE: Paul Grant, L. W. *Mail-Order Survey*, page not known.

Art Kemble

1st week	2d week	3d week	4th week	8th week	26th week
30%	58%	75%	84%	95%	100%

SOURCE: Art Kemble. *Direct Mail*, date not known.

Lawrence G. Chait & Co.
(From a mailing of 14 million, third-class bulk rate,
of a big-ticket nonimpulse mail-order item—
perhaps a camera or electronic item)

	Percentage of total orders	Cumulative percentage by week
2d week*	1.3	1.3
3d week	6.3	7.6
4th week	21.5	29.1
5th week	27.2	56.3
6th week	13.4	69.7
7th week	7.9	77.6
8th week	5.9	83.5
9th week	3.2	86.7
10th week	2.8	89.5
11th week	2.8	92.3
12th week	1.9	94.2
13th week	1.2	95.4
14th week	.9	96.3
15th week	.6	96.9
16th week	.6	97.5
17th week	.5	98.0
18th week	.4	98.4
19th week	.2	98.6
20th week	1.3	99.9

* Ed Burnett (who should know) swears that these weeks are dated from the mailing "drop" date, and the dating from the first order would push the schedule back about 2 weeks.
SOURCE: *Direct Marketing*, May 1970, p. 3.

Concerning the relative "pulls" of direct-mail and display ads, Bringe estimates that "generally you can multiply results by 12 when sending mail to the same people who have been exposed to your magazine ad."[29] But *please* remember that this is a *very* rough "guesstimate."

21

Especially about Direct-Mail Copy

by Paul Bringe

Paul Bringe has been writing effective, lively, and honest direct-mail copy for years from his shop in Hartford, Wisconsin. He also writes a monthly column on direct-mail copy for Direct Marketing.

Are there any "rules" for creating effective direct-mail copy? That's a frequently asked question for which there can be no positive answer. There are no rules that can be applied to all situations. There are no rules that have not been broken many times by experts with good results.

No hard and fast rules, but there are guidelines—a distillation of successful mail-selling experiences—which if applied intelligently can make a big difference in the pulling power of your mail-order copy.

Why Mail-Order Copy Is Different

All of us are exposed to printed and electronic advertising many hours of every day. Why can't we use as models the obviously successful magazine and newspaper advertising copy, or the spoken copy of radio and TV advertising? Many fledgling mail-order writers try just that, and usually with sad results.

Most such general media advertising does not pretend to do the entire selling job with one presentation. Much of it is aimed at bringing the prospect to a store or other point of sale, where the real selling will be done. And TV, because it has the advantage of animated illustration, places even less demands on copy.

Let's look first at the structure of mail-order copy.

1. You will want to use short words of one or two syllables. Longer words should be suspect and a shorter synonym substituted if possible.

2. Use short sentences that *average* about twelve words. The important word is *average*. Some of your sentences will be shorter, some longer.

3. Keep paragraphs short. Two sentences is usually long enough. Some paragraphs need be only one sentence.

4. Your mail-order or letter copy must look *easy to read.* It is possible to make very simple copy look like difficult reading. Keep yours inviting by using headlines, subheads, short paragraphs, and indented paragraphs. At times you may want to use drawings or photos right on your letterhead to help illustrate your story.

This recital of some of the basic "mechanics" of mail-order copy is to emphasize the importance of getting your message read. Reading is an acquired skill requiring many hours and years of study to master. Some people never learn to read. In the United States, it is estimated that about 28 percent of all adults are "functionally illiterate," unable to understand a product label or to complete an employment application.

Others, while able to read, do not enjoy the process. They read only what they must, preferring the ready-made stories offered by TV, which call for no imaginative input or even minimum thinking on the part of the viewer. This group, by far the largest part of any mail-order audience, must be enticed to read.

To hold these reluctant readers, written material must be interesting and always pointing to more interesting material to come with the turn of the page.

Now let's talk a bit about the structure of that "story" you are going to relate to your reader in your mail-order copy. It must be well planned. It must follow the thinking habits of your reader, habits acquired from reading thousands of stories.

1. You will promise your reader an immediate benefit in your headline. Your most important benefit should be the hook that stops your reader and makes him want to read more.

2. Assuming you have stopped your reader with an attractive benefit, you will want to tell him more about it. Build it up. That's what he expects to find by reading more.

3. Now spell out a detailed description of the product or service you are offering. Be specific, with all the details of size, color, smell, or beauty so your reader can create a mental image.

4. Tell about your customers, how pleased they are with your product. Quote their exact words. Testimonials sell!

5. Tell your reader what he might miss by not having your product or service, or what he might lose by not ordering.

6. Now as you approach the end of your sales message go over the benefits again, arranging them in order with the strongest first.

7. Finally, ask for the order and tell your reader why he should buy *now* rather than put off his decision. Urging your reader to act at once, with believable reasons, is very important. All of us find it easy to procrastinate. You might consider adding a "hurry up" incentive with an extra gift for an immediate order to make it more difficult for your reader to put off his decision.

You can follow this story guide very closely and still not write a strong sales message. There is nothing here that will put inspired words on your page. But keep your story within these guidelines and you will have the beginning of a strong sales message.

What Kind of Words?

There are certain words your reader will respond to much faster than to others, the kind of words the reader has in mind when he says, "Talk about me and I'll listen." They are words such as you and yours, and words that designate people, such as Aunt Matilda, sister, mother, and wife.

Your reader is not much interested in words that tell about your affairs, such as I, me, ours, us, or my, and therefore you will use them as little as possible. If your reader is interested in you, it will be only to the extent he thinks you can benefit him.

Keep your copy moving. You do this by liberal use of verbs, verbs, and more verbs. Your copy must create a moving picture in the mind of the reader. It must compete with TV and with the action of life itself.

Use few adjectives. About one adjective for every three verbs is a good mix. Adjectives modify nouns and pronouns and therefore slow up the reader. Better to say a "young girl" than a "young girl with red hair, wearing a blue dress." Let the reader construct in the mind's eye his or her own version of a young girl.

Use a narrative style. Mail-order copy should have a beginning, a middle, and an end. The story should have a logical sequence that fits the reader's expectations of how a story should unfold. No "flashbacks," or "jumps ahead," so often used by those who produce literature. Your object is to lead your reader to buying your product. Mental side excursions in your story won't help.

You may think that these suggestions will surely result in "copy for the simple minded," copy that will quickly bore the reasonably well-educated person. But this is not the case. Simple, straightforward copy will hold the well-educated to its message, providing that message is written from the reader's point of view.

The well-educated will read and understand your message faster than the ill-educated, but if you are "talking about the reader" he will continue reading, be it one page, five pages, or ten pages.

You Want an Order on the First Try!

The successful mail-order operator wants every mailing package to bring back enough orders to pay the cost of his ad and his mail, as well as the cost of his product, and show a good profit besides. The key word is profit. Don't ask what your rate of return should be, and fret about a 3 percent response that you think should be 4 percent.

All you need be concerned about is profit per thousand pieces mailed. If that is satisfactory, you keep going back to the well for more orders, and with the same mailing package, until the profit drops below a satisfactory level.

Because you want an order on the first try, you will give the reader complete facts about the product or service. You will answer in advance any and all questions that might be asked. You will anticipate objections, state them, and respond to them. You will show your reader benefits about your product that may never have occurred to him.

Since you are going to tell all about your product, it follows that you must know all about that product before you can write persuasively about it. So make it your business to study the product. Use it yourself, if possible, or talk to people who have used it. Ask users how it might be improved, what they especially like about it and what they dislike.

As you discover benefits for the user, list them on a sheet of paper. Later you might try numbering them in order of importance because it is in that order the benefits should be presented in your copy.

Some products will be more easily sold on a negative rather than a positive appeal. A burglar alarm, for example, or a fire extinguisher, are bought to forestall unpleasant events. For such products a legitimate sales approach is an opening that may frighten or threaten the reader with loss unless your product or service is available.

The Offer Is King

The good copywriter gives much attention to the offer he will make to the prospect. By offer I do not mean an advantageous price, though that might enter into some offers.

A good offer is one that states the sales proposition in a way that seems to be to the prospect's best advantage. A book-club offer, for example, might say, "Buy this book for $10 and select any four additional books free." It might say, "Introductory offer to new members only—select any five of these books for $10." Or it might say, "Select any three books, free to you if you agree to buy two additional books within the next 90 days at $5 each."

Economically these three offers are the same thing. Yet one will pull much better results than the other two. And so it is with anything you want to sell. How you state your offer can greatly affect the responses you will receive.

Writing Good Copy Is Not Just Putting Words on Paper

The successful copywriter must be 100 percent sales-minded. He or she must look at every product or service from all angles. Turn it over. Approach it from finished result and move back to first construction. Don't accept without question a manufacturer's or supplier's word for what a product is good for or can do for a buyer.

Many suppliers do not know all their product can do. You have an advantage. You have no preconceived notions, prejudices, or preferences to destroy before you can take an unbiased look. It is quite possible if you examine a product with a clear eye that you will see completely new consumer benefits that may never have occurred to the originator. Here is where the successful copywriter earns his money—by contributing his knowledge of how people react to problems and opportunities.

Your Copy Is Not Likely to Change a Mind—But It Can Help a Mind to Rationalize

A good salesman or a good politician, and certainly a good copywriter, will very seldom expect to put a new idea in a prospect's mind. Your prospect comes to you with a lifetime of experience, schooling, and training of various kinds deeply impressed on his mind.

In most cases he is a huge bundle of habits, which he has acquired to make life easier. He has certain attitudes, gained over the years, which enable him to cope, more or less successfully, with life's problems and opportunities. He is not going to change this very comfortable set of mental furniture to accommodate any new ideas you may have to offer.

Your task is to determine as closely as possible what kind of a bundle of preconceived ideas you are dealing with. Has your prospect ever bought by mail? Does he have sufficient spendable income? Is his demographic profile similar to that of your customers?

You must take your prospect as he is and where he is, fixed ideas and all, determine the direction in which he is moving, and put your proposition in his path. Don't expect your prospect to think for you. You must think for him, help him rationalize the purchase of your product so that it becomes easier for him to buy than not to buy.

A big order? Certainly. But if it was so easy to write successful mail-order copy the competition would be fierce. Of the thousands who try to write successful copy, very few succeed. You can be on the way to successful copywriting if you lay out the rules you will work with and stick to them.

Taking Advantage of Your Hidden Equipment

Successful ideas come from the subconscious. They do, that is, if you feed in the basic information necessary to produce ideas. Letting your subconscious do the creating is infinitely easier than anything you will consciously grind out. So how do you tap this great storehouse of brilliant ideas?

You do it by absorbing every scrap of information about the product or service you must write about, literally soaking up all the data you can possibly assemble. When you think you have it all, put the data away and don't go back to it for 3 or 4 days.

Then come back to the job and start to write. You begin writing *anything!* You don't need a specific idea to begin. If you have done a good job of feeding your subconscious, you will soon be writing good copy, copy that makes sense, copy that sells!

A final word. Proficiency in mail-order copywriting, like proficiency in anything, comes with practice. You must write a lot of copy, and as you write, you will become more skilled. But you don't have the opportunity to write much copy? You have the same opportunity that everyone else has. Read mail-order copy, lots and lots of it. And whenever you see a piece of copy, rewrite it to your satisfaction. A dull business? Not at all—not if you really want to write order-pulling mail-order copy.

Read product labels, read matchbook covers, and read as many ads as you can find time for. Be critical as you read. How would you say it? Rewrite it in your mind's eye. You don't need a typewriter or pen.

When the time comes that the sight of selling copy automatically stimulates you to do a rewrite, you will be writing good mail-order copy.

22

Direct-Mail
Lists

Brokers, Compilers, Managers, and Consultants /
Types of Lists / Direct-Mail List Rates and Data
(DMLRD) / How to Choose Lists / Duplication of
Names on Lists / List Building and Maintenance /
Extra Revenue by Renting Your List / When to
Mail / How Often to Remail to a List / How Long
to Keep an Inactive Customer on Your List

This fact bears repetition: The choice of lists is absolutely crucial in direct mail. A winning offer in a winning package will fall flat on its face when sent to the wrong list. If you ever sell mail-order products by direct mail, you'll learn this lesson for yourself sooner or later, and the lesson will be expensive.

Brokers, Compilers,
Managers, and Consultants

Effectively using the various types of firms in the list business is of vital importance to almost every mail-order operator. There are several types of functions that they perform, such as "broker," "compiler," and "consultant," but any given firm may do two or all three of these functions.

Consultants try to give you their best advice not only about the appropriate lists for you to use, but also about all aspects of your

direct-mail program, without being influenced by particular connections that they have to particular lists that they manage or compile—
though being human, their judgment might on occasion be influenced
by their own connections. They charge you by the hour, just like
any other consultant. They are especially valuable when you are just
getting your feet wet using direct mail. Though their fees may seem
steep, consultants may be a great bargain by keeping you from falling
into pitfalls. And you might consider it good economy to get a second
viewpoint from another consultant even if you have a very good
opinion of the first consultant.

List managers take charge of renting mail-order firms' customer
lists. Their job is to promote those particular lists as effectively as
possible on behalf of the owner. You should not expect them to be
impartial in that role.

List compilers work up lists of all kinds—say, all the bookkeeping
firms listed in the yellow pages of telephone books all over the United
States. These compiled lists are particularly valuable if you sell business
services, but they can sometimes be effective for some consumer goods
even though they are not lists of proved mail-order buyers. A sample
of such lists is shown in Figure 22-1. Appendix D contains the names
of several list brokers.

List brokers are of vital importance to almost every direct-mail
mail-order firm. It is their function to bring together the owners of
lists and the firms that want to rent lists. They usually get a flat 20
percent commission on the rental, and it is to their advantage that
each test list you rent is successful, because you will then use the
whole list and boost their fees. The broker does not make any money
on a test that fails.

Brokers have a wide knowledge about choosing lists, which they
pass on to you as part of their service. But brokers, like other people,
are fallible. Don't be afraid to let your judgment override the broker's
judgment on ocassion.

Brokers also may *own* compiled lists, which they rent to you outright
for their own account. There are many other firms that specialize in
compiled lists, too

Don't ever consider buying or renting the small, low-price lists of
names offered direct by tiny, unknown firms to anyone who runs a
classified ad or small display ad. Even if such lists were to prove
satisfactory, they are far too small to do you any good.

Consult a broker or a list manager about future rentals of your
own list, today. Do this *before* you have a big list because the broker's
advice may affect the way you maintain your list.

Code No.	Quantity	Description	Dollars Per Thousand
HORTICULTURE , cont.			
Ht 14	17,000	rose bush buyers	15.
Ht 15	95,228	garden supplies, seed and nursery item buyers	15.
Ht 16	40,000	plant food, planters & garden supply buyers	15.
Ht 17	82,000	seed, ornamental shrubs, and fruit plant buyers	15.
Ht 18	2,067,100	buyers of lawn care magazine, supplies	15.
Ht 19	209,000	women buyers of dutch bulbs (home owners)	15.
Ht 20	10,000	buyers of water plants, lily pool supplies	19.
Ht 21	17,000	former subscribers to famous horticulture magazine	17.
Ht 22	150,000	members of horticulture groups and societies	17.
Ht 23	30,000	persons interested in raising orchids	15.
Ht 24	7,725	subscribers to Tropical Homes & Gardens (Florida)	15.
Ht 25	40,000	90% women who sent money for iris bulbs	15.
Ht 26	1,689,290	bought products for lawn care (in central states)	14.
Ht 27	22,500	retail florists	20.
Ht 58	~~75,000~~	~~bought~~	~~15.~~
Ht 59	37,500	buyers of geraniums, violets, ivy plants	15.
Ht 60	11,850	bought tree & shrub seeds	15.
Ht 61	50,000	bought nursery products	15.
Ht 62	23,077	buyers of quality seeds	15.
Ht 63	30,000	seed, bulb, plant buyers	15.
Ht 64	56,000	75% are repeat buyers of fruit trees	15.
Ht 65	15,000	leading female flower growers & gardeners	15.
Ht 66	140,000	buyers of trees, roses, evergreens, shrubs, etc.	13.
Ht 67	125,904	buyers of fruit trees and other nursery items	14.
Ht 68	95,000	buyers of pompon, mums, azaleamums	15.
Ht 69	140,000	above average income home owners who bought fruit trees, berry plants, seed	15.

Page 72

Code No.	Quantity	Description	Dollars Per Thousand
Ht 70	12,000	members of Plant of Month Club, buyers of shrubs	15.
Ht 71	25,000	subscribers to Popular Gardening	15.
Ht 72	24,000	buyers of flower seeds, bulbs, rock gardens	15.
Ht 73	180,000	fine seed buyer list	15.
Ht 74	44,700	buyers of nursery items	15.
Ht 75	39,000	buyers of choice flowers (glads, etc.)	15.
Ht 76	32,000	women buyers of Hawaiian good luck plant	14.
Ht 77	14,200	hobbyists who purchased orchid plants	15.
Ht 78	29,117	orchid fanciers who bought catalog and growing instructions	15.
Ht 79	90,103	U.S. florists and nurserymen	15.
Ht 80	10,930	80% public spirited men, members of American Forestry Association	17.
Ht 81	30,000	buyers of horticulture supplies, violets	15.
Ht 82	13,000	catalog requests (50% women) for seeds, garden supplies	13.
Ht 83	135,000	buyers of perennial plants, lawn seeds, etc.	15.
Ht 84	50,000	buyers of grass seed, shears, garden hose	14.
HOUSEWARES			
Hs 1	25,900	buyers of aluminum cake molds	13.
Hs 2	100,000	buyers of electrical appliances	15.
Hs 32	117,000	bought thermal salad bowl	13.
Hs 33	119,000	buyers of personalized door mat	15.
Hs 34	49,000	99% women who buy household cutlery	15.
Hs 35	100,000	buyers of colorful plastic dinnerware	13.
Hs 36	69,900	buyers of many household items	14.
Hs 37	64,000	buyers of top quality home accessories, toys	15.
Hs 38	1,500,000	buyers of kitchen gadgets	15.
Hs 39	50,000	buyers of colored burlap	15.

Page 73

Figure 22-1

Once again, remember that list brokers have a great deal of precious knowledge about which offers have worked on which lists. Take advantage of their knowledge just as much as you can. Incidentally, a most valuable part of their knowledge is how to select the higher-responding parts of larger lists that on average may not be excellent, but which can be segmented effectively. This is a vital aspect of the art of list usage, Ed Burnett urges.

Consultants, brokers, compilers, and managers are conveniently listed in the classified pages of all the direct marketing periodicals—*Direct Marketing, ZIP, DMLRD, Catalog Age,* and so on. Therefore, I won't include a listing here, because it cannot be as current as those classified listings. You might also consult the yellow pages of the telephone book in your area to try to find local connections with whom you can work face to face. Finding competent and imaginative firms and individuals to work with you is as chancy here as in other aspects of life. You must use your best judgment, get advice from others, and recognize that your best choice will also depend on your own skills and personality.

Rental Means Rental. You use the names once and that's all. The owner of the list is protected by the criminal law against your stealing the list. You guard against stealing by placing "decoy" names on the list, made-up names which someone else couldn't know of without using your list. Decoy names are evidence in court.

The use of decoy names is absolutely crucial. It is legally binding evidence against anyone who might steal your list. For example, I was called as a witness by a firm whose sales manager had photocopied their entire list of industrial buyers and then moved over to a new competitor. The mail received from the competition at the old addresses was the basis for a legal settlement that ran near $100,000. (In that case the firm did *not* have coded names on the list but by a lucky accident there were some catchalls and a "COD account" with the firm's own address on the list, and the post office delivered the criminal firm's mail to that address!)

Not only must you put coded names and addresses on your customer file, but you must not reveal which ones they are to your employees. For example, in a case now in the courts, a top-salaried executive became disgruntled and took the customer list with him to a new employer.

Here are some details from Kenneth Emens on how to seed a list with decoy names:[1]

MARKING THE LIST

To seek recovery or injunctive relief should your list be stolen, it is necessary to prove that the list is your property. To prove this, your list must be marked in some manner.

Name and Address Modification. A list can be marked by placing unique, fictitious names and addresses in it. One approach commonly used is to misspell names in a unique manner. For example, my name and address is:

Kenneth L. Emens
39 Ridley Avenue
Aldan, PA 19018

The first line could be changed to Kenneth L. Emmens, K.Z. Emens, etc., to make the name unique.

However, placement of seed identifying data in the first line is not as good as the second or third line. First line data can be replaced randomly, rearranged, removed, or replaced with "Resident" or "Occupant." This would eliminate the uniqueness of the name and address without affecting mailability.

The second line can be "seeded" by using the technique described for the first line. In addition, other possibilities include:

1. Add a code behind the street address, e.g., 39 Ridley Ave. 18

2. Add a code in the second line disguised as an apartment number, e.g., 39 Ridley Ave., Apt. 18.

Completely Fictitious Seeds. Someone who stole your list could defeat the uniqueness of your seed in the above examples by scrambling and replacing letters and numbers on a random basis. Therefore, one of the best seeds is a completely fictitious person and/or address. This can be done by establishing a Post Office Box or using a non-existent street address. For example: Mickey Mouse, Box 99 or 139 Ridley Ave. where there is no 100 block. This might take a little cooperation from the local postmaster to open a Post Office Box in a fictitious name or from the postman to insure that mail to a non-existent address gets delivered properly.

List Dating. Seed identifying characteristics should be changed on a periodic basis. This allows a stolen list to be dated as well as identified. Such information can help establish who had access to the list.

For example: a seed could be set up with two initials and a surname such as A.A. Emens. The first initial could stand for a year (A = 1970, B = 1972, etc.); the second initial could stand for a month (A = January, B = February, etc.) or a biweekly period.

Another way to date lists is to include a date in the seed name and/or address. For example, the last four digits of the current Julian date could be appended to a surname or disguised as an apartment number. Two examples of Julian dates for given Grergorian dates follow. 1/13/76 would be 76013, 2/15/75 would be 75046. If labels or a list were produced on 1/13/76 (Julian 76013), the last four digits could be placed in a seed name as an apartment number such as 39 Ridley Ave., Apt. 6013.

Other Aspects of a Good Seed Program.

- The number of seeds should be adequate to cover each logically expected subset, for example each mailing segment, reel of magnetic tape or microfilm cassette. There is no hard and fast rule in this regard. The quality of the seeds is more important than the quantity.
- The seeds should be dispersed over the same geographic area as the list.
- Some seeds should be identifiable and be included in all lists, labels and other outputs created. These seeds are a protection against outsiders and some insiders.
- Automatic inclusion of the above seeds should be under computer program control if the list is computerized and be included in all mailings.
- Some seeds should not be identifiable as such. They should appear to be normal in all aspects. This would include the purchase of product, maintaining of an account balance or whatever. These seeds are a protection against insiders.
- The unidentified seeds should be maintained independently by at least two individuals. This would then necessitate collusion to obtain a totally seedless list.
- A positive feedback loop must be established with the seeds. Records of mailing should be maintained. Seeds should be provided with return envelopes and instructed to return *all* mail received in the seed name. Return from seeds should be recorded and exceptions investigated.
- Seeds should immediately inform the organization of any unexpected mail received in the seed name.
- Seeds should be tested from time to time by sending foreign or competitive literature to them under the seed name.

About the problem of checking that the mail really gets out as and when it is supposed to: U.S. Monitor Service (32 Maple Ave, New City, NY 10956) offers to receive and record delivery in 5, 10, or 25 cities, at addresses you can put on your mailing lists. These decoy names also check unauthorized use of your list.

Many list owners forgo considerable extra income by refusing to rent their lists, out of fear of theft. Their caution is understandable, because their lists are the most important assets of their businesses. But their caution is probably not justified, and costs them extra profits each year.

To arrange to rent lists, call or write one or more brokers. Tell the broker what you are selling, and if possible, include a mailing piece. The broker will recommend lists by sending you cards with full information about the lists he or she recommends.

The mechanics of renting lists vary, but they are always simple. The two most usual arrangements are: (1) You send your envelopes to the renter or to the renter's letter shop, which then returns the addressed envelopes to you. (2) The list owner sends you gummed labels to affix to your envelopes.

Types of Lists

There are three basic types of mailing lists: (1) compiled lists, (2) "response" lists of mail-order buyers, and (3) the "house list." They are very different, but all have their important uses.

Compiled lists are lists of people who have some characteristic in common. The common characteristic may be as simple as that the addresses are in the same area. (For example, the crisscross telephone directories that list people up and down the street, "occupant" lists, and "rural box holder" lists.) Or the common characteristic may be that the addresses all belong to the Interplanetary Study Society.

Compiled lists are derived from many sources—mostly records of trade organizations, professional organizations, and publicly available records. But even if the original material is available to you, you will usually find it more economical in the long run to use the services of a list compiler.

Mail-order buyer "response" lists are lists of people who have bought from particular mail-order firms. People on mail-order buyer lists have *two* things in common:

1. They have bought or expressed interest in a particular type of merchandise.
2. They are inclined to buy by mail.

The importance of 1 is obvious; 2 has been *proved* crucial, time after time. All else being equal, it is tremendously harder to sell by mail to people who have no record of buying by mail than to mail-order buyers.

Another distinction made in thinking about lists is whether the mail is sent to a home address or to a business address.

Despite the importance of the "response" nature of mail-order buyer lists, you should not prejudge a list's chances of success too completely. Some compiled lists work, many buyers lists do not. Ultimately, the only important distinction, Ed Burnett says, is between lists that work and lists that do not work.

The house list is the list of people who have bought from you in the past. Paul Bringe gives this example of the tremendous power of the house list.[2]

> The Republican Party is having good results with its fund raising by mail effort. First mailings last year brought an average 3% response of $11 each at a cost of 17½ cents per dollar collected. "Renewals" this year from last year's donors brought a 50% response at a cost of 1½ cents per dollar.
>
> This is a good demonstration of the great difference between a qualified list and a non-qualified list. The first year the Republican mailing was probably made, with the aid of census tract information, to upper income groups suspected but not known to be Republican.
>
> The second year's mailing went to known customers who, if they did not contribute, would have to admit to themselves that they made a mistake the first year. Such an admission is difficult for anyone to make. Doesn't this indicate that in many cases an outright loss the first year could prove mighty profitable thereafter? Magazine publishers have known it for years.

During the past few years there has been a noticeable increase in the use of fund-raising campaigns by mail by candidates of both Republican and Democratic parties.

According to Ed Burnett, test after test shows that lists do not decline in response if they are rented more often.

Figures 22-2*a*, 22-2*b*, 22-2*c*, and 22-2*d* provide an interesting example of such fund solicitations. Please notice the use of the name and address of the addressee in the body of the computerized letter.

Direct-Mail List Rates and Data (DMLRD)

Every mail-order operator should know about Standard Rate & Data Service's compilation of Direct Mail List Rates and Data (DMLRD). This volume comes out six times a year, published at 5201 Old Orchard Road, Skokie, IL 60076. The price of a yearly subscription is $170, as of 1985.

With the publication of DMLRD, you now have in front of you thousands of "compiled" lists and hundreds of lists of mail-order buyers. This compilation is valuable not only as a source of lists, but also as a way to get a general understanding of what is happening in the mail-order business.

In addition to mailing lists, DMLRD includes a compilation of cooperative mailings and package inserts, whereby you can send your direct-mail solicitation either together in an envelope with that of

GERALD R. FORD

WASHINGTON

December 4, 1975

Mrs. Julian Simon
1105 S. Busey St
Urbana, Illinois 61801

Dear Mrs. Simon,

I am writing you today to personally ask for your help in a
matter that is of great concern to me.

Since becoming President, I have tried to achieve many
things. Among them are holding the line of government spending to reduce inflation, a strong national defense, less
government regulation, and a national energy program to prevent us from being at the mercy of foreign energy suppliers.

As you know, many of these efforts and other positive steps
have been thwarted by a Congress heavily controlled by the
Democrats. In some instances, the Congress has turned a
deaf ear; in others it has written its own extravagant legislation.

I have had to employ the veto over 30 times to stem this tide
of irresponsible legislation.

However, Mrs. Simon, you and I know that this is only a temp-
orary solution.

What America needs is a Republican Congress working for
Republican goals. Unless more Republicans are elected in
1976, inflation and excessive deficit spending will continue.

That is why I have visited many regions of the country for
the Republican Party and Republican candidates. Though I
would prefer to contact you on one of these party-building
trips, time dictates a written message.

Democrats seem to believe that America is great because of
what government does for people and generally vote for more
government programs, more federal spending and taxing.
Republicans believe America is great because of what free
people do for themselves and generally vote for less government involvement. Democrats have controlled the Congress

"A copy of our report is filed with the Federal Election Commission and is available for purchase from the Federal Election Commission, Washington, D.C."
Absolutely no taxpayers' funds have been used in the preparation or mailing of this correspondence.

Figure 22-2a

Mrs. Julian Simon

for 40 of the last 45 years and have contributed to the many problems we face today.

The best way to begin overcoming such problems is to elect more Republicans to Congress in 1976. That is the best way to reduce wasteful government spending, cut back needless federal controls which are strangling our private enterprise system, and reform a welfare system that saps individual initiative and costs you and other taxpayers billions of dollars each year.

This is why I sincerely hope you will decide, today, to support the outstanding work of the National Republican Congressional Committee in its effort to elect Republicans in 1976.

This committee supports Republican candidates for the House of Representatives with direct campaign contributions and a wide variety of important campaign services.

From my own experience as a Member of Congress, I know that the Committee's support is invaluable in electing and re-electing Republicans to the House of Representatives.

Committee Chairman, Congressman Guy Vander Jagt, has told me a financial goal of $2,100,000 has been established for the 1976 GOP Victory Fund. I feel this sum is reasonable and necessary. It must be achieved.

You can play a major role by joining me and the Committee in our joint efforts to elect a Republican Congress by sending your maximum contribution in the enclosed envelope. In order to successfully reach this goal, we need virtually 100% participation by all friends and supporters of this Committee.

Without your help we simply cannot elect more Republicans to Congress.

I look forward to Chairman Vander Jagt's report to me on the results of this appeal, Mrs. Simon.

Thank you in advance for your assistance.

Sincerely,

Jerry Ford

Figure 22-2b

```
                                                        ┌─────────────────────┐
                                                        │ FIRST  CLASS        │
                                                        │ Permit No. 36350    │
                                                        │ Washington, D. C.   │
                                                        └─────────────────────┘

      Business Reply Mail No Postage Necessary If Mailed In The United States
      ─────────────────────────────────────────────────────────    ══════════════
                                                                    ══════════════
                  Postage will be paid by:                          ══════════════
                                                                    ══════════════
                  Gerald R. Ford                                    ══════════════
    PERSONAL      The White House                                   ══════════════
                  c/o G.O.P. 1976 Victory Fund
                  Box 2837
                  Washington, D.C. 20013
```

Figure 22–2c

other firms, or in the packages of merchandise sent out by other firms. These can be economical and powerful selling methods.

DMLRD also provides information about mailing-list brokers, list compilers, list managers, and a great many of the other people who supply services to the direct-mail-order industry such as consultants, sellers of letters, printing and computerized letters, and so on. DMLRD also contains the latest postal information. When you first begin to use it, read very carefully the "Suggestions on How to Use Direct Mail List Rates and Data" found in the front. This section will save you lots of confusion in figuring out what is included therein.

Each listing in the catalog is organized as follows: After the classification by industry or product or consumer-marketing program, there is the title of the list, the names of the owner and the broker, the description of the list including the average unit of sale, data on how you can get the list broken down by state or county or zip code if you wish, the source of the names for the list, the rental rate and commissions, and various technical data about how you actually use the lists (how they are delivered, what kind of addressing system, and so on).

How to Choose Lists

The following principles may help you to analyze lists for your offer:

1. Use the same lists, or the same types of lists, as your competition does. This is our old key principle, of course, of following along wherever success has been proven.

2. Use your competitor's lists themselves, if you can get permission. Many competitors exchange lists.

To: President Gerald R. Ford, c/o GOP VICTORY FUND
    P.O. Box 2837, Washington, D.C. 20013

Dear Mr. President:

   I agree. We must stop waste in government, cut bureaucratic rules and regulations,
fight inflation and recession and keep a strong U.S. Military Defense.

   I know you need 100% participation to reach your goal and I will do my share
to help. Enclosed is my contribution to the 1976 GOP VICTORY FUND in the amount
of:

☐ $———   ☐ $100   ☐ $75   ☐ $50

☐ $25   ☐ $15   ☐ $10

☐ CHECK ATTACHED   ☐ BILL ME $———   ☐ QUARTERLY   ☐ OTHER: ———

☐ I am sorry. I cannot contribute now. But please keep me informed of your 1976
   GOP Victory Fund Campaign plans for next year.
FROM:
Mr.
Mrs.
Miss
Ms.
_____
PLEASE PRINT YOUR NAME HERE

_____
PLEASE PRINT YOUR ADDRESS HERE

_____
PLEASE PRINT YOUR CITY OR POST OFFICE HERE   STATE   ZIP CODE

_____   _____
           OCCUPATION   PLACE OF BUSINESS

Please make checks payable to the GOP 1976 Victory Fund. Your personal letter of acknowledgment (a valid tax-deductible receipt) will be sent by return mail. Please indicate changes
of address necessary. Thank you!

Please return your check in the enclosed postage-paid envelope.

Corporate contributions are prohibited by law.

———————————

If you are a Federal employee or if you have a matter pending before a Federal regulatory
commission or a Federal agency, please disregard this appeal.

———————————

Figure 22-2d

3. A big list can give you the big volume that makes a heavy profit. On the other hand, there is some tendency for smaller lists to be of better quality.

4. Use *fresh* or *well-maintained* lists. The Direct Mail Marketing Association estimates that *each year* changes in address or name include 22 percent of householders, 23 percent of merchants, and 39 percent of advertising executives.[3] Stone estimates 20 to 30 percent annual changes on buyer lists.[4] And there was a 25 percent change in a single year in job addresses from a McGraw-Hill list.[5] But an old list that works is better than a fresh list that doesn't.

5. The longer the time since the customers on a list last bought from the list owner, the less likely they are to buy from either the list owner or another firm that rents the list. Stone estimates the deterioration as follows: If this year's customers will buy at a rate of 100 units, last year's customers will buy at a rate of 80 units, and 2-years-ago customers will buy at a rate of 60 units.[6]

6. Compiled lists are seldom as good as mail-order response lists for sales of consumer items by direct mail. But they are invaluable for commercial and industrial sales.

7. Inquiries versus purchasers of the same products: Purchaser lists will always do better because there are no "curiosity seekers" among them. The interest of a purchaser is bound to be higher than that of an inquirer.

8. Price of item bought: The higher the unit sale, the more money the customers obviously had to spend—and the more they are able to spend for your products, too—unless they are the kind of products purchased especially by low-income families.

9. "Class" of lists: High-class lists do very well for a variety of customers. The Diners' Club list is a favorite.

These further principles may help you:

1. Ask yourself, "Are these the kind of people who will be interested in this offer?" There is no replacement for sound intuition, experience, and knowledge in answering that question.

2. Rely on your list broker. He or she is on your side. The very nature of the financial transaction between the two of you means that his or her interests are your interests.

3. Consider whether you can use only *some of the states* on a list, or consider dropping out the cities. Often you can greatly increase

the average results from a list in this way because you are weeding out the areas that would drag the average down.

4. Mail to businesspersons' homes may pull better.

Direct-mail experts disagree on many points, but on this they are unanimous: *The best list is the list of your old customers.* It will pull 2 to 10 times better than any prospect list you can find. The people on your list know you and patronize you as they would patronize an old friend.

Second-best to the house list is a list of people who have purchased similar goods by mail. Third-best is a list of people who have purchased *anything* by mail. Next is a compiled list of people with some special characteristic to which your goods will appeal. Poorest of all is just any old list, such as the alphabetical telephone directory. Few and far between are the offers so good they will make money on such "unqualified" lists.

Exceptions to these rules are

1. *Commercial vendors.* If you sell steel in 10-ton lots, no list of mail-order buyers will do you any good. What you need is a list of manufacturers that use steel.

2. *Retailers.* The delicatessen around the corner in a big city is mainly limited to the store's neighborhood as a market, and therefore, it can only use the crisscross phone book (in which the listings run up and down the street, rather than alphabetically). And many a retailer has done well with this kind of direct mail. (Retailers can use other local lists, too, on occasion.)

It is prudent to get as much information as you can about the lists you might rent. For consumers lists (see Figure 22-3), find out exactly what was the offer that generated the list and how the names were acquired. For compiled lists, find out how the list was compiled. And in every case, find out enough to ensure that you're not renting a list you've rented before through a different broker (it happens).

Above all, don't rely on your judgment. Test! Often the results contradict your intuition, as in this experience of Bringe's:[7]

A fund raising letter for a girls college was sent to three groups: A-parents of previous students, B-parents of present students. C-people who had paid admission to public fund raising entertainment program the previous year.

Response: A-6½%, B-12½% and C-25%. The group with the weakest connection with the school responded the best. I have my own ideas

Figure 22-3

about why this happened but it illustrates a point—don't be too sure a list will not respond to your offer. Too often our own unsupported notions of what people will do stop us from testing. Uncle Remus says: "The answers always come after the askin'."

Duplication of Names
on Lists

Some names appear on many lists, of course, and it is to your advantage not to send six appeals to the same person on the same morning.

You can reduce duplication by mailing similar lists at different times. That way, your duplicated letter has several chances to sell the customer. The second and third letters are not completely wasted as they are if they arrive on the same day.

Sometimes the avoidance of duplication is more costly than are the wasted letters. But now that most lists have been put on computer cards and tape, in many cases it is possible to automatically eliminate duplication between the lists. This is done with what is called a "merge and purge" program, carried out by the computer-service organization to whom the lists are sent for processing. Ask your list broker about this when you order the lists.

Duplicates are not just a sign of waste, however. Duplicated names are likely to be particularly good prospects. In fact, if a list that is a candidate for rental has a high degree of duplication with your house list, that is a sign that the list is a particularly good prospect for you to use.

List Building and
Maintenance

You *must* have as big a house list of active customers as possible. You must build this list in any way you can and maintain it in tip-top shape. Your list is vital for rental income as well as for your own use. For some firms, list rental accounts for 25 percent of their annual gross, and list rental has a terrific profit margin.

The post office helps you maintain your list, though their help costs you money. The most important help is informing you of new customer addresses. And you *must* keep up to date with accurate addresses. There are several third-class list-correction methods offered by the post office, and you should ask about them on one of your visits there.

Another part of maintenance list is to scratch off the first-class nixies that are returned as unknown.

The post office helps in other ways, too, depending on what you request on the envelope. Check with your postmaster and use your *Postal Manual*, because procedures change from time to time. (By the way, a *Postal Manual* should be your first investment in your

USERS OF THE MONEYSWORTH LISTS

Alden's	Columbia Record Club	GEICO Insurance	Mother Earth News	Research Inst. of America
Ambassador Leather	Comml. Travelers Ins.	General Nutrition	NAACP	Rodale Press
Amer. Civil Liberties	Common Cause	Gulf Travel Club	National Wildlife Fed.	Saturday Review
American Express	Consumer Reports	Hammacher-Schlemmer	Nation's Business	F.A.O. Schwartz
American Heritage	Cosvetics Labs	Harper's Magazine	Nationwide Auto Ins.	Simon & Schuster
American Mngmnt. Assn.	Crown Publishers	Highlights for Children	Newsweek	Ski Magazine
Amoco Travel Club	Cue Magazine	Holt Executive Advisory	New West Magazine	Smithsonian Magazine
Amsterdam Printing	Danbury Mint	Hudson Vitamin Co.	New York Magazine	Southern Living Mag.
Atlantic Monthly	De Beers Diamonds	Instant Learning	Jay Norris Corporation	Spencer Gifts
Automated Learning	Democratic Natl. Comm.	ITT	Oklahoma Monthly	Spiegel, Inc.
Baxter International	Diners Club	Joseph Karbo	Oui Magazine	Standard & Poor's
H&R Block	Doubleday & Company	Kidney Foundation	Penthouse Magazine	Sunset House
Boardroom Reports	Dow Jones & Company	Kiplinger Letters	Philadelphia Magazine	Texas Monthly
Book Digest	Dow Theory Forecasts	Ladies Home Journal	Planned Parenthood	Thompson Cigar
Book-of-the-Month Club	The Dreyfus Corporation	LaSalle Extension Univ.	Playboy Book Club	Time-Life Books
Business Week	Dun & Bradstreet	McCall's Magazine	Prentice-Hall	Time Magazine
Calhoun Collectors Soc.	Esquire Magazine	McGraw-Hill Book Co.	Prevention Magazine	The Tog Shop
CARE	EXXON	Mason Shoes Company	Psychology Today	United Business Service
Carte Blanche	Figi's	Master Charge	Publishers Central Bureau	US News & World Report
Changing Times	Forbes Magazine	Mellinger Company	Pblshrs. Clearing House	Valley Forge Insurance
Cheeselovers Intl.	Fortune Magazine	Meredith Corporation	RCA Record Club	Value Line
Chilton Book Company	Friends of the Earth	Money Magazine	Reader's Digest	Volkswagen Auto Ins.
Collier Publishing	Funk & Wagnall's	Montgomery Ward	Republican Natl. Comm.	J.C. Whitney & Company

Figure 22-4

mail-order business, though your letter shop should be your first port of call when you need postal information.)

It is usually helpful in building a list to ask your customers for the names of their friends who may be interested in your products. Satisfied customers are glad to cooperate, especially if you offer them a small free gift. And be sure to tell the new people the names of the friends who suggested you write them.

Extra Revenue by Renting Your List

Not only is your house list worth a great deal to you in repeat sales, but you can boost your income greatly by renting your list to other mailers.

You can rent your list yourself by offering it to other mailers. Or you can use the services of a list broker to help you rent your list. List brokers usually take a 20 percent commission, and they are almost always worth it.

An advertisement for *Moneysworth* magazine provides interesting information about list rental. This is a list of firms that rented that firm's list (see Figure 22-4).

To get some idea of the extra revenue to be obtained with a list rental, consider that a representative list of 100,000 to 500,000 names had a rental fee of $16 to $30 and a rate of rental as high as two or three times a month. You might earn an extra $50,000 or even $500,000 yearly by renting your list if it is big enough and good enough. Some mail-order firms have made even more.[8] Figure 22-5 shows examples of list owners' advertisements.

One of the side benefits of renting your list to other firms is that you get new ideas about what *you* can sell to your customers. (For the same offer, the response *you* get from *your* list will be higher than the response another firm would obtain.)

When to Mail

If you mail first class, it may be wise to spot your mailing on a specific day. But third-class mailers can't depend upon any correlation between when third-class material is mailed and when it gets there. Tests show variation from 6 to 15 days in getting across the country.

In one test, one batch of catalogs was mailed in New York on March 26. They arrived in New York on March 27, in a suburb of New York on April 3, in Chicago on April 2, and in Los Angeles on April 3. Another batch of catalogs was mailed in Chicago on March 26. They arrived in New York on April 6, a New York suburb on April 9, in Chicago on April 2, and in Los Angeles on April 4.[9]

The only possible conclusion is that the speed of third-class mail is practically unpredictable. It averages about 11 days, but it varies from mailing to mailing and place to place.

The effect of the *month* on mail-order returns is discussed in Chapter 15. Stone says about direct mail: "Most mass mailers who test in the summer months get a 25 to 30 percent higher return during their mailing season" than during the summer test.[10] This drop-off in the summer is *less* than in display ads, especially from newsstand magazines. Periodicals have a lower *readership* in summer, *and* the actual readers purchase less.

You can obtain some indication of how good a month is from information about the number of mailings that are made in your particular product line in each month. (But don't fall into the error that thinking that the response is twice as good in one month as in another if twice as many mailings are made in the former month as in the latter.) Tables 22-1 and 22-2 show results of a seasonality study from the Kleid Company. Not only do the patterns differ considerably from product line to product line, but they even change somewhat from year to year. The best information for your own business will be your own result records, once you have been operating long enough to have enough data.

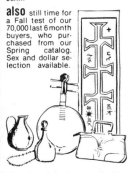
Figure 22-5

Table 22-1. Seasonality Study Category: General Reading—
Monthly % of Total Mailings

	1981–82	1982–83	1983–84	1984–85	1985–86
Mar.	3.5	11.4	10.1	4.8	8.5
Apr.	1.5	2.7	3.6	7.1	1.2
May	3.5	8.2	5.9	10.1	7.4
June	3.1	18.2	11.3	16.0	15.4
July	26.0	8.6	13.3	12.3	13.9
Aug.	2.4	3.5	2.8	2.3	5.1
Sept.	11.9	7.6	11.3	8.8	11.4
Oct.	0.1	0.9	3.0	1.7	3.4
Nov.	1.9	0.1	1.9	2.0	2.8
Dec.	22.6	21.4	25.8	20.4	22.8
Jan.	18.8	12.5	7.0	12.0	6.2
Feb.	4.7	4.9	4.0	2.5	2.0
Total	100	100	100	100	100

SOURCE: Kleid Company, 1986.

Table 22-2. Seasonality Study Category: Self Improvement—
Monthly % of Total Mailings

	1981–82	1982–83	1983–84	1984–85	1985–86
Mar.	2.2	5.8	6.7	4.8	6.1
Apr.	2.4	3.1	5.7	8.2	8.5
May	1.5	2.2	5.1	1.8	5.9
June	5.6	6.8	10.8	14.2	4.9
July	7.3	5.1	2.6	14.9	8.1
Aug.	9.0	10.8	11.0	3.6	3.6
Sept.	15.9	14.2	11.6	11.2	9.7
Oct.	1.3	7.3	7.0	6.3	6.1
Nov.	1.6	2.9	1.1	1.4	1.4
Dec.	30.8	16.3	14.9	19.5	32.7
Jan.	13.1	14.3	14.0	10.1	11.1
Feb.	9.3	11.2	9.5	4.0	1.9
Total	100	100	100	100	100

SOURCE: Kleid Company, 1986.

Snyder estimates the response in the various months for a nonseasonal item as follows, relative to a rating of 100 for January: January, 100; February, 96; March, 71; April, 71½; May, 71½; June, 67; July, 73; August, 87; September, 79; October, 90; November, 81; and December, 79.[11]

Seasonal gift mail must go out early. September, or even August, is not too soon for Christmas mailings.

How Often to Remail to a List

You will mail to your own house list of customers just as often as you can develop new products to sell them. *You can almost never mail too often to your own customers.* They will never tire of hearing from you about new products.

You can also mail more than once to cold lists. If you mail an offer to a rented list and the results are *far* above your break-even points, wait a while, then rent the same list again and mail the *same offer.*

A more difficult question is how often to mail your *catalog* to your house list. Should you mail once a year? Twice a year? Even four times a year? That is, we want to know the optimum frequency of mailing. If one mails too often, the response drops off. And the overall results may be even worse than the response to particular mailings suggests; this is because the mailings may be "borrowing" (sometimes called "stealing") sales from customers who would ordinarily reorder by themselves.

The only way to determine the optimum frequency of remailing is to *experiment.* And it makes terrific good sense to experiment with *samples* of your list rather than with the whole list at once. For example, a drug-products firm I worked with chose four samples of 1,000 names each. Each sample included people who had been customers of the firm for varying lengths of time, starting with brand-new customers who had just bought their first sample order from a space ad; the distribution of people by length of time since first order was thereby made the same for each sample. Then the four samples were sent catalogs on the following four schedules:

Schedule of Mailing Catalog

Group	Schedule
1	No catalog
2	Catalog every 3 months
3	Catalog every 6 months
4	Catalog every year

Then we kept track of the results over a period of 2 years, and at that time we calculated that it was most profitable to mail every 6 months, taking into account the sales revenue, the cost of servicing the orders, and the cost of mailing catalogs. Samuel Hall said that "if a large mailing of an entire list pulls as much as twice your break-even point, then you can safely remail to the entire list 45 days [Ed Burnett says 70 days] after you deposit your first remailing, without retesting."[12]

How Long to Keep an Inactive Customer on Your List

Perhaps the crucial question in list maintenance is how long to keep a customer on the list after his or her last order. Mailing "dead" customers is very costly indeed. But to drop a potentially live customer can be even more costly.

Emanuel Haldeman-Julius said that when the great depression of the 1930s hit in earnest, the expense of mailing to his huge list of 2 million buyers of "Little Blue Books" was killing him.[13] So he resolved to take heroic measures to pare the list of all except the really live customers. He then sent out a *half-price* offer. Every single person who didn't accept the half-price offer was dropped from the list.

Heroic and necessary as Haldeman-Julius's method may have been, there were almost surely better methods for the long and short run.

A reasonable procedure for inactive names is to separate them by length of time since last order—perhaps by 3- or 6-month periods. Whenever a person orders again, that person's name should be taken out of the inactive file and placed in the active list. Then treat each segment of the inactive list exactly as you would any other list to which you consider mailing, with the same break-even based on the same value of a customer. (Ed Burnett suggests dropping a segment to the inactive list when it no longer is better than the best outside list to which you can mail, but this strikes me as not being as reasonable a rule as the one I suggest above.)

23

Using Other Mail-Order Media

*Television / Radio / Matchbooks / Package
Stuffers / Bill Stuffers / Transit Advertising /Comic
Books / Daily Newspapers / Sunday Newspaper
Inserts / Other Media / Foreign Media / Telephone
Solicitations / Use a Variety of Media*

Mail-order people have always been ingenious and resourceful. At one time or another they have tested almost every medium except sky-writing and fluorescent raincoats to see if they would pull profitably.

Most products, most of the time, do best in the standard print media we have discussed so far. But in this chapter we shall talk briefly about the special media that can be of great importance under the right circumstances.

Television

Television is the new giant of mail order. But until recently it was little used by mail-order firms. Its terrific growth can be seen in the fivefold rise from $22.5 million in national advertising to $105 million over the short period from 1969 to 1973.[1]

Television is used in three ways to sell mail-order merchandise: (1) as a straightforward sales medium, like other mail-order advertising media; (2) to generate leads for future selling effort; and (3) in support of other media. We'll discuss them separately.

Television as a Complete Mail-Order Medium

Record and tape advertising dominates television. TV can be successful for special products that can tie the entertainment to the sales pitch. For example, a record company offered *Fifty Great Moments in Music.* The program itself played the musical excerpts as the camera focused on "appropriate" paintings. The entire program was a sales demonstration which only needed to be completed by the price, time element, and premium offer.

More recently, record and tape firms such as Dynamic House—which sells mostly popular records such as *The Greatest of Nat "King" Cole* and *The Greatest Hits of Rock and Roll*—have used straightforward commercial spots playing the music and showing the singer.[2] Television and mail-order selling has now come to be the most important medium for records and tapes.

The DMA *Fact Book* observes that a mail-order television ad is generally "a two-minute commercial, of which the last 30 seconds (the tag) is devoted to ordering information including a post office box or an 800 telephone number for C.O.D. or credit card options. . . . The maximum price at which one-shot merchandise can be sold on TV seems to range between $10 to $15."[3]

Record and tape mail-order sales are often PI (per-inquiry) deals between the record company and the television stations. The mail-order firm tapes the program, except for the station identification, and distributes the tape to the stations. The commercials ask that purchase orders and money be sent to the station. The station sends the letters on to the company, which then reimburses the station a fixed amount for each offer.

A commercial also will pull better if the address is a local station; this is because of the confidence that people feel in doing business with a local station as compared with a faraway, unknown firm.

Television as a Lead-Generating Device

Schools, encyclopedias, and other big-ticket items usually require a long selling job in person or in print. Television can be used to get people to inquire for more information. The DMA *Fact Book* observes that a 60-second commercial is usually long enough to do the job if you make sure that the tag-end is well done. "The action the viewer is asked to take must be spelled out completely and simply."[4]

Television in Support of Other Media

Television used in support of other media is a truly new role for television and accounts for a growing share of its mail-order advertising activity. "The commercial usually is 30-seconds long, and it usually begins running about four or five days prior to the anticipated delivery of the direct mail or the on-sale date of the space ad or newspaper preprint."[5]

> *Reader's Digest,* probably the first to experiment with this idea some 10 years ago, was back to support its massive, post-Christmas direct-mail drop (20 million-plus packages in the mail). But this year, RD departed from showing the traditional direct-mail package in the commercial. Danny Thomas was selected as spokesman. Thomas was shown talking with a painter in front of an outdoor poster. The comedian said, "Look for a mailing from *Reader's Digest.* You could win $100,000." This 30-second commercial ran on all three networks from January 2 to 7. Sharpe reported hearing that over $500,000 was spent on this TV support.
>
> Publishers Clearing House was back this year supporting its annual 20 million-plus direct-mail effort. PCH in their network spots also emphasized the sweepstakes offer in the mail, but presented past winners as testimonials to urge viewers to respond.
>
> Art DeMoss' National Liberty used Art Linkletter as campaign spokesman in its 30-second commercial to support newspaper preprints. Linkletter showed the preprint and said, "Watch for this in your weekend newspaper."

Full information on stations' addresses, rates, and other necessary data (except for PI deals) is found in *Standard Rate & Data.*

The use of television requires very close supervision on a day-to-day basis to check that the ads are pulling profitably—and that they are being run when you ordered them to be run. This is demanding because mail-order television time must be used on a local station-to-station basis rather than a network basis.

It is sales-test results that you must look at in evaluating television stations and time slots, not viewer ratings.

Radio

Radio carries a great deal of mail-order advertising because it costs much less per thousand listeners than does television. The offers which do best on radio are also those that tie in the program with the commercial. A health program can produce a lot of inquiries for vitamin catalogs. Disc jockeys can sell hit-record deals. One example is Sidney Walton's "Profit Research." Walton gives a talk on some money-saving or money-making topic; then he makes a pitch for his books in the same field of interest.

Another famous example years ago was the White House Company's "18 Top Hits" records. They sold up a storm of these records with a 15-minute radio show that they packaged for the stations they used. I have heard Standard & Poor's Corporation pitching its investment information services on Texas stations. Maybe the Texas millionaires make a good market for Standard & Poor's.

Per-inquiry (PI) deals constitute a good deal of radio mail-order advertising. If you have a product with radio possibilities, you must work up a sales letter to send to stations, pointing out how they can earn extra money with air time that would otherwise be without profit to them. Whether or not a station accepts your offer will depend on how persuasive you are in convincing them that the deal will be profitable, and it will also depend on station policy and the amount of air time they currently have available.

The advantages of radio are that you get results quickly and you don't tie up your money for long. Timeliness and short closing dates are other advantages. A disadvantage of purchased radio time (again except for PI) is that it requires extremely close watching and tight control. If your ads stop pulling and you don't notice for a while, you can lose your shirt.

Clear-channel stations—those that broadcast over a wide area of the country at night without interference from other stations—may be your best bets for a PI deal.

Mail-order offers have made money from radio, many of them on a straight time-purchase basis. A firm that sold "three maps for a dollar" did fabulously well on radio, if my memory serves me right.

One major disadvantage of both radio and television is the absence of a coupon that makes it "easy to order," but this obviously does not outweigh its advantages for some offers.

Descriptive data are in *Standard Rate & Data.*

Matchbooks

A large proportion of matchbooks that are distributed nationally carry mail-order advertising. Matchbooks are an excellent medium for offers that appeal to a mass audience rather than a specialized audience. Correspondence schools, especially those that offer high school-completion courses, use matchbooks a great deal. Address labels, Arizona and Florida land sales, insurance and auto-accessory firms, and stockbrokers use matchbooks. Surprising to me, at least one stamp firm appears to find matchbooks profitable.

Any offer with wide enough appeal should at least consider match covers. The big problem is that you can't test for less than a few thousand dollars. However, if your offer is well proved in other media, you can safely bet that even if the test is not a roaring success, you aren't likely to lose much, either.

A major advantage of matchbooks is that the entire inside cover makes a natural coupon. A frequent technique is to use a "reverse block" at the left of the inside cover as an arrow pointing to the fill-in lines.

Results come back slowly from matchbook advertising: 20 percent in the first 6 months, 75 percent in the first year, according to an industry source.

For further information, contact

Diamond Match Division, Diamond National Corporation, 733 Third Avenue, New York, NY 10017

Universal Match Corporation, 1 Penn Plaza, New York, NY 10001

Atlas Match Corporation, 1000 Avenue H.E., Arlington, TX 76011

Package Stuffers

Never send a package to customers without including an order blank for reorders and sales literature on other products. Package stuffers are the cheapest, yet most productive, medium for many mail-order firms.

Sometimes it is profitable to insert sales literature for drop-ship merchandise (i.e., merchandise that the wholesaler or manufacturer stocks for you). The manufacturer will often supply the sales literature to you. For example, White River Industries of Muskegon, Michigan, supplies complete sales literature for their branding iron, telling how it can be used to personalize items. Or you might even include an entire drop-ship catalog.

You should also consider including in your mailing one or more package inserts provided by others. Fingerhut carries six or eight outside pieces annually, and they net over $100,000 from these inserts alone.[6]

Bill Stuffers

If you have a proven mail-order offer that will offend no one's taste, you may be able to make a deal with department stores to include your sales literature, with their name and address on it, in the monthly bills they send to their customers. This is a per-inquiry, drop-ship arrangement. You pay them a fixed commission for every order they obtain, and you then ship the goods under their name.

A wide variety of mail-order merchandise has been sold in this way, especially the staples of mail-order. Personal stationery and address labels use this medium regularly. And there are several firms that specialize in selling magazine subscriptions through this medium. (The magazine-subscription firms go even further in making special arrangements. They print return envelopes, with an advertisement for the magazine inside the flap, for customers to return their monthly payments.)

Some big-ticket (i.e., high-unit-sale) merchandise, including cameras and optical equipment, has been sold through this technique.

Transit Advertising

This medium is known as "take-one" advertising, because the bus poster for a mail-order firm always includes coupons on a hook, with the caption, "take one."

A typical coupon is shown in Figure 23-1. Home-study courses for high school completion use a great deal of transit advertising, and it evidently is profitable for them. Transit advertising reaches a very wide mass market, which is good only for unspecialized mail-order products that interest all kinds of people.

Standard Rate & Data, Transportation Advertising Section, contains names and addresses of the media. The media will give you full details on what you need to know.

The fact that the bus company address is given on the coupon in Figure 23-1 leads me to think that it is a per-inquiry deal. You might check on this if you have an offer that would go well in transit advertising.

Another example of take-one advertising is the campus leave around shown in Figure 23-2.

Comic Books

Comic books are magazines, of course. But they deserve special mention here because they have such a special audience—ranging from

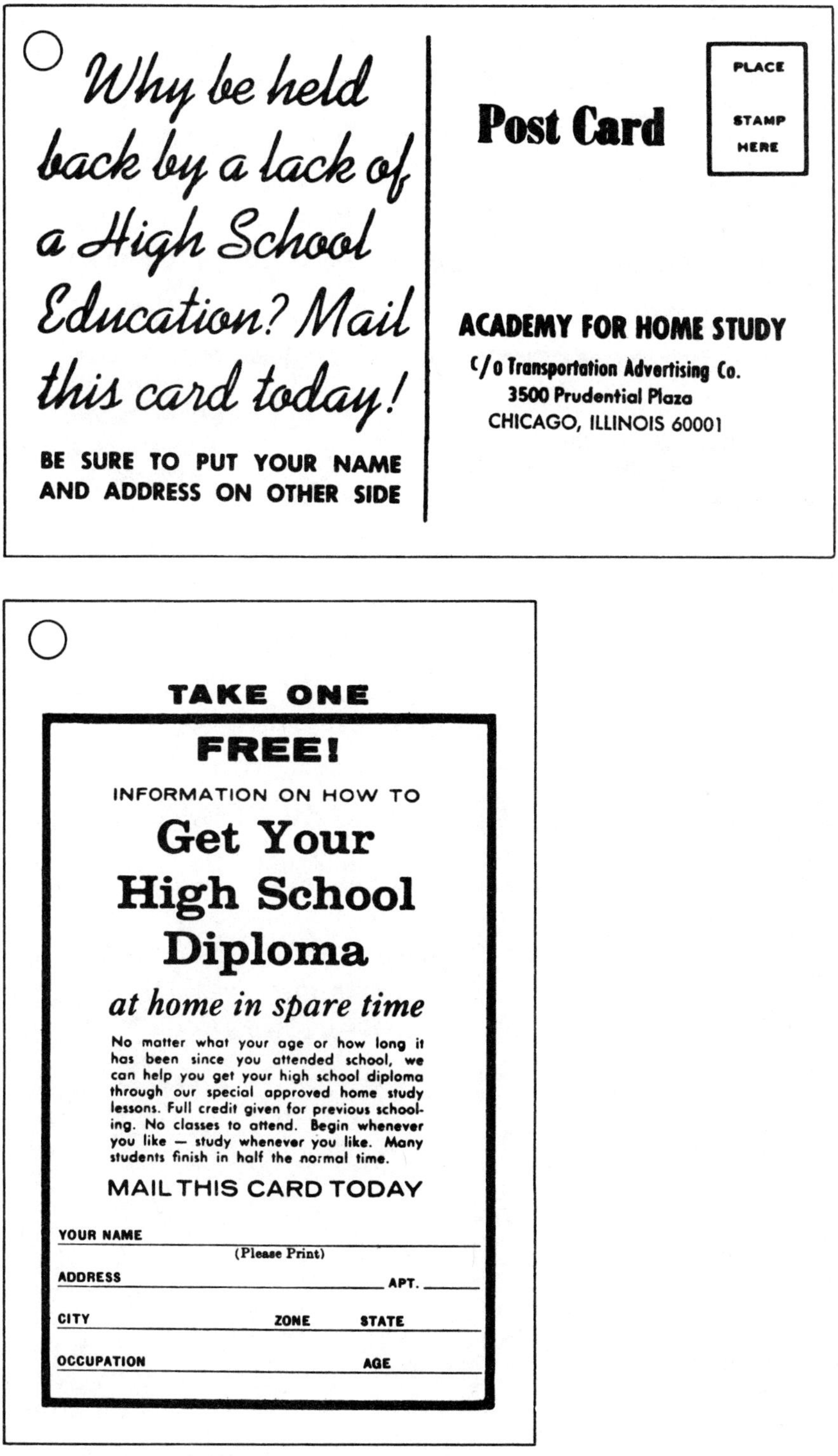

Figure 23-1 Example of transit "take-one" advertising.

BUSINESS REPLY MAIL
No postage stamp necessary if mailed in the United States
Postage will be paid by

FIRST CLASS
PERMIT NO. 22
CHICAGO, ILL.

TIME COLLEGE BUREAU
STUDENT SUBSCRIPTION SERVICE
301 EAST OHIO STREET
CHICAGO, ILLINOIS   60611

CAMPUS RATES

TIME: Please send me _____ issues for 25¢ an issue
and bill me later. Example: 40 issues/$10.00.
SPORTS ILLUSTRATED: Please send me _____ issues for
21¢ an issue and bill me later. Example: 40 issues/$8.40.
Minimum for TIME or SI subscription 25 issues; maximum 104.

FORTUNE: ☐ Please send 1 year for $11.
(12 monthly issues) (Payment must be enclosed.)

MONEY: ☐ Please send 1 year for $7.
(12 monthly issues)   65–159453

Continued service with prompt delivery guaranteed when you notify
us of your change of address.

Mr./Ms. _____
                          (please print)
Address _____ Apt. No. _____

City _____ State _____ Zip Code _____
                                      I am ☐ an undergraduate ☐ a graduate student.
Name of College or University _____
Year
studies end _____ **My major field of study is** _____ Please sign here _____

I am a ☐ faculty member ☐ administrator at ☐ elementary school ☐ high school ☐ college. Order not valid without
above information. Rates subject to change without notice. FORTUNE and MONEY are monthly magazines.
Please allow 60 days for shipment of your first issue. SI is published weekly except for a double issue at year end.

Figure 23-2 Examples of campus leave arounds.

Figure 23-2 (Continued)

bright 5-year-olds to uneducated adults. Advertisements for both children's goods (for example, BB guns) and adolescent and adult goods such as muscle-building and correspondence courses are run profitably in comic books. The Charles Atlas ad shown in Figure 23-3 is a long-running classic in comic books.

Daily Newspapers

Daily newspapers are not generally successful for mail-order offers. It is only the rare offer that can use them successfully. Almost always, it is a product that does not appeal to a specialized audience, but rather, a product whose purchasers must be drawn from the population as a whole.

The daily *New York Times* is apparently the only exception to the rule. On one Saturday there were, on one single page, large ads for

Figure 23–3 Famous example of comic book ad.

a digital thermometer; a fancy coat hanger; and filing cabinets, thermal shoes, plant pellets, and discount-price appliances. But in every one of these cases the firms also have retail outlets in or near New York, so the ads are selling both through mail order and through stores. It is doubtful that the mail-order sales alone could make these ads pay in *The New York Times.*

Correspondence courses in conversation improvement and English correction, antismoking remedies, seeds and nursery products, and special "health" clinics are examples of the successful users of daily newspapers.

Most of the examples given above use the "reading notice" form of ad. The ad looks like editorial matter and reads like a news story, offering further information at the bottom, without a coupon.

Big-city and small-city dailies are used by these offers at irregular intervals.

Some offers run ROP ("run of paper," i.e., wherever the newspaper finds it convenient to place the ad). Other offers specify sports page, garden page, etc.

Sunday Newspaper Inserts

One of the major developments since the first edition of this book has been the growth of mail-order advertising in inserts into Sunday newspapers.[7] These inserts are of various sorts: full-page inserts of four pages or more, smaller brochures of eight or sixteen pages, bound-in response cards, comic sections, and Sunday supplements. Let's start with the last.

There are three major syndicated Sunday supplements: *Family Weekly, Parade,* and *Sunday-Metro. Family Weekly* mostly goes into newspapers in many small cities, *Sunday-Metro* into about fifty of the biggest cities, and *Parade* into a hundred or so big and medium-sized cities. All of them carry a great deal of mail-order advertising. And they are favorite media for testing new offers because of the speed with which you can place an ad and get results. Testing can be done in selected cities. And *Parade* has a deal whereby you get a special discount if you run your mail-order advertising in "remnant" space, space in particular city editions where some package-goods advertisers don't want to advertise.

Inserts are really mail-order pieces prepared by the mail-order firm and carried by the newspaper distribution system instead of by the U.S. mail. Increases in postage costs have given a big boost to this growth because the cost of newspaper distribution of additional pages

✓ **CHECK YOUR SUBSCRIPTION SAVINGS**

One-year newsstand rate	$ 39
One-year subscription rate	$ 25
✓ **YOU SAVE**	**$ 14**
Two-year newsstand rate	$ 78
Two-year subscription rate	$ 42
✓ **YOU SAVE**	**$ 36**
Three-year newsstand rate	$117
Three-year subscription rate	$ 57
✓ **YOU SAVE**	**$ 60**

USE THIS HANDY CARD TO
ENTER YOUR MONEY-SAVING
SUBSCRIPTION TODAY.

HAVE ADVERTISING AGE EVERY MONDAY— and POCKET $14 TO BOOT !

Advertising Age: I like your saving ways. Enter my no-risk subscription as checked below. I understand that I may cancel at any time, and a FULL REFUND will be made for all unmailed copies.

□ 1 year (52 issues) $25. □ 2 years (104 issues) $42. □ 3 years (156 issues) $57. Europe & Middle East add $30 per year for jet-speeded delivery. Rate includes the monthly Advertising Age/EUROPE. All other foreign add $15 per year for surface delivery.

□ New subscription □ Renewal □ Bill me □ Bill company □ Payment enclosed.

Charge □ VISA □ Master Charge (Interbank No. _____)

Account No. _____ Exp. Date _____

Signature _____
SEND TO:
Name _____
                    PLEASE PRINT
Title _____

Firm _____

Type of Business _____

□ Busines □ Home Address _____

City _____ State _____ Zip _____

□ Send the monthly Advertising Age/EUROPE for just $16.
□ I would prefer not to receive information or advertising by mail from companies not affiliated with Crain Communications.

Figure 23-4   Example of magazine throw-in insert.

has grown less rapidly. There are twice as many of these self-standing stuffers in newspapers as the sum of all third-class mailings for mail-order prospects.[8]

The biggest users of inserts in Sunday newspapers have been firms whose products appeal to a very wide market: insurance companies, record and tape sellers, photo finishers, and catalog novelty firms such as Walter Drake. (The catalog novelty firms really put a section of their catalogs into the newspaper as a stuffer.)

Another type of insert is the magazine throw-in insert shown in Figure 23-4.

Other Media

Cooperative Mailings

Several offers can be mailed for the same bulk-rate postal charge. This naturally leads to the idea of splitting the cost among several different advertisers.

There are several firms that are in the business of organizing such mailings. For example, one day I received a mailing to "Occupant" containing offers from Colgate, United Film Club, and Ajax.

The R. H. Donnelley Marketing Corporation, 1235 N. Avenue, Nevada, IA 50201, operating under the trade name Carol Wright, has recently been doing a lot of co-op mailings, including photo, magazine, and appliance mail-order offers along with coupons for store-distributed products such as foods. An example is shown in Figure 23-5.

In the past, Shoppers Information Service, Inc., in New York, mailed huge quantities of a unique cooperative deal. For 10 cents the inquirer could get further information about any five offers that included correspondence courses, hearing aids, home-movie outfits, trips to Europe, insurance, franchises, and other offers that differ from mailing to mailing. The mail-order firms paid Shoppers Information Service a specified amount for each inquiry. Another firm used to send out cooperative mailings for firms that were seeking women agents for their products, or for women who wanted to work at home. Offers included Tandy Leather, H. B. Davis Catalog Sales, "Miracle Baskets," a candy-and-cake correspondence course, Christmas cards, etc.

Cooperative mailings can be categorized as follows:[9]

> What kind of co-ops are there? There are basically four kinds of co-ops in vogue today: mail-order co-ops; magazine co-ops; specialty co-ops; and mass consumer co-ops.
>
> 1. *The Mail Order Co-Op.*   A co-op mailing to a company's list of mail order buyers. A company will periodically mail its recent buyers list, usually with a covering letter. An example of this is the kind of mailing that is done by Ambassador Leather Goods to its list of mail order buyers—about two million names.
>
> 2. *Magazine Co-Op.*   A co-op which mails a magazine subscription list, the magazine itself being the entrepreneur, an example of this being the upcoming McCall's co-op.
>
> 3. *Specialty Co-Op.*   This is a co-op which is aimed at a specific age or demographic group. An example of this would be The Reuben H. Donnelley Young Family Co-Op to the new mother's list. Other examples are co-ops to college students, businessmen, and so forth. These can vary in size from just a few thousand to four or five million.
>
> 4. *Mass Consumer Co-Op.*   This is a co-op compiled from auto registration and telephone lists. It usually contains a combination of grocery cents-off coupons and mail-order offers. The Reuben H. Donnelley Carol Wright co-op, the only large mass-compiled co-op in the field currently mailing, mails about twenty-one million households seven or eight times a year.
>
> 5. *Co-Op Self-Standing Stuffers in Newspapers.*

FREE How to Pull Customers With Direct Mail

Gives You Tips the "Pros" Use . . . One of Today's Most Sought-After Guidebooks!

IT'S FREE—along with a 15-day Trial Examination of "THE CARR SPEIRS DIRECT MAIL ADVERTISING KIT"—

600 Letterheads with eye-catching art and striking headlines . . . 500 Attractive envelopes that get your letter sorted out from others . . . 60 Cards for short, sharp messages!

ONLY IF YOU ARE COMPLETELY SATISFIED with your Kit must you keep it for only $24.50, plus small shipping charge. Otherwise, return it at any time during your 15-day trial period, and PAY NOTHING!

Keep your FREE Guidebook in any case! FILL IN BELOW, DETACH AND RETURN THIS CARD!

NAME _____ FIRM _____

ADDRESS _____ CITY _____ STATE _____ ZIP_____
                                                                    CSDM-MBB 579

DON'T DROP THIS CARD IN THE MAIL!

Just pick up your phone and call us TOLL-FREE
800-621-5809
(In Illinois, 800-972-5858)

24 HOURS A DAY, 7 DAYS A WEEK
Ask for Allan Caplan

If you're short on time, tell us and we'll mail you complete information the same day. Naturally, there's no obligation.

MBB 3/79

Ring America™

6220 North California Ave. ★ Chicago, IL 60659

Figure 23-5 Examples of pack-of-cards co-op mailings.

6. *"Marriage Mail."* Two or more local offers combined in the same package.

A typical charge for a co-op mailing was $12.50 per thousand of your inserts that will be distributed. It was also sometimes possible to arrange a PI (per-inquiry deal). "A loose insert might run $12 to $15 per thousand for moderate distribution (the advertiser provides the insert). Substantial discounts are available for multimillion circulation. Post card circulation can range anywhere from $5.50 per thousand to $25 per thousand (including printing cost)."[10] For information on current co-op mailings, see the section in Standard Rate & Data Service's *Direct Mail Lists, Rates and Data,* and the classified advertising section of *Direct Marketing* magazine.

This recent news report is of interest:[11]

> MONTGOMERY WARD is selling advertising space to outsiders in its catalogs. The Mobil Corp. subsidiary began testing the idea a year or so ago with a few mail-order ads for RCA and Columbia phonograph records and for book clubs. Now, terming the tests a success, Ward plans to expand outside ad sales sharply. The company says it already has signed up $2 million of ads through 1979 and is "shooting for $4 million, though $3 million may be more realistic." Ward hopes to have one major auto maker's ads soon, plus those of non-competitive companies producing foods, pharmaceuticals and household products.
>
> Ward says the widely circulated catalogs are attractive to advertisers, because of whom and where they reach: A balanced readership of 55% female and 45% male with an annual average income of $19,800. Readers are heavily rural, where such advertising would be likely to have the biggest impact, says Ward.

Mass Consumer Magazines

For most mail-order firms, *Reader's Digest, TV Guide,* and similar magazines are not likely to be profitable. But there are some firms that use them profitably on scattered occasions. Some major mail-order firms go there first. These firms have offers that have a very wide market, involve considerable sums of money over the long haul, and have almost saturated their other mail-order markets.

Examples of such firms are the record and book clubs, La Salle Extension University's law courses, and film developing.

Analysis of profitable media and seasons in mass consumer magazines must be different from other mail-order media, because there are no competitive ads to check. Therefore, you must analyze readership, rates, and seasonal patterns just the way non-mail-order advertisers do. However, the second time you advertise, you will be able to use your own figures as a basis for your reckoning.

Assorted Minor Media

Mail-order people are ingenious, and they have successfully used many odd types of media from time to time. For example, Figure 23-6 shows an offer on a shopping bag handed out in drugstores. Insert cards in paperback books are an important medium for some advertisers, especially magazine-circulation offers.

Though we call these media "minor," any one of them can be major to you if your product fits the medium.

Figure 23-7 shows mail-order solicitations for film developing that are placed around the necks of catsup bottles sold in supermarkets. There are also mail-order advertisements on many food packages (especially cereals) which are often cooperative deals between the food brand and the mail-order advertiser, designed partly to sell mail-order merchandise and partly to promote sales of the brand ("send four labels plus $1 to. . . .").

Foreign Media

The United States is such a huge mail-order market that American marketers (for whom this book is mainly written) have in the past preferred to develop new offers for the American market rather than develop foreign markets for their well-established products. But in the last few years the foreign mail-order markets have grown so fast that professional American firms have aggressively begun to operate overseas.[12] Bell & Howell, for instance, has made the necessary changes in the cooperative deals it runs with U.S. credit-card list owners and has successfully exported the deals to several foreign countries. Diners Club has been in business in Europe for more than 20 years. Fingerhut began operations in France in 1972, and so on. Of course nationals of other countries have long had active mail-order businesses at home (see Figures 23-8 and 23-9) and also in other countries. For example, the London Educational Association (LEA) markets correspondence courses not only in Great Britain but also in countries in which a fairly large number of people speak English, and especially where there is an English newspaper such as the *Jerusalem Post* in Israel. Figure 23-10 shows three LEA ads from the *same page* of the *Jerusalem Post*. In Great Britain itself, the largest segment of the mail-order business is done by catalogs together with agents who call at peoples' homes. There is a big future for mail order in foreign markets.

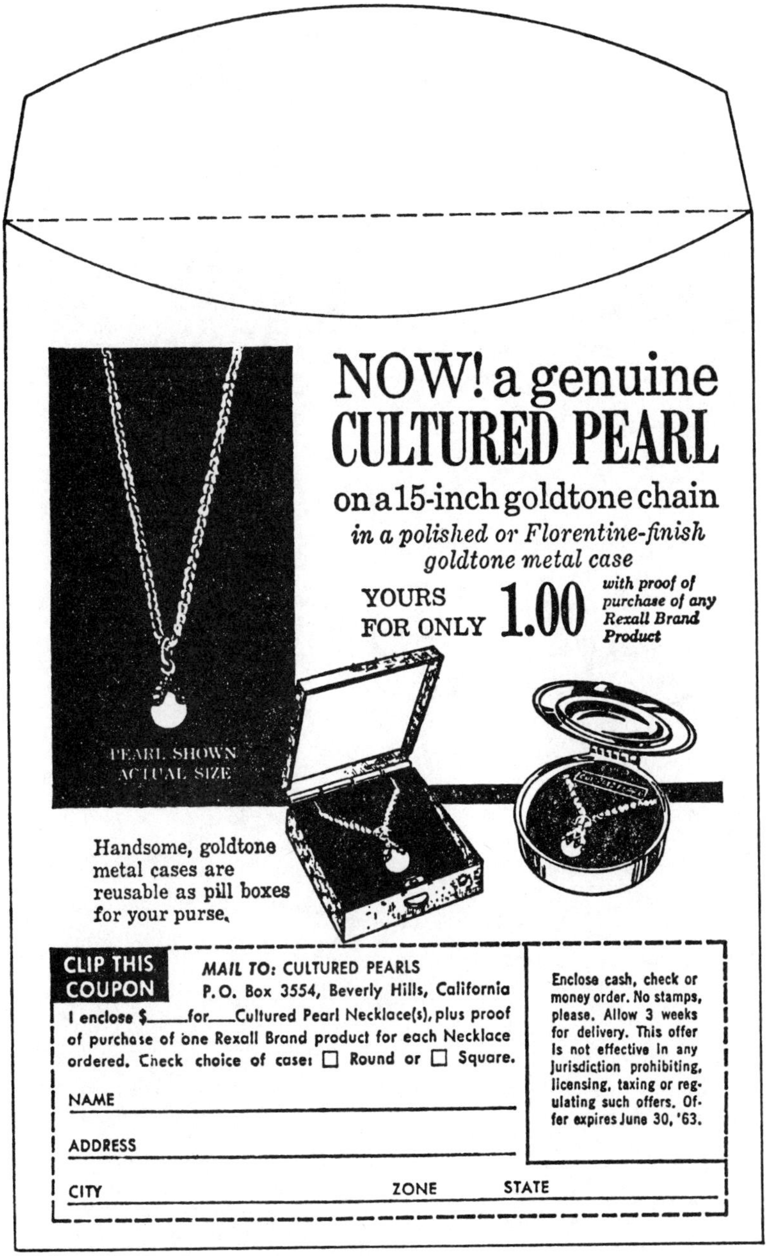

Figure 23-6 Example of shopping-bag offer.

Figure 23-7 Example of ad around catsup bottle.

Figure 23-8 Example of British mail order.

Figure 23-9 More advertising in British newspapers.

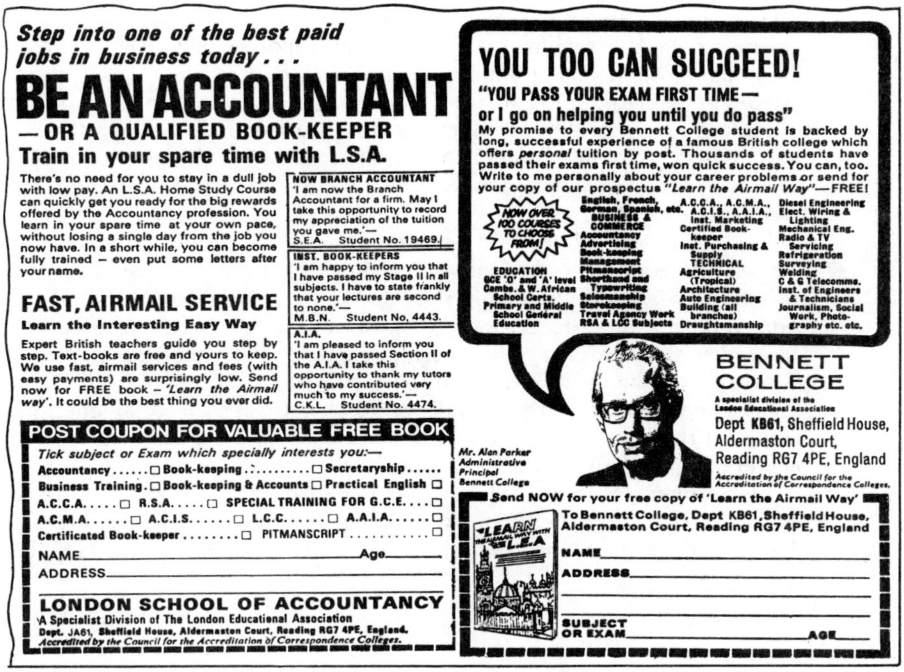

Figure 23-10   Ad for British school in Israeli paper.

Incidentally, the United States is a foreign market to firms outside this nation. And in some cases one can sell through mail order in the United States *from abroad*. A successful example is the Hong Kong clothing industry. There are about seventy firms that sell suits made in Hong Kong to American buyers, formerly through ships calling at Hong Kong and now through agents in this country and through mail-order catalogs.

The marketing systems used by mail-order firms are quite different in the three largest European mail-order markets, as described by a British writer:[13]

CATALOGUE SHOPPING SYSTEMS

In the UK, the majority of mail order sales are derived from some 3 million agents running catalogues (free to them but costing at least £3 each to produce). The agent gets a commission (normally 10 per cent in cash or 12½ per cent if taken in goods) on the catalogue price of everything she buys, either for herself and her family or friends and neighbours. The total number of catalogue customers is about 20 million. The companies send goods on two weeks' free approval and pay all the costs of postage and delivery, in both directions. There is no interest charge and no deposit is required for items which you can pay for in up to 38 weekly installments. Durables and more expensive items may be bought over two years at a reasonable rate of interest. Easy weekly payments and the convenience of choosing at home from a catalogue featuring up to 25,000 'product options' are the main reasons for the success of this £1,700 million per annum industry which accounts for nearly 9 per cent of all non-food retail sales, a proportion which has doubled since 1961.

France is a complete contrast. The customer runs the catalogue for herself but she has to pay for the privilege of owning it: the charge of around £1.50 being refundable after the first purchase from it. Catalogue companies are lucky to get more than three orders a year from an active customer. Cash trading is far more important than credit, thus there is little risk of bad debt. No commission is paid. Some people will buy a catalogue and never order at all, preferring to use the catalogue as a guide to the latest styles (Paris fashions are famous through the world), materials, merchandise and prices.

In Germany, both the agency and personal shopping systems are to be found in various degrees. Even though commission may on average be earned at only one half of the UK rate, this is nevertheless an important attraction in this market.

Telephone Solicitations

Soliciting orders by telephone is rather different from using the other media. For years the telephone has been used to generate leads by such firms as Encyclopaedia Britannica, where the sales representatives spend the morning telephoning people from up-and-down-the-street telephone lists. In recent years, as it has become possible to rent a WATS (wide-area or even nationwide) telephone line, firms have begun to make more solicitations by phone. An interesting new twist has been the use of taped messages from famous people; the operator gets the listener's permission to play the tape, and then afterward takes the order.

The telephone can also be valuable in confirming big orders that come in by mail. At the same time, additional business is solicited.

Use a Variety of Media

Though some media work better than do others for any given product, it is a rare product that can only use one medium profitably. And you may saturate any one given medium. Therefore, you must always think in terms of *many* media—space plus direct mail or space plus radio or matchbooks plus space and so on. And constantly keep on the lookout for additional media that may pay out for you.

24

How to Score
with Catalogs

*Fundamental Elements of Successful Catalogs /
Projecting Total Catalog Sales / How Much Will
the Catalog Cost? / The Key Decisions in Catalog
Selling /Order Forms / Postscript*

With every passing year, catalogs are increasingly the dominant aspect of the mail-order business. Therefore, no matter how you start out in business and how you get your initial orders—from magazine advertisements, classifieds, or direct mail—sooner or later (and preferably sooner) you are going to find yourself preparing and mailing a catalog of a line of products. In truth, operating without a catalog of offerings is likely to be impossible for most mail-order ventures.

Let's say that you have developed a single product that you are successfully selling by mail. The product could be a patented stretcher for emergency crews in fire and police departments. It could be a book on macramé that appeals to people because its instructions are so clear, or a book on how to make wine at home. Or it could be a film-developing service. All the people who started by selling these single products later expanded into selling related products with a catalog: emergency and safety equipment of all kinds, books of instructions for other crafts, and the ingredients and tools for making wine at home.

These examples illustrate one major route into mail-order catalog selling: Find a single product you can sell successfully, and then find related products that you can sell to the people who buy your original product. Then you must find additional products, either in or out of your current catalog, that you can use to attract new customers to your catalog, because any one single product tends to wear out as your new-customer seller (though you can often go back to it later).

(Sometimes you can go on and on with your original new-customer offer—as for example, the sampler packages of condoms or of fancy teas that continue to bring in new customers for catalog sellers of condoms and tea. Samplers are unusually effective in continuing to pull new customers to your catalog.)

Or, let's say that you are a retailer of foreign tires and wheels, art supplies, camping equipment, golf clubs, or office supplies. You have a good business, but your expansion is limited by the size of the community you are in. One possibility is to expand your retail operation into other cities or towns. But you might also consider selling your product attractively and cheaply by mail, while taking advantage of the inventory, warehouse facilities, and organization that you already maintain. Two quick examples discussed earlier: (1) Eddie DiNicolantonio branched out into mail-selling from his Atlantic City wholesale printed-T-shirt operation, and (2) Lou Burnett based his mail-order golf-equipment business on the pro-shop sales at his golf course in Warner Robins, Georgia.

Let's *not* say that you are an individual or a firm starting from scratch that decides to build a catalog of gift merchandise or even of specialty merchandise and dumps a flock of catalogs in the mail at Christmas. Let's not say it because you *should not do it*. Starting off from scratch with a mail-order catalog is an expensive ticket to going bust. I've been asked for advice dozens of times by people who have had this dream, and I've known secondhand about hundreds more. Some people took my advice to drop the idea. But of those who went ahead, I haven't heard of more than a small percentage who made good. It is just too tough a way to go.

Of course there are outstanding and well-publicized exceptions such as Roger Horchow, who started the Horchow Collection catalog of jewelry and other gifts, and who had perhaps $37 million in annual sales just four years after opening up.[1] But before starting that operation, Horchow had been a successful vice-president of mail-order activities at Neiman-Marcus department stores, and he had developed a mail-order operation at the Kenton Corporation. Furthermore, he reportedly dropped several million dollars in the first years he operated. So it doesn't pay to take such an exception as your model. To put it differently: A catalog operation should develop as an expansion of your other activities—your retail store, or your proved mail-order products.

Sometimes you can get around this start-up problem by finding a retail firm with whom you can make a deal to start a mail-order catalog operation. I once found an art-supplies store with a wonderful inventory that I could work with in starting a catalog operation, avoiding all inventory problems. And I was able to find firms that had parts of catalogs that I could combine into one large catalog, avoiding the heavy expense of catalog artwork and type. In that way I was able to get into the artist's supply business at acceptable cost, and try out various modes of doing business. But eventually you must either obtain your supplies from the retailer at a rock-bottom price, or you must go straight to the original suppliers yourself.

But now after having warned you of the hazards of breaking in with a catalog, I'm going to reverse my field completely and tell you that *some* kind of a catalog is usually *absolutely necessary for success* in a mail-order operation. The key point—as I've tried to stress at various other places—is that mail-order businesses must usually sell *an entire line of goods*, rather than just a single item. It is the *repeat business* that enables a mail-order business to make money even if it cannot make money (or even "loses money") on the initial sale. Of course there are a few firms that manage to jump from one successful novelty or big-ticket item to another, but they are scarce as hens' teeth. And that sort of business is super-competitive. So repeat sales are the key to success in the mail-order business. And a catalog is the key to repeat sales.

It is sometimes possible to generate repeat sales with the same item; this is how magazines operate, by selling subscription renewals. But for most other sorts of mail-order businesses, the repeat orders come from catalog sales.

So we have a dilemma! You can't do without the repeat business that a catalog provides, but you can't afford to jump right in with a catalog. What to do? How can you ease between the horns of this dilemma?

Luckily, the situation is not as bad as it seems. You can get your repeat sales without building a full-fledged catalog by backing your initial order with a small brochure that advertises related products, or with a bunch of loose package-stuffer offers, or with a packet of cards either sent with the order, or mailed afterwards. Examples of such packets of cards are shown in Figures 24-1 and 24-2. This "bounce back" business is likely to make the difference between success and failure.

"But a brochure is really no different from a catalog," you may say. Indeed, there is not a difference between a four-page brochure and a ninety-six-page catalog—except that one may cost 50 times as

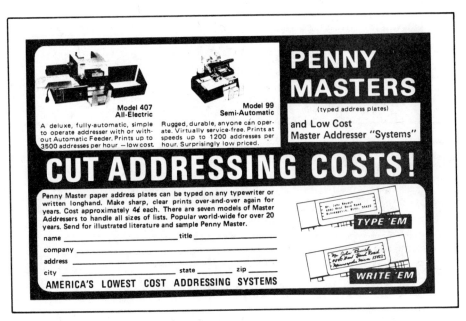

Figure 24-1 Two of the postpaid cards in the marketing and promotion bulletin board sent to lists of marketing executives.

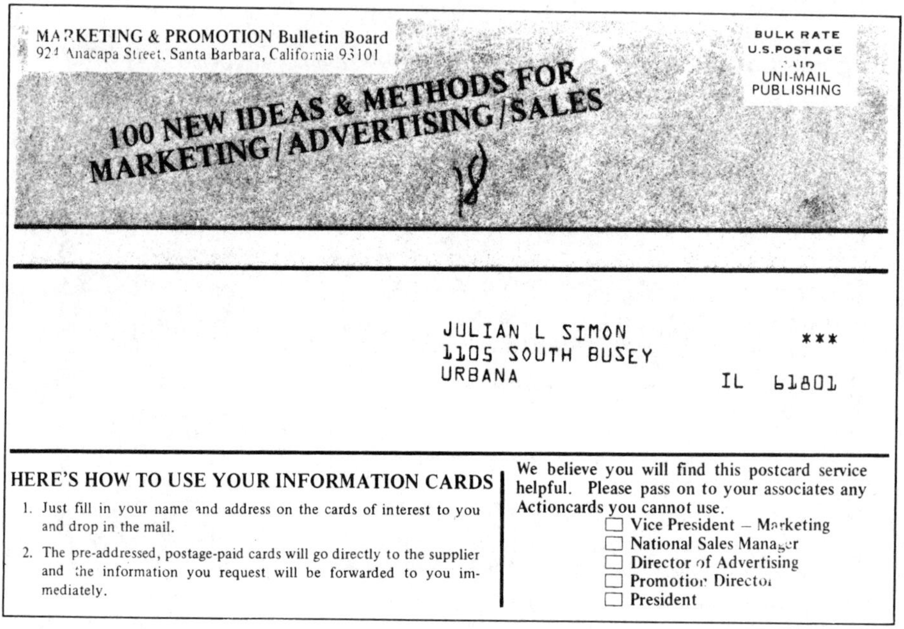

MARKETING & PROMOTION Bulletin Board
921 Anacapa Street, Santa Barbara, California 93101

BULK RATE
U.S.POSTAGE
PAID
UNI-MAIL
PUBLISHING

100 NEW IDEAS & METHODS FOR
MARKETING/ADVERTISING/SALES

JULIAN L SIMON   ***
1105 SOUTH BUSEY
URBANA   IL 61801

HERE'S HOW TO USE YOUR INFORMATION CARDS

1. Just fill in your name and address on the cards of interest to you and drop in the mail.

2. The pre-addressed, postage-paid cards will go directly to the supplier and the information you request will be forwarded to you immediately.

We believe you will find this postcard service helpful. Please pass on to your associates any Actioncards you cannot use.
☐ Vice President — Marketing
☐ National Sales Manager
☐ Director of Advertising
☐ Promotion Director
☐ President

Figure 24-2

much as the latter. It might cost you $100 to prepare 1,000 four-page 5½- × 8½-inch brochures in black and white, whereas 10,000 ninety-six-page catalogs might cost you—never mind, I don't want to scare you, and you get the idea.

Catalogs evolve out of brochures and package stuffers. Building a profitable catalog is usually a gradual process requiring a great deal of trial-and-error to learn about which products will sell well for you when they are combined in a catalog with your other products. Therefore you should think of your first brochures as the seeds of your future catalog. Then you should look at each successively larger and better catalog as a way station. After all, that's how Sears, Roebuck did it—most other successful catalog firms, too—and that's how Sears gradually made the transition to its present status of more than half of its catalogs being for specialties.

Before beginning work on a catalog of your own—or even on a small brochure—invest a lot of time in studying the catalogs of other firms. Write for a variety of them from advertisements in hunting-and-fishing magazines, "shelter" magazines, and the magazines in the trade that cover the range of products you are interested in. And save all the catalogs you get from being on direct-mail lists.

The management of a catalog mail-order operation can be divided into two general sets of activities:

1. *Marketing, or "the front end."* This includes all decisions about pricing, which items to put into the catalog and how much space to give them, how big the catalog will be, how often it will be mailed to which lists, and so on. These decisions are discussed in this chapter and also elsewhere in the book as they pertain to mail-order operations generally.

2. *Processing, or "the back end."* Aspects of order processing are discussed in Chapter 30 on computers.

Once more, like a broken record, comes my advice to focus your attention upon selling a product line to *businesses* rather than selling gifts and other consumer goods. Look at the catalog page reproduced in Figure 3-6. The catalog of Theta Industrial Products is sent to high school shop teachers. The catalog is very simple, and it can be produced very inexpensively. Yet it is quite sufficient to do its job. It would be much easier for you to get into a business like this one, and the competition probably would be much less cutthroat than in most lines of general consumer goods.

Figure 24-3 shows a catalog page from another sort of mail-order operation selling to business. Again, the catalog does not need to be nearly as slick and expensive as general consumer catalogs.

A happy new development for catalog sellers is the publication *Catalog Age*. In 1985 it is in its second year but already is a hefty publication full of informative articles and advertisements. And best of all, it is free to all catalog marketers. They are at 125 Elm Street, P.O. Box 4006, New Canaan, CT 06840-4006.

Fundamental Elements of Successful Catalogs

Here are some brief guidelines about what makes a catalog successful:

1. *More attractive, interesting, useful, and solid merchandise.* Your catalog has to be a place where people want to shop, a "store" that has merchandise they want to buy.

2. *Acceptable prices.* In some businesses, your appeal can be that your prices are lower than people can find elsewhere; an example is Burnett's cut-rate golf club business mentioned earlier. But the prices of the merchandise in most mail-order catalogs are not significantly lower than in other outlets. People shop through the catalogs, nevertheless, because (1) they find merchandise they can't conveniently find elsewhere, e.g., Sunset House novelties; (2) the catalog is a more

NEW ORDER PICKING TRUCK
1500 lb. capacity

Sloping shelves keep items secure!

Built to last a lifetime, ideal for sorting, picking and transporting parts, tools, assemblies, and much more! Open wire mesh provides easy visibility, reduces dust build-up. Sloped super-strong 14 gauge steel shelves hold up to 300 lbs. each. Full height center divider panel offers utmost storage flexibility. Bottom shelf has retaining lip to keep material from falling. Sturdy 1½" x 1½" angle posts for superior strength and stability. Optional hook-on clip board for easy logging of material. Easy-rolling 5" dia. hard rubber casters in a diamond pattern for tight turning capability. Rubber corner bumpers protect aisles and walls. Safety alert orange finish. 48"L x 28"W x 54"H overall.

Model 225100	$425.00
Model 225102 Optional Clip Board Shelf	$29.00

1500 lb. capacity

HI-END PLATFORM TRUCK
Save Time...Labor ...Money

Increase productivity...capable of handling more merchandise than several handtrucks and stock carts combined. Rugged steel bound wood deck or zinc plated galvanized steel deck. Two removable extra-high end handles prevent merchandise from falling off. Six wheel...full maneuverability, turns in its own radius. Two 8" rubber tired wheels and four 4" rubber wheel swivel casters.

	WOOD DECK				GALVANIZED STEEL DECK		
L" x W" x H"	Model	1-2	3+		Model	1-2	3+
48 x 16 x 61	168000	$153.00	$144.85		168004	$200.00	$189.95
60 x 16 x 61	168002	157.85	149.35		168006	204.65	193.65
48 x 24 x 58					168008	229.25	216.95
60 x 24 x 58					168010	247.50	233.95

NESTING PLATFORM TRUCK
1000 lbs. capacity

NEW

10 CARTS OCCUPY ONLY 14 FT. SPACE

Nests to less than ⅓ actual size!

Unique nesting feature saves valuable floor space. When not in use, deck rises to allow next truck to nest. Perfect for stockroom, production and other plant areas. Roomy 46" x 25" x 14"H deck allows easy-on and off material handling. Convenient 22" x 8" x 10"H wire utility basket. Heavy gauge all-welded steel frame for years of trouble-free service. Easy-rolling 5" dia. polyurethane casters, 2 swivel, 2 rigid. Handy offset handle for added maneuverability. Blue enamel finish. Shipped ready for immediate use. 57"L x 30"W x 40"H overall.

		Price	
Model	Description	1-2	3+
795100	Wood Deck	$251.50	$237.90
795102	Galvanized Deck	267.30	252.90

GALVANIZED STOCK CART

AS LOW AS $131.00

NEW

Rust and corrosion resistant galvanized steel 40" x 17" top shelf. Ideal for food and wet type operations. Unique all welded 1" tubular zinc plated steel "X" frame for maximum strength and ease of loading. Convenient push handle, 2 protective corner bumpers. Four 5" dia. rubber wheel casters, 2 swivel, 2 rigid, for easy mobility. Shipped ready for instant use. 32"H.

	1-2	3+
Model 795104	$138.80	$131.30

SEMI-LIVE SKID SYSTEM 2000 lbs. capacity

These semi-live skid platforms are ruggedly built, have small turning radius, seasoned hardwood platform, strengthened with cross battens. 8" x 2" rubber tired roller bearing wheels. One jack handle is sufficient for a number of platforms. Platforms conveniently stack in little space when not in use.

A single jack can easily be used to pull different platforms

Model	Size"	1-5	6-11	12+
952170	24 x 48	$112.00	$104.00	$ 95.00
952172	24 x 60	126.00	117.00	107.00
952174	30 x 48	130.00	121.00	111.00
952176	30 x 60	136.00	127.00	116.00
952178	36 x 60	148.00	138.00	126.00
952180	36 x 72	160.00	149.00	136.00
952182	Jack Handle	76.00	71.00	65.00

Figure 24-3 Example of mail order to businesses.

convenient way to shop, for example, doctor's office supplies by mail, or condoms in privacy by mail; or (3) the catalog offers a wider selection of merchandise than is available in local stores, for example, L. L. Bean's or Eddie Bauer's outdoor goods.

3. *The merchandise must have a common theme.* This is so that people who are interested in buying some of your merchandise will be likely to buy your other merchandise. Like any store, your catalog must appeal to people with particular interests, or to a particular part of their lives. For example, doctors' office supplies—stationary, forms, records of all kinds—all belong in the same catalog. You might also be able to include some medical instruments, too, but then again you might not be successful with them; it is even less likely that you would be able to profitably include a special golf-club offer, even though many doctors play golf.

Only Sears, Wards, Penney's, and Aldens can try to be full-line department stores in a catalog. Every other successful catalog firm is a specialist in one way or another, even the novelty and gift catalogs like Sunset House.

4. *You must display your merchandise well.* You must also tell enough about it so the reader understands exactly what you are selling. This doesn't mean fancy artwork; single black-and-white photos will do or even a listing, as in Montgomery Ward's catalog of 1875 (Figure 24-4), Carobil's catalog (Figure 24-5), or Morningside Bookshop's (Figure 24-6). But this does mean *facts,* not just glowing adjectives; the Sears catalog is the great masterpiece of this writing skill of giving people selling facts about merchandise.

5. *Give a solid money-back guarantee.* This will give new customers confidence in you and old customers will feel free to order and inspect.

6. *Include testimonials from satisfied customers.* Scatter them throughout the catalog, wherever you have a spare bit of white space. One of the few firm rules of mail order: testimonials help sell.

7. *Make your order blank as clear and easy to use as is humanly possible.* DON'T SKIMP ON ATTENTION TO THE ORDER BLANK—IT IS SUPREMELY IMPORTANT. Copy the best features of other firms' order blanks that will serve your purpose.

8. *Try offering free telephone service.* Don't decide against a WATS line or an 800 number unless you are *very* sure it doesn't pay for you. (Later we'll talk about how to decide.) A big advantage of telephone ordering is that it usually increases the size of the order, which is *very* important in the long-run profit picture.

Electronic catalogs and push-button ordering will be with us sometime—but they certainly are not important yet, even in Great Britain, where the technique is furthest advanced.

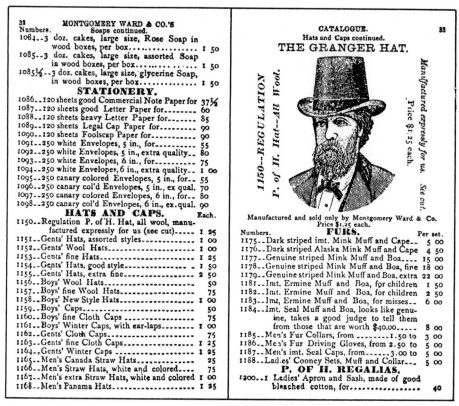

Figure 24-4 A page from Montgomery Ward's catalog of 1875.

9. *The overwrap.* This is a four-page sheet that goes on the outside of the catalog; it has come into much favor recently, and often seems to work well. On it you can easily vary the cover letter to the various market segments to which you send the catalog. And on it you can also try out various new offers with an eye to including them in the catalog later.

Projecting Total Catalog Sales

The heart of catalog-operation management is your analysis of the sales results after catalogs have been at work. We shall shortly be discussing how to make decisions about the size, frequency, and composition of the catalog on the basis of the results from the catalog as a whole and from particular items.

DWARF VARIETIES

These varieties generally grow to about 8 inches

$1.25 each

__AMBROSE (Stringer '66) fully double rosettes of creamy white flushed pale pink

__BANTAM, double, orange-salmon, dark foliage, bushy plant

__BUMBLEBEE, single, bright red flowers, deep green foliage

__BLACK DWARF, double, dark red flowers, dark green leaves

__CAROLYN, (our own) single, large salmon shading to a clear white edge

__DELICATE, double, white with light pink edges, light green foliage

__EMMA HOSSLER, double, light pink with white center, light green foliage

__EPSILON, single, large pinkish white with deeper pink ring, light green foliage

__FLIRT, double, blooms are creamy white flecked with salmon

__GRACIE WELLS, single mauve flowers with white base to the upper petals, dark foliage

__GREY SPRITE (Miller '69) dark green leaves with a narrow white border, single salmon-pink blooms

__GYPSY GEM, double, ruffled cherry red flowers, dark leaves

__JANET KERRIGAN, double, salmon-apricot, well-zoned foliage

__JAYNE EYRE (Stringer '68) a deep shade of lavender, double

__KEEPSAKE, double, light violet with a white eye, dark foliage

__KIRSTA, medium ball-shaped double flowers of mandarin red. Dark green foliage with a black zone

__LITTLE DARLING, single, bright pink flowers produced in abundance, bushy, light green leaves

__MASQUERADE (Duren) bushy plant covers itself with single soft rosy-salmon flowers with white centers on upper petals

__MEROPE, double dark red flowers with dark green leaves

__MISS WACKLES (Stringer '70) large deep red double flowers, outstanding English variety

__MR. EVERAARTS, double, medium rose-pink with white center, medium green leaves

__SUSIE BELLE, single salmon nicely veined flowers, well zoned leaves

__MEDLEY, double, white tinted with pink, dark leaves

__MOONBEAMS, single, large salmon flowers, dark foliage

__MORE MISCHIEF, double, creamy pink narrow twisted petals

__ORANGE GALORE, single, large bright orange flowers, dark leaves, very showy

__ORCHID PALOMA (Boone '75) double orchid-pink with a small red blotch on each petal

__PERKY, single, large bright red flower, white eye

__TIBERIUS, double, partly ruffled salmon-pink, bushy

Figure 24-5 The Carobil Farm's 20-page catalog offers customers over 400 different varieties of geraniums. It is mailed to a list of 12,000 during the months of January and February. No photographs are included in the catalog because, according to Bill Foster, most people on his list are aware of the kind of plant being offered. He also said photographs were eliminated to keep down production costs.

A Proposed Morningside Reprint

DYER: Compendium of the War of the Rebellion
This Volume printed in 1908 and reprinted in 1959 is an information packed volume of 1796 pages — we propose to reprint it on heavy paper and split it into 2 Volumes.
This contains a summary of troops furnished by States, Losses, Statistics, National Cemeteries, complete list of Regiments, Batteries raised by each state, a list of 900 regiments that lost 50 or more, The Military Divisions, the Organization of the Armies. The composition of all the Armies, East and West and almost 800 pages of short Histories of all the Federal Regiments, and very well indexed.
I can sell all the 1959 reprints I can get at $65.00, so here is a bargain that will be on heavy paper and sturdily bound. If you have never seen this book, ask a friend or any Librarian if you should own a copy at $48.00. After publication the price will be $60.00 at least.

Check the card and mail

Southern contingent particularly, will read with pleasure. Illustrations, maps, appendix, etc. (P. W. 5/26/75) 249 pp, dj, new. $8.95
378. **DAVIS, WM. C.: The Battle of Bull Run.** 298 pp, index, illus, maps. $9.95
379. **DAVIS, WILLIAM C. BRECKENRIDGE: Statesman, Soldier, Symbol.** The Complete Book that the Civil War student has waited years for— Vice President of the U. S. at 35 years of age, candidate for U. S. President in 1860, a Kentucky lawyer, a Congressman, a Brig. Gen. in C.S.A., one of the most fascinating careers in armies. 744 pp, L.S.U. Press. $17.50
J. C. Breckenridge was V.P. of the U. S. at age 35 and one of the candidates for President in 1860—a member of Pres. Davis' cabinet and a General in the field. Such a study of Breckenridge as Davis has done is long overdue.
380. **DAVIS, WILLIAM C., Duel Between the First Ironclads**, the famous Civil War battle at sea between the Union ironclad **Monitor** and the Confederacy's Virginia, the redesigned and rebuilt U.S.S. **Merrimack**, 201 pp., index, illus, 13.2x20.3 cm, dj, 1975. $8.95
381. **DAWSON, SARAH M.: A Confederate Girl's Diary.** Robertson, James I., ed. 1972. Repr. of 1960 ed. Lib. bdg. $19.75
382. **DAY, SAMUEL P.:** Down South; or an Englishman's Experience at the seat of the American War. 2 vols. (Research & Source Works Ser. No. 349) 1971. Repr. of 1862 ed. Set. Lib. bdg. $35.00
382A. **DAYTON, RUTH WOODS, The Diary of a Confederate Soldier**, James E. Hall, 141 pp, Charleston, 1961. $6.00
383. **DEBRAY, X. B., A Sketch of the History of Debray's 26th Regiment of Texas Cavalry.** $7.50
384. **DeFOREST, J. W.: Miss Ravenel's Conversion from Secession to Loyalty.** Gaicht, G. S., ed. $6.00
385. DEGLER, CARL N.: The Other South: Southern Dissenters in the 19th Century, 1974.   Paper $3.95
386. **DELANEY, CALDWELL: Confederate Mobile**, A Pictorial History, 360 pp, illus, cloth, 21x 27.7 cm, 1971. $25.00
387. **DELANEY, NORMAN C., John McIntosh Kell of the Raider Alabama**, 270 pp, index, photos, dj, 15x22.9 cm, 1973 Alabama. $8.50

388. **DE LEEIEW, ADELE**, Civil War Nurse **Mary Ann Bickerdyke**, 158 pp, index, 1973, New York, 13.6x20.8 cm, cloth. $6.00
389. **DeLEON, THOMAS COOPER, Four Years in Rebel Capital.** Orig. pub. Mobile, Ala. 1890, Reprinted 1975. 376 pp, frontis, 13.8x21.4 cm. $18.00
An inside view of life in the Southern Confederacy, from Birth to Death, from Original Notes, Collated in the Years 1861 to 1865, with Biographical Sketch of the Author by Louis de V. Chaudron.
390. **DeLEON, T. C.: Joseph Wheeler, The Man, The Statesman, The Soldier.** Facsimile reprint of rare 1899 edition. 13.8x18.6 cm, 142 pp, Kennesaw, Georgia 1960. $7.50
391. **DeLEON, THOMAS C.: Belles, Beaux & Brains of the 60's.** (Women in America Ser.) Illus, 1974. $27.00
391A. DeLEON, THOMAS C.: South Songs: From the Lays of Later Days, 1977. Repr. of 1866 ed., lib. bdg. $11.50
392. **DELL, CHRISTOPHER, Lincoln and The War Democrats**, The Grand Erosion of Conservative Tradition, introduction, 455 pp, index, bibliography, 15.2x23.5 cm, 1975, New Jersey. $18.50
393. **DENNIS, FRANK ALLEN, Ed.**, Foreword by Thomas L. Connelly. **Kemper County Rebel: The Civil War Diary of Robert Masten Holmes, C.S.A.** $5.00
Holmes was seventeen years of age when he enlisted in the Twenty-fourth Mississippi Regiment in 1861; he was barely twenty when he died of acute dysentry three years later in a federal prison. He won no fame and had little glory heaped on him. He was a cheerful lad who performed his duties loyally, and his diary reveals no hatred for the enemy. The worth of the journal is that it recognizes Robert Masten Holmes, a common soldier, and the thousands of others like him. His recognition is long overdue.
393A. DENNIS, FRANK L.; Lincoln-Douglas Debates. 1974. $6.95
394. DE VOTO, BERNARD: Year of Decision. 1850. $7.95
395. DEWEY, GEORGE: Autobiography. Illus. 1970. Repr. of 1913 ed. $12.50
396. **DICEY, EDWARD: Spectator of America**, a newly discovered document about Lincoln and Civil War America by a contemporary English correspondent. Intro. by Herbert Mitang, 318 pp, index, dj, 14.3x21 cm. $7.95

~~~~~~~~ *A MORNINGSIDE REPRINT* ~~~~~~~~
397. **DICKERT, CAPT. D. AUGUSTUS; History of Kershaw's Brigade.** $20.00
Kershaw's Brigade, one of the rarest of Civil War histories is again available as a reprint at a reasonable price.
Originally published in 1899 in a limited edition, the book promptly became even more restricted by accidental destruction of many copies prior to distribution. As a result it entered the ranks of hard to get books almost immediately and became so scarce in later years that it was valued on the rare book market at roughly $200 and seldom available at that.
Yet Dickert's work on Gen. Joseph Brevard Kershaw's brigade is perhaps the best of all Civil War unit histories. Moreover, it is an accurate, factual story of an important South Carolina unit that gave its best for the Confederacy throughout four years of war.
Beginning the story with South Carolina's secession Dec. 20, 1860, Dickert describes formation of the brigade and traces its history to surrender in North Carolina April 28, 1865.
Between activation and surrender this veteran unit saw almost continuous action and participated in most of the major engagements of the war including First (and Second) Manassas, Seven Pines, Harper's Ferry, Antietam, Fredericksburg, Chancellorsville, Gettysburg, Chickamauga, the Wilderness, Spotsylvania, Cold Harbor, Petersburg, the

Figure 24-6 A page from Morningside Bookshop's catalog.

You can't afford to wait until the last sale is in—which might be 2 years or even 10 years after the catalog goes out—before making decisions about your future catalogs. Therefore you must estimate total sales on the basis of partial sales results, just as with space ads and direct mail. The catalog "half-life" is a useful tool in making catalog sales projections. The half-life is the length of time after mailing that must pass before you get *half the total orders* that you can expect from the catalog.

Figure 24-7 shows what one writer finds to be a typical catalog response curve. From this figure you can compute the half life of the catalog: 4 percent of total sales in week 1, 14 percent in week 2, 16 percent in week 3, and 16 percent in week 4 neatly add to 50 percent, the half-life of the catalog.

Scharff's estimates for half-life of a catalog are as follows:[2]

Type of catalog	Half-life
Consumer merchandise	3 months
Educational merchandise	Almost 4 months
Industrial merchandise	4 months

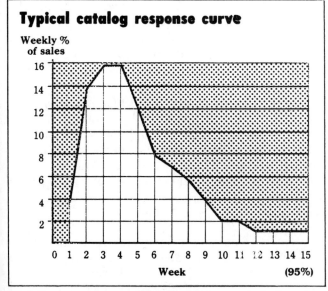

Developing response curves, which indicate the percent of sales for each week of the catalog response period, can be an effective way to gauge how much inventory is required for any given product. Often, the first week's response can give a reliable indication of final sales, especially for hot-selling items that will need to be reordered immediately.

Figure 24-7 Typical catalog response curve.

The half-life differs from firm to firm. And—obviously—it is influenced by the number of catalogs you send out; people throw away the old catalog when they get the new one. Also, the half-life is different for consumer-goods catalogs before holiday seasons than in other seasons. You will eventually have to estimate the half-life for your own catalog, but the figures given above can serve as a rough first guide.

How Much Will the Catalog Cost?

The most important aspect of estimating the cost of the catalog operation, and of particular items, is remembering to include every important item that affects total cost.

Here is a list of common elements of cost: (1) printing and paper, (2) photography, (3) typography, (4) envelope, (5) order blank, (6) inserting, (7) labeling, (8) list rental, (9) carrying cost for merchandise inventory, (10) the merchandise itself, of course, (11) warehousing of merchandise, (12) order-filling labor, (13) merchandise returns, (14) shipping, (15) supervisory overhead, and (16) rent and light.

You may be getting an advertising allowance from some firms whose goods you sell—"co-op money." But don't get so excited by the prospect of co-op money that you advertise products that won't make a profit for you.

How much does it cost to produce, print, and mail a catalog? The huge, color-filled 8½- × 11½-inch Sears catalog costs upwards of $2.00 apiece at 1979 prices, but keep in mind that they have the advantage of mailing millions. Eddie Bauer mailed over a million 5½- × 8½-inch catalogs of 84 to 120 pages at something more than 25 to 27 cents at 1979 prices. Ship's Wheel figured 23 cents per 80-page 5½- × 8½-inch catalog at 1976 prices to a list of around 100,000. At 1975 prices Kestnbaum estimated as follows:[3]

> Large catalogues, such as those used by Montgomery Ward or Sears Roebuck, cost $2 to $2.50 each, or $2000 to $2500 per thousand recipients. Medium-sized catalogues of 150 to 200 pages range in cost from $400 to $900 per thousand. Elaborate individual mailings with full colour brochures plus several extra inserts and small catalogues of up to ninety-six 5½ × 8½ inch pages tend to cost between $150 and $350 per thousand. At the low end of the spectrum, cooperative mailings, statement inserts, publication and broadcast advertisements generally cost between $3 and $25 per thousand.

The Key Decisions in Catalog Selling

Which Merchandise for the Catalog?

The importance of the merchandise was stressed above. But how do you decide which merchandise you should put into the catalog?

You begin selecting items with your intuition and your experience, plus the guidelines given above. (How to obtain the merchandise you want to sell is discussed in Chapter 28.) After that, you must *test* whether the merchandise will sell successfully or not. For your initial test you might run the merchandise in a display ad in one of the mail-order media in which you customarily advertise, or you might run an initial test on an overwrap or a package stuffer.

Once the item passes your initial test and you include it in the catalog, you must *continue* to measure its success on an ongoing basis. That is, you must continue to measure the results of each and every item in each and every issue of the catalog to find out whether it is losing money or making money, and how much.

NOW HEAR THIS! NOW HEAR THIS! The most important element in catalog management is keeping track of the sales made by each and every item, in each issue of the catalog, and then calculating the profitability of that item in that place. This calculation is done by making a tally for the sales of each item that resulted from the appearance in that *particular* catalog. (Of course there are always some orders that can't be traced to a particular catalog, but these can be apportioned just as with any other orders that come in without a key. Computerized record systems can spit out this information easily. For noncomputerized record systems, you must—that is, *must*— work out an accounting system that will give you this information.

With the sales figure for an item, plus the cost to you of the goods to fill the order and the cost of handling, you can calculate how much gross profit the item brought in. If this "gross item profitability measure" (GIFM) is more than the cost of that much catalog space— a cost to be discussed shortly—then the item is profitable; if not, it is not. We will be using the GIFM—and the *net* item profitability measure (NIFM), which is the GIFM with the catalog cost for the item subtracted out—again and again. To repeat, the GIFM and NIFM calculations are the cornerstone of catalog management. We'll discuss them in detail in a couple of pages.

Here is an example of a NIFM-type calculation for Lee Wards:[4]

Let's say we have a picture that requires four square inches of picture space and two and a half inches of copy space. Each square inch costs $237, giving us space cost of the item for $1,540. That is in mail order the advertising cost of an individual item and an individual catalog. We then put that together with the sales of an item. Let's say we have a selling price of $3.99, a cost of $1.91, a quantity of 1,544, which gives us total dollars $6,160 from which you subtract the cost of goods sold and an advertising cost and you'd get a marketing contribution, in this case $1,663, or 27% of sales.

When you have calculated the GIFMs and NIFMs for each item, write them for easy reference in heavy marker on your master copy of the catalog—each item's GIFM and NIFM right on the picture or description of the item itself.

How Much Space for an Item?

The more profitable an item, the more space you should give it. A sound general rule is that you should try to apportion space so that the *ratio* of the GIFM to the cost of that much space is the same for each item. To put the same rule differently, you should allocate space among products so that the GIFM per inch is the same for all products in the catalog.[5]

Please notice that the relevant numerator in the ratio is *not* the *gross sales* of the product, but rather the GIFM—gross sales *less* costs of goods and handling. There is no point in giving a lot of space (or any space at all, for that matter) to a product whose cost is such a high proportion of the price that there is little left over for catalog costs and profit. And don't forget the cost of warehouse space when you figure product cost. Big items take up more valuable space than do small items.

Now let's work an example to show how easy it is to implement this rule. The GIFM, catalog space cost, and ratio of GIFM to space cost are computed using an analysis such as is shown in Table 24-1, on the assumption that one twenty-fourth of a page of catalog space costs $81. We see that items 1318 and 2612 are bringing back very large returns per unit of space, and therefore they should get more space than in the past. Items 1319, 2613, 2614, 3499, and 3501 are losing money, and they either should be run in smaller space or dropped. The other items are somewhere in between and they might get less space if there are other worthy contenders elsewhere in the catalog.

Table 24-1

(1) Page no.	(2) Item no.	(3) Space allocation	(4) Dollar volume	(5) Product cost	(6) GIFM, 4−5	(7) Catalog space cost	(8) GIFM ÷ space cost, 6 ÷ 7
13	1318	1/2 pg.	6,699	1,608	5091	972	5.24
	1319	3/8	556	113	443	729	(.61)(loss)
47	2612	2/3	8,592	3,007	5585	1296	4.31
	2613	1/6	386	135	251	324	(.77)(loss)
	2614	1/6	193	68	125	324	(.39)(loss)
67	3499	1/2	817	531	286	972	(.29)(loss)
	3500	1/4	925	426	499	486	1.03
	3501	1/4	316	205	111	486	(.23)(loss)
69	4621	3/4	3,226	1,484	1742	1458	1.19
	4622	1/4	1,689	777	912	486	1.88

SOURCE: Adapted from Stone (1975, p. 227).

Here are some additional thoughts to improve the analysis:

1. Omitted from Table 24-1 is any systematic allowance for the effect of the present catalog on future sales. This is an important omission. We should make at least some allowance by adding some arbitrary percent to the dollar volume and profit for the catalog as a whole.

2. We are assuming that the sales pattern in the last catalog will continue to persist in the next catalog. If we have some reason to think otherwise, then we should make adjustments downward or upward in accord with our belief about the changes we would expect from one catalog to another.

3. We must be sure that a change is likely to provide us enough profit to be worth the cost of making the change. There is no point in bothering to switch from a 1-inch ad to a 1-1/16-inch ad.

4. Not all catalog positions are equally productive. For example, the back cover may produce twice as many sales for a given product than the average run-of-the-catalog page. If so, we should think in terms of results per *effective* or "weighted" inch rather than in terms of results per inch. We might give the back cover twice as much weight as we do an inner page. A reasonable estimate of the appropriate adjustment for special pages would be the amount of premium

that space media charge for the back cover, inside front, and inside back cover as compared to a regular page.

There may be some cases in which it is sensible to give items some small space in the catalog even though their NIFM does not justify it, in order to offer a complete selection of, say, office supplies. That is, some marginal items can be worthwhile because they increase sales for other items by making the catalog a place in which customers shop because they know they get all their needs fulfilled there. As Scharff put it:[6]

> At Edmund Scientific Company we sold metal detectors very nicely. We also carried books about metal detecting that did not earn their way by any means. However, we felt that we had to keep these books to get people interested in the hobby of metal detecting (by the way, it is a very interesting hobby). Also, sometimes you will have a line of merchandise that has three or four varieties. Do you drop the one variety that is not doing well if the others are doing very well? The answer is probably no if the item does not take up much space. In this case, you judge the sales and profits of the line overall and carry them all.

But you must be very careful with this practice lest too many of the items be money losers.

Most firms advertise many items on a page. Some, like Sears, will occasionally devote full pages to a single item, however. And the catalog of at least one firm—JS&A—contains nothing but half-page and full-page ads (see Figure 24-8). But this proves only that a full-page strategy may be good for JS&A; another firm also selling electronic gadgets may find that it does best with smaller space per item (see Figure 24-9).

How Big Should the Catalog Be?

The general answer about the best catalog length is easy: you should keep expanding the catalog until further expansion will not increase your *total* profit. But this answer is a bit too general to be helpful.

First off, I suggest that you expand your catalog *gradually,* perhaps by no more than 50 percent per increase—from, say, 16 to 24 pages, or from 24 to 36 pages. Few people have the skill or the heart to go from 24 to 72 pages in one jump. Go from 24 pages to 36 and see if the increase boosts profits before you go on to 48 pages, and so on.

The best way to evaluate the optimum catalog size scientifically would be to mail catalogs of several sizes to a random split of names in your list and then compare the responses. But because of the cost

Protect your car silently with a new breakthrough in auto protection.

Auto Surveillance Paging System

Car alarms have always caused problems. A false alarm might catch you inside a building where you are unable to hear your alarm while it wakes up the entire neighborhood. In a real robbery, an alarm only makes the burglar work faster.

The new Page Alert system is the first really smart and inexpensive way to protect your car. You carry a small 4-ounce paging unit with you similar to the familiar pocket pagers. If somebody breaks into your car, your pager beeps to alert you. You can then call the police or investigate the situation. Often the burglar can be caught as he unsuspectingly rum-

mages through your car, or the car thief can be stopped as he tries to cross your ignition wires.

The signal you receive is generated by a powerful 500 milliwatt transmitter that has a range of one-half mile. You can be in a house blocks away and still pick up the signal. The transmitter is just plugged into your cigarette lighter and a door sensor is stuck on the hinged portion of your door with pressure sensitive tape. You can install the complete system in less than a minute.

Each signal is individually coded with a dual tone sequential coding system. Since there are over 12,000 possible combinations, the

chances of someone else triggering your pager is highly unlikely.

When you leave your car, you have full confidence that your car is well protected. If you elect to attach a siren or horn, there is a connection that can be used for that purpose.

Owning a CB radio is no fun when you constantly have to remove it from your car. Now you can leave your radio or other possessions in your car knowing they will be protected without all the disadvantages of a typical alarm system. Order your Page Alert system from JS&A at no obligation today. Only **$99.95** (3.00 Order Nr **3070**)

Touch-Tap Light Switch

Just touch the light switch and your lights go off, keep touching the light switch and your lights dim. Here's a report on a major new lighting innovation.

Picture this. You tap your light switch and it turns on. You tap it again, and it turns off. But there's more.

Continue touching the new Levitan Sensitron light switch and the lights automatically dim and continue to dim until they darken, at which point they start to glow again.

The new light switch is a major new breakthrough in home lighting controls. Using the latest micro-electronic control technology, Levitan has created a light switch with no moving parts and made it easy enough so that anyone can install it.

Each switch is supplied with wire nuts and complete wiring instructions to make the installation easy and quick in any standard single-gang wall box.

There are distinct benefits to touch-tap light control. 1) The unit glows in the dark slightly so at night you can see the light switch. 2) You

can control every light in your home by dimmers which save electricity and add a charming glow to any room. And finally, 3) You save. Dimmers are expensive. The Levitan light switch is only $19.95 each.

There are four decorator colors. Put one in your entrance way or in your bedroom. If it doesn't provide more convenience than you expected, feel free to return it for a prompt and courteous refund.

The Levitan wall switches come in the following colors: Ivory with gold touch plate (**9220**), brown with gold touch plate (**9221**), black with silver touch plate (**9222**), and white with silver touch plate (**9223**). Add $2.50 per order for postage and handling. Just list the order number shown next to each wall switch, and we will promptly fill your order. If you like them order more. They're one of the year's major new breakthroughs in lighting controls.

23

Figure 24-8 Example of electronics catalog with only one or two items on a page.

LEXICON	$225.00	5 lbs.
LEXPORT (Portuguese)	65.00	2 lbs.
LEXSPAN (Spanish)	65.00	2 lbs.
LEXITAL (Italian)	65.00	2 lbs.
LEXGER (German)	65.00	2 lbs.
LEXFRENC (French)	65.00	2 lbs.

Pen not included.

Lexicon Translator breaks down communication Barriers when you are in a foreign country.

The Lexicon translator breaks down communication barriers when you are in a foreign country. Ideal for businessmen who travel abroad or for vacationers. This unit allows you to key in the question in English. It then does the translations for you. The memory bank contains the most used phrases. These are actuated by the first word. For example, if you need to know where the airport is, you key in "How" and then push P key. The dictionary goes down the words and phrases until you get to "How do I get to". That phrase is automatically entered into the memory. You then key in "the airport". The whole phrase is then translated into the appropriate language. Your choice of one language cassette (Spanish, French, German, Italian, Portuguese) with the unit.

ORDER NO. LEXICON
Shipping wt 5 lbs. **$225.00**

Astrology
At the touch of a button Astrology gives zodiac positions for the Sun, Mercury, Venus and Mars on the day of your birth. These planets affect your personality traits and the way you relate to others. Also can be used as a 4-function calculator.

ORDER NO. ASTROLOG
Shipping wt. 2 lbs.
Uses 2 batteries ERAA $1.50
$39.95

Not available until July 1, 1979

Elint Door Guard
Guard your family and household possessions with this attractive, easily-installed unit. The way it works is that only you and your family knows the secret code (first three digits of your license plate, birth date, etc.) When the connection is broken by the opening of a door, you have 7 seconds to key in the code. If it has not been keyed within that time or was keyed in incorrectly, the unit emits a piercing noise that will scare intruders away and alert your family to the intrusion.

ORDER NO. EL121
Shipping wt 4 lbs.
$24.95
Regularly $29.95

Kosmos
Biorhythm with lights and light up display. The most advanced hand held biorhythm computer on the market. Its unique traffic light system tells you good, mini-caution and caution days physically, intellectually, and emotionally. Also can be used as a 4 function calculator. Comes with book telling how biorhythms affected famous people.

ORDER NO. KOSMOS
Shipping wt 4 lbs.
Uses 3 batteries ERAA
(2 per pkg) $1.50
$34.95

Commodore Alarm Watch
Large easy read display. LCD, hours, minutes, seconds, month, date, full alarm!

ORDER NO. CM20403
Gold Tone
$29.95
Regularly $39.95

ORDER NO. CM2040S
Silver Tone
$27.95
Regularly $34.95   Shipping wt. 2 lbs.

31

Figure 24-9 Example of electronics catalog with multiple items per page.

of catalog preparation, you are likely instead to compare results of catalogs of different sizes in different periods. This is dangerous, but often must be done nevertheless.

If you are going from a smaller to a larger catalog, there are two benefits of the larger catalog which you may not see in the first couple of weeks of sales, as compared to the first couple of weeks of response of the smaller catalog the last time you mailed: (1) One benefit is that the half-life during which the catalog will continue to be used will be longer with a bigger catalog. You could easily fail to see this in an examination of the sales in the first few weeks. (2) The bigger catalog creates more customers who will be purchasing from *catalogs in the future.* That is, a larger catalog now means more sales for the catalogs to come. Just *how big* this effect is can only be guessed at, however, unless you can actually measure it.

Even after you have settled on the overall amount of space in your catalog, you must still decide on the page dimensions. For example, a 32-page catalog with each page 8½ × 11 inches has the same amount of space (actually more because there are fewer margins) than a 64-pager with pages 5½ × 8½ inches, and roughly the same cost. The smaller page size yields a thicker catalog, which (some experts think) feels more impressive, and hence may be held onto longer by customers. On the other hand, the small-page catalog may seem chintzy. You may test this, of course.

How Often Should You Send Out Catalogs?

If you don't send out catalogs often enough, you lose the chance to make some profitable sales, and you also let the bond between you and your customers grow weaker, thereby reducing future sales from future mailings. On the other hand, if you send out catalogs too often, the newest catalog "steals" too many sales from the previous catalog, thereby reducing the sales per catalog and hence its profitability. The question is: How often is just often enough?

The only way to answer this question satisfactorily is to *test* and *analyze.* This is the proper way to test: You take a sample of, say, the first 3,000—6,000 or 12,000 might be better sample sizes—names that are on your customer list as of January 1, and you put aside all their records so that they are not mailed any catalogs except as part of the test. Then you go down the 3,000 names and, starting with the first name, you (1) mark every third name "A," (2) start with the second name and mark every third name "B," and (3) starting with the third name, mark every third name with a "C." Then the As are mailed a catalog every 3 months, the Bs are mailed a catalog every 4 months, and the Cs are mailed a catalog every 6 months. At the end of about 15 months, you analyze the total sales and the total costs (including the costs of the catalog mailings) for each group, and determine which group yields the greatest total profit. *This is the ONLY way that you can ever make a satisfactory determination of the optimum frequency of mailing:* no nonexperimental analysis can give you a meaningful answer.

The central difficulty in executing this test—as with all other tests in the mail-order business—is making sure that the test procedure is actually carried out. It sounds easy when you first discuss and design the test, but in a frighteningly high proportion of tests, the procedure gets fouled up administratively. I remember too well trying to run a catalog-frequency test with one of my clients. The first time we tried it, the outfit that maintained the client's lists got the samples all mixed up, and we didn't find out until half a year had passed and we were getting peculiar results in our preliminary analysis. The next time we tried it, we decided to do it right at home in the client's offices. But the person in charge of the test quit halfway through, and no one remembered to continue the test procedures. And so it goes. Along with a sound design for the test, careful administrative supervision and record keeping is the most important element in arriving at reliable results about optimal frequency and other mail-order decisions.

Frequency and Customer Segments

It pays to mail more catalogs, more often, to better customers. LeeWards does this in a very sophisticated fashion as follows:[7]

> LeeWards divides its customers into approximately 2,400 individul cells based upon recency, frequency and monetary. We analyze each one of these 2,400 cells to determine how many catalogs those people will or can get. The more recent they are the more frequently customers purchase. If they are five years old and spent $10 and only bought from us once it may well be that they may only get one catalog. If they are two months old and spent $100 and bought from us six times in the last 24 weeks, they could get up to nine or 10 catalogs. They would get as many catalogs as we can print and mail.

A firm I counseled had been mailing an expensive "bulletin" or news articles plus advertising to its list of customers and prospects. It mailed six times a year to *each person on the list.* Based on purchase data, we figured out that by mailing nine times a year to purchasers, six times a year to recent inquirers, and three times a year to older inquirers, the firm could immediately increase its profit by $250,000 yearly.

Positioning and Grouping

After you have fixed the overall size of the catalog, you must make an interlocking set of decisions about which merchandise to put in the catalog, whether to run many items in small spaces or fewer items in larger spaces, whether to group similar merchandise or mix the types throughout the catalog, and where in the catalog to place the various items.

A really sound scientific analysis of this set of problems could be made, but it would be too complex for our purposes here. Therefore I'll make some simplifications and I'll give you some general observations, in place of the solid conclusions we could reach with careful testing plus complex analysis.

The page positions in the front of the catalog usually sell better than back pages. One gift seller analyzed this by rating each page of its catalog by whether the page's total sales were above or below the average. These were the results:[8]

Catalog pg. nos.	% above- average sales
1-9	58.0
10-19	60.0
20-29	55.0
30-39	47.5
40-49	37.5
50-59	35.0

You should put your better-selling items up front, just as you should give them more space—though you also want to make sure that the back pages have some exciting items, too.

Speaking of excitement, some firms go to great lengths to make it exciting to read the catalog. The most famous examples are Neiman-Marcus and Sakowitz. When the latter started its "Ultimate Gift" section[9]

> The initial offering was a *$125,000 dress* festooned with sapphires, rubies and emeralds. "More than one" was sold. Since then, its "ultimates" have been theme pages offering a variety of gifts at a variety of (big ticket) prices. Two of the most successful have been the "Gifts of Education" (wanta be a jockey—you can learn!) and "Dream Come True" (four sessions of sitting in on filming the Playboy centerfold were sold; one night of conducting the Houston Symphony Orchestra). In 1978, one bid has come through on the private lighthouse island and there have been a number of takers for the custom bound, blank page library. Nobody ordered the dinner party for 21 world-famous celebrities.

Such unusual items can also help your catalog sales by getting attention in the newspapers. A series of swimming lessons by Mark Spitz was an effective public-relations gimmick.

The need for excitement and surprise also is a sound reason for mixing up the types of merchandise throughout the catalog, if you are advertising gifts and "impulse" items. For the same reason you may vary the price range; Hammacher-Schlemmer makes a practice of putting one or more high-priced items on each page, as you can see in Figure 24-10.

If, however, you are selling merchandise for commercial purchase— say, office supplies or specialty goods such as camping or hardware items—you will want to group merchandise so that people can systematically shop for what they are looking for, rather than scatter the types of merchandise throughout the catalog.

Order Forms

The order form is all important in closing the sale. This is Stone's list of the elements of a satisfactory order form:[10]

1. Is there space to indicate how many, item number or style number, name of item, color if there is a choice, size if there is a choice, imprinting if offered, and the dollar amount?

2. Consistent with the total number of items called for on the average order, is there sufficient number of lines for listing the items desired? (It is always desirable to leave space for more than the average as an incentive for ordering more items.)

3. Are the items perfectly clear? If postage, insurance, and handling charges are extra, is the chart clear? If there are taxes to be added, is the percentage specified? If charge card privileges are offered, is there space to give the required identification numbers? If interest charges are applied to installment accounts, does the explanation comply with the Truth in Lending Law?

4. If drop shipments are solicited, is space allocated to provide for instructions?

5. If a discount is offered for exceeding minimum order requirements, is it clearly spelled out?

Figure 24-11 shows L. L. Bean's order form.

YOU MAY CHARGE TO YOUR HAMMACHER SCHLEMMER ACCOUNT, AMERICAN EXPRESS, MASTER CHARGE, DINER'S CLUB OR VISA.

53

Frigitote - Hot or Cold

The Wine Vault

FRIGITOTE - HOT OR COLD. Amazing new portable refrigerator. Electronic solid state cooling, freezing, or heating. Plugs into any 12 volt cigarette lighter; in your car, boat, airplane. Weighs only 5 lbs. yet holds six 12 oz. cans plus 3 sandwiches. Exterior size 11" long, 8" wide, 10¾" deep. Capacity 325 cu. inches. (11 pints. Constructed of high impact polystyrene. Beige and brown. Seamless, anodized aluminum liner wipes clean easily. Handy 2-way handle/shoulder strap. Ideal for salesmen, professional people, families, touring, camping, boating, flying. **Z64.** (6 lbs.). 129.95

THE WINE VAULT. A truly professional wine cellar for wine lovers. Made of quality-constructed, durable material. Interior walls lined with California redwood. It provides a natural environment with a temperature of 53-57°, proper humidity and darkness. All bottles are held in a horizontal position and thereby insure that wet corks keep air out. All bottles are instantly available and may be kept under lock and key. It plugs into 110 volt outlet, vibration proof. Patent locking panels permit easy assembly and disassembly for relocation. **PZ11.** (Exp.) **CHATEAU PETIT.** 312 bottles. 6'8"x4'x39" deep. Allow 4 to 5 weeks for delivery. . . . . 2995.00 Other sizes available from 156 bottles to 1,940 bottles. Prices and sizes upon request.

CIGAR ASHTRAY. The trouble is that cigars won't fit into cigarette ashtrays, so we have one of quality-lead solid crystal that's deep enough for the big cigar. A gift suggestion for your favorite smoker. **N5037.** (5 lbs.). 25.00

APPLE ICE BUCKET. Will hold 1½ quarts of ice cubes fresh and solid for hours. The removable plastic lining protects the inner glass lining from ice tongs and ice cubes. Made of bright apple-red high impact plastic. Ice tongs included. **NAJ1500.** (4 lbs.). 15.95

CELLARMASTER CORKSCREW. Removes corks quickly, easily from standard size bottles, magnums and double magnums. Black enamelled and chrome coated high grade steel for durability and efficiency. Fully 9¾" high; uncorks by lever-type action. **N45975.** (3 lbs.). 16.95

Cigar Ashtray

Cellarmaster Corkscrew

Apple Ice Bucket

Figure 24-10 Example of a catalog with at least one high-priced item per page.

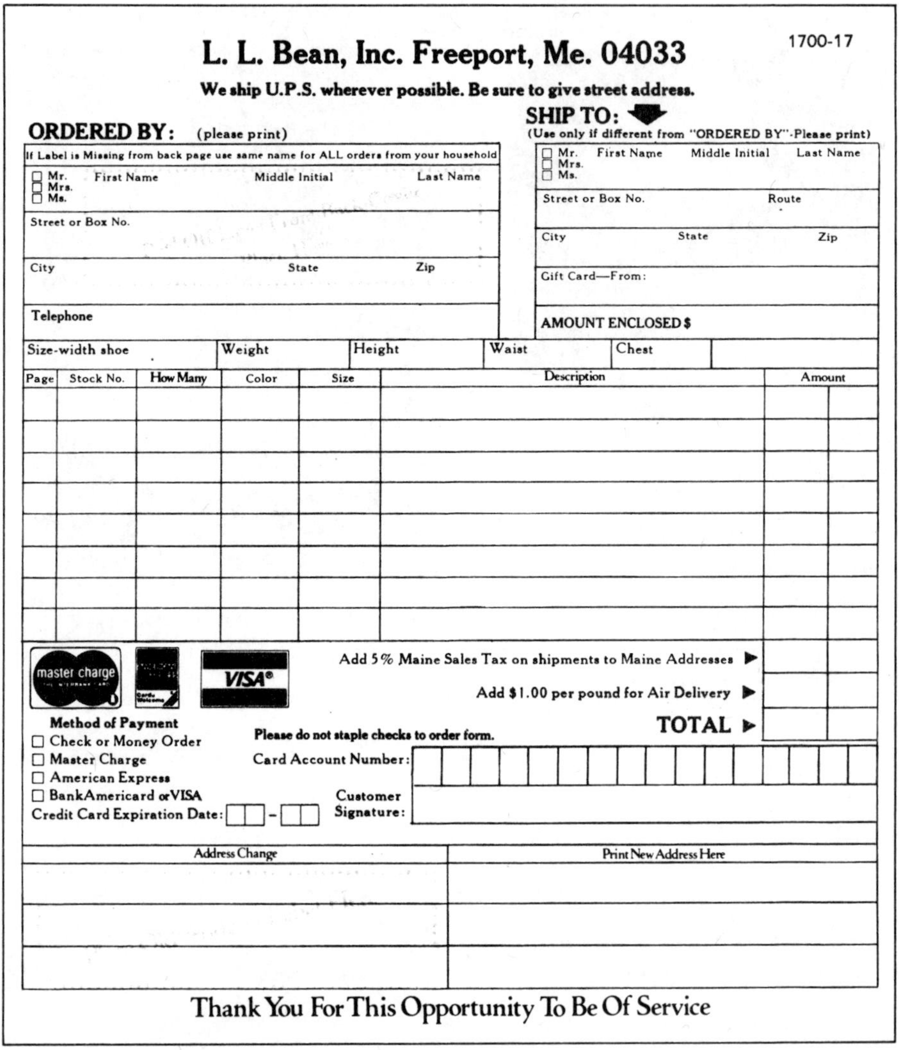

L. L. Bean, Inc. Freeport, Me. 04033   1700-17

We ship U.P.S. wherever possible. Be sure to give street address.

ORDERED BY: (please print)

SHIP TO: ➡

(Use only if different from "ORDERED BY"-Please print)

If Label is Missing from back page use same name for ALL orders from your household

☐ Mr.   First Name   Middle Initial   Last Name
☐ Mrs.
☐ Ms.

Street or Box No.

City   State   Zip

Telephone

☐ Mr.   First Name   Middle Initial   Last Name
☐ Mrs.
☐ Ms.

Street or Box No.   Route

City   State   Zip

Gift Card—From:

AMOUNT ENCLOSED $

Size-width shoe		Weight	Height	Waist		Chest	

Page	Stock No.	How Many	Color	Size	Description	Amount

master charge   **VISA®**

Add 5% Maine Sales Tax on shipments to Maine Addresses ▶

Add $1.00 per pound for Air Delivery ▶

TOTAL ▶

Method of Payment
☐ Check or Money Order
☐ Master Charge
☐ American Express
☐ BankAmericard or VISA
Credit Card Expiration Date: ☐☐ – ☐☐

Please do not staple checks to order form.

Card Account Number: ☐☐☐☐☐☐☐☐☐☐☐☐☐☐☐

Customer Signature:

Address Change	Print New Address Here

Thank You For This Opportunity To Be Of Service

Figure 24-11

Postscript

Before you actually embark on preparing a catalog, I suggest you look at Chapter 12 of Bob Stone's book, *Successful Direct-Marketing Methods* (1984 edition). It's the best guide to catalog preparation that I know of, and it is the best chapter in an excellent book. I've drawn some of the examples in this chapter from Stone.

25

Follow-up Letters to Inquirers

What to Send / How Many Follow-ups Should You Send? / When to Send the Follow-ups

In this chapter we assume that you have chosen to sell a high-priced product—perhaps a printing press or a correspondence course. The price is sufficiently high that you can't sell the product directly from the ad. Instead, your advertisements call for people to write for further information.

This chapter is about the information you send—in a series of letters—to people who inquire.

The purpose of follow-ups is quite different from the direct mail that you send to people on your *mailing list* when you sell stationery or food delicacies or other repeat items. Each letter in a follow-up series is designed to sell the *same item,* whereas you advertise a whole line of items in a repeat-business operation.

Furthermore, if you sell a line of repeat-purchase goods, all the people on your mailing list get the same direct mail from you at the *same time.* Follow-ups, on the other hand, go out on a schedule that starts the day the inquiry is received.

These are the questions about follow-ups that this chapter will help you answer:

1. *What* should you send?

2. How *many* follow-ups should you send?

3. How should you *space* the follow-ups?

The best way—and the only way—to understand follow-ups thoroughly is to study what successful operators do. Write to every correspondence school whose ads you can find in single issues of *Popular Science* and *Workbasket,* both the ads in display and those in classified. (A few salespeople will telephone you from the handful of biggest correspondence schools, but they won't bother you if you tell them you are not interested at present. Besides, hearing their pitches will be instructive to you.)

Many of the correspondence schools send beautiful brochures for their first follow-ups mail-out. But you are mainly interested in the series of letters after the first follow-up.

The first follow-up piece should almost always go out under first-class postage so that the inquirer's curiosity will not have time to cool. The dramatic difference in results between first-class and third-class mail to inquirers about a drug-products catalog can be seen in these data:

Test no.	Number mailed in sample	Number of conversions		Percent conversions
		First-class postage	Third-class postage	
1	200	85		42.5
1	200		71	35.5
2	200	86		43.0
2	200		55	27.5
3	500	173		35.0
3	500		136	27.2

After the first follow-up, subsequent follow-ups can go third class, so write the date on the envelope when each one arrives. Save everything that comes, of course, for your files.

Remember that follow-ups are not just an unnecessary frill to the business. If correspondence courses were limited to one mailing piece—or even to two follow-ups—many firms would have to go out of business. The first mailing for an experienced operator will only get about *half* the orders he or she will eventually develop with his or her entire series of follow-ups.

What to Send

Follow-ups are direct mail, and *good* follow-ups will obey the rules for good direct mail. Reread the preceding two chapters to refresh your memory on the subject.

The first follow-up provides no special problems about what to send. It will be a complete, hard-working mailing piece—exactly the same kind of mailing piece you would send even if there were no more follow-ups to come. But obviously, the second, third, fourth, and succeeding follow-ups must be related to the first piece and to one another, and that's what we discuss in this section.

The first follow-up will generally be longer and more complete than any subsequent follow-up. It will usually contain every major reason that will help persuade the prospect to buy.

Some mailers—particularly those who sell industrial goods and use automatically typed letters—find that a *carbon copy* of the first letter is very successful.

Each subsequent follow-up usually hammers away at a *single* major reason for buying, as explained in the following from *The New York Times:*[1]

> The first letter of the series may bring out the value of the article from a dollars-and-cents standpoint. The second may advance the theory that the article will pay for itself within a short time. The third may stress pride of ownership. The fourth may emphasize the enjoyment feature, and so on through the scale of selling appeals.

Or, different follow-ups can offer different sales terms. If the first follow-up offers $10 down and $10 per month, the second follow-up may offer $5 down and $7 per month. Or a follow-up may push the "Free Trial."

It is generally *not* wise to reduce the overall price of the merchandise, and few major firms do so. Customers may lose faith in firms that offer to cut their own price. And record keeping becomes more complicated and troublesome if you cut your price.

Some outfits reduce the price but "justify" the reduction to the consumer by giving an excuse for the reduction. One way to justify a price reduction is to offer the merchandise without some fringe benefit, i.e., without the consultation advice, or the customizing feature, or the fancy building.

Another way to justify the reduction is by offering "a few slightly soiled pieces at half price."

Still another practice is to set up another company name in another town and offer the same merchandise at a cheaper price.

Though almost everyone else is against this practice, Charles Atlas starts by offering his course at $25, and by the eighth follow-up he is down to $5. And Atlas has been a very successful operation.

In any case, never reduce the price until the customer must otherwise be considered dead.

In your last letter to otherwise-dead customers, you should throw in every gimmick and premium you have offered at any time. If that collection of appeals won't get them, nothing will.

Each follow-up should give the prospect a good reason why you are writing again. ("Perhaps my letter went astray," "Perhaps you were too busy," "I received this letter from a satisfied customer yesterday and I thought you would be interested," or "My boss authorized me to offer special terms at this time of the year.")

But, never forget that each letter must repeat the basic story line of what you are selling, why the prospect should want it, and how he or she can buy it immediately.

Each follow-up should *look* different from the others. Vary the color of the paper or the ink, or change the letterhead. Use a different shape of envelope. But retain the *basic identity* of the letters. Keep the trademark and the typography uniform. The letters should seem as if they are *different members of the same family.*

Some advertisers use a different signature, from a different "officer" of the firm, for each letter. I have never understood the logic of that practice, but it evidently is successful for some firms.

Change the testimonials in each follow-up. One of your follow-ups might consist almost *entirely* of new testimonials.

How Many Follow-ups Should You Send?

If the first letter doesn't sell the customer, then maybe the second letter will, or the sixth. Make up your mind that once you have a prospect who is least interested in your product, you won't stop soliciting him or her until a series of letters brings back less money than it actually costs—and that could be the tenth letter or a later one, depending on the product.

La Salle Extension University sends about ten follow-ups in its first series, at 1- or 2-week intervals. Then it sends two or three mailings each year for several years. It has made money on mailings to prospects who inquired as long as 5 years before !²

Here are a few case histories for which we have data:

- Charles Atlas closed one-third of his sales with his first letter and booklet. The other two-thirds were scattered over the next nine letters, each letter doing only slightly worse than the one before.

- Musselman mentions a correspondence course selling between $50 and $100.³ The mailings pulled this way:

1st follow-up	½%
2d	¼
3d	½
4th	¾ (easier terms)
5th	1 (reduced price)
6th	½ (reduced price)
7th	¼ (reduced price)

- At one time the New York Institute of Photography obtained inquiries for 56 to 70 cents each. A series of six letters went out over a 6-month period—the early letters at shorter intervals than the later letters. They closed 6 to 7 percent at a sales price of $88. More than half probably paid in full.

  I'd guess that the total of six mailings at that time cost perhaps $1, so the total cost of a prospect was about $1.65. The revenue per inquiry was above $2.75—a very nice profit, indeed.

- More than 70 years ago W. A. Shryer obtained these results in selling his credit-collection course:⁴

1st follow-up	0.012%	11th follow-up	0.0062%
2d	0.015	12th	0.0074
3d	0.011	13th	0.0031
4th	0.0106	14th	0.0071
5th	0.0106	15th	0.0052
6th	0.018	16th	0.0052
7th	0.013	17th	0.0032
8th	0.0046	18th	0.0025
9th	0.0033	19th	0.0039
10th	0.0038	20th	0.0009

Shryer's follow-up series consisted of five regular letters at short intervals, and then a special letter every 3 months. His results are an interesting demonstration that the basic principles of the mail-order business have not changed in a long, long time.

In general, each letter will pull slightly less than the preceding letter. If a later letter does better, it probably means that the copy and appeal are stronger than the preceding letter. You should then consider putting the stronger copy in the earlier letters.

Stop sending follow-ups when the cost of the follow-up is greater than the dollar returns it brings back. For example, if printing, postage, handling, and other costs add to $80 per thousand for a follow-up, and if you keep $75 after fulfillment costs for each $100 of revenue you receive, then each follow-up must bring back more than $106.67.

$$\frac{100}{75} \times \$80 = \$106.67$$

Stop the follow-up series when the results fall below $106.67.

The more expensive the item and the greater the net revenue (order margin) per unit, the more follow-ups you will find it profitable to send.

When to Send the Follow-ups

In general, the early letters go out at short intervals while the prospect is "hot." Grant writes of a successful series in which the second follow-up went out just *one day* after the first (though probably the second went out by third-class mail and therefore arrived several days later).[5]

The first letter, especially, must go out *immediately*—and by first-class mail. Time is absolutely of the essence. On one offer I first obtained better than a 10 percent response, sending letters out promptly and first class. This dropped to just above 8 percent when the printer made us several weeks late in getting them out, and when we sent them third class. (These are reliable data: over 200 replies in one case and over 380 in the other.)

Grant recommends the second follow-up a week after the first, and the other follow-ups 2 weeks apart—except for a price reduction, which should follow a considerable delay. He also states, "Never mail a follow-up in December or June."[6]

Another plan schedules first a 1-week delay, then a 2-week delay, then a 3-week delay, then a space of 1 month between letters.

The *best* policy will be to test various intervals for your own proposition, however.

26

The Vital Brain of Mail Order: Testing

What Is Testing All About / Testing in Periodical Advertising / Direct-Mail Testing Techniques / How to Select a Test Sample / Conclusions about Direct-Mail Testing

What Is Testing All About?

Mail order is something like poker. In poker you try to maneuver into a position in which you have a really good hand, and then you play the hand to the hilt. In mail order, you try like the dickens to find a big-winning proposition, and then you try to milk it for all it's worth. (But don't get me wrong. Mail order is much less of a gamble than most other types of business—at least, once you are established.)

Testing tells you whether or not you have a big winner and how much you can try to milk it for. Important? Testing couldn't be more important. If you don't understand testing, you'll never make a good buck in mail order.

(You may not have to understand some of the more complicated stuff I discuss in this chapter. Lots of successful mail-order people won't know what I'm talking about. I'm convinced, though, that they would be far more successful if they did understand and use all these ideas.)

Sometimes you will try a loser. Either it is a brand-new product and people don't want it, or it's an established product whose market is not big enough for you *and* the competition.

You would obviously prefer not to wind up with any costly stock on your hands in a situation in which you can't sell it. The fear of this keeps many people from testing good products.

But there is a partial answer. Large industrial manufacturing companies test a product—perhaps a new type of steel—by asking their customers in advance whether they can use it. Their customers are likely to give accurate answers.

Major concerns that sell direct to household consumers find that they cannot rely on their customers' answers. Consumers just cannot predict their own behavior in advance well enough to give you accurate information. So these concerns resort to many other stratagems, including motivation research.

The mail-order advertiser is less interested in the way that people react to the goods and more interested in the way they react to the advertising. What you *can* do, then, is to advertise before you have any merchandise, to find out how great the response will be.

This practice never really feels very good ethically. But on the other hand, it is not really bad, either. The worst that happens is that a customer wastes time and a postage stamp in writing to you. If you do put the product on the market, he or she merely has to wait awhile until you are ready. Whether or not the practice feels right to you, you should know that the late Bennet Cerf of Random House (one of America's largest publishers) asserted that this practice was a necessary and common trade practice, when he was in a discussion of the ethical relationships of publishers to booksellers.[1]

The Science of Mail Order

Mail-order selling is the most scientific business in the world. By that I mean *figuring* and *calculating* can control a firm's decisions more than in any other line of trade. Aside from the selection of the offer and the creation of copy, the "human factor" and other imponderables have a smaller effect in mail order than in any other business, no matter how large the business is.

For example, the split-run test (more about that later) is the most perfect experiment ever devised in the social sciences. Its accuracy and validity are fantastically greater than any psychologist, sociologist, or economist ever hopes to achieve in her work.

It would seem, then, that mail-order people would respond readily to improvements in methods of figuring. But alas, no, they're just not very much interested. Like everyone else, mail-order people are satisfied to get along. They're convinced that their knowledge is basically pretty complete. (As of 1986, though, mail-order people are becoming much more open to new ideas involving statistics and computer analyses.)

"Buying Information"

When you spend a quarter to call the Weather Bureau for the latest report, you are buying information. When you lay out $300 for an encyclopedia, you are also buying information—not books, mind you, but *information*.

Testing is also a way of buying information. You spend a little extra time and energy to obtain some factual data that you can then use to increase your profit. A test is good only if it costs less in money and hassle than the information is worth in the long run.

Here is an example. You have a proposition that has proved to be a winner in four out of the five magazines in which you have run. Now you are in a hurry to find the greatest number of magazines that will pull a profit for you.

In this situation, you should not be too cautious in your testing. You should take a chance on every magazine that has even a *reasonable* chance of paying out. Here's why. If you think you have a one-in-three chance of making a profit on a magazine, you should test in it. Based on your test of the five magazines above, you know that you won't lose your shirt. The most you can lose is some small part of the cost of the ad and the merchandise. If you *make* money, you can rerun the ad far more than three times. And more than two insertions in a paying magazine will more than cover the losses in two nonpaying magazines.

So it pays to think of testing as buying information that will allow you to build a profit in the future. Don't think of the test as an investment all by itself. If you understand this principle, you will test more freely and you can pyramid your profits remarkably fast.

What to Test

All through this manual I've been saying, "Test this" and "Test that" or "You'll have to test this for yourself."

You want to test all the factors that have an important effect upon the number of sales that you make. These factors are as follows: (1) *The offer*, which includes the product or service that you are selling, and the price at which you offer it, along with the other aspects of the proposition such as the guarantee. (2) *The copy,* including both the words that you use in the headline and body copy, and the artwork. (3) *The market* to which you are making your offer, which may be the audience of a magazine or radio show or the list to which you are mailing. (4) *The timing* of the offer, most importantly which month a magazine advertisement appears or your mailing goes out, but specific dates can be important, too, such as just before Christmas. (5) *The size* of the advertisement if in a magazine or on the air, or the type of package and the degree of expensive preparation if it is a direct-mail piece.

Test *only* the important things. Don't test petty things. Mail-order people have spent huge amounts of time and energy testing such trivial items as exact shades of color, one type face versus another typeface, etc., ad nauseam. Such tests spend more to buy information than the information is worth. The results don't make enough difference to matter much.

To paraphrase Victor Schwab:[2] Test for differences that *scream.* Don't test for differences that whisper. . . . Test for differences in headlines that could double your profit. Test for a price that could increase your take by 40 percent. Test a brochure that could increase sales 15 percent.

When you first put an offer on the market, your testing will be very different from the testing that you will do later on in the product history. Your first advertisement tests the offer, but it *also* tests the medium and the copy. If any one of those elements is bad, the whole test fails. That's when you have to exert judgment to decide whether to drop the whole thing, or to repair what you think is the faulty element.

Later on, after you *know* what your offer and copy will do, you can compare one magazine against another, and your test results will give you information purely about the magazines.

Or, you can change the copy but keep the same offer, and run in a medium in which you ran the old ad. In that case, the results give you a straight answer about the copy.

Testing has different meanings at the various stages of your mail-order campaign.

Does Scientific Testing Work?

People who don't understand testing don't trust its results. As an eye opener to direct-mail people, William Doppler and the Book-of-the-

Month Club tested random sampling on over *a million* letters. The results were just exactly as predicted by sampling theory.[3]

(Of course, statisticians knows—as Doppler did—that any such test was totally unnecessary and a waste of time and money. They would know that the results had to be the way they turned out.)

Is Testing Just Theory and Not Practice?

The practical man may wonder if scientific testing is not just ivory-tower stuff, a theoretical nicety not really done by businesses in a hurry to make profit. Not so. In the mail-order business one *has* to test, and the most profitable firms tend to do a lot of testing. For example, the vice-president of J. C. Penney, the second largest merchandiser in the United States after Sears, said this about Penney's catalog testing:[4]

> Which media alternatives are best for a particular item or promotion—mail, broadcast, print, telephone? We find out through testing. Which distribution alternatives are most efficient—mail, parcel post, united parcel? Which is more productive, color or black and white, for which categories of merchandise? Again, the answers come through testing.
>
> Decision-making is aided importantly by testing. Judgment, based on accumulated experience, will never go out of style, but in direct marketing, at least, it is not enough. Too often I have seen our best judgments overturned by a simple test result.

The most important thing in testing is to keep good records.

Testing in Periodical Advertising

A true split run is a perfect test for two pieces of copy. In a split run, two different ads are set up for a single issue of a publication. The test is arranged so that each ad is in exactly half the copies, appearing in every other copy in each pile of magazines or newspapers that leaves the printing plant.

The split-run ads are keyed differently, and the number of returns is a perfect test of whichever copy or price is better.

Several magazines and newspapers have true split-run facilities, for which there is an extra charge. *Standard Rate & Data* lists these publications.

There are also some publications that offer *regional* "split runs." In this setup all the copies going to the West, perhaps, have one ad, while all the copies going to the East have another ad. The results are not perfectly reliable because readers in different parts of the country may have different tastes and needs. This is not a true split-run test. Nevertheless, it can sometimes be useful.

Split runs usually test copy treatments and various offers against each other, but it is also possible to test color versus black and white, size of ad, position in the magazine, and other variables.

Problems in Testing

You need plenty of good judgment to interpret display-ad tests. As a matter of fact, how good your judgment of tests is may decide how successful a display advertiser you are. And I think that the trickiest job in mail order is to estimate, on the basis of one or more ads, how other ads or other media will pull.

These are some of the problems in judging test results:

1. If you test two different ads in two consecutive issues of a magazine, you must take account of the difference in pulling power in different months.

2. Two ads may appear in different positions in different issues. Good position can pull twice as well as poor position.

3. A given issue of a magazine may be especially attractive and sell extra copies on the newsstand, giving an extra boost to ads in that issue.

4. National events, such as a war scare, can affect results.

5. One issue may carry more competitive advertising than another issue.

These are some of the reasons why you must evaluate the results of a particular test very closely. Chapters 14 and 15 on display advertising give you information that should help improve your judgment of test results.

General Methods of Testing Ads and Media

1. If you have a piece of copy that you have used in many media before, you can use that copy to test new media. La Salle Extension University has used one piece of copy to test new publications for over 35 years.

2. You can get a fair comparison of two ads in the "crisscross" method. In this method you run ad A in medium X and ad B in medium Y in the first issue. In the next issue, ad A goes into medium Y, and ad B goes into medium X. The ad which pulls more total responses should be better. However, different conditions can still distort the picture, even though the crisscross reduces the likelihood of that happening.

3. If you have plenty of time you can alternate ads from month to month. After 4 to 6 months your results should be satisfactorily reliable.

4. Mail-order people are fond of saying that you can test only one thing at a time. That saying is not always true. Let's say that you have run your first test ad, and the results are highly satisfactory. Now you are in a great hurry to test out perhaps eight new media and perhaps eight forms of offer, price and copy.

I am convinced that your best bet in this case is to put a different ad into each different medium. The insertions that pull the very best suggest to you that *both* the ad and the medium are strong. The insertions that pull worst suggest the opposite.

On the next time around, place the ads from the better-result insertions into many media, including the media whose insertions pulled only middling well on the first test. But place no ads in the media in which the first insertions did poorly. After this second round, by a simple and obvious deduction, you can say with much greater accuracy which media are best and which ads are best.

The advantage of this approach is that you get a lot of information rapidly. The rationale depends on the fact that your offer is generally quite profitable, and for that reason it is possible and profitable to buy the further information.

And don't forget: Keep good records, *faithfully.*

One of the disadvantages of display advertising is that it takes a long time to get results. *Some* media give you a quick test, though. Chapter 14 also discusses the problem of guessing from one medium's results what the results in another medium will be.

Readership Reports

In mail order it is *orders* that count, not the number of people who read your ads.

Nevertheless, readership surveys can sometimes give you interesting data about the effectiveness of various *parts* of a magazine. They also can give you a faint clue to the effectiveness of competitors' ads.

Readership reports are available on request from many of the larger magazines.

Television and Radio Testing

Television and radio testing is not very different in principle from testing in periodicals. You should first try a few stations that usually seem to produce rather well and consistently for your prior offers. Then, if they show results that are good compared with prior tests and are profitable in absolute terms, you repeat in those stations and also go on to other stations. As Lawrence Crane, head of a large television record-seller, Dynamic House, describes it[5]

> We have five or six markets that we usually test in [at the same time]. They vary from time to time because we know from past experience what good results and what bad results come from that particular station. We look back at our previous records to see how well that package did. The key question I usually ask is how does it compare to a particular winner in that particular market. We can gauge just how well that package would do. And then we roll it out very slowly before we ever get to the 600 stations.

Direct-Mail Testing Techniques

Every self-respecting direct-mail tester should ask these two questions each and every time a test is run:

1. How do I design the best test for this particular direct-mail problem? One part—but only a part—of this question boils down to: How big a test sample should I use?

2. How do I evaluate the results of the test after the returns are in? This question *always* breaks into two subquestions:

   a. What is my *best guess* about what the test shows?

   b. How *accurate* is that best guess likely to be, given the test-sample size?

The answers to these questions will be different from test to test. There is no simple and easy set of rules you can follow blindly. There is no $2 board into which you can plug your jack for an automatic answer.

But even *before* those questions, as a direct-mail tester you must consider

1. What you are trying to find out from the test
2. What decisions will be influenced by the test results
3. How the test results can guide you in the decisions you have to make
4. How much money is involved

Depending on these considerations, the testing situation probably will fall into one of these three major categories:

1. Will this new offer make a profit?
2. How should I test *lists?*
3. How do I test one piece of copy against another?

We shall consider these major categories one by one.

Though at a particular moment you may be primarily interested in testing a new offer, you should also design the test so that it provides information on other variables as well. For example, if you are comparing a price of $149 against a price of $99, you should test the two prices on several lists—say four or five. You should *not* send the $149 offer to some lists and the $99 offer to others, because then you would not know whether the more successful mailing is due to better offer *or* to a better list; the results are then said to be "confounded." Rather, you want to split up *each* of the lists into two equal halves (by, say, taking every other name for each price offer) with one half getting the lower-priced offer and the other the higher-priced offer. I know that this takes extra trouble. But not only is it a necessary procedure, but it provides additional information of very great value.

If you were to test the two offers by splitting up just one fairly good-sized test list into equal halves, the test would not be confounded. But you would learn nothing about the excellence of that particular list. If you split your offer in each of several smaller-sized test lists, you not only learn which offer is better, but you also learn—at practically no additional cost—which lists are better for your offer.

And there is still another bonus in splitting your offer among several lists: It may be that the lower-priced offer is better in some markets—that is, when mailed to some lists—whereas the higher-priced offer is better in other list markets. You could never find that out if you split your offer within just one single list.

To carry the process one step further, you can also test various types of copy at the same time. If you want to test three copy treatments and two prices, you split up each test list into six parts, each part having a different combination of copy and price, and each going to every sixth name on each of several lists. And the best part about this sort of design is that you do not need a larger total test sample than if you were testing just two offers on one list, though the more complex design does cost more in printing and handling as well as in the time and trouble it takes you to execute it.

When splitting lists for testing, the size of each "cell"—that is, each group of names that receives a treatment different from other groups—should be the same.

Not many years ago, many people still believed that it was impossible to test more than one variable at a time. This is totally wrong scientifically. And by now direct-mail testers have become sufficiently sophisticated that they design tests as cleverly as the best-designed tests in agricultural research, a branch of science which has been the leader in experimental design for many decades.

This is as good a place as any to mention the importance of testing lists as compared with testing the offer and copy and direct-mail package. There is sometimes a tendency among inexperienced mail-order operators to focus their attention on the copy and offer, because they seem to be the more "creative" aspects of the business, and to use lists without much discrimination. This is a disastrous error. Pay at least as much attention to the choice of the list as to the other factors, because the variation in results among good and bad lists is at least as great as among good and bad offers, and probably much greater than among good and bad copy treatments. For example, Ed Burnett relates that he once tried 400 separate lists for a fund-raising appeal over the course of 4 years. All of these were lists that there was good reason to believe had a reasonable chance of succeeding, based on the judgment of Burnett, who is as knowledgeable as anybody in the field. The best list produced *10 times* as many responses as the worst list—and that worst list was not a dog to start with.

Warning: At this point I want to warn you that there is a *better* method of looking at these problems than the one I shall describe. That method is "decision theory," which takes into account not only the probabilities of various events taking place, but also the size of the monetary gains or losses that may take place, and the best guesses of the manager about what will happen.

That better method is described using an example of a direct-mail bookclub publisher, in Robert Schlaifer's book *Introduction to Statistics for Business Decisions.*[6] However, few mail-order operators are likely to be willing to follow through on Schlaifer's method. Most will boggle at estimating the monetary gains or losses that will follow as a result of various possible test outcomes.

Estimating how much risk you are willing to take obviously depends upon how much money is at stake. Nevertheless, many people are probably willing to state how much of a risk they want to take, even if they will not estimate the dollar amounts directly. And in that circumstance, the methods that I describe are the best that I know of.

Will This New Offer Make a Profit?

You want to know whether your product or offer is attractive enough for further investment. Commonly you tackle this problem by selecting several potentially good lists, writing the best possible copy, and mailing at a good time of the year. (You might mail in an off season if you know how much to upgrade the results you get.) You figure that if you have a winner, further experimentation will improve the techniques and unearth even better lists.

How big a test? How many tests? There is no stock answer. Are you selling a $5.95 product or one that goes for $5,950? Is it a one-shot solicitation, or is it a repeat-business operation?

Let's try an example. You want to sell an auto accessory priced at $15. For simplicity we'll say that it is a one-shot offer, though a sound analysis should include the future value of having the customers on your list for future solicitations. You figure that a 1.125 percent return will return your future solicitations. You figure that a 1.125 percent return will return your investment and leave something for overhead and profit. In other words, 1.125 percent is the break-even point you choose. If your offer pulls that well or better over the long haul, you'll consider the offer a success rather than a failure.

How big a test sample should you mail? Let's say that you want to be 85 percent sure that chance will make your test results no more than 25 percent higher than repeated mailings. You obviously don't care at all if follow-ups would be higher than the test results. You merely want protection against test results that are too high, leading you into unwise further investment.

(NOTE: When we say "85 percent sure," we mean that the right betting odds in a horse race would be 17 to 3. Note also that at this

Table 26-1

		Percent of drop-off* (The percentage difference between the estimated return and the break-even point; or the drop-off percentage you wish to guard against)			
		50%	25%	12½%	6¼%
The degree of surety (how	75%			29.2	116.8
sure you wish to be that	85		14.0	56.0	
the result will be over the	90		26.2	104.8	
break-even point)`	95	11.0	42.8		
	99	21.7	86.9		

* The numbers within the table represent the number of returns the test must be arranged to obtain in order to meet the drop-off requirement and the degree of certainty required. Note that this table, like the other tables in this chapter, is approximate. Note also that it holds only for return percentages under 10 percent.

point we are discussing the variation in results due only to chance factors. We shall discuss the fall-off effect later.)

You estimate that the offer will pull 1.5 percent. The difference between your estimate of 1.5 percent and your break-even point of 1.125 percent is 0.375 percent, which is 25 percent of 1.5 percent.

To find the correct sample size to satisfy your specifications, refer to Table 26-1. Go along the horizontal top line until you find 25 percent, the drop-off percentage you want to guard against. Then proceed down the 25 percent vertical column until you reach the 85 percent degree of surety you demand. The number in the box will be the number of returns you must set up your test sample to obtain. To find the correct sample size, divide the number of returns in the box (14 in this example) by the percent of return you expect (1.5 percent in this case): 14 divided by 0.015 equals 933. So try a test of 933, or around 1,000.

Perhaps you are selling a higher-priced product like kitchenware. Your experience leads you to expect a return of 0.5 percent. As in the previous example, you desire to guard against a drop-off of 25 percent from test results to continuation results, and you demand a surety of 85 percent. You therefore would need to get the same number of returns as in the previous example (14), and your sample size therefore is 14 divided by 0.5 percent, or 2,799. You would probably test-mail 2,500 or 3,000.

But if you expect 0.5 percent return and are willing to settle for 75 percent surety against a later drop-off of 25 percent or more, you need a test sample of 7.3 divided by 0.5 percent, or roughly 1,500. Let us return to the auto-accessory example.

So you run a test, expecting 1.5 percent on a test sample of 1,000, and you get results of 1.3 percent. Your *best guess* is that future mailings will pull 1.3 percent, provided the copy, list, seasonal conditions, etc., stay the same. (Don't snicker at this apparently simpleminded statement. The "best guess" is not always so obvious, and many mailers have run into difficulty because they made a wrong "best guess.")

But how sure are you that future results will be above your break-even mark of 1.125 percent? Certainly you are not as sure as you hoped to be after the test. However, those are the vagaries of testing.

The difference between what you obtained (1.3 percent) and your break-even point (1.125 percent) is 0.175 percent, which is roughly 13.5 percent of 1.3 percent. Use the figure of 13.5 percent to enter Table 26-2. Go across the horizontal top row to the column headed "15%," the closest to 13.5 percent. Then run down the column to 12.4, which is closest to the 13 returns you obtained. In the vertical column to the left you can read that you are roughly 70 percent sure that repeated tests will bring home an average return of better than your break-even point. (Actually, since the 13.5 percent figure you were working with is less than the 15 percent, you are even less than 70 percent sure.)

Given that information, you are probably *not* satisfied that your test results will support further heavy investment without further testing. Run another test, then, perhaps the same size as the first, or somewhat larger. Then combine the results of the *two* tests as if they were just one large test, and go back to Table 26-2, following the previous instructions. By this time you should have sufficiently unambiguous answers to either push forward with confidence or drop the project. (This combination technique is probably not logically waterproof, but it is simple, easy to communicate, and free of serious error.)

For the situation in which your test results fall *below* the break-even point and you wish to know the chances that repeated mailings would be *above* the break-even point, you can still use Table 26-2. Substitute break-even and test results for one another, and subtract the degree of surety in the table from 100 to find the desired figure.

Some top direct-mail consultants do not agree with this section because they believe that I do not sufficiently discourage small sample tests. But I think they are thinking *only* of major mailers testing consumer offers, whereas the advice I give here may also apply to, say, a new business testing a computer package for mail-order firms selling for $3,000, where the total market is in the tens of thousands

Table 26-2

		$\dfrac{\text{Observed return \%}-\text{break-even return \%}}{\text{Observed return \%}} \times 100 = \%$				
		10%	15%	20%	30%	50%
Degree of surety that future	60%	6.5				
return percentage will be	70	27.6	12.4	6.6	3.1	
above break-even	80	67.2	30.0	16.8	7.5	
percentage	90	163.8	73.0	40.9	18.2	6.6
	95		121.2	63.1	30.3	11.0

Each number in the table is the number of returns a test produced—irrespective of the sample size.

Note: Tables 26-1 and 26-2 contain the same type of statistical material. We include Table 26-2 only for the convenience of the different headings.

at most. In that case, an initial test of say 500 letters may yield valuable information.

On the other hand, for run-of-the-mine direct-mail testing situations, Ed Burnett's rule-of-thumb sample size—large enough to obtain 40 or 50 responses—probably provides good guidance. Try that unless you have a strong reason to choose another sample size.

How to Test a List

Assume that your product offer is already fixed, as is your copy. You are committed to selling the product, and you have been successful with other lists. What you want, then, is to mail to every list that gives you even a dollar of profit.

Note that in this situation you will compute overhead in a manner different from that used for the problems in the section above. When you are just *considering* a product, you must add *all* costs into overhead—including setup and organization costs—and apply them to each unit you mail. But when the question is, rather, "Do I or don't I mail *this* list?" you should only load your overhead calculations with the cost of the overrun of stock, postage, addressing, and direct handling costs. This is important because you may otherwise pass up mailing chances that would increase your total year-end profit.

How large is the entire list you want to test? The size of the list *should* affect the size of your test sample. But, contrary to popular notion, the size of the list does not affect the *accuracy* of your test, but only the *economics* of the test. On a test of 2,000, it matters little for accuracy whether the entire list is 10,000 or a million. As long as your test sample is less than one-fifth of the total list—as it always will be—the accuracy will be almost the same no matter what the list size.

To repeat this difficult-to-believe but absolutely true statement: The accuracy of a test depends only on the size of the sample and not at all on the size of the list—as long as the list is more than, say, 5 times bigger than the sample.

But—the larger the total list, the more *valuable* your test information will be, and therefore the more you should be willing to lay out for the test, i.e., the higher the degree of surety you should demand. If the entire list is 10,000 and you expect a profit of 5 cents per piece mailed, the most you can make from the list after your 2,000 test is 5 cents times 8,000, or $400. But if the list is a million, your potential profit is 5 cents times 998,000. So errors are much more expensive if the list is very large. *That's* why a larger test may be warranted for a larger list.

Next you must decide the break-even point with which you are going to work. Then estimate the percent of return you expect and how sure you want to be of your results. Example: You estimate the return will be 2 percent, and your break-even point is 1.5 percent. (The break-even estimate should be accurate, but the estimated return estimate can be off considerably without harming the calculation.) You state that if you *do* get a return of 2 percent on the test, you'd like to be 75 percent sure that subsequent mailings will be above 1.5 percent.

To find the proper sample size, read Table 26-1 down to 75 percent (because that is the surety you have chosen to demand), read across to 25 percent [because (2.0 minus 1.5) divided by 2.0 equals 25 percent], and the number in the block (7.3) tells you how many returns you need to get. Then divide the number in the block by the percent of return you expect. The result—365—is the sample size you need.

If you expect a 1 percent return, and you still don't want to fall below 25 percent of your expected return (i.e., your break-even point is 0.75 percent), you will work with the same block in the chart. You will still set your test up to get 7.3 returns, but the sample size will be twice as large—730.

But we all know very well that much more must go into this than straight statistics. With most lists you face the problem that when you go back to the list after the test, the returns will fall below the test mailing. We usually assume that this phenomenon results from tests that are not random samples of the whole list. Lewis Kleid's report "Importance of Stipulating Test Samples" gives excellent directions for obtaining random test samples.[7] If you follow those directions, you can prevent fall-off from this cause.

If you expect that follow-up will fall below the test results, there are two possible solutions:

1. You can go back to the list in several successive mailings. Each mailing should do worse than the last, and you keep mailing till you fall below your break-even point. The first remailing will be close to the test results, and you may use the technique above to predict what you will obtain.

2. If it is inconvenient for you to mail to the list in several sections, and if you can't bludgeon the list owner into giving you a random sample, your only recourse is to guess how much the entire list, on the average, will drop below the test. If you figure that the list will average 80 percent of a fair test, then reduce the test returns by 20 percent and go on from there in your calculations.

(A seller of professional books turned the fall-off effect to good advantage. He mailed test samples of 5,000 each to 50 different lists—with no intention of ever going back to any of the lists—and his overall results were pleasantly high. The same firm estimates that a mailing indirectly sells 3 times as many books in bookstores as through direct replies.)

To evaluate the test results *after* they are in, go back and use Table 26-2 in just the same way you did when testing a product offer. Find the blocks that contain numbers close to the total returns you received. Each block gives you a combination of a degree of surety and a boundary to your guess. If you received seven returns, you can be 60 percent sure that follow-up mailings will not fall more than 10 percent below the test average; *or*, you can be 80 percent sure that the follow-ups will not fall more than 30 percent below your test average. (Pay no attention to the coincidental sequencing of numbers. The two figures cannot be added or subtracted.)

Follow-up (continuation) mailings usually are 5 to 10 times the initial mailing size, Ed Burnett says. I hope that in the future someone will work out a careful analysis to evaluate this rule of thumb.

How to Test One Piece of Copy against Another

In the simple copy-testing situation the *costs* of both letter units being tested are the same. All you care about, then, is which letter unit pulls "better." And you need no calculations to tell you that you should go with whichever package shows up better on the test, no matter how small the margin between the two. Post-test calculating

Table 26-3

		The difference you care about: percent return, letter 1 minus % return, letter 2 (average percent return, letters 1 and 2)				
		4%	10%	20%	35%	50%
Degree of surety (how sure	75%	1,237.5	182	45.5	14.3	7
you want to be that the	85		424	106	34.7	17
test results indicate the	90		656	164	53.0	26
better letter)	95			272	86.7	43.5

Each number in the table shows the number of *returns* you must expect from the *average* of the two test samples. To obtain the sample size for *each* test sample, divide number of returns by estimated average return.

will only help you to decide whether your first test was conclusive, or whether you need to test further.

When the costs of the two letter units are different, the situation is more complex. Then you must balance the margin between them against the extra cost, using test results as your guide. The solution to that problem is beyond the scope of this discussion.

For the simple case, begin by asking yourself: How *big* a difference am I interested in? You obviously don't care if one letter unit is 1/10,000 better than the other, no matter how large your mailings will be. But you certainly do care if one mailing piece will bring in twice as many returns as the other, no matter how small your mailing will be. You must ask yourself at what point you cease caring, given the particular requirements of your situation.

As an example for discussion here, let's say that you wouldn't bother to test if you thought that the difference between the two proposed letter units would be less than 10 percent (of the average return).

Next you must ask yourself: *If* the difference is as big as, or bigger than, I care about, how *sure* do I want to be that the test will indicate which is the better letter unit? In other words, how sure do you want to be that the test will not mislead you? For example, here, let's say that you want to be 85 percent sure that the test indicates the better letter unit.

With those two values in mind, refer to Table 26-3. Read across to "10%," then down to "85%," and you find that you would require 424 returns to satisfy your requirements. You immediately decide that that would be too expensive, and you decide to scale down your demand for surety to 75 percent and to concern yourself only with differences of 20 percent or more of the average return. You then find that you need to get 45.5 returns. If you expect an *average* return of 2 percent for the two test samples, *each* test sample must then be 45.5 divided by 2 percent, or 2,275. In total, you need to mail 4,550 letters to satisfy your requirements in this case.

If the *real* difference between the letter units is even greater than you are testing for, you stand an even better chance of the test being right. If the real difference between them is less than you care about, you stand a greater chance of the best being wrong. But you have said that if the latter is the case, you are not concerned.

After the test is over and the results are in hand, you will probably *not* want to determine *how* sure you are that the test is right. If the difference between the mailing-piece returns is great, you need no further test. If the difference is slight, there isn't much point in further testing. Shoot the works with the letter that does better— no matter by how little it does better.

The fallacy has somehow gone abroad that you can test only one variable in a mailing. Not so. You can, in the same mailing, test headline, colors, copy, and other variables. Testing more than one variable at a time does require extreme caution and attention lest you go astray. But it also can give you a great deal of information at a relatively low testing cost.

Let's say that you want to test two headlines against each other, and you also want to test a pink versus a blue reply envelope. You will mail four equal-sized random test samples: headline 1, pink; headline 2, pink; headline 1, blue; headline 2, blue.

How big a test should you make? My recommendation is that you should use test samples just as large as if you were only testing headline 1 versus headline 2, pink versus blue. (See preceding pages for guidance on that problem.) So you are getting two tests (almost) for the price of one.

To analyze the test, look at the *total* numbers of pink versus blue, and headline 1 versus headline 2. See the example in Table 26-4.

Blue is the color that pulled the greatest total number of returns, and it is probably better. Similarly for headline 2, which pulled the greatest total number. But which *combination* is best is a difficult question. Apparently the combination of headline 2 and pink did better than any other combination. However, that could be a fluke of the sample. Unless you think that there is likely to be some *interaction* between the color and the headline, then you would disregard the highest-score combination. I do not think such interaction is likely, and hence I would bet that the combination of the best

Table 26-4. (Hypothetical Data)

	Headline 1	Headline 2	Color totals
Pink	40	60	100
Blue	50	58	108
Headline totals	90	118	208 (Overall total)

headline taken by itself and the best color taken by itself—headline 2 and blue—would be the best combination.

Proceed with great caution in multiple testing. You *cannot* use the tables shown here to help you with tests of three or more units that vary on the same dimension, i.e., when there are three or more different headlines, colors, or what have you. It is crucial to understand that the more variations you test on the same dimension—eight different headlines, for example—the more the variability you must expect in your results, and the larger the tests must therefore be. An analogy may help to make this clear. The more evenings you play poker, the more likely you are to come up with a royal flush—even though the chance of drawing it in any individual evening will remain the same. To test eight different headlines, *each* of the eight test samples will have to be *much* larger than *either* of the test samples when only two headlines are being tested.

Furthermore, if you test eight headlines, the percentage of returns for the *best* test sample is not—repeat, not—your best guess about what that headline will pull in the future. In Table 26-5, headline 4 is your best bet, but chances are that subsequent retests of the headline will not pull as high as 2.9 percent. I can't prove that statement here, and the body of theory is weak on this issue, but take my word for it anyway. (See technical note 6 in Appendix E for more discussion of this point.)

How to Select a Test Sample

There are two methods of choosing test samples that will give you satisfactory tests. (When I say "satisfactory," I mean that you will not obtain false information that can lead you into a costly or disastrously bad decision.)

One satisfactory method is to select a scientifically "random" sample of the names on the list. William Doppler made these interesting interview comments on random sampling.[8] They go back to the precomputer era, but they are still applicable to sampling the house list for firms that are not yet computerized.

Table 26-5

Headline	Return (%)
1	2.3
2	1.8
3	2.7
4	2.9
5	1.9
6	1.9
7	2.0
8	2.2

QUESTION: Many mailers consider that a list arranged alphabetically automatically gives you a representative sample. What are some of the factors that might influence response on an alphabetical list?

ANSWER: It is *not* correct to test an alphabetical list by taking the names in sequence. You must space the names in a random pattern. Alphabetical sequences give you unbelievable distortions. I would look upon results from such sampling with suspicion.

QUESTION: Bill, could you give me an example of "random" selection in testing a list arranged alphabetically?

ANSWER: Random means a situation where each name has an equal chance to be selected. Most random sampling is based on tables of random numbers. Under ideal circumstances, give each name a number and pull those which match with the random numbers in the book. Random samples are expensive. Random sampling takes a lot of time and labor.

QUESTION: It seems to me that scientific sampling is a very involved affair which requires a lot of clerical labor and tabulations. What does it cost to pull a scientific sample?

ANSWER: Let me give you a case history. We had a list filed alphabetically. The total number of names was 400,000. We figured the size of the sample based on expectation, error, and confidence and came up with 2,000 names. The next question was how are we going to select the 2,000 names. We had made some studies on alphabetical sequences and had learned that any group of names in alphabetical order gave us a distorted and, therefore, unpredictable sample.

We also had some experience with sampling in lots or batches. For example we could have divided the 2,000 names into 20 lots of 100 names, each lot in alphabetical sequence. Sampling by lots gave us a better sample than the alphabetical sequence, but still not a sample reliable enough to make predictions. So we decided to sample by individual cards. We decided to stand up every card at intervals of 200. We did not have to count the cards—we measured the distance between 200 cards, made a couple of wire gauges and went through the file drawers. When we got finished with the sampling job we had a sample which was a reasonably true cross section of the list. The cost of the sample was about $50 per 1,000 names. We used this sample over and over again for different kinds of tests [a somewhat dangerous tactic]. So the actual cost of the sample per test was not too bad. The results we obtained from the sample were confirmed by the mass mailings with an astounding degree of accuracy. Obviously, a mailer cannot expect to buy a true scientific sample at the standard rental addressing price of $15 per M.

With respect to rented lists, with the aid of the computer it is nowadays frequently possible to obtain a true random sample by taking every nth name or by using another scientific procedure. Talk to your list broker about this. However, it is not *always* possible to obtain a true random sample from a rented list. Alternatively, one tries to obtain a reasonable representative sample.

There are several methods of doing so. Lewis Kleid describes them this way:[9]

1. *Alphabetically Arranged Lists.* List owners should address an equal number of names from each of 5 sections of the list.
   A-E
   F-J
   K-O
   P-T
   U-Z

2. *Unarranged Lists.* List owner should address test names from at least three different parts of the list.

3. *Chronologically Arranged Lists.* List owner should address a proportionate quantity of names for each year or period covered by the list. He should be further cautioned *not* to address only the latest names.

4. *Geographically Arranged Lists.* Test cross sections should be worked out using the major eleven geographical sections of the country.

A good list broker should be able to help you work out the details of a satisfactory geographical sample or the other types of representative samples.

It is very important that you should not be satisfied simply to *ask* for "a fair sample." A fair sample is exactly what you won't get unless you *make sure* that you get a good test sample by specifying exactly what you want.

Conclusions about
Direct-Mail Testing

1. The more willing and able you are to make follow-up tests—the more time and patience you have—the smaller your original samples can be.

2. The higher the unit sale price—or better, the higher the net revenue (order margin) per order and therefore the smaller the percent of return needed to break even—the bigger the test sample you need to obtain the accuracy you choose to get.

3. Ever-larger test samples are not the necessary answer to your search for reliable information. Careful thought, together with *proper* test-sample sizes, is the answer. Very small samples can yield a great deal of information. An expert can often come to very important—and sound—conclusions on a test large enough to produce only ten or twenty-five responses.

4. The size of the list does not affect the *accuracy* of the test, hard as this is to believe. But it may influence the size of the *most economical* test nevertheless.

5. Extremely precise statistical methods are not necessary in direct-mail testing. This is true partly because test samples are often badly unrepresentative and partly because a mailer wants the *big* indications that make a big difference in the pocketbook. (Listen to differences that scream, not the differences that whisper.) Nevertheless, the *theory* of statistics plus crude rule-of-thumb approximations can be tremendously helpful in making and saving you money.

6. If you are testing many different variations of headline, color, etc., you must look for differences much bigger than if you were testing just one variation against another. (Just *how* much bigger is a tricky question.)

7. We have said nothing about the mechanics of splitting test samples "randomly." Most direct-mail people are aware of how easy it is to foul up a test by sending all one sample to one state and all the other sample to another state. The surest guarantee of a fair test, of course, is to send one letter to every other name on the list—no matter what the original order or disorder of the list. In any case, don't forget that if your lists are not reasonably randomly selected, all other technique is for nought.

The purpose of this section has been to give *some* of the benefits of statistical theory to direct-mail testers who don't wish to study statistics or the philosophy of science. But the wise will recognize the risks of this shortcut, and they will not look upon it as a substitute for expert advice when tricky problems arise.

A Reminder

This is the time for another reminder: Keep good records faithfully. So often one sets up a beautiful and expensive test and then forgets to keep the records that will allow one to draw conclusions. So remember your careful record keeping.

27

How to Produce and Print Mail-Order Advertising

The Many Ways of Putting Ink on Paper / Type and Typographers / How to Prepare an Ad for Letterpress / How to Prepare an Ad for Offset / Miscellaneous Printing Matters

Printing is a world in itself—a fascinating, technical world. The more you know about printing and the graphic arts, the more that printing will interest you and give you pleasure. Knowledge of printing processes will also benefit you in the mail-order business.

Our purpose in this chapter is to tell you only the bare facts about printing that you need to run a mail-order business. If your business grows big enough so that you have very long runs of catalogs or direct-mail pieces, you will need to hire a production specialist.

Here's a tip you are sure to forget and sure to regret forgetting: Take out the *very first piece* of any printing you buy and place it in a bound folio marked "Do not remove any page on pain of death." Then take out another five pieces and throw them into a junk file. Time after time you will need these old samples, and you'll curse and scream when you can't find the ones you need. Then your junk file can save you.

The Many Ways of Putting Ink on Paper

Letterpress

The letterpress process with movable type is what Gutenberg invented. The letterpress printer places metal type and/or engravings into a "chase" and then places the chase on the press. The printing press rolls ink across the raised type and then brings the type in contact with the paper.

Large sizes of type for headlines and special effects are set by hand from "fonts" that the typographer or printer has available. Small type for body copy is cast by automatic linotype machines that the printer operates like a typewriter.

Illustrations are printed in one of several ways, depending upon the type of artwork. Toned illustrations (illustrations with varying shades from white to black, rather than just light and dark) are most difficult. In general, illustrations are transformed into engraving by photographic means. Engravers are specialists who operate separately from printers.

Printing presses of the letterpress type come in all shapes and sizes.

Most newspapers and some magazines use the letterpress process. But more and more publications are shifting to offset printing, especially for the inside pages.

When you send a small ad to a letterpress publication, you can ask the publication to set the type for you. Chapter 14 discusses how to work with the magazine to get them to do what you want. Or you can send the publication a complete "cut" (engraving) of your ad which you have had made up by an engraver from typographer's type.

You yourself will probably not use the letterpress process very frequently in your daily work, except for envelopes and odd work like labels and some four-color brochures. Offset may be better for very long runs of envelopes and other pieces.

Letterpress has always been noted for its faithful reproduction and therefore is chosen for four-color printing. But recent improvements in offset printing have narrowed that difference.

Offset Lithography

"Offset," lithography," and "planograph" all refer to the same process. "Multilith" is the trade name for one brand of offset printing press.

In the offset process, the platemakers (or the offset printer, if they make their own plates) *photograph* the material that you want printed. Artwork is photographed separately, through a "screen." The image is then transferred from the photographic negative to a metal plate. The plate is treated with a chemical solution that reacts to light. Wherever light does not shine on the plate, ink will not stick to the plate because of subsequent treatment, in the same way that water or ink will not stick to greased areas of a piece of metal or glass.

Then an ink blanket rolls across the plate, and the ink remains on the plate only in the pattern of the original material to be printed. A rubber blanket rolls over the plate and picks up the picture in ink from the plate. The rubber blanket then rolls across the paper and prints the material. (The process is called "offset" because the picture is offset from the plate to the paper by means of a rubber blanket.)

The most complex lithographs are illustrations in full color (four color). If you understand the following description written by the lithographers' union,[1] you will understand all about one-color illustrations and "line" jobs, too.

HOW A LITHOGRAPH IS MADE

1. Using special high-precision camera equipment, the original color artwork is photographed four times—through four different color filters—to produce four color separation negatives, one for each of the primary colors, yellow, red and blue, plus one for the black.

2. These color separations are made on black and white film. Each negative now contains, in relative degrees of gray from white to black, the values of intensity of one of the four colors in the original.

3. Each color separation negative is now retouched by expert craftsmen before being inserted into a camera which operates on the principle of a photographic enlarger—projecting light through the negative onto unexposed film. In this second photographic process, however, a fine "screen" is inserted between the color separation negative and the unexposed film.

4. This screen is made of two large discs of optical glass on which have been scribed microscopically fine lines. Set at right angles to each other, these lines form a grid of minute squares. The number of these squares will range from 14,400 to 90,000 per square inch, depending upon the fineness of the screen.

5. In exposing each color separation negative through the screen to produce a "screen positive," diffusion of light by each square of the grid breaks the image into minute dots or squares. The sizes of these dots on the developed film positive vary according to the amount of light passing through each square. Thus, on the yellow film positive, each dot on the filmed image represents the intensity

of light projected from the yellow negative through its corresponding square of the screen: the greater the intensity, the larger the dot!

Note: Eventually these dots will be transferred onto metal plates—one plate for each color—to become ink-bearing surfaces. Because of this, the size of each dot will determine the volume of ink it will hold, and hence the intensity of the color it will print.

6. The dot sizes on each screened positive must therefore be exactly right. To make certain of this before the plates are made, the four screened positives now undergo a highly skilled process known as dot etching. Over a light table, each positive film is examined minutely. Using fine brushes and acid, master craftsmen work over the dots, adjusting them where necessary to the precise sizes that are correct for the color values required. To make a particular shade of brown, for instance, the dot etcher must know the precise dot sizes required on the yellow, the blue and the red positives—and adjust those dot sizes so that the correct volume of each color will be printed—dot by dot—to produce the color pattern that creates the original brown in the artwork.

7. Each of the four screened and color-corrected positives is now stripped into a master form sheet or "flat" composed of all the elements of art and typography that will appear on the four color plates. With the aid of master register marks—attached to the original copy and reproduced on each separation negative and positive—skilled craftsmen work to precisions measured in thousandths of an inch. A separate "flat" is made for each color.

8. We're now ready for platemaking. Light-weight, flexible metal plates are first coated with a light-sensitive emulsion in a centrifugal whirler, converting the surface into a "photographic" plate. (Plates also can be bought pre-sensitized.)

9. Each of the four master flats—one for each color—is placed against a light-sensitive plate under pressure and exposed to light.

10. It is this photo-process which makes possible one of the important economic advantages of lithography. Multiple exposures can be made on each plate, repeating the image as many times as the plate size permits. In this operation known as "Step & Repeat" or "Photo-Composing," these multiple exposures are made with all the precise registering between the different items and the different plates for each color automated in the platemaking stage to eliminate costly time on the press.

11. The exposed plate is now developed, and a grease-receptive lacquer is applied which adheres only to the image-bearing areas, making them water-repellent. For the principle of lithography is based upon the chemical fact that water and oil repel each other.

12. The four plates—one for each color—are now curved around the press cylinders, fastened, and adjusted for hairline register. Each minute dot on each plate is now an ink bearing surface which will

hold a precise volume of colored ink, in volume according to its size.

13. On press, each of the four plates comes in contact with three sets of rollers: the water roller which moistens all non-inkbearing surfaces—the ink roller which imparts the plate's particular color to the ink-bearing surfaces—and the rubber "offset" cylinder onto which the inked impression is transferred.

14. The rubber "offset cylinder" in turn transfers that impression onto the paper as it passes through the press. (Hence the term offset.)

Offset Prices on Job Printing.   For the standard 8½- by 11-inch, 16-pound sheet of white paper, you should pay no *more* (1986) than $26 for the first thousand, and much less for succeeding thousands. If no printer near you will approach those prices, you can do business by mail with New York or Chicago printers. The "Business Services" column of the classified ads in *The New York Times* Sunday Business Section usually carries several listings of printers who will handle your job for you.

Rotogravure

"Roto" is a photographic process in which the picture is actually etched *into* a metal plate. It provides very fine reproduction, and it is good for very long runs. That's why much rotogravure is used in Sears, Roebuck catalogs and in some Sunday newspaper sections.

You will have little contact with rotogravure at first. If you send copy to a rotogravure magazine, send the same material you would send for offset reproduction.

Mimeograph

In this process you type holes in a clothlike stencil. The stencil is then wrapped around an inky drum, and when the drum is rolled over paper, the ink feeds out through the impressions you made with your typewriter.

Mimeograph is a good reproduction process for short runs (under 5,000) of some kinds of sales literature. It has the advantage of being quick. A person can type a mimeograph stencil and run it off immediately. There is no costly type to set, and no platemaker to wait for. Mimeo is usually cheaper than offset for runs under 500.

A *good* mimeographing job of typewritten copy will look very nearly as good as an offset job. And now, new electronic scanning devices will transfer an illustration or a letterhead to the mimeograph stencil. (But the reproduction of illustrations by mimeograph is nowhere nearly as sharp as an offset job, and it is *not* cheap.

It's handy to have a mimeograph machine around your office. But chances are there is a professional letter shop near you that will do the job better and at lower true cost.

Automatic Typewriting

This process is used when it is essential that each letter look hand-typed. (There are very few times in mail order when this is necessary, however.)

The operator cuts a roll that looks like the roll in a player piano, and the rolls are then inserted into one or more automatic typewriters. The letter is typed out exactly like the original. You can leave blank spaces to type in later the name and address or any other special message you desire.

Hooven and Auto-typist (American Automatic Typewriter Company) are two systems of automatic typewriters on the market. You can find their addresses in the New York and Chicago telephone directories.

The cost of automatically typed letters is not low, but it is considerably less than the cost of having them typed by hand when you are having them done in quantity.

Computer-Typed Letters

Computer-typed letters not only look individually typed, but the name, address, and other details of the addressee may be typed in as they come from the computer tape. Such letters can pull better than letters that are not individually typed. But, they do not perform miracles. You can obtain more details by contacting one or more of the firms that advertise under the category "Computer Letter Services" in the classified advertising section of *Direct Marketing*. Eventually, your own computer and attached printer may do the job.

Type and Typographers

Every advertisement and direct-mail piece uses type—lots of type. You must learn to choose the typeface you want, and the arrangement of type; or, at least you must learn to be a good critic of whoever "specifies the type" for your ads.

A letterpress printer does set type. But for almost all your jobs you need more skill in typography and a wider variety of type faces than a job printer possesses. That's where the typographer comes in.

A typographer is a specialist who sets type for you according to your instructions, and then prints only a few "reproduction proofs," which you then photograph and convert into either an offset plate or a "cut" for letterpress.

All that you need to learn from this paragraph is *not* to expect a printer to do the job of a typographer, or you will be disappointed. The letterpress printer is seldom equipped to set type for the kind of printed pieces that you need to sell your product effectively.

Type for headlines can be any of very many different typefaces, some of which are shown in Figures 27-1 and 27-2. You will want a type that has a "personality" in keeping with the product you are advertising. You don't want the thickest, blackest, strongest type if you are advertising lingerie. The typographer's judgment may be good as to which type you should use, but an artist's judgment is likely to be much better.

Beware of typographers and artists who want to give you a "good-looking ad." Effective mail-order ads are seldom good to look at.

If you want to specify the type yourself, get a book of typefaces and look through it till you find what you want. If the typographer doesn't have that exact style, she or he can come pretty close in matching it.

The four basic kinds of type are

Old Style Roman

Modern Roman

Sans-serif (Gothic)

Special-purpose types

Caslon and Garamond are classic examples of Old Style Roman. Bodoni is a good example of Modern Roman. There are dozens more varieties of both. The various strokes in Modern Roman differ more from one another in width than in Old Style, and the "serifs"—the tiny strokes at right angles to the main stroke—are flat. Old Style serifs are round.

Sans-serif Gothic is just what it says: without serifs. Gothic headlines give you the most punch for your money. Most of your headlines will be in one or another of the Gothic families. Franklin Gothic is an example of this family.

THE SIX FACES OF TYPE

1. 𝕿𝖊𝖝𝖙   4. Gothic

2. Roman   4a. Sans Serif

2a. Oldstyle   4b. Sq. Serif

2b. Modern   5. *Script,* Cursives

2c. Mixed

3. *Italic*   6. NOVELTY

Figure 27-1

Not only are there various families of type, but there are also variations within a family. For example, a family may be condensed, extended, both, light, etc.

There are also *italic* faces in many families of type. Figure 27-3 shows some examples. Italics can sometimes be good for headlines, especially when you want the ad to look like editorial matter for a reading notice.

Don't use several different faces of type in your various headlines and subheads. Many different faces are confusing, and they are even uglier than a mail-order ad should be. (However, I have no data to *prove* that this dictum holds true in mail order.)

Use type as big as you can squeeze into the width of the space you have available. This is especially true for the overall heading. Reverse type (white on black) gives your headline even more punch. But never use it for body type or on the order form; it is too hard to read.

For the type in the *body* of your ad, follow your typographer's recommendation. Never use Gothic or italic, because they are hard to read. Generally, you will use a very small body type—sometimes smaller, in fact, than your printer has available. In that case, you can reduce the size of the type with a photostat.

But don't try to be *too* greedy and set your type *too* small. Five-point or six-point type is probably best for most situations you will run into. Follow the examples of good mail-order ads whose purpose is similar to what you are trying to do.

SOME REPRESENTATIVE TYPES

Cloister Black, h Goudy Text, h

Garamond, Te Caslon, TeA

Goudy Bold, Ei Cloister Oldstyle, T

Bodoni Book, Tt **Ultra Bodoni**

Cheltenham BC AGg Bulmer, T

Caslon Italic ***Bodoni Bold Italic***

R RR GOTHIC

Sans Serif BC Sans Serif Light

Spartan Ex B Sans Serif Bold

Stymie Light **Stymie Bold**

Brush Script *Coronet Cursive*

Hobo, ygpq LOMBARDIC

P. T. Barnum Typewriter Type

Figure 27-2

Typography service is expensive because of the large investment a typographer must make in type and equipment. It will pay you to get everything as clear as possible before the work starts, and then you should make as few changes as possible.

In recent years photographic typesetting has come strongly onto the market. In this process, the typesetter only has *one* size of each type face. You get the exact size you want by photographic enlargement. Photosetting is as sharp as ordinary typography, and it may be considerably cheaper for your needs. It's worth checking on.

Paste-up type is a quick and cheap substitute for typography. Sometimes it is very satisfactory. You buy an entire sheet of alphabet letters for about $1 to $5 in the typeface and size that you need. You lay the letters you want over a lined-off piece of paper, and rub the letters off the sheet and onto your apper. Repeat the process until you have your headline.

An even cruder method is to cut letters out of magazines. In a pinch, it can work just fine.

You should memorize these measurements: 14 agate lines = 1 inch; 6 picas = 1 inch; 72 points = 1 inch. You measure the width of an ad in picas or columns, the height in agate lines or points.

How to Prepare an Ad for Letterpress

Let's first talk about *magazine ads* in letterpress publications. (The rate card tells you which magazines use letterpress.)

A letterpress magazine *will* set type for your ad, if you desire. This can be an advantage. When you run the first test of an ad, you may not wish to shell out typographer's charges when you know you will be changing the ad.

On the other hand, the typesetting the magazine produces for you will be far inferior to that of a typographer. You are *not* likely to obtain exactly the effect you want. Your choice of typefaces will be limited, and the arrangement of the type will *not* be just as you wish.

Furthermore, most magazines will not make cuts of illustrations for you. (A few shopping-section magazines such as *House Beautiful* and *The New York Times Magazine* will do the whole job—because they get a lot of business from amateurs in the mail-order business.)

When your ad has been tested and you are reasonably sure that you will be inserting it repeatedly, you should perfect the ad in the way you want it, then have an original cut and duplicate cuts made. At this time you should call in an artist or use an advertising agency.

ABCDEFGHIJ SMALL CAPITALS abcdefghijklmnopqrstuvwx*abcdefghijklmnopqrstuv* 12 pt.

HERE ARE TEN POINT CAPITALS ABCD SMALL CAPITALS ABCDEFGHIJKLMNOPQRSTUVWXYZ ABCD
lower case abcdefghijklmnopqrstuvwxyz abcdefghij *ITALIC abcdefghijklmnopqrstuvwxyz abcdefghijklmno* 10 pt.

CASLON OLD FACE

HERE YOU SEE TEN POINT CAPS ABCD SMALL CAPS ABCDEFGHIJKLMNOPQRSTUVWXYP AB 10 pt.
lower case abcdefghijklmnopqrstuvwxyzabcdef *ITALIC CAPS Italic lower case abcdefghijklmnop*

HERE YOU SEE EIGHT POINT CAPS ABCDEFJ SMALL CAPS ABCDEFGHIJKLMNOPQRSTUVWXYP ABCDEFGHI 8 pt.
lower case abcdefghijklmnopqrstuvwxyzabcdefghijklm *ITALIC CAPS Italic lower case abcdefghijklmnopqrstuwwx*

GARAMOND

24 pt. T. S. ELIOT speaks with an *authority a*

18 pt. REX WARNER spins a sonnet or a *thoughtful ode and*

BODONI

ABCDEFGHIJKLMNOPQRS
TUVWXYZ& abcdefghijklm
Franklin Gothic

Figure 27-3

You need professional help to specify how each of the elements in the ad should look, and then to fit the entire ad together.

The first element in the ad will be the type. You will get a "reproduction proof" from the typographer with your exact requirements in choice of typeface, size of type, width of typesetting, and heading. If you don't get exactly what you want, explain your wishes to the typographer and get a second proof. Figure 27-4 shows the proofreaders' marks used in correcting your copy.

The second element in the ad will be the artwork—either a photograph or a dummy.

Then you paste up the artwork and the type into a "dummy" or "mechanical," which you send to the engraver. The engraver first makes an original plate of the ad and then makes duplicate plates. In most cases you will retain the original plate in case you want to make additional copies. You send the duplicate plates off to the various magazines in which you want to run.

Take your engraver's advice on the type of duplicate plates to use. There are many different kinds: electrotype, stereotype, plastic plates, and molded rubber plates.

Different types of media have different column widths. Newspapers are comparatively narrow, generally. Each different column width requires a different size plate. Of course you can "float" a small plate in a wider column, but that is not an economical use of space.

Width of columns is specified for each medium on its rate card and in *Standard Rate & Data.*

Multicolor letterpress jobs are too technical to discuss here. As we said before, you probably won't use letterpress much except for letterpress magazines and for special jobs.

How to Prepare an Ad for Offset

Offset is remarkably flexible. Anything you can put on a piece of paper can be printed easily and quickly in offset, without extra costs for engraving or special preparation. Preparation for the "camera" is the same for direct-mail pieces and for publication ads.

The simplest ads to prepare for offset are all-type ads, of course. You paste the headline down where you want it (using rubber cement). You paste the body copy where you want it. And that's all there is to it. You don't need to worry about minor imperfections because the camera won't pick them up.

Proofreaders' Marks

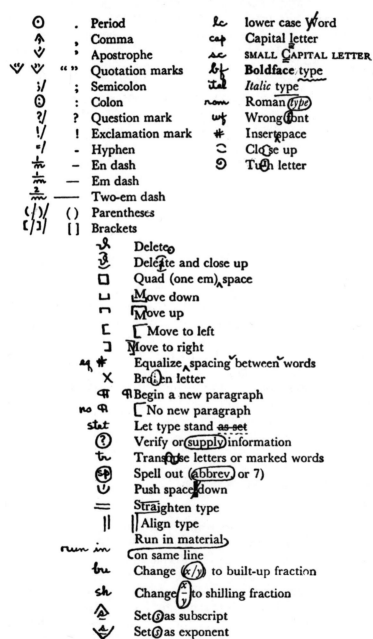

⊙	.	Period	lc	lower case Word
	,	Comma	cap	Capital letter
	'	Apostrophe	sc	SMALL CAPITAL LETTER
	" "	Quotation marks	bf	**Boldface** type
	;	Semicolon	ital	*Italic* type
	:	Colon	rom	Roman (type)
	?	Question mark	wf	Wrong font
	!	Exclamation mark	#	Insert space
	-	Hyphen	⊃	Close up
	–	En dash	⊕	Turn letter
	—	Em dash		
	——	Two-em dash		
	( )	Parentheses		
	[ ]	Brackets		

- Delete
- Delete and close up
- □ Quad (one em) space
- ⊔ Move down
- ⊓ Move up
- ⊏ Move to left
- ⊐ Move to right
- # Equalize spacing between words
- × Broken letter
- ¶ Begin a new paragraph
- no ¶ No new paragraph
- stet Let type stand as set
- (?) Verify or supply information
- tr Transpose letters or marked words
- sp Spell out (abbrev. or 7)
- ∪ Push space down
- = Straighten type
- ‖ Align type
- run in Run in material on same line
- bu Change (x/y) to built-up fraction
- sh Change (x/y) to shilling fraction
- Set as subscript
- Set as exponent

Figure 27–4

The camera won't pick up the full strength of any color except black unless you make special arrangements. And it won't pick up light blue at all, so you can use a light blue pencil to mark up the copy.

Rubber cement is invaluable. With rubber cement it is easy to position or remove elements in the ad. Stray drops rub off smoothly with a ball of dried cement or with your fingernail.

"Line drawings"—drawings that have no darks and lights but only straight ink lines—can also go onto any ordinary piece of offset copy. The camera picks up the lines in the drawing just the way it picks up type or pen lines.

"Tone" artwork must be "screened." The section on offset earlier in this chapter tells you about screening. After the artwork is screened, it is "stripped" into the negative along with the unscreened type elements.

One of the advantages of offset's flexibility is that you can easily experiment with your ad. You can paste in new headlines, paste on a border, increase the size of the headline, paste in a new price, etc.

An X-acto knife, a single-edged razor, a draftsman's T square, and a wooden drawing board are necessary and inexpensive tools of the trade. You can do much of this work very well after you have had a little practice, even if you are totally without art skills.

You will generally get body type for publication ads from a typographer. But in your direct-mail pieces, you will use typewriter type most of the time. This is one of the very great advantages of offset. You can type out a letter, get it to the offset shop, and often have them complete the job within an hour. At least one large offset shop in New York City does a great deal of its work on a "While-U-Wait" basis.

To type a page for offset, use the whitest, flattest paper you can find. The best bond paper is *not* good, because it is not flat. Paper from typewriter pads sold in stationery stores is best.

Make sure your typewriter keys are very clean and make a sharp impression. Use a new ribbon. An electric typewriter gives you the best-looking job, but it is not essential.

There are two typewriterlike machines that you can use for your body copy for publication ads. They are the Varityper and the Justowriter. With both of them you can insert many different typefaces. Also, they justify your copy. (That is, they space out the letters—on the second typing—so that all lines end at the right-hand margin.)

The IBM Selectric Composer typewriter also justifies your lines.

But for a direct-mail letter, you will do better with a ragged right-hand margin because it looks more informal and more like a letter. Never justify a letter.

If you find you have more to say than you can fit onto the page even with an elite (small-type) typewriter, have the printer *reduce* your ad photographically. Don't forget that when you plan on reduction, you should run wider on the width as well as deeper on the length. A 10 percent reduction—which means 10 percent reduction for both width *and* length—reduces the total area by 19 percent. This means you can increase the amount of copy by more than 23 percent with a 10 percent reduction.

You can "blow up" an ad, too. You will do that mostly for the artistic effect.

When you reproduce a letter by offset, you reproduce both the letterhead *and* the rest of the letter simply by pasting them up together. This is one of the great economies of the offset process for the mail-order person.

Miscellaneous Printing Matters

Envelopes

Buy your envelopes from an envelope maker and *not* from a printer. The envelope house will print your envelopes and charge you a fraction of the price a printer will charge.

Look for envelope suppliers in *The New York Times* Sunday Business Section, in classified, under "Business Services," or look in *Direct Marketing.*

There are dozens of types of trick envelopes that combine various elements of the direct-mail package. These cost more, but may be worth it in special situations.

For very long runs and for special copy printed on them, it will pay to have your envelopes run offset, and made up afterward. Check printers and prices on this.

Paper

There are many different kinds of paper available at many different prices. But nine times out of ten you will use the cheapest 16-pound or 20-pound paper. For two-side printing, 20-pound paper is a necessity.

Colored paper may be good for short runs to liven up your mailing. But for runs of more than a couple of thousand, use colored ink instead. It is cheaper.

For anything except long runs, buy paper through your printer, who purchases in large quantities and gets a much better price than you can get.

Miscellaneous Operations

Direct mail must be folded, inserted into the envelope, sealed, stamped, and perhaps sorted and tied into bundles. All these operations should be done mechanically, except in the smallest runs.

Printers can fold your letters for about $15.00 per thousand though in very large quantities it might get as low as $5.00 per thousand (8½ by 11). Unless you have inserting equipment yourself, you will do better to use a letter shop, preferably a letter shop that has a Phillipsburg or other model of automatic inserter. The inserter places all the pieces in the envelopes and seals them. If you use a letter shop, let them do the folding too.

For comparison purposes—assume you have a two-page letter and a business-reply envelope to go inside a no. 10 envelope. A good letter shop (in 1985) will do 5,000 pieces for a maximum of about $45 to $50 per thousand—folded, inserted, and sealed.

Most automatic postage meters will seal envelopes as well as apply postage. If you send follow-ups that must be keyed inside the envelope, you will need an automatic meter to seal the envelopes just before you send them out.

There are also plain envelope sealers available for under $200 new, and around $100 secondhand.

If you send out a great deal of direct mail, it is economical to take advantage of the bulk rate. But then you must sort the mail by destination. Many rented lists are already separated by geography. In that case, your letter shop will use an automatic tying machine to make bundles and deliver the mail directly to the post office. You should get a receipt from the post office—a receipt that records the number of pieces mailed and the amount paid.

How to Deal with Printers

When you want more than one sheet printed at a time, keep in mind that printing presses are of a few standard sizes, and the price will be cheapest if you can utilize all that printing area. This is the principle of "gang runs."

For example, if you want to print a sheet 5½ by 8½, you would probably make two identical pieces of copy, paste them on an 8½ by 11 sheet, have the printer run them on a small press, then cut them apart. In this way the price to you is for 1,000 pieces rather than 2,000.

You can also gang-up two or more different pieces of copy at the same time.

Purchasing printing so as to get quality *and* service *and* price is a real art. To begin with, let me give you some yardsticks of minimum prices (1986) for some basic units of printing:

1,000	8½ × 11	One side	20 lb.	$ 25.00
5,000	8½ × 11	One side	20 lb.	110.00
5,000	No. 10 envelopes			91.75
5,000	No. 6¾ business-reply envelopes			77.25

The prices shown are low because they are standard units and require no special adjustment to presses. They use standard-size paper fully.

Many printers will charge you twice as much as those prices and not be robbing you. If you can't find a local printer who will give you those prices, look in the back pages of *The New York Times* Business Section and write to the firms advertising there.

Dealing with printers so as to get the work you want by the date you want it is particularly difficult. Printers face great problems in scheduling their work. One day they have nothing to do; next day they're loaded with customers screaming for rush jobs. Unfortunately, few printers have the courage to turn down the customers whose work they can't complete by the date the customers request it. So they lie and stall, and you, the customer, find yourself way behind.

There are several ways to try to handle this problem with printers:

1. Be willing to pay extra for service. No one likes to do this, but sometimes you have to.

2. Be very smart in your scheduling and never need anything quickly. Then lie to the printer and say you need it a week earlier than you really need it. Few of us are smart enough to do the former. The latter is against my taste because I don't think it is fair to the printer.

3. Find a printer with whom you can form a relationship of trust, and then give him or her all of your business and treasure him or her like gold. Beware, though, of the honeymoon. Printers are irrationally willing to break their necks to satisfy a *new* customer. Then, once they have you, they often neglect you, raise prices to you, and finally drive you away. Why? I don't know.

I found a printer who studied industrial engineering in college and who runs his small shop like General Motors. I know he thinks straight, plans well, and doesn't *permit* situations that require alibis. (Well, practically never.) I'm so satisfied I don't even squawk when bills are too high.

This is a short checklist of instructions to cover when you tell your printer what you want to have done:

Name and type of piece to be printed

Size of piece

Color of stock

Paper texture and weight

Type faces and sizes

Placement of copy on page

Color(s) of ink

Printing process

Exact copy

28

Filling Orders

How to Find a Supplier / Drop Shipping versus
Consignment versus Cash Purchase / Buy It, or
Make It Yourself? / How to Handle Mail and
Orders / Addressing Systems / Handling
Complaints / Shipping Orders / Miscellaneous
Operations

This chapter is about almost everything in the mail-order business
except getting the order. The fact that we need only one chapter
for filling orders, in contrast with so many chapters for getting orders,
should emphasize the importance of the advertising in mail order.

How to Find a Supplier

There are no special sources of mail-order products. If you sell a
drug, you will obtain it either from a firm that already manufactures
it and will put it up for you under your own brand, or from a
manufacturing chemist who will make it up for you specially. If you
sell auto parts, you will buy them from distributors or manufacturers.
And so on.

Ingenuity and diligence will locate suppliers for you. The best place
to start is by examining the competitors' products for a manufacturer's
name printed on the product. Once you have the name of the maker,
the rest is easy.

There are several firms that sell directories of distributors who will
drop-ship, or sell outright, items that may work in mail-order catalogs.
I have no direct knowledge of how satisfactory these directories are,

but I am a little skeptical. Certainly you cannot make a profit in selling any one of those items alone.

The Manhattan classified phone directory is invaluable. Your local library will have one, or you can purchase a copy from the New York Telephone Company. Look under many different headings until you find what you want. If the product is foreign-made, look under "Importers." Then call firms on the phone or write to them, and if they can't supply what you want, be sure to ask them for their advice as to where you *can* get it. Such good-natured referrals will lead you to the right place more often than any other method.

Thomas' Directory and *Macrae's Blue Book* are other valuable sources. They list firms all over the United States. Again, if you don't find what you are looking for under the likeliest heading, look under three or four other headings.

Other useful source books: *Premium Suppliers' Directory (Blue Book Issue), Playthings Directory, Gift & Decorative Accessory Directory, Toys Buyers Directory.*

Trade associations can often help you. Almost every industry from steel to art materials has a trade association, and the staff can often guide you to the likeliest source of just what you want. For the names and addresses of associations, check the *Encyclopedia of Associations*[1] at your local library.

The purpose of the consulates of the various foreign countries is to inform you where you can buy products made in their countries. They will direct you to importers in this country or manufacturers abroad, whichever is appropriate. Use your common sense in choosing the likeliest consulates: Japan and not Ghana will probably sell you telescopes cheaply. The consulates will also advise you on tariffs in many cases. Or better yet, call the U.S. Customs Office for tariff information.

If you plan to sell books, manuals, information of any kind, or other printed products, you have a double supply problem: the written copy and the printing of the copy.

You yourself may write what you plan to sell. Or you can hire a ghostwriter to write for you. You can contact ghostwriters through ads in the literary sections of Sunday papers, in the *Saturday Review,* and in writers' magazines.

Printing the material is not a problem, but finding a cheap, reliable printer is a real art. Prices of printing can vary 100 percent and affect your profit margin greatly.

One outstanding advantage of selling information is that you have perfect control over your product. You are not at the mercy of any supplier. Furthermore, the copyright on your material (don't forget to get a copyright! See Appendix C) will present a barrier to competitors if the content is at all complex and difficult to reproduce.

Full-scale books and correspondence courses can also be ghostwritten. Frequently you can find a book that is out of copyright that will serve as is, or that can be brought up to date. Or you may find a book presently on the market whose publisher will give you an exclusive and guaranteed supply for some period of time.

Note that the seller of printed material pays less for the physical paper-and-ink product—as a percent of the sales price—than sellers of almost any other product. It is *information* that is really being sold, not paper and ink. The cost of the *information* is laid out only once, when the information is gathered and written down.

Drop Shipping versus Consignment versus Cash Purchase

Many suppliers will do business with you only if you buy outright, cash on the barrelhead.

If you can buy on consignment, it is always preferable to buying outright. Consignment buying has all the advantages of the outright purchase plus the privilege of return if you can't sell the merchandise.

Drop shipping *may* be better than purchasing outright or on consignment. When you sell with this method, your capital is not tied up in stock, you take no inventory risk, and you need no storage space.

Drop-ship arrangements are seldom available on anything but expensive merchandise. And drop-ship has disadvantages, too:

1. You usually pay more per unit when you buy on a drop-ship arrangement. The supplier is no dope. He or she knows that tying up *his* or *her* capital and warehouse space costs money, and you bear the burden in the price you pay.

2. Drop shipping is never as dependable as having the merchandise in your office. You *know* what you are going to do. You never know when the supplier's stock boy will take a day off.

3. Drop shipping introduces an extra step, and extra delay, between the customer's order and his or her receipt of the package. This extra delay makes the customer unhappy, and that costs you money in the long run in lost customers.

Drop shipping is most useful

1. When you are first testing merchandise and you have no idea how well it will go over
2. If you sell a very wide assortment of expensive units of merchandise

But a drop-ship operation is seldom a short cut to riches in mail order for people who have no investment capital.

Buy It, or Make It Yourself?

One of the common business fallacies is to set too low a cost on an item or service you render to yourself, usually because you don't include the cost of your own labor and overhead in the total cost. Let's say, for example, that you can either send material out to be mimeographed nearby for 60 to 80 cents per hundred copies, or you can buy a mimeograph machine and run things off in your own shop. If an employee of yours does the work on a mimeograph machine of your own, the cost may be only 30 cents for paper plus 15 cents for labor—a total of 45 cents, and apparently a saving of 15 or 25 cents per hundred sheets.

But when you figure the cost of supervision of the job, the cost of space to house the mimeograph, the amortized cost of the machine itself, and miscellaneous other overhead expenses, you will often find it much cheaper to send the work out.

The same argument will hold true for folding, sealing, and addressing and for most small manufacturing operations.

The primary advantage of doing the work in your own shop is that you have greater control over time of execution and better quality control.

The biggest corporations in the country, from General Motors on down, send out much work that they could do for themselves—but at a higher cost. Learn your lesson from them.

How to Handle Mail and Orders

These are the usual steps in a day's work in a smaller firm that does *not* use computer cards or tape. I will describe the steps very generally so that they will fit many types of businesses.

1. Sort incoming mail by key numbers.

2. Record returns—both inquiries and orders—for each day. (See Chapters 29 and 30)

3. Open mail.

4. Sort mail into piles of similar inquiries and similar orders.

5. Type address labels for each pile, making as many carbons as necessary for your particular needs. Key the labels in a way that reveals what the person ordered or inquired about. A crayon line that touches each label on a sheet of labels is often all you need.

6. Place labels on orders and inquiry follow-ups.

7. Put postage on orders and outgoing letters.

8. Place extra carbon labels on index cards, and file them.

9. Handle complaints, questions, and other nonroutine mail.

Remember that the routine varies greatly among businesses. Some kinds of businesses omit many of the steps above. Other firms include many more steps.

Opening the Mail.   Open the mail, probably after, but possibly before, sorting for key numbers. Your common sense will tell you which is better for your operation.

By all means get an *electric* letter-opener. You can buy a secondhand model for something over $100. I have found the Bircher Lightning a fine machine. An electric opener will justify its cost if you receive as few as fifty letters a day. Besides, it is fun for you or your employees to operate.

It is usually best to staple together the letter, the order, and the envelope. That saves all important information, including the crucial address. Often you will need the postmark to address the label correctly.

If you have thousands of cheap inquiries (costing under 25 cents apiece, for example), it may be economical to keep only whichever piece—letter or envelope—has a complete address. You will still need to save both envelope and letter in many cases, however.

Typing Labels.   Type labels for new customers or inquirers with as many carbons as are needed. Use the sets of two, three, or four sheets of labels that come with carbons. Or make address plates or other addressing-system cards.

If you receive large numbers of inquiries, you might consider using home typists. They need no office supervision and you pay for no fringe benefits (though you must pay taxes for them just as for other employees). And home typists supply their own typewriters, or even computers, nowadays.

Insist on reliable workers. Home typists are so plentiful (an ad in the newspaper brings in dozens) that you can hold out for the best.

A good average typist types 150 addresses an hour on labels. Have your typists save time by omitting periods after abbreviations like "Mrs," "NJ," "St," "Ms." This is a substantial saving in typing time.

Copy the address just the way the addressee writes it. Check all doubtful towns or states in the *Zip Code Directory of United States Post Offices.* (Get at least one copy from the Superintendent of Documents, Washington, DC 20402. This is almost the first thing you need in the mail-order business.)

Abbreviations. Never abbreviate the name of any city. Don't abbreviate such words as "Center," "Junction," "Spring," etc., or "North," "South," "East," and "West."

If you want to do business with the customer again in the future, don't abbreviate any part of her name. Write her name exactly as she writes it and *never* misspell it.

Two sets of state abbreviations are

Alabama	Ala	AL	Montana	Mont	MT
Alaska	Alaska	AK	Nebraska	Nebr	NE
Arizona	Ariz	AZ	Nevada	Nev	NV
Arkansas	Ark	AR	New Hampshire	NH	NH
California	Calif	CA	New Jersey	NJ	NJ
Colorado	Colo	CO	New Mexico	N Mex	NM
Connecticut	Conn	CT	New York	NY	NY
Delaware	Del	DE	North Carolina	N Car	NC
District of Columbia	DC	DC	North Dakota	N Dak	ND
Florida	Fla	FL	Ohio	Ohio	OH
Georgia	Ga	GA	Oklahoma	Okla	OK
Hawaii	Hawaii	HI	Oregon	Ore	OR
Idaho	Idaho	ID	Pennsylvania	Penna	PA
Illinois	Ill	IL	Rhode Island	RI	RI
Indiana	Ind	IN	South Carolina	S Car	SC
Iowa	Iowa	IA	South Dakota	S Dak	SD
Kansas	Kans	KS	Tennessee	Tenn	TN
Kentucky	Ky	KY	Texas	Tex	TX
Louisiana	La	LA	Utah	Utah	UT
Maine	Maine	ME	Vermont	Vt	VT
Maryland	Md	MD	Virginia	Va	VA
Massachusetts	Mass	MA	Washington	Wash	WA
Michigan	Mich	MI	West Virginia	W Va	WV
Minnesota	Minn	MN	Wisconsin	Wis	WI
Mississippi	Miss	MS	Wyoming	Wyo	WY
Missouri	Mo	MO			

Many firms now prefer to use the Post-Office-approved two-letter abbreviations for each state, and with zip code, that should now do the trick, avoiding confusion.

Addressing Systems

Nowadays, addressing is done by computer. It is the only way to go. If you have not yet gotten yourself onto computer, you may want to consult earlier editions of this book on precomputer addressing systems. But again—get onto that computer! I don't want to give you any advice about any other system that will delay your computerizing.

Handling Complaints

General rules for handling complaints are

1. Be as courteous as you possibly can. Expressing your irritation at a customer will cost you money in the long run.

2. But don't be a patsy for customers who want to cheat you. Let them know where you stand.

3. Honor requests for refunds *instantly* and *pleasantly,* expressing your regret. You can then convert a dissatisfied customer into a valuable, satisfied customer. But if the customer has no leg to stand on, and if the sum is large or if it is a one-shot deal, don't be afraid to stand on your rights.

4. Write as few individual letters or notes as possible. Set up form letters or postcards to handle all matters that come up often. After you send out the same message ten times, you will be ready to create a form postcard, and you'll know what to say.

5. The best way to handle complaints is to prevent them, by effective communication with your customers. The forms shown in Figures 28-1 and 28-2 are good examples of such effective complaint-preventing communications.

Always include on a form postcard "Please return this card (or letter) if your package does not arrive within a week," etc. That way you can deal with subsequent correspondence much more quickly.

Sawyer had this to say way back in 1900:[2]

> This is one of the unpleasant features of a mail-order enterprise. No mail business can be carried on without a reasonable number of complaints. These are the most common reasons that people kick up a fuss:

Delay in filling order

Sending goods not ordered, by error

Omitting part of order

Damage to goods in transit

Delay or loss of goods in transit

Loss or miscarriage of letter

Miscarriage of goods

Dissatisfaction as to goods received

Sometimes you get a complaint about money that was supposedly sent to you but that never reached your office or never was recorded in your records. *Esquire's* Mail Order Newsletter gives sage advice about this problem:[3]

Every mail order advertiser faces the problem of having cash remittances lost in the mail. A small percentage of chiselers attempt to make envelopes appear as though *cash remittances* were actually enclosed (pressure is put on envelopes to raise impressions and then coins are removed, the envelopes torn or slit to simulate tampering.)

But the great majority of lost remittances are actually lost or stolen and they are difficult to trace. The Post Office provides form 1510 for the filing of claims for lost remittances.

To shift the headaches and responsibility from the advertiser to the prospect and also to curb chiseling, here's what one large mail order firm does:

1. It immediately answers orders without remittances with its own form stating that the customer's letter was opened and there was no remittance, the letter apparently having been tampered with in the mails. It goes on to state the customer's letter and envelope is being returned to him *exactly* as received.

2. The Post Office form 1510 is also enclosed and the customer is asked to fill out and take it to the Post Master to file his claim. If the "customer" is a chiseler he will hesitate to file; if he is honest he will, of course, cooperate.

As long as we're quoting Sawyer in this chapter, read this delightful account of one mail-order nuisance:[4]

In the mail-order business, letters come without signature or insufficient address. Parcels sent to people in accordance with the address they give in their letters will sometimes fail to reach them and utimately come back to the sender. People sometimes return goods for exchange and fail to put their name on the wrapper of the package and also forget to write any letter to accompany same. Once in awhile, a dollar bill or

WHAT HAPPENS TO YOUR ORDER–

–STEP BY STEP

As soon as you mail your order, the post office gets to work getting it to us. First class mail generally gets here in one to five days, depending on where you live. Of course if you phone in your order, we start processing it immediately.

We meet the morning mail in Putney at 8:30 a.m. It's pretty handy for us since we're located on Main Street directly across from the post office.

Back in the office we start opening the morning mail immediately. I personally check your order to make sure that sizes, colors and quantities etc. are indicated. If there is any question about your order, or if there will be a delay, Brook Sherwood, our customer service manager, will pick up the phone and give you a call, or drop you a quick note. Once she's checked your order she passes it down the processing desk to Barbara Rose, who types your shipping label and takes your order into our warehouse. There the items you ordered are carefully selected from our shelves.

It's now about 10:30 and everything stops for our morning coffee break.

Right after coffee break, Sarah Bensonhaver starts packing orders for shipment. This takes a while because we want to pack each item very carefully so that it will arrive to you in perfect condition. Vicky Lyon does the gift wrapping on any items you've indicated. It's a big job and on busy days we all pitch in and give Sarah a hand.

We're working toward a 4:00 p.m. deadline so that we'll have your package ready when the United Parcel Service driver arrives. He takes your package directly to the UPS terminal (6 miles south of here) where your package is sorted and routed out that very evening, rolling down the highway toward your house before midnight.

So you can see that when we receive your order we do our best to get it on its way to you (or any gift recipient you've indicated) that very same day. We know that it's important to you, and we want you to know that it's important to us. Our business depends upon pleasing you—again and again and again.

Figure 28–1

---

new process company® ⓝⓟⓒ warren,pennsylvania 16366

Dear Mr. Simon:

The refund check above is for the merchandise which you returned.
We appreciated your order and are only sorry that we were unable
to completely please you.

I'm very much in hopes though, that you'll give us another chance
before too long. As always, you'll have the advantage of our
full week's free trial terms. Believe me, we'll try all the harder
to please!

RT RT-2

---

henniker's 779 Bush St., Box 7584, San Francisco, CA 94120

ABOUT YOUR ORDER

Dear Customer:

We have your order and we thank you very much. We wanted you to have this confirmation right away.

As you know, we are being buffeted right now by transportation strikes. Trucks do not move, the largest domestic air carrier is on strike, and the most important international carrier is about to go on strike and does not accept forward commitments. For "jurisdictional" reasons, quite a few ships are being picketed in port and cannot be unloaded.

All of this causes interruption in our supply of merchandise and in our ability to distribute it. Therefore, it is possible that your order may be delayed for two or three weeks or that we may be unable to fill it in just one delivery. We know how annoying this must be to you. I assure you that we share your frustration.

By the inevitable mechanics of our business, your check was deposited or your bankcard account debited, immediately upon receipt of your order. This may irritate you somewhat — we hope not too much. It is, however, an understandable procedure for a business in which virtually all orders are routinely filled immediately from ample stock. The transportation strikes have created an unexpected situation for which our systems do not really provide.

If you authorized charge to your bankcard, we would be grateful if you would not "dispute" the charge with your bank, even though you might receive your charge before your merchandise. To enter a "dispute" would give rise to much back-and-forth and much paperwork, for both you and us.

We wish to thank you once again for your order, but also for your confidence and for your forbearance, for two or three weeks.

Sincerely yours,

Chris Simpson   Chris Simpson Customer Services

C.S. 206

Figure 28-2

---

a quantity of stamps will come in an envelope without the scratch of a pen to show who sent them.

Sometimes a son writes a note of endearment to his mother, enclosing a photograph, and sends it to a mail-order house, the letter being signed, "Your loving son, John"; while a formal order, such as, "Please send twelve white bow ties, for which find twenty-five two cent stamps" may go to the loving mother. The mail-order house does not think it quite fair to throw away the letter containing the photograph, neither is it advisable to tear up that inquiry without the name or address nor should that returned package be cast aside without consideration. Therefore, a rendezvous for this kind of pieces is naturally created and generally resolves into a convenient box or drawer, where after awhile the envelope that contained the dollar bill matches a communication from the lady who forgot to enclose her letter; the box which came back enclosing the pair of opera glasses finds companionship with a complaint from the fellow who ordered them for a gift to his best girl, but who left for another town before they reached him, and John's letter with the photograph utimately finds its owner, through the course of John's mother writing John and John straightening things out.

Here are Fenvessy's suggestions on how to handle customer complaints:[5]

Sort mail by problem. Anyone who has managed a well-run large correspondence operation knows that "the secret is in the sort." Specifically, after the mail is dated, it should be sorted according to the nature of the complaint or inquiry. . . .

The nature of the business will dictate the categories of the sort. . . .

Mail which requires file look-up should be segregated from that which does not. Other common complaint categories: where is my order; requests for replacement or refund; pricing problems; and billing complaints. Serious complaints should be given quick special handling. . . .

Changes of patterns in customer correspondence provide valuable hints on your weaknesses in deliveries, deteriorating manufacturing quality, undersirable sales practices, computer errors, and other areas which obviously need improving. *Improve the research function.* . . .

Include an enclosure in each shipment giveing essential information about the shipment, with space and a checklist for the customer to state any problem or complaint. The customer is to complete and send the enclosure if he returns the merchandise or writes about it. Frequently the information on the enclosure is all that is needed to handle the transaction. . . .

Simplify the preparation of responses. We have found that 75% to 90% of all customer complaint correspondence can be answered with a prepared form reply. Carefully composed and appropriate form letters received quickly are just as appreciated as a dictated letter. A form letter can cost less than 35 cents compared to $3.50 for some dictated letters at current cost studies. . . .

Make the adjustment immediately. Making the adjustment promptly not only saves money but saves a customer. If an adjustment involves a relatively small sum or a reshipment, execute it promptly. (A "small sum" can vary between $5 and $50 depending upon the industry.)

Do not generate more expensive correspondence by writing for cancelled checks or proof of purchase. Experience has shown that the customer is fundamentally honest and is usually correct in his contention.

Handle nearby and serious complaints by telephone. The use of the telephone to handle customer complaints is on the threshold of major expansion. For instance, the consumer book division of a large publisher made 37,000 telephone calls to customers last year. The goodwill generated was simply amazing and the company saved money—even after paying the telephone bill—by reducing mail reading, answering and postage. . . .

When a customer sends you a complaint, she is rarely saying that she will no longer use your product or service. She is giving you another chance to retain her as a customer. How well your company responds to this challenge depends upon the professionalism of your customer service operation.

Shipping Orders

It is crucial to ship orders immediately upon receipt of the order. Every day that the order is delayed in your shop, the more complaints, cancellation, and COD refusals you will have.

It is often a good practice to send out a postcard on the day the order is received, stating that the order follows by parcel post, United Parcel Service, etc. The postcard keeps customers from worrying about their money and merchandise.

If the order is unavoidably delayed, send off a card explaining the delay and telling the customer how soon you will be able to ship.

If your article is light or heavy, you may find it cheaper and faster to ship by means other than parcel post. But if the article is very heavy or bulky, you *must* find some other means of transportation because the post office won't accept it. United Parcel Service (UPS) presently services forty-eight states and the District of Columbia. UPS is used a lot by mail-order businesses instead of parcel post. (Even the Government Printing Office has recently switched to UPS for shipments west of the Mississippi, because of lower price as well as better lost-order tracing.) Parcels are picked up by the truck at the shipper's address and, in general, UPS makes deliveries in less time than parcel post. They limit the maximum weight per package to 50 pounds and maximum weight of all packages to one consignee in one day to 100 pounds. Maximum size per package is 108 inches in length and girth combined. Rates are lower than parcel post and are based on the gross weight of the shipment and its contents. Unless a greater value is declared in writing on the pickup record, the shipper declares the released value of each package to be $100. Higher valuations carry an additional charge for coverage.

If you plan to sell a great many of a standard item, shipped alone, you should make careful packing plans. Always make up a model package in advance. And when you make up your model package, watch the weight so that you don't go one-eighth of an ounce into the next pound. On 1,000 or 5,000 packages, that slight difference can add up to a lot of money.

Which Way to Ship?

The various methods of shipping—airmail, first-class mail, parcel post, United Parcel Service, trucker, mule train—have disadvantages and advantages in speed, convenience, and cost. And the disadvantages and advantages change from time to time as, for example, when postage rates change. Therefore, the problem of how to ship comes back time and again.

One way to make easier the decision about how to ship is to ask your customers how they want their shipments sent—require that they pay the appropriate price for faster or slower shipment. But, beyond that, you must experiment to see how fast your packages arrive with, say, parcel post versus UPS, and how satisfied the customers are with each system as measured by the repeat-order rate of customers whose packages are sent various ways.

A last point: From time to time rethink your decision about how to ship. Conditions change.

Good Relations with the Post Office

It pays to have an amicable relationship with the post office. You can best keep the goodwill that you need by saving trouble and avoiding extra work for post office help. This includes

1. Deliver mail to the post office rather than dumping it in street boxes.
2. Keep outgoing letters faced in the same direction.
3. Use precanceled stamps. (You can obtain a free permit to do this.)

One of the extra services the post office can render you is to deliver your mail to you even if it is insufficiently addressed. When using a new address for the first time, try the post office out by sending yourself a few postcards using the new address and the possible variations on it.

Miscellaneous Operations

Checking Advertisements.   Either you or your agency must check to see that each ad you pay for *actually runs.* I have found the easiest checking method for a mail-order firm is to create a reply record sheet for each ad you pay for, indicating "Paid" and the amount on the sheet. Keep a separate file of pages containing your ads, in alphabetical order, as they come in. Start a new alphabetical file every once in a while. If replies come in to that key, you automatically know that the ad ran. If no replies arrive, you verify with your alphabetical file of advertising pages and demand your refund.

Applying Postage. Putting stamps on envelopes is tedious work. The easiest way is to rip the stamps into horizontal strips (rolls of stamps are hard to tear), stand a pile of envelopes upright against a box, wet five or ten stamps at a time, turn each envelope down as you press a stamp on, and rip it off with your thumb.

You can also buy or rent a small machine that applies stamps automatically. But by that time you're probably ready for a postage meter.

Postage meters are wonderful things. They speed stamping (and usually sealing, too), and they protect you from stamp theft. When you are ready for a meter, check prices and models with the local representative of *all* these firms:

Postalia Corp., 33-20 61st St., Woodside, NY 11377

Singer Business Machines, Friden Division, 211 E. 43rd St., New York, NY 10017

Pitney-Bowes, Inc., Stamford, CT 06905

Metered mail pulls replies just as well as, or better than, stamped mail. No problems from that source.

Gummed-Tape Machines. Gummed-tape machines are another necessity. Get one that takes tape up to 3 inches wide. You just pull a handle to get a length of tape. Secondhand shops very often have serviceable machines.

Envelope Sealer. An envelope sealer may be handy. But you will probably prefer a postage meter that has an envelope-sealing attachment.

29

Managing Your Information System without a Computer

The chapter after this one tells you more than you will probably want to know about the use of computers in a mail-order operation. This short chapter reviews the management of your information system without a computer. This information is intended to be useful to people in the very first throes of getting their business started. And it may also be a useful quick look at some of the tasks that the computer can do vastly better than you can ever do by hand. This chapter is a holdover from the days before I could recommend that everyone should computerize immediately. But I hope that you will not let this chapter delay you even 1 minute from getting your business onto a computer. We have now reached the state of technology and cost that it is absolutely essential to do so almost from the first day of the business.

The information stored in your records and files is crucial to running your business successfully. Right from the very first order you get, you must keep good records or you won't know how to proceed. So give plenty of attention to your information system. A mail-order business needs lots of information to make profitable decisions. And it has lots of data about its customers to use in making those decisions. When the business is very small, it is possible to manage with hand-kept record systems. But as the business gets larger and more complex, even the most sensible hand-kept record systems are expensive, become difficult to manage, and produce the necessary information only with enormous difficulty.

Conclusion: An established and growing mail-order business must computerize its record keeping. This means putting all the relevant information about each order on a computer disk or tape, making labels from the disk or tape, and then generating the necessary records from the computer disk or tape. The tape or disk can then be used for list rental.

Your files should be your slaves, not your master. Keep all the files and records that your particular type of business needs, and none other. The types of files you need will depend upon the type of business you run.

Customer files are the most crucial files in mail-order businesses. The following are some kinds of customer systems you might use.

One-Shot Business.   If your business is strictly a one-shot proposition, you probably would not want any customer file at all. You merely make an extra carbon of labels which will be the basis for a rental list, or you sell the original letters outright to a firm like William Stroh, Jr., 568 54th St., West New York, NJ 07043, in which case you need no record of customers at all.

You will hear from customers again only in case of complaints. Chapter 28 tells you how to deal with complaints. In a one-shot deal for under, say, $10 or $20, it is cheaper in almost every case to send out a duplicate shipment, rather than to check a file to determine the cause of complaint.

Repeat-Sales Business.   If your business depends on repeat sales to the same customers, you need a record of each purchase a customer makes. Usually 4- X 6-inch index cards do the trick. Figure 29-1 shows a standard form for the cards.

File these cards in alphabetical order until your list reaches a fairly large size. Then split them into "alpha-geo" order, filing by states and then alphabetically within each state.

Your customer list is the principal asset of your business. It is very wise to keep a duplicate set in a fireproof location somewhere other than at your business. Don't bother to keep that duplicate set "clean" or orderly, however.

If you use Elliott, Addressograph, or similar addressing systems, your addressing-plate file should be identical with your card file. Whenever you add or drop a name from the card file, you must bring the plate file up to date.

The alpha-geo system speeds name-searching. It also places outgoing mail in the proper sequence for sorting to take advantage of third-class bulk rates.

Spirit addressing systems make it possible to address directly from the back of the customer card. This saves you the extra clerical chore

| Name _____ Date of 1st inquiry or order _____ |
| Street Address _____ Key _____ |
| City, State, Zip _____ Other Customer Data ____ |

Date	Item	Price	Date	Item	Price

Figure 29-1

of keeping the address-plate file up to date. It also removes a dangerous source of error.

When you begin to use computer disk or tape, pull *all* the information *from each order* on a card. With the help of the computer you can later add the information onto the customer's master record. *Please* include *all* the *possibly* relevant information, even though you can't see immediately how you will use it; later on, you *will* use it.

Inquiry and Follow-ups. If you sell by repeated follow-ups to inquirers, you will need a tickler file system to tell you when to send out inquiries. One way to maintain a tickler file is to make up one sheet of carbon labels for each follow-up in your series. Set up a separate file for each follow-up letter, and file each sheet by the date it is to go out.

When an order comes in, you must remember to go through each follow-up file to cross off the name of the customer who has already bought. No point in sending further expensive solicitations!

Spirit-system addressing can also simplify this procedure. Each day's inquirer cards are punched, all together, with the dates of the follow-ups. Each day you sort for the follow-up to go out. And when a customer purchases you can stop the follow-up series by removing just that one card from your files.

Three basic information reports are shown in Figures 29-2, 29-3, and 29-4. Figure 29-2 shows the daily record sheet, which summarizes the incoming business each day. From Figure 29-2 you can prepare your weekly, monthly, and yearly reports which reveal how your business is doing, and which serve as the basis for your overall decisions.

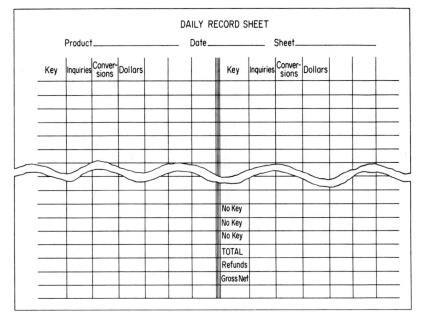

Figure 29-2

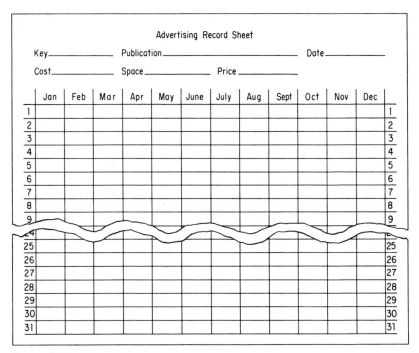

Figure 29-3

DIRECT MAIL LIST–RECORD SHEET

Purpose: _____

To Whom Mailed: _____

Mail Date(s): _____

Results: _____

Comparison To Which List: _____

Key _____

WK.	Response	Cumulative response	Projected total response	Projected percent return	Profit	Loss
(1)						

Figure 29-4

Figures 29-3 and 29-4 are record sheets for space ads and direct-mail tests, respectively. They are taken from two different businesses to illustrate two styles. These report forms serve as the basis for decisions about which ads and tests should be used in the future, and which policies that you test out are better.

Each day you fill out a Daily Record Sheet for each product that you sell, classifying the letters by the key they show.

Then you prepare an Advertising Record Sheet for each advertisement you run.

Each day you transfer the results for each day from the Daily Record Sheet to the Advertising Record Sheet.

Keep the records clearly and up to date, and never throw them away. The Daily Record Sheet is especially valuable for income-tax purposes.

30

Our Brand-New Miracle: The Computer*

Some Warnings in Advance / The Ideal Program and Computer / Comparison Checklist

Much of the information in the other chapters of this book is not new, even though it is quite up to date. You can find the most important ideas about the mail-order business in the better books on the subject that were published way back in the first three decades of this century. But this chapter—brand new in this edition and the first such chapter in any book on the mail-order business anywhere—contains material which not only is published here for the first time, but is about a true breakthrough for the mail-order business.

A mail-order business depends on numbers and quantitative analyses to a greater extent than does any other sort of business. And a mail-order operator's decisions require doing the right arithmetic on the right pieces of information more than do decisions in any other lines of business. In the past this meant having huge masses of written records and doing lots of tedious figuring. When the first mechanical-

* It is a pleasure to acknowledge the extensive help in preparing this chapter that came from Lloyd Merriam of CoLinear Systems and Michael Lindeburg of Professional Publications. I also benefited from reading the excellent article by William Dyke, "Automated Fulfillment: The Invisible Computer," *Direct Marketing*, May 1983, pp. 76–80, and some pages by Jack Beardsley of Beardsley & Associates. Dan Richards of Colwell Systems and his staff gave me a useful short seminar on their systems. And Philip Harvey and I spent several pleasant hours arguing about how to implement a computer system in a mail-order business.

electrical calculating machines came along before and after the Second World War, the big mail-order firms saw the opportunity, and they put computers to use. The same was true when the first electronic computers arrived in the 1950s and 1960s. But those old machines were too complex and expensive for most smaller firms. When computers became cheaper and more manageable about 1965 and 1970, many medium-sized firms went out and bought the "hardware." (I'll put into quotation marks the terminology about computers that you must learn.) But the machines in that earlier "generation" of computers were expensive. And even worse, the firms often had excruciating difficulties in obtaining satisfactory programming, the "software" that fitted their purposes. I once babysat with a firm as it struggled for 2 agonizing years to find a consultant-programmer who would give them what they really needed, rather than what the programmer incorrectly thought that they needed. Their experience was not at all unusual.

By now the situation has changed dramatically. The new "personal computers" with "hard disks" are able to handle the needs of firms that are just starting out, and the necessary combination of hardware and software is quite affordable for almost any firm. Best of all, it is now possible to purchase a "canned" program that is set up to handle the basic needs of a mail-order firm, so you know exactly what you get before you buy it. The least expensive program "packages" for the personal computer cost well under a thousand dollars, while some other packages with more features cost no more than about $3,000 or $4,000. The cost of the computer hardware is another $3,000 or so. So, for about one-third the cost of a clerk for just 1 year, you can purchase the hardware and software for a "turnkey operation" that will save you the labor of many many clerks, and, even more important, the computer will help you run your business in an efficient, rational, and enjoyable fashion.

Now do you understand why I consider personal computers and the associated programs the greatest breakthrough, for the beginner or for the established small mail-order firm, and the biggest new mail-order development in about 50 years? That's why this chapter alone may be worth to you many times the price of the book—because you cannot get this information elsewhere, and because it can save you so much money by not doing things in the old precomputer fashion.

When should you start your thinking about buying a computer system? You should *start* thinking about it from day 1 in the business so that you will be ready when the time comes. And the time to actually get to work acquiring a system is just as soon as you are sure enough that your early experiments in the business have been crowned with sufficient success that you can count on being in business for a while. This time may well be before you have any full-time employees. Yes, that soon. If you are running the business yourself from your kitchen table, the computer will enable you to put off hiring employees for a while; this is because you plus the computer can do all the clerical work vastly faster than employees can by hand. Every day that you delay getting on the computer probably will cost you a pretty penny in added costs in many directions. In the past, I recommended waiting considerably longer, but that was because no inexpensive canned programs for personal computers were available then.

How much knowledge about computers must you have before you start looking around to buy a system? None. Really. But I do not mean that you can and should plan to get by without *acquiring* knowledge about computers. Rather, you will need to acquire a fair amount of elementary knowledge, not of technical programming (you don't ever have to learn to do any programming) but rather general knowledge about computers and their capabilities. This does *not* mean that you have to go back to school to get a Ph.D. in computer science. But it *does* mean that you are going to have to sit still with your tail end firmly applied to a hard chair for some hours or days while the sellers of the computer systems explain to you how the system works, and as you study some manuals that come with the system. The simple fact is that computer systems represent an incredible amount of information-management capability, and it takes some time to find out what that capability is and how to manage it.

You are also going to have to learn some new words such as "hard disk drive," "boot up," and "software," as well as a host of code terms specific to the program that you purchase. All that terminology will seem bewildering at first. But these words and ideas will sort themselves out in a fairly short time. I guarantee it. And I don't guarantee many things in these days when you can successfully sue your clergyman (and maybe even the author of a book like this one) for malpractice. And keep in mind that literally millions of Americans with far less background and aptitude for computers than you probably possess already have mastered all this knowledge, and more, and are happy members of the computer-literate generation.

The most important qualities that you need in order to absorb the necessary knowledge are some patience, and a lack of fear of computers. Even if you are apprehensive now, your fear can be dispelled by struggling your way to some basic knowledge. Everything else that you need to know you already have in your head.

The computer system requirements of each mail-order business are different from those of all other businesses, even other mail-order businesses. And computer system requirements vary by general type of business; magazines have very different needs than do catalog firms, for example. In writing this chapter, I have tried to keep in mind a firm selling a variety of items through a catalog. The items might be woodworking tools or books or machine parts. I have chosen a catalog firm as the model because it has to deal with most of the complications that other mail-order firms must deal with.

Some Warnings in Advance

A few warnings in advance:

1. First and foremost, from the very first day that your computer is in operation, set up *and make sure you use* a supercareful security system for your data. One aspect of security is that no one can gain access to your data without your permission. This aspect of computer security is handled technically, and it should be discussed with whomever sells you the software package. It is not vital at the very beginning because you won't have anything worth stealing for a while.

A more important aspect of security is protecting against the very real danger that lightning, fire, or human error will destroy the most valuable asset of your business—your customer "database" and the results of your past business activities, especially the results of your past advertisements. You must protect against this danger by "backing up" your data from the very first order that you process with the computer. And you must stay with it and follow through on the security procedures every single business day, because the one day that you postpone backing up your data until tomorrow inevitably is the day that disaster hits.

At the end of every single day you must have a record of every customer purchase processed that day, not only on the hard disk which holds the "live" files with which you work each day, but also on another type of storage system, of which "floppy disks" are the type you are likely to begin with, though they are fast becoming outmoded for business purposes. You need two sets of floppy disk "backups." Call one set "blue" and keep it in your workplace after the first day's work. Call the other set "red" and keep it in another location to guard against the eventuality of a fire or other disaster destroying your workplace. If your workplace is your home at present, keep one set at a friend's house or office in another building. Because you will not be making changes in these daily records of consumer purchases, you can simply add each day's files to the set. Each set then constitutes your "archive." This material will later on become your primary source of data for complex analyses when you are ready to make them because, as we shall discuss below, the detailed purchase information will almost surely be consolidated and some of it erased from the hard disk because of lack of space there.

While we are talking of backups, you should use a somewhat different procedure when you are not only adding to, but also editing, a file from day to day. In that case, you must not only make blue and red sets of backups, but you must also alternate them every day so that the off-premise set is never more than a day out of date. That is the appropriate procedure for a manuscript in process, such as this book. A somewhat similar procedure is appropriate for your basic customer list, though the everyday backup and switch is less necessary because you can restore the information to your customer list from the records of customer purchases on the days since you last made a backup.

Still another sort of backup is also necessary, a periodic backup perhaps once a month. This is necessary because it is possible for something to go wrong with a file, such as your customer record, and have the defect go undiscovered for several days. If so, and if you erase the old backups and create new backups each day, you may be caught with nothing but defective backups in addition to a defective live file. A periodic backup reduces the likelihood of this danger.

If backing up *all* the material on your hard disk seems absolutely impossible that day, at least back up your *order file* for that day. With that day's order file plus your previous backups of the other files, you can recreate all the other files by reentering the order file, and loss or destruction of the live files would not be a devastating blow.

Yes, I know that all this backing-up of files is a tedious nuisance. But I also know that disaster is predictable unless you do it faithfully. No matter who swears up and down to the contrary and no matter how many safeguards (such as "surge protectors" against lightning damage) that you install, sooner or later something will happen to your hard disk that will destroy or render worthless all your precious data. And something can even happen to the set of back-up disks or tapes that you keep on the premises—say, theft or fire. That is why you *must* MUST protect yourself with a sound system of backups.

When working with creative materials such as catalog preparation, you need to follow still another safety measure: You must train yourself and everyone working with you to *frequently* "save" onto disks the material you are working with in computer memory. By "frequently" I mean less than every hour; even better, do it every time you pause to look out the window for a moment or take a call on the phone.

There are few things more frustrating than finishing a job on the computer and then having all that work lost because you did not save it, when some bug in the machine or in the power supply or some other minor foul-up causes you to lose all the work in memory. (This remark is not appropriate for order-processing work because the entries are automatically written on the hard disk in most systems, rather than kept in memory. But better check this with any system that you consider buying.)

A device that has recently come onto the market for quickly backing up long files is the "streaming cassette," which looks very much like an ordinary cassette; a related device uses a tape cartridge instead of a cassette. Its advantage is that its capacity is greater than a single floppy and the process therefore is much much faster than floppy disks, saving you lots of time and therefore money. The drawback of this device is that you must buy an additional drive to go with it, at a cost of perhaps $1,000 (July 1986), though this price will surely have fallen considerably by the time you read this.

While we are talking about preventing loss of your valuable records, make sure that you have a surge protector attached to your power line so that lightning or some other power failure cannot destroy the records on your hard disk, and perhaps blow out your computer completely. (Yes, it does happen. It happened to me, for example.)

I realize that you are not yet in a position to understand what I have written in the paragraphs above. You will be better prepared to understand the previous paragraphs after you read further in the chapter. But I place the warning about back-up security here at the top of the list to increase the chances that it will capture your attention, and that you will therefore come back and read it again when you are better equipped to understand what the paragraphs say.

2. Don't let anyone talk you into buying any computer—that is, any hardware—which is not compatible with the IBM-PC and other machines using the "operating system" called "MS-DOS." You don't need to understand that technical language now. But you do need to remember to ask that question of anyone with whom you are discussing software or hardware for your business. The most promising new software for small mail-order businesses is written for the group of machines that use MS-DOS. And the prospects are excellent that programs which run on the IBM-PC and use MS-DOS will be the standard in the field for a long time to come. When your business grows much larger and you move up to bigger machines, you will be able to transfer your system without hassle. (A footnote to this discussion: The Mail Order Pro system can convert files from the older

CP/M "environment" to the MS-DOS environment without difficulty. This enables you to buy an older, cheaper machine to get started with, if you like, and then move up to a new MS-DOS machine without having a problem with your older data.)

As to whether the machine that you eventually buy is an IBM-PC or another machine compatible with it, that question can be deferred for awhile, and how you answer it probably will not be crucial in the success or failure of getting your business computerized. So don't get panicked by the large number of possible choices of machine.

One warning about which machine you buy, however: You probably will do well to buy a machine made by a firm sufficiently large and well established that it will remain in business for the foreseeable future. Buying a machine that may become an "orphan" because the maker goes out of business can be a problem.

3. Don't let anyone convince you to have them write a custom program especially for you, instead of using the existing canned software. There are a zillion "bugs" that have to be ironed out in the development of a piece of business software. One of the biggest advantages of a canned program which has already been used by other firms for some time is that the worst bugs have been spotted and fixed as users experimented with the system and reported the bugs to the software seller. These bugs bedeviled mail-order firms in the past when they put their operations onto computers with custom-written programs.

A recent story in *The Wall Street Journal* should underline this warning about buying either a new and insufficiently tested program or a custom program. It was headed "Buyer Beware: Software Plagued by Poor Quality and Poor Service," and it continued, "In the market for personal computer software, the buyer had best beware. As thousands of customers already know, the typical $500 program is likely to have 'bugs'—it's just a matter of how bad. . . . One reason for the problems is that some software firms, pressed for cash and behind schedule, ship projects before the basic features are even finished."[1]

So, don't purchase a system until you have talked on the phone or in person to several satisfied users whose names the software seller should supply to you. (But try not to use too much of the satisfied-user's time. And express your appreciation for the important favor.) To repeat: When new, every computer system has bugs. You don't want to buy a system until the bugs have been exterminated. And it takes a good deal of operating time, by several users, to discover all the bugs.

4. The subject of this warning is the maintenance of complete information about customer purchases and advertising sources. And this subject requires that we must resolve some potential confusion about the term "file maintenance." The software developers will tell you—and correctly—that it is not possible to maintain all your information on the hard disk because of lack of space, and therefore it is necessary to delete all except some of the most important information, some of which may be summarized (such as the sum of the customer's purchases within the past year). Fine. But at the same time you must maintain a complete file—and when I say "complete" I mean with no information whatsoever deleted—in some sort of storage form on at least two sets of backups. With the information in such an archive, you can always transfer it to the hard disk on your machine, or on some other machine, and conduct such analyses as you wish upon the file, or upon a random sample of data drawn from it. So the warning is: Never let anyone talk you into not recording for your permanent records, or into deleting, any—and I mean *any*—information concerning transactions with customers from the file of customer purchases which you maintain in your archive. The information that you don't have surely will turn out to be the information that you desperately need for an analysis 2 years later. But on the other hand, recognize that no personal computer system whose cost is within the realm of feasibility at present has a storage capacity that can maintain on the hard disk all the information for a business of any size at all, along with the other material that must be stored on that disk.

5. Don't take your record-keeping task to a "fulfillment house"— a firm that is in the business of processing orders and keeping records—rather than doing your operations yourself. This is not a knock against the fulfillment firms, many of which are magnificently competent businesses. But they are mostly set up to handle the specialized needs of large firms, such as magazines, that have very large customer lists, keeping them up-to-date and unduplicated. In my experience, fulfillment houses usually are not well prepared to handle the needs of a small firm. Also, their standard procedures often do not allow you to maintain and analyze all the information which is crucial for you to run your business effectively. In the past, when computer systems were much more expensive and difficult to acquire, fulfillment houses often offered the only feasible alternative, but this is no longer the case.

6. Actually try out the program before you buy it, using a demonstration program ("demo") that the seller will send you. (The demo

is just like the full program except that it uses preprogrammed information, and it is "crippled" so that you cannot use the demo to do your own work. Crippling is the seller's protection against your using the software without paying for it.) You may also ask (and sometimes get) the seller for a trial period for use of the program, because a demo program is far from a full experience of how the system works.

7. Don't let yourself get snowed by glowing descriptions of a lot of fancy frills in the program. It is easy, and lots of fun for the programmer, to attach a bunch of "bells and whistles," that look impressive but that actually are not very valuable. Colors, musical tones, and "windows" are examples of such frills.

8. Check that the firm with which you are dealing commits itself to provide emergency consulting services over the phone for a substantial length of time—say 3 or 6 months or a year—and then provide consulting services indefinitely at some reasonable price. Even more important, check that the firm not only promises but actually *delivers* such services. The only way to check is by asking firms who have bought the system earlier.

Again, there are advantages in purchasing your software from a firm that is sufficiently well established that you have some protection against them going out of business and leaving you without a good source of support and without assistance in modifying the program. Maybe a firm that is not well established will work out a deal with you whereby you pay on the installment plan; this will give you some hold on them to ensure that they fulfill their promises of assistance down the road.

The Ideal Program and Computer

Let's begin the analysis by asking what a perfect program and computer would do for us. The most important characteristics also are the characteristics that most sharply distinguish among the various software packages. No program has all these characteristics, of course.

First, a perfect system would keep track forever of every piece of information an inquirer or customer provides to you.

The "customer database record" or "customer file" begins with a unique identification number for each customer. This number is assigned to the customer automatically by the computer when the customer first makes a purchase. In the case of businesses that have many inquiries for information but only some portion of the inquirers become customers, this identification number probably is best given when a person either makes an inquiry *or* a purchase.

The necessary information that comes from the user includes such basics as name; company name if not an individual; address; phone number; the discount the customer ordinarily receives; characteristics of the customer, such as the industry if the customer is a firm; whether the customer must be charged tax; information on every item the customer ever buys, including price, quantity, size, color, and so on; the date of every order; the dollar volume of every order; whether any items are returned; the profit from every order; and so on. (Not all of this information need remain in the customer file; but instead it may be stored in the archive, though as the cost of computer disk capacity falls, it will become feasible to store all of it in the main customer file.)

Ideally, the computer should check some of these pieces of information as they come from the customer, for example, whether the zip code is the correct one for that community and whether the credit card number has a typographical mistake in it (as many do). The information that is used for this checking comes from a variety of sources (for example, the post office department's handbook of zip codes), and it is stored in special files in the computer for comparison when the customer first orders.

One important use of the information contained in the customer database is to build your "house list," that is, the list of your own customers; this list always is by far the best source of additional orders. With information on types and volumes of prior purchases, you can select which customers to solicit, how often, and with which offers for which products; this selectivity allows you to "segment your market" in a manner that is crucial for mail-order selling. And when you rent your house list to other mail-order firms—an important source of revenue for a large number of firms—you can select the various segments of your list that other firms wish to rent, thereby making your house list more attractive for them to use.

For the purposes of market segmentation in list rentals, you can get by with less information on individual customers than is necessary for satisfactory marketing analysis for your own operations. But this should not serve as an excuse for you to have your system retain less than the fullest information possible on customers' purchases and of your advertising to them.

Second, a perfect system also would keep a record of every piece of *advertising* sent by you to each customer, and it would indicate which advertisement or catalog triggered each order.

If the customer originally replied to a space advertisement, or to a direct-mail piece, the record must indicate exactly which ad, in which medium, on which date, produced that first customer contact. And then the record must show which catalogs and subsequent direct-mail pieces were sent by you to each customer, as well as the "key" on the order form of each order received, so that you can establish the relationship between particular advertisements (and also the total volume of advertising) and the orders received. This sort of information also allows you to make crucial decisions, such as the size of the space given to an item in your catalog, based upon the volume of sales of that item.

Together with the basic information that the customer sends you and various other information that you collect, the information about the record of your advertising to the customer constitutes the customer database.

The information discussed in the first and second sections above is easy to collect, and much of it is recorded on the order form in even the least comprehensive computer program. But the storage capacity of the personal computer, even with a hard disk, is too small to accommodate a considerable amount of information about a fairly large number of customers (though this may not be true for the 30-megabyte and larger disks now coming onto the market as of 1986, but their cost may be prohibitive for a while). The programs economize on storage space by retaining only part of the customer information from one sale to the next, dropping out (say) the specific items which the customer purchased and coding only the categories, or maintaining detailed information only on the latest purchase and the total dollar amounts of the previous purchases, or dropping out records of all the catalogs sent to the customer, and so on. Later on, this information may be desperately needed for the various types of analyses that you need in order to decide where and when to advertise. As long as the information is in the archive of back-up files discussed earlier, there is no problem, however, because whichever information you need can then be obtained when necessary.

So to repeat for the nth time even though you are undoubtedly sick of hearing about it. *No one*—and I mean no one—should fail to utilize this procedure: Everyday, dump the information from every order record onto floppy disks or a streaming cassette, back up the files properly, and store the information. Later on you can figure out ways of getting back the information that you need. This procedure is cheap and easy and invaluable. Yet many people won't do it—and later on will kick themselves around the block for not doing so.

Third, a perfect system will supply analyses of existing records that tell you what you need to know to run your business well. The most important analyses, partly because they are the ones that are least likely to be handled well by canned programs, are those that tell you the results of various advertising patterns, ranging from simple analyses of the number of orders received from a single advertisement in a magazine, to complex analyses of the results of sending out say three versus four catalogs a year to various groups of customers. Some of these analyses may be programmed when you first install your computer system. But you cannot know in advance all the analyses that you will want to make as your business develops. Therefore, you must ensure that the system (1) retains all the necessary information, as discussed in the two paragraphs above, and (2) allows you to use standard packages of statistical techniques without altering the basic system. To repeat, the system cannot supply analyses that require detailed information on each customer's purchases and the advertisements received by each customer unless this information is retained somewhere in your system—which may be in your back-up archives.

Fourth, a perfect system would process every order received completely so that no additional paperwork operations are needed. That is, the perfect system would record all details about an order, check the inventory to make sure that all the items are in stock, deal with the items that are not in stock by making appropriate notations on the order, bring the inventory records up to date by noting the decreases in stocks caused by this order, prepare a "picking ticket" for the person(s) who will assemble the order that tells what to put in the package, prepare a shipping label that indicates the mode of transportation, and do a variety of other tasks that may be required for your specific business. This processing function is an especial godsend for catalog businesses that carry a wide line of items. More about this below.

All of the canned programs can be arranged to handle the processing function effectively, though various amounts of "customizing" may be necessary, depending upon the nature of your business. Here we might note that CoLinear Systems, the maker of Response, is prepared to do customizing at a price, whereas Professional Publications, the maker of the less-expensive Mail Order Pro, will not do customizing because of the initial low price.

Fifth, an ideal system will be easy to work with. That is, it will have lots of "help" subprograms, or "screens," as they are known. There will be effective "error messages" that appear when you make a mistake and tell you what to do next. The program will be easy for people to learn as you are training them. It will show material conveniently on the screen as operators are working on the orders. That is, it will be "user friendly."

Sixth, an ideal system will ensure that you do not have any duplicate names in your list, perhaps with different addresses. It will also allow you to use your own list together with rented lists in such fashion that you do not duplicate mailings.

Seventh, an ideal system will contain many built-in checks to prevent errors. For example, the address from the customer database should appear automatically so that it can be checked against the address on the order that just came in. For another example, if the operator enters a zip code for a state other than the one written on the order, or enters a color of an item which you do not carry, the program should immediately inform the operator of that error. It should also speed operations by automatically doing as many clerical operations as possible, for example, immediately indicating the price when the item and the discount "class" of customer—retail, wholesale, and so on—have been entered.

Eighth, the system should function sufficiently rapidly in its various operations so that operator's time is used as efficiently as possible without having to wait for the machine to proceed. It should also be sufficiently fast that it does not frustrate you by making you wait so long for a response that you get antsy, that is, it should have an effective "index" system to help you rapidly obtain information for reports as well as information on individual customers.

Ninth, the program should allow you to send out personalized letters automatically, the contents of which are determined by information in your customer records. This feature can be arranged for in all the available programs. It should also keep a record of which letters were sent to which people.

Tenth, the program should maintain records on each "advertising vehicle"—space advertisement, direct mailing, catalog, or whatever—employed by the firm, showing the sales response to each and every advertisement and catalog separately. Recording the initial responses—both inquiries and sales—is relatively straightforward. The program automatically takes the advertisement key from the purchase order, and it adds that response to the running tallies kept on the advertising vehicle or "media record." The purchase information on the media record should be complete—items purchased, dollar value of purchase, cost of items, profitability of the purchases, and so on.

The tricky part of the advertising vehicle response recording process is to properly allow for repurchases. An individual order usually comes in with the key from the latest catalog. But the person ordering may originally have been made a customer by a magazine advertisement say 3 years before, and that original magazine advertisement must get credit (though the subsequent catalogs and mailings may appropriately get credit, too) for the later purchases even though subsequent advertisements and catalogs helped make the sale. And the recent catalog must also be recorded as getting part of the credit.

The simplest, most inclusive, and totally correct (though incomplete) answer is that the key that comes with every purchase should be recorded along with that purchase, and all purchase-order information should be kept forever. It is then always possible to go back and recapture any information that you need, and to make judgments about the selling power of the various components of your advertising schedule when you need them. For day-to-day decisions, you will need to know at least the total volume of purchases that are eventually made as a result of the advertisement that first caused the customer's response, totaled over all the customers who responded to that advertisement. This means that the customer's purchases must be recorded on the record of the advertisement whose key is on the first order, which is a crucial piece of information in the customer record. More complex analyses and types of recording of response are beyond the scope of this paragraph.

Eleventh, an ideal system will allow you to link up several computers in such manner that if several clerks are working on orders at the same time, they do not interfere with each other. The inventory file should be continuously updated so that each clerk's orders are entered into the same inventory file, and the status of inventory is correctly reported to each clerk at all times. This link-up is called a "multiuser system."

Twelfth, an ideal system in coming years will have features that we can't even imagine right now. For example, it is now feasible (though certainly too costly for most beginners) to arrange a 24-hour telephone ordering service with the computer asking all the questions and taking all the information. About the only thing I can't believe that the computer will be doing in a few short years is making your management decisions for you.

Large businesses have large machines (though called "mini," in contrast to the truly large "mainframe" computers that only a few mail-order businesses are big enough to require) that can do a good many of these tasks, and do them very rapidly for tens of thousands of customers every day, storing all the information on disks or tapes. However, in fairness to the microcomputer programs that we are discussing here, the latter are catching up fast. The programs for many of these mini systems were written individually for those large businesses, often at great cost in money, time, and aggravation, though packages are now more available for minis than in the past. We need not discuss those systems further here except to note that installing such a system requires lots of expert help. A qualified consultant often can save you lots of time and money. But finding out who is qualified is not easy. I suggest that a firm might begin by contacting the consultants who advertise in the columns of *Direct Marketing*, talk to several, get the names of firms they have worked for, and talk to those references, as well as doing some as further checking around the industry. But most of this book's readers are not ready to investigate such large systems.

Amazingly, inexpensive systems for the personal computer can come very close to this ideal, using the basic canned program together with relatively little customizing for the individual customer. Let us consider two programs that are on the market, discussing how each of them compares with the ideal.

Comparison Checklist

The market is beginning to explode with new software for mail-order firms. Before you make a purchase, you should consult the most recent articles in the trade publications, some of which rate programs in various ways. (I do not offer ratings here because the field is changing so rapidly.) As of January 1986, the latest articles on the subject are Ernest H. Schell's "1985 Review: Catalog Management Software" covering programs for microcomputers in the December/January 1986 issue of *Catalog Age* (there was a review of minicomputer systems in the October/November 1985 issue) and "Software Systems Review, Part I" in *Direct Marketing*, January 1986, which covers both micro and minicomputer systems. Chances are that the same publications will have follow-up reviews in the same months' issues each year.

First will come a few words about the two systems that received the best ratings in their price classes in Schell's assessment; the characteristics of each system will also be noted below. Then will come the names and addresses of other systems, one of which might well be best for your purposes. Software selling for much above $2,000 is not included.

- Mail Order Pro (formerly called Mail Pro and Dispatch) is produced by Professional Publications, Inc., P.O. Box 199, San Carlos, CA 94070, 415-593-9119. It is relatively inexpensive—$395 for Mail Order Pro alone, and another $295 for the associated List Pro, or a total of $790—and it does an excellent job in order processing. It has the advantage of having been in use since 1981 in a good number of installations, which means that the main bugs have been discovered and remedied. Because of the low price, however, you cannot obtain additional customizing by the seller.

- Response is produced by CoLinear Systems, Inc., P.O. Box 11562, Atlanta, GA 30355, 404-433-3217. The cost of the basic package is about $3,000, and the extra cost to have the system adapted to your needs might be in the low hundreds of dollars. It has the advantage that the developer will customize various operations for you at reasonable cost. It has a great many useful features, seems to have been programmed in a sophisticated and advanced fashion so that you can process relatively many orders rapidly, and rivals the mini packages in many ways. Because it is newer than Mail Order Pro, there has been less opportunity for the rough spots to have been smoothed out, however.

    Response also comes in a scaled-down form—less capacity, fewer features—for $995. It can later be upgraded to the full system without greater cost than if you begin with the full system.

- MOMe (Mail Order Management Expert), produced by International Software Technology, Inc., 1112 7th Avenue, Monroe, WI 53566, 608-328-8870.

- MoM (Mail Order Manager), Data Absolute: The Computer Rescue Squad, 315 Main Street, Roseville, CA 95678, 916-786-5455.

- MOMS, Dash Data Systems, Inc., 1308 Doris Avenue, Ocean, NJ 07712, 201-531-7277.

- PC Mail Order System, Professional Business Solutions, 4719 W. 69th Terrace, Shawnee Mission, KS 66208, 913-677-1024.

- Perelman/Camis, P.O. Box 241758, Los Angeles, CA 90024, 213-207-9566.

- Accounting Publications, Inc., 4202 Spicewood Springs, Suite 118, Austin, TX 78759, 512-345-6165.

- Inquiry Services, Inc., 12842 Pennridge Industrial Drive, Bridgeton (St. Louis), MO 63044, 314-298-0599.

- Goldsmith & Associates, 48 Shattuck Avenue, Suite 86, Berkeley, CA 94704, 415-540-8396.

- Professional Publications, Inc., P.O. Box 199, San Carlos, CA 94070-0199, 415-593-9119.

Next follows a checklist of various characteristics of computer systems that are of interest to mail-order firms. The characteristics are clustered into groups according to the file in which they appear, but this classification is not watertight, and some characteristics appear in more than one place in the list so that they will receive your attention along with related characteristics.

Notations are made for the degree of importance of the characteristics—absolutely crucial (CRU); valuable, and worth having if the extra cost is not too much and if it is not ordinarily provided (VAL); a nice and perhaps useful frill (LUX). Of course, the importance of each characteristic depends upon your particular business.

An important purpose of this list is to serve as a checklist for you as you consider various software packages. You are not likely to know enough about your business or about computers to do a *good* job now in knowing which characteristics you need. But as they say—too soon old, too late smart; in the meantime, you do the best you can and muddle through. If you can get advice from someone else already in the mail-order business, you can benefit greatly at this juncture— as at many others.

The two mail-order software packages which I have examined in some detail, Response (Resp) and Mail Order Pro (Pro), are coded as follows: the feature is a standard part of the package (REG), they will supply it at slight additional cost (LO-OPT), they will supply it but only at non-negligible cost (CO), or it cannot be obtained with that package (N.A.).

Order File

The following characteristics may or may not be included in the "order file." The order file is the batch of material typed into the computer each day from the customer's order form or as it is received over the phone, as soon as possible after the order arrives. Each order is kept on disk in a "file record" that is later used to print out basic work forms such as the picking ticket, the list of items that are picked out from the inventory and packaged for shipment. The data in the order file also are transferred—either immediately or (less desirably) later on—to the all-important customer file or database, which stores the information for use in business analyses about where and when to advertise, among other things.

1. *Customer name.* May be typed in last name first, which is then automatically reversed when the shipping ticket or a computer letter to the customer is printed. CRU; Pro–REG; Resp–REG.

2. *Firm name* (if there is one). CRU; Pro–REG; Resp–REG.

3. *Customer account identification number.* An account identification (ID) number assigned to each customer when that person or firm buys from you the first time, which is then attached to each subsequent order received by the customer. The system should automatically assign the next sequential number to each new customer.

If the customer ID number is available to the operator from your label on the order form (and it is desirable that it be printed on your outgoing labels and also on the label on the order form, though this can be difficult in some cases), enter the ID number first, and check that the name is correct. CRU; Pro–REG; Resp–REG.

4. *Automatic retrieval of identification number when customer name is typed in, if previously a customer* (this characteristic is not a piece of information, but rather a characteristic of the system). It is absolutely vital that all the orders for a given customer be linked by the unique customer identification number. Therefore, if there has previously been a sale to this person or firm, the computer should respond with the customer identification number when the customer's name is typed in. And it is important that the system do a good job of identifying the customer even if the customer's name is typed in somewhat incorrectly, perhaps by cross-checking the address.

When you have found a previous record of either the customer ID number, the customer name, or the customer address, the system should automatically check that there is no other listing for this customer under another ID number, and that the address and name spelling is consistent in all cases.

Also to be retrieved automatically along with the customer ID number is any information about credit status that might cause the order shipment to be held up. DES; Pro–N.A.; Resp–REG.

5. *Order number.* A sequential number assigned automatically by the computer. CRU; Pro–REG; Resp–REG.

6. *Date of entering the order.* CRU; Pro–REG; Resp–REG.

7. *Date of receipt of order* (if known to be different from the date of entering this order record). DES; Pro–REG; Resp–LO-OPT. ($25.00)

8. *Date order must be shipped* (if the customer specifies a rush date or a special date for gift or other purposes). LUX; Pro–N.A.; Resp–LO-OPT ($25.00).

9. *Operator's initials or name.* Knowing who processed the order helps you check on the quality of each operator's work as well as to trace problems if they occur. This is easy to add one way or another if it does not come with the package. DES; Pro–REG; Resp–REG.

10. *Shipping address.* This should appear automatically along with the customer's identification number, if the customer has previously ordered, so that the operator need only check the address on the order. DES; Pro–REG; Resp–REG.

11. *Zip code operation.* You type in the zip code, and the city and state appear automatically, drawn from a sprecial file. If this does not square with the address written on the order, the error is to be checked out and corrected. DES; Pro–N.A.; Resp–REG.

12. *Billing address if different from shipping address.* Automatic (that is, it should appear when you type in the name). CRU; Pro–REG; Resp–REG.

13. *"Attention" name.* Automatic. CRU; Pro–REG; Resp–REG.

14. *Phone number* (including area code and extension). Automatic. CRU; Pro–REG; Resp–REG.

15. *Advertising vehicle or catalog code.* This is the key of the catalog or advertisement (space or direct mail) from which the order comes, coded (keyed) on the order form or on the envelope if the advertisement is a space ad. Some orders come without any key, as noted in Chapter 11 on keying, and then this variable is coded "No key." CRU; Pro–REG; Resp–REG.

16. *Salesperson* (if personal selling is involved). CRU; Pro–REG; Resp–REG.

17. *Shipping method requested* (if request made). CRU; Pro–REG; Resp–REG.

18. *Method of payment* (if order to be charged). CRU; Pro–REG; Resp–REG.

19. *Credit card number.*   It is possible to hook up a system that will automatically check the credit-card status of the customer, but this is a very advanced feature. LUX; Pro–REG; Resp–REG.

20. *Complete information on the order.*   This includes quantities, identification numbers of items ordered, prices, colors, sizes, and whatever else is appropriate for your line of business. Prices for items are automatically retrieved from the price file, which may differ depending upon the catalog from which the customer ordered. These prices may then be checked against those written by the customer on the order form. CRU; Pro–REG; Resp–REG.

21. *Discount percentage for this customer.*   Automatic. If it does not come up from customer database, it must now be assigned by the supervisor. DES; Pro–N.A.; Resp–REG.

22. *Profit on each item and on the order.*   This information is automatically retrieved from the price file along with the price of each item, and it is then summed for the order. LUX; Pro–N.A.; Resp–REG.

23. *Order entry prompt.*   Allows the order taker to provide customers with additional information, i.e., related products pertaining to the items they are purchasing. LUX; Pro–N.A.; Resp–REG.

24. *Gift instructions.*   Gifts present special problems, especially multiple gifts from a single person. The donor must be notified after the gifts have been sent. LUX; Pro–N.A.; Resp–LO-OPT (about $50.00).

25. *Incoming message.*   This allows for messages from the customer such as a request for a new catalog or a complaint about a prior purchase. LUX; Pro–N.A.; Resp–LO-OPT.

Customer Records in the Customer Database

The first batch of information in the order form—from the customer's name down to the phone number, plus the discount percentage—is automatically transferred to the customer record file from the first order record for the particular customer. See details in above discussion of order form for these other variables.

1. *Tax exempt status.*   This can be determined automatically from the state and city zip code. DES; Pro–REG; Resp–REG.

2. *Gift giver or receiver.* If the gift giver does not give gifts again to particular persons the next holiday season, you would like to solicit orders from the persons who received gifts. But you don't want to solicit if the donor gives gifts again to those persons. LUX; Pro–N.A.; Resp–LO-OPT.

3. *Characteristics of customer.* Examples are age, sex, religion, and industry code. The characteristics on which you seek data depend upon your business, but they might also depend upon the interests of the firms which might rent your list. This information must be obtained by asking the customer; in some cases the questions may be deemed unwelcome by the customer, in which case the information is not obtained. But the use of such customer information to segment marketing efforts is a major new direction of the mail-order business—both your own marketing efforts and the marketing efforts of firms to which you rent your database list—and it would be well to get started on this right at the outset. DES; Pro–REG; Resp–LO-OPT or CO.

4. *Credit information.* Bad credit record with you? Credit limits? DES; Pro–REG; Resp–REG.

5. *Advertising source of first order.* This is automatically transferred from the source of the customer's first order. CRU; Pro–REG; Resp–REG.

6. *Date of first purchase.* CRU; Pro–REG; Resp–REG.

7. *Date of last previous purchase.* This is the date of the most recent order entered. CRU; Pro–REG; Resp–REG.

8. *Complete information on ALL orders.* You must transfer the order file intact to the customer database *without deleting any information* (except perhaps such details on goods ordered as color and size). It is with respect to this aspect of the customer database that the biggest difficulty arises. The problem is that the order information requires a lot of storage space on the computer disk, so much that today's microcomputers cannot hold this information for any business other than the smallest on the hard disk. And the available programs have not been designed to store this information on floppy disks or streaming tape in such fashion that the information can be retrieved—even on a sample basis—for use in analyses. The available programs therefore throw away much of the invaluable information on the order records before updating the customer record in the database. The solution is to arrange to store the full information, which is not

a major problem to accomplish. But you must do it or you will be sorry later on.

A record of all correspondence with the customer must be maintained, also, in order to facilitate compliance with the Federal Trade Commission's Mail Order Rule (see Appendix B). CRU; Pro–N.A.; Resp–LO-OPT.

9. *Purchase amount this year.* The computer automatically sums up the amounts in the order that is presently being added to the customer file, together with previous orders during the current calendar (or fiscal) year. DES; Pro–REG; Resp–REG.

10. *Profit this year.* Automatically summed from the orders. DES; Pro–REG; Resp–REG.

11. *Number of purchases this year.* DES; Pro–REG; Resp–REG.

Order Processing

The next set of characteristics pertains to the handling of the order so that the order is (1) filled with maximum efficiency, and (2) special problems such as out-of-stock for some items, and insufficient payment, are taken care of effectively and courteously.

1. *For each item: Is it in stock?* The system automatically checks the inventory, and if the item is in stock, the item number and description and quantity and location are printed onto a picking ticket. If the packing slip is not the same as the picking ticket, the information is also printed onto the packing slip. DES; Pro–REG; Resp–REG.

2. *If item not in stock, make back-order notation.* If the item will not be shipped for 30 days, the customer must be notified in accord with Federal Trade Commission Rules (See Chapter 6). The system must respond when the item comes back into stock, and it must arrange for shipment then. If the item is no longer carried, the system must make allowance in payment calculations and print out a refund check if appropriate. (This feature may be attractive, but it is no substitute for a separate order confirmation procedure.) DES; Pro–REG; Resp–REG.

3. *If payment is by check, is the payment large enough to cover the order?* If the check falls short of the summed prices of goods ordered by more than a small amount (the definition of "small" being decided by management), the system should print a letter, informing the customer of that fact. There also must be a double check that the item really is out of stock before the order is completed. The system

can err on this, and such a mistake can be costly. DES; Pro–REG; Resp–REG.

4. *Does the system create shipping logs for UPS and post office?* DES; Pro–REG; Resp–(for UPS) LO-OPT ($75.00).

5. *Print out credit card forms.* The system should also have a provision for communicating charge information to credit card companies, electronically or in print. CRU; Pro–REG; Resp–REG.

6. *Print shipping label.* CRU; Pro–REG; Resp–REG.

7. *Calculate the best way to ship, taking account of cost and speed, and indicate charges.* This feature is probably beyond the range of most reasonably priced system. LUX; Pro–REG; Resp–N.A.

Inventory Control

The following characteristics pertain to the system's capacity to provide the proper messages about the state of the inventory.

1. *Deduct each item ordered (and presumably picked) from the inventory.* CRU; Pro–REG; Resp–REG.

2. *Indicate the level of the inventory after updating, compare the post-shipment inventory to some target inventory level, and indicate whether the item has been reordered, each time an item is ordered.* CRU; Pro–REG; Resp–REG.

3. *Keep track of product information.* This includes the name of the supplier of the item, the price paid to the supplier and the date purchased, the date last ordered by a customer, amount and location of space for item in catalog, the quantity on order, the quantity backordered, the size and weight of the item, and so on. DES; Pro–REG (for most of these); Resp–REG (for most of these).

4. *Report the rate of item sales.* This might include item sales each month, quarter, and year, together with information on catalog space and location to help calculate profitability and to enlighten decisions about the next catalog's makeup. This report might be considered one of the management reports to be discussed below. LUX; Pro–REG; Resp–REG or LO-OPT.

Reporting to Management

Thinking about reports in advance of purchasing a system is less crucial than thinking about some other elements of the system, especially customer list maintenance, because reports can be pro-grammed when you need them. Nevertheless, let us consider some of the more important standard reports.

1. *Daily (or whenever you want it) report of sales.*   Each day you want to know total sales and total number of orders and of inquiries. You should also receive data on the sales of each item. The dollar sales results should be compared against the bank deposits each day to see that they tally. CRU; Pro–REG; Resp–REG.

2. *Daily report of inventory.*   Status of each item, as discussed above in order file. CRU; Pro–REG; Resp–REG.

3. *Daily report of media results.*   The numbers of inquiries and sales generated by each space advertisement, by each list, and from each catalog, to date. CRU; Pro–REG; Resp–REG.

4. *Sales results by advertisement.*   This detailed report includes the dollar value of repeat business that comes from persons who originally purchased from each advertisement. Net revenue (that is, gross profit, or sales less merchandise cost) may be calculated, too. CRU; Pro–REG; Resp–LO-OPT.

5. *Connections with accounting reports.*   It is desirable that the sales reports be capable of transfer to the accounting systems, both for the purposes of accounting control and for tax and other auditing purposes. DES; Pro–REG; Resp–N.A. (Is expected available soon.)

6. *Credit reports.*   This is the accounts receivable section of the program. If you offer credit, you want to know the number of accounts outstanding and the dollar value of accounts receivable. You also want to have a report on bad debts. And you want the system to indicate when you have received duplicate payment. DES; Pro–REG; Resp–REG.

Strategic Analyses

In addition to the standard reports mentioned in the section above, you will from time to time be needing various strategic analyses. An example is an analysis of how often you want to mail your catalog to various segments of your list. This is not a question that any standard report can answer. Instead, you will need to think out and have programmed a special analysis. This sort of special complex analysis cannot be allowed for in advance by any canned package. The best that you can ask for is that the customer database and the advertisement vehicle files be sufficiently detailed, and sufficiently well organized, that you are able to make the special analyses that you need.

Appraisal of Package

Now that we have run over a list of desirable characteristics and indicated the characteristics possessed by the various packages, you will surely be asking for a comparative appraisal of the available systems. Before anything else is said, I think it is important for you to know that the developers of the two systems I have been in close contact with—Mail Order Pro and Response—are very proud of their systems. This is not just a business with them, but also a labor of love, and it shows up in fierce pride in what their systems can do. And they deserve to be proud because they have very good products at amazingly low prices.

As to which one, I cannot in good conscience, without knowledge of your business's needs, give you a definitive answer. For example, Mail Order Pro says that it is an appropriate system for businesses that process fewer than 300 orders per day, and Response is less limited in this respect. Furthermore, as long as you keep your customer data in an archive so that you can retrieve it later, you cannot go wrong with either system. Response provides more possibilities than does Mail Order Pro, and it does not lack any crucial elements possessed by Mail Order Pro, so far as I can tell. Whether you will consider it worth the extra money when you are buying your first system will depend upon you. One advantage to Mail Order Pro as of 1986 is that scores of its packages have been in operation long enough—in some cases, several years—for the users, and hence the developer, to become aware of bugs and to iron them out; Response's track record is much shorter.

It is not out of the question to buy Mail Order Pro and shift to another system later on, since Mail Order Pro contains a feature which converts its own database to a format usable by other systems, databases, and spreadsheets; the cost of Mail Order Pro which you would have already paid will not be the crucial factor, but rather the hassle in changing from one system to another—both in software and data conversion and also in the organization of your business—can be considerable. But it may be worth going that route, anyway. For that matter, Mail Order Pro and Response can also convert databases from other systems into a format usable by them.

My best recommendation is that you purchase the demonstration packages for these (and any other available) programs, test them out, and then make your decision. You are not likely to go badly wrong whichever way you go.

31

General Management of a Mail-Order Business

When you go looking for an advertising agency, an advertising consultant, or other people or organizations to help you in your mail-order business, don't expect to find a witch doctor or a miracle man. I can assure you that from New York to Los Angeles you won't find a single mail-order "expert" who will—for a small fee—take you in hand, give you a product, figure out a selling plan for you, make up the ads, and make money for you. The only people who will promise you those services are fakers whose help is about as desirable as the plague.

The truth is that every profitable mail-order scheme and campaign has to be hammered out from scratch. Every new scheme requires full attention and work. Nobody has a "machine" that will make mail-order profits.

It stands to reason, that the most talented and most experienced mail-order persons will put their skill to work for the biggest of mail-order firms—the record and book clubs, the correspondence schools, or the vitamin companies, because those outfits can pay the most for the expert's knowledge.

Furthermore, those big outfits have no guarantee of being profitable either. Sometimes they make a pile, sometimes they lose their shirts. They have to work and scrounge just as you do in order to make money.

Various Ways to Have Ads Written

Creating advertisements is not a job for an amateur. You yourself may become qualified to create ads if you study and work hard at it. But without some practice, you are unlikely to do a good job. And only good ads make money!

If you will be spending upward of $12,000 per year for advertising, or if you plan to run large ads, you can develop a relationship with a small advertising agency on a regular basis. They will be glad to have you and will provide full service to you.

Or if you have a product line or a plan that looks as if it has a good potential, you can probably persuade an agency to invest its time and effort in your early ads, even though the early ads won't be profitable to the agency.

The advantage of working through an agency is that their service is "free" to you. The standard system is for the agency to keep 15 percent of the charge made by magazines and other media. And unless you set up a "house agency," you will have to pay the full charges to the media whether or not you use an agency.

The disadvantage of using an agency is that unless your account is really large, you either won't get enough attention or will receive a second-rate job of creating advertisements and selecting media. After all, an agency is going to devote to you only the amount of service that your billing deserves.

Another way to obtain advertisements is by hiring free-lance copy-writers and layout artists. Free-lancers charge by the piece of work, and their fees are not chicken feed.

The classified telephone book in any large city will list free-lancers under "Writers" and "Artists." Most of those persons and firms listed know nothing about mail order, however, despite what they may say. Look instead in *Direct Marketing, Catalog Age, Zip, Direct Marketing News,* and *Advertising Age.*

Choosing a good free-lancer is not easy, of course. Use the same standards as for choosing an advertising agency, which I shall describe below.

How to Choose an Advertising Agency

If you intend to depend upon an agency for the preparation of your advertising, then the choice of an agency will be crucial. A fine agency that knows its business and is honest will bring plenty of returns for your advertising dollars. A poor agency will certainly create non-productive ads and may even lead you to overadvertise unprofitably so as to increase their commissions.

Keep these points in mind when choosing an agency:

1. Get an agency that specializes in mail-order work. There is a tremendous difference between mail-order and non-mail-order ads, and to use a non-mail-order agency is like using a heart surgeon to fill your teeth.

2. Get an agency that is small enough to take your business seriously. If the agency doesn't need the potential revenue you represent, you will never get first-class work from them.

The classic method of choosing a mail-order agency is to look for very good mail-order ads. Then find out who the agency was that did them. You can find the name of the agency either by looking up the client in *Standard Directory of Advertisers* or by writing to the advertiser.

The trouble with this method is that it depends upon your ability to spot good ads. I have severe doubts about *anyone's* ability to do this accurately, let alone a novice.

How to Set Up a House Agency

If you intend to use free-lance talent or create ads yourself, you might as well have the 15 percent commission instead of donating it to the media. Setting up a house agency can save the commission which can represent a good chunk of your profit.

Up until 1954, the magazines and newspapers were very strict about "recognizing" an agency as qualified to collect the commission. But the Federal Trade Commission moved in on the associations of publishers and "persuaded" them to abandon their old practices. Nowadays, the publishers cannot act together to prevent you from earning the commission.

This means that all you have to do is convince most magazines that you are a good credit risk, and they will "recognize" you as an advertising agency.

In fact, if you represent any sizable amount of revenue, you can place it direct with many magazines and save the 15 percent commission without even pretending to be an independent agency.

Setting up a house agency is not "shady." Some of the very biggest corporations in the country have set up house agencies, including drug companies that spend up to 60 percent of their total revenue on advertising.

Setting up a house agency is easy. About all you need is $20 worth of insertion orders, plus some stationery. Give your agency a name different from your mail-order firm's name, and then print up some forms like those shown in Figure 31-1a, 1b, 1c, and 1d—except that you insert your own name in the two marked places, of course.

When you send in your first orders, some of the magazines will accept your orders on credit, if the order is small, without doing any checking at all. No trouble there!

But some magazines and almost all newspapers will ask you for references of other magazines with whom you have placed advertisements. They may also ask you for a full financial statement.

One way to handle this—and a rather good way—is to offer to pay cash, less the commission, of course. After you have paid cash for a while, you will find it easy to get credit. And in the meantime, you can tell *other* magazines that you have placed ads with the magazines who accept your first insertions.

Another way to handle the credit problem is to deposit a good-sized sum in an agency bank account, admit that your agency is brand-

Order Blank For Publications

NAME OF AGENCY
Address

☐ If checked here this is a SPACE RESERVATION

☐ If checked here this is a FIRM SPACE ORDER and
   BINDING unless cancelled before closing date*

☐ If checked here this is CANCELLATION
   or change of: _____

To the publisher of:

ORDER NO. _____

Date _____

Advertiser _____

Product _____

Contract Year _____

Discount Level _____

Edition: (specify) National _____

               Regional _____

*Subject to conditions stated above and on back hereof

ISSUE DATE	SPACE	COLOR/BLEED	FREQUENCY	RATE

Position

Additional Instructions:

Copy instructions & material ☐ to follow   ☐ herewith

Address all other correspondence to:

_____

Less agency commission   on gross

        Cash discount   on net

Mail all invoices to:

_____
(Authorized Signature)

PLEASE FILL IN AND RETURN THIS ACKNOWLEDGMENT TO AGENCY

(NAME AND ADDRESS OF AGENCY)   ORDER NO. _____

This acknowledges that your order dated _____ covering advertising for _____

was received on (date) _____ and instructions thereon thoroughly understood.

American Association of Advertising Agencies, Inc.   PUBLICATION _____

        Copyright 1973   PER _____

Figure 31-1a

CONDITIONS

Approved 1973 by the American Association of Advertising Agencies, American Business Press, and the Magazine Publishers Association. Such approval does not mean that any parties contracting for advertising space are obligated to use this form or these conditions.

The advertising agency placing advertising covered by this order (hereafter called "Agency") and the publisher accepting this order (hereafter called "Publisher") hereby agree to be governed by the following conditions:

1. TERMS OF PAYMENT

(a) Liability

Agency agrees to pay for all advertising published by Publisher in accordance with Publisher's rate card. When cash discount is deducted, such payment shall be made on or before the cash discount date specified on said rate card.

Publisher agrees to render bills to Agency not less often than monthy and to hold Agency solely liable for payment (unless otherwise specified on the face of this form). Failure to bill at least monthly shall not constitute a breach of contract.

If Agency defaults in the payment of bills or if, in the judgment of Publisher, Agency credit becomes impaired, Publisher may require payment in advance.

(b) Shipping

Agency agrees to prepay transportation and import charges on all materials sent to Publisher. If such charges are not prepaid, Publisher may either reject the materials or accept them and pay the charges. In the latter case Agency shall promptly reimburse Publisher.

(c) Short Rate/Rebate

Publisher shall bill at the rate earned during the applicable 12-month period. Publisher shall adjust to the earned rate within 60 days after expiration or termination of the applicable 12-month period.

(d) Billing

Unless Agency makes written objection within 60 days after billing under this order, such bill shall be binding.

(e) Cancellation

Either Agency or Publisher may cancel this order prior to cancellation/closing date as stated on Publisher's rate card.

(f) Payment Date

The post mark date on the envelope containing the payment properly addressed to Publisher or Publisher's representative shall be considered the date when payment is made.

2. RATES

(a) "Publisher's Rate Card" shall mean the schedule of advertising rates prevailing at the time of each insertion. Publisher represents that all of his rates are published and shall furnish his rates to Agency if requested.

(b) Publisher represents that the rate applicable to the advertising placed hereunder is the lowest rate currently available for like space. If Publisher hereafter makes a lower rate for like space, such lower rate shall apply to advertising placed hereunder from the effective date of such lower rate.

3. ADVERTISING MATERIAL

(a) The subject matter, form, size, wording, illustration and typography of the advertising shall be subject to the approval of Publisher, but unless otherwise authorized in advance no change shall be made without the consent of Agency.

(b) If Publisher is unable to set any advertisement in the type or style requested, he may set such advertisement in such other type or style as in his opinion most nearly corresponds thereto, and the advertisement may be inserted without submission of proof unless proof before insertion is requested on the face of the order.

(c) Where material furnished by Agency occupies more space then specified in the insertion order, Publisher shall immediately communicate with Agency for definite instructions. If Publisher is unable to secure definite instructions from Agency, the advertising shall be omitted.

(d) If Agency has reserved space for a series of insertions in a publication, and before any closing date the insertion order and copy for next issue have not been received by Publisher, Publisher shall notify Agency and follow Agency's instructions.

(e) Advertisements ordered set in "space as required" shall be measured from office ad. rule to office ad. rule.

4. PROOF OF INSERTION

(a) Full Run

The page containing the advertising shall be supplied to Agency with the invoice for the insertion. At the request of Agency a copy of each issue in which its advertising appears shall be supplied.

(b) Less-Than-Full Run

A copy of the page containing the advertising and a statement by Publisher that the order for advertising was fulfilled shall be supplied to Agency with the invoice for the insertion. Publisher's Master Copy of each issue shall be available for inspection by Agency.

5. CIRCULATION

(a) Unless Publisher is a member of the Audit Bureau of Circulations or Business Publications Audit of Circulation, Agency shall be entitled, upon request, to a statement of circulation verified by a certified public accountant or other auditing organization. If further verification is requested, Publisher shall be required to open his circulation records for examination by Agency.

6. OMISSION OF ADVERTISING

(a) Unintentional or inadvertent failure by Publisher to publish the advertising covered by this order invalidates this order, but shall not constitute a breach of contract or affect any earned discounts.

Intentional omission by Publisher after closing date of the advertising covered by this order is permitted after consultation with Agency.

Figure 31-1*b*

NEWSPAPER CONTRACT

NAME OF AGENCY
Address

To the Publisher of:
City and State

ORDER NO. _____

Date _____

Please Publish Advertising of
(Advertiser)

For (Product)

SPACE TO BE ORDERED WITHIN ONE YEAR FROM _____ Through _____

———— SPACE* ————   ———— TIMES* ————   ———— DATES OF INSERTION* ————

POSITION	COPY
RATE	

LESS AGENCY COMMISSION	ON GROSS	LESS CASH DISCOUNT	ON NET

Subject to Conditions Stated Below and on Back Thereof:

* Only Necessary on Insertion Orders

Mail All Invoices to:

PER _____

ACCEPTED FOR NEWSPAPER ON _____   BY _____

DUPLICATE FOR ACKNOWLEDGEMENT
Please sign and return to agency

Copyright 1974
American Association of Advertising Agencies

Figure 31–1c

CONDITIONS

Approved 1974 by the American Association of Advertising Agencies and International Newspaper Advertising Executives. Such approval does not mean that any parties contracting for advertising space are obligated to use this form or these conditions.

The advertising agency placing advertising covered by this contract (hereinafter called "Agency") and the publisher accepting this contract (hereinafter called "Publisher") hereby agree that this contract shall be governed by the following conditions:

1. TERMS OF PAYMENT

[a]. Agency agrees to pay for all advertising published by Publisher in accordance with this contract. Agency shall make such payment at the office of Publisher or Publisher's authorized representative on or before the last day of the month following that in which the advertising is published, unless otherwise stipulated on Publisher's rate card. When cash discount is deducted, such payment shall be made on or before the cash discount date specified on said rate card, or if the cash discount date is not specified thereon, on or before the 15th of the month following.

Publisher agrees to hold Agency solely liable for payment, (unless otherwise specified on the face of this form) and to render bills to Agency not less often than monthly. Failure to bill at least monthly shall not constitute breach of contract.

[b]. If Publisher at request of Agency furnishes drawings, compositions, cuts or mats, Agency agrees to pay for same, in accordance with Publisher's rate card and in the manner specified in paragraph (a) above.

[c]. Agency agrees to prepay transportation and import charges on all advertising material sent to Publisher. If such charges are not prepaid, Publisher may either reject the advertising material or accept them and pay the charges. In the latter case Agency shall promptly reimburse Publisher.

[d]. If, at the end of the advertising period named in this contract or upon prior termination of this contract for any cause, Agency has not used the full amount of advertising contracted for, Agency agrees to pay to Publisher an additional sum on all advertising published, such sum to equal the difference, if any, between the amount due at the rate named in this contract and the amount due at the rate applicable to the quantity of space used as stated in Publisher's rate card. Such additional sum shall not be due unless Publisher renders a bill therefor within 60 days after such expiration or termination. Upon rendition of such a bill, such additional sum shall become immediately due and payable.

Subject to the payment of such additional sum for advertising published, Agency may cancel this contract at any time or may use less space than the amount contracted for.

[e]. Unless Agency makes written objection within 60 days from the rendering of any bill for advertising published under this contract, such bill shall be conclusive as to the correctness of the items therein set forth and shall constitute an account stated.

[f]. Publisher reserves the right to cancel this contract at any time upon default by Agency in the payment of bills or in the event of any other substantial breach of this contract by Agency. Upon such cancellation charges for all advertising published and all other charges payable under this contract, including the short rates defined in paragraph (d), shall become immediately due and payable by Agency upon rendition of bills therefor.

If Agency defaults in the payment of bills, or if in the judgment of Publisher its credit becomes impaired, Publisher shall have the right to require payment for further advertising under this contract upon such terms as he may see fit.

[g]. The post mark date on the envelope properly addressed to Publisher or to Publisher's representative shall be considered the date when payment is made.

2. RATES

[a]. Publisher represents that all of his rates are published. Publisher shall furnish his rates to Agency if requested.

[b]. "Publisher's rate card" shall be understood to mean the schedule of advertising rates of Publisher upon which this contract is based.

[c]. Publisher represents that the rate stated in the contract is the minimum rate at which an equal or less amount of space, for the same class of advertising, to be published in a like position, under the same conditions, within the same period of time, can be secured at the time this contract is entered into.

[d]. If additional space is used within the period covered by the contract, where Publisher has a schedule of graduated rates, any lower rate shall be given if earned, according to Publisher's rate card on which this contract is based.

3. ADVERTISING MATERIAL

[a]. The subject matter, form, size, wording, illustration and typography of the advertising shall be subject to the approval of Publisher but unless otherwise authorized in advance no change shall be made without the consent of Agency.

[b]. If Publisher is unable to set any advertisement in the type of style requested, he may set such advertisement in such other type or style as in his opinion most nearly corresponds thereto, and the advertisement may be inserted without submission of proof unless proof before insertion is requested on the face of the order.

[c]. Where materials furnished by Agency occupy more space than specified in the contract or insertion order, Publisher should communicate with Agency for definite instructions. If publisher is unable to secure definite instructions from Agency, the advertising shall be omitted.

[d]. If agency has contracted for a series of insertions in a publication, and before closing date insertion order and copy for next issue have not been received by Publisher, Publisher shall notify Agency and follow Agency's instructions.

[e]. Advertisements ordered set in "space as required" shall be measured from office ad. rule to office ad. rule.

4. PROOF OF INSERTION

[a]. The page containing the advertising or, at the request of Agency, a copy of each issue in which the advertising appears, shall be mailed or otherwise supplied to Agency, which shall be deemed to have received such copy or page unless Publisher is notified in writing of the non-receipt thereof within thirty days after the date of publication. Publisher may mail or otherwise supply an affidavit of publication in lieu of a second copy or page containing the advertisement. Failure to forward or furnish such copy, page or affidavit shall not constitute a breach of the contract.

5. CIRCULATION

[a]. Unless Publisher is a member of the Audit Bureau of Circulations, Agency shall be entitled, upon request, to a statement of net paid circulation verified by a certified public accountant, or in lieu thereof to the right to examine Publisher's circulation books.

6. OMISSION OF ADVERTISING

[a]. Failure by Publisher to insert in any particular issue or issues invalidates the order for insertion in the missed issue but shall not constitute a breach of contract.

The advertising must appear in all ordered regular editions issued on the date for which the advertising is ordered. Advertisements omitted from any particular edition or editions must be reported to Agency and if received in time and omitted through fault of Publisher must be made up or adjusted unless otherwise instructed.

Unless otherwise stipulated, Publisher shall have the right to omit any advertisement when the space allotted to advertising in the issue for which such advertisement is ordered has all been taken, and also to limit the amount of space an advertiser may use in any one issue.

7. GENERAL

[a]. In dealing with agencies, Publisher shall follow a uniform policy to avoid discrimination.

[b]. Unless later date is specified in Publisher's rate card, advertising shall begin within thirty days from the date of this contract, or contract becomes null and void.

[c]. A waiver by either party hereto of any default or breach by the other party shall not be construed as a waiver of any subsequent default or breach of the same or any other provisions hereof.

Figure 31-1*d*

new, and fill out the credit forms. Many media will give you credit on that basis.

Credit is so very important in placing ads because of the long time lag between closing dates and publication dates. Without credit you must pay months in advance, and that ties up a lot of your working capital.

It should be unnecessary to add that a touch of bluffing may aid you immeasurably in obtaining credit. If you can make any medium think your credit is good everywhere else, you have the problem licked.

If your advertising budget is too small to justify the exertion of setting up a house agency, you can often get an established agency to "clear" your account for you. They keep perhaps 5 percent for the trouble of billing you and other clerical work, and you keep the other 10 percent.

Merchandising Your Products

If you develop a good mail-order product that is not patented or copyrighted, you will have only a limited time to reap the profits before competition swarms in. If you merchandise the product to other firms, you can profit by the swarm of competition instead of being hurt by it. That way you will make a small profit on the large number of pieces your competitors will sell. And on their side, the competitors will prefer to deal with you because you already have developed the item and can make it available to them immediately, without the development costs they would otherwise incur.

These are various ways to merchandise the product:

1. If the product is a small novelty selling under $5, try the large novelty catalog firms. If you can show them good mail-order results, they will be glad to put it into their catalogs for a trial. Begin your campaign of merchandising to catalog mail-order dealers by going through an entire issue of *House Beautiful* and *House & Garden* and writing for catalogs from every advertiser in the shopping section. Those advertisers will be your prospects.

You must expect to sell the product to catalog houses at about 30 percent of the retail price on a $1 or $2 item, slightly more for more expensive items.

Don't rush to the catalog houses just as soon as you hit a winner. Wait until you have wiped up most of the gravy and until competition has had almost time enough to come in.

2. Contact firms that sell mail-order catalogs to other firms. Some stock the merchandise; others will want you to operate on a drop-ship basis. Some firms are listed under "Mail Order Drop-Ship Catalog and Merchandise" in the classified section of *Direct Marketing*.

3. Large mail-order firms may take your product and sell it through display advertising. Several firms get a low rate on newspaper and other space because they buy a lot of space. That cost advantage, plus their know-how, can make it profitable for them to move a lot more merchandise than you are able to do.

4. Chains of stores such as Whelan's often sell the mail-order type of merchandise. Try to sell to them.

Credit: To Customers and from Suppliers

Let's start with *your* credit. As we said earlier when we talked about setting up your own agency, credit with advertising media is probably more important than any other line of credit. If you use an advertising agency, credit with them is equally important.

Other suppliers will grant credit if you *sound* reliable and if you can furnish a few solid-sounding references, including a bank. The more business you give a single firm, the better the credit reference the firm will give for you to other people. This is an argument for using a few reliable suppliers rather than distributing your business widely among many firms.

If you can't get credit, you will have to develop it by paying cash at first.

If your character is good, and if you have a persuasive story to tell, you have a fighting chance to obtain credit anywhere!

Selling on credit is always a difficult problem. If you sell a big-ticket product to consumers, you must expect to sell on the installment plan; otherwise you will lose too many sales. Naturally, selling on credit requires working capital and extra bookkeeping, and you will inevitably have some credit losses. But these difficulties are a necessary part of doing business. Don't eat your heart out about unavoidable credit losses.

Mail-order firms doing business with consumers rarely check credit. The merchandise often costs only a small proportion of the selling price, and this makes it sensible to take a chance on any sale. Furthermore, the cost of checking credit is exorbitant.

If you sell to industrial or commercial accounts, you will follow normal credit-checking practices, however.

A good series of collection letters, sent out on a correctly timed schedule, is a mail-order operator's best friend. Model your letters after those of other mail-order firms.

Sometimes it is best to turn to a credit-collection specialist to help you collect your accounts, if individually they are big enough. At the time of writing, at least one such specialist advertises in *Direct Marketing's* classified directory.

Don't Spread Yourself Too Thin

You *cannot* successfully manage a *great many* mail-order products or several product lines. Everything that makes money for you requires attention—a lot more attention than you think. You must concentrate on the most profitable aspects of your business and push them hard. That's the only way to operate successfully.

You must keep a watchful eye on each ad's performance, and that takes energy and time. This is the only reason that big companies don't use the classified ads that they know will be a very profitable investment per dollar invested. They don't want to spend the necessary time and energy in management control. This is also why good ads don't spread everywhere immediately.

And you can't spread your ads too thin, either. Though it is true that you can put many different items into a *catalog,* Stone says this about direct mail:[2] "Paradoxically, few mailers are successful at advertising more than one product at a time. The simple fact seems to be that it is difficult to sell more than one idea at a time."

Banks

Mail-order businesses are not particularly desirable customers for a bank because of the large volume of small checks. Maintaining a large and constant balance in your account will go a long way to sweetening their humor, however.

Banks do not have the same rates for the important matter of the charge on check deposits.

Get checks that look businesslike. Use the form that has an invoice box at the left. And *never* mingle business funds with your personal account.

Why It's Easier to Get Rich in Mail Order

It's not just the money you *make;* it's the money you *keep.* And there is a unique characteristic of the mail-order business that permits you to keep more—for quite a while—than in most other businesses.

The tax law says you must pay taxes on earnings that you *invest,* but not on expenses. Therefore, every businessperson seeks to justify making an outlay into an expense rather than an investment.

The advertising you do to obtain repeat-business customers is customarily treated as an expense of doing business. But a considerable portion of that outlay is an investment that will pay off in future years! And you pay much lower taxes in the current period than if the outlay was treated as an investment. This is a terrific help in accumulating capital.

Magazines invest in a list of subscribers in this fashion also, though I believe the advertising cost is always treated as an expense.

Sooner or later, you must pay taxes on your extra profits. But the further into the future the tax occurs, the better for you.

32

How to Buy
or Sell
a Mail-Order
Business

How to Find Mail-Order Businesses That Are for Sale / How to Put a Price on a Business / How to Sell a Business

Three major topics make up this chapter. In the order in which we shall discuss them, these topics are (1) how to find mail-order businesses that are for sale; (2) how to put a price on a mail-order business, whether buying or selling it; and (3) how to find customers for a business that you wish to sell.

How to Find Mail-Order
Businesses That Are for Sale

Finding a mail-order business for sale is much like finding any other kind of business that is for sale. One difference is that there are fewer mail-order businesses than there are drugstores, say, and the fewer there are of anything, the harder it is to find them. Another difference is that mail-order businesses are really many different kinds of businesses, and you cannot reach them through the channels of any one particular trade, as you can reach all office-supplies firms through their trade magazine, for example.

The first step in seeking out a mail-order business is to read the "Business Opportunities" subsection of the newspaper classified columns. The "Business Opportunities" subsection of the Sunday issue of *The New York Times* is one of the best places to look for a mail-order business that is for sale, no matter where in the United States you live.

A second step is to contact business brokers. You can try those in your area, or you can write to business brokers in New York. However, any given business broker is not very likely to have a listing for a mail-order business at any given time. (When you talk or write to business brokers, try to make them understand what you mean when you say "mail-order business." Very often they will have listings of businesses that do most of their business by mail and really are mail-order businesses, but the business broker may have them classified under "Office Supplies" or "Stamps" or "Printing" or what have you.) The Direct Marketing Association has a service to help you sell a business, but I have no knowledge of how helpful it is.

A third method is to advertise in the "Business Opportunities" subsection of the Sunday paper, especially *The New York Times*. A three-line ad that I ran once brought me over fifty replies from people who wanted to sell businesses. Most of them were not real possibilities, but there were at least six good prospects in the lot. If I were again in the market for a business, I would immediately make this small investment, once a month or so, until I found a business.

You might also advertise in the classified columns of *Direct Marketing*. Many mail-order firms read that magazine.

A fourth method of finding a mail-order business is to write to many mail-order businesses, asking if they wish to sell. You can develop a list of prospects by watching mail-order ads and direct mail. Write to those firms that are in the line of business that interests you and that seem to be of a size that you wish to purchase. (But don't pay *too* much attention to size. It is very hard to guess the size of a mail-order business by its advertising. Once I was interested in a firm that sells printing by mail. I estimated its yearly gross at $100,000, but a Dun & Bradstreet report indicated yearly sales of $750,000. More often, however, firms are *smaller* than you would guess.)

Use business stationery when you write to firms, and write a letter that indicates that you mean business and that you are a good prospect to sell to. Give them plenty of details about you that will impress them with your reliability and financial capability. I won't give you a sample letter here. You should be able to write your own letter for a task like this.

How to Put a Price on a Business

The basic determinant of the value of a business is the amount that the business earns and/or the amount that it can earn under your management.

But the relationship of price to earnings varies with the size of a firm and with the type of business that it does. Very large firms (multimillions of dollars of sales per year) may be worth upward of 7 times earnings, perhaps as high as 20 times earnings. But if you are in the market for a firm of that size, I trust you will obtain additional advice.

A mail-order business that grosses perhaps $500,000 a year might be worth 5 times its yearly earnings. Note that "earnings" does not include the salary of the owner or owners. But how much to count as salary is a very difficult question that we shall not consider here.

A mail-order business that provides perhaps $50,000 to its owner yearly (in salary plus earnings, taken all together) might be worth a price approximately equal to that sum. However, you might pay half a year's earnings or twice a year's earnings, depending upon other desirable or undesirable characteristics of the firm, including its future potential, the pleasantness of the business, and the market at that time for mail-order businesses. The final price will reflect a lot of bargaining, how badly you want to buy, and how badly the owner wants to sell.

So far, so good. But there is a catch! It is very difficult to determine just how much a business earns or how much it provides to its owner. Tax returns are always adjusted to show the minimum possible net to the owner so that he or she will have to pay the minimum of taxes. And sometimes items that are included as expenses have value to him or her just as the earnings have value—a company car, for example.

Watch out for the person who shows you the records of a business that pays no taxes, or small taxes, and who tells you that the business is really earning a lot of money. First of all, if he or she is cheating the Internal Revenue Service, he or she may cheat you, too. Second, many of the expenses that are listed as expenses really must be expenses, even if you are told that they are not necessary. Third, if the owner has rigged the books so that they will pass the scrutiny of government investigators, how can you ever tell just how much the business is earning?

Watch out also for illegal businesses that are for sale. Unfortunately, there are many mail-order businesses that the government will close up sooner or later because they violate the law. Not only do you prefer to avoid being mixed up in such a business, but you should not take the chance of wasting your money in buying a business that won't be a business for very long.

The tax returns of a business are the best set of books for you to examine, because if they are wrong, the owner is liable to the United States government. Never believe any other records until you have seen the tax returns.

In any case, this is an absolute rule: Always get your own accountant to examine the records of a firm that you are considering buying.

Beyond the Tax Returns

Often the tax returns do not supply all the information you need, however. There are several possible reasons for needing to study other records, including the following:

An owner may wish to sell only part of a business. The tax returns may apply only to the entire business. You must then figure out how much of the entire firm's earnings come from the part of the business the owner wishes to sell.

You may have reason to believe that the business is being badly run, and that it could throw off much greater net profit under your management. (But don't be taken in by owners who tell you what a great future the business has, even though it is doing poorly at the moment. They invent a million reasons for this, including absentee ownership, disinterest in the business, arguments between partners, etc. The truth of the matter is that if the owner is having a hard time getting money out of the business, it is an excellent indication that it will not be easy for you to make a big profit, either.)

The business may be changing rapidly, or it may have been in existence too short a time for the tax returns to provide a clear indication.

You may not be satisfied that the tax records provide a satisfactory picture of the firm's operations and earnings.

Now I shall give you the outline of a method to estimate the future earnings of a business. These are the steps in the method:

1. Estimate the average volume of sales made to the average customer before she ceases purchasing, including all the sales made to her in future years. Then estimate the *gross* profit on that average volume of sales per customer by subtracting the cost of the goods and direct expenses of labor, etc., to you. This is the method described in Chapter 9 for finding the average value of putting a customer onto your books.

2. Determine the cost of creating the average new customer. You calculate this value by dividing the total cost of the advertising (or that part that creates new customers) in the past year by the number of new customers created in the past year. Subtract this value from the value of putting a customer onto your books, as found in item 1 above.

3. Multiply by the number of new customers added in the past year. This value will be the expected profit per year, when the firm's business levels off, before subtracting for overhead.

4. Subtract whatever you think appropriate for rent, telephone, insurance, and other overhead expenses. What is left is your expected salary plus profit.

5. If you believe that you can increase the size of the business by increasing the advertising, you might be right to include that potential in your figuring. But be sure not to forget that it will get more expensive to create new customers as you expand your advertising.

Despite the fact that you must pay for intangible organization and knowledge when you buy a business, it is often cheaper to purchase than to start fresh. It is surprisingly expensive to begin a business when you consider the amount of time that it takes you to get into action, and there are many hidden expenses that you can't figure in advance. Very often the owner sells you the intangibles for less than they cost him. And when you buy a going business, you avoid the very costly risk that the business you start from scratch may not succeed!

The advice of a person experienced in the mail-order business can be invaluable to you when you are considering buying a business. It is the same as when you ask a skilled mechanic to look over a car that you think you might buy, in order to check for hidden defects and to tell you if the price is fair.

Call a successful mail-order operator in your area and offer to pay a consultation fee for consultation time. If you pick a knowledgeable and successful person, he or she will be worth far more than anything that you pay. The operator can give you advice and knowledge that no accountant, lawyer, or general businessperson can give you. Or call a mail-order consultant.

Of course you should *also* consult an accountant and a lawyer before you buy a business! That should go without saying.

I recommend that you read Chapter 7, "Appraising a Going Concern," in *How to Organize and Operate a Small Business,* by Pearce

C. Kelley and Kenneth Lawyer.[1] The authors give you many helpful warnings and pointers. And while you're at it, look through the rest of the book, too. It contains lots of useful information for the person who intends to go into business for himself or herself.

Check on the *real* reason the present owner wants to sell. Don't accept at face value the statement that he or she has had a heart attack or is about to retire because he or she has made a fortune. The *real* reason may be that the seller has lost a lease, competition has just entered the field, or the seller is engaged in something shady. *Find out the truth.*

And, before purchasing, always obtain a sworn statement from the owner that he or she will not enter a competitive line of business for 2 or 3 years. Remind your lawyer of this before you sign any final papers.

How to Sell a Business

To find a customer for your business, just reverse the steps you should take to find a business that is for sale.

The biggest problem you face in selling a business, apart from convincing your prospective customers to buy, is the danger of giving out enough information about your business so that the prospective customer could use the information to start his or her own business. Your customer list is the most secret, of course. But your advertising methods are also an important secret of your business.

William J. Papp tells the story of an enterprising pharmacist who developed a neat little mail-order business peddling an educational device, and then decided to sell out.[2] In an effort to convince purchasers of the soundness of the business, the pharmacist gave them so much information that very soon several competitors began to advertise exactly the same offer in the best-pulling magazines.

Papp suggests these ways to avoid the worst dangers:

1. Do business through a third person—lawyer, broker, or banker. This person can conceal the name of your firm and can endorse its soundness.

2. Indicate whether you are willing to continue as a consultant to the owner.

3. Describe the potential of your firm.

4. After you supply preliminary information, ask that the potential buyer deposit a substantial sum of money in escrow with a bank

of his or her choice. If he or she enters competition with you, this money is forfeited. If he or she does not buy, and refrains from competing, the deposit is returned after a period of time. Or if your figures and claims prove incorrect, the deposit is given back.

This is the end of what I have to say. I wish you success and happiness in your mail-order adventures, and I hope that I have been of some help to you. Good luck!

How to Lose Money with Mail-Order Franchises and "Deals"

I'm sure you have seen those fascinating ads for "mail-order franchises," for "catalog mailing," and for "cooperative" deals of all kinds. Those ads make powerful promises indeed. And the literature the advertisers send you has headlines like "We Will Set You Up and Back You in a Profitable Mail-Order Business of Your Own" or "Get Rich by Mail." What about them?

Catalog-Mailing Deals

Arrangements to mail other firms' *catalogs* probably have no chance at all to make money for you unless you already have a customer list and are in the mail-order business. This goes for the best as well as the worst of them. *No* firm has yet presented any *facts* to show that the average individual comes anywhere near breaking even or that *any* of its "dealers" makes a significant profit—unless the dealer started out with a list of customers from prior mail-order or retail operations.

The basic reason for the failure of catalog-mailing plans is this: If there really was money to be made in mailing the catalogs to "cold" lists, the supplier would do the mailing. You might have some advantage in mailing to your friends (like an insurance agent who contacts all relatives first). But the number of such friends and acquaintances that you can mail to is very limited. After that, you are just pouring money into the supplier's pocket.

Or, at the very best, it may be possible to make money in the long run by mailing to *some* rented lists. But you can be sure that the supplier will mail to the best lists under his or her own name, and only the "dogs" will be left for you.

Don't get the idea that the "catalog-mailing" scheme is new. It isn't. It has been kicking around almost since the mail-order business began. This is what the author of a 1906 *Encyclopedia of the Mail-Order Business* wrote some 80 years ago:[1]

THE EVILS OF THE STOCK CATALOG

Lest the term "Stock Catalog" be misunderstood, let us explain that this phrase is used when speaking of a catalog that is issued in immense quantities by certain supply houses who carry or pretend to carry all the goods in stock that is listed in this catalog. These catalogs are offered to beginners with their own name and address printed on them, so that the recipient of the catalog would be led to believe that the beginner was really the publisher of this catalog. The argument of the promoter is that the beginner could not publish a catalog of this description unless he spend a great deal more money for this individual printing. Again they argue that the beginner need not carry goods in stock, but can forward the orders to the supply house, who in turn, would fill the order and ship the goods direct to the customer, in the beginner's own firm name. This all sounds very nice, but in all these years during which time countless thousands have been "started" in this way, the writer cannot find more than three or four who actually built up a little business by the use of this catalog, and these injected some originality of their own, to come out ahead of the game. Another inducement some of these promoters offer, is the furnishing of "a list of names" to whom to mail the catalog, or to place some "advertising" for them in "pulling" mediums. But all these schemes are failures. The writer has personally interviewed mail-order customers, he has travelled through the rural districts, stopped over in farm houses, and saw with his own eyes, no less than several identical "stock catalogs" in one house. The difference was the imprint on the different catalogs. As these promoters advertise everywhere for victims, the people in the rural district know all about the stock catalog, and do no more than bestow pitying glances on this literature—and either throw it into the fire, or give it to the baby to play with, as was the case in the farm house where I was stopping.

In debating with yourself the arguments for and against the use of the common and moss-backed stock catalog, just for a minute consider what sort of a reception it is likely to meet with at the hands of the people to whom it is mailed; particularly when as is often the case, the catalogs are sent to the list of names and addresses of "buyers" furnished by the same firm who sells you the catalogs. The result is that at some remote farmhouse day after day there will be copies of the same cheaply gotten up catalog coming by mail, the imprints of the senders being something like this: One day, The Royal Novelty Co., Squedunk Corners, Me., next day, Imperial Crescent Supply Co., Box 9, Frogs' Hole, Wis., the day following, The Associated Mail Order Manufacturers and Merchants, of Lock Box 12, Hoboes Landing, Perry Township, Fayette County, Mo., and so on and so forth in ridiculous repetition.

To sum up, your aim should be to get out of the beaten track and strike out a path to success for yourself. And of all beaten tracks the stock catalog is the one that stinks loudest in the nostrils of honest men and real Mail Order dealers. It is a track strewn with the bones and rotten carcasses of business hopes and mail order ideals that have been killed and strangled by the nefarious stock catalog and it is heavy with the smoke of money that has been burned in the vain hope of achieving success under the direction of the fakirs who operate under the guise of promoters who will point out the way to success to you. Keep away from that veritable Death Valley and don't let your hopes and your money be destroyed together in the burnt offerings of the misguided fools who in spite of countless warnings continue to keep the misplaced confidence game alive.

The stock catalog *can* be useful and profitable to you if you already have a list of people who buy other goods from you by mail. Gimbel's is said to purchase and mail millions of a stock catalog each year, evidently at a solid profit. The reason why stock catalogs can work if you have an existing list is this: Between 2 and 10 times as many people will buy from you if they have done business with you before as will buy if they have never heard of you. This is the difference between success and abysmal failure. So, if you are already in the mail-order business and if you have a mailing list of satisfied customers, you might well make money by sending them a stock catalog imprinted with your name.

In previous editions I gave the names of some organizations that supply catalogs and who either drop-ship or supply the names of individual drop-ship suppliers, and do not extort "franchise" fees. But since then I have had the impression that even these organizations actually solicit unwary beginners, and hence I'll not mention them here. Their direct-mail piece says "Yes, X has put *thousands* of individuals like yourself in the profitable and fascinating mail-order business overnight and with fantastically small capital outlay and risk." But they continue, "TESTIMONIALS ARE PLENTIFUL—but we do not publish them or ask permission to do so. This would be a violation of business privacy." That's garbage. If someone gives permission to use a testimonial, there is no invasion of privacy, and the deal therefore stinks. There are listings under "Mail Order Drop-Ship Catalog and Merchandise" in the classified section of *Direct Marketing*. Chances are pretty good that they are on the up-and-up.

There are many other reputable firms that supply catalogs that you can use to sell *in person* but that will not work at all by mail.

It is very, *very* unlikely that you can mail imprinted catalogs to any "cold" list of people who have never done business with you, and make money at it. Many "suckers" have reported substantial losses, and *Direct Marketing*—a leading trade magazine—has run article after article on the dangers of this practice.

Mail-Order "Setup" Plans

A sure-profit business is a very valuable commodity. A business that will earn $10,000 a year for your full-time effort is probably worth $15,000. So why should anyone sell you the "setup" for $5 or even $500?

Furthermore, it is certain that no one can crank out "setups" on a mass-production basis, as must be the case if those who advertise them for a small sum are to make money.

Geniuses like to be rich and famous, too. I can guarantee you that there is no genius with an almost magical inside knowledge of mail order, in Salt Lake City, Fandango, Maine, or anywhere else, who will "put you into" a profitable mail-order business for a small price. If there ever was such a genius, he or she is now selling his or her schemes to large companies for perhaps $25,000 per proposition.

"Cooperative Setup" Deals

Another scheme: You put up the capital for an already-developed ad, then purchase the products from the firm that developed the ad.

In other words, you "rent" the ad from the firm, and run it in a magazine at your expense. Any profit over and above your "rent" would belong to you.

In theory this plan sounds OK. If the ad pulls enough returns, you *could* make money. But the nature of the one-shot mail-order business forces your chances to be small because your "rent" is too high.

One firm that offered this deal took the first part of its rent in its advertising-agency commission. They argued that you would pay this commission even on your own advertising, but that is not necessarily true. When the firm runs the ad for its own account, it pays no commission, and that commission is an important part of its revenue.

The second part of the rent is the amount, much greater than cost, which you pay them for the merchandise.

But there is an even greater danger. It stands to reason that the firm will run the ad for its own account whenever it is relatively sure the ad will pull enough to be profitable. (And if it would be profitable for you, it will be even more profitable for them!) But they can rent you the ad to run in magazines that will *not* be profitable for them, and that way they take their profit out of your hide.

I come down hard on this plan not only because it is theoretically so bad, but also because the firm in question has shown no proof that there are people who have profited by the deal. If firms had such proof, they would certainly show it. (And I would not believe any proof except *consistent and repeated* successes. They could manufacture "proof" by letting a couple of their customers make money on choice media.)

Another firm, operating now, sells you packages of direct-mail materials at prices ranging from $63 to $340. This outfit has the unbelievable effrontery to demand that "your order must accompany signed honesty pledge." And the sales piece says

> "A few know it all characters" have written asking this same old worn out question, "If my method is such a fantastic money maker then why would I want to share it"? Now for those who consider this to be a reasonable question here is a reasonable answer, I need letter handler collection agents in the same manner that General Motors need independently franchised dealers to sell their cars—Surely you know that General Motors, a billion dollar corporation, does not sell direct-to-the-public, also for the same reason that such giant manufacturers as Pepsi Cola, Coca Cola, MacDonalds, Howard Johnson Restaurants, General Electric and virtually every other major firm in this country prefer to use local independent wholesalers, dealers and retailers to sell their merchandise.
>
> Then why don't these giant companies sell their own products? Simply because they as well as practically every prosperous business person knows that the easiest and quickest way to increase sales is by offering a hefty chunk of the profits to their independent agents.
>
> It's a known fact that for years this proven selling technique has worked profitably for General Motors and other billion dollar biggies and you can bet your boopy that I intend to let it work for me too. Obviously this is why I'm so interested in sharing my big money success only with agents who don't mind giving up some time and extra effort mailing out my tested advertisements.

If you believe that, you'll believe anything.

Then there are a couple of promoters who offer ready-made mail-order "plans." They promise to furnish you with a product (almost always a booklet) and advertising copy for display and/or direct-mail advertising.

If the "plan" really could make money for you, it could make much more for the promoter. One could make more with it than any inexperienced person, and also save the fees. Furthermore, the promoter usually sells you the product itself at a steep price, and this makes it even less likely that you can make any money with the scheme. This should persuade you that you will only lose more hard-earned money in that kind of deal.

Beware of anyone who offers you the opportunity to sell her mail-order-tested product through the mail. If *you* can sell it profitably, why can't she sell it even more profitably, because she keeps the markup on the sale to you? The mailing lists available to you as a beginner are available to her, and so on. The most recent offer of this sort I've seen is an outfit that sells debt-collection forms by mail, and offers to put you in the business of selling those forms by mail. Once again, I'll believe that you have a chance to make money with this deal only when I see proof that a fair sample of people have done so—and this offer doesn't even cite *one case* of a "distributor" making money.

Chain Schemes

One of the oldest mail-order rackets is the deal by which someone sells you the materials to make money in mail order by selling the same deal to someone else. Not only is this out-and-out illegal, but it doesn't even make money for anyone except the originator, who sells you the phony material at a very high markup.

Mail-order racketeers are ingenious, however. I just received a chain-letter offer which may (or may not) escape the law by offering a "report" in addition to the chain-letter scheme, which they claim makes the deal legal. That "deal" was shown in Figure 6-2, page 86 for your edification. Fascinating? Yes. And disgusting.

A Summing Up

It all adds up to this: There is no pie-in-the-sky scheme that will get you started profitably in mail order. You will just have to study and learn the business, follow the methods and instructions I give you in this book—which should give you a better chance in mail order than anyone ever had before—and take your chances like the rest of us. If you win, you will have a glorious and valuable prize. If you lose, most of what you lose will be your time, because mail-order money investments are characteristically small. And you'll have a great experience in any case. Good luck again!

Federal Trade Commission Summary of Types of Unfair Methods and Practices and the Mail-Order Rule

This appendix first gives you the FTC's description of mail-order customers' rights and protections from the point of view of the mail-order buyer. Then it gives the FTC's summary of the Mail-Order Rule from the point of view of the mail-order operator.

Mail-Order Customers' Rights and Protections

SHOPPING BY MAIL

Ordering merchandise by mail can be convenient; you may save time, effort, and money. Sometimes it's a way to buy an article you just can't find in a local store. But when you order merchandise by mail and it arrives late—or not at all—it can be a real headache.

It's clear that mail order purchases trouble many consumers. According to FTC records, the most frequent mail order problem is the failure of a merchant to get products to the buyer on time. In fact, at least 27% of all complaints logged in by the FTC during the period between October 1, 1977, and June 30, 1978, involved a purchase through the mail.

The Mail-Order Merchandise Rule. The Federal Trade Commission has a rule that gives you some rights when you order by mail. The mail order rule, adopted by the Commission in October, 1975, provides that . . .

. . . you must receive the merchandise when the seller says you will;

. . . if you are not promised delivery within a certain time period, the seller must ship the merchandise to you no later than 30 days after your order comes in; and

. . . if you don't receive it shortly after that 30-day period, you can cancel your order and get your money back.

How the Rule Works. The seller must notify you if the promised delivery date (or the 30-day limit) cannot be met. The seller must also tell you what the new shipping date will be and give you the option to either cancel the order and receive a full refund or agree to the new shipping date. The seller must also give you a free way to send back your answer, such as a stamped envelope or a postage-paid postcard. *If you don't answer, it means you agree to the shipping delay.*

The seller must tell you if the shipping delay is going to be more than 30 days. You then can agree to the delay or, if you do *not* agree, the seller must return your money by the end of the first 30 days of the delay.

If you cancel a prepaid order, the seller must mail you the refund within seven business days. Where there is a credit sale, the seller must adjust your account within one billing cycle.

It would be impossible, however, for one rule to apply uniformly to such a varied field as mail order merchandising. For example, the rule does *not* apply to mail order photo finishing, magazine subscriptions, and other serial deliveries (except for the initial shipment); to mail order seeds and growing plants; to COD orders; or to credit orders where the buyer's account is not charged prior to shipment of the merchandise.

Protect Yourself. Whenever you order anything through the mail, take these precautions:

1. Read the product description. Don't rely on pictures only. Make sure the product offered is what you really want.

2. If possible, investigate the advertiser's claims. Find out if the product will really do what the advertiser claims it will.

3. Note the delivery time stated. Allow plenty of delivery time before holidays or other special days so you won't be disappointed by a late delivery.

4. Find out the merchant's return policy. If it isn't stated anywhere, ask before you order.

5. Keep a copy of your order blank.

6. Make a note of the merchant's name and address and the date you sent in your order.

7. Hold on to your cancelled checks and charge account records. If you have a problem later, these papers would be necessary to prove your side of the case.

Unordered Merchandise. Have you ever received something in the mail you did *not* order? If so, you may *consider it a gift and keep it without paying for it.*

Only two kinds of merchandise can be sent legally through the mails without a consumer's prior consent: (1) free samples, clearly marked as such, and (2) merchandise mailed by a charitable organization for contributions. Even though unordered merchandise from charitable organizations can legally be sent to your house, the same rule applies: you don't have to pay for it.

It's illegal for the sender to pressure you to return unordered merchandise or to send you a bill for it. Just to be sure, you might write the sender and ask for proof that you placed the order. You might have forgotten you did. Or a friend may have ordered the merchandise for you as a gift and you were mistakenly billed for it as well. But if it was really unordered, you may keep it at no cost.

What to Do If You Have a Problem. If you have a complaint against a mail order company (non-delivery, misleading advertisements, damages because of poor wrapping), you may have trouble resolving it: the company may be in another state or not have a listed telephone number.

In any case, your first step is to write directly to the company (the address will be on that order blank copy you saved). Tell them about the problem. If it's not resolved, you can take further action:

- Call your local or state consumer protection office or Better Business Bureau. They may be able to help you.
- Contact the state or local consumer protection agency closest to the company. Ask for their assistance, also.
- Call your local postmaster. Ask for the name and address of the appropriate postal inspector-in-charge. That person may also be able to resolve your dispute.
- Contact the book, magazine, or newspaper publisher that carried the advertisement. Publishers often try to resolve problems between their readers and their advertisers.

Help Solve the Problem. Send copies of your correspondence to the FTC, Washington, D.C., 20580. Although the FTC generally can't resolve individual disputes, the information you provide may help show a pattern of practices requiring action by the Commission.

These are the methods and practices the FTC calls "unfair":

The use of false or misleading advertising concerning, and the misbranding of, commodities, respecting the materials or ingredients of which they are composed, their quality, purity, origin, source, attributes, or properties, or nature of manufacture, and selling them under such name and circumstances as to deceive the public. An important part of these include misrepresentation of the therapeutic and corrective properties of medicinal preparations and devices, and cosmetics, and the false representation expressly or by failure to disclose their potential harmfulness, that such preparations may be safely used.

Describing various symptoms and falsely representing that they indicate the presence of diseases and abnormal conditions which the product advertised will cure or alleviate.

Representing products to have been made in the United States when the mechanism or movements, in whole or in important part, are of foreign origin.

Making false and disparaging statements respecting competitors' products and business, in some cases under the guise of ostensibly disinterested and specially informed sources or through purported scientific, but in fact misleading, demonstrations or tests.

Passing off goods for products of competitors through appropriation or simulation of such competitors' trade names, labels, dress of goods, or counter-display catalogs.

Making use of false and misleading representations, schemes, and practices to obtain representatives and make contracts such as pretended puzzle-prize contests purportedly offering opportunities to win handsome prizes, but which are in fact mere "come-on" schemes and devices in which the "seller's true identity and interest are intially concealed . . .

Using merchandising schemes based on lot or chance, or on a pretended contest of skill.

Aiding, assisting, or abetting unfair practice, misrepresentation, and deception, and furnishing means or instrumentalities therefor; and combining and conspiring to offer or sell products by chance or by deceptive methods, through such practices as supplying dealers with lottery devices, or selling to dealers and assisting them in conducting content schemes as a part of which pretended credit slips or certificates are issued to contestants, when in fact the price of the goods has been marked up to absorb the face value of the credit slip; and the supplying of emblems or devices to conceal marks of country of origin of goods, or otherwise to misbrand goods as to country or origin. . . .

Sales plans in which the seller's usual price is falsely represented as a special reduced price for a limited time or to a limited class, or false claim of special terms, equipment, or other privileges, or advantages.

False or misleading use of the word "Free" in advertising.

Use of misleading trade names calculated to create the impression that a dealer is a producer or importer selling directly to the consumer, with resultant savings.

Offering of false "bargains" by pretended cutting of a fictitious "regular" price.

Use of false representations that an article offered has been rejected as nonstandard and is offered at an exceptionally favorable price, or that the number thereof that may be purchased is limited.

Falsely representing that goods are not being offered as sales in ordinary course, but are specially priced and offered as a part of a special advertising campaign to obtain customers, or for some purpose other than the customary profit.

Misrepresenting seller's alleged advantages of location or size, or the branches, domestic or foreign, or the dealer outlets he has. . . .

Alleged connection of a concern, organization, association, or institute with, or endorsement of it or its product or service by, the Government or nationally known organization, or representation that the use of such product or services is required by the Government, or that failure to comply with such requirement is subject to penalty.

False claim by a vendor of being an importer, or a technician, or a diagnostician, or a manufacturer, grower, or nurseryman, or a distiller, or of being a wholesaler, selling to the consumer at wholesale prices; or by a manufacturer of being also the manufacturer of the raw material entering into the product, or by an assembler of being a manufacturer.

Falsely claiming to be a manufacturer's representative and outlet for surplus stock sold at a sacrifice.

Falsely representing that the seller owns a laboratory in which the product offered is analyzed and tested.

Representing that an ordinary private commercial seller and business is an association, or national association, or connected therewith, or sponsored thereby, or is otherwise connected with noncommercial or professional organizations or associations or constitutes an institute, or, in effect, that it is altruistic in purpose, giving work to the unemployed.

Falsely claiming that a business is bonded, or misrepresenting its age or history, or the demand established for its products, or the selection afforded, or the quality or comparative value of its goods, or the personnel or staff of personages presently or theretofore associated with such business or the products thereof.

Claiming falsely or misleadingly by patent, trade-mark, or other special and exclusive rights.

Granting seals of approval by a magazine to products advertised therein and misrepresenting thereby that such products have been adequately tested, and misrepresenting by other means the quality, performance, and characteristics of such products. . . .

Misrepresenting that seller fills order promptly, ships kind of merchandise described, and assigns exclusive territorial rights within definite trade areas to purchasers or prospective purchasers.

Obtaining orders on the basis of samples displayed for customer's selection and failing or refusing to respect such selection thereafter in the filling of orders, or promising results impossible of fulfillment, or falsely making promises or holding out quarantis, or the right of return, or results, or refunds, replacements, or reimbursements, or special or additional advantages to the prospective purchasers such as extra credit or furnishing of supplies or advisory assistance; or falsely assuring the purchaser or prospective purchaser that certain special or exclusively personal favors or advantages are being granted him.

Concealing from prospective purchaser unusual features involved in purchaser's commitment, the result of which will be to require of purchaser further expenditure in order to obtain benefit of commitment and expenditure already made, such as failure to reveal peculiar or nonstandard shape of portrait or photographic enlargement, so as to make securing of frame therefor from sources other than seller difficult and impracticable, if not impossible.

Advertising a price for a product as illustrated or described and not including in such price all charges for equipment or accessories illustrated or described or necessary for use of the product or customarily included as standard equipment, and failing to include all charges not specified as extra.

Giving products misleading names so as to give them a value to the purchasing public which they would not otherwise possess, such as names implying falsely that:

The products were made for the Government or in accordance with its specifications and of corresponding quality, or that the advertiser is connected with the Government in some way, or in some way the products have been passed upon, inspected, underwritten, or endorsed by it; or

They are composed in whole or in part of ingredient or materials which in fact are present only to an extent or not at all, or that they have qualities or properties which they do not have; or

They were made in or came from some locality famous for the quality of such products, or are of national reputation; or

They were made by some well and favorably known process; or

They have been inspected, passed, or approved after meeting the tests of some official organization charged with the duty of making such tests expertly and disinterestedly, or giving such approval; or

They were made under conditions or circumstances considered of importance by a substantial part of the general purchasing public; or

. . .

They are of greater value, durability, and desirability than is the fact, as labeling rabbit fur as "Beaver"; or . . .

They are designed, sponsored, produced, or approved by the medical profession, health and welfare associations, hospitals, celebrities, educational institutions and authorities, such as the use of the letters "M.D." and the words "Red Cross" and its insignia and the words "Boy Scout". . . .

Misrepresenting, through salesmen or otherwise, products' composition, nature, qualities, results accomplished, safety, value, and earnings or profits to be had therefrom.

Falsely claiming unique status or advantages, or special merit therefor, on the basis of misleading and ill-founded demonstrations or scientific tests, or of pretended widespread tests, or of pretended widespread and critical professional acceptance and use.

Misrepresenting the history or circumstances involved in the making and offer of the products or the source of origin thereof (foreign or domestic), or of the ingredients entering therein, or parts thereof, or the opportunities brought to the buyer through purchase of the offering, or otherwise misrepresenting scientific or other facts bearing on the value thereof to the purchaser.

Falsely representing products as legitimate, or prepared in accordance with Government or official standards of specifications.

Falsely claiming Government or official or other acceptance, use, and endorsement of product, and misrepresenting success and standing thereof through use of false and misleading endorsements or false and misleading claims with respect thereto, or otherwise.

Making use of a misleading trade name and representing by other means that the nature of a business is different than is the fact. . . .

Misrepresenting fabrics or garments as to fiber content; and, in the case of wool products, failing to attach tags thereto indicating the wool, re-used wool, reprocessed wool, or other fibers contained therein, and the identity of the manufacturer or qualified reseller, as required by the Wool Products Labeling Act, or removing or mutilating tags required to be affixed to the products when they are offered for sale to the public.

One of the most difficult practices to judge is that of "dry testing," advertising merchandise (especially books) that have not yet been produced, and may never be produced. This is the FTC's latest—and surprisingly flexible—ruling on the subject:

The practice of soliciting mail orders for merchandise prior to making a decision as to whether or not to fill the orders may in certain circumstances be a lawful business practice. For example, in the book publishing business there is a practice called "dry testing" in which marketer disseminates promotional material to the general public soliciting subscriptions to a continuity book series before the books have been published. Whether or not the book series is actually published depends on the size of the response to the solicitation. The Commission has stated that it does not object to the use of dry testing a continuity book series to be sold by mail order where the solicitation does not have the capacity or tendency to mislead the public into believing that the books have been or will be published, the terms and conditions of the transaction and other material facts are clearly and conspicuously disclosed and persons who subscribe are given timely notice of the status of their orders.

The Mail-Order Rule

INTRODUCTION

What is the Mail Order Rule. The Mail Order Rule was issued by the Federal Trade Commission (FTC) to correct growing problems with late or undelivered mail order merchandise. Under this Rule, you have a duty to ship merchandise on time. You also must follow procedures that the Rule requires if you cannot ship ordered merchandise on time.

When there is a shipping delay, the Rule requires that you notify your customers of the delay and provide them with an option either to agree to the delay or to cancel the order and receive a prompt refund. For each additional delay, your customers must be notified that they must send you a signed consent to a further delay or a refund will be given. **Why Was the Rule Issued.** The Rule was issued after federal, state, and local consumer protection authorities received thousands of consumer complaints about mail order problems. The major complaints were:

failure to deliver merchandise, late delivery of merchandise, failure to make prompt refunds, and failure to answer customer inquiries about delayed or lost orders. For example:

- One consumer wrote about Christmas decorations she ordered in early October that were finally shipped the day before Christmas. This consumer wrote twice to the company about her order, the second time requesting a refund. Both inquiries were ignored.

- Another consumer complained about a company that failed to send a stereo component he ordered with payment in July. By late October, the only communication he received from the company was his canceled check.

The FTC received 3,200 similar consumer complaints prior to beginning its rulemaking process. In addition, the President's Office of Consumer Affairs (OCA) received over 1,000 complaints concerning mail order practices, 60% of which concerned non-delivery. OCA complaint statistics for mail order were second only to complaints about autos and auto services.

The rulemaking record contains more than 10,000 pages of complaints regarding mail order sales. State and local agencies urged the Commission to take action to correct these problems. Industry members provided valuable input as to the feasibility and practicality of a mail order rule.

On October 22, 1975, the FTC promulgated the Mail Order Rule, and it went into effect on February 2, 1976.

Why You Should Comply with the Rule.   When you comply with the Rule, you are being responsive to your customers. This is beneficial to you and to your customers because it promotes a positive industry image. Compliance creates consumer trust in buying by mail and fosters repeat mail order business. Of course if you ship on time, the requirements of the Rule pertaining to "option notices" do not apply.

Although most members of the mail order industry adhere to the Rule's requirements, there are some who do not. The FTC's Bureau of Consumer Protection monitors consumer complaints to ensure that businesses comply with the Rule. The FTC also provides compliance information, such as this manual, and assistance to all industry members.

HOW TO COMPLY WITH THE RULE

What to Know When You Make an Offer.   When you offer to sell merchandise by mail, the Rule requires you to have a "reasonable basis" for expecting to ship within the time stated in your solicitation.

For example, if you know before advertising your products that your suppliers are on strike and are likely to remain on strike for several months, you do not have a "reasonable basis" for expecting to ship within a month.

The shipping date, when provided in your offer, must be clearly and conspicuously stated:

ADVERTISEMENT
Cardigan Sweaters
S,M,L—Beige or Blue
$29.95 plus tax
Allow 5 weeks for shipment.

If you do not provide a shipping date, you must ship the merchandise within 30 days of receiving a "properly completed" order. An order is properly completed when you receive payment accompanied by all information you need to fill the order. Payment may be made by cash, money order, check, or credit card, according to your company policy. If a credit card is used for a purchase, the order is properly completed when you charge your customer's account.

When you cannot ship on time, you must provide your customer with an "option" notice. The notice must provide an option to cancel the order and receive a prompt refund, or to agree to a delay in shipping. And, as with the original date, you must have a reasonable basis for setting that shipping date.

You must also have a reasonable basis for telling your customers that you do not know when you can ship merchandise. In that case, you must provide the specific reasons for the shipping problem. For example, you could state that a fire destroyed the warehouse holding the goods and you are unable to provide a revised shipping date because you do not know how long it will take to replace the merchandise.

When You Should Send a First Notice. If a shipment is delayed, the Rule requires that you give your customers an option:

- to consent to a delayed, or
- to cancel the order and receive a prompt refund.

People in the trade often refer to the notice as a "delay" notice. More accurately, it should be called an "option" notice. You violate the Rule if you only provide a notice of delay without also providing an option to cancel the order.

Remember, you must send the notice after you first become aware that there will be a shipping delay. The notice must be sent:

- before the promised shipping date; or
- within 30 days after you receive the order (if no date was provided in your solicitation).

What a First Notice Must Say. If you provide a revised shipping date of 30 days or less, you must have a reasonable basis for making the change. The notice must inform your customers that non-response is considered consent to be a delay of 30 days or less.

If you are unable to provide a revised shipping date, your notice must state that you cannot determine when the merchandise will be shipped. It must also state that the order will be automatically canceled unless:

- you ship the merchandise within 30 days of the original shipping date and you have not received your customer's cancellation before shipment; or

- you receive within 30 days of the original date your customer's consent to the delay.

Your notice must provide this information if the definite revised shipping date is more than 30 days after the original date.

When you are unable to provide a revised shipping date, you must inform your customers of their continuing right to cancel the order by notifying you prior to actual shipment.

What Later Notices Must Say. If you are unable to ship the merchandise on or before your revised shipping date, you must notify your customers again. This is called a "renewed option" notice. This notice must inform your customers of their right to consent to a further delay, or to cancel the order and receive a prompt refund.

The renewed option notice must inform customers that if they do not agree in writing to this delay, their order will be canceled. Unless you receive your customer's express written consent to the second delay before the first delay period ends, you must cancel the order and provide a full refund.

Keep in mind that you do not have to offer a "renewed option" to customers who consent to an indefinite delay in response to the first option notice. But any customer who agrees to an indefinite delay has the continuing right to cancel the order at any time before the merchandise is shipped.

How You Should Send Notices. You should send any option notice by first class mail, and your notice should provide a written means for your customers to respond. A prepaid business mail reply or prepaid postage card meets this requirement.

The notice is most advantageous for you if at some point you have to prove that you complied with the Rule. If the FTC takes action against a company, the firm must be able to show that any other form of notice it used was equal to or better than the written form described in the Rule. For example, an "800" telephone number for customers' use in canceling orders is an adequate substitute, if you can prove that the system met the Rule's requirements. This would include being able to show that the 800 number could readily and consistently be used to cancel an order because you provided adequate and competent staff to take cancellations. You should keep records of all cancellations.

When You _May_ Cancel an Order. In some cases you can have an option to cancel an order or to send out another notice. You may make this decision when you are unable to ship merchandise on time or within the delay period to which your customer agreed. But if you decide to cancel the order, you must inform your customer of this decision and provide a prompt refund.

Whether you cancel or send another notice, you must inform your customer about it within a reasonable time after you know you cannot ship the merchandise.

When You _Must_ Cancel an Order. You must cancel an order and provide a prompt refund:

- when your customer does not agree to a delay and exercises the option to cancel an order before it has been shipped;
- when you notify your customer of your inability to ship the merchandise and of your decision to cancel the order.
- when you are unable to ship merchandise before the revised shipping date and you have not received your customer's consent to a further delay.
- when the delay is indefinite and you have not shipped the merchandise or received your customer's consent to an indefinite delay;
- when the definite revised shipping date in the first option notice is more than 30 days after the original shipping date, and you have not shipped the merchandise, nor received your customer's consent to the delay within 30 days of the original shipping date; or
- when you cannot ship on time and do not notify your customers of their options.

All refunds must be sent to the buyer by first class mail. If the buyer paid by cash, check, or money order, you must refund payment within seven (7) days after the order is canceled. For credit card sales, you must make refunds within one billing cycle after the order is canceled. Under no circumstances are you to substitute credit vouchers or script for a refund.

Why You Should Keep Records. If for some reason your company has problems in shipping on time, your customers may begin to file complaints with you, and with local, state, or federal law enforcement agencies. Because the Federal Trade Commission has enforcement jurisdiction under the Mail Order Rule, many complaints are forwarded to the FTC from other agencies.

When the FTC takes action against a company and alleges that it violated the Rule, the company must have records or other documentary proof that will show the steps it took to comply. Systems and procedures for complying with the Rule are carefully reviewed. Lack of such proof creates a rebuttable presumption that the company failed to comply. This means that the seller must be able to show that it used reasonable systems and procedures to comply with the Rule. Consequently, it is in your best interest to establish an accurate, up-to-date record-keeping system.

What the Rule Does Not Cover. The following mail order sales are exempt from the Rule:

- magazine subscriptions (and similar serial deliveries), except for the first shipment;
- sales of seeds and growing plants;
- orders made on a collect-on-delivery basis (C.O.D.);
- transactions covered by the FTC's Negative Option Rule (such as book and record clubs);

- mail order photo-finishing; or
- orders made by telephone and charged to a credit card account.

Where to Go for Help. For more information, contact:

- the Federal Trade
  Commission, Enforcement Division, B.C.P.,
  Washington, D.C. 20580, (202) 376-3475;
- the Direct Marketing Association, 1730 K Street, N.W., Washington, D.C. 20006.
- your local United States Postal Service; and
- your local consumer protection office.

State and local governments also may have requirements with which you must comply. You should consult each agency for information about laws that affect your operations.

Copyrights

Mail-order firms often need to know the law of copyright, in order to protect printed material that you write or have written for you, either sales literature or information that you sell. You may also need to know the law of copyright so that you can determine whether a piece of published material is in the public domain so that you can legitimately use it or sell it.

You should know that *any* material published by the federal government may be reproduced and sold by anyone. One firm reproduces government-written tax guides intact, and sells them commercially. Another firm apparently did well by reprinting the official English government report of the famous Christine Keeler scandal. More commonly, you may wish to include government-written material as part of a book or pamphlet. In the previous appendix, I did just that.

The most important thing you must know is exactly how to protect yourself from having work pirated from you. Prior to the new copyright law of January 1, 1978, you ran the risk of losing your rights unless you carried out the correct procedure. Now you have more protection, and hence we need not spell out the details here. Here are a few lawyer's sentences on the matter:[1]

> *Copyright Notices.* When a work is published by authority of the copyright owner, it should bear a notice of copyright. A typical notice would by the symbol © 1986 Author's Name. . . .
>
> Notice requirements are important. Errors or omissions can result in loss of copyright. However, provisions of the new law sometimes allow such a fatal consequence to be avoided.
>
> *Deposit of Copies.* Generally, when a work is published in the United States with notice of copyright, two copies should be deposited with the Copyright Office for the benefit of the Library of Congress. . . .
>
> *Registrations.* The law provides for registration of copyright claims [408]. Although registration is rarely absolutely essential, failure to reg-

ister early sometimes will mean that the full array of copyright protection will not be available against an infringer. Registration calls for the completion of an application, the payment of a $10 fee, and, usually, the deposit of two copies of the work. For more information, write to the Copyright Office, Library of Congress, Washington, D.C. 20025.

Mailing-List Brokers, Consultants, and Mail-Order Advertising Agencies

List Brokers

Previous editions of this book gave the names of some of the more prominent list brokers, list consultants, and advertising agencies specializing in mail order. But two developments in recent years have convinced me to delete the list from this edition. First, the number of such service firms has grown considerably. Second, there are excellent listings in several publications. These are the publications that contain listings and/or classified advertising sections:

Direct Marketing. Its classified advertising section is the most complete in the field, and it is available in a great many libraries. Or you can order a subscription from 224 Seventh Street, Garden City, NY 11530, 516-746-6700.

Catalog Age. The Marketplace section contains many classified listings. Available free to mail-order firms from 125 Elm Street, P.O. Box 4006, New Canaan, CT 06840-4006.

The Direct Marketing Market Place. A book published by Hilary House, 1033 Channel Drive, Hewlett Harbor, NY 11557, which lists all sorts of service forms and suppliers, though most of its space is devoted to a listing of mail-order firms.

ZIP Target Marketing.   Each month *ZIP* carries a large classified section of brokers, advertising agencies, consultants, and other kinds of suppliers. And each year its December issue is a "Who's Who of Direct Marketing," an extensive list of all kinds of service firms. Subscription available from North American Publishing Company, 401 N. Broad St., Philadelphia, PA 19108.

Direct Mail List Rates and Data.   This publication of Standard Rate and Data Service is discussed in Chapter 22 on lists. Each edition contains a directory of firms that have paid an editorial service fee to be listed, like a classified section. In addition to a list of mailing-list brokers, compilers, and managers (in most cases with the lists which they manage), there is an extensive list of many other kinds of suppliers. Figure D-1 will give you an idea of the variety of such services that is available. It is an index of these suppliers.

About Advertising Agencies and Consultants

Advertising agencies and consultants range from large, well-established organizations to firms that may or may not still be in business when you call them. Some will service you honestly and well, whereas, for others, you will be a mark from whom they can snatch a quick buck. In this as in all other business dealings, you must proceed with great caution until you have enough experience with an organization to know that the connection is good for you.

As to rates, and especially rates for advertising copy, let's quote Paul Bringe:[1]

WHAT'S THE COST FOR COMPOSING A SINGLE PAGE DIRECT MAIL LETTER?

I get queries similar to this month after month. It cannot be answered intelligently. The questioner may not *need* a letter but doesn't know it. And if he does need it, should it be one page? The product or service may take one, five or ten pages for an adequate selling job.

In any case, letters are not sold by the page or pound. They are priced, as is all sales effort, by the knowledge and skill necessary to do the job. Some products are difficult to sell and some easy—for a particular writer. His charges will reflect that difference.

Direct Mail Suppliers and Services Directory

A source of supply section designed to inform buyers of direct mail services, equipment, materials and supplies. The tabulation presents firms who have paid an editorial service fee to express their interest in rendering service to the users of Direct Mail List Rates and Data. There is an implication, also, that these firms listed are experienced in servicing of direct mail users.

The Directory Section is organized by nature of business classifications:

Within each sub-classification, Directory listings are sequenced alphabetically by state and alphabetically by company within each state.

Figure D-1

Technical Notes on Direct-Mail Testing

1. This discussion of direct-mail testing uses only one-tail tests. I don't believe that the direct-mail tester needs or cares about protection against test results being too low—except in the case in which the test results fall below the break-even point. Even then it would be a one-tail test, but in the other direction.

2. Rule-of-thumb Tables 26-1 through 26-3 all depend on the proposition that when the proportion of returns is very low (under 5 percent, say) and the sample size is large, the standard deviation will (approximately) depend only on the ratio of proportion of returns to sample size. This means that the standard deviation can be considered a function of the *number* of returns only.

3. Tables 26-1 and 26-2 are derived from $\sigma = \sqrt{pq/n}$ (where n is large and q is 1) and the cumulative normal distribution.

4. Table 26-3 flows from the following proposition, which, I believe, is novel: The probability that sample means from two populations with different means will be in a reverse order from the population means (i.e., that the lower sample mean will come from the population with the higher real mean) is the percentage of *one* of the populations that lies beyond the mean of the two population means. Robert J. Wolfson supplied a proof that this proposition holds when the sample sizes and standard deviations for the two samples are equal.[1] In direct-mail testing, the sample sizes are made equal almost as a matter of course. And with the return proportion that direct-mail testers deal with, we may, without any grave loss of accuracy, treat the standard deviations as being equal.

5. The 2 × 2 paradigm discussion of testing more than one variable at a time holds only where the variables are effectively independent. But such independence is the rule in direct-mail testing: price, headlines, colors, first- versus third-class mail, etc., are not likely to interact very much.

6. Multiple-variable tests are hard to evaluate. There are statistical methods of determining whether or not the variability is due to chance—i.e., whether the variables are really different from each other. But that isn't much help to the direct-mail tester who is concerned with *magnitudes* of differences. I think about the multivariate situations in this way: the greater the number of variables tested, the less the information the tester puts into the situation, and therefore the less he or she can get out of it with a given sample size. In terms of subjectivistic statistics, his or her prior hypotheses are much less sharp, and therefore when they are combined with the test results, they are of less help in arriving at a final decision.

Types of Successful Mail-Order Businesses

The purpose of this appendix is to list and describe for you a good many *specific* lines of mail-order businesses which might be profitable for you to compete with.

It is very important for you to understand that this appendix is not about mail-order *items*. There are literally millions of items sold by mail order, but very few of these items are a business in themselves. What I am trying to describe in this appendix are *lines of items*, or *lines of business*, that will constitute a real business year in and year out.

Let me try to explain the difference. One of the most successful mail-order items a few years ago was the flat-tire inflator can. It still sells by mail and will continue to sell, but in the catalogs of a dozen different firms. It may still be an entire business to its manufacturer, but it is only one item in a line of items for mail-order firms that sell it. The *lines of items* may be automotive accessories, or novelties. We shall talk only about *lines of items*.

Of course, many items do constitute a business all by themselves, e.g., correspondence courses.

Here are some other examples of *products* that sell well by mail order, but are not likely to constitute a business unless you combine them with a line of similar goods. Note how many of them appear in novelty catalogs, sooner or later.

Blackhead remover

Cuckoo clock

Address labels

Closet organizer

Cleaning cloths

Huge balloon

Needle threader

Paper playhouse

Confederate money

One-way-glass formula

Shrunken heads

Magnets

Supermarket cost counter

Hand vacuum cleaner

Pocket calculator

Examples of individual items, the first pages of extensive listings in *The Mail-Order Crafts Catalogue* and *The Directory of Mail Order Catalogs,* appear at the end of this section. You might want to look at the full listings in those publications for more ideas about products to sell.

This appendix is far from inclusive. If it even scratches the surface, I shall be satisfied. Where I describe one firm, there may be twenty. You will have to do most of the searching for yourself. These are some places to look:

1. The advertising media. Chapter 3 gives you full instructions about how and where to look.

2. The lines of products listed in mail-order list brokers' catalogs. Chapter 22 tells about those catalogs.

3. B. Klein's *Directory of Mail-Order Firms* gives some information on what firms sell.

4. The Standard Directory of Advertisers and *Standard Directory of Advertising Agencies* at your local library or a nearby advertising agency. Look under "Mail-Order," "Books," "Correspondence Courses," and similar listings.

5. Lee Mountain, Pisgah, AL, issues a catalog of used books and correspondence courses he sells by mail. This is a helpful source of ideas.

It is often helpful to have some idea of the size of firms in a business you are interested in. It is difficult to find out the size of a business. Publishers' Information Bureau, 575 Lexington Ave., New York, NY 10017, gives data on the amount that firms spend on advertising in the major consumer magazines. But in most cases, mail-order firms spend most or all of their advertising appropriations in direct-mail or unlisted display media. *Direct-Mail List Rates and Data* gives the size of the customer lists for many firms.

There is no special reason for the order of the listings in this appendix: I have tried to keep similar lines somewhere near each other. But you may find the same line or product popping up in several different places.

In this appendix there are a number of descriptions of businesses that have been quoted and paraphrased from *Direct Marketing's* series of "Ideas in Sound" interviews.

The full interviews are available on tape from *Direct Marketing*, 224 7th St., Garden City, NY. The code numbers for ordering are given at the end of each description. Most of the tapes cost $8 at 1980 prices.

[I am grateful to *Direct Marketing* and to Henry R. ("Pete") Hoke for permission to use this material.]

Examples of Mail-Order Product Lines

AGENT-SOLD PRODUCTS

Look through any of the salesmen's opportunity magazines to see perhaps 500 different lines in a single issue. I shall mention some of them when I list particular classes of products.

FOOD AND DRINK

Most of the food and drink that is sold by mail is gourmet stuff—special delicacies that are not easily obtainable in nearby stores, or very high-quality foods that gourmets are willing to pay a premium for.

There have been exceptions, but generally it is not possible to sell ordinary-quality foods by mail, even if you offer special price inducements. The cost of shipping is too high relative to the weight of the food to make it possible to offer real bargains.

Liquors, on the other hand, can be offered on a price basis under special circumstances, as we shall see.

There are many mail-order food ads in *Gourmet, Signature,* and similar magazines, especially before Christmas.

Meat.   Fancy steaks are shipped frozen, by the dozen, at fancy prices. Several firms in the Midwest ship all over the country.

Smoked Ham, Smoked Turkey

Fish. For many years the famous Frank Davis Company in Gloucester, MA, advertised its mackerel and other fish by direct mail and in magazines. What happened to the firm? I don't know. Maybe there is room for someone, or maybe the market is gone.

Lobsters and Seafood. A professor who got tired of teaching and who wanted to live on Cape Cod sells lobsters by mail order, far and wide.

Cheese. Cheese is a favorite mail-order food item. Distinctive cheeses are a specialty, and they travel well over long distances. Also, the price/weight ratio is good. There are several firms in the business, selling through different techniques. Some sell direct to the consumer all year long. Others do most of their business in Christmas gifts. Still others sell their cheeses as *business* gifts. And then there is at least one cheese-of-the-month club plan. One firm distributes over 10 million catalogs a year.

Fruit. I am continuously surprised that fruit can be sold successfully by mail order. And yet, it can.

One fruit firm is responsible for a famous headline in a big ad in *Fortune.* It went something like "Imagine Harry and me advertising our pears in *Fortune!*"

Mail-order fruit is usually remarkably large and juicy and commands a stiff price. One firm sells apples by mail that are good, but I can't tell them from the extra special apples I can buy in season right here in town (for less than half the price).

One of the most famous and successful advertising men of all time started up a mail-order fruit business, with plain and gift wrappings, after he retired from his old job.

Preserves. There's a little old lady in a dingy little store on a side street in New York who makes her own preserves by hand and sells them by mail. She has been written up in several major magazines and gets orders from all over the world.

Fruitcakes. Mary and Sam Lauderdale sell pecan fruitcakes. Sold 500 pounds first year, grossing $800, netting $400. Mary of Puddin Hill business started virtually on kitchen table at Puddin Hill, family homeplace of Mary Lauderdale whose ancestors received property as land grant in 1836 during the Texas war with Mexico. Cakes made in October for Christmas season. Couple had to store cakes in apartment during early days. Afterwards moved to 1,200 square foot plant; added 3,600 square feet and warehouse facilities including refrigeration. ("Ideas in Sound," #73022JH8)

Candy. Sold to organizations for resale to their members and others, as a fund-raising campaign.

Pastry. Available are fancy pastries and those made from special foreign recipes.

Pretzels. Pretzels are now sold in gift packages.

Doughnuts. Doughnuts can be ordered by dialing a computerized super-market.

Pecans. Sold direct to consumers, and also to organizations for fund raising.

Coffee and Tea. My first mail-order venture was selling fancy coffee by mail. It was an enjoyable business. But it could never be very big, so I turned it over to someone else, who let it run down and die.

There are still some companies in New York City advertising coffees. Herb teas and other special teas also are advertised.

Health Foods. Look at *Organic Farming, Let's Live,* and *Prevention* magazines to see the large numbers of firms, large and small, in this line.

Catalog/mail order business. . . . with chain of 170 retail outlets. . . . General Nutrition Corp. . . . opened first store in depths of depression, 1935. Range up $35 in sales first day, $25M first year. By 1960s grossed $5 million per year. Mail order accounted for 95%. Last three years, concentrated on opening stores. . . . Discovered that stores help mail order. Mail order helps stores. Mails tabloid 5 times year to promote store traffic. Store people register all new customers, send names to Pittsburgh for central data processing (some 350,000 so far this year). Mail-order customers receive 80-page catalog containing 3,000 items. Now shipping 35,000 orders a week. ("Ideas in Sound," 72 GNPH 12 C1)

Gourmet Foods, Full Line. There are several firms, including one on the West Coast that has a fabulous millionaire customer list, that sell a full line of fancy foods. This is probably not an easy business to enter.

Gourmet Food Business. Paprikas Weiss (1548 Second Ave., NY 10027) . . . started . . . 50 years ago. Original catalog sent out in Hungarian, German and English languages. Now catalog is English only as ethnic groups have moved and integrated into American melting pot. Recently published Hungarian Cookbook carries best selling items from catalog in back pages, plus order forms for food, spices and other gourmet treats not normally obtainable in retail stores. Advertisers book on wraparound catalog cover and as stuffer with own merchandise. Also uses space in such magazines as *New Yorker.* Space ads do not offer catalog, usually hardware only. The recipient receives catalog with package. ("Ideas in Sound," 72 EWJH 8 C1)

Gourmet Merchandise. Lady entrepreneur, probably largest in MO field, now mailing over 6MM catalogs/year, has 50M active customers from '72–'73 with average sale of $18. Lillian Katz, owner of Lillian Vernon's, and division. The Country Gourmet, start of business 22 years ago. Uses space extensively mostly in shelter magazines for individual items, but advertises only gourmet merchandise for The Country Gourmet, other merchandise for Lillian Vernon's. Results: gets two markets with one basic catalog. Space not only gets new customer, but keeps name in front of public, so when catalog arrives, recipient not unfamiliar with company name. Currently mails 5 catalogs/year starting heavy in August-September. Smallest mailing goes out from Easter to June to cream of list. Mostly personalized items such as door mat with name of family. Heavy in personalization for all merchandise "wherever we can get a name or initial." About half of merchandise offered at "$1.98 . . . 2 for $3.50" or similar. "People love a bargain." Uses service bureau with success for list maintenance. Computer Directions manages. ("Ideas in Sound," 73 0 363 JH 8.)

Wine and Liquor. In big cities there are very successful dealers who solicit orders by newspapers and direct-mail advertising. A natural for anyone in the liquor business who wants to branch out into mail order.

California Wine. Tiburon Vintners selling premium California wine by mail since '64. . . . Originally sold products only in California to distributors, but at same time offered wine by mail through rented lists in "two step" selling. Mail piece told story of Tiburon wines, offered to send additional information if recipient desired. Biggest selling point was offering printed, personalized labels to buyer for self, friends or as business gifts. Label reads "Selected Expressly for the Dining Pleasure of. . . ." Now, . . . company in process of expanding into national distribution. Law forbids winery selling direct to consumer outside California, so . . . setting up label program through wholesalers who buy in case lots, send names for personalization back to Tiburon, which prints, sends labels back to wholesaler who distributes them to retailer for affixing to bottles. . . . only property was retail roadside stand, no vineyards. Sales $15M. For past fiscal year ending July, sales $5.766MM. ("Ideas in Sound," 72-PFJH 8 C1)

Duty-Free Liquor. These firms solicit tourists before they go abroad. The liquor is delivered in the United States. (Shops are located in air terminals.)

SMOKING MATERIALS

Cigarettes. Several years ago several companies in New Jersey did a thriving business selling cartons of cigarettes by mail to people in states that had higher taxes on cigarettes. But after a long fight, the U.S. Supreme Court interfered with the practice. Now firms in North Carolina have found some new more-or-less legal way to sell cigarettes by mail. Be careful.

Cigarette-Rolling Equipment. This ad has appeared for years in the classified sections of various men's magazines, sure evidence of a profitable business: "Cigarettes—Make 20 plain or filter-tip for 9¢. Facts free. . . ."

Cigarettes, Imprinted. A New York firm runs a regular 1-inch ad in *The New York Times* and other media offering cigarettes specially imprinted with "Happy Birthday," "Good Luck Joe," or whatever else you want. This is a good example of offering *personalized* goods as mail-order items.

Cigars. Many of the firms that sold cigarettes by mail turned to selling cigars by mail, and several of them are now thriving. They offer bargain offers and free trials in cigar-length one-column ads in various Sunday newspapers and mail-order sections of magazines. Their profit comes in the repeat business over a long period of time. Cigar smokers like to try various types of cigars from time to time, and the firms make their offers to their lists by direct mail.

A customer list of 25,000 to 75,000 should support a very nice business. Connections with manufacturers of cigars are very helpful in entering this business.

Fancy Smoking Articles. At least two old and famous firms in Boston, and one in New York, issue mail-order catalogs of every conceivable article and tobacco a smoker could want.

Pipes. Look for the ad that says, "Don't give up smoking until you try my pipe." It's a great ad and shows what can be done in this line by mail order.

Tobacco. There are several farm-magazine classified advertisers who sell tobacco by the pound, by mail.

Lighters.

HEALTH AND MEDICAL PRODUCTS

Health and medical products, and information on these subjects, are great mail-order items. But be careful! Make sure that what you sell has real and scientifically proved value.

An advantage of this field is that most health preparations are easy to manufacture or to buy from a manufacturing chemist. But this advantage is also a disadvantage. Just as it is easy to break in, so it is easy for the competition to break in too, once it is apparent that you have a profitable line on the market.

Vitamins. Vitamins are a classic mail-order item. Fortunes have been made in this field. Large companies and tiny ones, too, have been successful. Again, however, be very careful about making claims for the effect of vitamins which you can't substantiate. (As a matter of fact, I doubt that *any* claim of benefits for vitamins to *any* potential customers is scientifically reasonable. I think it is all quackery except for obvious diseases, and they require medical treatment.)

Nevertheless, people want vitamins and will continue to purchase them by mail—and in large dollar amounts every year.

Vitamins can be purchased wholesale from a variety of places, in bulk or made up into packages. A little shopping will locate suppliers for you.

The usual marketing technique is to offer a bargain rate for a short-term supply—or even free samples.

You will have plenty of competition, for there are probably *hundreds* of firms selling vitamins by mail. But of course that also proves what a good potential business vitamins are.

Disease Cures. Several "clinics" of various healing persuasions offer their wares by mail. I suspect that some or all of these are quackery at its worst, but of course I can't say for sure (at least, not here).

Salve. There is a firm that sells a plain petroleum jelly salve. It advertises in comic books for small-boy agents. The owner nets $100,000 yearly and plays golf most of the day, according to the account given in a recent government investigation, I'm told.

Acne and Pimple Preparations.

Blackhead Removers.

Prescription Drugs. Several firms are already in the business of selling prescription drugs by mail at discount prices. I would guess that this will be a big, important, and respectable mail-order line in the future.

Hearing Aids. Several companies sell their hearing aids by mail, usually with the help of agents in the field.

Eyeglasses, Prescription. Look for the occasioinal—but successful—ad of a company in this field. It sells at prices far below neighborhood opticians. I bet there is room for many more such companies than there are now.

Good advertising media are those that go to areas in which many elderly folk live.

Eyeglasses, Magnifying. Simple and cheap magnifying spectacles. A best-seller for years. One firm sells a type that clips onto other eyeglasses for further magnification. Lighted magnifiers for special needs is another possible item.

False Teeth and Dentures.

Dental-Plate Repair or Reliner Kits.

Food Care Materials. A New York firm sells an entire line of devices for bunions, hammertoes, etc. Looks like a good field, to me.

Nose-Hair Scissors. Sold directly from ads as well as through other firms' novelty catalogs.

Reducing Preparations. If you can help people to reduce, you have a mail-order product. Dozens of different kinds of preparations have been sold. Most of them are clearly phony, and the government cracks down. Some of them have limited use, and are more or less within the law. My advice is that you don't go near this business with a 10-foot pole.

Reducing Books. Some reducing programs have real value and can be sold honestly. Others cater to the dreams of those who want a miracle way to lose weight fast. The history of mail order is replete with excursions into this field. All I can say is: Be careful; don't get sucked in by the lure of a quick buck.

Diets. There is always a market for appetizing but nonfattening meal plans.

Reducing, Exercise Equipment. Mechanical reducing ads range from $1.98 rubber-stretch gadgets to expensive exercycles. Don't try to sell massage equipment as an aid to reducing, because it just doesn't work.

Antismoking Aids. A rash of these items is hitting the market now, in the wake of recent scientific discoveries of tobacco dangers. Just what any drugs can or cannot do to stop or reduce smoking is questionable. You'll have to do a lot of research for yourself on this.

Antismoking Psychological "Programs." One book on how to stop smoking sold over 300,000 copies. There are several "programs" selling for up to $50.

Thermal Pads.   Warren F. Clark, 87, has been in direct mail for over 60 years, and is still going strong with newest enterprise, 5-year old Clark Solaray Corp . . . Company manufactures thermal pad for use under bed pad to keep sleeper warm, work out aches and pains and to improve circulation. Holder of over 50 patents, Clark rarely sells except through direct mail. Honesty in copy and good solid product best guiding principles. Comments that he hasn't seen much change in DM over the years. Biggest change . . . is in improvements in graphics and production. Over the years he has sold only one shot items. Will not use catalog or multi-mailer techniques. Gets 1–2% return on mailings of 50–100M per year. ("Ideas in Sound," 72-SCJH 8 C1)

Sleep.   One firm does well with a line of gadgets that help you sleep comfortably, read in bed, keep sound and light out, etc.

Birth-Prevention Devices.   Until recently, it was not clear what the law was on selling information or devices to prevent pregnancy. But then a courageous and socially motivated mail-order firm challenged the Postal Service on this and won. Now you can freely mail contraceptive devices.

A book on the rhythm system has done well, too. Lately, at least one reputable firm has brought out a mail-order book on birth prevention and artificial contraception.

Trusses for Rupture.   A classic mail-order item. One firm was already well-established in 1913, and it still does well. Its ads have changed little in that time.

Posture Braces, Slimming Garments, and Girdles.   Several firms make and/or sell various body braces. One firm sells an entire line, and it will sell you its catalog and drop-ship for you, if you have a customer list that you can use it for. They also run their own display ads.

Lately the gift catalogs are showing these devices.

Bedwetting-Prevention Systems for Children.

Medical Equipment.   Stethoscopes and similar small pieces of equipment are sold to laymen through display advertising. Often billed as "surplus."

Noise Preventers.

COSMETICS AND BEAUTY AIDS

You might guess that cosmetics would be an ideal mail-order line. They are high-markup, repeatedly bought products, easily shipped by mail. But despite these advantages, full-line cosmetics have shown little promise for mail order— probably because they require demonstration before women will buy them.

However, specialty cosmetics have succeeded in mail order, as have firms that sell through agents. In fact, two firms that sell cosmetics through agents are among the most flourishing mail-order firms.

Hair Removers (Depilatories and Devices).   Various methods of removing women's unwanted hair have done well in mail order. One firm that sells an electrolytic device has run practically the same ad for years and years in women's magazines, a sure sign of success. Another firm began in mail order and sold that way for years before converting its operation mostly to selling through drugstores.

Special Antiperspirant Products.

Fingernail Preservatives.

Age-Spot Removers.

Perfume. Sometimes sold in a basket of many small bottles of various scents. Suffers as a mail-order item because women want to try the scent before they buy.

Wigs. Women's wigs sold successfully by mail long before the recent craze hit the nation.

Toupees for Men. A specialized, high-priced, successful mail-order item.

Men's Hair-Coloring Preparations.

Cosmetics for Blacks. Special preparations, especially for the hair, sell well by mail to blacks. There is at least one large company, and many small ones, that specialize in this line. Look for their ads in magazines catering to blacks.

In-Shoe Height Raisers.

Shoe Air Conditioners for Sportsmen.

Electric Shavers. Must be at bargain prices.

CLOTHING

Clothing always has been, and always will be, one of the great mail-order lines. But the mail-order offer must be different from clothes offered in local stores, either in type of clothing or in price.

Women's Dresses. Johnny Appleseed . . . has "backbone" business of moderately priced women's ready-to-wear, plus Christmas catalog of gift items. Ready-to-wear catalogs sent January, March, July to total of 3MM. Christmas catalog mailed Sept. to 1M. . . . all catalogs full color, featuring artwork rather than photography. Because of style changes, new fabrics. . . . Changes 90% of items in each new catalog. His average sale of $35/order, up $5/order over past 2–3 years. Attributes increase to upgrading of quality of merchandise rather than inflation. Company provides 24 hour/day phone ordering service through local answering service. After four years, finds credit cards accounting for 15% of business, improving size, number of orders. Reorders, many from same catalog, also hold up sales volume now at $3MM/year from MO only. ("Ideas in Sound," 72 SBJH 8 C1)

A famous Pennsylvania firm offers unbelievable bargains in inexpensive women's dresses by direct mail.

Another huge firm sells frocks through agents that it recruits by a vast campaign of mail-order advertising in magazines and through direct mail.

Several exclusive dress shops sell some of their simpler styles through *The New York Times Magazine* and other media.

Bridal and Wedding Needs. [Joan Cook, Inc.] starting in '55 on Long Island, mailed Joan Cook's Bluebook for Brides, sending to newly engaged girls. At same time, published same basic catalog for bridal party shops, caterers, with individual imprint of various shops to stimulate wholesale business. Features wedding accessories, matches, gifts, decorations. Still mail half million throughout year on retail basis; have 1000 active wholesale accounts, but wedding business now only 20% of total. Seven years ago . . . began housewares, gift catalog. Most recent effort 96 pages, 32 in color in 5″ × 8″ format listing 500 items. Most consistent sellers: silver, silver plate serving pieces, with or without monograms. Mailed 1.5MM catalogs this year, up 300M over '71. Prospects through list rentals but each test has to return at least 35¢/catalog for continuation of list use. Average sale $25. Rents or trades own list. ("Ideas in Sound," 72 CAJH 8 C1)

Special-Size Women's Clothing. These lines are good examples of how and why mail order works. Many women throughout the country do not fit into the standard sizes of clothing offered at local stores. But the demand is not sufficient in most places for the stores to offer the additional sizes. A mail-order firm, however, can cater to the demand of these women all over the country, without having to fight local competition. In addition to dresses, coats and other clothing are sold.

Half sizes

Extra-large sizes. One major firm also has department stores in the largest cities.

Small sizes.

Maternity sizes.

Still another firm sells *used* dresses—twenty dresses for $3.50—and other used clothing.

Uniforms. Many types of uniforms are sold by mail—to nurses, waitresses, etc. Men's uniforms are also a good mail-order line.

Special Brassieres and Lingerie. One firm sells a fantastic assortment of padded, stuffed, and tapered women's underwear that appear to be marvels of engineering genius. The display pictures make your eyes pop out. Some people buy their 25-cent catalog for entertainment.

Other firms sell only special brassieres, not designed to be spectacular.

A girdle firm has a mailing list of over 150,000 mail-order girdle buyers.

Stockings. Two huge firms sell women's hosiery through agents. They claim special long-wearing properties for their products, and they use imaginative and varied merchandising devices.

Women's Shoes, Wide Sizes.

Furs, New and Used.

Fur-Coat Remodeling.

Miscellaneous Women's Clothing. Various firms sell various lines of bathrobes, bathing suits, and other occasional clothing. The trick, of course, is to build a list of women who like the styles you sell.

Men's Suits.   Several firms take orders for suits custom-made in Hong Kong. Other firms have sold custom-made men's suits through agents for years and years.

And there are many exclusive (or expensive) men's shops that circularize the people who have formerly bought from them. They send out two or more brochures or catalogs each year, illustrating the styles they carry.

Men's Suit Remodeling.   A specialty of at least two firms is cutting down old double-breasted suits into the up-to-date style. If you want to go into this business, you might work up an arrangement with a good tailor who wants to expand his or her business.

Men's Clothes, Large and Tall Sizes.   Small sizes probably would not work as a specialty because of male vanity.

Men's Slacks.   A famous New Jersey firm sold ties by mail for many years. Now, as far as I can tell, they are concentrating their energies on selling men's slacks. They send swatches of material in the direct-mail pieces, and offer pants made of DuPont material at bargain prices. It was probably their success that convinced Spiegel to jump into this line, in competition.

Men's Ties.   One of America's great advertising men had a hand in building a mail-order firm that sold ties made by hand by New Mexico Indians.

Men's Fancy Shirts.

Bathing Suits.

Men's Shirts, Custom-Made.

Men's Shoes.   Several big companies sell men's shoes through agents. They use direct mail, match books, space ads, and all other media to recruit salespeople. This is big business.

Men's Shoes, Large and Wide Sizes.

Men's Shoes, Imported.

Shoes by Mail from Hong Kong.   Lee Lee, owner of Lee Kee, well-thought-of shoemaker and retailer in Kowloon. 60% of business mail order, but not aggressively promoted. K.K. visitors have outline of foot and several measurements taken so that custom made shoes can be ordered by mail by simply tearing out any fashion ad in a magazine, sending it to Lee Kee to be copied for $14–$20, and mailed to U.S. Some 150–200 orders arrive each day in Hong Kong though Lee does little advertising. Depends on word of mouth and constant influx of new visitors. ("Ideas in Sound," 72 LKPH 6 C1)

A New Jersey fellow sells shoes imported from England. He advertises in classified and small display in *Saturday Review, The New York Times Magazine,* shelter magazines, etc. He also runs a retail store. I've been in there, and it is a nice little business. He sends out a beautiful printed catalog.

Men's Huaraches, Imported.

Moccasins.

Riding Boots.

Men's Uniforms.   Some firms sell through agents.

Robes and Gowns.   For ceremonial occasions, graduations, and ministers.

Men's Outdoor Clothing and Equipment.   There are at least two fine old firms that sell men everything they need to be dry, warm, and good-looking in the outdoors. They also sell related equipment along with the clothing.

Stadium Blankets.

Rain Suits.

Western Clothing, Men's.

Men's Work Clothes, Used.   Small ads in lower-class men's magazines sell reconditioned work clothing for an Ohio firm.

Belts.

Fabrics.   Several firms sell fabrics by the yard to women who sew at home. You probably need to be near a garment center to be in this business, in order to be close to your supplies.

Fabric Remnants.   Back in the 1920s, several firms did well selling remnants in large quantities at low prices. I would think there is still a good market for this proposition.

Wool.   A nice little business in Connecticut sells wool to women and men who weave at home.

Sewing Accessories.   There are a good many firms that sell women everything they need to sew at home. One firm specializes in dress dummies. Others sell a full line of notions. Look in *Workbasket* to see their offers.

JEWELRY

Diamonds.   One firm sells by mail and emphasizes the investment aspect of buying diamonds. It advertises in *The Wall Street Journal,* among other media.

Pearls.

Diamond Rings.   Several outfits specialize in selling to servicemen. Look in *Army Times* to see their ads.

Synthetic Gems.

Simulated Diamonds.   Simulated diamonds with constantly changing product line "bread and butter" of OGI International. . . . Uses newest "corundum" stone under trade name "Diamint" in promotions. Stone has 9 hardness on MOH jewelers scale, compared to 10 hardness for real diamond. Early stones only registered at 5–6, were easily scratched, chipped, broken. Later development of "yags" were harder, but intense competition dropped price/karat from $50 to about $4, he says. Shaw sells corundum stones at $22/karat including mounting, sizing.

Diamints also sold successfully through credit card promotions. . . . Also tested DM using rented lists. Results "very disappointing." Then tried space in many national magazines where two-step selling technique used, i.e., prospect wrote in "for more information." Shaw says he "just traded dollars and probably lost a few." Now "asks for the order" in full-color, full-page ads. ("Ideas in Sound," 73 0304 JH 8)

This is a flourishing mail-order business. Just make sure your advertisements tell exactly what you are selling.

Watches.   Richard Sears of Sears, Roebuck got his start selling watches by mail, and it's still a good mail-order business. You must offer a bargain, though.

Jewelry-Making Hobby Supplies.

AUTOS, BOATS, AND ACCESSORIES

Autos.   The automobile manufacturers speculate that in the future they may sell a lot of automobiles from catalogs and mail order. But that's not the business for you!

Car-Purchase Criteria and Information by Computer Service.

Midget Cars.

Miniature Models of Cars.

Miniature Cars, New and Old.   After several years of scraping by with little or no financing, David Sinclair, . . . Auto Miniatures, . . . today finds more money available than he needs, now that his company is well on the road to success. Prices of the miniatures range from $2.50 all the way up to $4250. Some are kits, most are not. Sinclair finds his repeat business is very good and many collectors look upon their expenditures as an investment. Advertising in "class" magazines, he qualifies prospects by selling his 72 page catalog for $1.00. Staying with high quality merchandise, Sinclair will expand into railroads, ships, cannons and antique machinery. Last year volume topped $200,000, and he expects $1 million in five years. He uses credit cards very effectively and does not use rented lists for prospecting. . . . Four employees do the complete job for Sinclair. ("Ideas in Sound," 72 DSJH 8 C1)

Trailers and Parts.

Motorcycles and Parts, Tool Bags, Models.

Hot-Rod and Custom Car Parts.

Auto Parts and Supplies.   Several firms issue huge catalogs of accessories for ordinary stock autos. Other firms sell parts for foreign cars, or to the hot-rod set. There is also at least one tiny mail-order business that sells parts for the Ford Model T.

Car Caddy.

Tires.   For trucks, cars, sports cars—all at prices said to be below wholesale.

Reconditioned Spark Plugs.   Also sold through agents.

Wheel Balancers.

Auto Seat Covers.   One firm solicits new-car buyers by direct mail from rental lists of new-car registrations.

Sun Glasses, Auto.   Guaranteed to prevent glare. Sold by direct mail.

Auto Polishing and Washing Cloths.

Car-Washing Cloths.   Kozak Auto Drywash, Inc. . . . started in 1926 when cloth for dry washing demonstrator cars of dealers was needed to circumvent expensive wet wash every night. Product line now up to 16 items for household use. Include: special sponges, chamois like cloths. Price range $2 to $18. Sales were first made through distributors, wholesalers and retailers. Turned to direct mail in 1950. Company does multiple mailings each year to segmented list of 1 million. Also buys $100M in space advertising. ("Ideas in Sound," 72 KAJH 8 C1)

A small-town firm sells nothing but this item, with remarkable success. They advertise by direct mail, and in display ads in such places as the Sunday garden page of *The New York Times.*

This is an example of what can be done in the mail-order business with a good basic item, or line of items, plus a great deal of mail-order imagination.

Windshield Fog-Cleaner Cloth.   This is one of the leading items in the line of a firm that sells various auto and home goods through agents.

Boats and Motors.   See the outdoor magazines for the full variety of firms in this market.

Boat Equipment.   Detectors for noxious gases in boats, campers, etc.

Canoes.

Boat Designs (How-to-Do-It).

Airplane Designs (How-to-Do-It).

Engines and Motors for Lawn Mowers.

MAGAZINE SUBSCRIPTIONS

Magazines.   Proverbial kitchen table and $1500 capital starting place 3½ years ago for John and Jane Shuttleworth, publishers of bimonthly The Mother Earth News, other publications which stress "consume less, enjoy it more" theme by getting back to land, basic living. Company now approaching $2MM level, but, says Shuttleworth, . . . "We're still working 12–14 hours a day, seven days a week." . . . Does big business in back issues. Ten months ago launched Lifestyle! "the magazine of alternatives." More oriented to urban groups. Published bimonthly to fill in odd months when "Mother" not published . . . At same time, Shuttleworth says, "We get paid to promote ourselves" via syndicated column 3 ×/week in 62 newspapers; radio broadcasts on ecology, related subjects, on 90 radio stations which Shuttleworth records himself in own "down home in Indiana" style. . . . In MO business with

Mother's Truck Store Catalog, "tools for living the satisfying life." Sells everything from old fashioned wood burning stoves, to candle making kits. ("Ideas in Sound," 73 0349 JH 8)

Almost every magazine publisher, from *Time* to *American Bee Journal,* is in the mail-order business of selling subscriptions. And these magazines are the biggest single users of third-class mail in the country. There are literally thousands of magazines in the mail-order business in the United States.

Magazines sell subscriptions to their own magazines. But there are also various types of mail-order firms that sell subscriptions essentially as agents for the magazines. One firm offers fifty different magazines at cut prices direct to consumers. It sells by direct mail and mails millions of pieces per year. It is a huge operation, run by the former circulation director of a major magazine. Reportedly, this operation required a large sum of money to organize, and it did not become profitable for quite a while. It makes its profits, like the magazines themselves, on reorders rather than on the initial subscriptions.

Other firms make deals with department stores to enclose stuffers advertising the magazines, along with monthly bills, or to print ads on the backs of return envelopes. These firms have apparently found that they do best when they offer only a few magazines at a time.

Still other firms sell through agents that they recruit by classified or display advertising.

All these operations are drop-ship operations. They handle no merchandise. All they do is solicit orders, collect money, and take out their commission before forwarding the money to the magazines. Naturally they must sell at bargain prices (though never less than half the listed rate, or the magazine does not get credit for the subscription). And they must get bedrock deals from the magazines. Since magazines themselves often expect to spend every cent they get in subscription revenues in soliciting subscriptions, it is likely that these firms are sometimes able to arrange to keep all the subscription revenue they take in.

Magazines and Newspapers, Back Date.

Racing Forms, Back Date.

Binders for Magazines. Some firms sell the binders. Others bind the magazines for the customer.

BOOKS

Book Clubs. From $5.5 million in '69 to $12 million in '71 is the record posted by publisher Fuller and Dees. . . . Two book clubs account for the greater portion of the mail order business and 7½ million pieces of mail out of a total of 12 million were sent in 1971 soliciting memberships in the clubs. Other products include customized cookbooks, a set of books for in-home sex education of children and a treasury of Bible stories. ("Ideas in Sound," 72 JPJH 8 C1)

There is considerable overlap between this section and the sections on Correspondence Courses and Information. Whether a piece of written material is a course or a book depends mostly on the price and the way it is presented. Most correspondence-course material is also sold as books.

Some books that are good mail-order items are also mentioned in our sections on health, sports, and other topics.

Selling books and pamphlets by mail order has many advantages and some disadvantages. Chief among the advantages is that once you know you have a salable product, you can either write the material or have it written for you. This gives you perfect control over your material and perfect independence from the vagaries of suppliers.

If you own the rights to the material, you are in a position to reap the second great advantage, that of selling books at low cost, as low as 2 cents on the sales dollar.

Books and pamphlets go through the mail very cheaply, partly because of their low weight-to-cost ratio, partly because of the preferential postal rates Congress has seen fit to legislate for books. This is one of the reasons that books and courses are the greatest of the classic mail-order items.

The greatest advantage to selling books and information is also its greatest disadvantage: the ease of entering the field. Just as it is very cheap for you to test out a printed product and then go at it full blast, so it also is very easy for competitors to get in and reap part of the profit as soon as it becomes obvious to them (by repetition of your ads) that you have a profitable item. This means that in the field of selling books and information more than in any other field, the profits will go to the most efficient operator and the best advertiser.

The best source of ideas for salable books is the mail-order ads, of course. The next best source is the catalog of the Little Blue Book Company (including the Big Blue Book catalog) of Girard, Kansas. The founder of "Little Blue Books," Emmanuel Haldeman-Julius, was one of the great mail-order people of all time, and each book in his huge series was selected with an eye to its mail-order sales appeal. The list covers practically every subject that will have mail-order appeal to a mass public. It is a gold mine of ideas, and it is also a source of books to sell while you are still testing and not ready to print your own.

Other sources of cheap books for the mail-order market include the Wholesale Book Corp., 902 Broadway, New York, NY 10010; Associated Booksellers, 147 McKinley Ave., Bridgeport, CT 06606; Book Sales Inc., 110 Enterprise Ave., Secaucus, NJ 07094.

Incidentally, Haldeman-Julius wrote a superb book that is a tremendous store of knowledge for all mail-order sellers. It is called *The First Hundred Million.* Unfortunately, the book is out of print.

Another source of ideas for books to sell by mail is the catalog of Lee Mountain, Pisgah, AL. Most of the books listed in his catalog, as well as the courses, have been successful mail-order items at one time or another. I'll mention some of the specific titles. These titles should give you a good idea of which types of books will and which won't make good mail-order items.

Sometimes you can find a good mail-order seller that is not outdated but that has fallen out of copyright. The book is then in the public domain, and you are perfectly free to duplicate it and sell it yourself without anyone's permission. See Appendix C for further information on copyright law.

Sex Books.   This class includes books of sexual knowledge, not pornography or fiction. It is a tremendous mail-order field.

One firm that sells a "marriage book" (perfectly respectable, of course) offered to rent its list of 140,000 buyers in 1962, 170,000 buyers in 1961, and 100,000 buyers in 1960. You can figure for yourself how much they grossed at $2.95 per copy. And that's only one of several items they sell. Their basic medium is display ads in men's magazines.

Other firms buy books from publishers and offer several books in their ads. Or they arrange with the publishers to drop-ship for them. All you have to do is persuade the publisher that you are a bookseller—several orders will prove that—and they will drop-ship the merchandise to your customers.

How-to-Do-It Books. Even how-to-do-it encyclopedias have sold well by mail.

Travel Books. Books on how to travel cheaply (by freighter, etc.), and how to retire cheaply in little-known places, are particularly good mail-order offers. One firm offers a line of these books.

Health Books.
How to Live Long
How to Stop Smoking
How to Reduce
"Science of Keeping Young"
Home Remedies
Home Medical Encyclopedias
"How to Live 365 Days a Year"
"How to Stop Killing Yourself"
Birth Prevention

Inspirational Books.

Books, Ethnic and Religious.

Business and Money-Making Books. Starting with $30,000 capital in 1971, Donald Dible, founder, Entrepreneur Press, Inc. . . . and author of "Up Your Organization—How to Start and Finance a New Business" tells . . . that sales for last year were $250,000, and he expects to do $500,000 in 1974. Book now in 5th printing after 26,000 copies sold at $14.95. Original price $24.95, but mail tests indicated greater profitability at reduced rate. Originally marketed book in space ads, but expanded to other media like co-ops, press reviews, mail, retail. Inquiries now costing about $2/piece. Converts about 30% to sales, depending on source. One-half of '73 books sold in retail trade. ("Ideas in Sound," 14-0015 JM)

You'll find a raft of these books advertised in classified space in the mechnical and outdoor magazines.

"Get Rich in Spite of Yourself" is a typical, successful title. This one sells at $1 from newspaper reading notices.
Handwriting Analysis (Graphology)
Cartooning
Show-Card Writing
Sign Painting
Restaurant Management
Shoe Repairing

"Cash from Sawdust, Coat Hangers, etc."
"990 Bizarre Businesses"
"609 Unusual, Successful Businesses"

Stock-and-Bond Record Books.

Baby Books, Wedding Books, Bar Mitzvah Books, Confirmation, and Graduation Books.

Miscellaneous. One fellow made a nice little business out of just one book—an adult stunt book of 101 best stunts.

Auto-Repair Books.

Atlases.

Maps.

Great Museums, Great Monuments, Milestones of History.

Almanacs.

Bibles. A great sold-by-agents business. Some Bibles also are sold directly by mail.

Self-Help Books.
 Bashfulness
 Sleep Learning
 Self-Hypnosis
 Voice and Speaking Improvement
 Dancing
 Penmanship. (This was a better seller before typewriters became so common.
  But one old firm still sells its instructions.)
 English
 Etiquette
 How to Get to Sleep
 Mathematics Made Easy
 Public Speaking
 Conversation Improvement
 Horse-Race Betting
 Shorthand Systems
 Fortune-Telling
 How to Stop Smoking
 Foreign Languages (also sold as records)
 Beauty for Women
 Body Building for Men (including isometrics)
 Fighting Methods (karate, boxing, wrestling, judo, etc.)
 Memory Improvement
 Musical Instruments (especially guitar)
 Personal Magnetism
 Personal Efficiency
 "Seven Keys to Popularity"
 "Self-Mastery"
 "The Knack of Remembering Names and Faces"

"Conquest of Fear"
Correct Breathing
Secrets of Strength
Psychology
Yoga
Hypnotism. (At least fifteen firms sell books and hypnotic aids.)
Methods of Success
"How to Put the Subconscious Mind to Work"
Personal Finances
Tax Saving
Social Security Benefits
Salesmanship
Handwriting Analysis
"70 Bible Lessons 25¢. Bulletin, Box 87. . . ." (A long-running classified ad.)
How to Buy Surplus from the Government. (Several firms sell these guides.)

Most self-help books are sold one at a time. However, there are several publishers who sell their whole line of books via consolidated ads in magazines. Some of them sell pamphlets at 50 cents (three for $1); others sell books at $2.

Textbooks, New and Used. When you think about mail order and books, you should remember that many, if not most, publishers of hard-cover books are in the mail-order business. This is especially true of university presses.

Coin Catalogs and Albums.

Photo Albums and Photo-Mounting Supplies.

Stamp Albums.

Book Clubs. The Book-of-the-Month Club started a business that has burgeoned. Now there is a book club, it seems, to suit every interest: intellectuals, mystery lovers, bargain lovers, etc.

The book-club business is specialized, however, and as a beginner you won't be attempting it.

Discount Books. On one of the back pages of the book-review section of *The New York Times* on Sunday, in the *Chicago Tribune,* and in other media, you will see the ads for several firms who advertise books at 25 to 30 percent off the list price. These outfits take your order, deduct the difference between your price and the publisher's wholesale price, and send money and your address to the publisher. That's all. No merchandise to carry. No investment. A nice repeat business.

I'm sure these businesses aren't getting rich. And they must be efficient to make money on their small margin.

Book Finders. The only ways to buy a book that is out of print is to get it from a secondhand bookstore or have a book finder get it for you. The book finders use several trade publications to locate the books. I don't know how they work, but I do know that at least ten of them advertise regularly in classified columns of book reviews and magazines.

Bookbinding.

CORRESPONDENCE SCHOOLS

Correspondence schools are another great mail-order product. Tens of millions of Americans have taken courses in the past, and many of them have been helped to live better lives. (Look at the International Correspondence Schools testimonials in their ads!) And millions of Americans are studying hundreds of different subjects at home right now.

Correspondence schools have the major advantage that the course work travels lightly and cheaply by mail. They sell products which often cannot be studied elsewhere, or cannot be studied locally in most areas. They offer real benefits to the student—either a better job, more money, or a richer life.

In addition to the correspondence schools, there are many resident schools that sell their services by mail. The auctioneering schools, for example, require that the student travel to the school, but all the selling is done by mail.

The listing of types of correspondence courses is nowhere near complete. Lee Mountain's catalog (Pisgah, AL) contains the fullest listing of past and present courses that I know of. The classified and display sections of *Popular Science, Workbasket,* and the various specialized magazines will give you the complete picture of what's on the market now.

Correspondence courses go on and on, year after year. Owners of a correspondence school are not constantly hunting up new items to put into their catalogs or sweating out the latest fad. They will be continuously experimenting with their advertising, year after year, but they can count on reasonably stable incomes from sales of their courses.

High School Home Study. A big field, and probably getting bigger even though more and more people graduate from high school.

The schools use many and various methods of promotion, including car cards and match books.

Full-Line Correspondence Schools. Most correspondence schools offer one or a few courses. Several offer five or ten related courses, such as the foreign-language schools. International Correspondence Schools and LaSalle are unique in offering many, many courses—over 250 by ICS.

"Do you make these mistakes in English?" is one of the most famous, and most effective, headlines ever written. The Sherwin Cody School has tried many other headlines and many other ads over a period of several decades. They always go back to using their original ad.

Self-Improvement.

  Handwriting Analysis
  Child Rearing for Parents
  Art. The art correspondence schools teach many different facets of art: commercial, cartooning, painting, advertising, etc.
  Music. One of the schools ran the most famous headline in advertising 40 years ago: "They Laughed when I Sat Down at the Piano—But when I Began to Play. . . ."
  You can learn any instrument at one or more of the schools. Other outfits offer just a single course. Guitar instruction is a best seller.
  English Improvement

Conversation Improvement
Memory Improvement
Voice and Speech Training
Body Building and Muscle Building for Men
Beauty for Women
Ventriloquism
Penmanship
Home Instruction for Children

Science of Personal Success (tape cassettes).

Technical Courses. There is a wide variety of technical courses sold by mail order, ranging from navigation to welding, but we shall not discuss them here. International Correspondence Schools offers many of them, and you can check their catalog. Advertisements in technical magazines will show you others.

Business, Job, and Money-Making Courses.

Bookkeeping. Instructions to set up your own local business. Government manuals, which are in the public domain, probably supply the backbone of at least one of these inexpensive courses.
Accounting
Accident Investigation
Auctioneering
Watchmaking
Gunsmithing
Detective Training. Detection equipment is also sold by the outfits that sell the courses.
Piano Tuning
Practical Nursing
Restaurant Management
Swedish Massage
Invisible Mending
Millinery Design
Locksmithing
Woodworking
Typewriter Repair
Television and Radio Servicing
Photograph Coloring
Interior Decoration
Baking
Landscaping
Forestry and Conservation
Doll Making and Repair
Dressmaking
Floristry
Orchid Raising
Accident Claim Investigation
Hotel Management
Watch Repair

Meat Cutting

Taxidermy. One school has been in business over 50 years with little change in its advertising.

Exterminating. This is a course that I have never seen available, but I think it would be a good bet.

Candy Making

Photography

Child Photography

Writing

Civil Service Examination Studies

Commercial Art

Commercial Writing

Law

Metal Plating

Mirror Silvering

Baby-Shoe Metallizing

Travel Agency. I'd guess this course would be a specially good bet today, when so many people are traveling.

Cleaning and Pressing

Printing

Real Estate

Insurance

Education by Mail. Education By Mail burgeoning business of Insurors Press. . . . Three-year-old company grossed $200M in '69–70; $458M in '71; expects to go over $1 million mark this year, with more than $2 million projected for '73. Publishing firm specializes in educational materials for insurance industry, but expanding rapidly into other fields such as industrial security, occupational health and safety, humor books for doctors, dentists . . . Follows up mailing with salesmen on WATS lines. If specific name known in company, salesman will sell 6 of 10; if name not known, sales drop to 3 of 10. ("Ideas in Sound," 72 IPJH 8 C1)

Salesmanship (sometimes with records)

Electric Appliance Repairing

Upholstering

Credit and Collection

Sign Painting

Silk-Screen Process

Flocking

General Business Training for Executives

INFORMATION SERVICES

Information services differ from books and courses in that the information must be *current and timely,* and therefore must constantly be new and up to date. Because of the high cost of gathering information, it is usually sold at a high price to a few subscribers. Information services sell their product for as high as $30,000 per year to a single firm. But most of the information services that we shall mention sell for from $2 to $100 yearly to individual or business subscribers.

Naturally enough, your information must not be easily available elsewhere, or no one will buy your service.

Information services have many similarities to magazines, and in fact, many magazines have started this way.

Stock-Market Advisory Services. Look at their ads in *The New York Times* Business Section. Some are very big, some very small. Taken as a whole, this is big business.

Make sure you really are in a position to provide true information. And get clear on the laws that regulate this business.

Business Newsletters. There are several "inside dope" newsletters that provide general tips. At least one of these is a huge business.

Most major industries also have weekly newsletters that collect industry gossip, promotions, hirings, firings, alarms, and anything else of interest to company executives. These letters are generally started by people who have a wide acquaintance in the industry. They have sources of information and know what executives want to know about.

Economic Information. One firm supplies leads for salespeople on all new businesses opening all over the country. Another tabulates references to economic forecasts made in all the trade magazines. A third, a huge company, provides information on new building permits.

Information Brokers. Some firms have developed an interesting trade in bringing together people who need tips on new business, mergers, etc., and people who can supply such information.

Social Security Information. Most of the information sold is extracted directly from uncopyrighted government publications in the public domain.

Retirement Information. Where to live cheaply.

Sermons for Ministers.

Dress Patterns.

Architects' Plans for Houses.

Boat and Airplane Construction Plans. Look for the ads in the mechanics magazines.

Plans for Home-Workshop Projects.

Employment and Job Information.

Directories. Several firms publish directories of various types of business information: names of firms in an industry, names of buyers, names of trade associations, etc.

PHONOGRAPH RECORDS

Records have much in common with books as mail-order products. Both are readily mailable, can be offered as bargains, and often have specialized audiences.

Record Clubs. Most of the clubs are run or controlled by manufacturers, and they have a cost advantage not available to outsiders.

Language Records.

Stereo Components.

Children's Records.

Teaching Records for Children.

Popular Hit Records, Stereo Tapes, and Cassettes. Combinations of the latest hits, on one record, have sold well from radio advertising. The commercial ties in with the program. A similar scheme has worked for classical themes on television.

Religious Records.

Poetry Recordings.

PHOTOGRAPHY

Moving Pictures and Slides. Respectable home movies are sold via catalogs. Also 35-millimeter slides and religious movies and filmstrips.

Photos of Movie Stars.

Wallet-Sized Photos. Some firms make copies of photographs. At least one firm has a recent list of 95,000 buyers.

Cameras and Equipment.

Cameras and Equipment Secondhand.

Correspondence Photography Courses.

Photograph-Club Plans. One firm worked up a dandy business selling gift subscriptions for children's pictures taken every year on the child's birthday, from age 1 to age 6. Then they franchised the plan to local studios.

Local Studio Photography. Photographers can increase their local businesses greatly with mail-order techniques.

Baby Pictures.

Film Developing.

Mail-Order Film Processing. Beacon Photo Service . . . mails about 2,500 orders/day. In '71 grossed $10 million, accounting for about 3% of total mail photo processing done in U.S. yearly. ("Ideas in Sound," 72 RBJH 8 C1)

There is a large number of firms that do this work at cut-rate prices by mail. Their gimmick is that they cut out the middleman drugstores and other pickup places from the economic chain. They advertise everywhere, in heavy volume, in many media.

GARDEN SUPPLIES, PLANTS, SEEDS, SPECIAL TOOLS FOR TERRARIUMS

Gardeners are good mail-order buyers. See garden magazines and garden sections of Sunday newspapers. Many large and small firms flourish in this field. One firm has a mailing list of 6 *million* customers. Another large firm sells through agents.

Garden-Supply-Club Plans. A different plant or seed is sent at regular intervals.

Bird Feeders and Houses.

Decorative Water Fountains.

Fountains by Mail. Roman Fountains, Inc. . . . turns to wholesale for bulk of yearly sales of $500M. Fountains bought principally by landscape architects and contractors, registered architects. Now testing real estate developers. . . . Most fountains sold by mail for hotels, office buildings, professional buildings, art and civic centers, shopping center malls. Smaller fountains sell for as little as $80; major jobs run as high as $50/M. Prints 80-page catalog listing 150 fountains. . . . ("Ideas in Sound," 72 JEJH 8 C1)

HOBBIES

Every year Americans have more free time and more money to spend on their hobbies. The growth of mail-order businesses in this area proves it.

Hobby Correspondence Courses. Taxidermy, Music, Horse Training, and many others.

Hobby Supplies and Tools.

Tools. Since 1967 when the company first went into catalog mailing, the Brookstone Company . . . has more than doubled its business each year. The product line is devoted almost exclusively to tools for the sophisticated hobbyist, miniature builders, engineer, outdoorsman. In 1971, the company realized over $1 million in sales with an average sale of $18. ("Ideas in Sound," 72 RCJH 8 C1)

Guns.

Air Rifles.

Antique Guns.

Gun Accessories and Supplies. Gunsmith supplies and hunting calls.

Blank Pistols for Training Dogs.

Archery Equipment.

Slingshots.

Animal Traps.

Fishing Tackle. Rods, reels, lures, tackle of all descriptions. Some firms sell direct from ads, some from catalogs.

Fish Lures and Scents.

Trophies.

Dogs.

Dog Equipment. Collars, kennels, shipping crates, "doors" into the house, dog "toys," etc.

Model Trains.

Model Planes.

Model Boats.

Model-Building Supplies.

Tents.

Sleeping Bags.

Backpacking Equipment.

Portable Flush Toilets. For camping and other outdoor activities.

Golf Equipment, Club Plans.

Golf Books.

Personalized Golf Balls.

Golf Shoes.

Golf Supplies. Ball warmers, hand dryers, club covers, etc.

Pneumatic Swimming Support. A German patent, brought here. Manufacturer sells to other mail-order companies, catalogs, etc.

Diving and Scuba Equipment.

Ski Supplies, Books, and Clothing.

Body Warmers (for skiers, backpackers or winter campers).

Barbells.

Contour Joggers (for jogging at home).

Body-Building Books and Courses.

Electronic Equipment, High Fidelity. Tape recorder tape and supplies.

Photography. Photo travel slides.

Telescopes.

Chronographs.

Binoculars and Optical Equipment. Domestic and imported.
   The Bushnel Optical Corp. . . . deals in sports optics, spectator viewing equipment, shooting and hunting scopes. The optical equipment is made in

Japan mostly under the design and supervision of Bushnell technicians. The cost vs. U.S. made products is one half or less. ("Ideas in Sound," 72 BOJH 8 C1)

Range Finders.

Scientific Hobby Equipment.   Edmund started his own business by selling damaged, chipped-edged lenses for $1 through $9 classified ad. Now has 5 million per year business, mainly mail order, specializing in photographic and scientific equipment and novelties. Average sale: $3. 55,000 people per month request 4,000 item free annual catalog. ("Ideas in Sound," 72 HMNE 8 C1)

Kites for Adults and Children.

Leatherwork Supplies.

Musical Instruments.   See the music magazines for a full display. Accordians, guitars, and chord organs are sold through mass consumer media.

Recorders.   One firm does well selling just this one instrument.

Astrological Horoscopes.

ART

Correspondence Art Courses.   Probably the most successful mail-order business in the art field.

Art Supplies.   Necessary to have a retail store also, to maintain the necessary stock. Cut-rate special supplies are sold successfully.

Pottery Wheels and Kilns.

Custom Paintings from Photos.

Prints, Reproductions, and Posters.   Over the past few years these lines finally seem to have had some success.

Paintings, Imported.   The firms mail out selections on approval, like stamps.

Sculpture.

Statue Reproductions.

Wood Carvings.

Posters.

Antiques.

Antique Reproductions.

Picture Moldings.

Commemorative or Art Medals and Commemorative Plates.

Origami Paper.

Stamps.   This is one of the great mail-order fields. There are far more than 100 firms in the field, many consisting of just one man working part time.

A recent issue of *Popular Science* carried ads for seventy outfits. But you'd better know the stamp game before you try this field. The larger stamp firms use many media, including match books.

Coins.   A booming field in the last 5 years, and it will probably continue to boom. Some firms make a dandy profit on their catalogs alone, but this may not be ethical.

Indian Relics.   This is just one tiny example of hundreds or thousands of types of little-known and specialized lines that mail-order firms sell at a neat profit. They advertise in out-of-the-way places, and you must really research the field to come up with those that will be good fields for you.

Ship Models.

Woodworking Supplies.

Jewelry-Making Supplies.

Needlework Designs and Supplies.

Braided-Rug Supplies.

Costume-Jewelry Supplies.

Sculptured and Fancy Candles.

TOYS

Toys are not a great mail-order item. Yet, under some conditions they do well. For example, the famous F.A.O. Schwartz Co. uses display advertising to solicit inquiries for its catalog before Christmas, and Penney's, among others, sends out a big catalog, too.

Electronic Computer Toys.

Science Kits for Children.

Dolls, 100 for $1.

Huge Balloons.

Balloons, 200 for $1.

Magic Tricks and Novelties.

PRINTING

This is a field of mail order which already thrives mightily, and which will grow even more in the future, I think, for this reason: If you went into a local printer and ordered 500 address labels, he or she would probably have to charge you $20. The shop would have to buy special paper, set up a press specially for the job, get the labels padded, etc. But a firm that makes a business of address labels can make a profit on them at 50 cents or $1. Why? Because they mass-produce them at a fantastic volume. It's the old American story, as simple as that.

The same idea holds for personal stationery, memo pads, calendars, office forms, envelopes, and a hundred other types of printing.

So, if you find a printed product that people want, and if you can operate efficiently and cut costs, this can be a mighty profitable field of endeavor.

Address Labels.   These are often sold as a "leader" to introduce people to a line of gifts or novelties. Other firms sell them through agents, and through stores and women's clubs as money-raising goods.

Fancy address labels with photographs of hobbies.

Personal Stationery.   Two firms sell 100 letters and 50 envelopes, good quality, at the fabulously low price of $1.50 and apparently make a nice profit. One of them was reported to gross $750,000 several years ago.

Greeting Cards.   Though cards are sold all year round, the major business is for Christmas. This is a big, solid business, done mostly through agents.

Greeting-Card Kits (for making own greeting cards).

Wedding Announcements.

Birth Announcements.

Greeting Cards for Business.   Office and commercial greeting cards for Christmas are a big business. One firm has a list of 110,000 commercial customers, very nice indeed.

Name Stamps, Rubber.   Name stamps are sold for pocket use, with the personal signature engraved on them, and also just plain rubber stamps. One firm has a recent customer list of 104,000.

Book Plates.

Embossing Machines.

Personalized Welcome Mats.   Sold direct and through agents.

Personal Signs.   Metal and plastic signs are sold for all kinds of purposes: mailboxes, desks, gardens, everything. People like to see their own names in print, and that's why this is such a flourishing mail-order business.

Business Cards.   Sold by mail at about $7 per thousand.

Letterheads.   One firm offers to design them and print them, too.

Office Forms.   Standard sales forms, invoices, etc. More complicated forms will probably continue to require a salesperson. The economies of the mail-order offer are in *standardized* forms.

Legal Forms.   Arizona lawyer giving up practice after 21 years to pursue new career in mail order. James E. Grant, . . . in MO part time for several years selling legal, semi-legal printed forms to other lawyers, office suppliers. Grant . . . says gross in past 12 months about $50M, but by going full time after July 1, he expects to double gross in year. So far, 75% of business in Arizona only. Difficult to sell same forms in other states because of complexities, variations in same basic laws. Now expanding into forms utilized in Federal laws such as bankruptcy sets, Federal court forms, odometer forms certifying mileage on used cars. ("Ideas in Sound," 73 0335 JH 8)

Postal Scales (pocket-size).

Job Printing.   One New York firm cuts its own low prices in its direct-by-mail, cash-with-offer deal.

Mimeographing.   A Chicago firm even does mimeographing for large firms whose business it solicited by mail, though I think its work is not outstanding nor its prices particularly low.

Envelopes.   Mail-order envelope firms offer real economies to large users of envelopes all over the country.

Collection Aids.   An entire big business has been built on collection aids and stickers for insurance offices and similar customers.

Memorandum Devices.   These are big sellers to business people. *Signature,* the Diners Club Magazine, is chock-full of large ads for various varieties— especially at the end of the year, of course.

Schedules and Calendars.

Advertising Novelties.   Many advertising novelties have the advertiser's name imprinted on the novelty.

Tarot Cards (fortune-telling).   An example of a small printed novelty that has sold for years. It has probably been too small a line for anyone to challenge, so one firm seems to have the whole market.

Book Matches, Imprinted.   Usually sold through agents.

Prepared Circulars and Stuffers.   Various firms prepare advertising materials for cleaners, florists, and other businesses, and sell them to one exclusive customer in each area.

Printing Devices.   A Connecticut firm has used the identical ad to sell its low-priced printing presses for 80 years. Another firm sells presses and accessories to commercial users. Another sells mimeograph machines through agents. Still a fourth sells a postcard mimeograph machine. And there are lots more.

MONEY

Money has an advantage for mail order: It is light in weight and easily mailable. It also has a disadvantage: The person with whom you are dealing is not close at hand.

Small Loans.   For a while small companies had this field to themselves. Recently a mail-order giant tested the field, and jumped in with both feet.

Business Loans.   A large commercial lender mails incessantly to supermarkets and other businesses to find prospects who want to borrow money for new equipment and fixtures. They close the sales in person, however.

Coins and Bullion.

Real Estate.

Life Insurance. Getting bigger every day.

Health and Casualty Insurance. Growing by leaps and bounds.

Burial Insurance.

Auto Insurance. I am intrigued by the "special offers" to those who say they don't drink.

Savings and Loan Associations. Dozens of them advertise for you to save with them. Two firms make a business of acting as mail-order broker for many savings and loan accounts. Stock-market firms also get into the act. One reported $60,000 in accounts for a $100 ad.

Stocks and Bonds. Regular accounts as well as voluntary investment plans for small investors.

Investment Advice and Market Letters.

Betting. Betting in English football pools grossing $3MM/week for Vernons Football Pool, subsidiary of Vernons Organisation. . . . Vernons, one of five privately owned pools in England, ranks #2, gets 30% of total bets. Average bet, about one U.S. dollar. Twenty percent of customers covered by mail every three weeks with envelope containing three coupons for betting following three weeks. Bettor sends in one coupon/week. Formerly mailed 1 coupon/week but as postal rates increased, frequency moved to every two weeks; now three. Each mail drop is 1.5MM pieces; returns 600M bets/week. Remaining 80% of bettors solicited weekly by "agents" in factories or door-to-door agents. . . . Football Pool marketing director, John Kennerly, says . . . that every street and address in England on computer. ("Ideas in Sound," 73 0338 JH 8)

Collection of Debts. One firm obtains collection clients through the agents it recruits by mail.

Credit Cards. Diners Club has done a remarkable mail-order job in obtaining subscribers. It has utilized car cards and take-one advertising of all kinds, among its media.

HOME-BUSINESS EQUIPMENT AND SUPPLIES

Bees and Beekeeping Materials.

Squabs. A gentleman named Elmer Rice made a remarkable mail-order success by putting people into the business of raising squabs. He was also the pet account of one of the three largest advertising agencies in the country.

Chicks and Chicken-Farming Equipment and Supplies. Years ago everyone thought it was impossible to sell chicks by mail order. Now the mails are full of them!

Fish, Partridges, Rabbits.

Vending Machines.

Baby-Shoe-Bronzing Equipment.

Electoplating Kits.

Rubber Stamp Machines.

Tennis-Racket-Restringing Equipment.

Printing Presses and Printing Supplies.

Welding Equipment.

Saw-Sharpening Machines.

Plastic Molding.

Synthetic Gem Making.

Doughnut Machines.

Rug-Cleaning Equipment.   Typically, one firm sells a franchise and marketing program along with the equipment.

Furniture-Cleaning Equipment.

Wall-Cleaning Equipment.

Sign-Making Machines.

SERVICES

When you think about what to sell by mail order, don't concentrate so much on products that you forget about services. There are many things that you can do *for* people and firms, and that can be arranged by mail—far more than you think. So search your own experience to see if you have a special knowledge that you can sell to people for profit, or if you can develop such a skill or knowledge.

Book Binding.   Mentioned earlier under "Books."

Vanity Publishing.

Blanket Weaving.   "Send us wool for blankets. Write. . . ." reads the ad.

Comforter Recovering.

Commercial Photography.

Advertisement Writing and Consultation.   Several hot direct-mail letter writers make a nice living this way, I'm told.

Commercial Artwork.   One fellow caters to mail-order firms and does small ad layouts for them. He has done it for years.

Collection Agencies.   Most of them do their collection entirely by mail. And some solicit all their clients by mail.

List Owners and List Brokers.   One of them advertises in foreign newspapers and does a direct-mail business with its catalog.

Patent Search.   You must be in Washington to render this service, I would guess.

Invention Marketing.

Glove and Leather Goods Repairs.

LOCAL SERVICES

Don't get the idea that a mail-order business must be national in scope. Many local businesses are run on mail-order principles, except that the customer calls or comes in person, or that delivery is limited to a small area. For example, a business that advertises firewood could never be national. But it might operate entirely by advertising and telephone orders, and have all the hallmarks of a mail-order business.

Local services are usually part mail-order-type, part straight retail. The two hands wash each other!

I will list only a few examples of the multitude of services that you can run this way.

Window Washing.

Auto Mechanics.

Rug, Furniture and Wall Cleaning.

Floor Sanding.   A dandy little business for some couples. He goes out and does the jobs while she minds the phone to answer the inquiries they get from newspaper classified advertising.

Duplicating and Photostat Work.

Travel Agency.   Some travel agents do considerable busines by mail outside the local area, too.

Flower Delivery.   In one major city two fellows started a successful weekly club plan. And I experimented with the idea in New York under the name "Flowers Every Friday." I gave it up in favor of another scheme at the time, though afterward I saw that it had excellent prospects. The plan was later developed for weekly delivery to banks.

Lawn and Tree Care and Treatment.

BUSINESS TO BUSINESSES

For some reason, beginners in mail order always focus on products and services for consumers, ignoring the huge field of mail-order sales to commercial and industrial firms. It will be very educational to have a friend in a small office collect and show you the mail the office receives over a short time. You'll be amazed at its volume. As an example, I will list just a few of the major types of mail-order offers that come into an ordinary insurance agency.

Office Equipment.   Kole Enterprises, Inc., . . . sells corrugated merchandise, mostly for industrial use. Line includes bins for parts storage, pull drawer and office files, corrugated boxes, cabinets, related items. ("Ideas in Sound," 72 GBJH 8 C1)

Office Supplies.   Everything from pencils to filing cabinets. One firm mails to a list of 3 million, among whom are a whopping 800,000 buyers.

Rubber Bands by the Pound.

Specialized Books.

Sales-Training Bulletins, Programs, and Records.

Letterhead.

Stationery.

Printing.

Janitor Supplies.   Ice-melting products, just for one example.

Building Maintenance.   Revere Chemical Corp. . . . built profitable business selling assortment of building maintenance products solely by mail. . . . Company distributes catalog to 100,000 customers. Careful attention to detail plus wide attention to telephone contacts, which account for 10% of sales a must. ("Ideas in Sound," 73 0352 PH 8)

Brushes, Industrial.   Some sell through agents.

Envelopes.

Collection Aids.

Specialized Magazines.

Typewriters, New and Used.

Adding Machines and Calculators.   Imported, usually.

Electronics.

Wall Charts and Display Boards.

Advertising Novelties.

Furniture for Institutions (Churches, Schools, etc.).

Machinery and Construction Equipment.   Of every size, shape, and description from chain hoists to printing presses.

Junkyard Equipment.   Selling junk car crushers, heavy equipment, down to small office supplies by mail to junk yard owners turns $300M/year into $5MM/year business in three years. . . . TeleCom Industries . . . three years ago sent small flyer to 40 junk yards in NY State offering piano wire to cut out windshields, other small items. Response good, so Diefendorf got lists from associations, other sources; expanded mailings into Northeast sector of country, then Eastern seaboard. Now mails nationally to 15M/month. In view of success, company plans on expanding market into Europe with Denmark office soon. Later, will expand market to include sales of heavy construction equipment by mail. ("Ideas in Sound," 73 0158 JH 8)

HOME FURNISHINGS AND HOMES

Farms.

Home Plots in Retirement Areas.

Precut (prefabricated) Houses.

Roofing (especially of aluminum).

House Plans (Architectural).

Lumber. For do-it-yourself builders especially.

Fuel Oil. A local business.

Awnings.

Hammocks.

Wallpaper.

Drapery.

Burlap for Home Decoration.

Custom-Made Drapes.

Bedspread Caddies.

Burglar Alarms. Also sold through agents.

Fire Alarms.

Pumps for Miscellaneous Uses.

Hardware Novelties. Door knockers, switch plates, etc.

Door Checks.

Home-Workshop Equipment.

Tools.

Welding Equipment (Do-It-Yourself).

Rugs.

Furniture. Chairs, tables, cabinets, garden furniture, all kinds of furniture.

Elevating Recliner (for handicapped or disabled).

Furniture Do-It-Yourself Kits.

Chair-Caning Supplies.

Bars.

Bar Supplies. Novelty glasses, mixers, bars, etc.

Cabinets and Drawers. One firm that specializes in old-American style reputedly does a large business, all drop-shipped.

Bed Massage Equipment.

Long-Life Light Bulbs.   Sold through agents.

Wireless Light Fixtures for Closets.

Miniature Chandeliers.

Fire Extinguishers.

Cookware.   A terrific amount of cookware is sold by agents through home "parties." Other stuff is sold directly through "unbelievable bargain" ads, some of which are phony "surplus" or "liquidation."

Gadgets.   Part-time, in-home catalog mail firm, Hendry House . . . still going strong after 17 years, says Mrs. Gay Hendry, owner. . . . Says she averages three-hour-day, grosses "under" $100M/year. . . . Ninety percent of 150 items shown in 32-page, 2-color 5½" × 8" catalog drop shipped. Remainder of fulfillment done by family of five Hendry children, friends, who pitch in when busy. Mails about 100M catalogs/year spread over average three mailings. . . . Uses NY Times, Parade, others for sale of single items. . . . Always lookout for "gadgety things;" new, unusual, exclusive items. Looks for items not found in other MO catalogs. ("Ideas in Sound," 73 0088 JH 8)

China.

Silverware.

Basketware.

Lamp Specialties.

Telephones and Telephone Equipment.

Plastic Freezer Containers.   One firm has a list of 50,000 customers whose average purchase is $15.

Cutlery.

Typewriters.

Calculators.   First direct marketing venture brought in over $20 million in sales for Hewlett-Packard's HP-35 pocket calculator which sold for $395 each. . . . Hewlett-Packard traditionally sold its line of 3000 products through its own sales force. For products selling from $1000 to $100,000, $50 to $200 cost per sales call could be justified. Lesser priced calculator prohibited individual sales calls except on volume basis. Company turned to. . . . a direct mail program. Result: mailing package costing 20¢ each. Mailing pieces went to cold prospects, rented list of engineers. Success of campaign induced Hewlett-Packard to use dm for all lower cost products. ("Ideas in Sound," 14-0046 KC)

Power Mowers.

Lawn Markers.

Lawn Furniture.

Candles, Decorative.

Dry Window Cleaner. Through agents.

Fabric-Mending Glue. Through agents. Also needle threader, eyeglass cleaner, etc.

Glue. Through agents.

GENERAL MERCHANDISE

Most firms in the mail-order business specialize in one or a few lines of merchandise. And I strongly advise everyone who is interested in mail order to start off with a specialty line, at least at the beginning. However, there are also a good number of firms that sell a variety of merchandise. These general merchandisers fall into a few major classes that we shall now describe.

Department-Store Type of Firms. Everyone is familiar with the Sears, Roebuck type of operation. 'Nuff said, except to mention that at least two major firms, J. C. Penney and Singer, have entered the field more recently, testimony to the vitality of mail-order selling today.

General Agents' Merchandise. There are several prosperous firms that sell a wide variety of merchandise through mail-order-recruited agents.

Novelty and Gift Merchandise. Since World War II there has been a fabulous growth in the firms that offer novelties priced from 88 cents to $10 through catalogs. They sell knickknacks that retail stores don't carry, new and gimmicky things that are fun for customers to buy and give away. Some of these firms have been terrific success stories. One of them has a customer list of 2.6 million, and in a short 16 years has grown from nothing to an annual volume of $7 million.

This is not a field for a beginner starting on a shoestring unless you possess considerable merchandising skill and experience. Capital, too.

These firms solicit new customers in one of two ways: (1) By offering a specially attractive bargain leader in space ads. They lose money on the initial order, but make it up in later purchases. (2) By sending their catalogs to lists rented from, or traded with, competitors in the same general field.

Assorted "Bargains" and "Surplus" Specialties. Klein's *Directory* lists about 3,000 firms, most of which are in this category. Many of those firms make little or nothing, however, and many are in the business for only a short time.

These firms work in a variety of ways. One method is to develop a customer clientele for real or apparent bargains of all types. The firm ordinarily advertises one or more of these bargains in space advertising, then follows it up with package stuffers and direct-mail flyers of from one to eight pages of similar merchandise.

Some of the merchandise is truly bargain, imported or domestic—the result of good merchandising ability on the part of the firm. Other merchandise is government surplus. Still other firms sell phony bargains and "liquidated" merchandise that can be bought just as cheaply at retail stores.

Some firms really are able to make money with a succession of one-shot items sold directly from space advertising. But such firms are few and far between. Mostly they must depend on repeat sales for profitable volume.

MISCELLANEOUS LINES

Religious Materials.

Dog Repellent.

Insects. Terry Taylor, an entomologist and owner sells Lepidiota Bimaculata from Thailand by mail to biologists, teachers, collectors, researchers, ad agencies, artists, and museums. Inventory of 3MM specimens and thousands of species in home-based laboratory. Taylor and wife operate business. ("Ideas in Sound," 73 0482 JH)

Plastic Custom Molds.

Chemicals.

Grave Monuments, $14.95 (pre-1970 price). These tombstones are made of concrete.

Bed and Sleep Furnishings.

Tear-Gas Guns.

Book Plates.

Coin-Bank Calendars.

Novelty Pets. Includes monkeys, horses, turtles.

Chalk-Talk Cartooning.

Old Gold Bought.

Fortune-Telling. I do not recommend this field.

Flagpoles.

Coats of Arms with Family Name. In pewter or wood shield, $7 or $14.50.

Marriage Brokers.

Employment Agencies. Teacher's employment agencies seem to do well by mail.

Transistor Radios.

Charm-and-Treasure Jewelry.

Slide Rules.

Plaques and Tables.

Church Furniture.

Children's Things. See mothers' magazines.

Ball-Point Pens and Refills.

Pest-Control Supplies.

Decorated T-Shirts.

Decorative Maps.

Trading Cards. There is something to be learned about the mail-order business from this example. You would never guess, from the advertising, that one firm, let alone several firms, does a very substantial volume in trading cards (baseball and other sports pictures) sold to children and collectors.

Only a few tiny ads appear each year in a couple of specialized media, accounting for only a tiny advertising budget. And yet I learned about one of these firms—a retired couple, whose large apartment was filled from wall to wall with trays of cards. The business, started as a hobby, was easily worth $25,000 when I saw it in the mid-1960s, despite the fact that many items were sold for a few cents each.

Precision Timers. The Meylan Stopwatch Corp . . . started selling regular watches by mail in 1921. However, keen competition led to stopwatch field. . . . First customers were largely sports enthusiasts or government personnel. In thirties they turned to industry where stop watches were used for time study use and industrial engineering. More recent catalog . . . includes sophisticated timers, counter, watches and time-study boards." ("Ideas in Sound," 72 MSJH 8 C1)

Canoe Trips.

Computers.

Computer Service. Selling $440/year computer information service subscription by phone, only successful method found after much testing. Subscription consists of three basic volumes totalling 1804 pages, monthly update of 120 pages, unlimited phone consultation. "Most authoritative reference work in the industry," says Kalbach. Gives complete information on all types of hardware, software, new developments. Market is any company owning, leasing computers, peripheral equipment. Kalbach started in '70 when sales $250M; now $2MM and growing. Renewals "better than 80%" sell at $330/year. ("Ideas in Sound," 73 0305 JH8)

Brand-Name Items on Credit.

Co-op Catalogs.

Phone Catalog Grocery Sales. Grocery delivery direct from warehouse to home via phone ordering service off and running in pilot operation. Galaxy Foods, Inc., Brooklyn, NY . . . has no walk-in business, delivers only within three-mile radius of warehouse, does not sell produce, all meats flash frozen. Minimum order $7 paid for at door. Customer orders day in advance, can specify delivery time in any two hour period from 8 a.m. to 10 p.m. . . . No membership fee, no freezer to buy, no contract, money back guarantee. First order taken on spot from loose leaf catalog of 3,500 items. When merchandise delivered, new catalog goes with order and customer number given. ("Ideas in Sound," 73 0223 JH 8)

Examples of Individual Mail-Order Items

The following product list is from the "A" items in *The Directory of Mail Order Catalogs,* Second Edition, Richard Gottlieb, General Editor, Grey House Publishing. It illustrates the variety of goods that can be sold by mail.

Product Index

The above listings in the "A" category illustrate the variety of items sold by mail. It might be worthwhile to examine the entire index as a source for product ideas.

The list that follows contains examples of individual items in the "A " category from *The Mail-Order Crafts Catalogue,* Margaret A. Boyd, Chilton Book Company, Radnor, PA., again illustrating what can be sold by mail.

Craft Item Index

abalone
Bishop's House of Gems; M. Nowotny
abrasive disks
Foredom Electric Co.
abrasive points
Foredom Electric Co.
accessories
Boin Arts & Crafts; Castolite; R.S. Duncan & Co.; Foam Fantasy; Knits'N That Yarn Shop; Merribee; Joan Moshimer; Sharon's Petite Sherre; Sign of the Arrow; Skil-Crafts Division; Straw Into Gold; The Thread Shed, Inc.
acetate
Dick Blick; Plaza Artists Materials, Inc.
acid dyes
Glen Black Handwoven Textiles.
acrylics
Bear Cave.
acrylic felt pens
Lillian Vernon.
acrylic in sheet form
Rohm & Haas Co.
acrylic items
Greentree Ranch Wools, Countryside Handweavers; Lillian Vernon.
acrylic modifier
Siphon Art Products.
acrylic yarn
Wonoco Yarn Co.
additives
Adhesive Products Corp.; Castolite; Westwood Ceramic Supply Co.
adhesive sprays
Walnut Hill Co.
adhesives
Art Mart, Inc.; Basic Crafts Co.; Arthur Brown & Bro., Inc.; The Ducketts; Holiday Craft; Skil-Crafts Division; W. Wooley & Co.
adjustable hairpin lace loom
Rosemond Hobbycraft.
adz
Elizabeth R. King.
aerosol finishes
Carnival Arts & Crafts.
afghans
Merribee.
African trading beads
Jewelart Inc.; Jeweler's Emporium.
agate cabochons
Adris Oriental Gem & Art Corp.; Tumblecraft.
agate carnelian
Murray American Corp.

agates
Aspen Lapidary; Biship's House of Gems; Mississippi Petrified Forest; Sandy Symons; The Treasure Chest; Tumblecraft; Twin Peaks Rock Shop; G. Weidinger.
aged documents.
Whittemore-Durgin Glass Co.
aida
The Hidden Village; Needlecraft Shop Inc.
airbrushes
Badger Air-Brush Co.; Dick Blick; Arthur Brown & Bro., Inc.; Douglas & Sturgess, Inc.; Newton's Potters Supply; Plaza Artists Materials, Inc.; Skil-Crafts Division.
alcohol burners
Gilman's
alcohol dyes
Fezandie & Sperrle, Inc.
alcohol lamps
Delco Craft Center, Inc.
alexandrite
De Lapa Mining Inc.; International Import Co.
alloyed gold
T.B. Hagstoz & Son.
alpaca
Colonial Textiles; Greentree Ranch Wools, Countryside Handweavers; The Hidden Village; KM Yarn Co.; Valley Handweaving Supply
alpencarpet
Greentree Ranch Wools, Countryside Handweavers.
alphabet beads
Bead Game; Jewelart Inc.
alphabet stencils
Sax Arts & Crafts.
aluminum
A 'N L's Hobbicraft, Inc.
aluminum circles
St. Louis Crafts Inc.
aluminum enamels
Ceramic Coating Co.
aluminum foils
Delco Craft Center, Inc.
aluminum molds for ornamental concrete
Concrete Machinery Co.
amazonite
Murray American Corp.
amazonite barroques
Jim's Rock Shop.
amber
Purcelli's Gems.
amber agate
M.W. Jackson & Assoc.

American Indian artifacts
Dover Scientific Co.
American Indian bead corn
Crowe & Coulter.
American Indian crafts
Boin Arts & Crafts; Craft Service; Magnus Craft Materials.; Sax Arts & Crafts; Tandy Leather Co.; Winona Trading Post
American Indian flower corn
Crowe & Coulter.
American Indian jewelry supplies
Panther International Ltd.
American Indian seed beads
Anne's Treasure Trove; The Beadcraft Corner/Beadcraft Club; Nicole Bead & Craft Co., Inc.
Americana samplers
J.L.T.; Northwest Handcraft House.
amethyst
Aspen Lapidary; Biship's House of Gems; Commercial Mineral Corp.; De Lapa Mining Inc.; Gem-O-Rama, Inc.; Inter-Ocean Trade Co.; International Import Co.; Melbourn Gem Co.; Murray American Corp.; Norlene Lapidary; M. Nowotny; Oceanside Gem Imports, Inc.; Purcelli's Gems; Syn-Crer Creations; Transworld Trading Co.; Treasure of the Pirates, Inc.; G. Weidinger; Weisz Import Export Corp.
andalusite
Commercial Mineral Corp.; De Lapa Mining Inc.; W.D. Hudson, Jr.; International Import Co.; Oceanside Gem Imports, Inc.; Purcelli's Gems.
angora yarn
Wonoco Yarn Co.
aniline dyes
Fezandie & Sperrle, Inc.
animal eyes
Sav-On-Crafts.
animal fossils
Geological Enterprises.
animal molds
Town & Country Crafts.
antique dolls
The Needle Works.
antique newspapers
Whittemore-Durgin Glass Co.
antiquing
Birchwood Casey; Carnival Arts & Crafts.
anvils
Frank Mittermeier Inc.
Apache tears
Panther International Ltd.
apatite
Norlene Lapidary.

appliques
Leman Publications; Lillian Vernon.
aquamarine
Harry Bookstone; Commercial Mineral Corp.; De Lapa Mining Inc.; Inter-Ocean Trade Co.; International Import Co.; Murray American Corp.; Norlene Lapidary; Oceanside Gem Imports, Inc.; Purcelli's Gems; Syn-Crer Creations; Weisz Import Export Corp.
arbors
Green's Rock & Lapidary Ltd.; Lindell Industries; Lortone Inc.
arc welding supplies
Wel-Dex Mfg. Co.
Arkansas minerals
Wright's Rock Shop
armatures
Delco Craft Center, Inc.; Plaza Artists Materials, Inc.; Sculpture Associates Ltd.
art foam
Dick Blick; Boin Arts & Crafts; Cleveland Leather Co.; Craft Service; Craftsman Supply House; Delco Craft Center, Inc.; Economy Handicrafts, Inc.; Foam Fantasy; The Handcraft Supply Corp.; Holiday Handicrafts, Inc.; House of Flowers; Hazel Pearson Handi Craft; Sax Arts & Crafts; Supreme Handicrafts; Zim's.
art foam patterns
Don's Hobby Co.
art metal
American Handicrafts.
art metal tools
Sax Arts & Crafts.
art paper
Delco Craft Center, Inc.; Skil-Crafts Division.
art prints
Supreme Handicrafts
art tape
Economy Handicrafts, Inc.
artificial flowers
Schrock's, The House of Hobbies & Crafts; Lee Wards.
artificial foliage
Boycan's Craft Supplies.
artificial fruits
Zim's.
artificial plants
Lee Wards.
artificial straw
House of Flowers.
artist portfolios
Framaway Co.

artist's dry colors
Fezandie & Sperrle, Inc.
artist's supplies
A 'N L's Hobbicraft, Inc.; Bergen Arts & Crafts, Inc.; Dick Blick; Bob's Arts & Crafts; Boin Arts & Crafts; Arthur Brown & Bro., Inc.; D.M. Campana Co.; Craft Service; Delco Craft Center, Inc.; Kraft Korner; Make It Happen Craft Studio; NASCO Arts & Crafts; Plaza Artists Materials, Inc.; Skil-Crafts Division.
asbestos tile cutters
Beno J. Gundlach Co.
ash splint
The Workshop.

ash tray inserts
Albert Constantine & Son Inc.
asphalt cutters
Beno J. Gundlach Co.
aurora borealis beads
The Beadcraft Corner/Beadcraft Club.
Australian chrysoprase
Australian Imports.
Australian gem rough
Minex Lapidary Supplies
Australian jade
Interlectric House of Fine Australian Opals.
Australian opals
Australian Exports; Australian Imports;

Appendix G

Reading about Mail Order

If you insist on learning your way in the mail-order business by your own experience alone, your future is not so rosy as it might be. Instead, learn by the experience of others. Learn what pitfalls to avoid, which devices will help you sell. The way to gain the experience of others is by reading what they have written about their experiences in mail order as well as by studying their operations through the ads that they run and rerun.

Of course, there is no law that will force you to read the books listed here. Other people have begun mail-order businesses without ever reading anything. But those people usually wish they had learned before they started. Either they lose a potful of money before getting into the black—money they would not have needed to lose if they had profited by the experience of others—or they make less profit than they could have made with a better grounding in the field.

So take my advice, and invest a little time and money in books before you begin. A hundred dollars in books will be the best investment you ever make. It may save you $50,000 in time.

Also, don't just skim through the books and put them away. Keep them around and reread them from time to time. You can appreciate the wisdom in these books only after you have gotten into the business.

Many of the books in the listing were written a long time ago. But don't turn your nose up at their old age. Most of the key ideas about mail order have been around a long time, and each time you reread about these ideas, something new sticks in your mind. Also, the older books often contain ideas that once were employed effectively but have now fallen out of use, in which case you can often bring them back profitably.

The main magazines relating to the mail-order business are listed in Appendix D. In addition, you might want to look at *Advertising*

Age, a general periodical on the advertising business, and *Folio,* which is mainly about the magazine industry.

Scholars who seek an extensive bibliography should refer to Emmett and Jeuck (included in list that follows).

This reading list does not cover all the works listed in the chapter references or all mail-order books. I have included some books that I have not read, many because they are not easily available. The books that I have read and can recommend I have annotated.

Alexander, Ken (Segal): *How to Start Your Own Mail-Order Business,* Stravon Publishers, New York, 1950.
Pretty fair introduction. Worth reading as a refresher.
Arco Editorial Board: *How to Win Success in the Mail-Order Business,* Arco Publishing Co., New York, 1966.
Asher, Louis E., and Edith Heal: *Send No Money,* Argus, Niles, IL 1942.
Baier, Martin: *Elements of Direct Marketing,* McGraw-Hill, New York, 1983.
Baker, Robert A.: *Help Yourself to Better Mail Order,* Printers' Ink Publishing Co., Inc., New York, 1953.
An excellent book for the small mail-order operator. Covers basic topics in copy, media, and product choice. Also contains excellent checklists and media lists, plus some good mail-order ads.
Bedell, Clyde: *How to Write Advertising That Sells,* 2d ed., McGraw-Hill, New York, 1952.
A top book on mail-order copy, slanted somewhat toward retail.
Bernstein, Ronald A. et al: *Successful Direct Selling,* Prentice-Hall, Englewood Cliffs, NJ, 1984.
Bird, Drayton: *Common Sense Direct Marketing,* The Printed Shop, London, 1982.
B.P. Foundation: *Mail-Order Operation,* Wehman.
Brann, Christian: *Direct Mail and Direct-Response Promotion,* Wiley, New York, 1972.
Brantley, C.: *One Hundred & Forty-four Ways to Sell Printing by Mail.* North American Publishing Co., 1972.
Bringe, Paul: *Briefs from Bringe,* privately published monthly; Hartford, WI.
An informative monthly newsletter, written as a house organ by a crack copywriter. Available from Bringe for a nominal buck a year. Write Paul Bringe, First National Bank Building, Hartford, WI.
Buckley, Earle A.: *How to Sell by Mail,* McGraw-Hill, New York, 1938.
Burstiner, Irving: *Mail Order Selling: How to Market Almost Anything by Mail,* Prentice-Hall, Englewood Cliffs, NJ, 1982.
Caples, John: *Tested Advertising Methods,* Harper & Row, New York, 1940.
An excellent book on mail-order copywriting.
———: *Making Ads Pay,* Dover, New York, 1966.
Cohen, William A.: *Direct Response Marketing: An Entrepreneurial Approach,* Wiley, New York, 1985.
Cohen, William A.: *Building a Mail Order Business: A Complete Manual for Success,* 2d ed., Wiley, New York, 1985.
An excellent text that covers some points not discussed in this book.
Collier, Robert: *The Robert Collier Letter Book,* Prentice-Hall, Englewood Cliffs, NJ, 1950.
Classic book on direct-mail copy.
Conklin, Lawrence: *Profitable Mail-Order Marketing,* International Ideas, 1976.
Cossman, E. Joseph: *How I Made $1,000,000 in Mail Order,* Prentice-Hall, Englewood Cliffs, NJ, 1963.
A few interesting tidbits, plus inspiration. But I think Cossman's advice is exactly wrong for beginners.
Dillon, John (ed.): *Handbook of International Direct Marketing.* McGraw Hill, New York, 1976.

Direct-Mail Advertising & Selling for Retailers, National Retail Merchants, 1978.
Direct Marketing (formerly *The Reporter of Direct-Mail Advertising*), Garden City, NY.
   A monthly trade magazine that often carries articles on mail-order businesses. Its ads are also of interest.
DMA Fact Book on Direct Marketing—1984, New York, 1984.
Emmet, Boris, and John Jeuck: *Catalogues and Counters,* The University of Chicago Press, Chicago, 1950.
   An excellent book on Sears, Roebuck. Contains a large bibliography on the mail-order business.
Ferrara, V.P.: *A Complete Course in the Mail-Order Business,* Nelson-Hall, Chicago, 1955.
   This is a very sound volume, from which the mail-order beginner can learn a lot, especially about selling books.
Foster, Lee: *Just Twenty-five Cents and Three Wheaties Box Tops,* Foster Publisher, Pacific Coast Publishing Co., Menlo Park, CA.
Friday Report, Published by Hoke Communications (weekly).
Gonzales, Andres: *Mail Order & Other Profitable Methods.* 1978.
Gottlieb, Richard: *The Directory of Mail Order Catalogs,* 2d ed., Grey House, 1983.
Graham, Irvin: *How to Sell Through Mail Order,* McGraw-Hill, New York, 1949.
   Very competent book on mail-order advertising. Extremely useful if you act as your own agency.
Grant, Paul: *L. W. Mail-Order Survey.*
   A sound course by a real old pro who is especially knowledgeable about correspondence courses.
Haldeman-Julius, Emanuel: *The First Hundred Million,* Simon & Schuster, New York, 1928.
   The best source material for a mail-order bookseller, or any other mail-order person, for that matter. Gives you an unparalleled chance to understand what really makes mail-order copy succeed or fail.
Hall, Samuel R.: *Mail-Order and Direct-Mail Selling,* McGraw-Hill, New York, 1928.
   Somewhat outdated.
Hodgson, Richard S.: *Direct Mail & Mail Order Handbook,* 2d ed., Dartnell, Chicago, 1964.
Hoge, Cecil Sr.: *Mail-Order Moonlighting,* Ten Speed Press, St. James, New York, 1978.
———:*Mail Order Know-How,* Ten Speed Press, Berkeley, CA 1982.
   Excellent book.
Holtz, Herman: *Mail Order Magic,* McGraw-Hill, New York, 1983.
Hopkins, Claude: *Scientific Advertising,* Moore, New York, 1952.
   A classic little book by the acknowledged greatest of all copywriters. Out of print, unfortunately.
Hotchkiss, G. B.: *Advertising Copy,* 3d ed., Harper & Row, New York, 1949.
   A fine book on copywriting in general.
Howard, James E.: *How to Use Mail Order for Profit,* Grosset & Dunlap, New York, 1963.
   Skimpy but sound.
Joffe, Gerardo: *How You Too Can Make at Least $1 Million (but Probably Much More) in the Mail-Order Business,* Advance, San Francisco, 1978.
Joffe, Gerardo: *How to Build A Great Fortune In Mail Order,* Harper & Row, New York, 1983.
Kelley, Pearce C., and Kenneth Lawyer: *How to Organize and Operate a Small Business,* 3d ed., Prentice-Hall, Englewood Cliffs, NJ, 1961.
   This is a good book to have in your library for reference when problems come up.
Kestnbaum, Robert: "Cost per Response and Evaluation of Results," in John Dillon (ed.), *Handbook of International Direct Marketing,* McGraw-Hill, New York, 1976, pp. 125–153.

Kleid, Lewis (ed.): *Mail-Order Strategy,* Direct Mail, Garden City, NY, 1956.
A good collection of articles on direct mail in mail order.
Klein, Bernard: *Mail-Order Business Directory,* yearly, B. Klein Publications, Inc., Coral Springs, FL.
Lists mail-order firms.
Kobs, Jim: *Profitable Direct Marketing,* Crain, 1979.
Lewis, Herschell Gordon: *Direct Mail Copy That Sells,* Prentice-Hall, Englewood Cliffs, NJ, 1984.
First-rate advice on writing copy.
Lustig, Edward: *Modern Mechanical Addressing Systems,* Circulation Associates, New York, 1963.
A detailed discussion of addressing.
Lyons, Delphine: *Armchair Shopper's Guide,* Simon & Schuster, New York, 1968.
Mail-Order Digest, National Mail-Order Association, Los Angeles, January, 1978.
Martin, Sean: *How to Start & Run a Successful Mail-Order Business,* McKay, 1971.
Mayer, Edward N., Jr., and Roy G. Ljungren: *The Handbook Of Business Direct Mail Advertising,* BPAA.
McLean, Ed: *Direct Mail Strategies for Sales & Marketing Executives,* Sales & Marketing Management, New York, 1978.
Melcher, Daniel, and Nancy Larrick: *Printing and Promotion Handbook,* McGraw-Hill, 3d ed., New York, 1966.
Moller, E. V.: *World Wide Mail Order Shopper's Guide*
Moran, John: *The Mail-Order Business,* MBA Business Associates, Syracuse, NY, 1949.
A hodgepodge of very useful material—facts, lists, anecdotes. Good for idea browsing, but not a text.
Musselman, Henry E.: *Mail-Order Dollars,* Publicity Publications,Kalamazoo, MI, 1954.
Contains useful information.
Nash, Edward L.,: *Direct Marketing: Strategy, Planning, Execution,* McGraw-Hill, New York, 1982.
Nash, Edward L.: *The Direct Marketing Handbook,* McGraw-Hill, New York, 1984.
Non-Store Marketing Report. Maxwell Sroge Publishing, Inc., Chicago, 1979.
Ogilvy, David: *Confessions of an Advertising Man,* Atheneum, New York, 1963.
A great book on creating advertising.
——:*Ogilvy On Advertising,* Crown, New York, 1983.
Ornstein, Edwin J.: *Mail-Order Marketing,* Beekman Publishers.
Posch, Robert J., Jr.: *The Direct Marketer's Legal Adviser,* McGraw-Hill, New York, 1983.
Powers, Melvin: *How to Get Rich in Mail Order,* Wilshire, North Hollywood, CA, 1980.
Pratt, Verneur E.: *Selling by Mail,* McGraw-Hill, New York, 1924.
Covers many topics in mail order, including catalogs and agents. Includes many illustrations. A valuable book, though dated.
Preston, Harold P.: *Successful Mail Selling,* Ronald, New York, 1941.
Competent discussion of basic mail-order topics.
Rheinstrom, Carroll: *Psyching the Ads,* Covici-Friede, New York, 1929.
A compilation of advertising copy tests, the study of which should help you learn to create good ads.
Roman, Murray: *Telemarketing Campaigns That Work!,* McGraw-Hill, New York, 1983.
——:*Telephone Marketing: How To Build Your Business By Telephone,* McGraw-Hill, New York, 1976.
Rosden, George, and Peter Rosden: *The Law of Advertising,* Matthew Bender, New York, 1974.
Sawyer, Samuel: *Secrets of the Mail-Order Trade,* 1900.
A fine book, if you can find it. Old, but not dead.
Schultz, Whitt N.: *How to Build Your Own Mail-Order Business,* How Co., Kenilworth, IL.

Schwab, Victor O.: "Successful Mail-Order Advertising," in Roger Barton (ed.), *Advertising Handbook,* Prentice-Hall, Englewood Cliffs, NJ, 1950
The best short article on display copy.
——: *How to Write a Good Advertisement,* Harper & Row, New York, 1962.
Excellent book on copy.
Schwartz, Eugene M.: *Mail Order! How to Get Your Share of the Hidden Profits that Exist in Your Business,* Boardroom, 1982.
Secrets & Top Tips of Mail-Order Advertising, World Merch. Import 1976.
Shinn, Duane: *How to Sell Your Product to Mail Order Houses by the Thousands,* 1976.
——: *How to Start Your Own Drop-Ship Mail-Order Business,* 1976.
Shryer, William A.: *Analytical Advertising,* Business Service Corporation, Detroit, MI, 1912.
The first great book about mail-order advertising or any advertising. My favorite, because it gives facts and figures.
Simon, Morton J.: *The Law for Advertising and Marketing,* Norton, New York, 1956.
The bible!
Sparks, Howard: *Amazing Mail-Order Business & How to Succeed in It,* Frederick Fell, Inc., New York, 1966.
Squire, Elizabeth: *The Mail-Order Shopping Guide,* Morrow, New York, 1965.
Steckel, Robert C.: *Profitable Telephone Sales Operations,* Arco Publishing Co., United States Institute of Marketing, Special Reports Division, Pittsburgh.
Stern, Alfred: *How Mail-Order Fortunes Are Made,* Arco, New York, 1970.
——: *Five Hundred Mail-Order Ideas,* Porter, 1978.
——: *How Mail-Order Fortunes Are Made,* Selective, Rev. Ed. 1974.
Stern, Ed: *The Direct Marketing Marketplace 1984,* Hillary House.
Stone, Bob: *Successful Direct Marketing Methods,* 3d ed., Crain Books, Chicago, 1979.
Stone, Robert: *Successful Direct-Mail Advertising and Selling,* Prentice-Hall, Englewood Cliffs, NJ, 1955.
An excellent book on direct mail in general and as used in mail order.
Sumner, G. Lynn: *How I Learned the Secrets of Success in Advertising,* Prentice-Hall, Englewood Cliffs, NJ, 1952.
Easy-to-read stories of mail-order successes; it also includes some basic factual information.
Swan, Carrol J.: *Which Ad Pulled Best?* Printers' Ink Publishing Co., Inc., New York, 1951.
Studying this book is good training in copy.
Swett, Arthur E.: *Principles of Mail-Order Business,* 4th ed., Swett Publishers, 1900.
Almost as useful now as when it was published 75 years ago. Also interesting for its views on patent-medicine advertising, listings and rates of mail-order media. (The line rate per 100,000 seems to have changed astonishingly little!) Shows old mail-order ads.
Telemarketing Magazine, published by Technology Marketing Corp. (bimonthly).
Vogel, Erwin: *How to Start Minding Your Own Mail Order, That Is, Business,* Box TA, Copywrite, 1865 77th St., Brooklyn, NY 1969.
Wadsworth, R. K.: *Handbook of Mail-Order Selling and Merchandising,* Dartnell, Chicago, 1928.
A good book, somewhat outdated.
Watson, Lewis, and Sharon Watson: *How to Start a Homestead Mail-Order Business,* Stonehouse 1978.
Whitney, Walter N.: *Building a Mail-Order Business,* Alexander Hamilton Institute, no date shown.
Yeck, John D., and John T. Maguire: *Planning and Creating Better Direct Mail,* McGraw-Hill, New York, 1961.
Excellent book on its subject.
Young, John T.: *Mail-Order Advertising Handbook,* Educators Publishing Service, Cambridge, Mass.,
Zip Magazine, North American Publishing Company (9 times a year).

References

Chapter 1 The Possibilities of Mail Order

1 *Establishing and Operating a Mail-Order Business,* U.S. Department of Commerce, Industrial Small Business Series, no. 46, p. 12.

2 Robert A. Baker, *Help Yourself to Better Mail Order,* Printers' Ink Publishing Co., Inc., New York, 1953, p. 4.

3 "Mail Order Business Booms," *Washington Post,* Feb. 4, 1985, pp. 1, 27.

4 "Mail Order Bicycle Firm with $1,000 Start-Up Grossed $6.5 Million in Last Fiscal Year," *Direct Marketing,* Feb. 15, 1984, p. 38.

5 "Using Labor Raises Response for Gifts-by-Mail Company," *Direct Marketing,* February 1974, pp. 55 ff.

6 "Texas Pair Saddles Career Selling Fruit Cakes by Mail," *Direct Marketing,* December 1973, pp. 24 ff.

7 "Successful Jewelry Sales by Non-Legendary Camelot," *Direct Marketing,* July 1974, pp. 55 ff.

8 Arthur E. Swett, *Principles of the Mail Order Business,* 4th ed., Swett Publishers, 1900, p. 1.

9 Advertisement in *Advertising Age,* Oct. 22, 1973, p. 137.

10 "Thousand Dollar Investment Brings Millions in Ten Years," *Direct Marketing,* October 1973, pp. 29 ff.

11 *Direct Mail Lists, Rates and Data* (DMLRD), July 2, 1973.

12 *Direct Marketing,* October 1973.

Chapter 2 What Is the Mail-Order Business?

1 Ed Burnett (correspondence).

2 *The New York Times,* Apr. 5, 1976.

3 "The World of Advertising," *Advertising Age*, special issue, Jan. 15, 1963, p. 137.

4 Arnold Fishman, "Rise and Fall of Big Books in World of Catalog Retailing," *Direct Marketing*, 1985.

5 Joseph H. Rhoads, *Selling by Mail with Limited Capital*, U.S. Small Business Administration, Small Business Bulletin, December 1958, p. 1.

6 Interview by Pete Hoke with Arnold Fishman, "Mail Order: Continuing Its Maturation, Competitiveness," *Direct Marketing*, July 1985, p. 70.
These estimates exclude all in-store sales and personal selling, but include orders placed by telephone or electronically. The estimates do not include sales induced by telephone solicitations, as I understand the matter.

7 Ed Burnett (correspondence).

8 DMMA, *Fact Book*, 1979, p. 3; U.S. *Statistical Abstract*, 1985, p. 549.

9 *Advertising Age*, Nov. 21, 1973, p. 116; Ed Burnett (correspondence).

10 U.S. *Statistical Abstract* 1974, pp. 758, 759; 1985, p. 786.

11 Arnold Fishman, "Business to Business Mail Order Sales Reached $31 B in '84," *Direct Marketing*, September 1985, p. 72 ff.

12 *The New York Times*, Aug. 3, 1985.

13 James P. McClane, "Here's How Corporation Giants Took Mail Order Giant Steps," *Direct Marketing*, August 1975, pp. 50–52.

14 *The New York Times*, Aug. 3, 1985.

15 *The Wall Street Journal*, Oct. 3, 1985, p. 33.

16 *The New York Times*, Aug. 24, 1975, Section 3, p. 1.

17 Arnold Fishman, *Direct Marketing*, July 1985; "Seasoned DM Techniques Key to 58% Sales Increase for L.L. Bean," *DM News*, July 15, 1983; C. Lehmann-Haupt, "Literary Bait for a Mail-Order Hook," *The New York Times*, Feb. 28, 1985.

18 *Advertising Age*, Jan. 15, 1979, p. 38.

19 *The New York Times*, Jan. 19, 1974.

20 Data on 1978 data from Maxwell Sroge Company in *Direct Marketing*, p. 6 of issue now lost. *Marketing News*, Nov. 19, 1976, p. 6.

21 "International Mail Order—Severe Handicap, High Costs, Tough Regulations," *Direct Marketing*, August 1985, pp. 58 ff; *The Wall Street Journal*, June 26, 1985, p. 30.

22 *The Wall Street Journal*, Jan. 10, 1979, pp. 1, 16.

23 *The New York Times*, Jan. 24, 1975, p. 11.

24 *Maxwell Sroge Company*, 1978, p. 5.

25 *The Wall Street Journal*, Oct. 6, 1978, pp. 1, 24.

26 *The Wall Street Journal*, Apr. 27, 1979, p. 2.

27 *Zip*, August 1985, p. 49.

Chapter 3 The Professional
Method of Finding Products

1 Paul Bringe, *Briefs from Bringe,* August 1962.

2 *Direct Marketing,* June 1977.

3 Gerardo Joffe, *How You Too Can Make at Least $1 Million in the Mail-Order Business,* Adriano, San Francisco, 1978.

4 *Advertising Age,* May 13, 1973, p. 48.

5 *Direct Marketing,* May 1978.

6 Ibid., p. 48.

7 *The Wall Street Journal,* Sept. 21, 1978, pp. 1, 21.

8 Emanual Haldeman-Julius, *The First Hundred Million,* Simon & Schuster, New York, 1928.

Chapter 4 More about Finding
Products to Sell

1 "Combine a Love of the Sea with True Mail Order Success," *Direct Marketing,* April 1976, pp. 44 ff.

2 "How to Succeed in Business Doing Something You Enjoy," *Direct Marketing,* March 1977, pp. 36 ff.

3 "Deva Puts Philosophy in the Mail," *Washington Post,* Feb. 4, 1985, p. 26.

4 "Ideas in Sound," catalog no. 72, LHJK 8C1, Direct Marketing, Garden City, NY.

5 Maurice Segall, "Mailers and Retailers Revving Up for Marketing Revolution," *Direct Marketing,* July 1973, p. 26.

6 *Direct Marketing,* June 1974, p. 56.

7 *Fact Book,* p. 44.

8 *Advertising Age,* Feb. 4, 1974, p. 14.

9 *Direct Marketing.*

10 Murray Raphel in *Direct Marketing,* July 1965, p. 66.

11 *Direct Marketing,* "Selling Golf Clubs by Mail Brings Discounts for Duffers," March 1977, pp. 46 ff.

12 "Manufacturer Sells Business to Go Into Mail-Order Sales," *Direct Marketing,* May 1977, p. 32 ff.

13 Frank Vos, "How to Choose or Reject New Mail Order Ventures," *Direct Marketing,* vol. 39, January 1977, pp. 22–26.

Chapter 5 Which Products Are
Best for You to Sell

1 *Advertising Age,* Feb. 3, 1964, p. 38.

2 John Moran, *The Mail Order Business*, MBA Business Associates, Syracuse, NY, 1949.

3 Reporter of *Direct Mail Advertising*, December 1961, pp. 22–27.

Chapter 6 What You May, and May Not, Do in Mail Order

1 *Newsweek*, Feb. 19, 1979, p. 36.

2 See Appendix G for fuller references.

3 Verneur E. Pratt, *Selling by Mail*, 1st ed., McGraw-Hill, New York, 1924, pp. 50–51.

4 Samuel Sawyer, *Secrets of the Mail Order Trade*, 1900, p. 23.

5 U.S. Postal Service, General Release 25, Mar. 26, 1974.

6 *Direct Marketing*, 1979(?), p. 6.

7 U.S. Chief Postal Inspector, *Mail Fraud*, Government Printing Office, Washington, 1967.

8 *Newsweek*, Dec. 22, 1975, p. 64.

9 Sawyer, op. cit.

10 Paul Bringe, *Direct Mail Briefs by Bringe*, March 1963.

11 *Direct Marketing*, September 1974, p. 56.

12 Morton J. Simon, *Advertising Truth Book*, Advertising Federation of America, Washington, D.C.

Chapter 7 Strategies of Mail-Order Selling

1 Ed Burnett (correspondence, 1983).

Chapter 8 The Tactical Decisions in Mail-Order

1 Business Information, Inc.

2 Victor O. Schwab, "Successful Mail-Order Advertising," in Roger Barton (ed.), *Advertising Handbook*, Prentice-Hall, Englewood Cliffs, NJ, 1950, p. 605.

3 Victor O. Schwab, "What 92 Split-Run Ads Tell Us," Part 1, *Advertising & Selling*, April 1948, p. 62.

4 Harold P. Preston, *Successful Mail Selling*, Ronald, New York, 1941, p. 12.

5 Verneur E. Pratt, *Selling by Mail*, 1st ed., McGraw-Hill, New York, 1924, p. 377.

6 Victor O. Schwab, in Roger Barton (ed.), *Advertising Handbook*, p. 605.

7 Robert A. Baker, *Help Yourself to Better Mail Order*, Printers' Ink Publishing Co., Inc., New York, 1953, p. 90.

8 *Esquire* Mail Order Newsletter, undated.

9 Victor O. Schwab, quoted in John Moran, *The Mail Order Business,* MBA Business Associates, Syracuse, NY 1949, p. 241.

10 Robert F. Stone, *Successful Direct Marketing Methods,* Crain Publishing Co., Chicago, 1975, p. 156.

11 Victor O. Schwab, "What 92 Split-Run Ads Tell Us," Part II, *Advertising & Selling,* May 1948, p. 74.

12 Paul Grant, L.W. Mail Order Survey, page not known.

13 Ibid., p. 82.

14 DMMA *Fact Book,* 1979, p. 78.

15 Ibid.

16 E. H. Barnes, *Barnes on Credit and Collection,* Prentice-Hall, Englewood Cliffs, NJ, 1961; John D. Little, *Complete Credit and Collection Letter Book,* Prentice-Hall, Englewood Cliffs, NJ, 1953; Richard H. Morris, *Credit and Collection Letters,* National Association of Credit Management, Channel Press, Great Neck, NY, 1960.

17 Stanley J. Fenvessy, "Importance of Fulfillment in Keeping Customers Happy," *Direct Marketing,* February 1974, p. 22.

18 *The New York Times,* March 21, 1974, p. 49.

19 *Direct Marketing,* January 1973, p. 26.

20 Ibid.

Chapter 9 Calculating the Dollar Value of a Customer

1 *The New York Times,* April 5, 1976.

2 *Direct Marketing,* August 1972, p. 25.

Chapter 10 Calculating Mail-Order Costs and the Order Margin

1 Klaus Reuge, "There's More to Selling by Mail than Counting Coupons," *Direct Marketing,* January 1973, pp. 32–36.

2 Julian L. Simon, *Applied Managerial Economics,* Prentice-Hall, Englewood Cliffs, NJ, 1975, pp. 282–287.

Chapter 13 How to Test and Run Classified Ads

1 Readex survey quoted in Robert A. Baker, *Help Yourself to Better Mail Order,* Printers' Ink Publishing Co., Inc., New York, 1953, p. 103.

Chapter 14 Display-Advertising Procedure and Testing

1 John Caples, *Tested Advertising Methods,* Harper & Row, New York, 1940.

2 Victor O. Schwab, *How to Write a Good Advertisement,* 1st ed., Harper & Row, New York, 1962.

3 Clyde Bedell, *How to Write Advertising That Sells,* 2d ed., McGraw-Hill, New York, 1952.

4 G. B. Hotchkiss, *Advertising Copy,* 3d ed., Harper & Row, New York, 1949.

5 David Ogilvy, *Confessions of an Advertising Man,* Antheneum, New York, 1963.

6 G. Lynn Summer, *How I Learned the Secrets of Success in Advertising,* Prentice-Hall, Englewood Cliffs, NJ, 1952, p. 86.

7 Robert A. Baker, *Help Yourself to Better Mail Order,* Printers' Ink Publishing Co., New York, 1953, p. 73.

8 Paul Grant, L. W. Mail Order Survey, page not known.

9 S. D. Cates, quoted in John Moran, *The Mail Order Business* , MBA Associates, Syracuse, NY, 1949, p. 137.

10 Robert F. Stone, *Successful Direct Marketing Methods,* Crain Publishing Co., Chicago, 1975, p. 94.

11 Irvin Graham, *How to Sell Through Mail Order,* McGraw-Hill, New York, 1949, pp. 335–337.

12 G. Lynn Summer, loc. cit.

13 H.K. Simon, *Mail Order Profits and Pitfalls,* H. K. Simon Co., 1961.

14 Ken Alexander (pseudonym for Alexander Segal), *How to Start Your Own Mail Order Business,* Stravon Publishers, New York, 1950.

15 J. L. Simon, Urbana, IL, private data.

16 Robert D. Kestnbaum, ibid.

17 Robert Stone, *Successful Direct Mail Advertising and Selling,* Prentice-Hall, Englewood Cliffs, NJ, 1955, p. 50.

18 John Moran, *The Mail Order Business,* p. 493.

Chapter 15 Profitable Display—Advertising Operation

1 Robert F. Stone, *Successful Direct Marketing Methods,* Crain Books, Chicago, 1984, p. 140.

2 Ibid., 1975, p. 93.

3 William A. Shryer, *Analytical Advertising,* Business Service Corp., Detroit, 1912, p. 347.

4 Victor O. Schwab, "Successful Mail-Order Advertising," in Roger Barton (ed.), *Advertising Handbook,* Prentice-Hall, Englewood Cliffs, NJ, 1950, p. 612.

5 John Moran, *The Mail Order Business,* MBA Associates, Syracuse, NY, 1949, p. 150.

6 Elon Borton, "Tested Facts Produce One Million Sales for La Salle in 37 Years," *Printers' Ink,* Aug. 10, 1945, pp. 19–20.

7 *Esquire* Mail Order Newsletter, undated.

8 *Direct Marketing.*

9 Emmanuel Haldeman-Julius, in John Moran, op. cit., p. 467.

Chapter 16   The Display Advertisement

1 Victor O. Schwab, "What 92 Split-Run Ads Tell Us," Part II, *Advertising & Selling,* May 1948, p. 38.

2 Harold P. Preston, *Successful Mail Selling,* Ronald, New York, 1941, p. 44.

3 Ibid., p. 48.

4 Victor O. Schwab, "What 92 Split-Run Ads Tell Us," Part I, *Advertising & Selling,* April 1948, p. 33.

5 John Caples, "Headlines: Your First Try Should Not Be the Only One," *Direct Marketing.*

6 Schwab, "92 Split-Run Ads," Part I, p. 60, and Part II, p. 38.

7 John Moran, *The Mail Order Business,* MBA Associates, Syracuse, NY, 1949, p. 63.

8 Henry E. Musselman, *Mail Order Dollars,* Publicity Publications, Kalamazoo, MI, 1954, p. 174.

9 David Ogilvy, *Confessions of an Advertising Man,* Atheneum, New York, 1963.

10 Schwab, "92 Split-Run Ads," Part I, p. 62.

11 Robert A. Baker, *Help Yourself to Better Mail Order,* Printers' Ink Publishing Co., Inc., New York, 1953, p. 42.

12 Stanley Rapp, "Mail-Order Inserts Increase Sales Four Times," *Media/Scope,* September 1961, pp. 79–83.

13 Schwab, "92 Split-Run Ads," Part I, p. 60.

14 William A. Shryer, *Analytical Advertising,* Business Service Corp., Detroit, 1912, p. 171.

15 Baker, op. cit., p. 49.

16 John Caples, *Making Ads Pay,* Doon Publishing Co., 1966, paperback, pages not known.

17 Baker, op. cit., p. 48.

18 D. B. Lucas and S. H. Britt, *Advertising Psychology and Research,* McGraw-Hill, New York, 1950, p. 248.

19 Verneur E. Pratt, *Selling by Mail,* 1st ed., McGraw-Hill, New York, 1924, p. 352.

20 Elon P. Borton, "Tested Facts Produce One Million Sales for La Salle in 37 Years," *Printers' Ink*, Aug. 10, 1945, pp. 19–20.

21 Lucas and Britt, op. cit., pp. 234–236.

22 Borton, loc. cit.

23 Daniel Starch, "Do Inside Positions Differ in Readership?" *Media / Scope*, February 1962, p. 44.

24 Schwab, "Successful Mail-Order Advertising," p. 598.

25 Personal conversation with forgotten informant.

26 Schwab, "Successful Mail-Order Advertising," p. 598.

27 Robert Stone, "Where to Start, How to Test, in Direct Response Magazine Ads," *Advertising Age*, Oct. 22, 1973, p. 119.

28 Ken Alexander (pseudonym for Alexander Segal), *How to Start Your Own MailOrder Business*, Stravon Publishers, New York, 1950, p. 39.

29 G. Lynn Sumner, *How I Learned the Secrets of Success in Advertising*, Prentice-Hall, Englewood Cliffs, NJ, 1952, p. 63.

Chapter 17   How to Write Potent Copy

1 *Scientific American*, October 1962.

Chapter 20   The Direct-Mail Piece, Postage, and Results

1 Robert Stone, *Successful Direct-Mail Advertising and Selling*, Prentice-Hall, Englewood Cliffs, NJ, 1955.

2 Robert Collier, *The Robert Collier Letter Book*, Prentice-Hall, Englewood Cliffs, NJ, 1950.

3 John D. Yeck and John T. Maguire, *Planning and Creating Better Direct Mail*, McGraw-Hill, New York, 1961.

4 Robert Stone, "How to Get the Most Out of Your Direct-Mail Advertising Dollar," in Roger Barton (ed.), *Advertising Handbook*, Prentice-Hall, Englewood Cliffs, NJ, 1950, pp. 571–596.

5 Paul Bringe, *Direct Mail Briefs from Bringe*, August 1973.

6 Stone, *Successful Direct-Mail Advertising and Selling*, p. 71.

7 Ibid., p. 70.

8 John Moran, *The Mail-Order Business*, MBA Business Associates, Syracuse, NY, 1949, p. 418.

9 Stone, *Successful Direct-Mail Advertising and Selling*, p. 72.

10 Ibid., p. 71.

11 Ibid., p. 70.

12 B. M. Mellinger, Mail-Order Course, published by its author, Los Angeles.

13 Stone, *Successful Direct-Mail Advertising and Selling*, p. 71.

14 Paul Bringe, *Direct Mail Briefs from Bringe*, November 1978.

15 *Direct Marketing*, December 1974, p. 20.

16 *Esquire* Mail Order Newsletter, undated.

17 Stone, *Successful Direct-Mail Advertising and Selling*, p. 70.

18 Ibid., p. 73.

19 Ibid., p. 71.

20 Harold P. Preston, *Successful Mail Selling*, Ronald, New York, 1941, p. 103.

21 Robert A. Baker, *Help Yourself to Better Mail Order*, Printers' Ink Publishing Co., Inc., New York, 1953, p. 164.

22 Henry E. Musselman, *Mail-Order Dollars*, Publicity Publications, Kalamazoo, MI, 1954, p. 173.

23 Paul Bringe, op. cit., February 1979.

24 Moran, op. cit., p. 245.

25 Stone, *Successful Direct-Mail Advertising and Selling*, p. 71.

26 Ibid.

27 Paul Bringe, *Briefs from Bringe*, June 1962, quoting from Lewis Kleid, Inc., Research Report No. 48.

28 Paul Grant, L. W. Mail-Order Survey, page not known.

29 Paul Bringe, *Direct Mail Briefs from Bringe*, March 1979.

Chapter 22 Direct-Mail Lists

1 Kenneth L. Emens, "How to Institute an Efficient Mailing List Security Program," *Direct Marketing*, February 1978, pp. 43–44.

2 Paul Bringe, *Briefs from Bringe*, April 1963.

3 Business Information, Inc.

4 Robert Stone, *Successful Direct-Mail Advertising and Selling*, Prentice-Hall, Englewood Cliffs, NJ, 1955, p. 26.

5 Ibid.

6 Robert F. Stone, *Successful Direct-Marketing Methods*, Crain Books, Chicago, 1975, p. 49.

7 Paul Bringe, *Direct Mail Briefs from Bringe*, August 1973.

8 Advertisement in *Direct Marketing*.

9 *Direct Mail*, June 1962, p. 5.

10 Robert F. Stone, op. cit., p. 59.

11 Ray Snyder, quoted in Robert F. Stone, op. cit., p. 49.

12 Samuel R. Hall, *Mail-Order and Direct-Mail Selling*, McGraw-Hill, New York, 1928, p. 17.

13 Emanuel Haldeman-Julius, in Moran, op. cit., p. 467.

Chapter 23   Using Other Mail-Order Media

1 Robert F. Stone, *Successful Direct-Marketing Methods*, Crain Books, Chicago, 1975, p. 100.

2 "Spot TV Sales Promotion Draws High Viewer Response," *Direct Marketing*, December 1973, pp. 47 ff.

3 DMMA, *Fact Book*, p. 49.

4 Ibid.

5 Ibid.

6 Ed Burnett (correspondence).

7 Robert Stone, "How the Newspaper Medium Is Working for Direct-Response Advertisers," *Advertising Age*, Nov. 12, 1973, p. 67.

8 Ed Burnett (correspondence).

9 Bob Stone, "Co-op Mailers Grow in Stature: Unique Medium Can Boost Sales," *Advertising Age*, December 20, 1976.

10 Philip N. Dresden, "Rethinking Direct Response, A Real Economic Necessity," *Direct Marketing*, October 1974, p. 60.

11 *Wall Street Journal*, July 6, 1978, p. 1.

12 Robert Stone, "50 Million Frenchmen Can't Be Wrong About Direct Marketing," *Advertising Age*, May 7, 1973.

13 Michael Owdersmith, "Catalogue Shopping in France, West Germany and U.K.," *Quarterly Review of Marketing*, vol. 3, 1978.

Chapter 24   How to Score with Catalogs

1 *The New York Times*, November 24, p. D4.

2 Jack Scharff, "Scharff Emphasizes Concept of Catalog Being a 'Store'," *Direct Marketing*, 1977.

3 Robert Kestnbaum, "Cost Per Response and Evaluation of Results," in John Dillon (ed.), *Handbook of International Direct Marketing*, 149: McGraw-Hill, New York, 1976, pp. 125–153.

4 Ward E. Beck, "Changing Economy Is Affecting Mail-Order Catalog Companies," *Direct Marketing*, June 1976, p. 38.

5 Vithala Rao and Julian L. Simon, "Optimal Allocation of Space in Retail Advertisements and Catalogs," mimeo, 1978.

6 Scharff, op. cit., p. 64

7 *Direct Marketing*, June 1976, p. 38.

8 Edward C. Bursk and Stephen A. Greyser, *Advanced Cases in Marketing Management*, Prentice-Hall, Englewood Cliffs, NJ, 1966, p. 95.

9 William A. Robinson, "Wishbooks: Those Big Books of Dreams, Updated," *Advertising Age*, Jan. 15, 1979, p. 54.

10 Stone, pp. 225–226.

Chapter 25 Follow-up Letters to Inquirers

1 Verneur E. Pratt, *Selling by Mail*, 1st ed., McGraw-Hill, New York, 1924, p. 251.

2 Elon P. Borton, "Tested Facts Produce One Million Sales for La Salle in 37 Years," *Printers' Ink*, August 10, 1945, pp. 19–28.

3 Henry E. Musselman, *Mail-Order Dollars*, Publicity Publications, Kalamazoo, MI, 1954, p. 66.

4 William A. Shryer, *Analytical Advertising*, Business Service Corp., Detroit, 1912, p. 221.

5 Paul Grant, L. W. Mail-Order Survey, page not known.

6 Ibid.

Chapter 26 The Vital Brain of Mail Order: Testing

1 Source not known.

2 Victor O. Schwab, "What 92 Split-Run Ads Tell Us," Part I, *Advertising & Selling*, April 1948, p. 33.

3 William A. Doppler, "A Mail-Order Test to End All Tests . . . ," *Direct Mail*, September 1957, p. 40.

4 Donald Seibert, "Exciting Concepts Are Tested in Competition for Consumers," *Direct Marketing*, June 1974, p. 58.

5 "Spot TV Sales Promotion Draws High Viewer Response," *Direct Marketing*, December 1973, p. 47.

6 Robert Schlaifer, *Introduction to Statistics for Business Decisions*, McGraw-Hill, New York, 1961.

7 Lewis Kleid, Inc., Bulletin, undated.

8 William Doppler, in Lewis Kleid, Inc., Lewis Kleid Reports, March 1954.

9 Lewis Kleid, Report.

Chapter 27 How to Produce and Print Mail-Order Advertising

1 Amalgamated Lithographers of America, Local 1 of Greater New York, 113 University Place, New York 10003, 1963.

Chapter 28 Filling Orders

1 *Encyclopedia of Associations,* 8th ed., Gale Research Co., Detroit, 1973.

2 Samuel Sawyer, *Secrets of the Mail-Order Trade,* 1900, p. 25.

3 *Esquire* Mail-Order Newsletter, undated.

4 Sawyer, op. cit., p. 34.

5 Stanley J. Fenvessy, "How to Handle Customer Complaints," *Sales Management Magazine,* 1972.

Chapter 30 Our Brand New Miracle: The Computer

1 *Wall Street Journal,* Oct. 2, 1985, p. 33.

Chapter 31 General Management of a Mail-Order Business

1 Robert Stone, *Successful Direct-Mail Advertising and Selling,* Prentice-Hall, Englewood Cliffs, NJ, 1955, p. 87.

Chapter 32 How to Buy or Sell a Mail-Order Business

1 Pearce C. Kelley and Kenneth Lawyer, *How to Organize and Operate a Small Business,* 3d ed., Prentice-Hall, Englewood Cliffs, NJ, 1961.

2 William J. Papp, "Pitfalls to Avoid in Selling Your Mail-Order Business," *Direct Mail,* March 1963, p. 29.

Appendix A How to Lose Money with Mail-Order Franchise, and "Deals"

1 William Berkwitz, *Encyclopedia of the Mail-Order Business,* 1906.

Appendix C Copyrights

1 Donald F. Johnston, *Copyright Handbook,* Bowker, New York, 1978, p. 5.

Appendix D Mailing-List Brokers, Consultants, and Mail-Order Advertising Agencies

1 Paul Bringe (in a long-lost issue of his newsletter).

Appendix E Technical Notes on Direct-Mail Testing

1 Robert J. Wolfson (correspondence).

Index

ABOUT THE AUTHOR

Currently Professor of Business Administration at the University of Maryland, Julian L. Simon started, successfully operated, and profitably sold his own mail-order firm. He has been a consultant on mail order and other aspects of business and economics to some of the largest firms in the United States, as well as many small firms just getting started. He has also advised many U.S. and foreign government agencies. Dr. Simon is the author of hundreds of articles and many books on business and economics, several of which have been used as texts at almost every major U.S. university, and his writings have been translated into fifteen languages. He has appeared on national network television many times in the United States, France, Germany, Brazil, Israel, and other countries.